Childhood

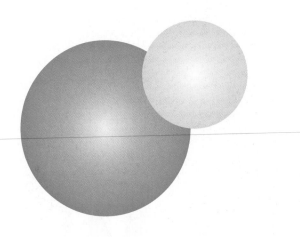

Childhood

Voyages in Development

THIRD EDITION

Spencer A. Rathus

New York University

THOMSON
WADSWORTH

Australia • Brazil • Canada • Mexico • Singapore
• Spain • United Kingdom • United States

THOMSON

WADSWORTH

Publisher: Michele Sordi

Development Editor: Kate Barnes

Assistant Editor: Rachel Guzman

Editorial Assistant: Erin Miskelly

Technology Project Manager: Amy Cohen

Marketing Manager: Sara Swangard

Marketing Assistant: Melanie Cregger

Marketing Communications Manager: Linda Yip

Project Manager, Editorial Production: Mary Noel

Creative Director: Rob Hugel

Art Director: Vernon T. Boes

Print Buyer: Judy Inouye

Permissions Editor: Bob Kauser

Production Service: Joan Keyes, Dovetail Publishing Services/G&S

Text Designer: Cheryl Carrington

Photo Researcher: Eric Schrader

Copy Editor: Kathleen Lafferty

Cover Designer: Cheryl Carrington

Cover Image: Digital Vision/Getty Images

Compositor: G&S Book Services

For more information about our products, contact us at:

Thomson Learning Academic Resource Center

1-800-423-0563

For permission to use material from this text or product, submit a request online at http://www.thomsonrights.com.

Any additional questions about permissions can be submitted by e-mail to thomsonrights@thomson.com.

Library of Congress Control Number: 2007939602

Student Edition:

ISBN-13: 978-0-495-50390-3

ISBN-10: 0-495-50390-8

Loose-leaf Edition:

ISBN-13: 978-0-495-50458-0

ISBN-10: 0-495-50458-0

Thomson Higher Education

10 Davis Drive

Belmont, CA 94002-3098

USA

Credits:

A Closer Look: Glowimages/Getty Images; Active review chapters 1–7: © PhotoDisc/Getty Images; Active review chapters 8–10: © Maya Barnes/The Image Works; Active review chapters 11–13: © Royalty-Free/CORBIS; Developing in a World of Diversity, left: Camille Tokerud/Getty Images; Developing in a World of Diversity, middle: Peter Cade/Getty Images; Developing in a World of Diversity, right: Russell Underwood/Getty Images; Lessons in Observation, Video Camera: Paul Tearle/Getty Images; Lessons in Observation, Book: Siede Preis/Getty Images; Lessons in Observation, screen shots: From *Childhood and Adolescence, Voyages in Development* 2nd edition by RATHUS, 2006. Reprinted with permission of Wadsworth, a division of Thomson Learning: www.thomsonrights.com. Fax 800-730-2215.

For Lois

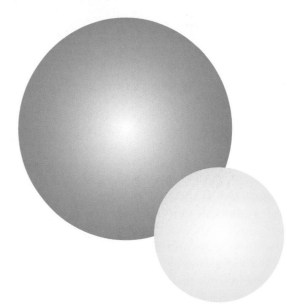

About the Author

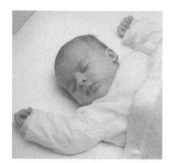

Numerous personal experiences enter into Rathus's textbooks. For example, he was the first member of his family to go to college. He found college textbooks to be cold and intimidating, and when his opportunity came to write college textbooks, he wanted them to be different—warm and encouraging, especially to students who were also the first generation in their families to be entering college.

Rathus's first professional experience was teaching high school English. Part of the task of the high school teacher is to motivate students and make learning fun. Through this experience he learned the importance of humor, and personal stories, which later became part of his textbook approach. Rathus wrote poetry and novels while he was an English teacher—and some of the poetry was published in poetry journals. The novels never saw the light of day (which is just as well, Rathus admits).

Rathus earned his Ph.D. in psychology and then entered clinical practice and teaching. He has published research articles in journals such as *Adolescence, Behavior Therapy, Journal of Clinical Psychology, Behaviour Research and Therapy, Journal of Behavior Therapy and Experimental Psychiatry,* and *Criminology.* His research interests lie in the areas of human growth and development, psychological disorders, methods of therapy, and psychological assessment.

Foremost among his research publications is the Rathus Assertiveness Schedule, which remains widely used in research and clinical practice. Rathus has since poured his energies into writing textbooks, while teaching at Northeastern University, St. John's University, and, currently, New York University. His introductory psychology textbook, *Psychology: Concepts and Connections,* is in its ninth edition.

Rathus is proud of his family. His wife Lois is a successful author and a professor of art at The College of New Jersey. His daughter Allyn graduated New York University's Tisch School of the Arts and is in theater management. His daughter Jordan also graduated from NYU's Tisch School of the Arts and is a production coordinator in film/video. Rathus's youngest daughter, Taylor, an eleventh grader, can dance the pants off of both of them. Rathus's eldest daughter, Jill, is a psychologist and teaches at C. W. Post College of Long Island University.

The author is shown at various stages of development in the four photos on this page.

Brief CONTENTS

CONTENTS

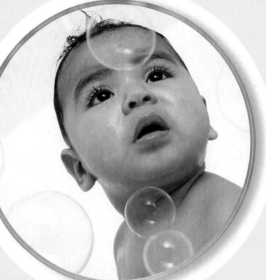

Part 2 | Beginnings

2 Heredity and Conception

3 Prenatal Development

4 Birth and the Newborn Baby: In the New World

Part 3 | Infancy

5 Infancy: Physical Development

6 Infancy: Cognitive Development

7 Infancy: Social and Emotional Development

Part 4 | Early Childhood

8 Early Childhood: Physical Development

10 Early Childhood: Social and Emotional Development

Part 5 | Middle Childhood

11 Middle Childhood: Physical Development

12 Middle Childhood: Cognitive Development

13 Middle Childhood: Social and Emotional Development

Chapter 5—Infancy: Physical Development

- Updated research on failure to thrive
- Update on breast-feeding versus bottle-feeding: advantages and disadvantages for the health of the child, politics, and trends.
- Updated research on the effects of myelination of the brain
- Updated research on the effects of fetal malnutrition on brain development
- Updated research on infant preferences for human faces
- Updated research on development of coordination of the senses

Chapter 6—Infancy: Cognitive Development

- Updated research on the priming of infants' memory
- Update on the possibility that newborns have "memory neurons" that facilitate imitation and bonding
- A revised critical look at testing intelligence in infancy
- Updated research on a "sensitive period" for language development

Chapter 7—Infancy: Social and Emotional Development

- New "A Closer Look" feature: *Prevention of Sexual Abuse of Children*
- New "A Closer Look" feature: *The Latest Shoe to Drop on Day Care from the NICHD* (results of research reported in 2007)
- Updated research on secure attachment and stability of attachment
- Updated research on incidence and biological correlates of autism spectrum disorders
- Updated research on social referencing
- Updated research on sex differences in infant's behavior

Chapter 8—Early Childhood: Physical Development

- Update on nutritional needs in early childhood
- New table on a diet that avoids excess sugar and excess fats for a 4-year-old
- Updated (2007) CDC version of "Ten Things You Need To Know About Immunizations"
- Updated figure: "Recommended Immunization Schedule for Persons Aged 0–6 Years, United States, 2007"
- Revised "A Closer Look" feature: *Assessing and Minimizing the Risk of Lead Poisoning*
- New table on leading causes of death for children aged 2 to 6
- Updated "Developing in a World of Diversity" feature: *Cross-Cultural Differences in Sleeping Arrangements*

Chapter 9—Early Childhood: Cognitive Development

- Updated information on the effects of Head Start
- Updated information on the effects of educational television
- Updated information on the "couch-potato" effect

Chapter 10—Early Childhood: Social and Emotional Development

- Updates on dimensions of child rearing
- Updates on the correlates of birth order
- Updates in evolutionary and hormonal factors in aggression
- New "A Closer Look" feature: *When* Doom *Leads to . . . Doom—What Children Learn from Violent Video Games*
- New "Developing in a World of Diversity" feature: *Where Are the Missing American Fathers?*
- Revised "A Closer Look" feature: *Helping Children Cope with Fears*

Chapter 11—Middle Childhood: Physical Development

- Complete revision of section on childhood obesity, "re-emerging" as a section on "Overweight in Children"
- New coverage of ethnicity and percent of children and adolescents who are overweight
- Updating of "A Closer Look" feature: *Helping Overweight Children Manage Their Weight*
- New coverage of the "Traffic Light Diet"
- New case description on attention-deficit/hyperactivity disorder
- Updating of literature on causes of attention-deficit/hyperactivity disorder, with emphasis on role of dopamine
- Updating of literature on dyslexia, including focus on the double-deficit hypothesis

Chapter 12—Middle Childhood: Cognitive Development

- New discussion of "social intelligence"
- Revised discussion of ethnic differences in intelligence
- New coverage of languages other than English spoken in the home in the United States, and how well people who speak another language in the home speak English

Chapter 13—Middle Childhood: Social and Emotional Development

- New "A Closer Look" feature: *How to Answer a 7-Year-Old's Questions about—Gulp—Sex*
- New coverage of Japanese research on factors in life satisfaction among mothers in the workplace
- New coverage of cyberbullying

New! Annotated Instructor's Edition

Child and adolescent development has many applications to teaching, everyday life, and different careers. As such, we have created a new Annotated Instructors Edition designed to help instructors identify and teach these important areas of development. Written by Debra Schwiesow of Creighton University, the new annotated instructor's edition contains the following Teaching Tips:

- Teaching Tip (for general development students)
- Teaching Tip: Parenting & Family Studies
- Teaching Tip: Education
- Teaching Tip: Social Work & Helping Professions
- Teaching Tip: Nursing & Health
- Technology Tip (suggestions for useful websites that relate to the chapter topics)

New Pedagogical Features

Reflect Items in "A Closer Look" and "Diversity" Features

Each "A Closer Look" and "Developing in a World of Diversity" feature now ends with at least one **Reflect** item. As used elsewhere in the text, **Reflect** items help students learn more effectively because they encourage students to think more deeply about the subject matter. Psychologists refer to reflection on subject matter as *elaborative rehearsal,* which helps students both understand and remember the subject matter.

Reflect: How closely did your parents pay attention to your height and weight? Did they chart it? When did you begin to think that you were average or above or below average in height and weight? What effect did your size have on your self-concept and self-esteem?

- Chapter 8: *Ten Things You Need To Know About Immunizations*
- Chapter 9: *Helping Children Use Television Wisely* (including teaching children *not* to imitate the violence they observe in the media)
- Chapter 10: *Helping Children Cope with Fears*

The following features share developmental information especially related to those studying to be child educators:

- Chapter 6: *Teaching Sign Language to Infants*
- Chapter 7: *What to Do If You Think a Child Has Been the Victim of Sexual Abuse*
- Chapter 10: *Helping Children Cope with Fears*
- Chapter 13: *Bullying—An Epidemic of Misbehavior and Fear*

An Enhanced Pedagogical Package: PQ4R

PQ4R discourages students from believing that they are sponges who will automatically soak up the subject matter in the same way that sponges soak up water. The PQ4R method stimulates students to *actively* engage the subject matter. Students are encouraged to become *proactive* rather than *reactive*.

PQ4R is the acronym for Preview, Question, Read, Reflect, Review, and Recite, a method that is related to the work of educational psychologist Francis P. Robinson. PQ4R is more than the standard built-in study guide. It goes well beyond a few pages of questions and exercises that are found at the ends of the chapters of many textbooks. It is an integral part of every chapter. It flows throughout every chapter. It begins and ends every chapter, and it accompanies the student page by page.

Preview

Chapter previews are provided in the form of chapter outlines intended to help shape students' expectations. It enables them to create mental templates or "advance organizers" into which they categorize the subject matter. Each chapter of *Childhood and Adolescence: Voyages in Development* previews the subject matter with a "Truth or Fiction" section and a chapter "Preview." The "Truth or Fiction" items stimulate students to delve into the subject matter by challenging folklore and common sense (which is often common *non*sense). "Truth-or-Fiction Revisited" sections in the chapter inform students as to whether or not they were correct in their assumptions. The *Preview* outlines the material in the chapter, creating mental categories that guide students' reading.

Following is a sample of challenging "Truth or Fiction" items from various chapters:

 You can carry the genes for a deadly illness and not become sick yourself.

 More children die from sudden infant death syndrome (SIDS) than from cancer, heart disease, pneumonia, child abuse, AIDS, cystic fibrosis and muscular dystrophy combined.

 Infants need to have experience crawling before they develop fear of heights.

 It is dangerous to awaken a sleepwalker.

 Three-year-olds usually say "Daddy goed away" instead of "Daddy went away" because they *do* understand rules of grammar.

 Children who watch 2 to 4 hours of TV a day will see 8,000 murders and another 100,000 acts of violence *by the time they have finished elementary school.*

Question

Devising questions about the subject matter before reading it in detail is another feature of the PQ4R method. Writing questions gives students goals: They attend class or read the text *in order to answer the questions.* Questions are placed in all primary sections of the text to help students use the PQ4R method most effectively. They are printed in *blue*. When students see a question, they can read the following material in order to answer that question. If they wish, they can also write the questions and answers in their notebooks, as recommended by Robinson.

Read

Reading is the first "R" in the PQ4R method. Although students will have to read for themselves, they are not alone. The text helps by providing:

- Previews of the chapter that help students organize the material
- "Truth or Fiction" sections that stimulate students by challenging common knowledge and folklore
- Presentation of the subject matter in clear, stimulating prose
- A running glossary that defines key terms in the margin of the text, near where the terms appear
- Development of concepts in an orderly fashion so that new concepts build on previously presented concepts

I have chosen a writing style that is "personal." It speaks directly to the student and employs humor and personal anecdotes designed to motivate and stimulate students.

Review

The second "R" in PQ4R stands for review. Regular reviews of the subject matter help students learn. There are two types of review features in *Childhood and Adolescence: Voyages in Development*. The first review feature is the "Concept Review." Because reviewing the subject matter is so important, and because of the value of visual cues in learning, "Concept Reviews" are found throughout the text (see page xxviii of this preface). The second type of review feature is the "Active Review." These features follow each major section in the text.

"Active Reviews" contain two types of items that foster active learning, retention, and critical thinking. Fill-in-the-blanks are the first type of item. The fill-in-the-blank format challenges students to *produce*, not simply *recognize*, the answer. Items are numbered and answers are found at the end of each chapter. For example, an "Active Review" from the chapter on "Heredity and Conception" has the following fill-in-the-blanks items:

13. The sets of traits that we inherit are referred to as our (Genotypes or Phenotypes?).
14. The actual traits that we display at any point in time are the product of genetic and environmental influences and are called our (Geno- types or Phenotypes?).
15. Parents and children have a _____ percent overlap in their genetic endowments.
16. _____ (MZ) twins share 100% of their genes.
17. _____ (DZ) twins have a 50% overlap, as do other siblings.

Reflect & Relate

Students learn more effectively when they *reflect* (the third "R" in PQ4R), on or *relate* to the subject matter. Psychologists who study learning and memory refer to reflection on subject matter as *elaborative rehearsal*. One way of reflecting on a subject is to *relate* it to things they already know about, whether it be academic material or events in their own lives. Reflecting and relating to the material makes it meaningful and easier to remember. It also makes it more likely that students will be able to *apply* the information to their own lives. Through effective reflection, students can embed material firmly in their memory so that rote repetition is unnecessary.

- Ethnic differences in chromosomal and genetic disorders (p. 57)
- The possible evolution of reflexes (p. 132)
- Pain as adaptive (p. 139)
- Nature and nurture in the development of the brain (pp. 165–166)
- Nature and nurture in motor development (pp. 169–170)
- Are humans prewired to prefer human stimuli to other stimuli? (p. 172)
- Nature and nurture in perceptual development (pp. 180–181)
- Imitation as adaptive (p. 199)
- Nature and nurture in language development (pp. 209–216)
- The nativist view of language development (p. 213)
- Nature and nurture in theories of attachment development (pp. 226–229)
- Genetic factors in handedness (pp. 275–276)
- Evolutionary theory of aggression (p. 350)
- Genetic/hormonal factors in aggression (p. 350)
- The possible roles of evolution and heredity in sex differences (pp. 359–360)
- Organization of the brain (pp. 360–361)
- Genetic factors in obesity (p. 375)
- Genetic factors in dyslexia (pp. 388–389)
- Genetic influences on intelligence (pp. 428–429)
- The possible role of evolution in step-families (p. 453)
- Possible genetic factors in conduct disorder (p. 465)
- Depression and serotonin (p. 467)

Applications

- Problems associated with use of punishment (pp. 14–15)
- Ways of reversing infertility (p. 68)
- Choosing the sex of one's child (p. 69)
- Maternal nutrition during pregnancy (pp. 93–94)
- Effects of maternal health problems on the embryo and fetus (pp. 94–97)
- Effects of environmental hazards on the embryo and the fetus (pp. 102–104)
- Using the Lamaze method to decrease fear and pain during delivery (pp. 118–119)
- Using C-section to avoid disease transmission from mother to infant (pp. 119–120)
- How interaction, talking, and stimulation can help preterm infants develop (p. 126)
- How a woman can work to get beyond postpartum depression (pp. 128–129)
- Understanding visual accommodation (p. 136)
- How to soothe an infant and ease crying (p. 143)
- How to introduce infants to new food (p. 158)
- Where women can go to learn more about breast-feeding (p. 161)
- Teaching sign language to infants (pp. 206–207)
- "Motherese" (pp. 212–213)
- Establishing attachment (p. 224)
- How child abuse may lead to psychological disorders in adulthood (p. 237)
- What to do if you think a child has been the victim of sexual abuse (p. 239)
- Neurological differences in autistic children (p. 242)
- Finding day care you and your child can live with (p. 247)
- How to comfort a child who doesn't know you (p. 251)
- Brain development and visual skills (pp. 267–268)

- Right brain/left brain (p. 268)
- Plasticity of the brain (p. 268)
- Teaching a child to enjoy healthy food (pp. 276–278)
- Ten things you need to know about immunizations (p. 279)
- Assessing and minimizing the risk of lead poisoning (p. 282)
- What to do about bed-wetting (p. 288)
- Watching how children show (or don't show) conservation (pp. 300–301)
- Memory strategies (pp. 318–319)
- Techniques for restricting children's behavior (pp. 333–334)
- Techniques parents can use to help control their children's behavior (p. 336)
- Helping children cope with fears (p. 357)
- Piaget's theory applied to education (pp. 399, 401)
- Rehearsal strategies for memory (pp. 410–411)
- How to ask children questions that elicit truthful answers (p. 412)
- How teachers can help motivate students (pp. 462–463)
- How to help children with conduct disorders (p. 465)
- How parents and teachers can help children with mild depression (p. 467)
- How parents and teachers can help children with school phobia (p. 471)

The Package

Childhood Voyages in Development is accompanied by a wide array of supplements prepared for both the instructor and student.

For the Instructor

Instructor's Manual (0-495-51029-7)

By Gwynn Morris of North Carolina State University. Available to adopters of Rathus' text, this comprehensive manual offers learning objectives, chapter outlines, chapter summaries, lecture topics, student exercises (such as Internet activities), film and videotape suggestions, activities for the Observing Children video series, and the Resource Integration Guide.

Test Bank (0-495-51030-0)

By Kimberly Dechman of George Mason University. For each chapter of the text, this Test Bank includes 130 multiple-choice questions, 20 matching questions, 15 true/false questions, 10 fill-in-the-blank questions, and 5 essay questions with model answers.

Observation Worksheets (0-495-51047-5)

By Debra Schwiesow of Creighton University. Perfect for homework or small group assignments, these Observation Worksheets encourage students to directly apply their knowledge and experience to their work as parents, counselors, caretakers, and teachers. The easy-to-complete, hands-on activities guide students through the process of observing, recording, and analyzing the behavior of children they encounter in the real world. For each chapter of the text, there is one individual activity and one small group activity.

PowerLecture with *JoinIn*™ and *ExamView*® CD-ROM (0-495-51031-9)

This one-stop lecture and class preparation tool contains ready-to-use Microsoft® PowerPoint® slides by Robin Musselman of LeHigh Carbon Community College, and allows you to assemble, edit, publish, and present custom lectures for your course. PowerLecture lets you bring together text-specific lecture outlines along

Childhood

1

History, Theories, and Methods

Truth or Fiction?

 During the Middle Ages, children were often treated as miniature adults. p. 6

 Children come into the world as "blank tablets," without inborn differences in intelligence and talents. p. 6

 Nail biting and smoking cigarettes are signs of conflict experienced during early childhood. p. 10

 Some theorists contend that children actively strive to understand and take charge of their worlds, whereas other theorists argue that children respond passively to environmental stimulation. p. 17

 Research with monkeys has helped psychologists understand the formation of attachment in humans. p. 37

 To learn how a person develops over a lifetime, researchers have tracked some individuals for more than 50 years. p. 37

Preview

© photographer's choice/First Light

 Go to

http://www.thomsonedu.com/psychology/rathus
for an interactive version of this "Truth or Fiction" feature.

This book has a story to tell. An important story. A remarkable story. It is your story. It is about the remarkable journey you have already taken through childhood. It is about the unfolding of your adult life. Billions of people have made this journey before. You have much in common with them. Yet you are unique, and things will happen to you, and because of you, that have never happened before.

Development of children is what this book is about. In a very real sense, we cannot hope to understand ourselves as adults—we cannot catch a glimpse of the remarkable journeys we have taken—without understanding children.

In this chapter, we explore some of the reasons for studying child development. We then take a brief tour of the history of child development. It may surprise you that until relatively recent times, people were not particularly sensitive to the ways in which children differ from adults. Next, we examine some controversies in child development, such as whether there are distinct stages of development. We see how theories help illuminate our observations and how theories help point the way toward new observations. Then we consider methods for the study of child development. Scientists have devised sophisticated methods for studying children, and ethics helps to determine the types of research that are deemed proper and improper. But first, let us embark on our search for ourselves by considering a basic question. ***Question: What is child development?***

What Is Child Development? Coming to Terms with Terms

You have heard the word *child* all your life, so why bother to define it? We do so because words in common usage are frequently used inexactly. A **child** is a person undergoing the period of development from *infancy* to *puberty*, two more familiar words that are frequently used inexactly. The term **infancy** derives from Latin roots meaning "not speaking," and infancy is usually defined as the first 2 years of life, or the period of life before the development of *complex* speech. We stress the word *complex* because many children have a large vocabulary and use simple sentences before their second birthday.

Researchers commonly speak of two other periods of development that lie between infancy and adolescence: early childhood and middle childhood. Early childhood encompasses the ages from 2 to 5 years. Middle childhood generally is defined as the years from 6 to 12. In Western society, the beginning of this period usually is marked by the child's entry into first grade. To study development, we must also look further back to the origin of sperm and ova (egg cells), the process of **conception**, and the **prenatal period**. Yet even that is not far enough to satisfy scientists. We also describe the mechanisms of heredity that give rise to traits in both humans and other animals.

Development is the orderly appearance of physical structures, psychological traits, behaviors, and ways of adapting to the demands of life over time. The changes brought on by development are both *qualitative* and *quantitative*. Qualitative changes are changes in type or kind. Consider **motor development**. As we develop, we gain the abilities to lift our heads, sit up, crawl, stand, and walk. These changes are qualitative. However, within each of these qualitative changes are quantitative developments, or changes in *amount*. After babies begin to lift their heads, they lift them higher and higher. Soon after children walk, they begin to run. Then they gain the capacity to run faster.

Development occurs across many dimensions: physiological, cognitive, social, emotional, and behavioral. Development is spurred by internal factors, such as genetics, and it is shaped by external factors, such as nutrition and culture.

child A person undergoing the period of development from infancy through puberty.

infancy The period of very early childhood, characterized by lack of complex speech; the first 2 years after birth.

conception The process of becoming pregnant; the process by which a sperm cell joins with an ovum to begin a new life.

prenatal period The period of development from conception to birth. (From roots meaning "prior to birth.")

development The processes by which organisms unfold features and traits, grow, and become more complex and specialized in structure and function.

motor development The development of the capacity for movement, particularly that made possible by changes in the nervous system and the muscles.

growth The processes by which organisms increase in size, weight, strength, and other traits as they develop.

4 •••

The terms *growth* and *development* are not synonymous, although many people use them interchangeably. **Growth** is usually used to refer to changes in size or quantity, whereas development also refers to changes in quality. During the early days following conception in the fallopian tube, the fertilized egg cell develops rapidly. It divides repeatedly, and cells begin to take on specialized forms, yet it does not "grow" in that there is no gain in mass. Why? Because the developing mass of cells has not yet become implanted in the uterus and therefore is without any external source of nourishment. Language development refers to the process by which the child's use of language becomes progressively more sophisticated and complex during the first few years of life. Vocabulary growth, by contrast, refers to the simple accumulation of new words and their meanings.

Child development, then, is a field of study that tries to understand the processes that govern the appearance and growth of children's biological structures, psychological traits, behavior, understanding, and ways of adapting to the demands of life.

Professionals from many fields are interested in child development. They include psychologists, educators, anthropologists, sociologists, nurses, and medical researchers. Each brings his or her own brand of expertise to the quest for knowledge. Intellectual cross-fertilization enhances the skills of developmentalists and enriches the lives of children.

© Photodisc/First Light

Motor Development
This infant has just mastered the ability to pull herself up to a standing position. Soon she will be able to stand alone, and then she will begin to walk.

Why Do We Study Child Development?

Question: Why do researchers study child development? An important motive for studying child development is curiosity and the desire to learn about children. Curiosity may be driven by the desire to answer questions about development that remain unresolved. It may also be driven by the desire to have fun. (Yes, children and the study of children can be fun.) There are other motives described below.

To Gain Insight into Human Nature

For centuries, philosophers, scientists, and educators have argued over whether children are aggressive or loving, whether children are conscious and self-aware, whether they have a natural curiosity that demands to unravel the mysteries of the universe, or whether they merely react mechanically to environmental stimulation. The quest for answers has an effect on the lives of children, parents, educators, and others who interact with children.

To Gain Insight into the Origins of Adult Behavior

How do we explain the origins of empathy in adults? Of antisocial behavior? How do we explain the assumption of "feminine" and "masculine" behavior patterns? The origins of special talents in writing, music, athletics, and math?

To Gain Insight into the Origins of Sex Differences and Gender Roles, and the Effects of Culture on Development

How do **gender roles**—that is, culturally induced expectations for stereotypical feminine and masculine behavior—develop? Are there sex differences in cognition and behavior? If so, how do they develop?

To Gain Insight into the Origins, Prevention, and Treatment of Developmental Problems

Fetal alcohol syndrome, **PKU, SIDS**, Down syndrome, autism, hyperactivity, dyslexia, and child abuse are but a handful of the buzzwords that stir fear in parents and parents-to-be. A major focus in child development research is the search for the causes of such problems so that they can be prevented and, when possible, treated.

gender roles Complex clusters of behavior that are considered stereotypical of females and males.

PKU Phenylketonuria. A genetic abnormality in which a child cannot metabolize phenylalanine, an amino acid, which consequently builds up in the body and causes mental retardation. If treated with a special diet, retardation is prevented.

SIDS Sudden infant death syndrome (discussed in Chapter 5).

To Optimize Conditions of Development

Most parents want to provide the best in nutrition and medical care so that their children will develop strong and healthy bodies. Parents want their infants to feel secure with them. They want to ensure that major transitions, such as the transition from the home to the school, will be as stress-free as possible. Developmentalists therefore undertake research to learn about issues such as:

- The effects of various foods and chemicals on the development of the embryo
- The effects of parent–infant interaction immediately following birth on bonds of attachment
- The effects of bottle feeding versus breast feeding on mother–infant attachment and the baby's health
- The effects of day-care programs on parent–child bonds of attachment and on children's social and intellectual development
- The effects of various patterns of child rearing on development of independence, competence, and social adjustment

The Development of Child Development

Child development as a field of scientific inquiry has existed for little more than a century.

*Question: **What views of children do we find throughout history?*** In ancient times and in the Middle Ages, children often were viewed as innately evil and discipline was harsh. Legally, medieval children were treated as property and servants. They could be sent to the monastery, married without consultation, or convicted of crimes. Children were nurtured until they were 7 years old, which was considered the "age of reason." Then they were expected to work alongside adults in the home and in the field. They ate, drank, and dressed as miniature adults. **Truth or Fiction Revisited:** Children were also treated as miniature adults throughout most of the Middle Ages. (For much of the Middle Ages, artists depicted children as small adults.) However, that means more was expected of them, not that they were given more privileges.

The transition to the study of development in modern times is marked by the thinking of philosophers such as John Locke and Jean-Jacques Rousseau. **Truth or Fiction Revisited:** Englishman John Locke (1632–1704) believed that the child came into the world as a *tabula rasa*—a "blank tablet" or clean slate—that was written on by experience. Locke did not believe that inborn predispositions toward good

A View of Children as Perceived in the 1600s
Centuries ago, children were viewed as miniature adults. In this 17th-century painting, notice how the body proportions of the young princess (in the middle) are similar to those of her adult attendants.

© Erich Lessing/Art Resource, NY

or evil played an important role in the conduct of the child. Instead, he focused on the role of the environment or of experience. Locke believed that social approval and disapproval are powerful shapers of behavior. Jean-Jacques Rousseau (1712–1778), a Swiss–French philosopher, reversed Locke's stance. Rousseau argued that children are inherently good and that, if allowed to express their natural impulses, they will develop into generous and moral individuals.

During the Industrial Revolution, family life came to be defined in terms of the nuclear unit of mother, father, and children rather than the extended family. Children became more visible, fostering awareness of childhood as a special time of life. Still, children often labored in factories from dawn to dusk through the early years of the 20th century.

In the 20th century, laws were passed to protect children from strenuous labor, to require that they attend school until a certain age, and to prevent them from getting married or being sexually exploited. Whereas children were once considered the property of parents to do with as they wished, laws now protect children from the abuse and neglect of parents and other caretakers. Juvenile courts see that children who break the law receive fair and appropriate treatment in the criminal justice system.

Pioneers in the Study of Child Development

Various thoughts about child development coalesced into a field of scientific study in the 19th and early 20th centuries. Many individuals, including Charles Darwin, G. Stanley Hall, and Alfred Binet, contributed to the emerging field.

Charles Darwin (1809–1882) is perhaps best known as the originator of the theory of evolution, but he was also one of the first observers to keep a *baby biography* in which he described his infant son's behaviors in great detail. G. Stanley Hall (1844–1924) is credited with founding child development as an academic discipline. He adapted the questionnaire method for use with large groups of children so that he could study the "contents of children's minds." The Frenchman Alfred Binet (1857–1911), along with Theodore Simon, developed the first standardized intelligence test near the beginning of the 20th century. Binet's purpose was to identify public school children who were at risk of falling behind their peers in academic achievement. By the start of the 20th century, child development had emerged as a scientific field of study. Within a short time, major theoretical views of the developing child had begun to emerge, proposed by such developmentalists as Arnold Gesell, Sigmund Freud, John B. Watson, and Jean Piaget. We next describe their theories of child development and those of others.

© Bettmann/Corbis

A Young Child Laborer
Children often worked long days in factories up through the early years of the 20th century. A number of cultures in the world today still use child labor.

Active Review

1. A child is a person undergoing the period of development from *infancy* to _____.
2. _____ is the orderly appearance of structures, traits, and behaviors over time.
3. The word *growth* is usually used to refer to changes in size or quantity, whereas the term _____ also refers to changes in quality.

Reflect & Relate: Do you believe that children are "wild"? Do you believe that children must be "tamed"? Do you see dangers (to children) in answering yes to either question? Explain.

Go to

http://www.thomsonedu.com/psychology/rathus

for an interactive version of this review.

Sigmund Freud
Freud is the originator of psychoanalytic theory. He proposed five stages of psychosexual development and emphasized the importance of biological factors in the development of personality.

unconscious In psychoanalytic theory, not available to awareness by simple focusing of attention.

psychosocial development Erikson's theory, which emphasizes the importance of social relationships and conscious choice throughout the eight stages of development.

Freud theorized three parts of the personality: *the id, ego*, and *superego*. The id is present at birth and while **unconscious**. It represents biological drives and demands instant gratification, as suggested by a baby's wailing. The ego, or the conscious sense of self, begins to develop when children learn to obtain gratification for themselves, without screaming or crying. The ego curbs the appetites of the id and makes plans that are in keeping with social conventions so that a person can find gratification yet avoid the disapproval of others. The superego develops throughout infancy and early childhood. It brings inward the wishes and morals of the child's caregivers and other members of the community. Throughout the remainder of the child's life, the superego will monitor the intentions and behavior of the ego and hand down judgments of right and wrong. If the child misbehaves, the superego will flood him or her with guilt and shame.

According to Freud, childhood has five stages of psychosexual development: *oral, anal, phallic, latency*, and *genital*. If a child receives too little or too much gratification during a stage, the child can become *fixated* in that stage. For example, during the first year of life, which Freud termed the *oral stage*, "oral" activities such as sucking and biting bring pleasure and gratification. If the child is weaned early or breast-fed too long, the child may become fixated on oral activities such as nail biting or smoking, or even show a "biting wit." **Truth or Fiction Revisited:** There is actually no research evidence that nail biting and smoking cigarettes are signs of conflict experienced during early childhood, even though these beliefs are consistent with Freudian theory.

In the second, or anal, stage, gratification is obtained through control and elimination of waste products. Excessively strict or permissive toilet training can lead to the development of anal-retentive traits, such as perfectionism and neatness, or anal-expulsive traits, such as sloppiness and carelessness. In the third stage, the *phallic stage*, parent–child conflict may develop over masturbation, which many parents treat with punishment and threats. It is normal for children to develop strong sexual attachments to the parent of the other sex during the phallic stage and to begin to view the parent of the same sex as a rival. Girls in this stage may express the wish to marry their fathers when they grow up. Boys are likely to have similar designs on their mothers.

By age 5 or 6, Freud believed, children enter a *latency stage* during which sexual feelings remain unconscious, children turn to schoolwork, and they typically prefer playmates of their own sex. The final stage of psychosexual development, the *genital stage*, begins with the biological changes that usher in adolescence. Adolescents generally desire sexual gratification through intercourse with a member of the other sex. Freud believed that oral or anal stimulation, masturbation, and male–male or female–female sexual activity are immature forms of sexual conduct that reflect fixations at early stages of development.

Evaluation   Freud's theory has had much appeal and was a major contribution to modern thought. It is a rich theory of development, explaining the childhood origins of many traits, and stimulating research on attachment, development of gender roles, and moral development. Freud's views about the anal stage have influenced child-care workers to recommend that toilet training not be started too early or handled punitively. His emphasis on the emotional needs of children has influenced educators to be more sensitive to the possible emotional reasons behind a child's misbehavior.

Yet Freud's work has been criticized on many grounds. For one thing, Freud developed his theory on the basis of contacts with patients (mostly women) who were experiencing emotional problems (Schultz & Schultz, 2008). He also concluded that most of his patients' problems originated in childhood conflicts. It is possible that he might have found less evidence of childhood conflict had his sample consisted of people drawn at random from the population. He was also dealing with recollections of his patients' pasts rather than observing children directly. Such recollections are subject to errors in memory. Freud may also have inadvertently guided patients into expressing ideas that confirmed his views.

Some of Freud's own disciples, including Erik Erikson and Karen Horney, believe that Freud placed too much emphasis on basic instincts and unconscious motives. They argue that people are motivated not only by drives such as sex and aggression but also by social relationships and conscious desires to achieve, to have aesthetic experiences, and to help others.

Once we have catalogued our criticisms of Freud's views, what is left? A number of things are. Freud pointed out that childhood experiences can have far-reaching effects. He noted that our mental processes can be distorted by our efforts to defend ourselves against anxiety and guilt. If these ideas no longer impress us as unusual, perhaps it is because they have been widely accepted since Freud gave voice to them.

Erik Erikson's Theory of Psychosocial Development

Question: How does Erikson's theory differ from Freud's? Erik Erikson (1902–1994) modified and expanded Freud's theory. Erikson's theory, like Freud's, focuses on the development of the emotional life and psychological traits. But Erikson also focuses on the development of self-identity. Out of the chaos of his own identity problems, Erikson forged a personally meaningful life pattern, and Erikson's social relationships had been more important than sexual or aggressive instincts in his development. Therefore, Erikson speaks of **psychosocial development** rather than of *psychosexual development.* Furthermore, it seemed to Erikson that he had developed his own personality through a series of conscious and purposeful acts. Consequently, he places greater emphasis on the ego, or the sense of self.

Erikson (1963) extended Freud's five developmental stages to eight to include the changing concerns throughout adulthood. Rather than label his stages after parts of the body, Erikson labeled stages after the **life crises** that the child (and then the adult) might encounter during that stage. Erikson's stages are compared with Freud's in Concept Review 1.1.

Erikson proposed that our social relationships and physical maturation give each stage its character. For example, the parent–child relationship and the infant's utter dependence and helplessness are responsible for the nature of the earliest stages of development. The 6-year-old's capacity to profit from the school setting reflects the cognitive capacities to learn to read and to understand the basics of math, and even the ability to sit still long enough to focus on schoolwork.

According to Erikson, early experiences affect future developments. With proper parental support early on, most children resolve early life crises productively. Successful resolution of each crisis bolsters their sense of identity—of who they are and what they stand for—and their expectation of future success.

Stages of Psychosocial Development Each stage in Erikson's theory carries a specific developmental task. Successful completion of this task depends heavily on the nature of the child's social relationships at each stage (see Concept Review 1.1).

Erikson's views, like Freud's, have influenced child rearing, early childhood education, and child therapy. For example, Erikson's views about an adolescent **identity crisis** have entered the popular culture and have affected the way many parents and teachers deal with teenagers. Some schools help students master the crisis by means of life-adjustment courses and study units on self-understanding in social studies and literature classes.

Evaluation Erikson's views have received much praise and much criticism. They are appealing in that they emphasize the importance of human consciousness and choice and minimize the role—and the threat—of dark, poorly perceived urges. They

Courtesy of Renate Horney

Karen Horney
Horney, a follower of Freud, argued that Freud placed too much emphasis on sexual and biological determinants of behavior while neglecting the importance of social factors.

Sarah Putnam/Index Stock/PhotoLibrary

Erik Erikson with his wife, Joan Erikson

life crisis An internal conflict that attends each stage of psychosocial development. Positive resolution of early life crises sets the stage for positive resolution of subsequent life crises.

identity crisis According to Erikson, a period of inner conflict during which one examines one's values and makes decisions about one's life roles.

B. F. Skinner

Skinner, a behaviorist, developed principles of operant conditioning and focused on the role of reinforcement of behavior.

conditioned stimulus (CS)
A previously neutral stimulus that elicits a response because it has been paired repeatedly with a stimulus that already elicited that response.

conditioned response (CR)
A learned response to a previously neutral stimulus.

operant conditioning A simple form of learning in which an organism learns to engage in behavior that is reinforced.

reinforcement The process of providing stimuli following a response, which has the effect of increasing the frequency of the response.

positive reinforcer A reinforcer that, when applied, increases the frequency of a response.

negative reinforcer A reinforcer that, when removed, increases the frequency of a response.

extinction The cessation of a response that is performed in the absence of reinforcement.

punishment An unpleasant stimulus that suppresses behavior.

deal of emotional learning is acquired through classical conditioning. For example, touching a hot stove is painful, and one or two incidents may elicit a fear response when a child looks at a stove or considers touching it again.

In classical conditioning, children learn to associate stimuli so that a response made to one is then made in response to the other. But in **operant conditioning** (a different kind of conditioning), children learn to do something because of its effects. B. F. Skinner introduced the key concept of **reinforcement**. Reinforcers are stimuli that increase the frequency of the behavior they follow. Most children learn to adjust their behavior to conform to social codes and rules to earn reinforcers such as the attention and approval of their parents and teachers. Other children, ironically, may learn to misbehave because misbehavior also draws attention. Any stimulus that increases the frequency of the responses preceding it serves as a reinforcer. Most of the time, food, social approval, and attention serve as reinforcers.

Skinner distinguished between positive and negative reinforcers. **Positive reinforcers** increase the frequency of behaviors when they are *applied*. Food and approval usually serve as positive reinforcers. **Negative reinforcers** increase the frequency of behaviors when they are *removed*. Fear acts as a negative reinforcer in that its removal increases the frequency of the behaviors preceding it. For example, fear of failure is removed when students study for a quiz. ● Figure 1.2 compares positive and negative reinforcers.

Extinction results from repeated performance of operant behavior without reinforcement. After a number of trials, the operant behavior is no longer shown. In many cases, children's temper tantrums and crying at bedtime can be extinguished within a few days by simply having parents remain out of the bedroom after the children have been put to bed. Previously, parental attention and company had reinforced the tantrums and crying. When the reinforcement of the problem behavior was removed, the behavior was eliminated.

Punishments are aversive events that suppress or *decrease* the frequency of the behavior they follow. (● Figure 1.3 on page 16 compares negative reinforcers with punishments.) Punishments can be physical (such as spanking) or verbal (e.g., scolding or criticizing) or the removal of privileges. Punishments can rapidly suppress undesirable behavior and may be warranted in emergencies, such as when a child tries to

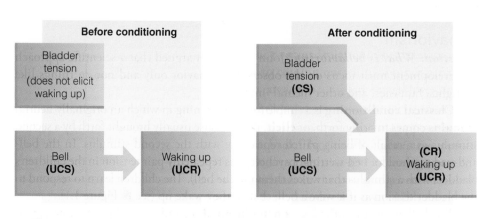

● **Figure 1.1** Schematic Representation of Classical Conditioning

Before conditioning, the bell elicits waking up. Bladder tension, a neutral stimulus, does not elicit waking up. During conditioning, bladder tension always precedes urination, which in turn causes the bell to ring. After conditioning, bladder tension has become a conditional stimulus (CS) that elicits waking up, which is the conditioned response (CR).

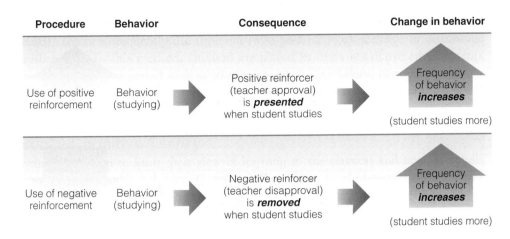

Procedure	Behavior	Consequence	Change in behavior

Use of positive reinforcement → Behavior (studying) → Positive reinforcer (teacher approval) is **presented** when student studies → Frequency of behavior **increases** (student studies more)

Use of negative reinforcement → Behavior (studying) → Negative reinforcer (teacher disapproval) is **removed** when student studies → Frequency of behavior **increases** (student studies more)

● **Figure 1.2** Positive versus Negative Reinforcers

All reinforcers *increase* the frequency of behavior. In these examples, teacher approval functions as a positive reinforcer when students study harder because of it. Teacher *disapproval* functions as a negative reinforcer when its *removal* increases the frequency of studying.

A Closer Look

Operant Conditioning of Vocalizations in Infants

A classic study by psychologist Harriet Rheingold and her colleagues (1959) demonstrated how reinforcement and extinction can influence the behavior—in this case, vocalization—of infants. A researcher first observed the subjects, 3-month-old infants, for about half an hour to record baseline (preexperimental) measures of the frequency of their vocalizing. Infants averaged 13–15 vocalizations each. During the conditioning phase of the study, the researcher reinforced the vocalizations with social stimuli, such as encouraging sounds, smiles, and gentle touches. There was a significant increase in the frequency of vocalizing throughout this phase. By the end of an hour of conditioning spread over a 2-day period, the average incidence of vocalizations had nearly doubled to 24–25 within a half-hour. During the extinction phase, as during the baseline period, the researcher passively observed each infant, no longer reinforcing vocalization. After two half-hour extinction periods, average vocalizing had returned to near baseline, 13–16 per half hour.

Reflect: Rheingold changed the frequency of vocalizations of infants. In what other kinds of learning do infants engage?

Courtesy of Dr. Arnold Rheingold

Conditioning Verbalizations in Infants
In this historic photo, Harriet Rheingold observes as a mother attempts to condition verbalizing in her infant.

Jean Piaget

Piaget's cognitive-developmental theory is a stage theory that focuses on the ways children adapt to the environment by mentally representing the world and solving problems. Piaget's early training as a biologist led him to view children as mentally assimilating and accommodating aspects of their environment.

Despite the demonstrated effectiveness of behavior modification, learning-theory approaches to child development have been criticized in several ways. First, there is the theoretical question of whether the conditioning process in children is mechanical or whether it changes the ways that children mentally represent the environment. In addition, learning theorists may underestimate the importance of maturational factors (Schultz & Schultz, 2008). Social cognitive theorists seem to be working on these issues. For example, they place more value on cognition and view children as being active, not as merely reacting mechanically to stimuli. Now let us turn to theories that place cognition at the heart of development.

The Cognitive Perspective

Cognitive theorists focus on children's mental processes. They investigate the ways in which children perceive and mentally represent the world, how they develop thinking, logic, and problem-solving ability. One cognitive perspective is **cognitive-developmental theory** advanced by Swiss biologist Jean Piaget (1896–1980). Another is information-processing theory.

Jean Piaget's Cognitive-Developmental Theory

During adolescence, Piaget studied philosophy, logic, and mathematics, but years later he took his Ph.D. in biology. In 1920, he obtained a job at the Binet Institute in Paris, where research on intelligence tests was being conducted. Piaget tried out items on children in various age groups. The task became boring, but then Piaget became interested in children's *wrong* answers. Someone else might have shrugged them off and forgotten them, but Piaget realized that there were methods to the children's madness. Their wrong answers reflected consistent—although illogical—mental processes. Piaget looked into the patterns of thought that led to the wrong answers.

Piaget wrote dozens of books and articles on these patterns, but his work was almost unknown in English-speaking countries until the 1950s. For one thing, Piaget's writing is difficult to understand, even to native speakers of French. (Piaget joked that he had the advantage of *not* having to read Piaget.) For another, Piaget's views differed from those of other theorists. Psychology in England and the United States was dominated by behaviorism and psychoanalysis, and Piaget's ideas had a biological-cognitive flavor. But today they are quite popular.

Behaviorists, such as John B. Watson, focus on learning observable behavior. They see children as "blank slates" that are written upon by experience. Freud's psychoanalytic theory focuses on personality and emotional development. It portrays children as largely irrational and at the mercy of instinctive impulses. ***Question: What are Jean Piaget's views on development?*** Piaget, by contrast, was concerned with how children form concepts or mental representations of the world and how they work with concepts to plan changes in the external world. But, like the behaviorists, he recognized that thoughts cannot be measured directly, so he tried to link his views on children's mental processes to observable behavior.

Piaget believed that that cognitive development largely depends on the maturation of the brain. He regarded maturing children as natural physicists who actively intend to learn about and take intellectual charge of their worlds. In the Piagetian view, children who squish their food and laugh enthusiastically are often acting as budding scientists. In addition to enjoying a response from parents, they are studying the texture and consistency of their food. (Parents, of course, often prefer that their children practice these experiments in the laboratory, not the dining room.)

Piaget's Basic Concepts   Piaget used concepts such as *schemes, adaptation, assimilation, accommodation,* and *equilibration* to describe and explain cognitive development. Piaget defines the **scheme** as a pattern of action or a mental structure that is involved in acquiring or organizing knowledge. Babies are said to have sucking

cognitive-developmental theory The stage theory that holds that the child's abilities to mentally represent the world and solve problems unfold as a result of the interaction of experience and the maturation of neurological structures.

scheme According to Piaget, an action pattern or mental structure that is involved in the acquisition and organization of knowledge.

schemes, grasping schemes, and looking schemes. (Others call these *reflexes*.) Newborn babies suck things that are placed in their mouths, grasp objects placed in their hands, and visually track moving objects. Piaget would say that infants' schemes give meaning to objects. Infants are responding to objects as "things I can suck" versus "things I can't suck" and as "things I can grasp" versus "things I can't grasp." Among older children, a scheme may be the inclusion of an object in a class. For example, the mammal class, or concept, includes a group of animals that are warm-blooded and nurse their young. The inclusion of cats, apes, whales, and people in the mammal class involves schemes that expand the child's knowledge of the natural world.

Adaptation refers to the interaction between the organism and the environment. According to Piaget, all organisms adapt to their environment; it is a biological tendency. Adaptation consists of assimilation and accommodation, which occur throughout life. In biology, assimilation is the process by which food is digested and converted into the tissues that compose an animal. Cognitive **assimilation** refers to the process by which someone responds to new objects or events according to existing schemes or ways of organizing knowledge. Infants, for example, usually try to place new objects in their mouths to suck, feel, or explore them. Piaget would say that the child is assimilating (fitting) a new toy or object into the sucking-an-object scheme. Similarly, 2-year-olds who refer to sheep and cows as "doggies" or "bowwows" can be said to be assimilating these new animals into the doggy (or bowwow) scheme.

Sometimes, a novel object or event cannot be made to fit (i.e., it cannot be assimilated into an existing scheme). In that case, the scheme may be changed or a new scheme may be created to incorporate the new event. This process is called **accommodation**. Consider the sucking reflex. Within the first month of life, infants modify sucking behavior as a result of experience sucking various objects. The nipple on the bottle is sucked one way, the thumb in a different way. Infants accommodate further by rejecting objects that are too large, that taste bad, or that are of the wrong texture or temperature.

Piaget theorized that when children can assimilate new events to existing schemes, they are in a state of cognitive harmony, or equilibrium. When something that does not fit happens along, their state of equilibrium is disturbed and they may try to accommodate. The process of restoring equilibrium is termed **equilibration**. Piaget believed that the attempt to restore equilibrium is the source of intellectual motivation and lies at the heart of the natural curiosity of the child.

Piaget's Stages of Cognitive Development

Piaget (1963) hypothesized that children's cognitive processes develop in an orderly sequence, or series, of stages. As with motor development, some children may be more advanced than others at particular ages, but the developmental sequence remains the same. Piaget identified four major stages of cognitive development: sensorimotor, preoperational, concrete operational, and formal operational. These stages are described in Concept Review 1.2 and are discussed in subsequent chapters.

Because Piaget's theory focuses on cognitive development, its applications are primarily in educational settings. Teachers following Piaget's views would engage the child actively in solving problems. They would gear instruction to the child's developmental level and offer activities that challenge the child to advance to the next level. For example, 5-year-olds learn primarily through play and direct sensory contact with the environment. Early formal instruction using workbooks and paper may be less effective than other methods in this age group (Crain, 2000).

Evaluation

Many researchers, using a variety of methods, have found that Piaget may have underestimated the ages when children are capable of doing certain things. It also appears that cognitive skills may develop more gradually than Piaget thought and not in distinct stages. Here, let us simply note that Piaget presented a view of

adaptation According to Piaget, the interaction between the organism and the environment. It consists of two processes: assimilation and accommodation.

assimilation According to Piaget, the incorporation of new events or knowledge into existing schemes.

accommodation According to Piaget, the modification of existing schemes to permit the incorporation of new events or knowledge.

equilibration The creation of an equilibrium, or balance, between assimilation and accommodation as a way of incorporating new events or knowledge.

Concept Review 1.2   Jean Piaget's Stages of Cognitive Development

Stage	Approximate Age	Comments	
Sensorimotor	Birth to 2 years	At first, the child lacks language and does not use symbols or mental representations of objects. In time, reflexive responding ends, and intentional behavior—as in making interesting stimulation last—begins. The child develops the object concept and acquires the basics of language.	©Doug Goodman/Photo Researchers Inc.
Preoperational	2 to 7 years	The child begins to represent the world mentally, but thought is egocentric. The child does not focus on two aspects of a situation at once and therefore lacks conservation. The child shows animism, artificialism, and objective responsibility for wrongdoing.	
Concrete operational	7 to 12 years	Logical mental actions—called operations—begin. The child develops conservation concepts, can adopt the viewpoint of others, can classify objects in series, and shows comprehension of basic relational concepts (such as one object being larger or heavier than another).	
Formal operational	12 years and older	Mature, adult thought emerges. Thinking is characterized by consideration of various possibilities (mental trial and error), abstract thought, and the formation and testing of hypotheses.	

children that is different from the psychoanalytic and behaviorist views, and he provided a strong theoretical foundation for researchers concerned with sequences in children's cognitive development.

Information-Processing Theory

Another face of the cognitive perspective is information processing (Flavell et al., 2002; Siegler & Alabali, 2005). *Question: What is information-processing theory?* Psychological thought has long been influenced by the status of the physical sciences of the day. For example, Freud's psychoanalytic theory was related to the development of the steam engine—which can explode when too much steam builds up—in the 19th century. Many of today's cognitive psychologists are influenced by computer science. Computers process information to solve problems. Information is encoded so that it can be accepted as input and then fed ("inputted") into the computer. Then it is placed in working memory (RAM) while it is manipulated. The information can be stored more permanently on a storage device, such as a hard drive. Many psychologists also speak of people as having working or short-term memory and a more permanent long-term memory (storage). If information has been placed in long-term memory, it must be retrieved before we can work on it again. To retrieve information from computer storage, we must know the code or name for the data file and the rules for retrieving data files. Similarly, note psychologists, without the cues to retrieve information from our own long-term memories, the information may be lost.

Thus, many cognitive psychologists focus on information processing in people—the processes by which information is encoded (input), stored (in long-term memory), retrieved (placed in short-term memory), and manipulated to solve problems (output). Our strategies for solving problems are sometimes referred to as our "mental programs" or "software." In this computer metaphor, our brains are the "hardware" that runs our mental programs. Our brains—containing billions of brain cells called *neurons*—become our most "personal" computers.

When psychologists who study information processing contemplate the cognitive development of children, they are likely to talk in terms of the *size* of the child's short-term memory at a given age and of the *number of programs* a child can run simultaneously.

The most obvious applications of information processing occur in teaching. For example, information-processing models alert teachers to the sequence of steps by which children acquire information, commit it to memory, and retrieve it to solve problems. By understanding this sequence, teachers can provide experiences that give students practice with each stage.

We now see that the brain is a sort of biological computer. Let us next see what other aspects of biology can be connected with child development.

The Biological Perspective

Question: What is the scope of the biological perspective? The biological perspective directly relates to physical development: to gains in height and weight; development of the brain; and developments connected with hormones, reproduction, and heredity. Here we consider one biologically oriented theory of development, *ethology*.

Ethology: "Doing What Comes Naturally"

Ethology was heavily influenced by the 19th-century work of Charles Darwin and by the work of 20th-century ethologists Konrad Lorenz and Niko Tinbergen (Washburn, 2007). *Question: What is ethology?* Ethology is concerned with instinctive, or inborn, behavior patterns.

The nervous systems of most, and perhaps all, animals are "prewired" or "preprogrammed" to respond to some situations in specific ways. For example, birds raised in isolation from other birds build nests during the mating season even if they have never seen a nest or seen another bird building one. Nest-building could not have been learned. Birds raised in isolation also sing the songs typical of their species. Salmon spawned in particular rivers swim out into the vast oceans and then, when mature, return to their own river to spawn. These behaviors are "built in," or instinctive. They are also referred to as inborn **fixed action patterns (FAPs)**.

During prenatal development, genes and sex hormones are responsible for the physical development of female and male sex organs. Most theorists also believe that

ethology The study of behaviors that are specific to a species.

fixed action pattern (FAP) A stereotyped pattern of behavior that is evoked by a "releasing stimulus." An instinct.

in many species, including humans, sex hormones can "masculinize" or "feminize" the embryonic brain by creating tendencies to behave in stereotypical masculine or feminine ways. Testosterone, the male sex hormone, seems to be connected with feelings of self-confidence, high activity levels, and—the negative side—aggressiveness (Archer, 2006; Davis et al., 2005; Geary, 2006).

Evaluation   Most theorists with an ethological perspective do not maintain that human behaviors are as mechanical as those of lower animals. Moreover, they tend to assume that instinctive behaviors can be modified through learning. Research into the ethological perspective suggests, however, that instinct may play a role in human behavior. Two questions that research seeks to answer are, What areas of human behavior and development, if any, involve instincts? and How powerful are instincts in people?

The Ecological Perspective

Ecology is the branch of biology that deals with the relationships between living organisms and their environment. *Question: What is the ecological systems theory of child development?* The **ecological systems theory** of child development addresses aspects of psychological, social, and emotional development as well as aspects of biological development. Ecological systems theorists explain child development in terms of the interaction between children and the settings in which they live (Bronfenbrenner & Morris, 2006).

According to Urie Bronfenbrenner (1917–2005), we need to focus on the two-way interactions between the child and the parents, not just maturational forces (nature) or parental child-rearing approaches (nurture). For example, some parents may choose to feed newborns on demand, whereas others may decide to stick to feedings that occur 4 hours apart. Some babies, however, will be more accepting than others, and some will never be comfortable with a strict schedule. That is the point: Parents are a key part of the child's environment and have a major influence on the child, but even babies have inborn temperaments that affect the parents.

Bronfenbrenner (Bronfenbrenner & Morris, 2006) suggested that we can view the setting or contexts of human development as consisting of multiple systems, each embedded within the next larger context. From narrowest to widest, these systems are the microsystem, the mesosystem, the exosystem, the macrosystem, and the chronosystem (● Figure 1.4).

The **microsystem** involves the interactions of the child and other people in the immediate setting, such as the home, the school, or the peer group. Initially, the microsystem is small, involving care-giving interactions with the parents or others, usually at home. As children get older, they do more, with more people, in more places.

The **mesosystem** involves the interactions of the various settings within the microsystem. For instance, the home and the school interact during parent–teacher conferences. The school and the larger community interact when children are taken on field trips. The ecological systems approach addresses the joint effect of two or more settings on the child.

The **exosystem** involves the institutions in which the child does not directly participate but which exert an indirect influence on the child. For example, the school board is part of the child's exosystem because board members put together programs for the child's education, determine what textbooks will be acceptable, and so forth. In similar fashion, the parents' workplaces and economic situations determine the hours during which they will be available to the child, what mood they will be in when they are with the child, and so on. For example, poverty and unemployment cause psychological distress in parents, which affects their parenting (Kaminski & Stormshak, 2007). As a result, children may misbehave at home and in school. Studies that

ecology The branch of biology that deals with the relationships between living organisms and their environment.

ecological systems theory The view that explains child development in terms of the reciprocal influences between children and the settings that make up their environment.

microsystem The immediate settings with which the child interacts, such as the home, the school, and one's peers (from the Greek *mikros*, meaning "small").

mesosystem The interlocking settings that influence the child, such as the interaction of the school and the larger community when children are taken on field trips (from the Greek *mesos*, meaning "middle").

exosystem Community institutions and settings that indirectly influence the child, such as the school board and the parents' workplaces (from the Greek *exo*, meaning "outside").

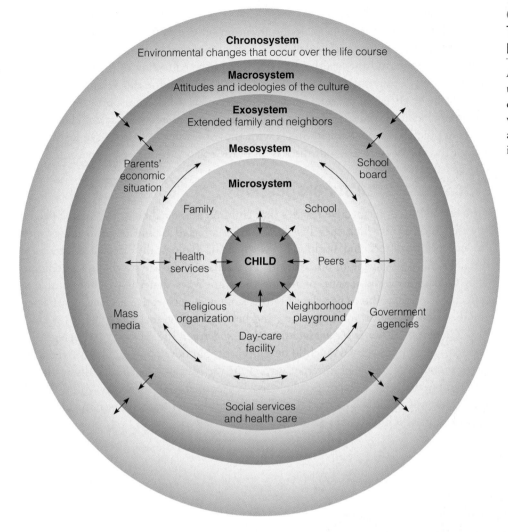

● **Figure 1.4**
The Contexts of Human Development

According to ecological systems theory, the systems within which children develop are embedded within larger systems. Children and these systems reciprocally influence each other.

address the effects of housing, health care, TV programs, church attendance, government agencies, or even iPods on children examine the interactions of the exosystem with the child (Kaminski & Stormshak, 2007).

The **macrosystem** involves the interaction of children with the beliefs, values, expectations, and lifestyles of their cultural settings. Cross-cultural studies examine children's interactions with their macrosystem. Macrosystems exist within a particular culture as well. For example, in the United States, the two-wage-earner family, the low-income single-parent household, and the family with father as sole breadwinner describe three different macrosystems. Each has its lifestyle, set of values, and expectations (Bronfenbrenner & Morris, 2006; Silbereisen, 2006). One issue affecting children is multiculturalism. A study of 258 Mexican American eighth- to eleventh-graders found that those who perceived their environment to be multicultural found school to be easier, obtained higher grades, and were more likely to stay in school (Tan, 1999).

The **chronosystem** considers the changes that occur over time. For example, the effects of divorce peak about a year after the event, and then children begin to recover (see Chapter 13). The breakup has more of an effect on boys than on girls. The ecological approach broadens the strategies for intervention in problems such as prevention of teenage pregnancy, child abuse, and juvenile offending, including substance abuse (Kaminski & Stormshak, 2007).

macrosystem The basic institutions and ideologies that influence the child, such as the American ideals of freedom of expression and equality under the law (from the Greek *makros*, meaning "long" or "enlarged").

chronosystem The environmental changes that occur over time and have an effect on the child (from the Greek *chronos*, meaning "time").

Evaluation

Ecological systems theory helps focus attention on the shifting systems with which children interact as they as they develop. The health of the infant requires relationships between parents and the health-care system, and the education of the child requires relationships between parents and schools. At the level of the exosystem, researchers look into the effects of parents' work lives, welfare agencies, transportation systems, shopping facilities, and so on. At the level of the macrosystem, we may compare child-rearing practices in the United States with those in other countries. We learn more about the role of culture in our discussion of the sociocultural perspective.

The Sociocultural Perspective

The sociocultural perspective teaches that children are social beings who are affected by the cultures in which they live. Yes, we are affected by biochemical forces such as neurotransmitters and hormones. We may be biologically "prewired" to form attachments and engage in other behaviors. Perhaps there are psychological tendencies to learn in certain ways, or maybe there are ways that the psychological past affects the present. But as noted within the ecological perspective, we are also affected by the customs, traditions, languages, and heritages of the societies in which we live.

Question: What is the sociocultural perspective? The sociocultural perspective overlaps other perspectives on child development, but developmentalists use the term *sociocultural* in a couple of different ways. One way refers quite specifically to the *sociocultural theory* of Russian psychologist Lev Semenovich Vygotsky (1896–1934). The other way broadly addresses the effect on children of human diversity, including such factors as ethnicity and gender.

Developing in a
World of Diversity

Influence of the Macrosystem on the Development of Independence

Cross-cultural studies provide interesting insights into the way children interact with their macrosystems. Consider the development of independence. Among the !Kung people of Namibia, babies are kept in close contact with their mothers during the first year (Konner, 1977). !Kung infants are frequently carried in slings across their mothers' hips that allow the mothers to nurse at will, literally all day long. The !Kung seem to follow the commandment "The infant shall not go hungry," not even for 5 seconds. In every way, !Kung mothers try to respond at once to their babies' cries and whims. By Western standards, !Kung babies are "spoiled." However, overindulgence does not appear to make !Kung babies overly dependent on their mothers. By the time the babies are capable of walking, they do. They do not cling to their mothers. In comparison to Western children of the same age, !Kung children spend less time with their mothers and more time with their peers.

Also compare Urie Bronfenbrenner's (1973) observations of child rearing in the United States and Russia. Russian babies, as a group, are more likely than U.S. babies to be cuddled, kissed, and hugged. Russian mothers are not quite so solicitous as their !Kung counterparts, but they are highly protective compared with U.S. mothers. However, Russian children are taught to take care of themselves at younger ages than U.S. children. By 18 months of age, Russian children are usually learning to dress themselves and are largely toilet trained.

Vygotsky's Sociocultural Theory

Whereas genetics is concerned with the biological transmission of traits from generation to generation, Vygotsky's (1978) theory is concerned with the transmission of information and cognitive skills from generation to generation. The transmission of skills involves teaching and learning, but Vygotsky does not view learning in terms of the conditioning of behavior. Rather, he focuses on how the child's social interaction with adults, largely in the home, organizes a child's learning experiences in such a way that the child can obtain cognitive skills—such as computation or reading skills—and use them to acquire information. Like Piaget, Vygotsky sees the child's functioning as adaptive (Kanevsky & Geake, 2004), and the child adapts to his or her social and cultural interactions.

Question: What are the key concepts of Vygotsky's sociocultural theory? Key concepts in Vygotsky's theory include the *zone of proximal development* and *scaffolding*. The word *proximal* means "nearby" or "close," as in the words *approximate* and *proximity*. The **zone of proximal development (ZPD)** refers to a range of tasks that a child can carry out with the help of someone who is more skilled. It is similar to an apprenticeship. Many developmentalists find that observing how a child learns when working with others provides more information about that child's cognitive abilities than does a simple inventory of knowledge (Meijer & Elshout, 2001). When learning with other people, the child tends to internalize—or bring inward—the conversations and explanations that help him or her gain the necessary skills (Ash, 2004; Umek et al., 2005; Vygotsky, 1962). In other words, children not only learn the meanings of words from teachers but also learn ways of talking to themselves about solving problems within a cultural context (Murata & Fuson, 2006). Outer speech becomes inner speech. What was the teacher's becomes the child's. What was a social and cultural context becomes embedded within the child.

A *scaffold* is a temporary skeletal structure that enables workers to fabricate a building, bridge, or other more permanent structure. In Vygotsky's theory, teachers and parents provide children with problem-solving methods that serve as cognitive **scaffolding** while the child gains the ability to function independently. For example, a child's instructors may offer advice on sounding out letters and words that provide a temporary support until reading "clicks" and the child no longer needs the device. Children may be offered scaffolding that enables them to use their fingers or their toes to do simple calculations. Eventually, the scaffolding is removed and the cognitive structures stand alone. A Puerto Rican study found that students also use scaffolding when they are explaining to one another how they can improve school projects, such as essay assignments (Guerrero & Villamil, 2000). Vygotsky's theory points out that children's attitudes toward schooling are embedded within the parent–child relationship.

The Sociocultural Perspective and Human Diversity

The field of child development focuses mainly on individuals and is committed to the dignity of the individual child. *Question: What is the connection between the sociocultural perspective and human diversity?* The sociocultural perspective asserts that we cannot understand individual children without awareness of the richness of their diversity (Fouad & Arredondo, 2007). For example, children diverge or differ in their ethnicity, gender, and socioeconomic status.

Children's **ethnic groups** involve their cultural heritage, their race, their language, and their common history. ● Figures 1.5 and ● 1.6 highlight the population shifts under way in the United States as a result of reproductive patterns and immigration. The numbers of African Americans and Latino and Latina Americans (who

Lev Semonovich Vygotsky
Vygotsky is known for showing how social speech becomes inner speech and how "scaffolding" by others assists children in developing the cognitive skills to succeed.

Archives of the History of American Psychology—The University of Akron

zone of proximal development (ZPD) Vygotsky's term for the situation in which a child carries out tasks with the help of someone who is more skilled, frequently an adult who represents the culture in which the child develops.

scaffolding Vygotsky's term for temporary cognitive structures or methods of solving problems that help the child as he or she learns to function independently.

ethnic groups Groups of people distinguished by cultural heritage, race, language, and common history.

● **Figure 1.5**

Numbers of Various Racial and Ethnic Groups in the United States, Year 2000 versus Year 2050 (in millions)

The numbers of each of the various racial and ethnic groups in the United States will grow over the next half-century, with the numbers of Latino and Latina Americans and Asian Americans and Pacific Islanders growing most rapidly.

Source: U.S. Bureau of the Census (2004).

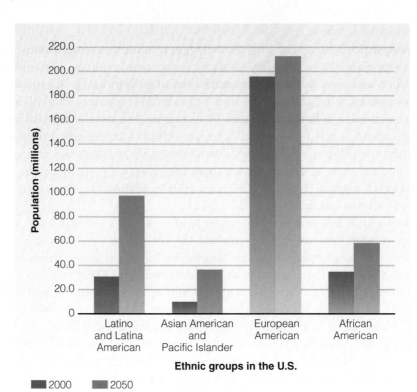

● **Figure 1.6**

Percentages of Various Racial and Ethnic Groups in the United States, Year 2000 versus Year 2050

Although European Americans are projected to remain the most populous ethnic group in the United States in the year 2050, the group's percentage of the population will diminish from 72% to 53%. But because of general population growth, there will still be more European Americans in the United States in 2050 than there are today.

Source: U.S. Bureau of the Census (2004).

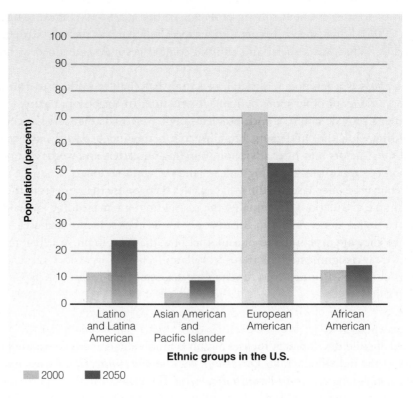

may be White, Black, or Native American in racial origin) are growing more rapidly than those of European Americans (U.S. Bureau of the Census, 2006). The cultural heritages, languages, and histories of ethnic minority groups are thus likely to have an increasing effect on the cultural life of the United States. Yet it turns out that the dominant culture in the United States has often disparaged the traditions and languages of people from ethnic minority groups. For example, it has been considered harmful to rear children bilingually, although research suggests that bilingualism broadens children, as we see in Chapter 12.

Studying diversity is also important so that children have appropriate educational experiences. To teach children and guide their learning, educators need to understand children's family values and cultural expectations. Many professionals—psychologists, teachers, social workers, psychiatrists, and others—are called on to help children and families who are having problems in school or in the community. Professionals may need special training to identify the problems of children and families from ethnic minority groups and to treat them in culturally sensitive ways (Constantine, 2007; Fu et al., 2007; Torres & Rollock, 2007).

Throughout the text, we consider many issues that affect children from various ethnic groups. A handful of them include bilingualism, ethnic differences in intelligence test scores, the prevalence of suicide among members of different ethnic minority groups, and patterns of child rearing among parents of various ethnic minority groups.

Gender is another aspect of human diversity. Gender is the psychological state of being male or being female, as influenced by cultural concepts of gender-appropriate behavior. The French have a saying, *Vive la différence* ("Long live the difference!"), which celebrates the difference between females and males. The French expression exudes the excitement people may feel when they are interacting with individuals of the other sex, but, unfortunately, it also alludes to the problem that females and males are often polarized by cultural expectations. That is, the differences may be exaggerated, as in the case of intellectual abilities. Put it this way: Males may very well differ from females in some respects, but history has created more burdens for women than men as a result. Gender-role expectations affect children's self-esteem and limit their hopes and dreams for the future.

Historically, girls have been discouraged from careers in the sciences, politics, and business. Women today are making inroads into academic and vocational spheres—such as medicine, law, engineering, and the military—that were traditionally male preserves. Today, most college students in the United States are female, but it is worth noting that girls were not considered qualified for education until relatively recent times. Who, for example, is Lucinda Foote? She was a brilliant young woman who is known to us only because of her rejection letter from Yale University in 1792, which confirmed that she was qualified for Yale in every way *except* for her sex (Leon, 2001). It may surprise you to learn that women were not admitted to college in the United States until 1833, the year that Oberlin College opened its doors to women. Even today, however, there remain many—many!—parts of the world in which women are prevented from obtaining an education.

Opportunities for women are crucial to the development of girls. Opportunities for adults give children their sense of what is possible for them. Just as many children from ethnic minority groups wonder whether they can experience the rewards and opportunities they see in the dominant culture, so do girls wonder whether the career and social roles they admire are available to them. I was surprised to learn that my daughters once thought that the presidency of the United States was open only to men. The effects of cultural expectations on girls' self-concepts and motivation are clear and compelling.

In this book, the focus on human diversity extends beyond ethnicity and gender to include children with various sexual orientations and disabilities. This approach broadens our understanding of all children as they experience the developmental changes brought about by quite different influences of heredity and experience.

Concept Review 1.3 summarizes similarities and differences among the perspectives on child development.

gender The psychological state of being female or male, as influenced by cultural concepts of gender-appropriate behavior. Compare and contrast the concept of gender with *anatomic sex*, which is based on the physical differences between females and males.

Active Review

4. _____ are intended to allow us to explain, predict, and control events.

5. _____ hypothesized five stages of psychosexual development.

6. Erikson extended Freud's five stages of development to _____.

7. Behaviorism sees children's learning as mechanical and relies on classical and _____ conditioning.

8. According to _____, children assimilate new events to existing schemes or accommodate schemes to incorporate novel events.

9. Information-_____ theory focuses on the processes by which information is encoded, stored, retrieved, and manipulated.

10. The _____ systems theory explains child development in terms of the interaction between children and the settings in which they live.

11. Vygotsky's _____ theory is concerned with the transmission of information and cognitive skills from generation to generation.

Reflect & Relate: How have your ethnic background and your sex influenced your development? Consider factors such as race, country of origin, language, nutrition, values, and the dominant culture's reaction to people of your background.

Go to

http://www.thomsonedu.com/psychology/rathus

for an interactive version of this review.

Controversies in Child Development

The discussion of theories of development reveals that developmentalists can see things in very different ways. Let us consider how they react to three of the most important debates in the field.

The Nature–Nurture Controversy

Question: Which exerts the greater influence on children, nature or nurture? Think about your friends for a moment. Some may be tall and lanky, others short and stocky. Some are outgoing and sociable, others more reserved and quiet. One may be a good athlete, another a fine musician. What made them this way? How much does inheritance have to do with it, and how much does the environment play a role?

Researchers are continually trying to sort out the extent to which human behavior is the result of **nature** (heredity) and of **nurture** (environmental influences). What aspects of behavior originate in our **genes** and are biologically programmed to unfold in the child as time goes on, as long as minimal nutrition and social experience are provided? What aspects of behavior can be traced largely to such environmental influences as nutrition and learning?

Scientists seek the natural causes of development in children's genetic heritage, the functioning of the nervous system, and in maturation. Scientists seek the environmental causes of development in children's nutrition, cultural and family backgrounds, and opportunities to learn about the world, including cognitive stimulation during early childhood and formal education.

Some theorists (e.g., cognitive-developmental and biological theorists) lean heavily toward natural explanations of development, whereas others (e.g., learning the-

nature The processes within an organism that guide that organism to develop according to its genetic code.

nurture The processes external to an organism that nourish it as it develops according to its genetic code or that cause it to swerve from its genetically programmed course. Environmental factors that influence development.

genes The basic building blocks of heredity.

orists) lean more heavily toward environmental explanations. But today nearly all researchers agree that nature and nurture play important roles in nearly every area of child development. Consider the development of language. Language is based in structures found in certain areas of the brain. Thus, biology (nature) plays a vital role in language development. But children also come to speak the languages spoken by their caretakers. Parent–child similarities in accent and vocabulary provide additional evidence for the role of learning (nurture) in language development.

The Continuity–Discontinuity Controversy

Question: Is development continuous or discontinuous? Do developmental changes occur gradually (continuously), the way a seedling becomes a tree? Or do changes occur in major qualitative leaps (discontinuously) that dramatically alter our bodies and behavior, the way a caterpillar turns into a butterfly?

Some developmentalists view human development as a continuous process in which the effects of learning mount gradually, with no major sudden qualitative changes. In contrast, other theorists believe that a number of rapid qualitative changes usher in new stages of development. Maturational theorists point out that the environment, even when enriched, profits us little until we are ready, or mature enough, to develop in a certain way. For example, newborn babies will not imitate their parents' speech, even when parents speak clearly and deliberately. Nor does aided practice in "walking" during the first few months after birth significantly accelerate the emergence of independent walking. They are not ready to do these things.

Stage theorists such as Sigmund Freud and Jean Piaget saw development as discontinuous. They saw biological changes as providing the potential for psychological changes. Freud focused on the ways in which biological developments might provide the basis for personality development. Piaget believed maturation of the nervous system allowed cognitive development.

Certain aspects of physical development do occur in stages. For example, from the age of 2 years to the onset of puberty, children gradually grow larger. Then the adolescent growth spurt occurs as rushes of hormones cause rapid biological changes in structure and function (as in the development of the sex organs) and in size. Psychologists disagree on whether developments in cognition occur in stages.

The Active–Passive Controversy

Question: Are children active (prewired to act on the world) or passive (shaped by experience)? Broadly speaking, all animals are active. But in the field of child development, the issue has a more specific meaning.

Historical views of children as willful and unruly suggest that people have generally seen children as active, even if mischievous (at best) or evil (at worst). John Locke introduced a view of children as passive beings (blank tablets); experience "wrote" features of personality and moral virtue on them.

At one extreme, educators who view children as passive may assume that they must be motivated to learn by their instructors. Such educators are likely to provide a traditional curriculum with rigorous exercises in spelling, music, and math to promote absorption of the subject matter. They are also likely to apply a powerful system of rewards and punishments to keep children on the straight and narrow.

© Mark Richards/PhotoEdit

Stages of Physical Development
Certain aspects of physical development seem to occur in stages. Girls usually spurt in growth before boys. The girl and boy who are dancing are the same age.

At the other extreme, educators who view children as active may assume that they have a natural love of learning. Such educators are likely to argue for open education and encourage children to explore an environment rich with learning materials. Such educators are likely to listen to the children to learn about their unique likes and talents and then support children as they pursue their own agendas.

These examples are extremes. Most educators probably agree that children show individual differences and that some children require more guidance and external motivation than others. In addition, children can be active in some subjects and passive in others. Whether children who do not actively seek to master certain subjects are coerced tends to depend on how important the subject is to functioning in today's society, the age of the child, the attitudes of the parents, and many other factors.

Urie Bronfenbrenner (Bronfenbrenner & Morris, 2006) argued that we miss the point when we assume that children are entirely active or passive. Children are influenced by the environment, but children also influence the environment. The challenge is to observe the ways in which children interact with their settings. Albert Bandura (2006a, 2006b) also refers to the two-way influences between children and the environment.

empirical Based on observation and experimentation.

These debates are theoretical. Scientists value theory for its ability to tie together observations and suggest new areas of investigation, but they also follow an **empirical** approach. That is, they engage in research methods, such as those described in the next section, to find evidence for or against various theoretical positions.

Active Review

12. Researchers in child development try to sort out the effects of _____ (heredity) and nurture (environmental influences).
13. Learning theorists tend to see development as continuous, whereas stage theorists see development as _____.

Reflect & Relate: Consider the active–passive controversy. Do you see yourself as being active or passive? Explain.

Go to

http://www.thomsonedu.com/psychology/rathus

for an interactive version of this review.

How Do We Study Child Development?

What is the relationship between children's intelligence and their achievement? What are the effects of maternal use of aspirin and alcohol on the fetus? How can you rear children to become competent and independent? What are the effects of parental divorce on children? We may have expressed opinions on such questions at one time or another. But scientists insist that such questions be answered by research. Strong arguments or reference to authority figures are not evidence. Scientific evidence is obtained only by the scientific method. *Question: What is the scientific method?*

The Scientific Method

The scientific method is a systematic way of forming and answering research questions. It allows scientists to test the theories discussed in the previous section. The scientific method has five steps.

Step 1: Forming a Research Question

Our daily experiences, theory, and even folklore help generate questions for research. Daily experience in using day-care centers may stimulate us to wonder whether day care affects children's intellectual or social development or the bonds of attachment between children and parents. Reading about observational learning may suggest research into the effects of TV violence.

Step 2: Developing a Hypothesis

The second step is the development of a hypothesis. A **hypothesis** is a specific statement about behavior that is tested through research. One hypothesis about day care might be that preschool children placed in day care will acquire better skills in getting along with other children than will preschoolers who are cared for in the home. A hypothesis about TV violence might be that elementary school children who watch more violent TV shows will behave more aggressively toward other children.

Step 3: Testing the Hypothesis

The third step is testing the hypothesis. Psychologists test the hypothesis through carefully controlled information-gathering techniques and research methods, such as **naturalistic observation**, the case study, correlation, and the experiment.

For example, we could introduce two groups of children—children who are in day care and children who are not in day care—to a new child in a college child-research center and see how each group acts toward the new child. Concerning the effects of TV violence, we could have parents help us tally which TV shows their children watch and rate the shows for violent content. Then we could ask the children's teachers to report how aggressively the children act toward classmates. We could do some math to determine whether more aggressive children also watch more violence on TV. We describe research methods such as these later in the chapter.

The Scientific Method
What is the cause of this girl's aggression? Would she behave differently if the other child reacted to her with anger instead of fear? How does the scientific method help us answer this type of question?

Step 4: Drawing Conclusions about the Hypothesis

The fourth step is drawing conclusions. Psychologists draw conclusions about the accuracy of their hypotheses from their research results. When research does not bear out their hypotheses, the researchers may modify the theories from which the hypotheses were derived. Research findings often suggest new hypotheses and new studies.

In our research on the effects of day care, we would probably find that children in day care show somewhat greater social skills than children cared for in the home (see Chapter 7). We would probably also find that more aggressive children spend more time watching TV violence, as we shall see in Chapter 10. But we will also see in the following pages that it might be wrong to conclude from this kind of evidence that TV violence *causes* aggressive behavior.

Step 5: Publishing Findings

Scientists publish their research findings in professional journals and make their data available to scientists and the public at large for scrutiny. Thus, they give other scientists the opportunity to review their data and conclusions to help determine the accuracy of the research.

hypothesis (high-POTH-uh-sis) A Greek word meaning "groundwork" or "foundation" that has come to mean a specific statement about behavior that is tested by research.

naturalistic observation A method of scientific observation in which children (and others) are observed in their natural environments.

Now let us consider the information-gathering techniques and the research methods used by developmentalists. Then we will discuss ethical issues concerning research in child development.

Gathering Information

Developmentalists use various methods to gather information. For example, they may ask children to keep diaries of their behavior, ask teachers or parents to report on the behavior of their children, or use interviews or questionnaires with children themselves. They also directly observe children in the laboratory or in the natural setting. Let us discuss two ways of gathering information: the naturalistic-observation method and the case-study method.

Naturalistic Observation

Question: What is naturalistic observation? Naturalistic-observation studies of children are conducted in "the field," that is, in the natural, or real-life, settings in which they happen. In field studies, investigators observe the natural behavior of children in settings such as homes, playgrounds, and classrooms and try not to interfere with it. Interference could affect or "bias" the results. Researchers may try to "blend into the woodwork" by sitting quietly in the back of a classroom or by observing the class through a one-way mirror.

A number of naturalistic-observation studies have been done with children of different cultures. For example, researchers have observed the motor behavior of Native American Hopi children who are strapped to cradle boards during the first year. They have observed language development in the United States, Mexico, Turkey, Kenya, and China—seeking universals that might suggest a major role for maturation in the acquisition of language skills. They have also observed the ways in which children are socialized in Russia, Israel, Japan, and other nations in an effort to determine what patterns of child rearing are associated with development of behaviors such as attachment and independence.

The Case Study

Another way of gathering information about children is the case-study method. *Question: What is the case study?* The **case study** is a carefully drawn account of the behavior of an individual. Parents who keep diaries of their children's activities

case study A carefully drawn biography of the life of an individual.

standardized test A test of some ability or trait in which an individual's score is compared to the scores of a group of similar individuals.

What Is the Relationship Between Intelligence and Achievement?
Does the correlational method allow us to say that intelligence causes or is responsible for academic achievement? Why or why not?

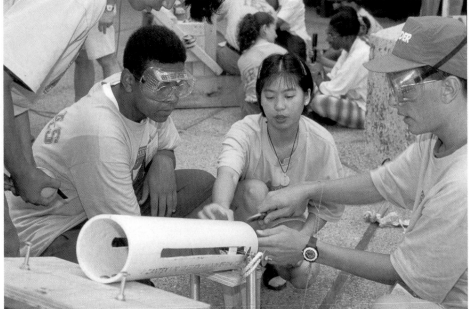

© Bob Daemmrich/The Image Works

are involved in informal case studies. Case studies themselves often use a number of different kinds of information about children. In addition to direct observation, case studies may include questionnaires, **standardized tests**, and interviews with the child and his or her parents, teachers, and friends. Information gleaned from school and other records may be included. Scientists who use the case-study method take great pains to record all the relevant factors in a child's behavior, and they are cautious in drawing conclusions about what leads to what.

Jean Piaget used the case-study method in carefully observing and recording the behavior of children, including his own (see Chapter 6). Sigmund Freud developed his psychoanalytic theory largely on the basis of case studies. Freud studied his patients in great depth and followed some of them for many years.

Correlation: Putting Things Together

Question: What does it mean to correlate information? Correlation is a mathematical method that researchers use to determine whether one behavior or trait being studied is related to, or correlated with, another. Consider, for example, the **variables** of intelligence and achievement. These variables are assigned numbers such as intelligence test scores and academic grade averages. Then the numbers or scores are mathematically related and expressed as a correlation coefficient. A **correlation coefficient** is a number that varies between +1.00 and −1.00.

Numerous studies report **positive correlations** between intelligence and achievement. In general, the higher children score on intelligence tests, the better their academic performance is likely to be. The scores attained on intelligence tests are positively correlated (about +0.60 to +0.70) with overall academic achievement.[1]

There is a **negative correlation** between children's school grades and their commission of delinquent acts. The higher a child's grades in school, the less likely the child is to engage in criminal behavior. ● Figure 1.7 illustrates positive and negative correlations.

Limitations of Correlational Information

Correlational information can reveal relationships between variables, but they do not show cause and effect. For example, children who watch TV shows with a lot of violence are more likely to show aggressive behavior at home and in school. It may seem logical to assume that exposure to TV violence makes children more aggressive. But it may be that children who are more aggressive to begin with prefer violent TV shows. The relationship between viewing violence and behaving aggressively may not be so clear-cut.

Similarly, studies in locations as far-flung as the United States and China report that children (especially boys) in divorced families sometimes show more problems than do children in intact families (Greene et al., 2006; Lansford et al., 2006). However, these studies do not show that divorce causes these adjustment problems. It could be that the factors that led to divorce (such as parental disorganization or conflict) also led to adjustment problems among the children (Hetherington, 2006). Or it may be that having a child with problems might put a strain on the parents' marriage and ultimately be a factor contributing to divorce.

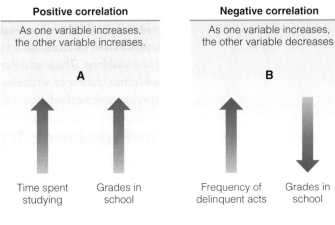

Positive correlation	Negative correlation
As one variable increases, the other variable increases.	As one variable increases, the other variable decreases.
A	B
Time spent studying — Grades in school	Frequency of delinquent acts — Grades in school

● **Figure 1.7**
Examples of Positive and Negative Correlations

When two variables are correlated *positively*, one increases as the other increases. There is a positive correlation between the amount of time spent studying and grades, as shown in Part A. When two variables are correlated *negatively*, one increases as the other decreases. There is a negative correlation between the frequency of a child's delinquent acts and his or her grades, as shown in Part B. As one's delinquent behavior increases, grades tend to decline.

variables Quantities that can vary from child to child or from occasion to occasion, such as height, weight, intelligence, and attention span.

correlation coefficient A number ranging from +1.00 to −1.00 that expresses the direction (positive or negative) and strength of the relationship between two variables.

positive correlation A relationship between two variables in which one variable increases as the other variable increases.

negative correlation A relationship between two variables in which one variable increases as the other variable decreases.

---

[1]Of course, +0.60 is the same as +.60. We insert the zeros to help prevent the decimal points from getting lost.

Concept Review 1.4   Comparison of Cross-Sectional and Longitudinal Research

	Cross-Sectional Research	Longitudinal Research
Description	• Studies children of different ages at the same point in time	• Studies the same children repeatedly over time
Advantages	• Can be completed in short period of time • No drop-out or practice effects	• Allows researchers to follow development over time • Studies the relationships between behavior at earlier and later ages
Disadvantages	• Does not study development across time • Cannot study relationship between behavior displayed at earlier and later ages • Is prey to cohort effect (subjects from different age groups may not be comparable)	• Expensive • Takes a long time to complete • Subjects drop out • Subjects who drop out may differ systematically from those who remain in the study • Practice effects may occur

Is Surfing the Internet an Activity That Illustrates the Cohort Effect?
Children and adults of different ages experience cultural and other events unique to their age group. Such experience is known as the cohort effect. For example, today's children—unlike their parents—are growing up taking video games, the Internet, and rap stars for granted.

touch as the years pass; others die. Also, those who remain in the study tend to be more motivated than those who drop out. The researchers must be patient. To compare 3-year-olds with 6-year-olds, they must wait 3 years. In the early stages of such a study, the idea of comparing 3-year-olds with 21-year-olds remains a distant dream. When the researchers themselves are middle-aged or older, they must hope that the candle of yearning for knowledge will be kept lit by a new generation of researchers.

Cross-Sectional Studies

Because of the drawbacks of longitudinal studies, most research that compares children of different ages is cross-sectional. In other words, most investigators gather data on what the "typical" 6-month-old is doing by finding children who are 6 months old today. When they expand their research to the behavior of typical 12-month-olds, they seek another group of children, and so on.

A major challenge to cross-sectional research is the **cohort effect**. A cohort is a group of people born at about the same time. As a result, they experience cultural and other events unique to their age group. In other words, children and adults of different ages are not likely to have shared similar cultural backgrounds. People who are 70 years old today, for example, grew up without TV. (Really, there was a time when television did not exist.) People who are 60 years old today grew up before people landed on the Moon. Nor did today's 50-year-olds spend their earliest years with *Sesame Street*. And today's children are growing up taking iPods and the Internet for granted. In fact, for today's children, Jennifer Lopez is an older woman.

Children of past generations also grew up with different expectations about gender roles and appropriate social behavior. Women in the Terman study generally chose motherhood over careers because of the times. Today's girls are growing up with female role models who are astronauts, government officials, and athletes. More-

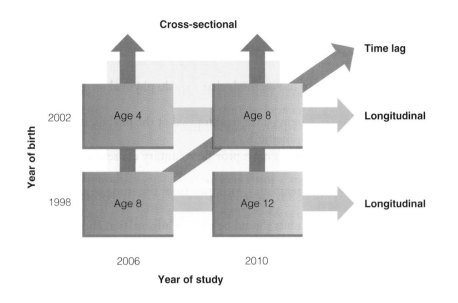

● **Figure 1.8**
Example of Cross-Sequential Research

Cross-sequential research combines three methods: cross-sectional, longitudinal, and time lag. The child's age at the time of testing appears in the boxes. Vertical columns represent cross-sectional comparisons. Horizontal rows represent longitudinal comparisons. Diagonals represent time-lag comparisons.

over, today the great majority of mothers are in the workforce, and their attitudes about women's roles have changed.

In other words, today's 75-year-olds are not today's 5-year-olds as seen 70 years later. The times change, and their influence on children changes also. In longitudinal studies, we know that we have the same individuals as they have developed over 5, 25, even 50 years or more. In cross-sectional research, we can only hope that they will be comparable.

Cross-Sequential Research

Cross-sequential research combines the longitudinal and cross-sectional methods so that many of their individual drawbacks are overcome. In the cross-sequential study, the full span of the ideal longitudinal study is broken up into convenient segments (see ● Figure 1.8). Assume that we wish to follow the attitudes of children toward gender roles from the age of 4 through the age of 12. The typical longitudinal study would take 8 years. However, we can divide this 8-year span in half by obtaining two samples of children (a cross-section) instead of one: 4-year-olds and 8-year-olds. We would then interview, test, and observe each group at the beginning of the study (2006) and 4 years later (2010). By the time of the second observation period, the 4-year-olds would have become 8 years old and the 8-year-olds would have become 12.

An obvious advantage to this collapsed method is that the study is completed in 4 years rather than 8 years. Still, the testing and retesting of samples provides some of the continuity of the longitudinal study. By observing both samples at the age of 8 (a **time-lag** comparison), we can also determine whether they are, in fact, comparable or whether the 4-year difference in their birthdates is associated with a cohort effect, that is, cultural and other environmental changes that lead to different attitudes.

Ethical Considerations

Researchers adhere to ethical standards that are intended to promote the dignity of the individual, foster human welfare, and maintain scientific integrity. These standards also ensure that they do not use methods or treatments that harm subjects. *Question: What ethical guidelines are involved in research in child development?*

Various professional groups, such as the American Psychological Association and the Society for Research in Child Development, and government review

cohort effect Similarities in behavior among a group of peers that stem from the fact that group members are approximately of the same age. (A possible source of misleading information in cross-sectional research.)

cross-sequential research An approach that combines the longitudinal and cross-sectional methods by following individuals of different ages for abbreviated periods of time.

time lag The study of developmental processes by taking measures of children of the same age group at different times.

11.	**What is the scope of the biological perspective?**	The biological perspective refers to heredity and to developments such as formation of sperm and ova, gains in height and weight, maturation of the nervous system, and the way hormones spur the changes of puberty.
12.	**What is ethology?**	Ethology involves instinctive, or inborn, behavior patterns, termed *fixed action patterns (FAPs)*. Many FAPs, such as those involved in attachment, occur during a *critical period* of life.
13.	**What is the ecological systems theory of child development?**	Bronfenbrenner's ecological theory explains development in terms of the *reciprocal interaction* between children and the settings in which development occurs. These settings are the *microsystem, mesosystem, exosystem, macrosystem*, and *chronosystem*.
14.	**What is meant by the sociocultural perspective?**	The sociocultural perspective emphasizes that children are social beings who are influenced by their cultural backgrounds.
15.	**What are the key concepts of Vygotsky's sociocultural theory?**	Vygotsky's key concepts are the *zone of proximal development (ZPD)* and *scaffolding*. Children internalize conversations and explanations that help them gain skills. Children learn ways of solving problems within a cultural context.
16.	**What is the connection between the sociocultural perspective and human diversity?**	The sociocultural perspective addresses the richness of children's diversity, as in their ethnicity and sex. Understanding the cultural heritages and historical problems of children from various ethnic groups is necessary for education and psychological intervention.
17.	**Which exerts the greater influence on children, nature or nurture?**	Development would appear to reflect the interaction of nature (genetics) and nurture (nutrition, cultural and family backgrounds, and opportunities to learn about the world).
18.	**Is development continuous or discontinuous?**	Maturational, psychoanalytic, and cognitive-developmental theorists see development as discontinuous (occurring in stages). Aspects of physical development, such as the adolescent growth spurt, do occur in stages. Learning theorists tend to see development as more continuous.
19.	**Are children active ("prewired" to act on the world), or are they passive (shaped by experience)?**	Bronfenbrenner and Bandura do not see children as entirely active or entirely passive. They believe that children are influenced by the environment but that the influence is reciprocal.
20.	**What is the scientific method?**	The scientific method is a systematic way of formulating and answering research questions that includes formulating a research question, developing a hypothesis, testing the hypothesis, drawing conclusions, and publishing results.
21.	**What is naturalistic observation?**	Naturalistic observation is conducted in "the field," in the actual settings in which children develop.

22. **What is the case study?**	The case study is a carefully drawn account or biography of the behavior of a child. Information may be derived from diaries, observation, questionnaires, standardized tests, interviews, and public records.
23. **What does it mean to correlate information?**	Correlation enables researchers to determine whether one behavior or trait is related to another. A correlation coefficient can vary between $+1.00$ and -1.00. Correlational studies reveal relationships but not cause and effect.
24. **What is an experiment?**	In an experiment, an experimental group receives a treatment (independent variable), whereas another group (a control group) does not. Subjects are observed to determine whether the treatment has an effect.
25. **How do researchers study development over time?**	Longitudinal research studies the same children repeatedly over time. Cross-sectional research observes and compares children of different ages. A drawback to cross-sectional research is the cohort effect. Cross-sequential research combines the longitudinal and cross-sectional methods by breaking down the full span of the ideal longitudinal study into convenient segments.
26. **What ethical guidelines are involved in research in child development?**	Ethical standards promote the dignity of the individual, foster human welfare, and maintain scientific integrity. Researchers are not to use treatments that may do harm. Subjects must participate voluntarily.

Key Terms

child, 4
infancy, 4
conception, 4
prenatal period, 4
development, 4
motor development, 4
growth, 4
gender roles, 5
PKU, 5
SIDS, 5
behaviorism, 8
maturation, 8
theory, 8
psychosexual development, 9
stage theory, 9
unconscious, 10
psychosocial development, 10
life crisis, 11
identity crisis, 11
behavior modification, 13
classical conditioning, 13
stimulus, 13

elicit, 13
unconditioned stimulus (UCS), 13
unconditioned response (UCR), 13
conditioned stimulus (CS), 14
conditioned response (CR), 14
operant conditioning, 14
reinforcement, 14
positive reinforcer, 14
negative reinforcer, 14
extinction, 14
punishment, 14
time out, 16
shaping, 16
socialization, 16
social cognitive theory, 17
observational learning, 17
cognitive-developmental theory, 18
scheme, 18
adaptation, 19
assimilation, 19
accommodation, 19

equilibration, 19
ethology, 21
fixed action pattern (FAP), 21
ecology, 22
ecological systems theory, 22
microsystem, 22
mesosystem, 22
exosystem, 22
macrosystem, 23
chronosystem, 23
zone of proximal development (ZPD), 25
scaffolding, 25
ethnic groups, 25
gender, 27
nature, 30
nurture, 30
genes, 30
empirical, 32
hypothesis, 33
naturalistic observation, 33
case study, 34

Active Learning Resources

Childhood & Adolescence Book Companion Website

http://www.thomsonedu.com/psychology/rathus

Visit your book companion website, where you will find more resources to help you study. There you will find interactive versions of your book features, including the Lessons in Observation video, Active Review sections, and the Truth or Fiction feature. In addition, the companion website contains quizzing, flash cards, and a pronunciation glossary.

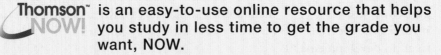 is an easy-to-use online resource that helps you study in less time to get the grade you want, NOW.

http://www.thomsonedu.com/login

Need help studying? This site is your one-stop study shop. Take a Pre-Test and ThomsonNOW will generate a Personalized Study Plan based on your test results. The Study Plan will identify the topics you need to review and direct you to online resources to help you master those topics. You can then take a Post-Test to determine the concepts you have mastered and what you still need to work on.

2

Heredity and Conception

Truth or Fiction?

T F Your father determined whether you are female or male. p. 49

T F Brown eyes are dominant over blue eyes. p. 51

T F You can carry the genes for a deadly illness and not become sick yourself. p. 52

T F Girls are born with all the egg cells they will ever have. p. 64

T F Approximately 120 to 150 boys are conceived for every 100 girls. p. 65

T F Sperm travel about at random inside the woman's reproductive tract, so reaching the ovum is a matter of luck. p. 65

T F Extensive athletic activity may contribute to infertility in the male. p. 67

T F "Test-tube" babies are grown in a laboratory dish throughout their 9-month gestation period. p. 68

Preview

Go to

http://www.thomsonedu.com/psychology/rathus
for an interactive version of this "Truth or Fiction" feature.

© Paul Kuroda/Super Stock

et's talk about the facts of life. Here are a few of them:

- People cannot breathe underwater (without special equipment).
- People cannot fly (without special equipment).
- Fish cannot learn to speak French or dance an Irish jig, even if you raise them in enriched environments and send them to finishing school.

We cannot breathe underwater or fly because we have not inherited gills or wings. Fish are similarly limited by their heredity. *Question: What is meant by heredity?* **Heredity** defines one's nature, which is based on the biological transmission of traits and characteristics from one generation to another. Because of their heredity, fish cannot speak French or do a jig.

In this chapter, we explore heredity and conception. We could say that development begins long before conception. Development involves the origins of the genetic structures that determine that human embryos will grow arms rather than wings, lungs rather than gills, and hair rather than scales. Our discussion thus begins with an examination of the building blocks of heredity: genes and chromosomes. Then, we describe the process of conception and find that the odds against any one sperm uniting with an ovum are quite literally astronomical.

The Influence of Heredity on Development: The Nature of Nature

Heredity makes possible all things human. The structures we inherit make our behavior possible and place limits on it. The field within the science of biology that studies heredity is called **genetics**.

Genetic (inherited) influences are fundamental in the transmission of physical traits, such as height, hair texture, and eye color. Genetics also appears to play a role in intelligence and in traits such as activity level, sociability, shyness, anxiety, empathy, effectiveness as a parent, happiness, even interest in arts and crafts (Johnson & Krueger, 2006; Knafo & Plomin, 2006; Leonardo & Hen, 2006). Genetic factors are also involved in psychological problems such as schizophrenia, depression, and dependence on nicotine, alcohol, and other substances (Farmer et al., 2007; Hill et al., 2007; Metzger et al., 2007; Riley & Kendler, 2005).

Chromosomes and Genes

Heredity is made possible by microscopic structures called chromosomes and genes. *Question: What are chromosomes and genes?* **Chromosomes** are rod-shaped structures found in cells. A normal human cell contains 46 chromosomes organized into 23 pairs. Each chromosome contains thousands of segments called genes. **Genes** are the biochemical materials that regulate the development of traits. Some traits, such as blood type, appear to be transmitted by a single pair of genes, one of which is derived from each parent. Other traits, referred to as **polygenic**, are determined by combinations of pairs of genes.

We have 20,000 to 25,000 genes in every cell of our bodies (International Human Genome Sequencing Consortium, 2006). Genes are segments of large strands of **deoxyribonucleic acid (DNA)**. DNA takes the form of a double spiral, or helix, similar in appearance to a twisting ladder (see ● Figure 2.1). In all living things, from one-celled animals to fish to people, the sides of the "ladder" consist of alternating segments of phosphate (P) and simple sugar (S). The "rungs" of the ladder are attached to the sugars and consist of one of two pairs of bases, either adenine with thymine

heredity The transmission of traits and characteristics from parent to child by means of genes.

genetics The branch of biology that studies heredity.

chromosomes Rod-shaped structures composed of genes that are found within the nuclei of cells.

gene The basic unit of heredity. Genes are composed of deoxyribonucleic acid (DNA).

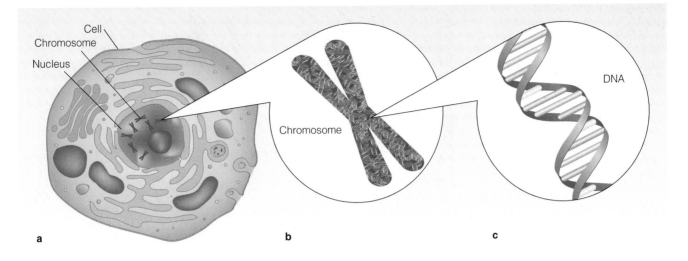

Cell
Chromosome
Nucleus

Chromosome

DNA

a

b

c

● **Figure 2.1**   The Double Helix of DNA

DNA consists of phosphate, sugar, and a number of bases. It takes the form of a double spiral, or helix.

(A with T) or cytosine with guanine (C with G). The sequence of the rungs is the genetic code that will cause the developing organism to grow arms or wings, skin or scales.

Mitosis and Meiosis

We begin life as a single cell, or zygote, that divides again and again. *Question: What happens during cell division?* There are two types of cell division: mitosis and meiosis. **Mitosis** is the cell-division process by which growth occurs and tissues are replaced. Through mitosis, our genetic code is carried into new cells in our bodies. In mitosis, strands of DNA break apart, or "unzip" (see ● Figure 2.2). The double helix then duplicates. The DNA forms two camps on either side of the cell, and then the cell divides. Each incomplete rung combines with the appropriate "partner" element (i.e., G combines with C, A with T, and so on) to form a new complete ladder. The two resulting identical copies of the DNA strand move apart when the cell divides, each becoming a member of one of the newly formed cells. As a consequence, the genetic code is identical in new cells unless **mutations** occur through radiation or other environmental influences. Mutations are also believed to occur by chance, but not often.

Sperm and ova ("egg cells") are produced through **meiosis**, or *reduction division*. In meiosis, the 46 chromosomes within the cell nucleus first line up into 23 pairs. The DNA ladders then unzip, leaving unpaired chromosome halves. When the cell divides, one member of each pair goes to each newly formed cell. As a consequence, each new cell nucleus contains only 23 chromosomes, not 46. Thus, a cell that results from meiosis has half the genetic material of a cell that results from mitosis.

When a sperm cell fertilizes an ovum, we receive 23 chromosomes from our father's sperm cell and 23 from our mother's ovum, and the combined chromosomes form 23 pairs (● Figure 2.3). Twenty-two of the pairs are **autosomes**, that is, pairs that look alike and possess genetic information concerning the same set of traits. The 23rd pair consists of the **sex chromosomes**, which look different from other chromosomes and determine our sex. We all receive an X sex chromosome (so called because of its X shape) from our mothers. **Truth or Fiction Revisited:** It is true that your father determined whether you are female or male, either by supplying a Y or an X sex

polygenic Resulting from many genes.

deoxyribonucleic acid (DNA) Genetic material that takes the form of a double helix composed of phosphates, sugars, and bases.

mitosis The form of cell division in which each chromosome splits lengthwise to double in number. Half of each chromosome combines with chemicals to retake its original form and then moves to the new cell.

mutation A sudden variation in a heritable characteristic, as by an accident that affects the composition of genes.

meiosis The form of cell division in which each pair of chromosomes splits so that one member of each pair moves to the new cell. As a result, each new cell has 23 chromosomes.

● **Figure 2.2**
Mitosis

(a) A segment of a strand of DNA before mitosis. (b) During mitosis, chromosomal strands of DNA "unzip." (c) The double helix is rebuilt in the cell as each incomplete "rung" combines with appropriate molecules. The resulting identical copies of the DNA strand move apart when the cell divides, each joining one of the new cells.

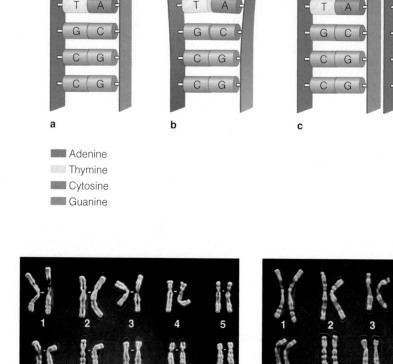

Bonds break

a   b   c

■ Adenine
■ Thymine
■ Cytosine
■ Guanine

● **Figure 2.3**
The 23 Pairs of Human Chromosomes

People normally have 23 pairs of chromosomes. Females have two X chromosomes, whereas males have an X and a Y sex chromosome.

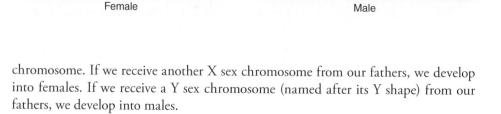

Female

Male

Both: © CNRI/SPL/Photo Researchers, Inc.

autosome A member of a pair of chromosomes (with the exception of sex chromosomes).

sex chromosome A chromosome in the shape of a Y (male) or X (female) that determines the sex of the child.

monozygotic (MZ) twins Twins that derive from a single zygote that has split into two; identical twins. Each MZ twin carries the same genetic code.

dizygotic (DZ) twins Twins that derive from two zygotes; fraternal twins.

chromosome. If we receive another X sex chromosome from our fathers, we develop into females. If we receive a Y sex chromosome (named after its Y shape) from our fathers, we develop into males.

Identical and Fraternal Twins

Question: How are twins formed? Now and then, a zygote divides into two cells that separate so that each subsequently develops into an individual with the same genetic makeup. These individuals are known as identical twins, or **monozygotic (MZ) twins**. If the woman produces two ova in the same month and they are each fertilized by a different sperm cell, they develop into fraternal twins, or **dizygotic (DZ) twins**.

There are 14 to 15 singleton pregnancies for each twin pregnancy, and of these, about two thirds are of DZ twins (Office of National Statistics, 2006). MZ twins occur with equal frequency in all ethnic groups, but Black people are most likely to have DZ twins and Asians are least likely to do so.

DZ twins run in families. If a woman is a twin, if her mother was a twin, or if she has previously borne twins, the chances rise that she will bear twins (Office of National Statistics, 2006). Similarly, women who have borne several children have an increased likelihood of twins in subsequent pregnancies.

As women reach the end of their child-bearing years, **ovulation** becomes less regular, resulting in a number of months when more than one ovum is released. Thus, the chances of twins increase with parental age (National Guideline Clearinghouse, 2007). Fertility drugs also enhance the chances of multiple births by causing more than one ovum to ripen and be released during a woman's cycle (National Guideline Clearinghouse, 2007).

Dominant and Recessive Traits

Question: How do genes determine traits? Traits are determined by pairs of genes. Each member of a pair of genes is referred to as an **allele**. When both of the alleles for a trait, such as hair color, are the same, the person is said to be **homozygous** for that trait. (*Homo*, in this usage, derives from the Greek root meaning "same," not the Latin root meaning "man.") When the alleles for a trait differ, the person is **heterozygous** for that trait.

Gregor Mendel (1822–1884), an Austrian monk, established a number of laws of heredity through his work with pea plants. Mendel realized that some traits result from an "averaging" of the genetic instructions carried by the parents. When the effects of both alleles are shown, there is said to be incomplete dominance or codominance.

Mendel also discovered the "law of dominance." When a *dominant* allele is paired with a *recessive* allele, the trait determined by the dominant allele appears in the offspring. For example, the offspring from the crossing of purebred tall peas and purebred dwarf peas were tall, suggesting that tallness is dominant over dwarfism. We now know that many genes determine **dominant traits** or **recessive traits**.

Truth or Fiction Revisited: Brown eyes, for instance, are dominant over blue eyes. If one parent carried genes for only brown eyes and if the other parent carried genes for only blue eyes, the children would invariably have brown eyes. But brown-eyed parents can also carry recessive genes for blue eyes, as shown in ● Figure 2.4. Similarly, the offspring of Mendel's crossing of purebred tall and purebred dwarf peas were not pure. They carried recessive genes for dwarfism.

If the recessive gene from one parent combines with the recessive gene from the other parent, the recessive trait will be shown. As suggested by Figure 2.4, approximately 25% of the offspring of brown-eyed parents who carry recessive blue eye color will have blue eyes. Mendel found that 25% of the offspring of parent peas that carried recessive dwarfism would be dwarfs. ■ Table 2.1 shows a number of dominant and recessive traits in humans.

Our discussion of eye color has been simplified. The percentages are not always perfect because other genes can alter the expression of the genes for brown and blue eyes, producing hazel, or greenish, eyes. Some genes also switch other genes "on" or "off" at various times during development. For example, we normally reach reproductive capacity in the teens and not earlier, and men who go bald usually do so during adulthood. Similarly, the heart and the limbs develop at different times in the embryo, again because of the switching on or off of certain genes by other genes.

People who bear one dominant gene and one recessive gene for a trait are said to be **carriers** of the recessive gene. In the cases of recessive genes that give rise to serious

ovulation The releasing of an ovum from an ovary.

allele A member of a pair of genes.

homozygous Having two identical alleles.

heterozygous Having two different alleles.

dominant trait A trait that is expressed.

recessive trait A trait that is not expressed when the gene or genes involved have been paired with dominant genes. Recessive traits are transmitted to future generations and expressed if they are paired with other recessive genes.

carrier A person who carries and transmits characteristics but does not exhibit them.

● **Figure 2.4**
Transmission of Dominant
and Recessive Traits

Two brown-eyed parents each
carry a gene for blue eyes.
Their children have an equal
opportunity of receiving genes
for brown eyes and blue eyes.

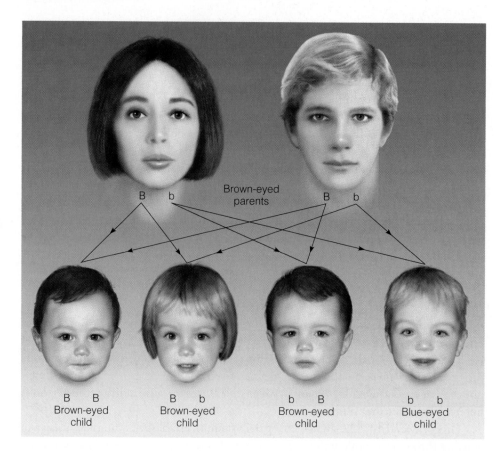

● Figure 2.4
Transmission of Dominant and Recessive Traits

B   b   Brown-eyed
parents   B   b

B   B   B   b   b   B   b   b
Brown-eyed   Brown-eyed   Brown-eyed   Blue-eyed
child   child   child   child

illnesses, carriers of those genes are fortunate to have dominant genes that cancel their
effects. **Truth or Fiction Revisited:** Therefore, it is true that you can carry the genes
for a deadly illness and not become sick yourself. This situation occurs when genes are
recessive and dominant genes cancel their effects.

Chromosomal or genetic abnormalities can cause health problems. Some chromosomal disorders reflect abnormalities in the 22 pairs of autosomes (such as Down syn-

■ **Table 2.1** Examples of Dominant and Recessive Traits

Dominant Trait	Recessive Trait
Dark hair	Blond hair
Dark hair	Red hair
Curly hair	Straight hair
Normal color vision	Red–green color blindness
Normal vision	Myopia (nearsightedness)
Farsightedness	Normal vision
Normal pigmentation	Deficiency of pigmentation in skin, hair, and retina (albinism)
Normal sensitivity to touch	Extremely fragile skin
Normal hearing	Some forms of deafness
Dimples	Lack of dimpling
Type A blood	Type O blood
Type B blood	Type O blood
Tolerance of lactose	Lactose intolerance

drome); others reflect abnormalities in the 23rd pair, the sex chromosomes (e.g., XYY syndrome). Some genetic abnormalities, such as cystic fibrosis, are caused by a single pair of genes; others are caused by combinations of genes. Diabetes mellitus, epilepsy, and peptic ulcers are **multifactorial problems**; that is, they reflect both a genetic predisposition and environmental contributors. Chromosomal and genetic abnormalities are discussed in the following sections and are summarized in Concept Review 2.1.

Chromosomal Abnormalities

People normally have 46 chromosomes. Children with more or fewer chromosomes usually experience health problems or behavioral abnormalities. The risk of chromosomal abnormalities rises with the age of the parents (American Fertility Association, 2007). *Question: What kinds of disorders are caused by chromosomal abnormalities?*

Down Syndrome

Down syndrome is usually caused by an extra chromosome on the 21st pair, resulting in 47 chromosomes. The probability of having a child with Down syndrome varies positively with the age of the parents: Older parents are more likely to bear children with the syndrome (see ■ Table 2.2 on page 56).

Children with Down syndrome have characteristic facial features that include a rounded face, a protruding tongue, a broad, flat nose, and a sloping fold of skin over the inner corners of the eyes (● Figure 2.5). Children with Down syndrome usually die from cardiovascular problems by middle age, although modern medicine has extended life appreciably. The children show deficits in cognitive development, including language development (Rondal & Ling, 2006), and in motor development (Virji-Babul et al., 2006). They encounter frequent disorders of the ear, nose, and throat, which also contribute to academic problems (Virji-Babul et al., 2006).

As you can imagine, children with Down syndrome have adjustment problems in school and in the community at large (King et al., 2000). Other children are not always sensitive to their needs and feelings and may poke fun at them. Children with Down syndrome and other problems also tend to need more attention from their parents. Parental response is variable; some parents are overwhelmed and a few are abusive, but many parents report that the special needs of their children have contributed to their own self-esteem and self-worth (Gowers & Bryan, 2005). We can make the generalization that parents who want their children usually do a better job of parenting, and this same principle applies when their children have special needs.

Sex-Linked Chromosomal Abnormalities

A number of disorders stem from an abnormal number of sex chromosomes and are therefore said to be **sex-linked chromosomal abnormalities**. Most individuals with an abnormal number of sex chromosomes are infertile. Beyond that common finding, there are many differences, some of them associated with "maleness" or "femaleness" (Wodrich, 2006).

Approximately 1 male in 700–1,000 has an extra Y chromosome. The Y chromosome is associated with maleness, and the extra Y sex chromosome apparently heightens male secondary sex characteristics. For example, XYY males are somewhat taller than average and develop heavier beards. For these kinds of reasons, males with XYY sex chromosomal structure were once referred to as "supermales." But the prefix *super-* often implies superior, and it turns out that XYY males tend to have more problems than XY males. For example, they are often mildly delayed, particularly in language development. As part of their "excessive maleness," it was once thought that XYY males were given to aggressive criminal behavior. When we examine prison populations, we find that the number of XYY males is "overrepresented" relative to their number in the population. However, it may be that the number of XYY males in

multifactorial problems Problems that stem from the interaction of heredity and environmental factors.

Down syndrome A chromosomal abnormality characterized by mental retardation and caused by an extra chromosome in the 21st pair.

sex-linked chromosomal abnormalities Abnormalities that are transmitted from generation to generation, carried by a sex chromosome, usually an X sex chromosome.

Concept Review 2.1 Chromosome and Genetic Disorders

Health Problem	Incidence	Comments	Treatment
Chromosomal Disorders			
Down syndrome www.ndss.org	1 birth in 700–800 overall; risk increases with parental age.	A condition characterized by a third chromosome on the 21st pair. A child with Down syndrome has a characteristic fold of skin over the eye and mental retardation.	No treatment, but educational programs are effective; usually fatal as a result of complications by middle age.
Klinefelter syndrome www.klinefelter syndrome.org	1 male in 500–900	A disorder affecting males that is characterized by an extra X sex chromosome and that is connected with underdeveloped male secondary sex characteristics, gynecomastia, and mild mental retardation, particularly in language skills.	Hormone (testosterone) replacement therapy; special education.
Turner syndrome www.turner-syndrome-us.org	1 girl in 2,500	A disorder that affects females, characterized by single X-sex-chromosomal structure and associated with infertility, poorly developed ovaries, underdevelopment of female secondary sex characteristics, and problems in visual-spatial skills and mathematics.	Hormone (estrogen) replacement therapy; special education.
XXX syndrome www.triplo-x.org	1 girl in 1,000	A sex-chromosomal disorder that affects females and that is connected with mild mental retardation.	Special education.
XYY syndrome http://www.aaa.dk/turner/engelsk/index.htm	1 male in 700–1,000	A sex-chromosomal disorder that affect males—sometimes referred to as "supermale syndrome"—and that is connected with heavy beards, tallness, and mild mental retardation, particularly in language development.	None.
Genetic Disorders			
Cystic fibrosis www.cff.org	1 birth in 2,000 among European Americans; 1 birth in 16,000 among African Americans.	A genetic disease caused by a recessive gene in which the pancreas and lungs become clogged with mucus, impairing the processes of respiration and digestion.	Physical therapy to loosen mucus and prompt bronchial drainage; antibiotics for infections of respiratory tract; management of diet.

Health Problem	Incidence	Comments	Treatment
Duchenne muscular dystrophy **www.mdausa.org**	1 male birth in 3,000–5,000	A fatal sex-linked degenerative muscle disease caused by a recessive gene, usually found in males and characterized by loss of ability to walk during middle childhood or early adolescence.	None; usually fatal by adolescence because of respiratory infection or cardiovascular damage.
Hemophilia **www.hemophilia.org**	1 male in 4,000–10,000	A sex-linked disorder in which blood does not clot properly.	Transfusion of blood to introduce clotting factors; proactive avoidance of injury.
Huntington's disease **www.hdsa.org**	1 birth in 18,000	A fatal neurological disorder caused by a dominant gene; onset occurs in middle adulthood.	None; usually fatal within 20 years of onset of symptoms.
Neural tube defects **ibis-birthdefects .org/start/ntdfact .htm**	1 birth in 1,000	Disorders of the brain or spine, such as *anencephaly*, in which part of the brain is missing, and *spina bifida*, in which part of the spine is exposed or missing. Some individuals with spina bifida survive for years, albeit with handicaps.	None for anencephaly, which is fatal; surgery to close spinal canal in spina bifida.
Phenylketonuria (PKU) **www .pkunetwork.org**	1 birth in 8,000–10,000	A disorder caused by a recessive gene in which children cannot metabolize the amino acid phenylalanine, which builds up in the form of phenylpyruvic acid and causes mental retardation. PKU is diagnosable at birth.	Controlled by special diet, which can prevent mental retardation.
Sickle-cell anemia **www.ascaa.org**	1 African American in 500	A blood disorder caused by a recessive gene that mostly afflicts African Americans; deformed blood cells obstruct small blood vessels, decreasing their capacity to carry oxygen and heightening the risk of occasionally fatal infections.	Transfusions to treat anemia and prevent strokes; antibiotics for infections; anesthetics; fatal to about half of those with disorder before adulthood.
Tay-Sachs disease **www.ntsad.org**	1 Jewish American of Eastern European origin in 3,000–3,600	A fatal neurological disorder caused by a recessive gene that primarily afflicts Jews of Eastern European origin.	None; usually fatal by age 3–4.
Thalassemia (Cooley's anemia) **www .thalassemia.org**	1 birth in 400–500 among Mediterranean American children	A disorder caused by a recessive gene that primarily afflicts people of Mediterranean origin and causes weakness and susceptibility to infections; usually fatal in adolescence or young adulthood.	Frequent blood transfusions; usually fatal by adolescence.

■ **Table 2.2** Risk of Giving Birth to an Infant with Down Syndrome, According to Age of the Mother

Age of Mother	Probability of Down Syndrome in the Child
20	1 in 1,667
30	1 in 953
40	1 in 106
49	1 in 11

Sources: American Fertility Association (2007) and Centers for Disease Control and Prevention (2002b).

● **Figure 2.5**
Down Syndrome

The development and adjustment of children with Down syndrome are related to their acceptance by their families. Children with Down syndrome who are reared at home develop more rapidly and achieve higher levels of functioning than those who are reared in institutions.

Klinefelter syndrome A chromosomal disorder found among males that is caused by an extra X sex chromosome and that is characterized by infertility and mild mental retardation.

testosterone A male sex hormone produced mainly by the testes.

Turner syndrome A chromosomal disorder found among females that is caused by having a single X sex chromosome and is characterized by infertility.

estrogen A female sex hormone produced mainly by the ovaries.

prisons reflects their level of intelligence rather than aggressiveness. Most XYY males in prison have committed crimes against property (e.g., stealing) rather than crimes against persons (e.g., assault and battery). And when we examine XYY individuals in the general population, most do not have records of aggressive criminal behavior (Wodrich, 2006).

Approximately 1 male in 500 has **Klinefelter syndrome**, which is caused by an extra X sex chromosome (an XXY sex chromosomal pattern). XXY males produce less of the male sex hormone—**testosterone**—than normal males. As a result, male primary and secondary sex characteristics—such as the testes, deepening of the voice, musculature, and the male pattern of body hair—do not develop properly. XXY males usually have enlarged breasts (*gynecomastia*) and are usually mildly mentally retarded, particularly in language skills (van Rijn et al., 2006). XXY males are typically treated with testosterone replacement therapy, which can foster growth of sex characteristics and elevate the mood, but the therapy does not reverse infertility.

Approximately 1 girl in 2,500 has a single X sex chromosome and as a result develops what is called **Turner syndrome**. The external genitals of girls with Turner syndrome are normal, but their ovaries are poorly developed and they produce little of the female sex hormone **estrogen**. Girls with this problem are shorter than average and infertile. Because of low estrogen production, they do not develop breasts or menstruate. Researchers have connected a specific pattern of cognitive deficits with low estrogen levels: problems in visual–spatial skills, mathematics, and nonverbal memory (Hart et al., 2006). Some studies find them to be more extroverted and more interested in seeking novel stimulation than other girls (e.g., Boman et al., 2006).

Approximately 1 girl in 1,000 has an XXX sex chromosomal structure, *Triple X syndrome*. Such girls are normal in appearance, but they tend to show lower-than-average language skills and poorer memory for recent events. Development of external sexual organs appears normal enough, although there is increased incidence of infertility (Wodrich, 2006).

Genetic Abnormalities

A number of disorders have been attributed to defective genes. *Question: What kinds of disorders are caused by genetic abnormalities?*

Phenylketonuria

The enzyme disorder **phenylketonuria (PKU)** is transmitted by a recessive gene, and affects about 1 child in 8,000. Therefore, if both parents possess the gene, PKU will be transmitted to one child in four (as in Figure 2.4). Two children in four will possess the gene but will not develop the disorder. These two, like their parents, will be carriers of the disease. One child in four will not receive the recessive gene. Therefore, he or she will not be a carrier.

Children with PKU cannot metabolize an amino acid called phenylalanine. As a consequence, the substance builds up in their bodies and impairs the functioning of the central nervous system. The results are serious: mental retardation, psychological disorders, and physical problems. There is no cure for PKU, but PKU can be detected in newborn children through analysis of the blood or urine. Children with PKU who are placed on diets low in phenylalanine within three to six weeks after birth develop normally. The diet prohibits all meat, poultry, fish, dairy products, beans, and nuts. Fruits, vegetables, and some starchy foods are allowed (Brazier & Rowlands, 2006). Pediatricians recommend staying on the diet at least until adolescence, and some encourage staying on it for life.

Huntington's Disease

Huntington's disease (HD) is a fatal, progressive degenerative disorder and is a dominant trait. Physical symptoms include uncontrollable muscle movements (Jacobs et al., 2006). Psychological symptoms include loss of intellectual functioning and personality change (Robins Wahlin et al., 2007). Because the onset of HD is delayed until middle adulthood, many individuals with the defect have borne children only to discover years later that they and possibly half their offspring will inevitably develop it. Fortunately, the disorder is rare, affecting approximately 1 American in 18,000. Medicines are helpful with some of the symptoms of HD, but they do not cure it.

Sickle-Cell Anemia

Sickle-cell anemia is caused by a recessive gene. Sickle-cell anemia is most common among African Americans but also occurs in people from Central and South America, the Caribbean, Mediterranean countries, and the Middle East. Nearly 1 African American in 10 and 1 Latino or Latina American in 20 is a carrier. In sickle-cell anemia, red blood cells take on the shape of a sickle and clump together, obstructing small blood vessels and decreasing the oxygen supply. The lessened oxygen supply can impair cognitive skills and academic performance (Hogan et al., 2005; Ogunfowora et al., 2005). Physical problems include painful and swollen joints, jaundice, and potentially fatal conditions such as pneumonia, stroke, and heart and kidney failure.

Tay-Sachs Disease

Tay-Sachs disease is also caused by a recessive gene. It causes the central nervous system to degenerate, resulting in death. The disorder is most commonly found among children in Jewish families of Eastern European background. Approximately 1 in 30 Jewish Americans from this background carries the recessive gene for Tay-Sachs. Children with the disorder progressively lose control over their muscles. They experience visual and auditory sensory losses, develop mental retardation, become paralyzed, and die toward the end of early childhood, by about the age of 5.

Cystic Fibrosis

Cystic fibrosis, also caused by a recessive gene, is the most common fatal hereditary disease among European Americans. Approximately 30,000 Americans have the disorder, but another 10 million (1 in every 31 people) are carriers (Cystic Fibrosis Foundation, 2007). Children with the disease suffer from excessive production of thick mucus that clogs the pancreas and lungs. Most victims die of respiratory infections in their 20s.

Sex-Linked Genetic Abnormalities

Some genetic defects, such as **hemophilia**, are carried on only the X sex chromosome. For this reason, they are referred to as **sex-linked genetic abnormalities**. These defects also involve recessive genes. Females, who have two X sex chromosomes, are less likely than males to show sex-linked disorders because the genes that cause the

phenylketonuria (PKU) (fee-nill-key-toe-NOOR-ee-uh) A genetic abnormality in which phenylalanine builds up and causes mental retardation.

Huntington's disease A fatal genetic neurologic disorder whose onset is in middle age.

sickle-cell anemia A genetic disorder that decreases the blood's capacity to carry oxygen.

Tay-Sachs disease A fatal genetic neurological disorder.

cystic fibrosis A fatal genetic disorder in which mucus obstructs the lungs and pancreas.

hemophilia (he-moe-FEEL-yuh) A genetic disorder in which blood does not clot properly.

sex-linked genetic abnormalities Abnormalities resulting from genes that are found on the X sex chromosome. They are more likely to be shown by male offspring (who do not have an opposing gene from a second X chromosome) than by female offspring.

disorder would have to be present on both of a female's sex chromosomes for the disorder to be expressed. Sex-linked diseases are more likely to afflict sons of female carriers because males have only one X sex chromosome, which they inherit from their mothers. Queen Victoria was a carrier of hemophilia and transmitted the blood disorder to many of her children, who in turn carried it into a number of the ruling houses of Europe. For this reason, hemophilia has been dubbed the "royal disease."

One form of **muscular dystrophy**, Duchenne muscular dystrophy, is sex-linked. Muscular dystrophy is characterized by a weakening of the of the muscles, which can lead to wasting away, inability to walk, and sometimes death. Other sex-linked abnormalities include diabetes, color blindness, and some types of night blindness.

Genetic Counseling and Prenatal Testing

It is now possible to detect the genetic abnormalities that are responsible for hundreds of diseases. *Question: How do health professionals determine whether children will have genetic or chromosomal abnormalities?*

In an effort to help parents avert these predictable tragedies, **genetic counseling** is becoming widely used. Genetic counselors compile information about a couple's genetic heritage to explore whether their children might develop genetic abnormalities. Couples who face a high risk of passing along genetic defects to their children sometimes elect to adopt or not have children rather than conceive their own.

In addition, **prenatal** testing can indicate whether the embryo or fetus is carrying genetic abnormalities. Prenatal testing includes amniocentesis, chorionic villus sampling, ultrasound, and blood tests.

Amniocentesis

Amniocentesis is usually performed on the mother at about 14–16 weeks after conception, although many physicians now perform the procedure earlier ("early amniocentesis"). In this method, the health professional uses a syringe (needle) to withdraw fluid from the amniotic sac (● Figure 2.6). The fluid contains cells that are sloughed off by the fetus. The cells are separated from the amniotic fluid, grown in a culture, and then examined microscopically for genetic and chromosomal abnormalities.

Amniocentesis has become routine among American women who become pregnant past the age of 35 because the chances of Down syndrome increase dramatically as women approach or pass the age of 40. But women carrying the children of aging fathers may also wish to have amniocentesis. Amniocentesis can detect the presence of well over 100 chromosomal and genetic abnormalities, including sickle-cell anemia, Tay-Sachs disease, **spina bifida**, muscular dystrophy, and Rh incompatibility in the fetus. Women (or their partners) who carry or have a family history of any of these disorders are advised to have amniocentesis performed. If the test reveals the presence of a serious disorder, the parents may decide to abort the fetus. Or, they may decide to continue the pregnancy and prepare themselves to raise a child who has special needs.

Amniocentesis also permits parents to learn the sex of their unborn child through examination of the sex chromosomes, but most parents learn the sex of their baby earlier by means of ultrasound. Amniocentesis carries some risk of miscarriage (approximately 1 woman in 100 who undergo the procedure will miscarry), so health professionals would not conduct it to learn the sex of the child.

Chorionic Villus Sampling

Chorionic villus sampling (CVS) is similar to amniocentesis but offers the advantage of diagnosing fetal abnormalities earlier in pregnancy. CVS is carried out between the 9th and 12th week of pregnancy. A small syringe is inserted through the vagina into the **uterus**. The syringe gently sucks out a few of the threadlike projections (villi) from the outer membrane that envelops the amniotic sac and fetus. Re-

muscular dystrophy (DIS-truh-fee) A chronic disease characterized by a progressive wasting away of the muscles.

genetic counseling Advice concerning the probabilities that a couple's children will show genetic abnormalities.

prenatal Before birth.

amniocentesis (AM-nee-oh-sent-TEE-sis) A procedure for drawing and examining fetal cells sloughed off into amniotic fluid to determine the presence of various disorders.

spina bifida A neural tube defect that causes abnormalities of the brain and spine.

chorionic villus sampling (CORE-ee-AH-nick VILL-us) A method for the prenatal detection of genetic abnormalities that samples the membrane enveloping the amniotic sac and fetus.

uterus The hollow organ within females in which the embryo and fetus develop.

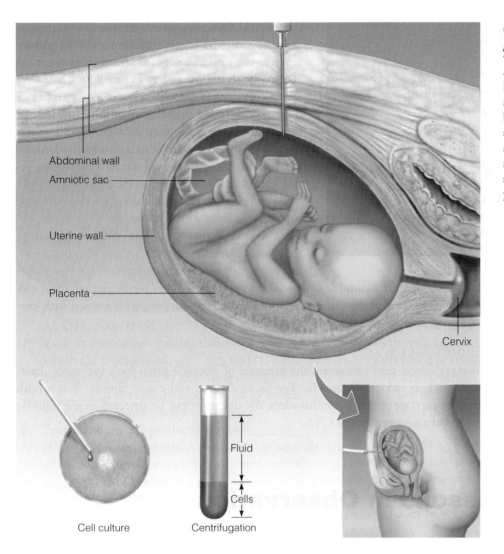

Amniocentesis allows prenatal identification of certain genetic and chromosomal disorders by examining genetic material sloughed off by the fetus into amniotic fluid. Amniocentesis also allows parents to learn the sex of their unborn child. Would you want to know?

Abdominal wall

Amniotic sac

Uterine wall

Placenta

Cervix

Cell culture

Centrifugation

Fluid

Cells

sults are available within days of the procedure. CVS has not been used as frequently as amniocentesis because many studies have shown that CVS carries a slightly greater risk of spontaneous abortion.

Consideration of the relative risks of amniocentesis and CVS is a highly controversial issue. Some studies have suggested that the risks of the procedures are about equivalent (Simpson, 2000). However, there are two types of amniocentesis—"late" and "early"—and there are also different types of CVS. More recent studies suggest that both amniocentesis and CVS increase the risk of miscarriage and that the risks might *not* be equal (Alfirevic et al., 2003; Philip et al., 2004). Another factor to consider, sad to say, is that some practitioners are better at carrying out these procedures than others. If you are considering having CVS or amniocentesis, ask your doctor for the latest information about the risks of each procedure. Also ask around to make sure that your doctor is the right doctor to carry out the procedure.

Ultrasound

For more than half a century, the military has been using sonar to locate enemy submarines. Sonar sends high-frequency sound waves into the depths of the ocean, and the waves bounce back from objects such as submarines (and whales and schools of fish and the ocean floor) to reveal their presence. Within the past generation, health professionals have also innovated the use of (very!) high-frequency sound waves to obtain information about the fetus. The sounds waves are too high in frequency to be heard by the human ear and are called **ultrasound**. However, they are reflected by

ultrasound Sound waves too high in pitch to be sensed by the human ear.

potential Shakespeare who is reared in poverty and never taught to read or write will not create a *Hamlet*. Our traits and behaviors represent the interaction of heredity and environment. The sets of traits that we inherit from our parents are referred to as our **genotypes**. Our actual sets of traits are called our **phenotypes**. Our phenotypes develop because of both genetic and environmental influences.

Researchers have developed a number of strategies to help sort out the effects of heredity and the environment on development. *Question: What kinds of research strategies do researchers use to sort out the effects of genetics and environmental influences on development?*

Kinship Studies: Are the Traits of Relatives Related?

Researchers study the distribution of a particular behavior pattern among relatives who differ in degree of genetic closeness. The more closely people are related, the more genes they have in common. Parents and children have a 50% overlap in their genetic endowments, and so do siblings (brothers and sisters), on average. Aunts and uncles have a 25% overlap with nieces and nephews, and so do grandparents with their grandchildren. First cousins share 12.5% of their genetic endowment. So, if genes are implicated in a physical trait or behavior pattern, people who are more closely related should be more likely to share the pattern. You probably look more like a parent or brother or sister than like a cousin, and you probably look very little like a stranger.

Twin Studies: Looking in the Genetic Mirror

Monozygotic (MZ) twins share 100% of their genes, whereas dizygotic (DZ) twins have a 50% overlap, just as other siblings do. If MZ twins show greater similarity on some trait or behavior than DZ twins do, a genetic basis for the trait or behavior is indicated.

MZ twins resemble each other more closely than DZ twins on a number of physical and psychological traits. MZ twins are more likely to look alike and to be similar in height, and they may even have more similar cholesterol levels than DZ twins (Plomin, 2002). This finding holds even when the MZ twins are reared apart and the DZ twins are reared together (Bouchard & Loehlin, 2001). Other physical similarities between pairs of MZ twins may be more subtle, but they are also strong. For example, research shows that MZ twin sisters begin to menstruate about 1 to 2 months apart, whereas DZ twins begin to menstruate about 1 year apart. MZ twins are more alike than DZ twins in their blood pressure, brain wave patterns, their speech patterns, gestures, and mannerisms (Plomin, 2002; Bouchard & Loehlin, 2001). Heredity even has an effect on their preference for coffee or tea (Luciano et al., 2005).

MZ twins resemble one another more strongly than DZ twins in intelligence and in personality traits such as sociability, anxiety, friendliness, conformity, and even happiness and the tendency to choose marriage over the single life (Hur, 2005; Johnson et al., 2004; McCrae et al., 2000). David Lykken and Mike Csikszentmihalyi (2001) suggested that we inherit a tendency toward a certain level of happiness. Despite the ups and downs of life, we tend to drift back to our usual levels of cheerfulness or irritability. It seems that our bank accounts, our levels of education, and our marital status are less influential than genes as contributors to happiness. Heredity is also a key contributor to psychological developmental factors such as cognitive functioning, and early signs of attachment (e.g., smiling, cuddling, and expression of fear of strangers) (Plomin, 2002). MZ twins are more likely than DZ twins to share psychological disorders such as **autism**, depression, schizophrenia, and even vulnerability to alcoholism (Belmonte & Carper, 2006; Plomin, 2002; Ronald et al., 2006).

genotype The genetic form or constitution of a person as determined by heredity.

phenotype The actual form or constitution of a person as determined by heredity and environmental factors.

autism A developmental disorder characterized by failure to relate to others, communication problems, intolerance of change, and ritualistic behavior.

Of course, twin studies are not perfect. MZ twins may resemble each other more closely than DZ twins partly because they are treated more similarly. MZ twins frequently are dressed identically, and parents sometimes have difficulty telling them apart.

One way to get around this difficulty is to find and compare MZ twins who were reared in different homes. Any similarities between MZ twins reared apart cannot be explained by a shared home environment and would appear to be largely a result of heredity. In the fascinating Minnesota Study of Twins Reared Apart (T. J. Bouchard et al., 1990; DiLalla et al., 1999; Lykken, 2006), researchers have been measuring the physiological and psychological characteristics of 56 sets of MZ adult twins who were separated in infancy and reared in different homes. The MZ twins reared apart are about as similar as MZ twins reared together on a variety of measures of intelligence, personality, temperament, occupational and leisure-time interests, and social attitudes. These traits thus would appear to have a genetic underpinning.

Adoption Studies

Adoption studies in which children are separated from their natural parents at an early age and reared by adoptive parents provide special opportunities for sorting out nature and nurture. As we see in discussions of the origins of intelligence (Chapter 12) and of various problem behaviors (Chapters 10 and 13), psychologists look for the relative similarities between children and their adoptive and natural parents. When children who are reared by adoptive parents are nonetheless more similar to their natural parents in a trait, a powerful argument is made for a genetic role in the appearance of that trait.

Traits are determined by pairs of genes. One member of each pair comes from each parent. ***Question: What process brings together the genes from each parent?*** That process is called conception. In the following section, we talk about the birds and the bees and the microscope to understand how conception works.

Active Review

13. The sets of traits that we inherit are referred to as our (Genotype or Phenotype?).
14. The actual traits that we display at any point in time are the product of genetic and environmental influences and are called our (Genotypes or Phenotypes?).
15. Parents and children have a _____% overlap in their genetic endowments.
16. _____ (MZ) twins share 100% of their genes.
17. _____ (DZ) twins have a 50% overlap, as do other siblings.

Reflect & Relate: Do you know sets of twins? Are they monozygotic or dizygotic? How are they alike? How do they differ?

Go to

http://www.thomsonedu.com/psychology/rathus

for an interactive version of this review.

It is no secret that most people in most cultures would prefer that their child, or at least their first child, be a boy. According to traditional gender roles, boys carry on the business of the family and represent continuity of a family's lineage (Ding & Hesketh, 2006; Sullum, 2007). They also pass on the family name. In less developed nations such as China and India, especially in rural areas, sons also represent protection from neglect and poverty in the later years. These attitudes are reflected in verses from the ancient Chinese *Book of Songs*, written some three thousand years ago:

> When a son is born,
> Let him sleep on the bed,
> Clothe him with fine clothes,
> And give him jade with which to play. . . .
> When a daughter is born,
> Let her sleep on the ground,
> Wrap her in common wrappings,
> And give her broken tiles with which to play. . . .

When Mao Zedong took power in 1949, his Communist government replaced family support in old age with state support and also rejected male superiority. There remained a balance in the numbers of males and females in the population throughout most of the 1970s. But beginning in 1979, China attempted to gain control of its mushrooming population of more than one billion by enforcing strict limits on family size. One child per family is allowed in urban areas. A second child is usually allowed in rural areas after 5 years have passed, especially if the first child is a girl (Li, 2004). Because Chinese families, like the families of old, continue to prefer boys,

the ratio of boys to girls began to change with the limitations on family size (Ding & Hesketh, 2006).

As noted in ■ Table 2.3, the desirability of having small families has generally caught on in the Chinese population. That is, the great majority of women interviewed in a recent survey expressed the desire to have either one or two children. However, there were some differences according to the woman's age, her area of residence, and her level of education. How would you account for such differences?

Because more boys than girls die in infancy, a "normal" ratio of boys to girls is about 106 to 100, which characterized China in the 1970s. The ratio was about 108.5 boys to 100 girls in the early 1980s, 111 to 100 in 1990, and 117 to 100 in 2000, and it is now at least 120 boys for every 100 girls and as high as 123 to 100 by some estimates (Ding & Hesketh, 2006).

Therefore, a great shortage of Chinese women is being created, which may not be much of a problem for parents but which will certainly be a problem for men seeking mates in future years. Chinese officials are concerned that the shortfall will result in millions of men with no prospect of getting married and thereby settling down when they are of age. Thus, they fear that this shortfall of women will result in an increased likelihood of social unrest, which can become political dissent as well as ordinary crime (Festini et al., 2006; Potts, 2006).

Prenatal Sex Selection

How do the Chinese have so many more sons than daughters? Once upon a time in places

like China and India, much of the answer lay in infanticide, that is, in the killing of unwanted female babies. More recently, according to the International Planned Parenthood Federation (Hesketh & Xing, 2006), the main answer is the selective abortion of female fetuses, as identified by inexpensive, portable ultrasound scanners and backstreet abortion clinics. It is estimated that some seven million abortions are performed in China each year and that 70% percent of them are of female fetuses (Hesketh & Xing, 2006).

The director of China's National Population and Family Planning Commission admitted that the gender gap created by the country's population policy has created a very serious challenge for the country (Festini et al., 2006; Sullum, 2007). China, however, does not intend to loosen its constraints on population growth. Instead, the government will experiment with educational campaigns, penalties for sex-selective abortions, and bonuses for parents who have girls (Sullum, 2007; Zhu, 2003).

Reflect:

- *Do you believe that there are any circumstances under which a government such as China's has the right to limit family size? Why or why not?*

- *How would you explain the relationship between the number of children a Chinese woman desires and her age? Her area of residence (urban or rural)? Her level of education?*

- *What sources of error might distort the results in Table 2.3?*

■ **Table 2.3** Preferred Number of Children among Chinese Women (Percent Expressing Preference)

	No children	1 child	2 children	3 or more children
Age of woman				
15–19	2.1	49	45	1.9
20–29	1.3	47	48	2.1
30–39	0.8	32	60	6.1
40–49	1.0	27	62	11
Area of residence				
Urban	3.1	52	43	1.5
Rural	0.4	30	61	7.5
Level of Education				
Illiterate or semi-literate	0.4	17	67	14
Primary school	0.3	25	65	8.5
Secondary school	2.1	46	47	2.5
College	4.0	49	44	2.2

Source: National Family Planning and Reproductive Health Survey, reported in Q. J. Ding & T. Hesketh (2006), Family size, fertility preferences, and sex ratio in China in the era of the one child family policy: Results from National Family Planning and Reproductive Health Survey, *British Medical Journal, 333*(7564), 371–373.

Note: Number of women interviewed: 39,344

Active Review

18. The union of an ovum and a sperm cell is called _____ .

19. Each month, an ovum is released from its follicle and enters a nearby _____ tube.

20. Low _____ count is the most common infertility problem in the male.

21. Failure to _____ is the most frequent infertility problem in women.

Reflect & Relate: What methods do people use to try to select the sex of their children? Do you believe that it is right or proper to attempt to select the sex of one's child? Support your point of view.

Go to

http://www.thomsonedu.com/psychology/rathus

for an interactive version of this review.

1. **What is meant by heredity?**

   Heredity defines one's nature, as determined by the biological transmission of traits and characteristics from one generation to another. Heredity is fundamental in the transmission of physical traits and is also involved in psychological traits, including psychological disorders.

2. **What are chromosomes and genes?**

   Chromosomes are rod-shaped structures found in cell nuclei. People normally have 46 chromosomes organized into 23 pairs. Each chromosome contains thousands of genes, the biochemical materials that regulate the development of traits. Genes are segments of strands of DNA, which takes the form of a twisting ladder.

3. **What happens during cell division?**

   In mitosis, strands of DNA break apart and are rebuilt in the new cell. Sperm and ova are produced by meiosis—or reduction division—and have 23 rather than 46 chromosomes.

4. **How are twins formed?**

   If a zygote divides into two cells that separate and each develops into an individual, monozygotic (MZ) twins, which are identical, develop. If two ova are each fertilized by a different sperm cell, they develop into dizygotic (DZ) twins, which are fraternal twins. DZ twins run in families.

5. **How do genes determine traits?**

   Traits are determined by pairs of genes. Mendel established laws of heredity and realized that some traits result from an "averaging" of the genetic instructions carried by the parents. However, genes can also be dominant (as in the case of brown eyes) or recessive (blue eyes). When recessive genes from both parent combine, the recessive trait is shown. People who bear one dominant gene and one recessive gene for a trait are carriers of the recessive gene. Some genetic abnormalities are caused by a single pair of genes, others by combinations of genes.

6. **What kinds of disorders are caused by chromosomal abnormalities?**

   Chromosomal abnormalities become more likely as parents age. Mental retardation is common in many such disorders. Down syndrome is caused by an extra chromosome on the 21st pair. Children with Down syndrome have characteristic facial features, including a downward-sloping fold of skin at the inner corners of the eyes, and various physical health problems. Disorders that arise from abnormal numbers of sex chromosomes are called sex-linked. They include XYY males and girls with a single X sex chromosome.

7. **What kinds of disorders are caused by genetic abnormalities?**

   Phenylketonuria (PKU) is a metabolic disorder transmitted by a recessive gene. Huntington's disease is a fatal progressive degenerative disorder and a dominant trait. Sickle-cell anemia is caused by a recessive gene and is most common among African Americans. Tay-Sachs disease is a fatal disease of the nervous system that is caused by a recessive gene and is most common among children in Jewish families of Eastern European origin. Cystic fibrosis is caused by a recessive gene and is the most common fatal hereditary disease among European Americans. Sex-linked genetic abnormalities are carried only on the X sex chromosome and include hemophilia, Duchenne muscular dystrophy, diabetes, and color blindness.

8. **How do health professionals determine whether children will have genetic or chromosomal abnormalities?**

Prenatal testing procedures can determine the presence of various genetic and chromosomal abnormalities. Such tests include amniocentesis, chorionic villus sampling, ultrasound, and parental blood tests.

9. **What is the difference between our genotypes and our phenotypes?**

Our genotypes are the sets of traits that we inherit. However, inherited traits vary in expression, depending on environmental conditions. One's actual set of traits at a given point in time is one's phenotype.

10. **What research strategies do researchers use to sort out the effects of genetics and environmental influences on development?**

Researchers can study the distribution of a trait among relatives who differ in degree of genetic closeness. Parents and children have a 50% overlap in genes, as do brothers and sisters, with the exception of MZ twins, who have 100% overlap. MZ twins resemble each other more closely than DZ twins on physical and psychological traits, even when reared apart. If adopted children are closer to their natural than to their adoptive parents on a physical or psychological trait, that trait is likely to have a strong genetic basis.

11. **What process brings together the genes from each parent?**

The process is the union of a sperm and an ovum, or conception. Fertilization normally occurs in a fallopian tube. If the egg is not fertilized, it is discharged. Men typically ejaculate hundreds of millions of sperm. More boys are conceived than girls, but male fetuses have a higher rate of spontaneous abortion. Chromosomes from the sperm cell align with chromosomes in the egg cell, combining to form 23 new pairs.

12. **What are the causes of infertility?**

Male fertility problems include low sperm count and motility, infections, and trauma to the testes. Female fertility problems include failure to ovulate, infections such as PID, endometriosis, and obstructions.

13. **How are couples helped to have children?**

Fertility drugs help regulate ovulation. Artificial insemination can be done with the sperm from multiple ejaculations of a man with a low sperm count or with the sperm of a donor. In vitro fertilization (IVF) can be used when the fallopian tubes are blocked. An embryo can also be transferred into a host uterus, as when the mother cannot produce ova.

14. **How do people attempt to select the sex of their children?**

The only reliable method for prenatal sex selection of a child is preimplantation genetic diagnosis.

Key Terms

Active Learning Resources

Childhood & Adolescence Book Companion Website

http://www.thomsonedu.com/psychology/rathus

Visit your book companion website, where you will find more resources to help you study. There you will find interactive versions of your book features, including the Lessons in Observation videos, Active Review sections, and the Truth or Fiction feature. In addition, the companion website contains quizzing, flash cards, and a pronunciation glossary.

 is an easy-to-use online resource that helps you study in less time to get the grade you want, NOW.

http://www.thomsonedu.com/login

Need help studying? This site is your one-stop study shop. Take a Pre-Test and ThomsonNOW will generate a Personalized Study Plan based on your test results. The Study Plan will identify the topics you need to review and direct you to online resources to help you master those topics. You can then take a Post-Test to determine the concepts you have mastered and what you still need to work on.

ack in 1938, when rapping was still something that hurt the knuckles, L. W. Sontag and T. W. Richards reported the results of a study in fetal behavior. They stimulated pregnant women with methods such as ringing a bell and measured the results on the heart rate of the fetus, as assessed by an instrument on the mother's abdomen. Many of the mothers smoked, and the researchers assessed the effects of smoking on the fetal heart rate. They also got the fetus all shook up by placing a vibrator against the mother's abdomen.

Sontag and Richards learned that powerful vibrations usually induced faster heart rates in the fetus (big surprise?), but maternal smoking had less predictable effects on the fetus. Cigarette smoke contains nicotine, which is a stimulant, but smoke also reduces the supply of oxygen in the bloodstream, and oxygen is needed to fuel bursts of activity. How could the researchers spend their time assessing the effects of maternal smoking rather than warning the mothers that their smoking was placing their fetuses at risk for low birth weight, prematurity, short attention span, academic problems, or hyperactivity? It was 1938, and little was known of the harmful effects of smoking.

In any event, Sontag and Richards also discovered that fetuses are sensitive to sound waves during the last months of pregnancy, which has led to a wave of more recent research, including research into whether **neonates** are "loyal" and prefer their mothers' voices to those of strangers and whether listening to classical rather than heavy metal music during pregnancy has noticeable effects (on the neonate's brain as well as heart rate). Stay tuned. Researchers are finding that the most rapid and dramatic human developments are literally "out of sight" and take place in the uterus. Within 9 months, a fetus develops from a nearly microscopic cell to a neonate about 20 inches long. Its weight increases a billionfold.

We can date pregnancy from the onset of the last menstrual period before conception, which makes the normal gestation period 280 days. We can also date pregnancy from the assumed date of fertilization, which normally occurs 2 weeks after the beginning of the woman's last menstrual cycle. With this accounting method, the gestation period is 266 days.

Soon after conception, the single cell formed by the union of sperm and egg begins to multiply, becoming two cells, then four, then eight, and so on. During the weeks and months that follow, tissues, organs, and structures begin to form, and the fetus gradually takes on the unmistakable shape of a human being. By the time a fetus is born, it consists of hundreds of billions of cells, more cells than there are stars in the Milky Way galaxy. Prenatal development is divided into three periods: the germinal stage (approximately the first 2 weeks), the embryonic stage (the third through the eighth weeks), and the fetal stage (the third month through birth). Health professionals also commonly speak of prenatal development in terms of three trimesters of 3 months each.

The Germinal Stage: Wanderings

Question: What happens during the germinal stage of prenatal development? Within 36 hours after conception, the zygote divides into two cells. It then divides repeatedly as it proceeds on its journey to the uterus. Within another 36 hours, it has become 32 cells. It takes the zygote 3 to 4 days to reach the uterus. The mass of dividing cells wanders about the uterus for another 3 to 4 days before it begins to become implanted in the uterine wall. Implantation takes another week or so. The period from conception to implantation is called the **germinal stage** (see ● Figure 3.1).

A few days into the germinal stage, the dividing cell mass takes the form of a fluid-filled ball of cells called a **blastocyst**. A blastocyst already shows cell differentiation.

neonate A newborn baby.

germinal stage The period of development between conception and the implantation of the embryo.

blastocyst A stage within the germinal period of prenatal development in which the zygote has the form of a sphere of cells surrounding a cavity of fluid.

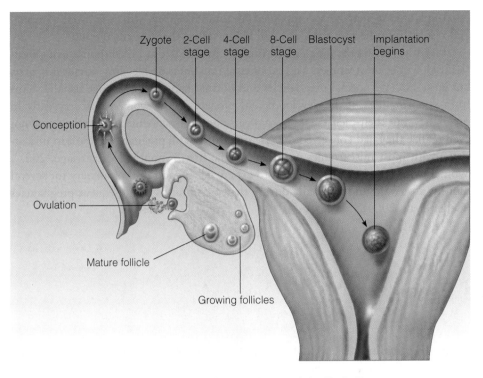

See your student companion website for an interactive version of Figure 3.1.

● **Figure 3.1** The Ovarian Cycle, Conception, and the Early Days of the Germinal Stage

The zygote first divides approximately 36 hours after conception. Continuing division creates the hollow sphere of cells termed the blastocyst. The blastocyst normally becomes implanted in the wall of the uterus.

Cells begin to separate into groups that will eventually become different structures. The inner part of the blastocyst has two distinct layers of cells that form a thickened mass of cells called the **embryonic disk**. These cells will become the embryo and eventually the fetus.

The outer part of the blastocyst, or **trophoblast**, at first consists of a single layer of cells, but it rapidly differentiates into four membranes that will protect and nourish the embryo. One membrane produces blood cells until the embryo's liver develops and takes over this function. Then that membrane disappears. Another membrane develops into the **umbilical cord** and the blood vessels of the **placenta**. A third develops into the amniotic sac, and the fourth becomes the chorion, which will line the placenta.

Without Visible Means of Support . . .

Question: If the dividing mass of cells is moving through a fallopian tube and then "wandering" through the uterus for another few days, how does it obtain any nourishment?

Although people are not chickens, the dividing cluster of cells that will become the embryo and then the fetus is at first nourished only by the yolk of the egg cell, just like a chick developing in an egg. **Truth or Fiction Revisited:** It is true that newly fertilized egg cells survive without any nourishment from the mother for more than a week. They are nourished by the yolk of the ovum until they implant in the wall of the uterus. Therefore, they make no gains in mass. A blastocyst gains mass only when it receives nourishment from the outside. For that to happen, it must be implanted in the wall of the uterus.

embryonic disk The platelike inner part of the blastocyst that differentiates into the ectoderm, mesoderm, and endoderm of the embryo.

trophoblast The outer part of the blastocyst from which the amniotic sac, placenta, and umbilical cord develop.

umbilical cord A tube that connects the fetus to the placenta.

placenta (pluh-SEN-tuh) An organ connected to the uterine wall and to the fetus by the umbilical cord. The placenta serves as a relay station between mother and fetus for the exchange of nutrients and wastes.

Sexual Differentiation

By 5 to 6 weeks, the embryo is only one-quarter to one-half inch long. Nevertheless, nondescript sex organs, including the internal and external genital organs, will already have formed, as shown in ● Figures 3.3 and ● 3.4. Both female and male embryos possess a pair of sexually undifferentiated gonads and two sets of primitive duct structures, the so-called Müllerian (female) ducts and the Wolffian (male) ducts. At this stage of development, both the internal and the external genitals resemble primitive female structures.

By about the seventh week, the genetic code (XY or XX) begins to assert itself, causing sex organs to differentiate. Genetic activity on the Y sex chromosome causes the testes to begin to differentiate. The ovaries begin to differentiate if the Y chromosome is *absent*. By about 4 months after conception, males and females show distinct external genital structures.

Sex Hormones and Sexual Differentiation

androgens Male sex hormones (from roots meaning "giving birth to men").

testosterone A male sex hormone—a steroid—that is produced by the testes and that promotes growth of male sexual characteristics and sperm.

Prenatal sexual differentiation requires hormonal influences as well as genetic influences. Male sex hormones—**androgens**—are critical in the development of male genital organs. **Truth or Fiction Revisited:** Without androgens, all people whether genetically female or male would develop external sex organs that look like those of females. However, apparent "females" with an XY sex chromosomal structure would be infertile.

Once the testes have developed in the embryo, they begin to produce androgens, the most important of which is **testosterone**. Testosterone spurs the differentiation of the male (Wolffian) duct system (see ● Figure 3.3) and remains involved in sexual development and activity for a lifetime. Each Wolffian duct develops into a complex

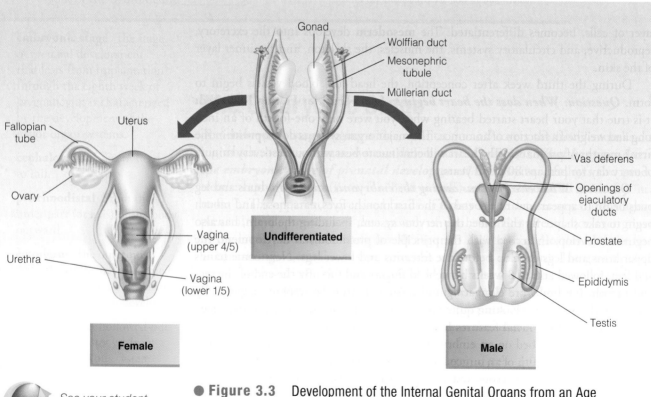

See your student companion website for an interactive version of Figure 3.3.

● **Figure 3.3**   Development of the Internal Genital Organs from an Age of 5–6 Weeks Following Conception

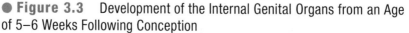

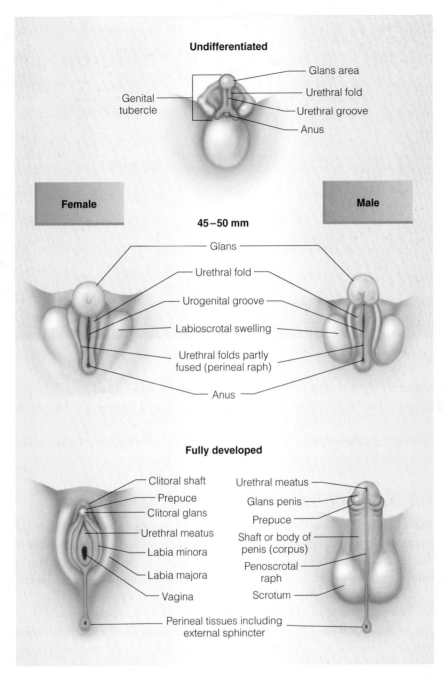

See your student companion website for an interactive version of Figure 3.4.

● **Figure 3.4** Development of the External Genital Organs from an Undifferentiated Stage at 5–6 Weeks Following Conception

maze of ducts and storage facilities for sperm. At about the eighth week of prenatal development, another androgen, dihydrotestosterone (DHT), spurs the formation of the external male genital organs, including the penis. Yet another testicular hormone, secreted somewhat later, prevents the Müllerian ducts from developing into the female duct system. That hormone is labeled Müllerian inhibiting substance (MIS).

Female embryos and fetuses do produce small amounts of androgens, but they are usually not enough to cause sexual differentiation along male lines. However, they do play important roles in the development of some secondary sexual characteristics in adolescence, such as the appearance of pubic hair and underarm hair. Androgens are also important in the sex drive of females for a lifetime (Morley & Perry, 2003;

A Human Embryo at 7 Weeks
At this late part of the embryonic stage, the major organ systems except for the sex organs have already become differentiated.

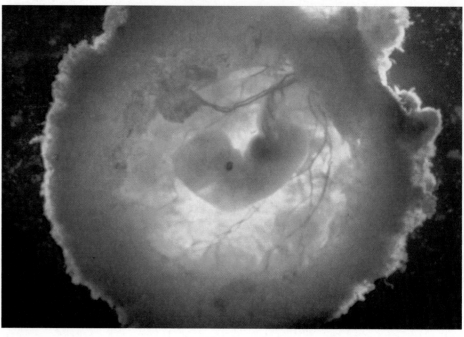

Nyunt, et al., 2005). But in the female embryo and fetus, low levels of androgens are connected with degeneration of the Wolffian ducts and further development of female sexual organs. The Müllerian ducts develop into fallopian tubes, the uterus, and the inner part of the vagina. The presence of the female sex hormones is not necessary for these developments to occur, although they will become crucial in puberty.

The Amniotic Sac: A Shock Absorber

The embryo and fetus develop suspended within a protective **amniotic sac** in the uterus. This sac is surrounded by a clear membrane and contains **amniotic fluid**. The fluid serves as a kind of natural air bag, allowing the embryo and fetus to move around without injury. It also helps maintain an even temperature in the sac.

Questions: How does the embryo get nourishment from its mother? How does it eliminate waste products? The answers to these questions involve the placenta and the umbilical cord. The placenta is a mass of tissue that permits the embryo (and, later on, the fetus) to exchange nutrients and wastes with the mother. The placenta is unique in origin. It grows from material supplied by both the mother and the embryo. The fetus is connected to the placenta by the umbilical cord. The mother is connected to the placenta by the system of blood vessels in the uterine wall.

The Placenta: A Filtration System

Question: Do germs or drugs in the mother pass through the placenta and affect the embryo? In one of the more fascinating feats of prenatal engineering, it turns out that the mother and embryo have separate circulatory systems. The mother's bloodstream is hers, and the embryo's bloodstream is the embryo's. The pancake-shaped placenta contains a membrane that acts as a filter, and only certain substances can pass through it. The membrane permits oxygen and nutrients to reach the embryo from the mother. It also permits carbon dioxide (which is the gas you breathe out and plants "breathe" in) and waste products to pass to the mother from the embryo. Once the mother has them, she eliminates them through her lungs and kidneys. That is the good part. It also happens that a number of harmful substances can sneak through

amniotic sac The sac containing the fetus.

amniotic fluid Fluid within the amniotic sac that suspends and protects the fetus.

the placenta, including various "germs" (microscopic disease-causing organisms), such as the ones that cause syphilis (a bacterium called *Treponema pallidum*), German measles, and, to some degree, AIDS. The good news here is that most pregnant women who are infected with HIV (the virus that causes AIDS) do not transmit it to the embryo through the placenta. HIV is more likely to be transmitted through childbirth. But some drugs—aspirin, narcotics, alcohol, tranquilizers, and others—do cross the placenta and can affect the fetus in one way or another.

The placenta also secretes hormones that preserve the pregnancy, prepare the breasts for nursing, and stimulate the uterine contractions that prompt childbirth. Ultimately, the placenta passes from the woman's body after the child is delivered. For this reason, it is also called the afterbirth.

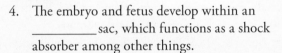

Active Review

4. The embryo and fetus develop within an _____ sac, which functions as a shock absorber among other things.
5. Development follows two general trends: cephalocaudal and _____.
6. The (Inner or Outer?) layer of cells of the ectoderm develops into the nervous system, sensory organs, and the outer layer of skin.
7. Without sex hormones, all embryos would develop the appearance of being (Males or Females?).

8. The _____ permits the embryo to exchange nutrients and wastes with the mother.
9. The embryo and fetus are connected to the placenta by the _____.

Reflect & Relate: Are you surprised at how early the heart begins to beat and at the size of the embryo at the time? Explain.

Go to

http://www.thomsonedu.com/psychology/rathus

for an interactive version of this review.

The Fetal Stage

The **fetal stage** lasts from the beginning of the third month until birth. *Question: What happens during the fetal stage of prenatal development?* The fetus begins to turn and respond to external stimulation at about the ninth or tenth week. By the end of the first trimester, all the major organ systems have been formed. The fingers and toes are fully formed. The eyes can be clearly distinguished, and the sex of the fetus can be determined visually.

The second trimester is characterized by further maturation of fetal organ systems and dramatic gains in size. The brain continues to mature, contributing to the fetus's ability to regulate its own basic body functions. During the second trimester, the fetus advances from 1 ounce to 2 pounds in weight and grows four to five times in length, from about 3 inches to 14 inches. Soft, downy hair grows above the eyes and on the scalp. The skin turns ruddy because of blood vessels that show through the surface. (During the third trimester, fatty layers will give the skin a pinkish hue.)

By the end of the second trimester, the fetus opens and shuts its eyes, sucks its thumb, alternates between periods of wakefulness and sleep, and perceives light and

fetal stage The stage of development that lasts from the beginning of the ninth week of pregnancy through birth; it is characterized by gains in size and weight and by maturation of the organ systems.

A Human Fetus at 12 Weeks

By the end of the first trimester, formation of all the major organ systems is complete. Fingers and toes are fully formed, and the sex of the fetus can be determined visually.

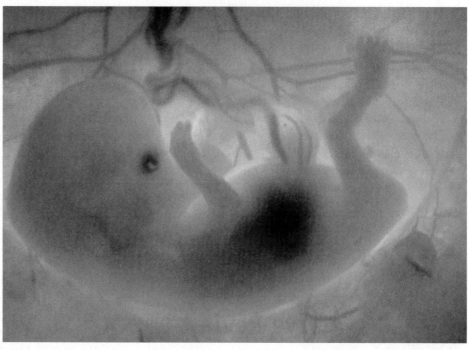

© Claude Edelmann/Photo Researchers, Inc.

sounds. **Truth or Fiction Revisited:** There are also sharp spasms of the diaphragm, or fetal hiccups, which may last for hours (ask a weary pregnant woman).

About half of babies who are born at 22 to 25 weeks of gestation will survive, and the survival rate is connected with the quality of the medical care they receive (Rogowski et al., 2004).

During the third trimester, the organ systems of the fetus continue to mature. The heart and lungs become increasingly capable of sustaining independent life. The fetus gains about 5½ pounds and doubles in length. Newborn boys average about 7½ pounds and newborn girls about 7 pounds.

During the seventh month, the fetus normally turns upside down in the uterus so that delivery will be head first. By the end of the seventh month, the fetus will have almost doubled in weight, gaining another 1 pound, 12 ounces, and will have increased another 2 inches in length. If born now, chances of survival are nearly

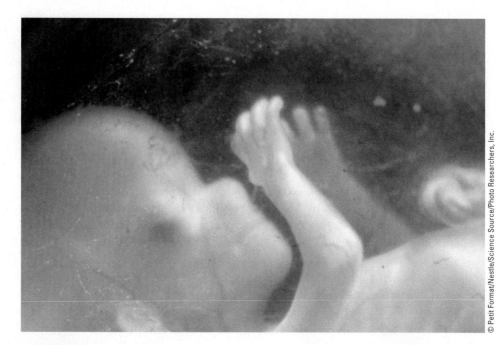

A Human Fetus at 4½ Months

At this midway point between conception and birth, the fetus is covered with fine, downy hair, called lanugo.

© Petit Format/Nestle/Science Source/Photo Researchers, Inc.

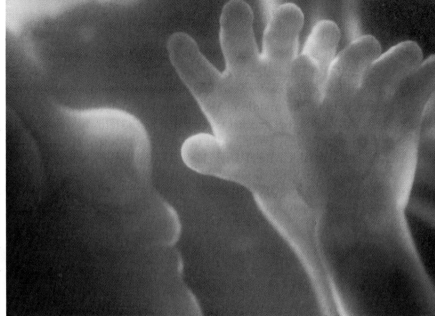

The Hands of a Human Fetus at 5 Months

By 5 months of age, the hands have been fully formed for a month or so. At this age, the fetus may occasionally suck its thumb.

© Petit Format/Nestle/Science Source/Photo Researchers, Inc.

90%. If born at the end of the eighth month, the odds are overwhelmingly in favor of survival.

Fetal Perception: Bach at Breakfast and Beethoven at Brunch?

Question: Why did my Aunt Margaret play classical music (and put the speakers near her abdomen) when she was 7 months pregnant? I never met your Aunt Margaret, so I can't be sure about the answer, but I'll share something with you. When I was a beginning graduate student and thought I knew everything, I was astounded by what I thought was the naïveté of parents-to-be who listened to Bach or Beethoven or who read Shakespeare aloud to promote the cultural development of their fetuses. But in more recent years, I admit that my wife and I have made more of an effort to expose our fetuses to good music as well.

Why? Classic research shows that by the 13th week of pregnancy, the fetus responds to sound waves. In research cited at the beginning of the chapter—and repeated here so that you cannot complain I sent you searching—Sontag and Richards (1938) rang a bell near the mother, and the fetus responded with movements similar to those of the startle reflex shown after birth. During the third trimester, fetuses respond to sounds of different frequencies through a variety of movements and changes in heart rate, suggesting that by this time they can discriminate pitch (Lecanuet et al., 2000).

An experiment by Anthony DeCasper and William Fifer (1980) is even more intriguing. In this study, women read the Dr. Seuss book *The Cat in the Hat* out loud twice daily during the final month and a half of pregnancy. After birth, their babies were given special pacifiers. Sucking on these pacifiers in one way would activate recordings of their mothers reading *The Cat in the Hat*, and sucking on them in another way would activate their mothers' readings of another book—*The King, the Mice, and the Cheese*—which was written in very different rhythms. The newborns "chose" to hear *The Cat in the Hat*. Using similar research methods, DeCasper and his colleagues also found that newborns prefer the mother's voice to that of their father or an unfamiliar woman (DeCasper & Prescott, 1984; DeCasper & Spence, 1986, 1991). Fetal learning may be one basis for the development of attachment to the mother (Krueger et al., 2004; Lecanuet, et al., 2005; Roth et al., 2004).

Developing in a World of Diversity

Let's have a look at some history and some pre-history—that is, some guesstimates of events that might have occurred before records were made. According to the U.S. Census Bureau[1] (http://www.census .gov/ipc/www/worldhis.html), which was *not* distributing questionnaires at the time, some 5 million humans walked the Earth about 10,000 years ago. It took another 5,000 years for that number to expand to 14 million. Skipping ahead 3,000 years to the year 1, humans gained a stronger foothold on the planet, and the number increased tenfold, to some 170 million. By 1900 the number increased ten- to twentyfold

(*continued, page 92*)

■ **Table 3.1** Fertility Rates and Related Factors Around the World

Nation	Fertility Rates	Rate of Usage of Modern Methods of Contraception (%)	Literacy Rates (%)		Years of Education	
			Men	Women	Men	Women
Afghanistan	7.48	3.6	43	13	9	4
Algeria	2.53	50.1	80	60	13	13
Angola	6.75	4.5	83	54	4	3
Argentina	2.35	a	97	97	15	16
Australia	1.75	72.2	a	a	20	20
Bolivia	3.96	34.9	93	81	a	a
Brazil	2.35	70.3	88	89	14	14
Cambodia	4.14	18.5	85	64	11	9
Canada	1.51	73.3	a	a	15	16
Chile	2.00	a	96	96	14	14
China	1.70	83.3	95	87	11	11
Colombia	2.62	67.6	93	93	11	12
Congo	6.70	4.4	81	54	4[b]	4[b]
Costa Rica	2.28	70.7	93	93	a	a
Cuba	1.61	72.1	100	100	14	14
Denmark	1.75	72.0	a	a	16	17
Dominican Republic	2.73	65.8	87	87	12	13
Equador	2.82	50.1	92	90	a	a
Egypt	3.29	56.5	83	59	12[b]	12[b]
France	1.87	69.3	a	a	15	16
Germany	1.32	71.8	a	a	16	16
Ghana	4.39	18.7	66	50	8	7
Greece	1.25	a	98	94	15	16
Guatemala	4.60	34.4	75	63	10	9
Honduras	3.72	50.8	80	80	11	12
India	3.07	42.8	73	48	11	9
Indonesia	2.37	56.7	94	87	12	12

(*continued on page 91*)

■ **Table 3.1** (continued)

Nation	Fertility Rates	Rate of Usage of Modern Methods of Contraception (%)	Literacy Rates (%)		Years of Education	
			Men	Women	Men	Women
Iran	2.12	56.0	84	70	13	12
Iraq	4.83	10.4	84	64	11	8
Ireland	1.94	a	a	a	18	18
Israel	2.85	51.9	98	96	15	16
Italy	1.28	38.9	99	98	16	16
Jamaica	2.44	62.6	74	86	11	12
Japan	1.33	51.0	a	a	15	15
Jordan	3.53	41.2	95	85	13	13
Kenya	5.00	31.5	78	70	10	10
Lithuania	1.28	30.5	100	100	15	16
Mali	6.92	5.7	27	12	6	5
Mexico	2.40	59.5	92	90	13	13
Morocco	2.76	54.8	66	40	11	9
Nicaragua	3.30	66.1	77	77	11	11
Pakistan	4.27	20.2	63	36	7	5
Palestinian Territories	5.57	37.1	97	88	13	14
Peru	2.86	50.4	93	82	14	14
Philippines	3.22	33.4	93	93	12	12
Russia	1.33		100	99	13	14
Saudi Arabia	4.09	28.5	87	69	10	10
Spain	1.27	67.4	a	a	16	17
Syria	3.47	28.3	86	74	a	a
Thailand	1.93	69.8	95	91	13	13
Turkey	2.46	37.7	95	80	12	10
Viet Nam	2.32		94	87	11	10
United Kingdom	1.66	81.0	a	a	16	17
United States of America	2.04	70.5	a	a	15	16

Sources: United Nations Department of Economic and Social Affairs, Demographic and Social Statistics, Social Indicators. Available at http://unstats.un.org/unsd/demographic/products/socind/default.htm (accessed April 1, 2007). Total fertility rate estimates from Population Division of the United Nations Secretariat, *World Population Prospects: Various Editions* (United Nations, Department of Economic and Social Affairs, Population Division, 2005), *World Contraceptive Use 2005, CD-ROM Edition*; data in digital form (POP/DB/CP/Rev. 2005); supplemented by contraceptive use data published by ORC Macro, available at http://www.measuredhs.com (accessed July 17, 2006). UNESCO Institute for Statistics, Table 8: School life expectancy (approximation method). Data on school life expectancy (years) from primary to tertiary by country and sex, available from UIS website, http://www.uis.unesco.org (last updated June 20, 2006).

[a]Data missing or unavailable at the United Nations website. It is not possible to draw conclusions of any kind.

[b]Number of years is for males and females combined because the numbers provided by the nation did not permit categorization by sex.

Developing in a World of Diversity

Birth Rates around the World (*continued*)

again, to more than 1.7 billion. In 1950 estimates place the number at about 2.5 billion, and today—with the increase in the food supply, sanitary water supplies, and vaccinations—the number is estimated to be at about 6.7 billion.

Therefore, we are in the middle of a population explosion, are we not? The answer would seem to depend on where one happens to be. **Truth or Fiction Revisited:** For example, if you check out ■ Table 3.1, you will readily see that it is not true that parents in wealthy nations have more children. Parents need to have slightly in excess of two children to reproduce themselves because some children are lost to illness, accidents, or violence. The table will show you that in countries such as Spain, Greece, Italy, Japan, Canada, Russia, and the United Kingdom, parents are not coming close to reproducing themselves. In some cases,

the national birth rates mask major differences within a country. In Israel, for example, the minorities of Orthodox Jews and Arabs outreproduce the majority of less religious or non-religious Jews, providing an overall somewhat inflated birth rate.

Also consider factors related to birth rates, such as use of modern means of contraception, literacy rates, and education, as measured by numbers of years spent in school. Consider the extremes. How do the birth rates of countries where 30% or fewer of the population use modern means of contraception compare with those where 60% or more use modern means? Similarly, what are the relationships between literacy and birth rate? Between education and birth rate?

I will now ask you to reflect upon some questions but I will not "spoon feed" you the answers. You

can develop your own views on the basis of your moral values or research.

[1]U.S. Census Bureau. Historical estimates of world population. http://www.census.gov/ipc/www/worldhis.html. Accessed 2 April, 2007.

Reflect:

- *How would you judge whether a particular birth rate in a particular nation is a good thing or a bad thing? If it is a bad thing, what can be done about it? Explain your views.*
- *Why do parents in wealthier nations tend to have fewer children? What are your feelings about this? Explain your views.*
- *Does the information in Table 3.1 show cause and effect? Why or why not?*

Active Review

10. The fetal stage is characterized by _____ of organ systems and gains in size and weight.
11. Research shows that fetuses respond to sound waves by about the _____ week of pregnancy.
12. Mothers usually detect fetal movements during the _____ month of pregnancy.

Reflect & Relate: During the fourth month, when the fetus's movements can be detected, many women have the feeling that their babies are "alive." What is your view on when the baby is alive? What standard or standards are you using to form your opinion?

Go to

http://www.thomsonedu.com/psychology/rathus

for an interactive version of this review.

Environmental Influences on Prenatal Development

Yes, the fetus develops in a protective "bubble," the amniotic sac. Nevertheless, the developing fetus is subject to many environmental hazards. Scientific advances have made us keenly aware of the types of things that can go wrong and what we can do to prevent these problems. In this section, we consider some environmental factors that can affect prenatal development.

Nutrition

Question: How does the nutrition of the mother affect prenatal development?
We quickly bring nutrition inside, but nutrition originates outside. Therefore, it is one environmental factor in prenatal (and subsequent) development.

It is a common misconception that fetuses "take what they need" from their mothers. If that were true, pregnant women would not have to be highly concerned about their diets, but malnutrition in the mother, especially during the last trimester when the fetus should be making rapid gains in weight, has been linked to low birth weight, prematurity, stunted growth, retardation of brain development, cognitive deficiencies, behavioral problems, and even cardiovascular disease (Giussani, 2006; Guerrini et al., 2007; Morton, 2006).

Fortunately, the effects of fetal malnutrition can sometimes be overcome by a supportive, care-giving environment. Experiments with children who suffered from fetal malnutrition show that enriched day-care programs enhance intellectual and social skills by 5 years of age (Ramey et al., 1999). Supplementing the diets of pregnant women who might otherwise be deficient in their intake of calories and protein also shows modest positive effects on the motor development of the women's infants (Morton, 2006).

On the other hand, maternal obesity is linked with a higher risk of **stillbirth** (Fernandez-Twinn & Ozanne, 2006). Obesity during pregnancy also increases the likelihood of neural tube defects. In a study reported in the *Journal of the American Medical Association*, women who weighed 176 to 195 pounds before pregnancy were about twice as likely as women who weighed 100 to 130 pounds to bear children with neural tube defects; women who weighed 242 pounds or more were four times as likely to have children with neural tube defects (Shaw et al., 1996). Note that these findings were for obese women only. Very tall women normally weigh more than shorter women, so the study's findings must be considered in terms of women's desirable weights for a given height. In Shaw's study, folic acid supplements did not appear to prevent neural tube defects in the babies of women who weighed more than 154 pounds.

What Should a Pregnant Woman Eat?

Pregnant women require the following food elements to maintain themselves and to give birth to healthy babies: protein, which is heavily concentrated in red meat, fish, poultry, eggs, beans, milk, and cheese; vitamin A, which is found in milk and vegetables; vitamin B, which is found in wheat germ, whole grain breads, and liver; vitamin C, which is found in citrus fruits; vitamin D, which is derived from sunshine, fish-liver oil, and vitamin D–fortified milk; vitamin E, which is found in whole grains, some vegetables, eggs, and peanuts; iron, which is concentrated heavily in meat (especially liver), egg yolks, fish, and raisins; the trace minerals zinc and cobalt, which are found in seafood; calcium, which is found in dairy products; and, yes, calories. Research also demonstrates the importance of consuming folic acid, which is found in leafy green vegetables. Women who eat a well-rounded diet do not require food

stillbirth The birth of a dead fetus.

supplements, but most doctors recommend them to be safe (Balluz et al., 2000). Pregnant women who take folic acid supplements reduce the risk of giving birth to babies with neural tube defects, which can cause paralysis and death (Honein et al., 2001; Lawrence et al., 2003).

How Much Weight Should a Pregnant Woman Gain?

Women can expect to gain quite a bit of weight during pregnancy because of the growth of the placenta, amniotic fluid, and the fetus itself. Women who do not restrict their diet during pregnancy normally will gain 25 to 35 pounds. Overweight women may gain less, and slender women may gain more. Regular weight gains of about 0.5 pound per week during the first half of pregnancy and 1 pound per week during the second half are most desirable. Sudden large gains or losses in weight should be discussed with the doctor.

Over the years, the pendulum has swung back and forth between views of ideal weight gains during pregnancy. Early in the 20th century, it was believed that greater weight gains would ensure proper nutrition for both the mother and the fetus. During the 1960s and part of the 1970s, pregnant women were advised to watch their weight. It was believed that excess weight posed risks for the mother and might be hard to take off following pregnancy, concerns with some basis in fact. But now the pendulum has swung back again. It is now known that inadequate weight gain in pregnancy increases the chances of having a premature or low-birth-weight baby (Bhutta et al., 2002; Christian et al., 2003; Hynes et al., 2002). Women who gain 25 to 35 pounds during pregnancy are more likely to have healthy babies than those who gain less. But a woman in the seventh or eighth month who finds herself overshooting a weight-gain target of, say, 25–30 pounds, should avoid a crash diet, especially when the fetus is making its most dramatic gains in weight.

Teratogens and Health Problems of the Mother

Most of what the mother does for the embryo is not only remarkable but also healthful. There are exceptions, however. Consider the case of teratogens. **Teratogens** (the word derives from frightening roots meaning "giving birth to monsters") are environmental agents that can harm the embryo or fetus. Teratogens include drugs that the mother ingests, such as thalidomide (connected with birth deformities) and alcohol, and substances that the mother's body produces, such as Rh-positive antibodies. Another class of teratogens is the heavy metals, such as lead and mercury, which are toxic to the embryo. Hormones are healthful in countless ways—for example, they help maintain pregnancy. However, excessive quantities of hormones are harmful to the embryo. If the mother is exposed to radiation, that radiation can harm the embryo. Then, of course, disease-causing organisms—also called pathogens—such as bacteria and viruses are also teratogens. When it comes to pathogens, bigger is better for the embryo. That is, larger pathogens are less likely to pass through the placenta and affect the embryo, but smaller pathogens sneak through, including those that cause mumps, syphilis, measles, and chicken pox. Some disorders, such as toxemia, are not transmitted to the embryo or fetus, but instead they adversely affect the environment in which it develops.

Critical Periods of Vulnerability

Question: Does it matter when, during pregnancy, a woman is exposed to a teratogen? Exposure to particular teratogens is most harmful during **critical periods** that correspond to the times when organs are developing. **Truth or Fiction Revisited:** Therefore, the same disease organism or chemical agent that can do serious damage to a 6-week-old embryo may have no effect on a 4-month-old fetus. For example, the heart develops rapidly in the third to fifth weeks after conception. As you can see

teratogens Environmental influences or agents that can damage the embryo or fetus (from the Greek *teras*, meaning "monster").

critical period In this usage, a period during which an embryo is particularly vulnerable to a certain teratogen.

in ● Figure 3.5, the heart is most vulnerable to certain teratogens at this time. The arms and legs, which develop later, are most vulnerable in the fourth through eighth weeks. Because the major organ systems differentiate during the embryonic stage, the embryo is generally more vulnerable to teratogens than the fetus. Even so, many teratogens are harmful throughout the entire course of prenatal development.

Question: What are the effects of maternal health problems? Let us consider the effects of various health problems of the mother. We begin with sexually transmitted infections (STIs).

Sexually Transmitted Infections

The **syphilis** bacterium can cause miscarriage, stillbirth, or **congenital** syphilis. Routine blood tests early in pregnancy can diagnose syphilis. The syphilis bacterium is vulnerable to antibiotics, and rates of syphilis are currently low in Western nations. In addition, the bacterium does not readily cross the placental membrane early in pregnancy. The fetus will probably not contract syphilis if an infected mother is treated with antibiotics before the fourth month of pregnancy. However, an infected woman has about a 40% chance of having a child who is stillborn or dies shortly after birth (Centers for Disease Control and Prevention, 2006a). If the mother is not treated, the baby has a 40% to 70% chance of being infected in utero and of developing congenital syphilis. Approximately 12% of those infected die.

syphilis A sexually transmitted infection that, in advanced stages, can attack major organ systems.

congenital Present at birth; resulting from the prenatal environment.

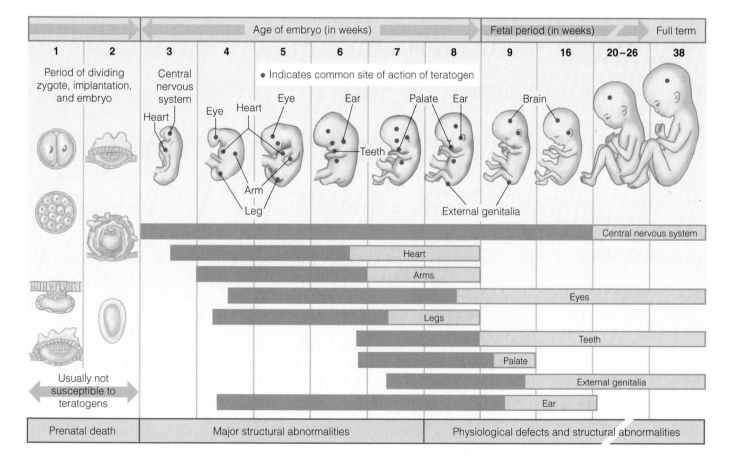

● Figure 3.5   Critical Periods in Prenatal Development

Knowledge of the sequences of prenatal development allows one to understand why specific teratogens are most harmful during certain periods of prenatal development. Major structural abnormalities are most likely to occur when teratogens strike during the embryonic period.

Infected babies may show no symptoms when they are born, but they may develop symptoms within a few weeks if they are not treated. The symptoms of congenital syphilis include skin sores, a sometimes bloody (and infectious) runny nose, slimy patches in the mouth, inflamed bones in the arms and legs, a swollen liver, jaundice, anemia, and a small head. Congenital syphilis can impair vision and hearing, damage the liver, or deform the bones and teeth. Untreated babies may develop mental retardation or have seizures.

HIV/AIDS (human immunodeficiency virus/acquired immunodeficiency syndrome) disables the body's immune system and leaves victims prey to a variety of fatal illnesses, including respiratory disorders and cancer. HIV/AIDS is lethal unless treated with a combination of antiviral drugs. Even then, the drugs do not work for everyone, and the eventual outcome remains in doubt (Rathus et al., 2008).

HIV can be transmitted by sexual relations, blood transfusions, sharing hypodermic needles while shooting up drugs, childbirth, and breast feeding. About one-fourth of babies born to HIV-infected mothers become infected themselves (Coovadia, 2004). During childbirth, blood vessels in the mother and baby rupture, enabling an exchange of blood and transmission of HIV. HIV is also found in breast milk. An African study found that the probability of transmission of HIV through breast milk was about 1 in 6 (16.2%) (Nduati et al., 2000).

Children from ethnic and racial minority groups are at greater risk of being infected with HIV. African Americans account for more than half of the pediatric cases of HIV/AIDS, and Latino and Latina Americans (especially those of Puerto Rican origin) account for almost one-fourth. Inner-city neighborhoods, where there is widespread intravenous drug use, are especially hard hit (Centers for Disease Control and Prevention, 2006a). Death rates resulting from AIDS are higher among African American and Puerto Rican children than among European American children (Centers for Disease Control and Prevention, 2004), apparently because African Americans and Puerto Ricans have less access to health care.

Rubella

Rubella (German measles) is a viral infection. Women who are infected during the first 20 weeks of pregnancy stand at least a 20% chance of bearing children with birth defects such as deafness, mental retardation, heart disease, or eye problems, including blindness (Food and Drug Administration, 2004; Reef et al., 2004).

Many adult women had rubella as children and became immune in this way. Women who are not immune are best vaccinated before they become pregnant, although they can be inoculated during pregnancy, if necessary. Inoculation has led to a dramatic decline in the number of American children born with defects caused by rubella, from approximately 2,000 cases in 1964–1965 to 21 cases in 2001 (Food and Drug Administration, 2004; Reef et al., 2004).

Toxemia

Toxemia is a life-threatening disease characterized by high blood pressure that may afflict women late in the second or early in the third trimester. Women with toxemia often have **premature** or undersized babies. Toxemia is also a cause of pregnancy-related maternal deaths (Rumbold et al., 2006). Toxemia appears to be linked to malnutrition, but the causes are unclear. Women who do not receive prenatal care are much more likely to die from toxemia than those who receive prenatal care (Scott, 2006).

Rh Incompatibility

In **Rh incompatibility**, antibodies produced by the mother are transmitted to a fetus or newborn infant and cause brain damage or death. Rh is a blood protein found in the red blood cells of some individuals. Rh incompatibility occurs when a woman

HIV/AIDS HIV stands for a virus, the human immunodeficiency virus, which cripples the body's immune system. AIDS stands for acquired immunodeficiency syndrome. HIV is a sexually transmitted infection that can also be transmitted in other ways, such as sharing needles when shooting up drugs. AIDS is caused by HIV and describes the body's state when the immune system is weakened to the point where it is vulnerable to a variety of diseases that would otherwise be fought off.

rubella A viral infection that can cause retardation and heart disease in the embryo. Also called German measles.

toxemia A life-threatening disease that can afflict pregnant women; it is characterized by high blood pressure.

premature Born before the full term of gestation. Also referred to as preterm.

Rh incompatibility A condition in which antibodies produced by the mother are transmitted to the child, possibly causing brain damage or death.

who does not have this factor—and is thus Rh negative—is carrying an Rh-positive fetus, which can happen if the father is Rh positive. The negative–positive combination occurs in approximately 10% of American couples and becomes a problem in some resulting pregnancies. Rh incompatibility does not affect a first child because women will not have formed Rh antibodies. The chances of an exchange of blood are greatest during childbirth. If an exchange occurs, the mother produces Rh-positive antibodies to the baby's Rh-positive blood. These antibodies can enter the fetal bloodstream during subsequent deliveries, causing anemia, mental deficiency, or death.

If an Rh-negative mother is injected with Rh immunoglobulin within 72 hours after delivery of an Rh-positive baby, she will not develop the antibodies. A fetus or newborn child at risk of Rh disease may receive a blood transfusion to remove the mother's antibodies.

Drugs Taken by the Parents

Rh antibodies can be lethal to children, but many other substances can have harmful effects. *Question: What are the effects of drugs taken by the mother on prenatal development?* In this section, we discuss the effects of various drugs—prescription drugs, over-the-counter drugs, and illegal drugs—on the unborn child. Even commonly used medications, such as aspirin, can be harmful to the fetus. If a woman is pregnant or thinks she may be, it is advisable for her to consult her obstetrician before taking any drugs, not just prescription medications. A physician usually can recommend a safe and effective substitute for a drug that could potentially harm a developing fetus.

A CLOSER LOOK

Preventing One's Baby from Being Infected with HIV

Pregnant women who are infected with HIV or any other sexually transmitted disease should discuss this issue with their physicians. Measures can be taken that will help prevent their babies from being infected. Current recommendations concerning transmission of HIV from mother to baby include highly active antiretroviral therapy (HAART), a combination of three drugs that decrease the amount of HIV in the bloodstream; cesarean section (C-section); and formula feeding. C-sections help prevent transmission of HIV to the fetus because it is not exposed to the mother's blood during vaginal delivery, when blood vessels rupture. HIV is also found in breast milk (hence the recommendation for formula feeding). All in all, the combination of HAART, C-section, and formula feeding has reduced mother-to-infant transmission of HIV from about 25% to 1–2% (Coovadia, 2004).

For up-to-date information on HIV/AIDS, call the National AIDS Hotline at 1-800-342-AIDS. If you want to receive information in Spanish, call 1-800-344-SIDA. You can also explore the Centers for Disease Control and Prevention website at http://www.cdc.gov. Once you are there, you can click on "Health Topics A–Z" and then on "AIDS/HIV."

Reflect: What have you done—or what will you do—to try to protect your babies from being infected with HIV and any other disease organism?

Thalidomide

Thalidomide was marketed in the 1960s as a treatment for insomnia and nausea. It was available in Germany and England without prescription. Within a few years, more than 10,000 babies with missing or stunted limbs were born in these countries and elsewhere as a result of their mothers using thalidomide during pregnancy (Ances, 2002). Thalidomide is still in use today and is used to treat disorders as various as dermatological problems and Kaposi's sarcoma, a form of cancer that affects many people with HIV/AIDS (Chaudhry et al., 2002).

Thalidomide provides a dramatic example of critical periods of vulnerability to various teratogens. A fetus's extremities undergo rapid development during the second month of pregnancy (see Figure 3.5). Thalidomide taken during this period almost invariably causes birth defects.

Antibiotics

Several antibiotics may be harmful to the fetus. Tetracycline, which is frequently prescribed for bacterial infections, can lead to yellowed teeth and bone abnormalities. Other antibiotics are implicated in hearing loss.

Hormones

Women at risk for miscarriages have been prescribed hormones to help maintain their pregnancies. For example, **progestin** is chemically similar to male sex hormones and can masculinize the external sex organs of female embryos. Prenatal progestin has also been linked to aggressive behavior and masculine-typed behaviors in females (Keenan & Soleymani, 2001; Molenda-Figueira et al., 2006).

DES (short for diethylstilbestrol), a powerful estrogen, was given to many women during the 1940s and 1950s to help prevent miscarriage, but it has caused cervical and testicular cancer in some of the offspring. Among daughters of DES users, about 1 in 1,000 will develop cancer in the reproductive tract. Daughters are also more likely to have babies who are premature or low in birth weight. Daughters and sons of mothers who took DES have high rates of infertility and immune system disorders (Centers for Disease Control and Prevention, 2005).

Vitamins

Although pregnant women are often prescribed multivitamins to maintain their own health and to promote the development of their fetuses, too much of a good thing can be dangerous. High doses of vitamins A and D have been associated with central nervous system damage, small head size, and heart defects (National Institutes of Health, 2002).

Heroin and Methadone

Maternal addiction to heroin or methadone is linked to low birth weight, prematurity, and toxemia. Narcotics such as heroin and methadone readily cross the placental membrane, and the fetuses of women who use them regularly can become addicted (Lejeune et al., 2006). **Truth or Fiction Revisited:** It is true that babies can be born addicted to narcotics and other substances used regularly by their mothers.

Addicted newborns may be given the narcotic or a substitute shortly after birth so that they will not suffer serious withdrawal symptoms. The drug is then withdrawn gradually. Addicted newborns may also have behavioral effects. For example, infants exposed to heroin in utero show delays in motor and language development at the age of 12 months (Bunikowski et al., 1998).

Marijuana (Cannabis)

Smoking marijuana during pregnancy apparently poses a number of risks for the fetus, including slower fetal growth (Hurd et al., 2005) and low birth weight (Visscher et al., 2003). These and the following risks are all proportional to the amount of

thalidomide A sedative used in the 1960s that has been linked to birth defects, especially deformed or absent limbs.

progestin A hormone used to maintain pregnancy that can cause masculinization of the fetus.

DES Abbreviation for diethylstilbestrol, a powerful estrogen that has been linked to cancer in the reproductive organs of children of women who used the hormone when pregnant.

marijuana smoked; that is, women who smoke more, or who inhale more secondary smoke (that is, smoke from others who are smoking), place their fetuses at relatively greater risk. The babies of women who regularly used marijuana show increased tremors and startling, suggesting immature development of the nervous system (Huestis et al., 2002).

Research into the cognitive effects of maternal prenatal use of marijuana shows mixed results. Some studies suggest that there may be no impairment (Fried & Smith, 2001). Others suggest that cognitive skills, including learning and memory, may be impaired (Huizink & Mulder, 2006). One study assessed the behavior of 10-year-olds who had been exposed prenatally to maternal use of marijuana (Goldschmidt et al., 2000). The study included the children of 635 mothers, age 18 to 42. Prenatal use of marijuana was significantly related to increased hyperactivity, impulsivity, and problems in paying attention (as measured by the Swanson, Noland, and Pelham checklist); increased delinquency (as measured by the Child Behavior Checklist); and increased delinquency and aggressive behavior (as measured by teacher report). The researchers hypothesized that the pathway between prenatal marijuana exposure and delinquency involves the effects of marijuana on attention, impairing the abilities to learn in school and to conform to social rules and norms. A Swedish study also suggests that fetal exposure to marijuana may impair systems in the brain that regulate emotional behavior (Wang et al., 2004).

Researchers have also found that maternal use of marijuana predisposes offspring to dependence on opiates (narcotics derived from the opium poppy). The fetal brain, like the adult brain, has cannabinoid receptors—called CB-1 receptors—and other structures that are altered by exposure to marijuana. The alterations make the individual more sensitive to the reinforcing properties of opiates, even in adulthood (Moreno et al., 2003). In any event, longitudinal research with 763 women recruited in the fourth month of pregnancy found that prenatal exposure to maternal marijuana smoking is a reasonably good predictor of whether or not the child will smoke marijuana at the age of 14 (Day et al., 2006).

Cocaine

There is little doubt that prenatal exposure to cocaine can harm the child. Pregnant women who abuse cocaine increase the risk of stillbirth, low birth weight, and birth defects. The infants are often excitable and irritable, or lethargic. The more heavily exposed to cocaine they are in utero, the more problems they have with jitteriness, concentration, and sleep (Schuetze et al., 2006). There are suggestions of delays in cognitive development even at 12 months of age (Singer et al., 2005).

Children who are exposed to cocaine prenatally also show problems at later ages. One study compared 189 children at 4 years of age who had been exposed to cocaine in utero with 185 other 4-year-olds who had not on the Clinical Evaluation of Language Fundamentals—Preschool (CELF-P) test (Lewis et al., 2004). The children exposed to cocaine had much lower expressive language scores and somewhat lower receptive language scores than those not exposed to cocaine. That is, the relative ability of children exposed to cocaine to express themselves was affected more than their ability to understand language. The study controlled for prenatal exposure to cigarette smoke, alcohol, and marijuana.

A study of 473 children who were 6 years old compared children who were exposed to cocaine in utero (204) with those who were not (Delaney-Black et al., 2004). The study found effects for the amount of cocaine used by the mother and the sex of the child. Boys, first of all, were more likely to be affected than girls. According to teacher reports, boys whose mothers used cocaine regularly were likely to be rated as hyperactive and indifferent to their environment and to show deficits in cognitive skills. The study controlled for maternal use of alcohol and illegal drugs other than cocaine while pregnant.

The studies with humans are correlational. That is, mothers are not randomly assigned to use cocaine; instead, they make the choice themselves. This problem is technically termed a selection factor. Thus, it may be that the same factors that lead mothers to use cocaine also affect their children. To overcome the selection factor, numerous experiments have been conducted with laboratory animals (Buxhoeveden et al., 2006; Chelonis et al., 2003). In one study, randomly selected pregnant rats were given cocaine during days 12–21 of gestation, whereas control rats received no cocaine (Huber et al., 2001). The rat pups were then exposed to stressors such as cold-water swimming and tail flicks. The pups exposed to cocaine showed less tolerance of the stressors—as measured by behaviors such as tail twitches and convulsions—than the control subjects. Another study found that such group differences in response to stressors endure into rat adulthood, that is, 90–120 days of age (Campbell et al., 2000).

Some investigators have also exposed rabbit embryos to cocaine during various periods of prenatal brain development (Gabriel et al., 2003; Stanwood et al., 2001; Thompson et al., 2005). The researchers found deficiencies in learning in the offspring and that a structure in the brain called the anterior cingulate cortex (ACC) shows changes in development. The ACC is involved in attention and self-control.

Alcohol

No drug has meant so much to so many as alcohol. Alcohol is our dinnertime relaxant, our bedtime sedative, our cocktail-party social lubricant. We use alcohol to celebrate holy days, applaud our accomplishments, and express joyous wishes. Millions of adolescents assert their maturity with alcohol. Alcohol is used at least occasionally by the majority of high school and college students (Johnston et al., 2006). Alcohol even kills germs on surface wounds.

Because alcohol passes through the placenta, however, drinking by a pregnant woman poses risks for the embryo and fetus. Heavy drinking can be lethal to the fetus and neonate. It is also connected with deficiencies and deformities in growth. Some children of heavy drinkers develop **fetal alcohol syndrome (FAS)** (Floyd et al., 2005; Connor et al., 2006). Babies with FAS are often smaller than normal, and so are their brains. Such babies have distinct facial features: widely spaced eyes, an underdeveloped upper jaw, a flattened nose. There may be malformation of the limbs, poor coordination, and cardiovascular problems. A number of psychological characteristics are connected with FAS and appear to reflect dysfunction of the brain: mental retardation, hyperactivity, distractibility, lessened verbal fluency, and learning disabilities (Guerrini et al., 2007; Connor et al., 2006). There are deficits in speech and hearing, practical reasoning, and visual–motor coordination (Connor et al., 2006).

The facial deformities of FAS diminish as the child moves into adolescence, and most children catch up in height and weight, but the intellectual, academic, and behavioral deficits of individuals with FAS persist. Academic and intellectual problems relative to peers range from verbal difficulties to deficiency in spatial memory (Guerrini et al., 2007). Studies find that the average academic functioning of adolescents and young adults with FAS was at the second- to fourth-grade level. Maladaptive behaviors such as poor judgment, distractibility, and difficulty perceiving social cues are common (Schonfeld et al., 2005).

FAS is part of a broader group of fetal alcohol–related problems referred to as fetal alcohol spectrum disorders (Connor et al., 2006). **Truth or Fiction Revisited:** It cannot be guaranteed that one glass of wine a day is harmless to the embryo and

© George Steinmetz

Fetal Alcohol Syndrome (FAS)
The children of many mothers who drank alcohol during pregnancy exhibit FAS. This syndrome is characterized by developmental lags and such facial features as an underdeveloped upper jaw, a flattened nose, and widely spaced eyes.

fetal alcohol syndrome (FAS) A cluster of symptoms shown by children of women who drank heavily during pregnancy, including characteristic facial features and mental retardation.

fetus. Although some health professionals allow pregnant women a glass of wine with dinner, research suggests that even moderate drinkers place their offspring at increased risk for a less severe set of effects known as **fetal alcohol effect (FAE)**. Pregnant women who have as few as one or two drinks a day may be more likely to miscarry and have growth-delayed babies than pregnant women who do not drink alcohol (Newburn-Cook et al., 2002; Ornoy, 2002).

The reported effects of maternal alcohol use, as with the effects of maternal use of cocaine, are based on correlational evidence. No researcher would randomly assign some pregnant women to drinking and others to abstention. However, researchers have randomly assigned experimental animals to intake of alcohol, and the results support the correlational evidence with humans. For example, research with animals finds that exposure to alcohol during gestation is connected with retarded growth, facial malformations characteristic of FAS, deficiencies in the immune system, and structural and chemical differences in the central nervous system (Lugo et al., 2006; Ponnappa & Rubin, 2000).

Caffeine

Many pregnant women consume caffeine in the form of coffee, tea, soft drinks, chocolate, and nonprescription drugs. Research findings on caffeine's effects on the developing fetus have been inconsistent. Some studies report no adverse findings, but other studies (e.g., Cnattingius et al., 2000) suggest that pregnant women who take in a good deal of caffeine may be more likely than nonusers of caffeine to have a miscarriage or a low-birth-weight baby. Because of such findings, many obstetricians recommend that pregnant women are well advised to be moderate in their caffeine intake.

Perhaps the best review of the literature to date is by Lisa Signorello and Joseph McLaughlin (2004). They carefully reviewed—perhaps I should say "ripped apart"—15 epidemiologic studies on caffeine and miscarriage, paying specific attention to the kinds of methodological problems that can lead to inaccurate results, such as selection factors in the sampling, problems in women's recall of exactly how much caffeine they used or in the measurement of exposure to caffeine, and the timing of the loss of the embryo or the fetus. They concluded that (1) each study was flawed and (2) there was no way to compare the results of the studies to one another, even though most studies reported a link between the intake of caffeine by the mother and the risk of miscarriage.

The evidence, apparently, is a train wreck, so what can I advise? Simply that until we have better evidence, pregnant women are well advised to be moderate in their caffeine intake.

Cigarettes

Cigarette smoke contains many ingredients, including the stimulant nicotine, the gas carbon monoxide, and hydrocarbons ("tars"), which are carcinogens. Fortunately, only the first two, the nicotine and the carbon monoxide, pass through the placenta and reach the fetus. That's the end of the fortunate news. Nicotine stimulates the fetus, but its long-term effects are uncertain. Carbon monoxide is toxic; it decreases the amount of oxygen available to the fetus. Oxygen deprivation is connected with cognitive and behavioral problems, including impaired motor development. The cognitive difficulties include academic delays, learning disabilities, and mental retardation. Not all children of smokers develop these problems, but many do not function as well as they would have if they had not been exposed to maternal smoking.

Pregnant women who smoke are likely to deliver smaller babies than nonsmokers (Bernstein et al., 2005). In addition, their babies are more likely to be stillborn or to die soon after birth (Cnattingius, 2004). The combination of smoking and drinking

fetal alcohol effect (FAE)
A cluster of symptoms less severe than those of fetal alcohol syndrome shown by children of women who drank moderately during pregnancy.

Smoking during pregnancy hurts the fetus. The only question is, "How much?"

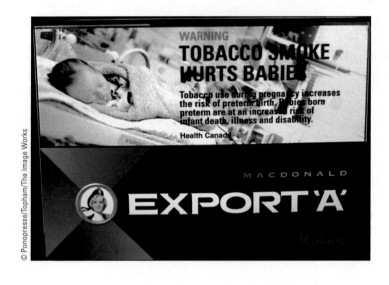

alcohol places the child at greater risk of low birth weight than either practice alone (Spencer, 2006).

Maternal smoking may also have long-term negative effects on development. Children whose mothers smoke during pregnancy are more likely to show short attention spans, hyperactivity, lower cognitive and language scores, and poor grades (Secker-Walker & Vacek, 2003).

Smoking during pregnancy obviously poses significant threats to the fetus. So why do pregnant women do it? Are they ignorant of the risks to their children? Perhaps. Despite decades of public education efforts, some women remain unaware that smoking will hurt the fetus. But most American women are aware of the threat, yet they say that they can't quit or that they can't suspend smoking until the baby is born. Why? Some claim that they are under too much stress to stop smoking, although cigarette smoking actually contributes to stress; it's not a one-way ticket to relaxation. Others smoke to fight feelings of depression (nicotine is a stimulant and depression is, well, depressing), because "everybody" around them smokes (often, "everybody" translates to "partner"), or because they just don't have the willpower (or perhaps I should say, the "won't power") to deal with the withdrawal symptoms of quitting (Cnattingius, 2004; Spencer, 2006). Some parents simply deny that their smoking is likely to harm their children, despite knowledge to the contrary. They reason: Why worry about quitting smoking? I could be run over by a truck tomorrow. (Yes, dear reader, one could be run over by a truck, but one can also look both ways before crossing the street, and one can choose to act as if one is in control of one's life.)

Secondhand smoke also holds dangers. Men who smoke are more likely to produce abnormal sperm. Babies of fathers who smoke have higher rates of birth defects, infant mortality, lower birth weights, and cardiovascular problems (Goel et al., 2004).

Environmental Hazards

Mothers know when they are ingesting drugs, but there are many other substances in the environment they may take in unknowingly. These substances are environmental hazards to which we are all exposed, and we refer to them collectively as pollution. *Question: What are the effects of environmental hazards during pregnancy?*

Prenatal exposure to heavy metals such as lead, mercury, and zinc threatens the development of children. Longitudinal research finds that newborns who have mildly elevated levels of lead in their umbilical cord blood show delayed mental development at 1 and 2 years of age (Heindel & Lawler, 2006). However, their cognitive functioning can improve if there is no longer lead in the home.

One study of the effects of prenatal exposure to lead recruited 442 children in Yugoslavia (Wasserman et al., 2000). Some of the children lived in a town with a smelter, and the others did not. (Smelting, or the melting of lead-bearing scrap metal into metallic lead, is a major source of lead fume emissions.) The children received intelligence testing at the ages of 3, 4, 5, and 7, using Wechsler and other scales. The researchers found that the children from the town with the smelter obtained somewhat lower intelligence test scores. It is conceivable, of course, that people who choose to live in a town without a smelter differ from those who live near one.

Experiments with rodents support the correlational findings with humans. For example, mice exposed to lead in utero do not form memories as well as those who are free of prenatal exposure to lead (de Oliveira et al., 2001). Research with rats has found that prenatal exposure to lead decreases the levels of neurotransmitters (the chemical messengers of the brain) in all areas of the brain, but especially in the hippocampus. The hippocampus is involved in memory formation.

The devastating effects of mercury on the fetus were first recognized among the Japanese who lived around Minimata Bay. Industrial waste containing mercury was dumped into the bay and accumulated in local fish, which were a major food source for local residents. Children born to women who had eaten the fish during pregnancy often were profoundly retarded and neurologically damaged (Vorhees & Mollnow, 1987). Prenatal exposure to even small amounts of mercury and other heavy metals such as cadmium and chromium can produce subtle deficits in cognitive functioning and physical health (Heindel & Lawler, 2006).

Polychlorinated biphenyls (PCBs) are chemicals used in many industrial products. Like mercury, they accumulate in fish that feed in polluted waters. Newborns whose mothers had consumed PCB-contaminated fish from Lake Michigan were smaller and showed poorer motor functioning and less responsiveness than newborns whose mothers had not eaten these fish. Furthermore, even those PCB-exposed infants who appeared normal at birth showed deficits in memory at 7 months and at 4 years of age (Jacobson et al., 1992).

An unfortunate natural experiment in the effects of prenatal exposure to PCBs took place in Taiwan during the late 1970s, when a group of people accidentally ingested contaminated rice. Children born to mothers who ate the rice had characteristic signs of PCB poisoning, including hyperpigmented skin. The researchers (Lai et al., 2001) had the opportunity to compare the cognitive development of 118 children born to exposed mothers with other children in the community. The children were all followed through the age of 12 and were tested with instruments that included the Bayley Scale for Infant Development, the Chinese version of the Stanford–Binet IQ Test, and two nonverbal intelligence tests. The children of mothers who ate the contaminated rice scored lower than the control children on each of these methods of measurement throughout the observation period. It appears that prenatal exposure to PCBs has long-term harmful effects on cognitive development.

Experiments with mice show that fetal exposure to radiation in high doses can cause defects in a number of organs, including the eyes, central nervous system, and skeleton (e.g., Hossain et al., 2005). Pregnant women who were exposed to atomic radiation during the bombings of Hiroshima and Nagasaki in World War II gave birth to babies who were more likely to be mentally retarded in addition to being physically deformed (Sadler, 2005). Pregnant women are advised to avoid unnecessary exposure to x-rays. (Ultrasound, which is not an x-ray, has not been shown to be harmful to the fetus, but women may question what appears to them to be excessive use of ultrasound.)

Research suggests that men exposed to heavy metals and radiation can also produce children with abnormalities. For example, children of fathers employed in jobs with high exposure to lead had three times more kidney tumors than children whose fathers were not exposed (Davis, 1991). Another study found a higher incidence of leukemia among children whose fathers worked in nuclear plants, where they were exposed to high levels of radiation before the children's conception ("British Study Finds," 1990).

The risks of radiation and other environmental agents to the embryo and fetus are summarized in Concept Review 3.2.

Maternal Stress

Although pregnancy can be a time of immense gratification for women, it can also be a time of stress. The baby might be unplanned and unwanted. Parents might not have the financial resources or the room for the child. The mother might be experiencing physical discomforts because of the pregnancy. *Question: What, then, are the apparent effects of maternal stress on the child?*

How does a mother's emotional state affect her fetus? Emotions are psychological feeling states, but they also have physiological components. For example, they are linked to the secretion of hormones such as adrenaline. **Adrenaline** stimulates the mother's heart rate, respiratory rate, and other bodily functions. Hormones pass through the placenta and also have an effect on the fetus.

Parents' Age

Question: Is the parents' age connected with the outcome of pregnancy?

Older fathers are more likely to produce abnormal sperm. The mother's age also matters. From a biological vantage point, the 20s may be the ideal age for women to bear children. Teenage mothers have a higher incidence of infant mortality and children with low birth weight (Phipps et al., 2002; Save the Children, 2004b). Girls who become pregnant in their early teens may place a burden on bodies that may not have adequately matured to facilitate pregnancy and childbirth. Teenage mothers also are less educated and less likely to obtain prenatal care than older mothers. These factors are associated with high-risk pregnancy (Berg et al., 2003).

What about women older than 30? Women's fertility declines gradually until the mid-30s, after which it declines more rapidly. Women beyond their middle 30s may have passed the point at which their reproductive systems function most efficiently. Women possess all their ova in immature form at birth. Over 30 years, these cells are exposed to the slings and arrows of an outrageous environment of toxic wastes, chemical pollutants, and radiation, thus increasing the risk of chromosomal abnormalities such as Down syndrome (Behrman et al., 2000). Women who wait until their 30s or 40s to have children also increase the likelihood of having stillborn or preterm babies (Berg et al., 2003). However, with adequate prenatal care, the risk of bearing a premature or unhealthy baby still is relatively small, even for older first-time mothers (Berg et al., 2003). This news should be encouraging for women who have delayed, or plan to delay, bearing children until their 30s or 40s.

Whatever the age of the mother, the events of childbirth provide some of the most memorable moments in the lives of parents. In Chapter 4, we continue our voyage with the process of birth and the characteristics of the newborn child.

adrenaline A hormone that generally arouses the body, increasing the heart and respiration rates.

Concept Review 3.2 Risks of Various Agents to the Embryo and Fetus

Agent	Risks
Prescription Drugs[a]	
Accutane (used to treat acne; repeated blood tests required to show that one is not pregnant or encountering drug-related problems)	Stillbirth, malformation of limbs and organs
Bendectin	Cleft palate, malformation of the heart
Carbamazepine (and other anticonvulsant drugs)	Spina bifida
Diethylstilbestrol (DES; once used to help maintain pregnancy)	Cancer of the cervix or testes
Strong general anesthesia during labor (sedation that goes beyond normal medical practice)	Anoxia, asphyxiation, brain damage
Progestin (a synthetic version of the natural hormone progesterone, which is sometimes used to help maintain pregnancy)	Masculinization of the sex organs of female embryos, possible development of "masculine" aggressiveness
Streptomycin (an antibiotic)	Deafness
Tetracycline (an antibiotic)	Malformed bones, yellow teeth
Thalidomide (several uses, including sedation)	Malformed or missing limbs
Other Drugs	
Alcohol	Fetal death, low birth weight, addiction, academic and intellectual problems, hyperactivity, distractibility, fetal alcohol syndrome (FAS, including characteristic facial features)
Aspirin (high doses)	Bleeding, respiratory problems
Caffeine (the stimulant found in coffee, tea, colas, chocolate)	Stimulates fetus (not necessarily a problem in itself), miscarriage, low birth weight
Cigarette smoke (the stimulant nicotine and carbon monoxide are transmitted through the placenta)	Stimulates fetus (not necessarily a problem in itself), premature birth, low birth weight, fetal death, academic problems, hyperactivity and shirt attention span
Opiates (heroin, morphine, others)	Low birth weight, premature birth, addiction, toxemia
Marijuana	Tremors, startling, premature birth, birth defects, neurological problems
Vitamins[b]	
Vitamin A (high doses)	Cleft palate, damage to the eyes
Vitamin D (high doses)	Mental retardation
Pathogens (disease-causing agents)	
HIV (the virus that causes AIDS)	Physical deformity, mental retardation
Rubella (German measles)	Neurological impairment involving sensation and perception (vision, hearing), mental retardation, heart problems, cataracts
Syphilis (a sexually transmitted infection caused by the *Treponema pallidum* bacterium)	Infant mortality, seizures, mental retardation, sensory impairment (vision, hearing), liver damage, malformation of bones and teeth
Environmental Hazards	
Heavy metals (lead, mercury, zinc)	Mental retardation, hyperactivity, stillbirth, problems in memory formation
Paint fumes (heavy exposure)	Mental retardation
PCBs (polychlorinated biphenyls), dioxin, other insecticides and herbicides	Stillbirth, low birth weight, cognitive impairment, motor impairment
X-rays	Deformation of organs
Biochemical Incompatibility with Mother	
Rh antibodies	Infant mortality, brain damage

[a]Normally healthful, even life-saving drugs can be harmful to the embryo and fetus. Women should inform their physicians when they are pregnant, may be pregnant, or are planning to become pregnant.

[b]Adequate intake of vitamins is essential to the well-being of the mother and the embryo and fetus. Most obstetricians advise pregnant women to take vitamin supplements, but too much of a good thing can be harmful. In brief, don't do "megavitamins" and, when in doubt, ask your obstetrician.

Active Review

13. Mothers who ingest folic acid reduce the risk of giving birth to babies with _____ tube defects.

14. _____ are environmental agents that can harm the developing embryo or fetus.

15. Women (Can or Cannot?) be successfully treated for syphilis during pregnancy.

16. Toxemia is mainly characterized by high _____ pressure.

17. In _____ incompatibility, antibodies produced by the mother are transmitted to a fetus or newborn infant and cause brain damage or death to the infant.

18. _____ was prescribed to help women maintain their pregnancies, but it caused cervical and testicular cancer in some of their children.

19. The babies of women who regularly used _____ during pregnancy have been found to show increased tremors and startling.

20. Heavy maternal use of alcohol is linked to _____ alcohol syndrome (FAS).

21. Women who smoke during pregnancy deprive their fetuses of _____, sometimes resulting in stillbirth and persistent academic problems.

22. Fetal exposure to the heavy metals lead and mercury can (Slow or Accelerate?) mental development.

Reflect & Relate: How will your knowledge of critical periods of prenatal development allow you to predict—and possibly prevent—the effects of various agents on the embryo and fetus? How difficult do you think it would be for you or someone you know to give up drinking alcohol or smoking during pregnancy? Would looking on the "sacrifice" as temporary make it easier?

Go to

http://www.thomsonedu.com/psychology/rathus

for an interactive version of this review.

RECITE: *An Active Summary*

1. **What happens during the germinal stage of prenatal development?**

During the germinal stage, the zygote divides repeatedly, but it does not gain in mass. It travels through a fallopian tube to the uterus, where it implants. It then takes the form of a blastocyst. Layers of cells form within the embryonic disk. The outer part of the blastocyst differentiates into membranes that will protect and nourish the embryo.

2. **If the dividing mass of cells is moving through a fallopian tube and then "wandering" through the uterus for another few days, how does it obtain any nourishment?**

Before implantation, the dividing cluster of cells is nourished by the yolk of the original egg cell. Once implanted in the uterine wall, it obtains nourishment from the mother.

3. **What happens during the embryonic stage of prenatal development?**

The embryonic stage lasts from implantation until the eighth week of development, during which the major organ systems differentiate. Development follows cephalocaudal and proximodistal trends. The outer layer of the embryonic disk develops into the nervous system, sensory organs, nails, hair, teeth, and skin. Two ridges form the neural tube, from which the nervous system develops. The inner layer forms the digestive and respiratory systems, liver, and pancreas. The middle layer becomes the excretory, reproductive, and circulatory systems, the muscles, the skeleton, and the inner layer of the skin.

4. **When does the heart begin to beat?**

The heart begins to beat during the fourth week.

5. **What else happens during the embryonic stage?**

Toward the end of the first month, arm and leg buds appear and the face takes shape. The nervous system has also begun to develop. By the end of the second month, limbs are elongating, facial features are becoming distinct, teeth buds have formed, the kidneys are working, and the liver is producing red blood cells.

6. **How do some babies develop into girls and others into boys?**

By 5 to 6 weeks, the embryo has undifferentiated sex organs that resemble female structures. Testes produce male sex hormones that spur development of male genital organs and the male duct system.

7. **How does the embryo get nourishment from its mother? How does it eliminate waste products?**

The embryo and fetus exchange nutrients and wastes with the mother through a mass of tissue called the placenta. The umbilical cord connects the fetus to the placenta.

8. **Do germs or drugs in the mother pass through the placenta and affect the baby?**

Many do, including the germs that cause syphilis and rubella. Some drugs also pass through, including aspirin, narcotics, and alcohol.

9. **What happens during the fetal stage of prenatal development?**

The fetal stage lasts from the end of the embryonic stage until birth. The fetus begins to turn in the ninth or tenth week. The second trimester is characterized by maturation of organs and gains in size. By the end of the second trimester, the fetus opens and shuts its eyes, sucks its thumb, alternates between wakefulness and sleep, and responds to light and sounds. During the third trimester, the heart and lungs become increasingly capable of sustaining independent life.

10. **Why did my Aunt Margaret play classical music (and put the speakers near her abdomen) when she was 7 months pregnant?**

I can't explain exactly why your Aunt Margaret played classical music, but the fetus responds to sound waves by the 13th week of pregnancy. Newborn babies prefer their mother's voice to that of other women, apparently because of prenatal exposure.

11.	**When does the mother begin to detect fetal movements?**	The mother usually detects fetal movements during the fourth month. By the end of the second trimester, the fetus turns somersaults.
12.	**How does the nutrition of the mother affect prenatal development?**	Malnutrition in the mother has been linked to low birth weight, prematurity, stunted growth, retardation of brain development, cognitive deficiencies, and behavioral problems. Folic acid reduces the risk of neural tube defects.
13.	**Does it matter when, during pregnancy, a woman is exposed to a teratogen?**	Yes. Exposure to particular teratogens is most harmful during critical periods, the times when certain organs are developing. The embryo is generally more vulnerable than the fetus because the major organ systems are differentiating.
14.	**What are the effects of maternal health problems?**	Women who contract rubella may bear children who suffer from deafness, mental retardation, heart disease, or cataracts. Syphilis can cause miscarriage, stillbirth, or congenital syphilis. Babies can be infected with HIV in utero, during childbirth, or by breast feeding. Toxemia is characterized by high blood pressure and is connected with preterm or undersized babies. In Rh incompatibility, antibodies produced by the mother are transmitted to a fetus or newborn infant and cause brain damage or death.
15.	**What are the effects of drugs taken by the mother on prenatal development?**	Thalidomide causes missing or stunted limbs in babies. Tetracycline can cause yellowed teeth and bone problems. DES leads to high risk of cervical and testicular cancer. High doses of vitamins A and D are associated with nervous system damage and heart defects. Maternal addiction to narcotics is linked to low birth weight, prematurity, and toxemia, and fetuses can be born addicted themselves. Marijuana may cause tremors and startling in babies. Cocaine increases the risk of stillbirth, low birth weight, and birth defects. Maternal use of alcohol is linked to death of the fetus and neonate, malformations, growth deficiencies, and fetal alcohol syndrome (FAS). Caffeine is connected with miscarriage and low birth weight. Maternal cigarette smoking is linked with low birth weight, stillbirth, and mental retardation.
16.	**What are the effects of environmental hazards during pregnancy?**	Prenatal exposure to heavy metals threatens cognitive development. Prenatal exposure to mercury is connected with neurological damage. Prenatal exposure to PCBs is connected with babies that are smaller, less responsive, and more likely to develop cognitive deficits. Fetal exposure to radiation can cause neural and skeletal problems.
17.	**What are the apparent effects of maternal stress on the child?**	Maternal stress is linked to the secretion of hormones such as adrenaline, which pass through the placenta and affect the baby. Maternal stress may be connected with complications during pregnancy and labor, preterm or low-birth-weight babies, and irritable babies.
18.	**Is the parents' age connected with the outcome of pregnancy?**	Yes. Teenage mothers have a higher incidence of infant mortality and children with low birth weight. Women older than the age of 30 run an increasing risk of chromosomal abnormalities and of having stillborn or preterm babies.

Key Terms

neonate, 78
germinal stage, 78
blastocyst, 78
embryonic disk, 79
trophoblast, 78
umbilical cord, 78
placenta, 78
embryonic stage, 80
cephalocaudal, 80
proximodistal, 80
ectoderm, 80
neural tube, 80

endoderm, 80
mesoderm, 81
androgens, 82
testosterone, 82
amniotic sac, 84
amniotic fluid, 84
fetal stage, 85
stillbirth, 93
teratogens, 94
critical period, 94
syphilis, 95
congenital, 95

HIV/AIDS, 96
rubella, 96
toxemia, 96
premature, 96
Rh incompatibility, 96
thalidomide, 98
progestin, 98
diethylstilbestrol (DES), 98
fetal alcohol syndrome (FAS), 100
fetal alcohol effect (FAE), 101
adrenaline, 104

Active Learning Resources

Childhood & Adolescence Book Companion Website

http://www.thomsonedu.com/psychology/rathus

Visit your book companion website, where you will find more resources to help you study. There you will find interactive versions of your book features, including the Lessons in Observation video, Active Review sections, and the Truth or Fiction feature. In addition, the companion website contains quizzing, flash cards, and a pronunciation glossary.

 is an easy-to-use online resource that helps you study in less time to get the grade you want, NOW.

http://www.thomsonedu.com/login

Need help studying? This site is your one-stop study shop. Take a Pre-Test and ThomsonNOW will generate a Personalized Study Plan based on your test results. The Study Plan will identify the topics you need to review and direct you to online resources to help you master those topics. You can then take a Post-Test to determine the concepts you have mastered and what you still need to work on.

4

Birth and the Newborn Baby:
In the New World

Truth or Fiction?

 The fetus signals its mother when it is ready to be born. p. 113

 After birth, babies are held upside down and slapped on the buttocks to stimulate independent breathing. p. 116

T F The way the umbilical cord is cut determines whether the baby's "belly button" will be an "innie" or an "outie." p. 116

T F Women who give birth according to the Lamaze method do not experience pain. p. 119

T F In the United States, nearly 3 of every 10 births are by cesarean section. p. 120

T F It is abnormal to feel depressed following childbirth. p. 128

T F Parents must have extended early contact with their newborn children if adequate bonding is to take place. p. 129

T F More children die from sudden infant death syndrome (SIDS) than from cancer, heart disease, pneumonia, child abuse, AIDS, cystic fibrosis, and muscular dystrophy combined. p. 143

Preview

Go to

http://www.thomsonedu.com/psychology/rathus
for an interactive version of this "Truth or Fiction" feature.

© Don Mason/CORBIS

uring the last few weeks before she gave birth, Michele explained: "I couldn't get my mind off the pregnancy—what it was going to be like when I finally delivered Lisa. I'd had the amniocentesis, so I knew it was a girl. I'd had the ultrasounds, so all her fingers and toes had been counted, but I was still hoping and praying that everything would turn out all right. To be honest, I was also worried about the delivery. I had always been an A student, and I guess I wanted to earn an A in childbirth as well. Matt was understanding, and he was even helpful, but, you know, it wasn't him.

"My obstetrician was bending over backwards—she could bend, I couldn't—being politically correct and kept on talking about how *we* had gotten pregnant and about how we were going to have the baby. Toward the end there, I would have been thrilled if it had really been we. Or I would even have allowed Matt to do it all by himself. But the fact is it was me, and I was worrying about how I could even reach the steering wheel of the car in those days, much less deliver a perfect healthy child. On TV, of course, they do it without even disturbing their mascara, but I was living in the real world. And waiting, waiting, waiting. And, oh yes, did I mention waiting?"

Nearly all first-time mothers struggle through the last weeks of pregnancy and worry about the mechanics of delivery. Childbirth is a natural function, of course, but so many of them have gone to classes to learn how to do what comes naturally! They worry about whether they'll get to the hospital or birthing center on time ("Is there gas in the car?" "Is it snowing?"). They worry about whether the baby will start breathing on its own properly. They may wonder if they'll do it on their own or need a C-section. They may also worry about whether it will hurt, and how much, and when they should ask for anesthetics, and, well, how to earn that A.

Close to full **term**, Michele and other women are sort of front-loaded and feel bent out of shape, and guess what? They are. The weight of the fetus may also be causing backaches. Will they deliver the baby, or will the baby—by being born—deliver them from discomfort? "Hanging in and having Lisa was a wonderful experience," Michele said. "I think Matt should have had it."

---

term A set period of time, such as the typical period of time between conception and the birth of a baby.

Braxton-Hicks contractions The first, usually painless, contractions of childbirth.

prostaglandins (pross-tuh-GLAN-dins) Hormones that stimulate uterine contractions.

oxytocin (ok-see-TOE-sin) A pituitary hormone that stimulates labor contractions (from the Greek *oxys*, meaning "quick," and *tokos*, meaning "birth").

neonate A newborn child (from the Greek *neos*, meaning "new," and the Latin *natus*, meaning "born").

Countdown . . .

Question: What events occur just before the beginning of childbirth? Early in the last month of pregnancy, the head of the fetus settles in the pelvis. This process is called dropping or lightening. Because lightening decreases pressure on the diaphragm, the mother may, in fact, feel lighter.

The first uterine contractions are called **Braxton-Hicks contractions**, or false labor contractions. They are relatively painless and may be experienced as early as the sixth month of pregnancy. They tend to increase in frequency as the pregnancy progresses and may serve to tone the muscles that will be used in delivery. Although Braxton-Hicks contractions may be confused with actual labor contractions, real labor contractions are more painful and regular and are also usually intensified by walking.

A day or so before labor begins, increased pelvic pressure from the fetus may rupture superficial blood vessels in the birth canal so that blood appears in vaginal secretions. The mucous tissue that had plugged the cervix and protected the uterus from infection becomes dislodged. At about this time, about 1 woman in 10 has a rush of warm liquid from the vagina. This liquid is amniotic fluid, and its discharge means that the amniotic sac has burst. The amniotic sac usually does not burst until the end of the first stage of childbirth, as described later. Indigestion, diarrhea, an ache in the small of the back, and abdominal cramps are also common signs that labor is beginning.

Truth or Fiction Revisited: The fetus may actually signal the mother when it is "ready" to be born, that is, when it is mature enough to sustain life outside the uterus. The adrenal and pituitary glands of the fetus may trigger labor by secreting hormones (Snegovskikh et al., 2006).

Fetal hormones stimulate the placenta (which is a gland as well as a relay station for nutrition and wastes between mother and fetus) and the uterus to secrete **prostaglandins**. Prostaglandins are the main culprits when women experience uncomfortable cramping before or during menstruation; they also serve the function of exciting the muscles of the uterus to engage in labor contractions. As labor progresses, the pituitary gland releases **oxytocin**, another hormone. Oxytocin stimulates contractions that are powerful enough to expel the baby.

In this chapter, we discuss the events of childbirth and the characteristics of the **neonate**. Arriving in the new world may be a bit more complex than you had thought, and it may also be that neonates can do a bit more than you had imagined.

The Stages of Childbirth

Regular uterine contractions signal the beginning of childbirth. Developmentalists speak of childbirth as occurring in three stages.

The First Stage

Question: What happens during the first stage of childbirth? In the first stage of childbirth, uterine contractions **efface** and **dilate** the cervix. This passageway needs to widen to about 4 inches (10 centimeters) to allow the baby to pass. Dilation of the cervix is responsible for most of the pain during childbirth. If the cervix dilates rapidly and easily, there may be little or no discomfort.

The first stage is the long stage. Among women undergoing their first deliveries, this stage may last from a few hours to more than a day. One-half a day to one day is about average, but some long stages are much briefer and some last up to a couple of days. Subsequent pregnancies take less time and may be surprisingly rapid, sometimes between 1 and 2 hours. The first contractions are not usually all that painful and are spaced 10 to 20 minutes apart. They may last from 20 to 40 seconds each.

As the process continues, the contractions become more powerful, frequent, and regular. Women are usually advised to go to the hospital or birthing center when the contractions are 4 to 5 minutes apart. Until the end of the first stage of labor, the mother is usually in a labor room with her partner or another companion.

If the woman is to be "prepped"—that is, if her pubic hair is to be shaved—it takes place now. The prep is intended to lower the chances of infection during delivery and to facilitate the performance of an **episiotomy** (described later). A woman may be given an enema to prevent an involuntary bowel movement during labor. However, many women find prepping and enemas degrading and seek obstetricians who do not perform them routinely.

During the first stage of childbirth, **fetal monitoring** may be used. One kind of monitoring is an electronic sensing device strapped around the woman's abdomen. It can measure the fetal heart rate as well as the frequency, strength, and duration of the mother's contractions. An abnormal heart rate alerts the medical staff to possible fetal distress so that appropriate steps can be taken, such as speeding up the delivery by **forceps**, a **vacuum extraction tube**, or other means. The forceps is a curved instrument that fits around the baby's head and allows the baby to be pulled out of the mother's body. The vacuum extraction tube relies on suction to pull the baby through the birth canal.

efface To rub out or wipe out; to become thin.

dilate To make wider or larger.

episiotomy (ih-pee-zee-AH-tuh-mee) A surgical incision in the area between the birth canal and the anus that widens the vaginal opening, preventing random tearing during childbirth.

fetal monitoring The use of instruments to track the heart rate and oxygen levels of the fetus during childbirth.

forceps A curved instrument that fits around the head of the baby and permits it to be pulled through the birth canal.

vacuum extraction tube An instrument that uses suction to pull the baby through the birth canal.

When the cervix is nearly fully dilated, the head of the fetus begins to move into the vagina, or birth canal. This process is called **transition**. During transition, which lasts about 30 minutes or less, contractions usually are frequent and strong.

The Second Stage

The second stage of childbirth follows transition. *Question: What occurs during the second stage of childbirth?* The second stage begins when the baby appears at the opening of the vagina (now referred to as the "birth canal"; see ● Figure 4.1). The second stage is briefer than the first stage. It may last minutes or a few hours and culminates in the birth of the baby. The woman may be taken to a delivery room for the second stage of childbirth.

transition The initial movement of the head of the fetus into the birth canal.

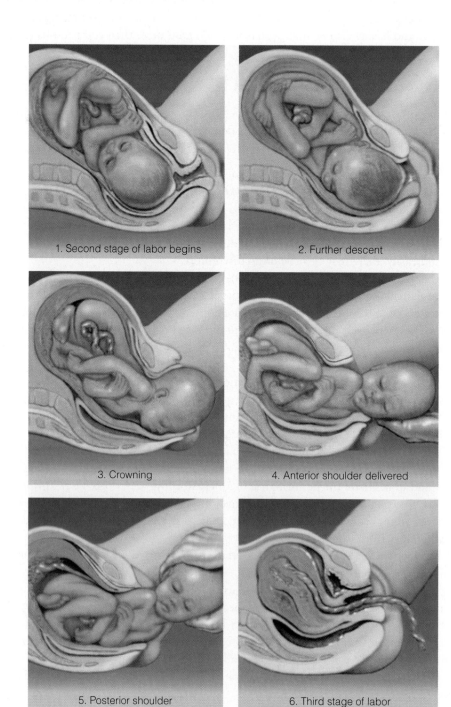

1. Second stage of labor begins

2. Further descent

3. Crowning

4. Anterior shoulder delivered

5. Posterior shoulder

6. Third stage of labor

● **Figure 4.1**
The Stages of Childbirth

In the first stage, uterine contractions efface and dilate the cervix to about 4 inches so that the baby may pass. The second stage begins with movement of the baby into the birth canal and ends with birth of the baby. During the third stage, the placenta separates from the uterine wall and is expelled through the birth canal.

The contractions of the second stage stretch the skin surrounding the birth canal farther and propel the baby farther along. The baby's head is said to have crowned when it begins to emerge from the birth canal. Once crowning has occurred, the baby normally emerges completely within minutes.

The physician, nurse, or midwife may perform an episiotomy once crowning takes place. The purpose of the episiotomy is to prevent random tearing when the area between the birth canal and the anus becomes severely stretched. Women are unlikely to feel the incision of the episiotomy because the pressure of the crowning head tends to numb the region between the vagina and the anus. The episiotomy, like prepping and the enema, is controversial and is not practiced in Europe. The incision may cause itching and discomfort as it heals. The incidence of the use of episiotomy in the United States dropped from about 70% in 1983 to 19% in 2000 (Goldberg et al., 2002). Many health professionals believe that an episiotomy is warranted when the baby's shoulders are quite wide or if the baby's heart rate declines for a long period of time. The strongest predictor of whether a practitioner will choose to use episiotomy is not the condition of the mother or the baby, but rather whether the physician normally performs an episiotomy.

Whether or not the physician performs an episiotomy, the passageway into the world outside is a tight fit, and the baby squeezes through. Mothers may be alarmed at

Lessons in Observation
Birth

To watch this video, visit your book companion website. You can also answer the questions and e-mail your responses to your professor.

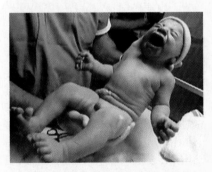

Lee delivers a healthy baby boy named Carter after laboring for more than 9 hours. The appearance of a newborn does not fit most people's definition of a "cute baby."

Learning Objectives

- What are the different birthing options available to expectant mothers?
- What are the different stages of birth?
- What does a newborn baby look like?
- What does a newborn baby act like?
- What does the Apgar scale test for in newborn babies?
- Why do health-care providers use the Apgar scale?

Applied Lesson

Describe the stages of birth. What stage is highlighted in the video?

Critical Thinking

If a baby scores low on the Apgar scale, what treatment options do parents and health-care providers have? Does the Apgar score predict the future health of a baby?

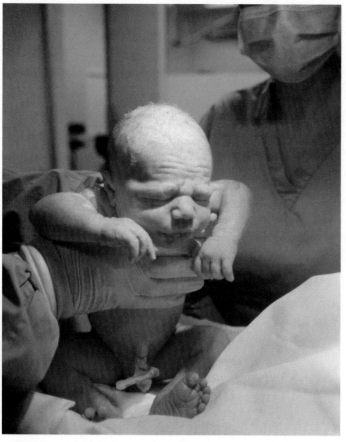

● **Figure 4.2   A Clamped and Severed Umbilical Cord**

The stump of the cord dries and falls off in about 10 days.

the visual results of the tight fit. Sometimes the baby's head and facial features are quite bent out of shape. The baby's head can wind up elongated, its nose can be flattened or pushed to the side, and the ears can be contorted, as though this little thing had gotten caught up in a vicious prizefight. My wife and I sometimes joke that our second child was born with her nose apparently coming out the side of her cheek. Parents understandably wonder whether their baby's features will "pop up" properly or return to a more normal shape. Usually they need not worry.

Don't wait for the baby to be held upside down and slapped on the buttocks to spur breathing on its own. That happens in old movies but not in today's hospitals and birthing centers. Today, to clear the passageway for breathing from any obstructions, mucus is suctioned from the baby's mouth as soon as the head emerges from the birth canal. The procedure may be repeated when the baby has fully emerged. **Truth or Fiction Revisited:** It is not true that newborn babies are held upside down and slapped on the buttocks to stimulate independent breathing.

When the baby is breathing adequately on its own, the umbilical cord is clamped and severed about 3 inches from the baby's body (● Figure 4.2). At approximately 266 days after conception, mother and infant have finally become separate beings. The stump of the umbilical cord will dry and fall off on its own in about 7 to 10 days. There are exceptions. My daughter Allyn, nearly 2 at the time, yanked off the umbilical cord of her newborn sister Jordan, causing a crisis in the family but no particular harm to Jordan.

Truth or Fiction Revisited: It is not true that the way the umbilical cord is cut determines whether the baby's "belly button" will be an "innie" or an "outie." Your belly-button status—that is, whether you have an outie or an innie—is unrelated to the methods of your obstetrician.

You might think that it would be nice for mother and baby to hang out together for a while at this juncture, but the baby is frequently whisked away by a nurse, who will perform various procedures, including footprinting the baby, supplying an ID bracelet, putting antibiotic ointment (erythromycin) or drops of silver nitrate into the baby's eyes to prevent bacterial infections, and giving the baby a vitamin K injection to help its blood clot properly if it bleeds (newborn babies do not manufacture vitamin K). While these procedures go on, the mother is in the third stage of labor.

The Third Stage

The third stage of labor is also referred to as the placental stage. It lasts from minutes to an hour or more. *Question: What happens during the third stage of childbirth?* During the third stage, the placenta separates from the wall of the uterus and is expelled through the birth canal along with fetal membranes. Bleeding is normal at this time. The uterus begins to shrink, although it will take some weeks for it to approximate its prepregnancy size. The obstetrician now sews the episiotomy, if one has been performed.

Active Review

1. The first uterine contractions are "false" and are called _____ contractions.
2. A day or so before delivery, about 1 woman in 10 has a rush of _____ fluid from the vagina.
3. In the first stage of childbirth, uterine contractions cause the cervix to become effaced and _____.
4. _____ occurs when the cervix is nearly fully dilated and the head of the fetus begins to move into the birth canal.
5. When the baby is breathing adequately, the _____ cord is clamped and severed.
6. During the third stage, the _____ separates from the uterine wall and is expelled.

Reflect & Relate: How do you feel about the routine performance of "prepping" and episiotomy? Why are these issues often controversial and personal?

Go to

http://www.thomsonedu.com/psychology/rathus

for an interactive version of this review.

Methods of Childbirth

Think of old movies in which a woman is giving birth in her home on the prairie and a helpful neighbor emerges from the bedroom, heralding the good news to the anxious father and members of the community. Perhaps prairies have not hosted the majority of childbirths over the millennia, but childbirth was once a more intimate procedure that usually took place in the woman's home and involved her, perhaps a **midwife**, and family. This pattern is followed in many less developed nations today, but only rarely in the United States and other developed nations. Contemporary American childbirths usually take place in hospitals, where physicians who use sophisticated instruments and **anesthetics** to protect mother and child from complications and discomfort oversee the birth. There is no question that modern medicine has saved lives, but childbearing has also become more impersonal. Some argue that modern methods wrest control from women over their own bodies. They even argue that anesthetics have denied many women the experience of giving birth, although many or most women admit that they appreciate having the experience "muted."

In the next section, we consider a number of contemporary methods for facilitating childbirth.

Anesthesia

Painful childbirth has historically been seen as the standard for women, but the development of modern medicine and effective anesthetics has led many people to believe that women need not experience discomfort during childbirth. Today, at least some anesthesia is used in most American deliveries. *Questions: How is anesthesia used in childbirth? What are its effects on the baby?*

General anesthesia achieves its anesthetic effect by putting the woman to sleep by means of a barbiturate that is injected into a vein in the hand or arm. Other drugs in common use are **tranquilizers**, oral barbiturates, and narcotics. These drugs are not anesthetics per se, but they may reduce anxiety and the perception of pain without causing sleep.

midwife An individual who helps women in childbirth (from Old English roots meaning "with woman").

anesthetics Agents that produce partial or total loss of the sense of pain (from Greek roots meaning "without feeling").

general anesthesia The process of eliminating pain by putting the person to sleep.

tranquilizer A drug that reduces feelings of anxiety and tension.

General anesthesia can have negative effects on the infant, including abnormal patterns of sleep and wakefulness and decreased attention and social responsiveness shortly after birth (Caton et al., 2002). The higher the dosage of anesthesia, the greater the effect. But there is little evidence that these anesthetics have long-term effects on the child (Caton et al., 2002).

Regional or **local anesthetics** deaden pain without putting the mother to sleep. With a pudendal block, the mother's external genitals are numbed by local injection. With an epidural block and the spinal block, anesthesia is injected into the spinal canal or spinal cord, temporarily numbing the body below the waist. Local anesthesia has minor depressive effects on the strength and activity levels of neonates shortly after birth, but when administered properly, the effects have not been shown to linger (Caton et al., 2002; Eltzschig et al., 2003).

In contrast to the use of anesthesia is a trend toward **natural childbirth**. In natural childbirth, a woman uses no anesthesia. Instead, a woman is educated about the biological aspects of reproduction and delivery, encouraged to maintain physical fitness, and taught relaxation and breathing exercises.

Prepared Childbirth

Question: What is prepared childbirth? Most women who are pregnant for the first time expect pain and discomfort during childbirth. Certainly the popular media image of childbirth is one in which the woman sweats profusely and screams and thrashes in pain. When French obstetrician Fernand Lamaze visited Russia, he discovered that many Russian women bore babies without anesthetics or pain. He studied their relaxation techniques and brought these techniques to Western Europe and the United States, where they became known as the **Lamaze method**, or pre-

local anesthetic A method that reduces pain in an area of the body.

natural childbirth A method of childbirth in which women use no anesthesia and are educated about childbirth and strategies for coping with discomfort.

Lamaze method A childbirth method in which women are educated about childbirth, learn to relax and breathe in patterns that conserve energy and lessen pain, and have a coach (usually the father) present during childbirth. Also called prepared childbirth.

© Masterfile

An Exercise Class for Pregnant Women
Years ago, the rule of thumb was that pregnant women were not to exert themselves. Today, it is recognized that exercise is healthful for pregnant women because it promotes cardiovascular fitness and increases muscle strength. Fitness and strength are assets during childbirth, and at other times.

pared childbirth. Lamaze (1981) contended that women could engage in breathing and relaxation exercises that would lessen fear and pain by giving them something to do and distracting them from discomfort.

In the Lamaze method, women do not go it alone. The mother-to-be attends Lamaze classes with a "coach"—most often, her partner—who will aid her in the delivery room by doing things such as massaging her, timing the contractions, offering social support, and coaching her in patterns of breathing and relaxation. The woman is taught to breathe in a specific way during contractions. She is taught how to contract specific muscles in her body while remaining generally relaxed. The idea is that she will be able to transfer this training to the process of childbirth by remaining generally at ease while her uterine muscles contract. The training procedure tones muscles that will be helpful in childbirth (such as leg muscles) and enables a woman to minimize tension, conserve energy, and experience less anxiety.

The woman is also educated about the process of childbirth, and the father-to-be or another coach is integrated into the process. As a result, the woman receives more social support than pregnant women who do not go through Lamaze training. **Truth or Fiction Revisited:** It is not true that women who give birth according to the Lamaze method do not experience pain. They do, however, apparently report less pain and ask for less medication when others, such as their partner, are present (Meldrum, 2003).

Social support during labor can be provided by individuals other than a woman's partner. A mother, sibling, or friend also can serve as a coach. Studies also demonstrate the benefit of continuous emotional support during labor by an experienced but nonprofessional female companion known as a doula (Guzikowski, 2006). Women with doulas present during the birth appear to have shorter labors than women without doulas (Campbell et al., 2006).

Cesarean Section

There are many controversies about the **cesarean section**. The first that comes to my mind is the proper spelling. Years ago, the term was spelled *Caesarean* section, after the Roman emperor Julius Caesar, who was thought to have been delivered in this

cesarean section A method of childbirth in which the neonate is delivered through a surgical incision in the mother's abdomen. (Also spelled Caesarean.)

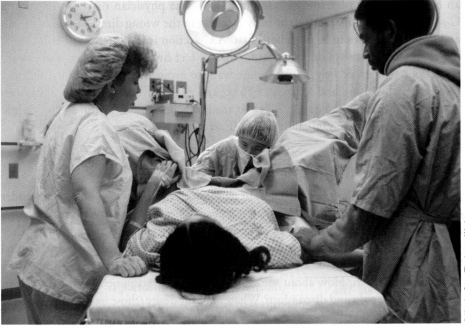

Partner in the Delivery Room
Today, the woman's partner is usually integrated into the process of childbirth. In this case, the father and mother take pride in "their" accomplishment of childbirth.

Treatment of Preterm Babies

Question: How are preterm infants treated following birth? Because of their physical frailty, preterm infants usually remain in the hospital and are placed in **incubators**, which maintain a temperature-controlled environment and afford some protection from disease. The babies may be given oxygen, although excessive oxygen can cause permanent eye injury.

Parents and Preterm Neonates

One might assume that parents would be more concerned about preterm babies than babies who have gone to full term and thus would treat them better. Ironically, that is not the case. Parents often do not treat preterm neonates as well as they treat full-term neonates. For one thing, preterm neonates are less attractive than full-term babies. Preterm infants usually do not have the robust, appealing appearance of many full-term babies. Their cries are more high pitched and grating, and they are more irritable (Bugental & Happaney, 2004; Eckerman et al., 1999). The demands of caring for preterm babies can be depressing to mothers (Davis et al., 2003; Drewett et al., 2004). Mothers of preterm babies frequently report that they feel alienated from their babies and harbor feelings of failure, guilt, and low self-esteem. They respond less sensitively to their infants' behavior than mothers of full-term babies (Bugental & Happaney, 2004). Mothers of preterm infants also touch and talk to their infants less and hold them at a greater distance during feeding. Fear of hurting preterm babies can further discourage parents from handling them, but encouraging mothers to massage their preterm infants can help them cope with fear of handling their babies and with feelings of helplessness and hopelessness (Feijó et al., 2006).

Once they come home from the hospital, preterm infants remain more passive and less sociable than full-term infants (Larroque et al., 2005; McGrath et al., 2005), so they demand less interaction with parents. However, when their parents do interact with them during the first year, the parents are more likely to poke at preterm babies, caress them, and talk to them, perhaps in an effort to prod them out of their passivity. Mothers of preterm babies report feeling overprotective toward them, which may in part explain why 1-year-old preterm infants explore less and stay closer to their mothers than do full-term babies of the same age.

Preterm infants fare better when they have responsive and caring parents. Longitudinal research shows that preterm children who are reared in attentive and responsive environments attain higher intelligence test scores, have higher self-esteem, show more positive social skills, and have fewer behavioral and emotional problems in childhood than do preterm children reared in less responsive homes (Dieterich et al., 2004; Lawson & Ruff, 2004).

Intervention Programs

A generation ago, preterm babies were left as undisturbed as possible. For one thing, concern was aroused by the prospect of handling such a tiny, frail creature. For another, preterm babies would not normally experience interpersonal contact or other sources of external stimulation until full term. However, experiments carried out over the past two decades have suggested that preterm infants profit from early stimulation just as full-term babies do. Preterm babies benefit from being cuddled, rocked, talked to, and sung to, being exposed to recordings of their mothers' voices, and having mobiles placed within view. Recent studies have shown the value of live and recorded music in the preterm infant's environment (Arnon et al., 2006; Hunter & Sahler, 2006; Lai et al., 2006). Other forms of stimulation include massage (Field et al., 2006) and "kangaroo care" (Lai et al., 2006), in which the baby spends several hours a day lying skin to skin, chest to chest, with one of its parents. By and large, preterm infants exposed to stimulation tend to gain weight more rapidly, show fewer

incubator A heated, protective container in which premature infants are kept.

respiratory problems, and make greater advances in motor, intellectual, and neurological development than control infants (Caulfield, 2000; Dombrowski et al., 2000)(see ● Figure 4.3).

Other intervention programs help parents adjust to the birth and care of a low-birthweight infant. One such program involved 92 preterm infants at three sites (Als et al., 2003). The following factors contributed to superior cognitive and motor development in the infants and better adjustment in the parents: early discontinuation of intravenous feeding, hospitalization with intensive care for digestive and other problems, and individualized counseling to foster appreciation of the infant.

As we see in the nearby "Developing in a World of Diversity" feature, maternal and infant mortality remain serious problems in many—perhaps most—parts of the world.

● **Figure 4.3**
Stimulating a Preterm Infant

It was once believed that preterm infants should be left as undisturbed as possible. Today, however, it is recognized that preterm infants usually profit from various kinds of stimulation.

Louie Psihoyos/Getty Images

Active Review

11. Prenatal _____ deprivation can impair the development of the fetus's central nervous system, leading to cognitive and motor problems and even psychological disorders.
12. A baby is considered to be _____ when birth occurs at or before 37 weeks of gestation.
13. A baby has a low _____ when it weighs less than 5.5 pounds (about 2,500 grams).

14. Research suggests that it is (Helpful or Harmful?) to stimulate preterm infants.

Reflect & Relate: If you had a preterm infant, do you think you would want to handle him or her as much as possible or would you tend to leave him or her alone? Explain.

Go to

http://www.thomsonedu.com/psychology/rathus
for an interactive version of this review.

The Postpartum Period

Postpartum derives from roots meaning "after" and "birth." The **postpartum period** refers to the weeks following delivery, but there is no specific limit. "Parting is such sweet sorrow," Shakespeare has Juliet tell Romeo. The "parting" from the baby is also frequently a happy experience. The family's long wait is over. Concerns about pregnancy and labor are over, fingers and toes have been counted, and despite some local discomfort, the mother finds her "load" to be lightened, most literally. However, according to the American Psychiatric Association (2000, p. 423), about 70% of new mothers have periods of tearfulness, sadness, and irritability that the association refers to as the "baby blues." In this section, we discuss two issues of the postpartum period: maternal depression and bonding.

postpartum period The period that immediately follows childbirth.

Maternal Depression

Question: What kinds of problems in mood do women experience during the postpartum period? These problems include the "baby blues" and more serious mood disorders ("postpartum-onset mood episodes"), which occasionally include "psychotic features" (American Psychiatric Association, 2000).

Truth or Fiction Revisited: Actually, it is normal to feel depressed following childbirth. The baby blues affect most women in the weeks after delivery (American Psychiatric Association, 2000). Baby blues and other postpartum mood problems are so common that they are statistically normal (Gavin et al., 2005). These problems are not limited to the United States or even to developed nations. They are far-flung, and researchers find them in China, Turkey, Guyana, Australia, and South Africa with similar frequency (Bloch et al., 2006; Cohen et al., 2006). Researchers believe that the baby blues are common because of hormonal changes that follow delivery (Kohl, 2004).

The baby blues last about 10 days and are generally not severe enough to impair the mother's functioning. Don't misunderstand; the baby blues are seriously discomforting and not to be ignored as in, "Oh, you're just experiencing what most women experience." The point is that most women can handle the baby blues, even though they are awful at times, partly because the women know that they are transient.

A minority of women but perhaps as many as one in five encounter the more serious mood disorder frequently referred to as **postpartum depression (PPD)**. PPD begins about a month after delivery and may linger for weeks, even months. PPD is technically referred to as a major depressive disorder with postpartum onset. As in other major depressive disorders, it is characterized by serious sadness, feelings of hopelessness and helplessness, feelings of worthlessness, difficulty concentrating, and major changes in appetite (usually loss of appetite) and sleep patterns (frequently insomnia). There can also be severe fluctuations in mood, with women sometimes feeling elated. Some women show obsessive concern with the well-being of their babies at this time. PPD can also interfere with the mother–baby relationship in the short term (Stanley et al., 2004).

Many researchers have suggested that PPD is caused by the interactions of physiological (mainly hormonal) and psychological factors, including a sudden drop in estrogen (Kohl, 2004). Feelings of depression before getting pregnant or during pregnancy are a risk factor for PPD, as are concerns about all the life changes that motherhood creates, marital problems, and having a sick or unwanted baby. But today the focus is on physiological factors because of the major changes in body chemistry during and after pregnancy and because women around the world seem to experience similar disturbances in mood, even when their life experiences and support systems are radically different from those found in the United States (Cohen et al., 2006).

According to the American Psychiatric Association (2000), postpartum mood episodes are accompanied by "psychotic features" in as many as 1 woman in 500. A psychotic feature may mean a break with reality. Mothers with these features may have delusional thoughts about the infant that place the infant at risk of injury of death. Some women experience delusions that the infant is possessed by the devil. Some women have "command hallucinations" to kill the infant and experience a command to kill the infant as though it is coming from the outside—perhaps from a commanding person or some kind of divine or evil spirit—even though the idea originates from within. Because these women may not be able to tell the difference between hallucinations and reality, the infant may be in serious jeopardy. Remember that these psychotic features are rather rare, however, and that when they occur, they need not always place the baby at risk.

Women who experience PPD usually profit from social support and a general history of high self-esteem. They may profit from counseling even if it does little more

postpartum depression (PPD) Severe, prolonged depression that afflicts 10–20% of women after delivery and that is characterized by sadness, apathy, and feelings of worthlessness.

than explain that many women encounter PPD and it usually eases and ends as time goes on. Drugs that increase estrogen levels or act as antidepressants may help. Most women will resolve PPD without professional help. At the very least, women should know that the problem is common and does not necessarily mean that something is wrong with them or that they are failing to live up to their obligations.

Bonding

Bonding—that is, the formation of bonds of attachment between parents and their children—is essential to the survival and well-being of children. Since the publication of controversial research by Marshall Klaus and John Kennell in the 1970s, many have wondered about the importance of bonding. *Question: How critical is parental interaction with neonates in the formation of bonds of attachment?*

Klaus and Kennell (1978) argued that the first hours postpartum provided a special—even a necessary—opportunity for bonding between parents and neonates. They labeled these hours a "maternal-sensitive" period during which the mother is particularly disposed, largely because of hormone levels, to form a bond with the neonate. In their study, one group of mothers was randomly assigned to standard hospital procedure in which their babies were whisked away to the nursery shortly after birth. Throughout the remainder of the hospital stay, the babies visited their mothers during

bonding The process of forming bonds of attachment between parent and child.

A Closer Look

Have We Found the Daddy Hormones?

Are oxytocin and vasopressin the "Daddy hormones"? Perhaps so, at least in meadow voles, which are a kind of tailless mouse, and sheep. These hormones are connected with the creation of mother–infant bonds in sheep, pair bonds in monogamous voles, and bonds of attachment between vole fathers and their young. **Truth or Fiction Revisited:** Experimental research shows that increasing vasopressin levels transforms an indifferent male into a caring, monogamous, and protective mate and father (Lim et al., 2004; Lim & Young, 2006).

Oxytocin and vasopressin are secreted by the pituitary gland, which secretes many hormones that are involved in reproduction and the nurturing of young. For example, prolactin regulates maternal behavior in lower mammals and stimulates the production of milk in women. Oxytocin stimulates labor but is also involved in social recognition and bonding. Vasopressin enables the body to conserve water by inhibiting urine production when fluid levels are low; however, it is also connected with paternal behavior patterns in some mammals. For example, male

prairie voles form pair-bonds with female prairie voles after mating with them (Lim et al., 2004; Lim & Young, 2006). Mating stimulates secretion of vasopressin, and vasopressin causes the previously promiscuous male to sing "I only have eyes for you."

Given their effects on voles, we may wonder how oxytocin and vasopressin may be connected with the formation of bonds between men and women, and men and children. Will perfume makers be lacing new scents with these hormones?

Reflect: In your own experience and in the portrayals of men and women you see in the media, what are the apparent sex differences in "cuddling," parenting, and tendencies toward monogamy? To what extent do you think that these differences may be the result of cultural influences or the result of chemistry, that is, chemicals such as oxytocin and vasopressin? Explain.

feeding. The other group of mothers spent 5 hours a day with their infants during the hospital stay. The hospital staff encouraged and reassured the group of mothers who had extended contact. Follow-ups over 2 years suggested that extended contact benefited both the mothers and their children. Mothers with extended contact were more likely than control mothers to cuddle their babies, soothe them when they cried, and interact with them.

Critics note that the Klaus and Kennell studies are fraught with methodological problems. For example, we cannot separate the benefits of extended contact from benefits attributable to parents' knowledge that they were in a special group and from the extra attention of the hospital staff. In short, the evidence that the hours after birth are critical is tainted. Consider the millions of solid adoptive parent–child relationships in which parents did not have early access to their children.

Parent–child bonding has been shown to be a complex process involving desire to have the child; parent–child familiarity with one another's sounds, odors, and tastes; and caring. On the other hand, serious maternal depression can delay bonding with newborns (Klier, 2006), and a history of rejection by parents can interfere with women's bonding with their own children (Leerkes & Crockenberg, 2006).

Truth or Fiction Revisited: Despite the Klaus and Kennell studies, which made a brief splash a generation ago, it is not true that parents must have extended early contact with their newborn children if adequate bonding is to take place. Researchers now view the hours after birth as only one element—and not even an essential element—in a complex and prolonged bonding process.

Active Review

15. Research suggests that the (Majority or Minority?) of new mothers experience periods of depression.
16. Postpartum depression has been connected with a precipitous decline in the hormone _____.
17. Research (Does or Does not?) show that early parental interaction with neonates is critical in the formation of bonds of attachment.

Reflect & Relate: Pretend for a minute that you visit a friend who has just had a baby. She is weepy and listless and worries that she doesn't have the "right" feelings for a new mother. What would you say to her? Why?

Go to

http://www.thomsonedu.com/psychology/rathus
for an interactive version of this review.

Characteristics of Neonates

Many neonates come into the world looking a bit fuzzy, but even though they are utterly dependent on others, they are probably more aware of their surroundings than you had imagined. Neonates make rapid adaptations to the world around them. In this section, we see how health professionals assess the health of neonates and describe the characteristics of neonates.

Assessing the Health of Neonates

Question: How do health professionals assess the health of neonates? The neonate's overall level of health is usually evaluated at birth according to the **Apgar scale**, developed by Virginia Apgar in 1953. Apgar scores are based on five signs of health,

Apgar scale A measure of a newborn's health that assesses appearance, pulse, grimace, activity level, and respiratory effort.

as shown in ■ Table 4.2. The neonate can receive a score of 0, 1, or 2 on each sign. The total Apgar score can therefore vary from 0 to 10. A score of 7 or above usually indicates that the baby is not in danger. A score below 4 suggests that the baby is in critical condition and requires medical attention. By 1 minute after birth, most normal babies attain scores of 8 to 10 (Clayton & Crosby, 2006).

The acronym APGAR is commonly used as an aid to remember the five criteria of the Apgar scale:

A: the general **a**ppearance or color of the neonate
P: the **p**ulse or heart rate
G: **g**rimace (the 1-point indicator of reflex irritability)
A: general **a**ctivity level or muscle tone
R: **r**espiratory effort, or rate of breathing

The **Brazelton Neonatal Behavioral Assessment Scale**, developed by pediatrician T. Berry Brazelton, measures neonates' reflexes and other behavior patterns. This test screens neonates for behavioral and neurological problems by assessing four areas of behavior: motor behavior, including muscle tone and most **reflexes**; response to stress; adaptive behavior; and control over physiological state.

Reflexes

If soon after birth you had been held gently for a few moments with your face down in comfortably warm water, you would not have drowned. Instead of breathing the water in, you would have exhaled slowly through your mouth and engaged in swimming motions. (We urge readers not to test babies for this reflex. The hazards are obvious.) This swimming response is "prewired"—innate or inborn—and is just one of the many reflexes shown by neonates. ***Questions: What are reflexes? What kinds of reflexes are shown by neonates?***

Reflexes are simple, unlearned, stereotypical responses that are elicited by certain types of stimulation. They do not require higher brain functions; they occur automatically, without thinking. Reflexes are the most complicated motor activities displayed by neonates. Neonates cannot roll over, sit up, reach for an object they see, or raise their heads.

Brazelton Neonatal Behavioral Assessment Scale A measure of a newborn's motor behavior, response to stress, adaptive behavior, and control over physiological state.

reflex An unlearned, stereotypical response to a stimulus.

■ **Table 4.2** The Apgar Scale

Points	0	1	2
Appearance:			
Color	Blue, pale	Body pink, extremities blue	Entirely pink
Pulse:			
Heart rate	Absent (not detectable)	Slow—below 100 beats/minute	Rapid—100–140 beats/minute
Grimace:			
Reflex irritability	No response	Grimace	Crying, coughing, sneezing
Activity level:			
Muscle tone	Completely flaccid, limp	Weak, inactive	Flexed arms and legs; resists extension
Respiratory effort:			
Breathing	Absent (infant is apneic)	Shallow, irregular, slow	Regular breathing; lusty crying

have had a chance to see or touch it. In one experiment, Macfarlane placed nursing pads above and to the sides of neonates' heads. One pad had absorbed milk from the mother, the other was clean. Neonates less than 1 week old spent more time turning to look at their mothers' pads than at the new pads.

Neonates will also turn toward preferred odors. In the second phase of this research, Macfarlane suspended pads with milk from the neonates' mothers and from strangers to the sides of babies' heads. For the first few days following birth, the infants did not turn toward their mothers' pads. However, by the time they were 1 week old, they turned toward their mothers' pads and spent more time looking at them than at the strangers' pads. It appears that the babies learned to respond positively to the odor of their mothers' milk during the first few days. Afterward, a source of this odor received preferential treatment even when the infants were not nursing.

Breast-fed 15-day-old infants also prefer their mother's axillary (underarm) odor to odors produced by other lactating (milk-producing) women and by nonlactating women. Bottle-fed infants do not show this preference (Cernoch & Porter, 1985; Porter et al., 1992). Investigators of such practices explain this difference by suggesting that breast-fed infants may be more likely than bottle-fed infants to be exposed to their mother's axillary odor. That is, mothers of bottle-fed infants usually remain clothed when feeding their babies. Axillary odor, along with odors from breast secretions, might contribute to the early development of recognition and attachment.

Taste

Neonates are sensitive to different tastes, and their preferences, as suggested by their facial expressions in response to various fluids, appear to be similar to those of adults (Werner & Bernstein, 2001). Neonates swallow without showing any facial expression suggestive of a positive or negative response when distilled water is placed on their tongues. Sweet solutions are met with smiles, licking, and eager sucking, as in ● Figure 4.13a (Rosenstein & Oster, 1988). Neonates discriminate among solutions with salty, sour, and bitter tastes, as suggested by reactions in the lower part of the face (Rosenstein & Oster, 1988). Sour fluids (Figure 4.13b) elicit pursing of the lips, nose wrinkling, and eye blinking. Bitter solutions (Figure 4.13c) stimulate spitting, gagging, and sticking out the tongue.

Sweet solutions have a calming effect on neonates (Blass & Camp, 2003). One study found that sweeter solutions increase the heart rate, suggesting heightened arousal, but also slow down the rate of sucking (Crook & Lipsitt, 1976). Researchers interpret this finding to suggest an effort to savor the sweeter solution, to make the flavor last. Although we do not know why infants ingest sweet foods more slowly than other foods, this difference could be adaptive in the sense of preventing overeating. Sweet foods tend to be high in calories; eating them slowly gives infants' brains more time to respond to bodily signals that they have eaten enough and thus to stop eating. Ah, to have the wisdom of a neonate!

Touch and Pain

The sense of touch is an extremely important avenue of learning and communication for babies. Not only do the skin senses provide information about the external world, but the sensations of skin against skin also appear to provide feelings of comfort and security that may be major factors in the formation of bonds of attachment between infants and their caregivers, as we see in Chapter 7.

Neonates are sensitive to touch. As noted earlier in this chapter, many reflexes—including the rooting, sucking, Babinski, and grasping reflexes, to name a few—are activated by pressure against the skin.

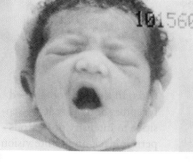

a–c: Rosenstein, D.S. & Oster, H. (1988). Differential facial responses to four basic tastes in newborns. *Child Development*, 59, 1555–1568.

● **Figure 4.13**
Facial Expressions Elicited by Sweet, Sour, and Bitter Solutions

Neonates are sensitive to different tastes, as shown by their facial expressions when tasting (a) sweet, (b) sour, and (c) bitter solutions.

It has been widely believed for many years that neonates are not as sensitive to pain as older babies are. Considering the squeezing that takes place during childbirth, relative insensitivity to pain would seem to be adaptive. However, this belief has recently been challenged by health professionals (e.g., Royal Australasian College of Physicians, 2006). What would appear to be accurate enough is that neonates are not cognitively equipped to fret about pain that may be coming or to ruminate about pain they have experienced. But they are certainly conditionable, meaning that if they perceive themselves to be in a situation that has brought them pain in the past, we should not be surprised if they shriek—and shriek and shriek. Health professionals now recommend that neonates and older infants be given anesthetics if they are going to undergo uncomfortable procedures, such as circumcision.

Learning: Really Early Childhood "Education"

Question: Can neonates learn? The somewhat limited sensory capabilities of neonates suggest that they may not learn as rapidly as older children do. After all, we must sense clearly those things we are to learn about. However, neonates do seem capable of at least two basic forms of learning: classical conditioning and operant conditioning.

Classical Conditioning of Neonates

In classical conditioning of neonates, involuntary responses are conditioned to new stimuli. In a typical study (Lipsitt, 2002), neonates were taught to blink in response to a tone. Blinking (the unconditioned response) was elicited by a puff of air directed toward the infant's eye (the unconditioned stimulus). A tone was sounded (the conditioned stimulus) as the puff of air was delivered. After repeated pairings, sounding the tone caused the neonate to blink (the conditioned response). Thus, neonates are equipped to learn that events peculiar to their own environments (touches or other conditioned stimuli) may mean that a meal is at hand (more accurately, at mouth). One neonate may learn that a light switched on overhead precedes a meal. Another may learn that feeding is preceded by the rustling of a carpet of thatched leaves. The conditioned stimuli are culture specific; the capacity to learn is universal.

Operant Conditioning of Neonates

Operant conditioning, like classical conditioning, can take place in neonates. In Chapter 3, we described an experiment in which neonates learned to suck on a pacifier in such a way as to activate a recording of their mothers reading *The Cat in the Hat* (DeCasper & Fifer, 1980; DeCasper & Spence, 1991) (● Figure 4.14), which the mothers had read aloud during their final weeks of pregnancy. In this example, the infants' sucking reflexes were modified through the reinforcement of hearing their mothers read a familiar story.

The younger the child, the more important it is that reinforcers be administered rapidly. Among neonates, it seems that reinforcers must be administered within 1 second after the desired behavior is performed if learning is to occur. Infants of age 6–8 months can learn if the reinforcer is delayed by 2 seconds, but if the delay is 3 seconds or more, learning does not take place (Millar, 1990). Although there are individual differences in conditionability in neonates, these differences do not correspond to differences in the complex cognitive abilities we later refer to as intelligence.

Sleeping and Waking

As adults, we spend about one-third of our time sleeping. *Question: What patterns of sleep are found among neonates?* Neonates greatly outdo us, spending two-thirds of their time, or about 16 hours per day, in sleep. And, in one of life's basic challenges to parents, neonates do not sleep their 16 hours consecutively.

tain amount of activity for the creation of proteins that are involved in the development of neurons and synapses (Dang-Vu et al., 2006). Brain activity can be stimulated by internal or external sources. In older children and adults, external sources of stimulation are provided by activity, a vast and shifting array of sensory impressions, and, perhaps, thought processes during the waking state. The neonate, however, spends its brief waking periods largely isolated from the kaleidoscope of events of the world outside and is not likely to be lost in deep thought. Thus, in the waking state, the brain may not be provided with the needed stimulation. Perhaps the neonate compensates by spending relatively more time in REM sleep, which most closely parallels the waking state in terms of brain waves. While infants are in REM sleep, internal stimulation spurs the brain on to appropriate development. Preterm babies spend an even greater proportion of their time in REM sleep than full-term babies, perhaps—goes the argument—because they require relatively greater stimulation of the brain.

Crying

No discussion of the sleeping and waking states of the neonate would be complete without mentioning crying, a comment that parents will view as an understatement. I have known first-time parents who have attempted to follow an imaginary 11th commandment: "The baby shall not cry." **Question: Why do babies cry?**

The main reason babies cry seems to be simple enough. Studies suggest that a one-word answer often suffices: pain (Gormally et al., 2001; Zeifman, 2004).

Some parents have entered into conflict with hospital nurses who tell them not to worry when their babies are crying on the other side of the nursery's glass partition. Nurses often tell the parents that their babies must cry because crying helps clear their respiratory systems of fluids that linger from the amniotic sac and also stimulates the circulatory system.

Whether crying is healthful and necessary remains an open question, but at least some crying among babies seems to be universal. Some scholars have suggested that crying may be a primitive language, but it is not. Languages contain units and groupings of sounds that symbolize objects and events, and crying does not. Still, crying appears to be both expressive and functional. It serves as an infant's expressive response to unpleasant feelings and also stimulates caretakers to do something to help. Crying thus communicates something, even though it is not a form of language. Crying may also communicate the identity of the crier across distance. Cries have multiple markers of individuality, and they may signal parents and other caretakers as to the location of their infant in a group.

Before parenthood, many people wonder whether they will be able to recognize the meaning of their babies' cries, but it usually does not take them long. Parents typically learn to distinguish cries that signify hunger, anger, and pain. A sudden, loud, insistent cry associated with flexing and kicking of the legs may indicate colic, that is, pain resulting from gas or other sources of distress in the digestive tract. The baby may seem to hold its breath for a few moments, then gasp and begin to cry again. Crying from colic can be severe and persistent; it may last for hours, although cries generally seem to settle into a pattern after a while (Barr et al., 2005). Much to the relief of parents, colic tends to disappear by the third to sixth month, as a baby's digestive system matures.

Parents and other people, including children, have similar bodily responses to infant crying, such as increases in heart rate, blood pressure, and sweating (Reijneveld et al., 2004). Infant crying makes others feel irritated and anxious and motivates them to run to the baby to try to relieve the distress. The pitch of an infant's cries appears to provide information (Zeifman, 2004). Adults perceive high-pitched crying to be more urgent, distressing, and sick sounding than low-pitched crying (Zeifman, 2004).

Certain high-pitched cries, when prolonged, may signify health problems. For example, the cries of chronically distressed infants differ from those of nondistressed infants in both rhythm and pitch. Patterns of crying may be indicative of such problems as chromosomal abnormalities, infections, fetal malnutrition, and exposure to narcotics (Zeifman, 2004). A striking example of the link between crying and a health problem is the syndrome called cri du chat, French for "cry of the cat." This genetic disorder produces abnormalities in the brain, atypical facial features, and a high-pitched, squeaky cry.

There are certain patterns of crying. For example, peaks of crying appear to be concentrated in the late afternoon and early evening (McGlaughlin & Grayson, 2001). Although some cries may seem extreme and random at first, they tend to settle into a pattern that is recognizable to most parents. Infants seem to produce about the same number of crying bouts during the first 9 months or so, but the duration of the bouts grows briefer, by half, during this period (Ijzendoorn & Hubbard, 2000). The response of the mother apparently influences infants' crying. It turns out that the more frequently mothers ignore their infants' crying bouts in the first 9 weeks, the less frequently their infants cry in the following 9-week period (Ijzendoorn & Hubbard, 2000). This finding should certainly not be interpreted to mean that infant crying is best ignored. At least at first, crying communicates pain and hunger, and these are conditions that it is advisable to correct. Persistent crying can strain the mother–infant relationship (Reijneveld et al., 2004).

Soothing

Question: What will stop an infant from crying? For one thing, sucking seems to function as a built-in tranquilizer. Sucking on a **pacifier** decreases crying and agitated movement in neonates who have not yet had the opportunity to feed (Field, 1999). Therefore, the soothing function of sucking need not be learned through experience. Sucking (drinking) a sweet solution also appears to have a soothing effect (Stevens et al., 2005). (Can it be that even babies are programmed to enjoy "comfort food"?)

Parents find many other ways to soothe infants: picking them up, patting them, caressing and rocking them, swaddling them, and speaking to them in a low voice. Parents then usually try to find the specific cause of the distress by offering a bottle or pacifier or checking the diaper. These responses to a crying infant are shown by parents in many cultures, including those of the United States, France, and Japan.

Learning occurs quickly during the soothing process. Parents learn by trial and error what types of embraces and movements are likely to soothe their infants, and infants learn quickly that crying is followed by being picked up or other forms of intervention. Parents sometimes worry that if they pick up the crying baby quickly, they are reinforcing the baby for crying. In this way, they believe, the child may become spoiled and find it progressively more difficult to engage in self-soothing to get to sleep.

Fortunately, as infants mature and learn, crying tends to become replaced by less upsetting verbal requests for intervention. Among adults, of course, soothing techniques take very different forms—a bouquet of flowers or admission that one started the argument.

© Photodisc/First Light

Soothing
How can a crying baby be soothed? Picking the baby up, talking to it quietly, patting, stroking, and rocking all seem to have calming effects.

Sudden Infant Death Syndrome (SIDS)

Truth or Fiction Revisited: It is true that more children die from sudden infant death syndrome (SIDS) than die from cancer, heart disease, pneumonia, child abuse, AIDS, cystic fibrosis, and muscular dystrophy combined (Lipsitt, 2003). ***Questions: What is SIDS? What are the risk factors for SIDS?***

pacifier An artificial nipple, teething ring, or similar device that, when sucked, soothes babies.

Sudden infant death syndrome (SIDS)—also known as crib death—is a disorder of infancy that apparently strikes while a baby is sleeping. In the typical case, a baby goes to sleep, apparently in perfect health, and is found dead the next morning. There is no sign that the baby struggled or was in pain.

SIDS is more common among the following (Hunt & Hauck, 2006; Paterson et al., 2006):

- Babies age 2–4 months
- Babies who are put to sleep in the prone position (on their stomachs) or their sides
- Premature and low-birth-weight infants
- Male babies
- Babies in families of lower socioeconomic status
- Babies in African American families (African American babies are twice as likely as European American babies to die of SIDS)
- Babies of teenage mothers
- Babies whose mothers smoked during or after pregnancy or whose mothers used narcotics during pregnancy

Studies have found a higher risk of SIDS among babies who sleep on their stomachs (Lipsitt, 2003). These findings led the American Academy of Pediatrics to recommend putting babies down to sleep on their back. A recent national survey revealed that before the recommendation, 43% of infants were usually placed to sleep on their stomachs (prone) and 27% on their back. By 2000, however, only 17% were placed in the prone position, and 56% were placed on their back (Willinger et al., 2000).

Home monitoring systems to alert parents to episodes of apnea and to give them time to intervene—for example, by using artificial respiration—have been developed. However, there is little evidence that SIDS rates have been reduced as a result of using monitors (SIDS Network, 2001).

The incidence of SIDS has been declining, but some 2,000–3,000 infants in the United States still die each year of SIDS. It is the most common cause of death in infants between the ages of 1 month and 1 year, and most of these deaths occur between 2 and 5 months of age (Paterson et al., 2006). New parents frequently live in dread of SIDS and check regularly through the night to see if their babies are breathing. It is not abnormal, by the way, for babies occasionally to suspend breathing for a moment. The intermittent suspension of respiration is called **apnea**, and the buildup of carbon dioxide usually spurs a return to breathing. Lewis Lipsitt (2003) noted that any theory of the causes of SIDS must include that it tends to occur between the second and fourth months, when reflexive behavior is weakening. He suggests that babies who are less likely to move reflexively and vigorously to obtain air when their air passageways are occluded are at higher risk of SIDS. Although it is known that SIDS does not result from suffocation or from choking on regurgitated food, its causes have remained largely obscure.

The Children's Hospital Boston Study

Perhaps the most compelling study to date about the causes of SIDS was led by health professionals at the Children's Hospital Boston and published in the *Journal of the American Medical Association* (Paterson et al., 2006). The study focused on an area in the brainstem called the **medulla** (● Figure 4.16), which is involved in basic functions such as breathing and sleep-and-wake cycles. Among other things, the medulla causes us to breathe if we are in need of oxygen. Researchers compared the medullas of babies who had died from SIDS with those of babies who had died at the same ages

sudden infant death syndrome (SIDS) The death, while sleeping, of apparently healthy babies who stop breathing for unknown medical reasons. Also called crib death.

apnea (AP-nee-uh) Temporary suspension of breathing (from the Greek *a-*, meaning "without," and *pnoie*, meaning "wind").

medulla A part of the brain stem that regulates vital and automatic functions such as breathing and the sleep–wake cycle.

serotonin A naturally occurring brain chemical that is involved in transmission of messages from one brain cell to another, the responsiveness of the medulla, emotional responses such as depression, and motivational responses such as hunger.

from other causes. They found that the medullas of the babies who died from SIDS were less sensitive to the brain chemical **serotonin**, a chemical that helps keep the medulla responsive. The problem was particularly striking in the brains of the boys, which could account for the sex difference in the incidence of SIDS.

What should *you* do about SIDS? Bear in mind that the prevention of SIDS begins during pregnancy. Smoking and using other drugs during pregnancy increase the risk of SIDS. Obtain adequate nutrition and health care during pregnancy. Place your baby to sleep in the supine position (on its back). Keep current with research data on SIDS by checking with your pediatrician and exploring websites such as those of the Centers for Disease Control and Prevention (http://www.cdc.gov/) and the SIDS Network (http://www.sids-network .org/). Perhaps within a few years we will have a screening test for SIDS and a method for preventing or controlling it.

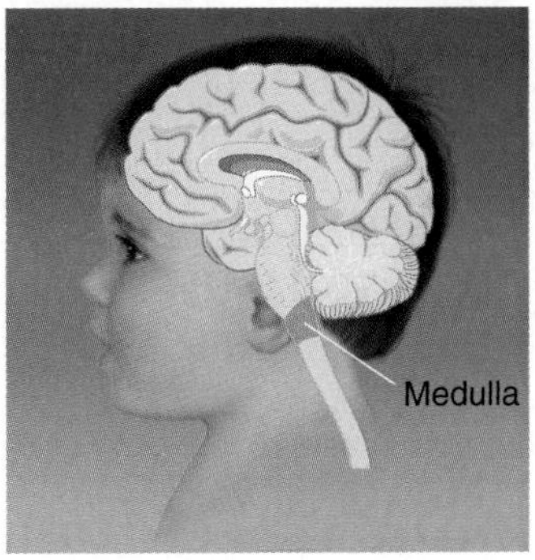

● **Figure 4.16**
The Medulla
....
Research by a team at the Children's Hospital Boston suggests that sudden infant death syndrome (SIDS) may be caused by a relatively low level of sensitivity of the medulla to the brain chemical serotonin.

Active Review

18. In the United States today, the neonate's overall level of health is usually evaluated at birth according to the _____ scale.

19. In the _____ reflex, the baby turns the head and mouth toward a stimulus that strokes the cheek, chin, or corner of the mouth.

20. Neonates are rather (Nearsighted or Farsighted?).

21. Neonates (Do or Do not?) prefer their mothers' voices to those of other women.

22. As babies mature, they spend a (Greater or Smaller?) percentage of their time sleeping in REM sleep.

23. _____ is the most common cause of death in infants between the ages of 1 month and 1 year.

Reflect & Relate: Have you or a family member had to adjust to the waking and sleeping patterns of a baby? Do you think that it is normal to occasionally resent being awakened repeatedly through the night? Explain.

Go to

http://www.thomsonedu.com/psychology/rathus

for an interactive version of this review.

1. **What events occur just before the beginning of childbirth?**

The first uterine contractions are called Braxton-Hicks contractions, or false labor contractions. A day or so before labor begins, some blood spotting can occur in vaginal secretions. At about this time, 1 woman in 10 has a rush of amniotic fluid from the vagina. The initiation of labor may be triggered by secretion of hormones by the fetus. Maternal hormones stimulate contractions strong enough to expel the baby.

2. **What happens during the first stage of childbirth?**

Childbirth begins with the onset of regular contractions of the uterus, which cause the cervix to become effaced and dilated. The first stage may last from a few hours to more than a day. During transition, the cervix is nearly fully dilated and the head of the fetus moves into the birth canal.

3. **What occurs during the second stage of childbirth?**

The second stage begins when the baby appears at the opening of the birth canal. It ends with the birth of the baby. Once the baby's head emerges from the mother's body, mucus is suctioned from its mouth so that breathing is not obstructed. When the baby is breathing on its own, the umbilical cord is clamped and severed.

4. **What happens during the third stage of childbirth?**

During this stage, the placenta separates from the uterine wall and is expelled along with fetal membranes.

5. **How is anesthesia used in childbirth? What are its effects on the baby?**

General anesthesia puts the woman to sleep, but it decreases the strength of uterine contractions and lowers the responsiveness of the neonate. Regional or local anesthetics deaden pain in parts of the body without putting the mother to sleep.

6. **What is prepared childbirth?**

Prepared childbirth teaches women to dissociate uterine contractions from pain and fear by associating other responses, such as relaxation, with contractions. A coach aids the mother in the delivery room.

7. **What is a C-section? Why is it so common?**

A cesarean section (C-section) delivers a baby surgically through the abdomen. C-sections are most likely to be advised if the baby is large or in distress or if the mother's pelvis is small or she is tired or weak. Herpes and HIV infections in the birth canal can be bypassed by C-section.

8. **How can a woman decide where to deliver her baby?**

Women have choices in childbirth, such as home delivery, birthing suites, or traditional labor rooms. Birthing suites provide homelike surroundings with immediate hospital backup available.

9. **What are the effects of oxygen deprivation at birth?**

Prenatal oxygen deprivation can be fatal if prolonged; it can also impair development of the nervous system, leading to cognitive and motor problems.

10. **What is meant by the terms *prematurity* and *low birth weight*?**

A baby is preterm when birth occurs at or before 37 weeks of gestation. A baby has a low birth weight when it weighs less than 5½ pounds (about 2,500 grams). A baby who is low in birth weight but born at full term is said to be small for dates. The risk of having preterm babies rises with multiple births.

11. **What risks are connected with being born prematurely or low in birth weight?**

Risks include infant mortality and delayed neurological and motor development. Preterm babies are relatively thin and often have vernix on the skin and lanugo. Sucking and breathing reflexes may be weak. The walls of air sacs in the lungs may stick together, leading to respiratory distress.

12. **How are preterm infants treated following birth?**

Preterm babies usually remain in the hospital in incubators. Preterm infants profit from early stimulation just as full-term babies do. Parents often do not treat preterm neonates as well as they treat full-term neonates, perhaps because preterm infants are less attractive and have irritating, high-pitched cries.

13. **What kinds of problems in mood do women experience during the postpartum period?**

Women may encounter the baby blues, postpartum depression, and postpartum psychosis. These problems are found around the world and probably reflect hormonal changes following birth, although stress can play a role. High self-esteem and social support help women manage these adjustment problems.

14. **How critical is parental interaction with neonates in the formation of bonds of attachment?**

It may not be critical. Research by Klaus and Kennell suggested that the first few hours after birth present a "maternal-sensitive" period during which the mother's hormone levels particularly dispose her to "bond" with her neonates. The study confounded the effects of extra time with their babies with special attention from health professionals, however.

15. **How do health professionals assess the health of neonates?**

The neonate's overall health is usually evaluated according to the Apgar scale. The Brazelton Neonatal Behavioral Assessment Scale also screens neonates for behavioral and neurological problems.

16. **What are reflexes? What kinds of reflexes are shown by neonates?**

Reflexes are simple, unlearned, stereotypical responses that are elicited by specific stimuli. The rooting and sucking reflexes are basic to survival. Other key reflexes include the startle reflex, the grasping reflex, the stepping reflex, the Babinski reflex, and the tonic-neck reflex. Most reflexes disappear or are replaced by voluntary behavior within months.

17. **How well do neonates see, hear, and so on?**

Neonates are nearsighted. They visually detect movement, and many track movement. Fetuses respond to sound months before they are born. Neonates are particularly responsive to the sounds and rhythms of speech. The nasal preferences of neonates are similar to those of older children and adults. Neonates prefer the taste of sweet solutions and find them soothing. The sensations of skin against skin are also soothing and may contribute to formation of bonds of attachment.

18. **Can neonates learn?**

Yes. Neonates are capable of classical and operant conditioning. For example, they can be conditioned to blink their eyes in response to a tone.

19. **What patterns of sleep are found among neonates?**

Neonates spend two-thirds of their time in sleep. Nearly all neonates distribute sleep through naps. Neonates spend about half their time sleeping in REM sleep, but as time goes on, REM sleep accounts for less of their sleep. REM sleep may be connected with brain development.

20. Why do babies cry?

Babies cry mainly because of pain and discomfort. Crying may communicate the identity of the crier across distance, as well as hunger, anger, pain, and the presence of health problems.

21. What will stop an infant from crying?

Pacifiers help because sucking is soothing. Parents also try picking babies up, patting them, caressing and rocking them, and speaking to them in a low voice.

22. What is SIDS? What are the risk factors for SIDS?

SIDS is a disorder of infancy that apparently strikes while a baby is sleeping. It is the most common cause of death in infants between the ages of 1 month and 1 year. SIDS is more common among babies who are put to sleep in the prone position, preterm and low-birth-weight infants, male infants, and infants whose mothers smoked during or after pregnancy or whose mothers used narcotics during pregnancy.

Key Terms

Active Learning Resources

Childhood & Adolescence Book Companion Website

http://www.thomsonedu.com/psychology/rathus

Visit your book companion website, where you will find more resources to help you study. There you will find interactive versions of your book features, including the Lessons in Observation video, Active Review sections, and the Truth or Fiction feature. In addition, the companion website contains quizzing, flash cards, and a pronunciation glossary.

 is an easy-to-use online resource that helps you study in less time to get the grade you want, NOW.

http://www.thomsonedu.com/login

Need help studying? This site is your one-stop study shop. Take a Pre-Test and ThomsonNOW will generate a Personalized Study Plan based on your test results. The Study Plan will identify the topics you need to review and direct you to online resources to help you master those topics. You can then take a Post-Test to determine the concepts you have mastered and what you still need to work on.

Concept Review 5.1   Sequences of Physical Development

Cephalocaudal Development

Cephalocaudal means that development proceeds from the "head" to the "tail," or, in the case of humans, to the lower parts of the body. Cephalocaudal development gives the brain an opportunity to participate more fully in subsequent developments.

This photo shows that infants gain control over their hands and upper body before they gain control over their lower body.

Proximodistal Development

Proximodistal means that development proceeds from the trunk or central axis of the body outward. The brain and spine make up the central nervous system along the central axis of the body and are functional before the infant can control the arms and legs.

In this photo you can see that the infant's arm is only slightly longer than her head. Compare this to the length of your own head and arm.

Differentiation

As children mature, physical reactions become less global and more specific. This infant engages in diffuse motor activity. Within a few months, he will be grasping for objects and holding onto them with a more and more sophisticated kind of grasp.

This photo shows that infants engage in diffuse motion before they begin to reach and grasp.

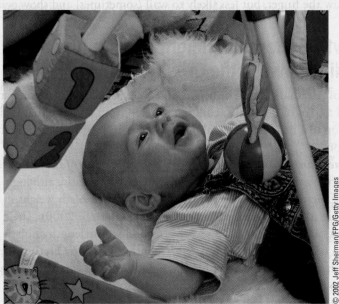

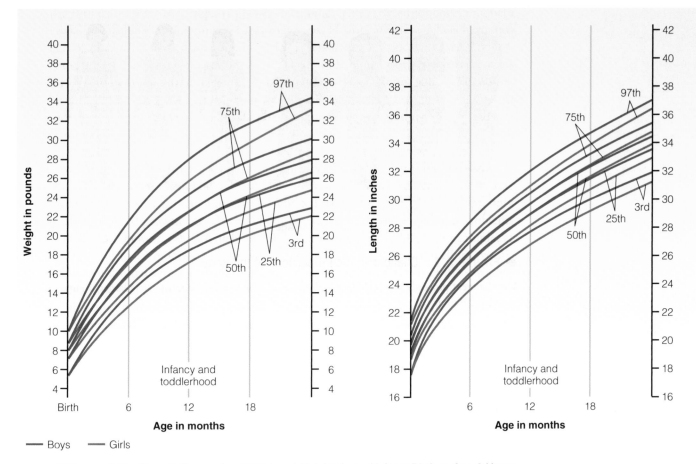

● **Figure 5.1** Growth Curves for Weight and Height (Length) from Birth to Age 2 Years

The curves indicate the percentiles for weight and length at different ages. Lines labeled 97th show the height and weight of children who are taller and heavier than 97% of children of a particular age. Lines marked 50th indicate the height and weight of the average child of a given age: Half their agemates are shorter and lighter, and half are heavier and taller. Lines labeled 3rd designate children who are taller and heavier than only 3% of children their age, and so on.

Source: Kuczmarski et al. (2000, Figures 1–4).

● Figure 5.1, but research suggests that infants actually grow in spurts. About 90%–95% of the time, they are not growing at all. One study measured the height of infants throughout their first 21 months (Lampl et al., 1992). The researchers found that the infants would remain the same size for 2 to 63 days and then would shoot up in length from one-fifth of an inch (0.5 centimeter) to a full inch (2.5 centimeters) in less than 24 hours. Parents who swear that their infants sometimes consume enormous amounts of food and grow overnight may not be exaggerating.

Infants grow another 4 to 6 inches during the second year and gain another 4 to 7 pounds. Boys generally reach half their adult height by their second birthday. Girls, however, mature more quickly than boys and are likely to reach half their adult height at the age of 18 months (Tanner, 1989). The growth rates of taller-than-average infants, as a group, tend to slow down. Those of shorter-than-average infants, as a group, tend to speed up. I am not suggesting that there is no relationship between infant and adult heights or that we all wind up in an average range. Tall infants, as a group, wind up taller than short infants, but in most cases not by as much as seemed likely during infancy.

are more likely than other children to display signs of poor nutrition, such as anemia and FTT (National Center for Children in Poverty, 2004). For more information on children in poverty, go to www.nccp.org. *Question: What are the nutritional needs of infants?*

From birth, infants should be fed either breast milk or an iron-fortified infant formula. The introduction of solid foods is not recommended until the infant can indicate hunger by leaning forward and fullness by turning away from food. These behaviors normally occur at 4 to 6 months of age, although the American Academy of Pediatrics recommends that infants be fed breast milk throughout the first year and longer if possible (American Academy of Pediatrics, 2007). For more information, go to the website of the American Academy of Pediatrics at www.aap.org. The first solid food is usually iron-enriched cereal, followed by strained fruits, then vegetables, and finally meats, poultry, and fish. Whole cow's milk is normally delayed until the infant is 9 to 12 months old. Finger foods such as teething biscuits are introduced in the latter part of the first year.

Here are some useful guidelines for infant nutrition (Infant and Toddler Nutrition, 2007):

- Build up to a variety of foods. Introduce new foods one at a time, if possible, to determine whether they make a difference in the infant's behavior. (The infant may be allergic to a new food, and introducing foods one at a time helps isolate a new food's possible effects on the infant.)
- In general, pay attention to the infant's appetite to help avoid overfeeding or underfeeding. (If the infant seems to have a poor appetite, discuss it with the pediatrician.)
- Do not restrict fat and cholesterol too much. (For example, do not substitute skim milk for whole milk.) Infants need calories and some fat.
- Do not overdo high-fiber foods.
- In general, avoid items with added sugar and salt.
- Encourage eating of high-iron foods; infants need more iron, pound for pound, than adults do.

When in doubt, parents should check with a pediatrician. What is good for adults is not good for infants. Parents who are on low-fat, high-fiber diets to ward off cardiovascular problems, cancer, and other health problems should not assume that the same diet is healthful for infants.

Breast Feeding versus Bottle Feeding: Pros and Cons, Biological and Political

In many developing nations, women have no choice: If their infants are going to be nourished, mothers will have to breast-feed. Even in developed nations, where formula is readily available, breast milk today is considered by most health professionals to be the "medical gold standard" and by many, perhaps most, mothers to be the "moral gold standard" (Knaak, 2005). Perhaps for this reason, popular magazines in the United States, including magazines that aim at African American mothers, tend to carry more articles on breast feeding than on bottle feeding (Frerichs et al., 2006).

Breast feeding, of course, is the "natural" way to nourish a baby. Infant formulas were developed in the 1930s. Over the next several decades, breast feeding declined because women were entering the workforce, bottle feeding was seen as "scientific," and the women's movement encouraged women to become liberated from traditional roles (Sloan et al., 2006). Breast feeding thus has political and social aspects as well as nutritional aspects (Knaak, 2005). *Question: How do women decide to bottle-*

feed or to breast-feed their children? Much of the decision of whether or not to breast-feed has to do with domestic and occupational arrangements, day care, social support, reactions to public breast feeding, and beliefs about mother–infant bonding (Sloan et al., 2006).

A survey of 35 African American and Latina American mothers or pregnant adolescents (age 12 to 19) found that those who recognized the benefits of breast feeding were more likely to do it (Hannon et al., 2000). They reported benefits such as promoting mother–infant bonding and the infant's health. Barriers to breast feeding include fear of pain, embarrassment by public exposure, and unease with the act itself. An influential person, such as the woman's partner or mother, often successfully encourages the mother to breast-feed, however (Sloan et al., 2006). Community support through volunteer workers and visiting nurses also encourages women to breast-feed (Fetrick et al., 2003; Graffy et al., 2004). Better-educated women are more likely to breast-feed, even among low-income women (Sloan et al., 2006).

In any event, breast feeding has become more popular during the past generation, largely because of increased knowledge of its health benefits, even among women at the lower end of the socioeconomic spectrum (Sloan et al., 2006). Today, most American mothers—more than 70%—breast-feed their children for at least a while, but only about two women in five continue to breast-feed after 6 months, and only one in five is still breast feeding after 1 year (Breastfeeding, 2006). The American Academy of Pediatrics (2007) recommends that women breast-feed for 1 year or more.

Many women bottle-feed because they return to work after childbirth and therefore are unavailable to breast-feed. Their partners, extended families, nannies, or child-care workers give their children bottles during the day. Some mothers pump their milk and bottle it for their children's use when they are away. Some parents bottle-feed because it permits both parents to share in feeding, around the clock. The father may not be equipped to breast-feed, but he can bottle-feed. Even though bottle feeding requires preparing formulas, many women find it to be less troublesome than breast feeding.

Question: What are the advantages and disadvantages of breast milk? Let us begin with the positive (American Academy of Pediatrics, 2007):

- Breast milk conforms to human digestion processes (i.e., it is unlikely to upset the infant's stomach).
- Breast milk alone is adequate for the first 6 months after birth. Water, juice, and other foods are generally unnecessary. Even if babies enjoy discovering new tastes and textures, solid foods should not replace breast feeding, but merely supplement breast milk through the first year (Breastfeeding, 2006).
- As the infant matures, the composition of breast milk changes to help meet the infant's changing needs.
- Breast milk contains the mother's antibodies; when they are transmitted to the infant, they help to prevent problems ranging from ear infections, pneumonia, wheezing, bronchiolitis, and tetanus to chicken pox, bacterial meningitis, and typhoid fever.
- Breast milk helps protect against the form of cancer known as childhood lymphoma (a cancer of the lymph glands).
- Diarrhea can be a persistent and deadly disease for millions of infants in developing countries, and breast milk decreases the likelihood of developing serious and lingering cases of diarrhea.
- Infants who are nourished by breast milk are less likely to develop allergic responses and constipation than infants who are bottle-fed.

Active Review

1. Cephalocaudal development describes the processes by which development proceeds from the _____ to the lower parts of the body.
2. The _____ principle means that development proceeds from the trunk outward.
3. Infants usually double their birth weight in about _____ months and triple it by the first birthday.
4. Mothers of infants with failure to thrive, compared with mothers of healthy infants, show fewer (Positive or Negative?) feelings toward their infants.
5. After illness or dietary deficiency, children show _____, which is a tendency to return to their genetically determined pattern of growth.

6. Breast milk contains _____ that can prevent problems such as ear infections, meningitis, tetanus, and chicken pox.

Reflect & Relate: How closely did your parents pay attention to your height and weight? Did they chart it? When did you begin to think that you were average or above or below average in height and weight? What effect did your size have on your self-concept and self-esteem?

Go to

http://www.thomsonedu.com/psychology/rathus
for an interactive version of this review.

Development of the Brain and Nervous System

When I was a child, I did not think that it was a good idea to have a nervous system. Who, after all, wants to be nervous? But then I learned that the nervous system is a system of **nerves** involved in heartbeat, visual–motor coordination, thought and language, and so on. The human nervous system is more complex than that of other animals. Although elephants and whales have heavier brains, our brains make up a larger proportion of our body weight.

Development of Neurons

The basic units of the nervous system are **neurons**. *Questions: What are neurons? How do they develop?* Neurons are cells that receive and transmit messages from one part of the body to another. The messages transmitted by neurons account for phenomena as varied as reflexes, the perception of an itch from a mosquito bite, the visual–motor coordination of a skier, the composition of a concerto, and the solution of a math problem.

People are born with about 100 billion neurons, most of which are in the brain. Neurons vary according to their functions and locations in the body. Some neurons in the brain are only a fraction of an inch in length, whereas neurons in the leg can grow several feet long. Each neuron possesses a cell body, dendrites, and an axon (see ● Figure 5.3). **Dendrites** are short fibers that extend from the cell body and receive incoming messages from up to 1,000 adjoining transmitting neurons. The **axon** extends trunklike from the cell body and accounts for much of the difference in length in neurons. An axon can be up to several feet in length if it is carrying messages from the toes upward. Messages are released from axon terminals in the form

nerves Bundles of axons from many neurons.

neurons Nerve cells; cells found in the nervous system that transmit messages.

dendrites The rootlike parts of a neuron that receive impulses from other neurons (from the Greek *dendron*, meaning "tree" and referring to the branching appearance of dendrites).

axon A long, thin part of a neuron that transmits impulses to other neurons through small branching structures called axon terminals.

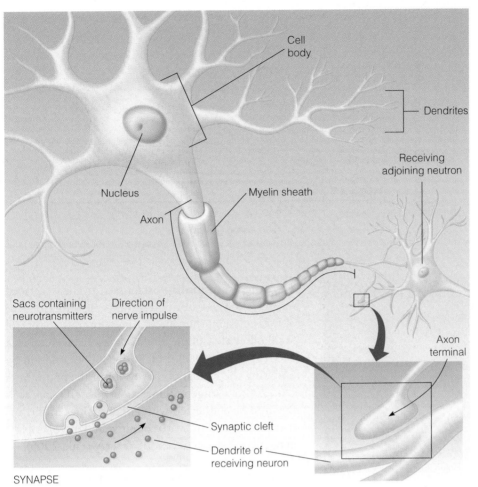

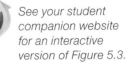

See your student companion website for an interactive version of Figure 5.3.

Cell body

Dendrites

Nucleus

Receiving adjoining neutron

Myelin sheath

Axon

Sacs containing neurotransmitters

Direction of nerve impulse

Axon terminal

Synaptic cleft

Dendrite of receiving neuron

SYNAPSE

● **Figure 5.3** Anatomy of a Neuron

"Messages" enter neurons through dendrites, are transmitted along the axon, and then are sent through axon terminals to muscles, glands, and other neurons. Neurons develop by means of proliferation of dendrites and axon terminals and through myelination.

of chemicals called **neurotransmitters**. These messages are then received by the dendrites of adjoining neurons, muscles, or glands. As the child matures, the axons of neurons grow in length, and the dendrites and axon terminals proliferate, creating vast interconnected networks for the transmission of complex messages.

Myelin

Many neurons are tightly wrapped with white, fatty **myelin sheaths** that give them the appearance of a string of white sausages. The high fat content of the myelin sheath insulates the neuron from electrically charged atoms in the fluids that encase the nervous system. In this way, leakage of the electric current being carried along the axon is minimized, and messages are conducted more efficiently.

The term **myelination** refers to the process by which axons are coated with myelin. Myelination is not complete at birth, but rather is part of the maturation process that leads to the abilities to crawl and walk during the first year after birth. Incomplete myelination accounts for some of the helplessness of neonates. Myelination of the brain's prefrontal matter continues into the second decade of life and is connected with advances in working memory and language ability (Aslin & Schlaggar, 2006; Pujol et al., 2006). Breakdown of myelin is believed to be associated with Alzheimer's disease, a source of cognitive decline that usually begins in middle to late adulthood (Bartzokis, 2004; Connor, 2004).

neurotransmitter A chemical substance that enables the transmission of neural impulses from one neuron to another.

myelin sheath (MY-uh-lin) A fatty, whitish substance that encases and insulates neurons, permitting more rapid transmission of neural impulses.

myelination The process by which axons are coated with myelin.

● **Figure 5.4**
Growth of Body Systems as a Percentage of Total Postnatal Growth

The brain of the neonate weighs about one-fourth of its adult weight. In keeping with the principle of cephalocaudal growth, the brain will triple in weight by the infant's first birthday, reaching nearly 70% of its adult weight.

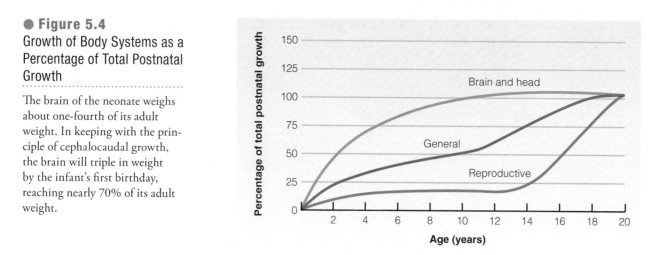

● **Figure 5.5**
Structures of the Brain

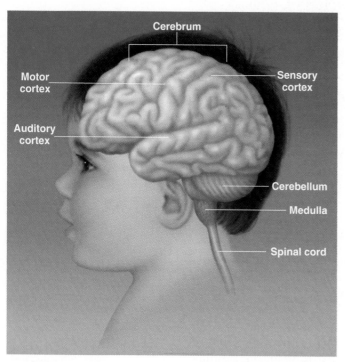

The convolutions of the cortex increase its surface area and, apparently, its intellectual capacity. (In this case, wrinkles are good.) The medulla is involved in vital functions such as respiration and heartbeat; the cerebellum is involved in balance and coordination.

See your student companion website for an interactive version of Figure 5.5.

In the disease **multiple sclerosis,** myelin is replaced by a hard, fibrous tissue that disrupts the timing of neural transmission, thus interfering with muscle control (Stankoff et al., 2006). The disorder phenylketonuria (PKU; see Chapter 2) leads to mental retardation by inhibiting the formation of myelin in the brain (Sirrs et al., 2007). Congenital infection with HIV has been shown to be connected with abnormalities in the formation of myelin and with cognitive and motor impairment (Blanchette et al., 2001; Thierry et al., 2005).

Development of the Brain

Questions: What is the brain? How does the brain develop? The brain is the command center of the developing organism. (If you like computer analogies, think of the brain as the central processing unit.) It contains neurons and provides the basis for physical, cognitive, and personal and social development.

The brain of the neonate weighs a little less than a pound, or nearly one-fourth its adult weight. **Truth or Fiction Revisited:** In keeping with the principles of cephalocaudal growth, an infant's brain reaches about 50% of its adult weight by the second birthday (see ● Figure 5.4). Let us look at the brain, as shown in ● Figure 5.5, and discuss the development of the structures within.

Structures of the Brain

Many nerves that connect the spinal cord to higher levels of the brain pass through the **medulla.** The medulla is vital in the control of basic functions, such as heartbeat and respiration. The medulla is part of an area called the brain stem, which may be implicated in sudden infant death syndrome (SIDS; see Chapter 4).

Above the medulla lies the **cerebellum,** which is Latin for "little brain." The cerebellum helps the child maintain balance, control motor behavior, and coordinate eye movements with bodily sensations.

The **cerebrum** is the crowning glory of the brain. It makes possible the breadth and depth of human learning, thought, memory, and language. Only in human beings does the cerebrum constitute such a large proportion of the brain. The surface of the cerebrum consists of two hemispheres—left and right—that become increasingly wrinkled as the child develops, coming to show ridges and valleys called fissures. This surface is the cerebral cortex. The wrinkles allow a great deal of surface area to be packed into the brain. **Truth or Fiction Revisited:** Yes, the cerebral cortex is only one-eighth of an inch thick, yet it is here that thought and reasoning occur. It is here that we display sensory information from the world outside and command muscles to move.

Growth Spurts of the Brain

The brain makes gains in size and weight in different ways. One way is in the formation of neurons, a process completed by birth. The first major growth spurt of the brain occurs during the fourth and fifth months of prenatal development, when neurons proliferate. A second growth spurt in the brain occurs between the 25th week of prenatal development and the end of the second year after birth. Whereas the first growth spurt of the brain is due to the formation of neurons, the second growth spurt is due primarily to the proliferation of dendrites and axon terminals (see ● Figure 5.6).

Brain Development in Infancy

There is a clear link between what infants can do and the myelination of areas within the brain. At birth, the parts of the brain involved in heartbeat and respiration, sleeping and arousal, and reflex activity are fairly well myelinated and functional.

Myelination of motor pathways allows neonates to show stereotyped reflexes, but otherwise neonates' physical activity tends to be random and ill-organized. Myelination of the motor area of the cerebral cortex begins at about the fourth month of prenatal development. Myelin develops rapidly along the major motor pathways from the cerebral cortex during the last month of pregnancy and continues after birth. The development of intentional physical activity coincides with myelination as the unorganized movements of the neonate come under increasing control. Myelination of the nerves to muscles is largely developed by the age of 2 years, although research using magnetic resonance imaging, or MRI, suggests that myelination continues to some degree into adolescence (Wozniak & Lim, 2006).

Although neonates respond to touch and can see and hear quite well, the areas of the cortex that are involved in vision, hearing, and the skin senses are less well myelinated at birth. As myelination progresses and the interconnections between the various areas of the cortex thicken, children become increasingly capable of complex and integrated sensorimotor activities (Wozniak & Lim, 2006).

Neonates whose mothers read *The Cat in the Hat* aloud during the last few weeks of pregnancy show a preference for this story (see Chapter 3). It turns out that myelination of the neurons involved in the sense of hearing begins at about the sixth month of pregnancy, coinciding with the period in which fetuses begin to respond to sound. Myelination of these pathways is developing rapidly at term and continues until about the age of 4 years.

Although the fetus shows some response to light during the third trimester, it is hard to imagine what use the fetus could have for vision. It turns out that the neurons involved in vision begin to myelinate only shortly before full term, but then they complete the process of myelination rapidly. Within a short 5 to 6 months after birth, vision has become the dominant sense.

Nature and Nurture in the Development of the Brain

Development of the areas of the brain that control sensation and movement begins as a result of maturation, but sensory stimulation and physical activity during early infancy also spur the development of these areas. *Question: How do nature and nurture affect the development of the brain?* Experience interacts with the unfolding of the genetic code to produce the brain—and intellectual functioning—as seen by a snapshot at a given point in time (Güntürkün, 2006; Posner & Rothbart, 2007).

Neonate   **Six months**   **Two years**

● **Figure 5.6**

Increase in Neural Connections in the Brain

A major growth spurt in the brain occurs between the 25th week of prenatal development and the end of the second year after birth. This growth spurt is due primarily to the proliferation of dendrites and axon terminals.

Source: Conel (1959).

multiple sclerosis A disorder in which myelin is replaced by hard fibrous tissue that impedes neural transmission.

medulla (muh-DUH-luh) An oblong-shaped area of the hindbrain involved in heartbeat and respiration.

cerebellum (ser-uh-BEH-lum) The part of the hindbrain involved in muscle coordination and balance.

cerebrum (seh-REE-brum) The large mass of the forebrain, which consists of two hemispheres.

Research with animals shows how sensory stimulation sparks growth of the cortex. Researchers have been given complex environmental exposure, in some cases rat "amusement parks" with toys such as ladders, platforms, and boxes to demonstrate the effects of enriched environments. In these studies, rats exposed to more complex environments develop heavier brains than control animals. The weight differences in part reflect more synapses per neuron than other rats (Briones et al., 2004). On the other hand, animals reared in darkness show shrinkage of the visual cortex, impaired vision, and impaired visual–motor coordination (Klintsova & Greenough, 1999). If they don't use it, they lose it?

Human brains also are affected by experience. Infants actually have more connections among neurons than adults do. Connections that are activated by experience survive; the others do not (Tsuneishi & Casaer, 2000; Weinberg, 2004).

The great adaptability of the brain appears to be a double-edged sword. Adaptability allows us to develop different patterns of neural connections to meet the demands of different environments, but lack of stimulation—especially during critical early periods of development (as we will see later)—can impair adaptability.

Brain nourishment, like early experience, plays a role in the brain achieving what is permitted by the child's genes. Inadequate fetal nutrition, especially during the prenatal growth spurt of the brain, has several negative effects such as smallness in the size of the brain, the formation of fewer neurons, and less myelination (Guerrini et al., 2007; Massaro et al., 2006).

Active Review

7. _____ are the basic units of the nervous system.
8. Each neuron possesses a cell body, dendrites, and a(n) _____.
9. The brain reaches nearly _____% of its adult weight by the first birthday.
10. The wrinkled part of the brain, called the _____, enables the child to maintain balance and to control physical behavior.

Reflect & Relate: Are you surprised that there is such a close connection between experience and development of the brain? How does the information presented in this section fit with the adage "Use it or lose it"?

Go to

http://www.thomsonedu.com/psychology/rathus
for an interactive version of this review.

Motor Development: How Moving

"Allyn couldn't walk yet at 10 months, but she zoomed after me in her walker, giggling her head off." "Anthony was walking forward and backward by the age of 13 months."

These are some of the types of comments parents make about their children's motor development. ***Questions: What is motor development? How does it occur?*** Motor development involves the activity of muscles, leading to changes in posture, movement, and coordination of movement with the infant's developing sensory apparatus. Motor development provides some of the most fascinating changes in infants, in part because so much seems to happen so fast, and so much of it during the first year.

Like physical development, motor development follows cephalocaudal and proximodistal patterns and differentiation. Infants gain control of their heads and upper torsos before they can effectively use their arms. This trend illustrates cephalocaudal development. Infants also can control their trunks and shoulders before they can use their hands and fingers, demonstrating the proximodistal trend.

Lifting and Holding the Torso and Head: Heads Up

Neonates can move their heads slightly to the side. They can thus avoid suffocation if they are lying face down and their noses or mouths are obstructed by bedding. At about 1 month, infants can raise their heads. By about 2 months, they can also lift their chests while lying on their stomachs.

When neonates are held, their heads must be supported. But by 3 to 6 months of age, infants generally manage to hold their heads quite well so supporting the head is no longer necessary. Unfortunately, infants who can normally support their heads cannot do so when they are lifted or moved about in a jerky manner; infants who are handled carelessly can thus develop neck injuries.

Control of the Hands: Getting a Grip on Things

The development of hand skills is a clear example of proximodistal development. Infants will track (follow) slowly moving objects with their eyes shortly after birth, but they will not generally reach for them. They show a grasp reflex but do not reliably reach for the objects that appear to interest them. Voluntary reaching and grasping require visual–motor coordination. By about the age of 3 months, infants will make clumsy swipes at objects, failing to grasp them, because their aim is poor or they close their hands too soon or too late.

Between the ages of 4 and 6 months, infants become more successful at grasping objects (Piek, 2006; Santos et al., 2000). However, they may not know how to let go and may hold an object indefinitely, until their attention is diverted and the hand opens accidentally. Four to 6 months is a good age for giving children rattles, large plastic spoons, mobiles, and other brightly colored hanging toys that can be grasped but are harmless when they wind up in the mouth.

Grasping is reflexive at first. Voluntary grasping (holding) replaces reflexive grasping by the age of 3 to 4 months. Infants first use an **ulnar grasp**, in which they hold objects clumsily between their fingers and their palm (Butterworth et al., 1997). By the age of 4 to 6 months, they can transfer objects back and forth between hands. The oppositional thumb comes into play at about the age of 9 to 12 months. Use of the thumb gives infants the ability to pick up tiny objects in a **pincer grasp** (● Figure 5.7). By about 11 months of age, infants can hold objects in each hand and inspect them in turn.

Between the ages of 5 and 11 months, infants adjust their hands in anticipation of grasping moving targets. They also gather information from the objects' movements to predict their future location and catch them (Wentworth et al., 2000). Think of the complex concepts it requires to explain this behavior and how well infants perform it, without any explanation at all! Of course, I am not suggesting that infants solve problems in geometry and physics to grasp moving objects; that interpretation, as developmental psychologist Marshall M. Haith (1998) would describe it, would put a "cog in infant cognition."

Another aspect of visual–motor coordination is stacking blocks. On average, children can stack two blocks at 15 months, three blocks at 18 months, and five blocks at 24 months (Wentworth et al., 2000). At about 24 months of age, children can also copy horizontal and vertical lines.

Locomotion: Getting a Move On

Locomotion is movement from one place to another. Children gain the capacity to move their bodies through a sequence of activities that includes rolling over, sitting up, crawling, creeping, walking, and running (see ● Figure 5.8). There is much variation in the ages at which infants first engage in these activities. Although the sequence

● **Figure 5.7**
Pincer Grasp

Infants first hold objects between their fingers and palm. Once the oppositional thumb comes into play at about 9 to 12 months of age, infants are able to pick up tiny objects using what is termed a pincer grasp.

ulnar grasp A method of grasping objects in which the fingers close somewhat clumsily against the palm.

pincer grasp The use of the opposing thumb to grasp objects between the thumb and other fingers.

locomotion Movement from one place to another.

© Mike Greenlar/The Image Works

A Native American Hopi Infant Strapped to a Cradle Board

Researchers have studied Hopi children who are strapped to cradle boards during their first year to see whether their motor development is delayed significantly. Once released from their boards, Hopi children make rapid advances in motor development, suggesting the importance of maturation in motor development.

building, and stair climbing from early infancy. The other twin was allowed to develop on his own. At first, the trained twin had better skills, but as time passed, the untrained twin became just as skilled.

Although the appearance of motor skills can be accelerated by training (Adolph & Berger, 2005; Zelazo, 1998), the effect seems slight. Practice in the absence of neural readiness has limited results. There is also little evidence that early training leads to superior motor skills.

Although being strapped to a cradle board did not permanently prevent the motor development of Hopi infants, Wayne Dennis (1960) reported that infants in an Iranian orphanage were significantly retarded in their motor development. In contrast to the Hopi infants, the institutionalized infants were exposed to extreme social and physical deprivation. Under these conditions, they grew apathetic, and all aspects of development suffered. But there is also a bright side to this tale of deprivation. The motor development of similar infants in a Lebanese orphanage accelerated dramatically in response to such minimal intervention as being propped up in their cribs and being given a few colorful toys (Dennis & Sayegh, 1965).

Nature provides the limits—the "reaction range"—for the expression of inherited traits. Nurture determines whether the child will develop skills that reach the upper limits of the range. Even as fundamental a skill as locomotion is determined by a complex interplay of maturational and environmental factors (Adolph & Berger, 2005). There may be little purpose in trying to train children to enhance motor skills before they are ready. Once they are ready, however, teaching and practice do make a difference. One does not become an Olympic athlete without "good genes," but one also usually does not become an Olympic athlete without high-quality training. And because motor skills are important to the self-concepts of children, good teaching is important.

Active Review

11. Infants can first raise their heads at about the age of _____ month(s).
12. Infants first use a(n) (Ulnar or Pincer?) grasp for holding objects.
13. Developmentalists assess infants' ability to stack blocks as a measure of their _____-motor coordination.
14. Infants (Sit up or Crawl?) before they (Sit up or Crawl?).
15. As children mature, their bones (Increase or Decrease?) in density.
16. Research reveals that both maturation and _____ play indispensable roles in motor development.

17. Arnold Gesell (Did or Did not?) find that extensive training in hand coordination, block building, and stair climbing gave infants enduring advantages over untrained infants in these skills.

Reflect & Relate: "When did your baby first sit up?" "When did he walk?" Why are people so concerned about when infants do what? Imagine that you are speaking to a parent who is concerned that her child is not yet walking at 14 months. What would you say to the parent? When should there be cause for concern?

Go to

http://www.thomsonedu.com/psychology/rathus

for an interactive version of this review.

Sensory and Perceptual Development: Taking in the World

What a world we live in: green hills and reddish skies; rumbling trucks, murmuring brooks, and voices; the sweet and the sour; the acrid and the perfumed; the metallic and the fuzzy. What an ever-changing display of sights, sounds, tastes, smells, and touches. The pleasures of the world, and its miseries, are known to us through sensory impressions and the organization of these impressions into personal inner maps of reality. Our eyes, our ears, the sensory receptors in our noses and our mouths, our skin senses—these are our tickets of admission to the world.

In Chapter 4, we examined the sensory capabilities of the neonate. *Question: How do sensation and perception develop in the infant?* In this section, we see how infants develop the ability to integrate disjointed **sensations** into meaningful patterns of events termed **perceptions**. We see what captures the attention of infants, and we see how young children develop into purposeful seekers of information selecting the sensory impressions they choose to capture. We focus on the development of vision and hearing, because most of the research on sensory and perceptual development in infancy has been done in these areas.

We will see that many things that are obvious to us are not so obvious to infants. You may know that a coffee cup is the same whether you see it from above or from the side, but make no such assumptions about the infant's knowledge. You may know that an infant's mother is the same size whether she is standing next to the infant or approaching from two blocks away, but do not assume that the infant agrees with you.

We cannot ask infants to explain why they look at some things and not at others. Nor can we ask them if their mother appears to be the same size whether she is standing close to them or far away. But investigators of childhood sensation and perception have devised clever methods to answer these questions, and their findings provide us with fascinating insights into the perceptual processes of even the neonate. They reveal that many basic perceptual competencies are present early in life.

Development of Vision: The Better to See You With

Development of vision involves development of visual acuity or sharpness, development of peripheral vision (seeing things off to the sides while looking straight ahead), visual preferences, depth perception, and perceptual constancies, such as knowing that an object remains the same object even though it may look different when seen from a different angle. (You knew that, didn't you?)

Development of Visual Acuity and Peripheral Vision

Newborns are extremely nearsighted, with vision beginning at about 20/600. The most dramatic gains in visual acuity are made between birth and 6 months of age, with acuity reaching about 20/50 (Cavallini et al., 2002; Haith, 1990; Skoczenski, 2002). Gains in visual acuity then become more gradual, approximating adult levels (20/20 in the best cases) by about 3 to 5 years of age.

Neonates also have poor peripheral vision (Cavallini et al., 2002; Skoczenski, 2002). Adults can perceive objects that are nearly 90 degrees off to the side (i.e., directly to the left or right), although objects at these extremes are unclear. Neonates cannot perceive visual stimuli that are off to the side by an angle of more than 30 degrees, but their peripheral vision expands to an angle of about 45 degrees by the age of 7 weeks. By 6 months of age, their peripheral vision is about equal to that of an adult.

Let us now consider the development of visual perception. In so doing, we will see that infants frequently prefer the strange to the familiar and will avoid going off the deep end—sometimes.

sensation The stimulation of sensory organs such as the eyes, ears, and skin and the transmission of sensory information to the brain.

perception The process by which sensations are organized into a mental map of the world.

Visual Preferences: How Do You Capture an Infant's Attention?

Questions: What captures the attention of infants? How do visual preferences develop? Neonates look at stripes longer than at blobs. This finding has been used in much of the research on visual acuity. Classic research found that by the age of 8 to 12 weeks, most infants also show distinct preferences for curved lines over straight ones (Fantz et al., 1975).

Robert Fantz (1961) also wondered whether there was something intrinsically interesting about the human face that drew the attention of infants. To investigate this question, he showed 2-month-old infants the six disks illustrated in ● Figure 5.11. One disk contained a caricature of human features, another contained newsprint, and still another contained a bull's-eye. The remaining three disks were featureless but were colored red, white, and yellow. In this study, the infants fixated significantly longer on the human face.

Some studies suggest that the infants in Fantz's (1961) study may have preferred the human face because it had a complex, intriguing pattern of dots (eyes) within an outline and not because it was a face. But theorists such as Michelle de Haan and Margrite Groen (2006) assert that "reading" faces is particularly important to infants because they do not understand verbal information as communicated through language. Thus, it would make evolutionary sense for infants to orient toward the human face and perceive the difference be-

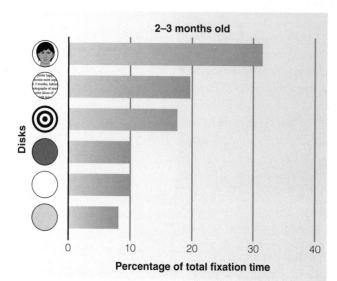

● Figure 5.11
Preferences for Visual Stimuli in 2-Month-Olds

Infants appear to prefer complex to simple visual stimuli. By the time they are 2 months old, they also tend to show a preference for the human face. Researchers continue to debate whether the face draws attention because of its content (i.e., being a face) or because of its stimulus characteristics (complexity, arrangement, etc.).

tween some facial expressions at very early ages.

Researchers therefore continue to investigate infants' preferences for the human face. They ask whether humans come into the world "prewired" to prefer human stimuli to other stimuli that are just as complex, and—if so—just what it is about human stimuli that draws attention. Some researchers—unlike de Haan and Groen—argue that neonates do not "prefer" faces because they are faces per se but because of the structure of their immature visual systems (Simion et al., 2001). A supportive study of 34 neonates found that the longer fixations on facelike stimuli resulted from a larger number of brief fixations (looks) rather than from a few prolonged fixations (Cassia et al., 2001). The infants' gaze, then, was sort of bouncing around from feature to feature rather than "staring" at the face in general. The researchers interpreted the finding to show that the stimulus properties of the visual object are more important than the fact that it represents a human face. Even so, of course, the "immature visual system" would be providing some "prewired" basis for attending to the face.

Learning clearly plays a role. Neonates can discriminate their mother's face from a stranger's after 8 hours of mother–infant contact spread over 4 days (Bushnell, 2001). By 3 to 5 months of age, infants respond differently to happy, surprised, and sad faces (Muir & Hains, 1993). Moreover, infants as young as 2 months prefer attractive faces to unattractive faces (Ramsey et al., 2004). This preference is more deeply ingrained by 6 months of age (Ramsey et al., 2004). Do standards of attractiveness have an inborn component, or are they learned (very!) early?

Neonates appear to direct their attention to the edges of objects. This pattern persists for the first several weeks (Bronson, 1991). When they are given the opportunity to look at human faces, 1-month-old infants tend to pay most attention to the "edges," that is, the chin, an ear, or the hairline. The eye movements of two-month-old infants move in from the edge, as shown in ● Figure 5.12. The infants focus particularly on the eyes, although they also inspect other inner features, such as the mouth and nose (Nelson & Ludemann, 1989).

Some researchers (e.g., Haith, 1979) explain infants' tendencies to scan from the edges of objects inward by noting that for the first several weeks of life, infants seem to be essentially concerned with *where* things are. Their attention is captured by movement and sharp contrasts in brightness and shape, such as those found where the edges of objects stand out against their backgrounds. But by about 2 months of age, infants tend to focus on the *what* of things. They may locate objects by looking at their edges, but now they scan systematically within the boundaries of objects (Bronson, 1990, 1997).

Development of Depth Perception: On *Not* Going Off the Deep End

Infants generally respond to cues for depth by the time they are able to crawl (6 to 8 months of age or so), and most have the good sense to avoid "going off the deep end," that is, crawling off ledges and tabletops into open space (Campos et al., 1978). ***Question: How do researchers determine whether infants will "go off the deep end"?***

In a classic study on depth perception, Eleanor Gibson and Richard Walk (1960) placed infants of various ages on a fabric-covered runway that ran across the center of a clever device called a visual cliff (see ● Figure 5.13). The visual cliff is a sheet of Plexiglas that covers a cloth with a high-contrast checkerboard pattern. On one side, the cloth is placed immediately beneath the Plexiglas; on the other, it is dropped about 4 feet below. Because the Plexiglas alone would easily support the infant, it is a visual cliff rather than an actual cliff. In the Gibson and Walk study, 8 out of 10 infants who had begun to crawl refused to venture onto the seemingly unsupported surface, even when their mothers beckoned encouragingly from the other side.

Psychologists can assess infants' emotional responses to the visual cliff long before infants can crawl. For example, Joseph Campos and his colleagues (1970) found that 1-month-old infants showed no change in heart rate when placed face down on the "cliff." They apparently did not perceive the depth of the cliff. At 2 months, infants showed decreases in heart rate when so placed, which psychologists interpret as a sign of interest. But the heart rates of 9-month-olds accelerated on the cliff, which is interpreted as a fear response. The study appears to suggest that infants profit from some experience crawling about (and, perhaps, accumulating some bumps) before they develop fear of heights. The 9-month-olds but not the 2-month-olds had had such experience. Other studies support the view that infants usually do not develop fear of heights until they can move around (Bertenthal & Campos, 1990). Newly walking infants are highly reluctant to venture out onto the visual cliff, even when their mothers signal them to do so (Sorce et al., 2000; Witherington et al., 2005).

Infants' tendencies to avoid falling off a cliff are apparently connected with their body positions at the time (Adolph, 2000; Adolph & Berger, 2005). Infants generally sit before they crawl, and by 9 months of age, we can think of most of them as experienced sitters. Crawling enters the picture at about 9 months. Karen Adolph

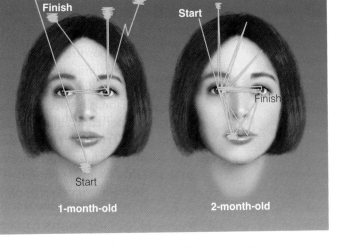

● **Figure 5.12**
Eye Movements of 1- and 2-Month-Olds

One-month-olds direct their attention to the edges of objects. Two-month-olds "move in from the edge." When looking at a face, for example, they focus on the eyes and other inner features. How do researchers explain this change?

Source: Salapatek (1975).

● **Figure 5.13**
The Visual Cliff

This young explorer has the good sense not to crawl out onto an apparently unsupported surface, even when mother beckons from the other side. Do infants have to experience some of life's "bumps" before they avoid "going off the deep end"?

1 month of age (Bushnell, 1993). One experiment demonstrating such understanding in 5-month-olds takes advantage of the fact that infants of this age tend to look longer at novel rather than familiar sources of stimulation. Julie Féron and her colleagues (2006) first allowed 5-month-old infants to handle (become manually familiar with) groups of either two or three objects, when they were presented one by one, to their right hand. The infants were then shown visual displays of either two or three objects. The infants looked significantly longer at the group of objects that differed from the one they had become manually familiar with, showing a transfer of information from the sense of touch to the sense of vision.

The Active–Passive Controversy in Perceptual Development

Question: Do children play an active or a passive role in perceptual development? Newborn children may have more sophisticated sensory capabilities than you expected. Still, their ways of perceiving the world are largely mechanical, or passive. The description of a stimulus capturing an infant's attention seems quite appropriate. Neonates seem to be generally at the mercy of external stimuli. When a bright light

A Closer Look

Effects of Early Exposure to Garlic, Alcohol, and—Gulp—Veggies *(continued)*

recently drunk alcohol. In fact, they ingest more breast milk once the alcohol is out of the mother's system, apparently to compensate for the lessened calorie intake at the previous feeding.

A related study by Mennella and a colleague, Pamela Garcia (2000), showed that early exposure to the odor of alcohol may also be something of a turnoff to infants. In this study, Mennella and Garcia compared the preferences of children who had been exposed to alcohol around the house during infancy with those of children who had not. All the children were about 4 to 6 years of age at the time of testing. Children who had been exposed to alcohol early were significantly more likely than the other children to dislike the odor of a bottle containing alcohol.

I would not suggest that parents drink alcohol to discourage their children from drinking later on, but the findings do seem to contradict what one might have expected.

And What About Encouraging Children to Eat Their Veggies during Infancy?

Many parents in the United States understand the benefits of eating vegetables and bring out the jars of vegetable baby food when they are feeding their infants. Does early exposure to these foods encourage or discourage the infants to eat them?

Early exposure generally seems to have a positive effect on children's appetites for vegetables. Consider a study of 4- to 7-month-old infants by Leann Birch and her colleagues (1998). The investigators repeatedly exposed infants to vegetables such as peas and green beans in the form of baby food to see whether they would subsequently eat more or less of them. Thirty-nine infants were fed the target foods once a day for 10 consecutive days. During that period, their consumption of the vegetables doubled from an average of 35 grams to an average of 72 grams. Moreover, the infants became more likely to eat similar foods, that is, other vegetables. Julie Mennella and her colleagues have also found that the infants of mothers who eat more diverse diets are more willing to eat a variety of foods (cited in Azar, 1998). Moreover, studies of rodents, pigs, and sheep show that once they are weaned, young animals prefer the flavors to which they were exposed through their mothers' milk. Early exposure to the foods that are traditional within a culture may be a key to shaping an infant's food preferences.

Reflect: Do you have any "ethnic" food preferences? Can you trace them to early experiences in the home or the neighborhood?

strikes, they attend to it. If the light moves slowly across the plane of their vision, they track it.

As time passes, broad changes occur in the perceptual processes of children, and the child's role in perception appears to become decidedly more active. Developmental psychologist Eleanor Gibson (1969, 1991) noted a number of these changes:

1. Intentional action replaces "capture" (automatic responses to stimulation). As infants mature and gain experience, purposeful scanning and exploration of the environment take the place of mechanical movements and passive responses to potent stimulation.

    Consider the scanning "strategies" of neonates. In a lighted room, neonates move their eyes mostly from left to right and back again. Mechanically, they sweep a horizontal plane. If they encounter an object that contrasts sharply with the background, their eye movements bounce back and forth against the edges. Even when neonates awaken in a dark room, they show the stereotypical horizontal scanning pattern, with about two eye movements per second (Haith, 1990).

    The stereotypical quality of these initial scanning movements suggests that they are inborn. They provide strong evidence that the neonate is neurologically prewired to gather and seek visual information. They do not reflect what we would consider a purposeful, or intentional, effort to learn about the environment.

2. Systematic search replaces unsystematic search. Over the first few years of life, children become more active as they develop systematic ways of exploring the environment. They come to pay progressively more attention to details of objects and people and to make finer and finer discriminations.

3. Attention becomes selective. Older children become capable of selecting the information they need from the welter of confusion in the environment.

Lessons in Observation

Sensation and Perception in Infancy

To watch this video, visit the book companion website. You can also answer the questions and e-mail your responses to your professor.

Learning Objectives

- What types of tests do doctors perform to test newborn and infant senses?
- What visual preferences do newborns have?
- Do visual preferences change as a newborn becomes an infant?

Applied Lesson

Describe the different tests doctors use to check the senses in newborns and infants.

Critical Thinking

How can a newborn's capacities for vision and hearing be considered adaptive? Hint: Think about Carter's initial interaction with his mother in this video.

Vision is the least mature of a newborn's senses, but infants have a strong preference for patterns with strong contrasts and prefer human faces above all else. Here, 2-month-old Giuseppina fixates on a drawing of a face.

For example, when older children are separated from their parents in a department store, they have the capacity to systematically scan for people of their parents' height, hair color, vocal characteristics, and so on. They are also more capable of discriminating the spot where the parent was last seen. A younger child is more likely to be confused by the welter of voices and faces and aisles and to be unable to extract essential information from this backdrop.

4. Irrelevant information becomes ignored. Older children gain the capacity to screen out or deploy their attention away from stimuli that are irrelevant to the task at hand. That might mean shutting out the noise of cars in the street or radios in the neighborhood so as to focus on a book.

In short, children develop from passive, mechanical reactors to the world about them into active, purposeful seekers and organizers of sensory information. They develop from beings whose attention is diffuse and "captured" into people who make decisions about what they will attend to. This process, as with so many others, appears to depend on both maturation and experience.

Let us now screen out distractions and turn our attention to consideration of the importance of maturation (the development of nature) and experience (nurture) in perceptual development.

Nature and Nurture in Perceptual Development

The nature–nurture issue is found in perceptual development, just as it is in other dimensions of development. *Question: What is the evidence for the roles of nature and nurture in perceptual development?*

Evidence for the Role of Nature

Compelling evidence supports the idea that our inborn sensory capacities play a crucial role in our perceptual development. For one thing, neonates have already come into the world with a good number of perceptual skills. They can see nearby objects quite well, and their hearing is usually fine. They are also born with tendencies to track moving objects, to systematically scan the horizon, and to prefer certain kinds of stimuli. Preferences for different kinds of visual stimuli appear to unfold on schedule as the first months wear on. Sensory changes, as with motor changes, appear to be linked to maturation of the nervous system.

For these reasons, it seems clear that we do have certain inborn ways of responding to sensory input—certain "categories" and built-in limits—that allow us to perceive certain aspects of the world of physical reality.

Evidence for the Role of Nurture

Evidence that experience plays a crucial role in perceptual development is also compelling. We could use any of hundreds of studies with children and other species to make the point, but let us limit our discussion to a couple of examples of research with kittens and human infants.

Children and lower animals have critical periods in their perceptual development. Failure to receive adequate sensory stimulation during these critical periods can result in permanent sensory deficits (Greenough et al., 2002). For example, newborn kittens raised with a patch over one eye wind up with few or no cells in the visual area of the cerebral cortex that would normally be stimulated by light that enters that eye. In effect, that eye becomes blind, even though sensory receptors in the eye itself may fire in response to light. On the other hand, if the eye of an adult cat is patched for the same amount of time, the animal will not lose vision in that eye. The critical period apparently will have passed. Similarly, if health problems require that a child's eye must be patched for an extensive period of time during the first year, the child's visual acuity in that eye may be impaired.

Consider a study of visual acuity among 28 human infants who had been deprived of all patterned visual input by cataracts in one or both eyes until they were treated at 1 week to 9 months of age (Maurer et al., 1999). Immediately following treatment, their visual acuity was no better than that of normal neonates, suggesting that their lack of visual experience has impaired their visual development. However, their visual acuity improved rapidly over the month following treatment. They showed some improvement in as little as 1 hour following visual input.

So, with perceptual development as with other dimensions of development, nature and nurture play indispensable roles. Today, few developmentalists would subscribe to either extreme. Most would agree that nature and nurture interact to shape perceptual development. Nature continues to guide the unfolding of the child's physical systems. Yet nurture continues to interact with nature in the development of these systems. We know that inborn physical structures, such as the nature of the cortex of the brain, place limits on our abilities to respond to the world. But we also know that experience continues to help shape our most basic physical structures. For example, sensorimotor experiences thicken the cortex of the brain. Sensory experiences are linked to the very development of neurons in the cortex, causing dendrites to proliferate and affecting myelination.

In the next chapter, we see how nature and nurture influence the development of thought and language in infants.

Active Review

18. At 2 months of age, infants tend to fixate longer on a (Scrambled or Real?) face.
19. Neonates direct their attention to the (Center or Edges?) of objects.
20. Researchers have studied depth perception in infants through use of the visual _____.
21. Research suggests that infants have developed size constancy by about _____ months.
22. As infants develop, they have (Greater or Lesser?) ability to screen out meaningless sounds in their native languages.
23. As time passes during infancy, one change in perceptual development is that intentional action

replaces _____ (automatic responses to stimulation).
24. Research shows that both nature and _____ are essential to perceptual development.

Reflect & Relate: What do you think it would mean if infants came into the world "prewired" to prefer the human face to other equally complex visual stimulation? Can you explain the evolutionary advantage that such prewiring would provide?

Go to

http://www.thomsonedu.com/psychology/rathus
for an interactive version of this review.

6 Infancy: Cognitive Development

Truth or Fiction?

T F For 2-month-old infants, "out of sight" is "out of mind." p. 193

T F A 1-hour-old infant may imitate an adult who sticks out his or her tongue. p. 199

T F Psychologists can begin to measure intelligence in infancy. p. 201

T F Infant crying is a primitive form of language. p. 204

T F You can advance children's development of pronunciation by correcting their errors. p. 211

T F Children are "prewired" to listen to language in such a way that they come to understand rules of grammar. p. 214

Preview

Victoria Snowber/Getty Images

 Go to

http://www.thomsonedu.com/psychology/rathus
for an interactive version of this "Truth or Fiction" feature.

aurent . . . resumes his experiments of the day before. He grabs in succession a celluloid swan, a box, etc., stretches out his arm and lets them fall. He distinctly varies the position of the fall. Sometimes he stretches out his arm vertically, sometimes he holds it obliquely, in front of or behind his eyes, etc. When the object falls in a new position, he lets it fall two or three times more on the same place, as though to study the spatial relation; then he modifies the situation.

Is this description one of a scientist at work? In a way, it is. Although Swiss psychologist Jean Piaget (1963 [1936]) was describing his 11-month-old son Laurent, children of this age frequently act like scientists, performing what Piaget called "experiments in order to see."

In this chapter, we chronicle the developing thought processes of infants and toddlers—that is, their cognitive development. We focus on the sensorimotor stage of cognitive development hypothesized by Piaget. Then, we examine infant memory and imitation. We next explore individual differences in infant intelligence. Finally, we turn our attention to a remarkable aspect of cognitive development: language.

Cognitive Development: Jean Piaget

Cognitive development focuses on the development of children's ways of perceiving and mentally representing the world. Piaget labeled children's concepts of the world **schemes**. He hypothesized that children try to use **assimilation** to absorb new events into existing schemes, and when assimilation does not allow the child to make sense of novel events, children try to modify existing schemes through **accommodation**.

Piaget (1963 [1936]) hypothesized that children's cognitive processes develop in an orderly sequence, or series, of stages. As with motor and perceptual development, some children may be more advanced than others at particular ages, but the developmental sequence does not normally vary (Flavell et al., 2002; Siegler & Alibali, 2005). Piaget identified four major stages of cognitive development: sensorimotor, preoperational, concrete operational, and formal operational. In this chapter, we discuss the sensorimotor stage.

The Sensorimotor Stage

Question: What is the sensorimotor stage of cognitive development? Piaget's sensorimotor stage refers to the first 2 years of cognitive development, a time when these developments are demonstrated by means of sensory and motor activity. Although it may be difficult for us to imagine how we can develop and use cognitive processes in the absence of language, children do so in many ways.

During the sensorimotor stage, infants progress from responding to events with reflexes, or ready-made schemes, to goal-oriented behavior that involves awareness of past events. During this stage, they come to form mental representations of objects and events, to hold complex pictures of past events in mind, and to solve problems by mental trial and error.

Question: What are the parts or substages of the sensorimotor stage? Piaget divided the sensorimotor stage into six substages, each of which is characterized by more complex behavior than the preceding substage. But there is also continuity from substage to substage. Each substage can be characterized as a variation on a theme in which earlier forms of behavior are repeated, varied, and coordinated. The approximate time periods of the substages and some characteristics of each are summarized in Concept Review 6.1.

scheme Within Piaget's cognitive view of development, an action pattern (such as a reflex) or a mental structure that is involved in the acquisition or organization of knowledge.

assimilation According to Piaget, the incorporation of new events or knowledge into existing schemes.

accommodation According to Piaget, the modification of existing schemes so as to incorporate new events or knowledge.

Concept Review 6.1   The Six Substages of the Sensorimotor Stage, According to Piaget

	Substage	Comments
	**1. Simple reflexes (0–1 month)**	Assimilation of new objects into reflexive responses. Infants "look and see." Inborn reflexes can be modified by experience.
	**2. Primary circular reactions (1–4 months)**	Repetition of actions that may have initially occurred by chance but that have satisfying or interesting results. Infants "look in order to see." The focus is on the infant's body. Infants do not yet distinguish between themselves and the external world.
	**3. Secondary circular reactions (4–8 months)**	Repetition of schemes that have interesting effects on the environment. The focus shifts to external objects and events. There is initial cognitive awareness that schemes influence the external world.
	4. Coordination of secondary schemes (8–12 months)	Coordination of secondary schemes, such as looking and grasping to attain specific goals. There is the beginning of intentionality and means–end differentiation. We find imitation of actions not already in infants' repertoires.
	5. Tertiary circular reactions (12–18 months)	Purposeful adaptation of established schemes to specific situations. Behavior takes on an experimental quality. There is overt trial and error in problem solving.
	**6. Invention of new means through mental combinations (18–24 months)**	Mental trial and error in problem solving. Infants take "mental detours" based on cognitive maps. Infants engage in deferred imitation and symbolic play. Infants' cognitive advances are made possible by mental representations of objects and events and the beginnings of symbolic thought.

© Praefice/G&J/Stockphoto/Black Star

© Picture Partners/Alamy

© Matt Brasier/Masterfile

© Laura Dwight/Photo Edit

© David Mendelsohn/Masterfile

Photo by Stephen Ausmus/Courtesy of the USDA

Simple Reflexes

At birth, neonates assimulate objects into reflexive responses. But even within hours after birth, neonates begin to modify reflexes as a result of experience. For example, they adapt sucking patterns to the shape of the nipple. (But don't be too impressed; porpoises are born swimming and "know" to rise to the surface of the ocean to breathe.)

Simple Reflexes

The first substage covers the first month after birth. It is dominated by the assimilation of sources of stimulation into inborn reflexes such as grasping, visual tracking, crying, sucking, and crudely turning the head toward a sound.

At birth, reflexes have a stereotypical, inflexible quality. But even within the first few hours, neonates begin to modify reflexes as a result of experience. For example, infants will adapt (accommodate) patterns of sucking to the shape of the nipple and the rate of flow of fluid.

During the first month or so, infants apparently make no connection between stimulation perceived through different sensory modalities. They make no effort to grasp objects that they visually track. Crude turning toward sources of sounds and smells has a mechanical look about it that cannot be considered purposeful searching.

Primary Circular Reactions

The second substage, primary circular reactions, lasts from about 1 to 4 months of age and is characterized by the beginnings of the ability to coordinate various sensorimotor schemes. In this substage, infants tend to repeat stimulating actions that first occurred by chance. For example, they may lift their arm repeatedly to bring it into view. A circular reaction is a behavior that is repeated. **Primary circular reactions** focus on the infant's own body rather than on the external environment. Piaget noticed the following primary circular reaction in his son Laurent:

> At 2 months 4 days, Laurent by chance discovers his right index finger and looks at it briefly. At 2 months 11 days, he inspects for a moment his open right hand, perceived by chance. At 2 months 17 days, he follows its spontaneous movement for a moment, then examines it several times while it searches for his nose or rubs his eye.
>
> At 2 months 21 days, he holds his two fists in the air and looks at the left one, after which he slowly brings it toward his face and rubs his nose with it, then his eye. A moment later the left hand again approaches his face; he looks at it and touches his nose. He recommences and laughs five or six times in succession while moving the left hand to his face. . . . He laughs beforehand but begins to smile again on seeing the hand.
>
> —Piaget (1963 [1936], pp. 96–97)

Thus, Laurent, early in the third month, visually tracks the behavior of his hand, but his visual observations do not seem to influence their movement. At about 2 months 21 days, Laurent can apparently exert some control over his hands because he seems to know when a hand is about to move (and entertain him), but the link between looking at and moving the hands remains weak. A few days later, however, his looking "acts" on the hands, causing them to remain in his field of vision. Sensorimotor coordination has been achieved. An action is repeated because it stimulates the infant.

In terms of assimilation and accommodation, the child is attempting to assimilate the motor scheme (moving the hand) into the sensory scheme (looking at it). But the schemes do not automatically fit. Several days of apparent trial and error pass, during which the infant seems to be trying to make accommodations so that they will fit.

Goal-directed behavior makes significant advances during the second substage. During the month after birth, infants visually track objects that contrast with their backgrounds, especially moving objects. But this ready-made behavior is largely automatic, so that the infant is "looking and seeing." But by the third month, infants may examine objects repeatedly and intensely, as Laurent did. It seems clear that the infant is no longer simply looking and seeing but is now "looking in order to see." And by the end of the third month, Laurent seems to be moving his hands just to look at them.

Because Laurent (and other infants) will repeat actions that allow them to see, cognitive-developmental psychologists consider sensorimotor coordination self-

Primary Circular Reactions

In the substage of primary circular reactions, infants repeat actions that involve their bodies. The 3-month-old in this picture is also beginning to coordinate visual and sensorimotor schemes; that is, looking at the hand is becoming coordinated with holding it in the field of vision.

reinforcing. Laurent does not seem to be looking or moving his hands because these acts allow him to satisfy a more basic drive such as hunger or thirst. The desire to prolong stimulation may be just as basic.

Secondary Circular Reactions

The third substage lasts from about 4 to 8 months and is characterized by **secondary circular reactions**, in which patterns of activity are repeated because of their effect on the environment. In the second substage (primary circular reactions), infants are focused on their own bodies, as in the example given with Laurent. In the third substage (secondary circular reactions), the focus shifts to objects and environmental events. Infants may now learn to pull strings in order to make a plastic face appear or to shake an object in order to hear it rattle.

Although infants in this substage track the trajectory of moving objects, they abandon their searches when the objects disappear from view. As we see later in this chapter, the object concepts of infants are quite limited at these ages, especially the age at which the third substage begins.

Coordination of Secondary Schemes

In the fourth substage, infants no longer act simply to prolong interesting occurrences. Now they can coordinate schemes to attain specific goals. Infants begin to show intentional, goal-directed behavior in which they differentiate between the means of achieving a goal and the goal or end itself. For example, they may lift a piece of cloth to reach a toy that they had seen a parent place under the cloth earlier. In this example, the scheme of picking up the cloth (the means) is coordinated with the scheme of reaching for the toy (the goal or end).

This example indicates that the infant has mentally represented the toy placed under the cloth. Consider another example. At the age of 5 months, one of Piaget's daughters, Lucienne, was reaching across her crib for a toy. As she did so, Piaget obscured the toy with his hand. Lucienne pushed her father's hand aside but, in doing so, became distracted and began to play with the hand. A few months later, Lucienne did not allow her father's hand to distract her from the goal of reaching the toy. She moved the hand firmly to the side and then grabbed the toy. The mental representation of the object appears to have become more persistent. The intention of reaching the object was also maintained, and so the hand was perceived as a barrier and not as another interesting stimulus.

During the fourth substage, infants also gain the capacity to copy actions that are not in their own repertoires. Infants can now imitate many gestures and sounds that they had previously ignored. The imitation of a new facial gesture implies that infants have mentally represented their own faces and can tell what parts of their faces they are moving through feedback from facial muscles. For example, when a girl imitates her mother sticking out her tongue, it would appear that she has coordinated moving her own tongue with feedback from muscles in the tongue and mouth. In this way, imitation suggests a great deal about the child's emerging self-concept.

Tertiary Circular Reactions

In the fifth substage, which lasts from about 12 to 18 months of age, Piaget looked on the behavior of infants as characteristic of budding scientists. Infants now engage in **tertiary circular reactions**, or purposeful adaptations of established schemes to specific situations. Behavior takes on a new experimental quality, and infants may vary their actions dozens of times in a deliberate trial-and-error fashion to learn how things work.

Piaget reported an example of tertiary circular reactions by his daughter Jacqueline. The episode was an experiment in which Piaget placed a stick outside Jacqueline's playpen, which had wooden bars (Piaget, 1963 [1936]). At first, Jacqueline grasped the stick and tried to pull it sideways into the playpen. The stick was too long and could not fit through the bars. Over a number of days of trial and error, however, Jacqueline

Secondary Circular Reactions
In the substage of secondary circular reactions, patterns of activity are repeated because of their effect on the environment. This infant shakes a rattle to produce an interesting sound.

Coordination of Secondary Schemes
During this substage, infants coordinate their behaviors to attain specific goals. This infant lifts a piece of cloth to retrieve a toy that has been placed under the cloth.

primary circular reactions
The repetition of actions that first occurred by chance and that focus on the infant's own body.

secondary circular reactions
The repetition of actions that produce an effect on the environment.

tertiary circular reactions
The purposeful adaptation of established schemes to new situations.

Information Processing

The information-processing approach to cognitive development focuses on how children manipulate or process information coming in from the environment or already stored in the mind (Siegler & Alibali, 2005). *Question: What are infants' tools for processing information?* One is memory. Another is imitation.

Infants' Memory

Many of the cognitive capabilities of infants—recognizing the faces of familiar people, developing object permanence, and, in fact, learning in any form—depend on one critical aspect of cognitive development: their memory (Daman-Wasserman et al., 2006; Hayne & Fagen, 2003; Pascual-Leone, 2000). Even neonates demonstrate memory for stimuli to which they have been exposed previously. For example, neonates adjust their rate of sucking to hear a recording of their mother reading a story she had read aloud during the last weeks of pregnancy (DeCasper & Fifer, 1980; DeCasper & Spence, 1991). Remember, too, that neonates who are breast-fed are able to remember and show recognition of their mother's unique odor (Cernoch & Porter, 1985).

Memory improves dramatically between 2 and 6 months of age and then again by 12 months (Pelphrey et al., 2004; Rose et al., 2001). The improvement may indicate that older infants are more capable than younger ones of encoding (i.e., storing) information, retrieving information already stored, or both (Hayne & Fagen, 2003).

A fascinating series of studies by Carolyn Rovee-Collier and her colleagues (Rovee-Collier, 1993) illustrates some of these developmental changes in infant memory (see ● Figure 6.4). One end of a ribbon was tied to a brightly colored mobile suspended above the infant's crib. The other end was tied to the infant's ankle, so that when the infant kicked, the mobile moved. Infants quickly learned to increase their rate of kicking. To measure memory, the infant's ankle was again fastened to the mobile after a period of 1 or more days had elapsed. In one study, 2-month-olds remembered how to make the mobile move after delays of up to 3 days, and 3-month-olds remembered for more than a week (Greco et al., 1986).

Infant memory can be improved if infants receive a reminder before they are given the memory test (Bearce et al., 2006). In one study that used a reminder ("priming"), infants were shown the moving mobile on the day before the memory test, but they were not allowed to activate it. Under these conditions, 3-month-olds remembered how to move the mobile after a 28-day delay (Rovee-Collier, 1993).

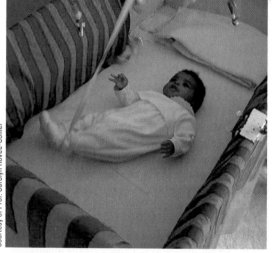

Courtesy of Prof. Carolyn Rovee-Collier

● **Figure 6.4**
Investigating Infant Memory

In this technique, developed by Carolyn Rovee-Collier, the infant's ankle is connected to a mobile by a ribbon. Infants quickly learn to kick to make the mobile move. Two- and 3-month-olds remember how to perform this feat after a delay of a few days. If given a reminder of simply viewing the mobile, their memory lasts for 2 to 4 weeks.

Imitation: Infant See, Infant Do?

Imitation is the basis for much of human learning. Deferred imitation—that is, the imitation of actions after a time delay—occurs as early as 6 months of age (Barr et al., 2005; Campanella & Rovee-Collier, 2005). To help them remember the imitated act, infants are usually permitted to practice it when they learn it. But in one study, 12-month-old infants were prevented from practicing the behavior they imitated. Yet they were able to demonstrate it 4 weeks later, suggesting that they had mentally represented the act (Klein & Meltzoff, 1999).

But infants can imitate certain actions at a much earlier age. Neonates only 0.7 to 71 hours old have been found to imitate adults who open their mouths or stick out their tongues (Meltzoff & Prinz, 2002; Rizzolatti et al., 2002) (see ● Figure 6.5).

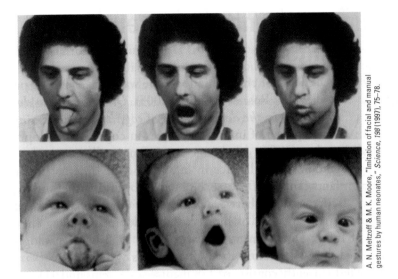

A. N. Meltzoff & M. K. Moore, "Imitation of facial and manual gestures by human neonates," *Science, 198* (1997), 75–78.

● **Figure 6.5**
Imitation in Infants

These 2- to 3-week-old infants are imitating the facial gestures of an adult experimenter. How are we to interpret these findings? Can we say that the infants "knew" what the experimenter was doing and "chose" to imitate the behavior, or is there an another explanation?

Before you become too impressed with this early imitative ability of neonates, you should know that some studies have not found imitation in early infancy (Abravanel & DeYong, 1991). One key factor may be the infants' age. The studies that find imitation generally have been done with very young infants—up to 2 weeks old—whereas the studies that do not find imitation have tended to use older infants. Therefore, the imitation of neonates is likely to be reflexive. Thus, imitation might disappear when reflexes are "dropping out" and re-emerge when it has a firmer cognitive footing. **Truth or Fiction Revisited:** It is true that a 1-hour-old infant may imitate an adult who sticks out his or her tongue, but such imitation is reflexive. That is, the infant is not observing the adult and then deciding to stick out his or her tongue.

Why might newborns possess some sort of imitation reflex? Answers lie in the realm of speculation. One possibility is that such a built-in response would contribute to the formation of caregiver–infant bonding and the survival of the newborn (Meltzoff & Prinz, 2002). Some theorists speculate that the imitation reflex is made possible by "mirror neurons" that are found in human brains. Such neurons are maintained by evolutionary forces because they enhance the probability of survival as a result of caregiving (Oztop et al., 2006; Rizzolatti et al., 2002).

Active Review

8. The _____-processing approach to cognitive development focuses on how children manipulate or process information.
9. _____ improves dramatically between the ages of 2 and 6 months.
10. The imitation of actions after a time delay is called _____ imitation.

Reflect & Relate: Why do adolescents and adults stick their tongues out at infants? (Why not ask a few—a few adolescents and adults, that is?)

Go to

http://www.thomsonedu.com/psychology/rathus

for an interactive version of this review.

months to achieve a vocabulary of 10 to 30 words. Children's first words are mostly nominals. Children with a referential language style use language mainly to label objects. Those with an expressive language style mainly seek social interactions. Infants often extend the meaning of a word to refer to things and actions for which they do not have words.

11. How do infants create sentences?

Infants' early sentences are telegraphic. Two-word sentences show understanding of syntax. The kinds of two-word sentences are the same among children from diverse linguistic environments.

12. How do learning theorists account for language development?

Learning theorists explain language development in terms of imitation and reinforcement, but children resist imitating sentences that do not fit with their awareness of grammar.

13. What is the nativist view of language development?

The nativist view holds that innate or inborn prewiring causes children to attend to and acquire language in certain ways. Psycholinguistic theory considers that language acquisition involves the interaction between environmental influences and prewiring. Chomsky argues that languages share a "universal grammar" that children are prewired to perceive and use.

14. What parts of the brain are involved in language development?

Key biological structures are based in the left hemisphere for most people: Broca's area and Wernicke's area. Damage to either area may cause a characteristic aphasia.

15. What is meant by a *sensitive period* for language development?

This theory proposes that plasticity of the brain provides a sensitive period for learning language that begins at about 18 to 24 months and lasts until puberty.

Key Terms

scheme, 188
assimilation, 188
accommodation, 188
primary circular reactions, 191
secondary circular
    reactions, 191
tertiary circular reactions, 191
object permanence, 192
deferred imitation, 195
visual recognition
    memory, 201
prelinguistic, 204
cooing, 205
babbling, 205

echolalia, 205
intonation, 205
receptive vocabulary, 205
expressive vocabulary, 205
referential language
    style, 208
expressive language style, 208
overextension, 208
telegraphic speech, 208
mean length of utterance
    (MLU), 208
morpheme, 208
holophrase, 209
syntax, 209

models, 210
extinction, 211
shaping, 211
psycholinguistic theory, 214
language acquisition device
    (LAD), 214
surface structure, 214
deep structure, 214
aphasia, 214
Broca's aphasia, 215
Wernicke's aphasia, 215
sensitive period, 215
American Sign Language
    (ASL), 216

Active Learning Resources

 Childhood & Adolescence Book Companion Website
http://www.thomsonedu.com/psychology/rathus

Visit your book companion website where you will find more resources to help you study. There you will find interactive versions of your book features, including the Lessons in Observation video, Active Review sections, and the Truth or Fiction feature. In addition, the companion website contains quizzing, flash cards, and a pronunciation glossary.

 is an easy-to-use online resource that helps you study in less time to get the grade you want—NOW.

http://www.thomsonedu.com/login

Need help studying? This site is your one-stop study shop. Take a Pre-Test and ThomsonNOW will generate a Personalized Study Plan based on your test results. The Study Plan will identify the topics you need to review and direct you to online resources to help you master those topics. You can then take a Post-Test to determine the concepts you have mastered and what you still need to work on.

7

Infancy:
Social and Emotional
Development

Truth or Fiction?

 Infants who are securely attached to their mothers do not like to stray from them. p. 224

 You can estimate how strongly infants are attached to their fathers if you know how many diapers per week their fathers change. p. 225

 Child abusers have frequently been the victims of child abuse themselves. p. 236

 Autism is caused by the mercury in measles-mumps-rubella vaccine. p. 242

 Autistic children may respond to people as though they were pieces of furniture. p. 242

 Children placed in day care are more aggressive than children who are cared for in the home. p. 246

 Fear of strangers is abnormal among infants. p. 250

 All children are "born" with the same temperament. Treatment by caregivers determines whether they are difficult or easygoing. p. 255

 Girls prefer dolls and toy animals, and boys prefer toy trucks and sports equipment only after they have become aware of the gender roles assigned to them by society. p. 257

 Go to

http://www.thomsonedu.com/psychology/rathus
for an interactive version of this "Truth or Fiction" feature.

© Masterfile

t the age of 2, my daughter Allyn almost succeeded at preventing publication of a book on which I was working. When I locked myself into my study, she positioned herself outside the door and called, "Daddy, oh Daddy." At other times she would bang on the door or cry. When I would give in (several times a day) and open the door, she would run in and say, "I want you to pick up me," and hold out her arms or climb into my lap. How would I ever finish the book? Being a psychologist, solutions came easily. For example, I could write outside the home, but this solution had the drawback of distancing me from my family. Another solution was to ignore my daughter and let her cry. If I refused to reinforce crying, crying might become extinguished. (And research does suggest that ignoring crying discourages it [IJzendoorn & Hubbard, 2000].) There was only one problem with this solution: I didn't want to extinguish her efforts to get to me. **Attachment**, you see, is a two-way street.

Attachment is one of the key issues in the social and personality development of the infant. If this chapter had been written by the poet John Donne, it might have begun, "No children are islands unto themselves." Children come into this world fully dependent on others for their survival and well-being.

This chapter is about some of the consequences of that absolute dependency. It is about the social relationships between infants and caregivers and about the development of the bonds of attachment that usually—but not always—bind them. It is about the behaviors of infants that prompt social and emotional responses from adults and about the behaviors of adults that prompt social and emotional responses from infants. It is also about infants' unique and different ways of reacting socially and emotionally.

Let us first consider the issue of attachment and the factors that contribute to its development. Next, we examine some circumstances that interfere with the development of attachment: social deprivation, child abuse, and autism. Then, we turn to a discussion of day care. Finally, we look at the development of emotions and personality in infancy, including the self-concept, temperament, and sex differences.

Attachment: Bonds That Endure

Question: What is meant by "attachment"? Attachment is what most people refer to as affection or love. Mary Ainsworth (1989), one of the preeminent researchers on attachment, defines attachment as an emotional tie formed between one animal or person and another specific individual. Attachment keeps organisms together and tends to endure. John Bowlby believes that attachment is essential to the very survival of the infant (Bowlby, 1988; Ainsworth & Bowlby, 1991). He argues that babies are born with behaviors—crying, smiling, clinging—that elicit caregiving from parents.

Babies and children try to maintain contact with caregivers to whom they are attached. They engage in eye contact, pull and tug at them, and ask to be picked up. When they cannot maintain contact, infants show behaviors suggestive of **separation anxiety**. They may thrash about, fuss, cry, screech, or whine. Parents who are seeking a few minutes to attend to their own needs sometimes see these behaviors as manipulative, and, in a sense, they are. That is, children learn that the behaviors achieve desired ends. But what is wrong with "manipulating"—or influencing—a loved one to end distress?

Patterns of Attachment

Mary Ainsworth and her colleagues (1978) identified various patterns of attachment. Broadly, infants show either **secure attachment** or insecure attachment. Ainsworth and other investigators have found that most infants, older children, and adults in the United States are securely attached (Belsky, 2006a; McCartney et al., 2004).

Mary D. Salter Ainsworth

attachment An affectional bond between individuals characterized by a seeking of closeness or contact and a show of distress upon separation.

separation anxiety Fear of being separated from a target of attachment, usually a primary caregiver.

secure attachment A type of attachment characterized by mild distress at leave-takings, seeking nearness to an attachment figure, and being readily soothed by the figure.

Question: What does it mean for a child to be "secure"? Think of security in terms of what infants do. Ainsworth developed the strange-situation method as a way of measuring the development of attachment (● Figure 7.1). In this method, an infant is exposed to a series of separations and reunions with a caregiver (usually the mother) and a stranger who is a confederate of the researchers. In the strange situation, securely attached infants mildly protest their mother's departure, seek interaction upon reunion, and are readily comforted by her.

Question: What, then, is "insecurity"? There are two major types of insecurity, or "insecure attachment": They are **avoidant attachment** and **ambivalent/resistant attachment**. Babies who show avoidant attachment are least distressed by their mothers' departure. They play without fuss when alone and ignore their mothers upon reunion. Ambivalent/resistant babies are the most emotional infants. They show severe signs of distress when their mothers leave and show ambivalence upon reunion by alternately clinging to and pushing away their mothers. Additional categories of insecure attachment have been proposed, including **disorganized–disoriented attachment**. Babies showing this pattern appear dazed, confused, or disoriented. They may show contradictory behaviors, such as moving toward the mother while looking away from her.

Question: Is it better for an infant to be securely attached to its caregivers? Sure it is. Securely attached infants and toddlers are happier, more sociable with unfamiliar adults, and more cooperative with parents, get along better with peers, and are better adjusted in school than insecurely attached children (Belsky, 2006a; McCartney et al., 2004; Spieker et al., 2003). Insecure attachment at the age of 1 year predicts psychological disorders at the age of 17 (Sroufe, 1998; Steele, 2005). Infants use the mother as a secure base from which to venture out and explore the environment (Belsky, 2006a). Secure attachment is also connected with the experiencing of fewer negative emotions toward members of out-groups (Mikulincer & Shaver, 2001). Thus, security encourages children to explore interactions with unfamiliar

avoidant attachment A type of insecure attachment characterized by apparent indifference to the leave-takings of and reunions with an attachment figure.

ambivalent/resistant attachment A type of insecure attachment characterized by severe distress at the leave-takings of and ambivalent behavior at reunions with an attachment figure.

disorganized–disoriented attachment A type of insecure attachment characterized by dazed and contradictory behaviors toward an attachment figure.

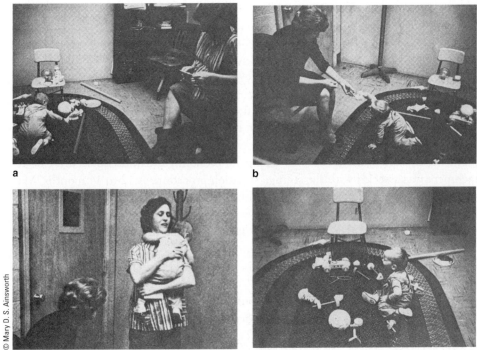

© Mary D. S. Ainsworth

a

b

c

d

● **Figure 7.1**
The Strange Situation

These historic photos show a 12-month-old child in the strange situation. In (a), the child plays with toys, glancing occasionally at mother. In (b), the stranger approaches with a toy. While the child is distracted, mother leaves the room. In (c), mother returns after a brief absence. The child crawls to her quickly and clings to her when picked up. In (d), the child cries when mother again leaves the room. What pattern of attachment is this child showing?

people, broadening their horizons. **Truth or Fiction Revisited:** Thus, infants who are securely attached to their mothers are likely to "stray" from them in the sense that they use them as a secure base for exploration of the environment.

Securely attached toddlers also have longer attention spans, are less impulsive, and are better at solving problems than insecurely attached toddlers (Granot & Mayseless, 2001; Spieker et al., 2003). At ages 5 and 6, securely attached children are better liked by peers and teachers, are more competent, are less aggressive, and have fewer behavior problems than insecurely attached children (Belsky, 2006a; Coleman, 2003).

Question: What are the roles of the parents in the formation of bonds of attachment?

Establishing Attachment

Attachment is one measure of the quality of care that infants receive (Belsky, 2006a; Coleman, 2003). The parents of securely attached infants are more affectionate, cooperative, and predictable in their caregiving than parents of insecurely attached infants. These parents respond more sensitively to their infants' smiles, cries, and other social behaviors (Harel & Scher, 2003).

A Japanese study found evidence for the "intergenerational transmission of attachment" from mother to child (Kazui et al., 2000). For example, the children of secure mothers showed the most secure patterns of attachment themselves, as assessed by various means. The children of secure mothers interacted positively both with their mothers and with strangers, so their pattern of attachment provided a secure base for exploration.

Providing economically stressed families with support services can enhance their involvement with their infants and increase secure attachment. In one study, low-income women received child-care information and social support from home visitors during pregnancy and through the child's third year (Spieker et al., 2005). The visitors first worked with the mothers on how they conceptualized their fetuses. Following childbirth, the home visitors helped the mothers accurately interpret their babies' cues and respond to them. They also encouraged mother–infant interaction and play, by and large resulting in appropriate maternal responsiveness and secure attachment between infant and mother.

Insecure attachment occurs more often among infants whose mothers are mentally ill or abusive (Cicchetti et al., 2006; McCartney et al., 2004). It is found more often among infants whose mothers are slow to meet their needs or meet them coldly (Steele et al., 2003).

Research by Marinus van IJzendoorn and his colleagues (2000) suggests that siblings tend to develop similar attachment relationships with their mother. The study pooled data on sibling attachment from research groups in the United States, the Netherlands, and Canada to form 138 pairs of siblings. Children's security of attachment was assessed with the strange-situation procedure at 12 to 14 months. Maternal sensitivity to infants' needs was also observed. Broad sibling attachment relationships (secure or insecure, but not necessarily the kinds of insecurity) with the mother were found to be significantly alike. It was also found that siblings of the same sex are more likely to form similar attachment relationships with their mother than are girl–boy pairs. Mothers, that is, may behave differently with daughters and sons.

Although it is tempting to seek the sources of attachment in caregivers' behavior and personalities, that is not the whole story. Security is also connected with the baby's temperament (Belsky, 2006a; Kerns et al., 2007). Babies who are more active and irritable and who display more negative emotion are more likely to develop insecure attachment. Such babies may elicit parental behaviors that are not conducive to the development of secure attachment. For example, mothers of "difficult" children are less responsive to their children and report that they feel less emotionally close to them (Morrell & Steele, 2003; Stams et al., 2002). Caregivers respond to babies' behavior, just as the babies respond to caregivers' behavior. The process of attachment is a two-way street.

Involvement of Fathers

Truth or Fiction Revisited: It is true that you can predict how well babies are attached to their fathers if you know how many diapers the fathers change each week. Gail Ross and her colleagues (1975) found that the more diapers the father changed, the stronger the attachment. There is no magical connection between diapers and love, but the number of diapers the father changes roughly reflects his involvement in child rearing.

How involved is the average father with his children? The brief answer, in developed nations, is more so than in the past. Gender roles are blurring to some degree, and fathers, as well as mothers, can rear infants competently and sensitively (Grossmann et al., 2002). But studies of parents in the United States show that father–child interactions differ qualitatively and quantitatively from mother–child interactions (Laflamme et al., 2002). Mothers engage in far more interactions with their infants. Most fathers spend much less time on basic child-care tasks, such as feeding and diaper changing, than mothers do. Fathers are more likely to play with their children than to feed or clean them (Laflamme et al., 2002). Fathers more often than mothers engage in physical rough-and-tumble play, such as tossing their babies into the air and poking them. Mothers are more likely to play games like patty-cake and peekaboo and to play games involving toys (Laflamme et al., 2002).

How strongly, then, do infants become attached to their fathers? The answer depends on the quality of the time that the father spends with the baby (R. A. Thompson et al., 2003). The more affectionate the interaction between father and infant, the stronger the attachment (R. A. Thompson et al., 2003). Infants under stress still seek out mothers more than fathers (Lamb et al., 1992b). But when observed at their natural activities in the home and other familiar settings, infants seek to be near to and touch their fathers about as often as their mothers.

© Laura Dwight/Photo Edit

Fathers and Attachment: The "Diaper Index"
The number of diapers a father changes reflects his involvement in child rearing. Children develop strong attachments to fathers as well as mothers, especially if the father interacts positively and affectionately with the child.

Stability of Attachment

Patterns of attachment tend to persist when care-giving conditions remain consistent (Ammaniti et al., 2005; Karavasilis et al., 2003). But attachment patterns can change when child care changes. Byron Egeland and Alan Sroufe (1981) followed a number of infants who were severely neglected and others who received high-quality care from 12 to 18 months of age. Attachment patterns remained stable (secure) for infants receiving fine care. However, many neglected infants changed from insecurely to securely attached over the 6-month period, sometimes because of a relationship with a supportive family member, sometimes because home life grew less tense. Children can also become less securely attached to caregivers when the quality of home life deteriorates (Belsky, 2006a).

Concept Review 7.1   Theories of Attachment

Theory	Characteristics
Cognitive theory (proponent: Alan Sroufe)	• Emotional development is connected with and relies on cognitive development. • Infant must have developed object permanence before attachment to a specific other becomes possible. • Infant must be able to discriminate familiar people from strangers to develop fear of strangers.
Behaviorism (proponent: John B. Watson)	• Caregiver is a conditioned reinforcer; attachment behaviors are learned through conditioning. • Caregivers meet infants' physiological needs; thus, infants associate caregivers with gratification. • Feelings of gratification associated with meeting needs generalize into feelings of security when the caregiver is present.
Psychoanalytic theory (proponents: Sigmund Freud, Erik Erikson, Margaret Mahler)	• Caregiver is a love object who forms the basis for future attachments. • Infant becomes attached to the mother during infancy because she primarily satisfies the infant's needs for food and sucking (Freud). • First year is critical in developing a sense of trust in the mother, which, in turn, fosters feelings of attachment (Erikson).
Contact comfort (proponents: Harry and Margaret Harlow)	• Caregiver is a source of contact comfort. • Experiments with rhesus monkeys suggest that contact comfort is more crucial than feeding to attachment.

Ethological theory
(proponents: Konrad Lorenz, Mary Ainsworth, John Bowlby)
	• Attachment is an inborn fixed action pattern (FAP) that occurs in the presence of a species-specific releasing stimulus during a critical period of development (Lorenz).
	• Waterfowl become attached to the first moving object they encounter (Lorenz).
	• The image of the moving object becomes "imprinted" on the young animal (Lorenz).
	• Caregiving in humans is elicited by infants' cries of distress (Bowlby).
	• The human face is a releasing stimulus that elicits a baby's smile (Bowlby).
	• Smiling helps ensure survival by eliciting caregiving and feelings of affection (Bowlby).
	• Attachment in humans is a complex process that continues for months or years (Ainsworth).
	• The quality of attachment is related to the quality of the caregiver–infant relationship (Ainsworth).
	• Attachment in humans occurs in stages or phases (Ainsworth):
	  1. The initial-preattachment phase: birth to about 3 months; indiscriminate attachment
	  2. The attachment-in-the-making phase: 3 or 4 months; preference for familiar figures
	  3. The clear-cut-attachment phase: 6 or 7 months; intensified dependence on the primary caregiver.

Social Deprivation

Studies of children reared in institutions where they receive little social stimulation from caregivers are limited in that they are correlational. In other words, family factors that led to the children's placement in institutions may also have contributed to their developmental problems. Ethical considerations prevent us from conducting experiments in which we randomly assign children to social deprivation. However, experiments of this kind have been undertaken with rhesus monkeys, and the results are consistent with those of the correlational studies of children. Let us first examine these animal experiments and then turn to the correlational research involving children.

Experiments with Monkeys

The Harlows and their colleagues conducted studies of rhesus monkeys that were "reared by" wire-mesh and terry-cloth surrogate mothers. In later studies, rhesus monkeys were reared without even this questionable "social" support. They were reared without seeing any other animal, whether monkey or human.

Question: What are the findings of the Harlows' studies on the effects of social deprivation on monkeys? The Harlows (Harlow et al., 1971) found that rhesus infants reared in this most solitary confinement later avoided contact with other monkeys. They did not engage in the characteristic playful chasing and romping. Instead, they cowered in the presence of others and failed to respond to them. Nor did they attempt to fend off attacks by other monkeys. Rather, they sat in the corner, clutching themselves and rocking back and forth. Females who later bore children tended to ignore or abuse them.

Can the damage done by social deprivation be overcome? When monkeys deprived for 6 months or more are placed with younger, 3- to 4-month-old females for a couple of hours a day, the younger monkeys make efforts to initiate social interaction with their deprived elders (see ● Figure 7.5). Many of the deprived monkeys begin to play with the youngsters after a few weeks, and many of them eventually expand their social contacts to other rhesus monkeys of various ages (Suomi et al., 1972). Perhaps of greater interest is the related finding that socially withdrawn 4- and 5-year-old children make gains in their social and emotional development when they are provided with younger playmates (Furman et al., 1979).

Question: What do we know about the effects of social deprivation on humans?

Studies with Children

Institutionalized children whose material needs are met but who receive little social stimulation from caregivers encounter problems in their physical, intellectual, social, and emotional development (Ganesh & Magdalin, 2007; Rutter, 2006a). René A. Spitz (1965) noted that many institutionalized children appear to develop a syndrome

● **Figure 7.5**
Monkey Therapists

In the left-hand photo, a 3- to 4-month-old rhesus monkey "therapist" tries to soothe a monkey who was reared in social isolation. The deprived monkey remains withdrawn. She clutches herself into a ball and rocks back and forth. The right-hand photo was taken several weeks later and shows that deprived monkeys given young "therapists" can learn to play and adjust to community life. Socially withdrawn preschoolers have similarly profited from exposure to younger peers.

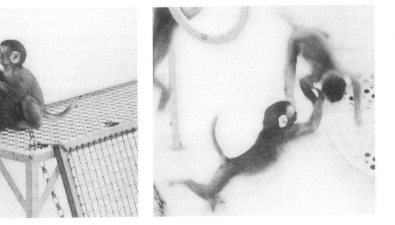

Harlow Primate Laboratory, University of Wisconsin

characterized by withdrawal and depression. They show progressively less interest in their world and become progressively inactive. Some of them die.

In one institution, infants were maintained in separate cubicles for most of their first year to ward off infectious diseases (Provence & Lipton, 1962). Adults tended to them only to feed and change their diapers. As a rule, baby bottles were propped up in the infants' cribs. Attendants rarely responded to the babies' cries, and the infants were rarely played with or spoken to. By the age of 4 months, the infants in this institution showed little interest in adults. They rarely tried to gain the adults' attention, even when in distress. A few months later, some of them sat withdrawn in their cribs and rocked back and forth, almost like the Harlows' monkeys. Language deficiencies were striking. As the first year progressed, little babbling was heard within the infants' cubicles. None were speaking even one word at 12 months.

Why do children whose material needs are met show such dramatic deficiencies? Is it because they do not receive the love and affection of a human? Or is it because they do not receive adequate sensory or social stimulation?

The answer may depend, in part, on the age of the child. Classic studies by Leon Yarrow and his colleagues (Yarrow et al., 1971; Yarrow & Goodwin, 1973) suggest that deficiencies in sensory stimulation and social interaction may cause more problems than lack of love in infants who are too young to have developed specific attachments. But once infants have developed specific attachments, separation from their primary caregivers can lead to problems.

In the first study, the development of 53 adopted children was followed over a 10-year period (Yarrow et al., 1971). The researchers compared the development of three subgroups: (1) children who were transferred to their permanent adoptive homes almost immediately after birth, (2) children who were given temporary foster mothers and then transferred to permanent adoptive homes before they were 6 months old, and (3) children who were transferred from temporary foster mothers to their permanent adoptive homes after they were 6 months old. At the age of 10, children in the first two groups showed no differences in social and emotional development. However, children in the third group showed significantly less ability to relate to other people. Perhaps their deficits resulted from being separated from their initial foster mothers after they had become attached to them.

In the second study, Yarrow and Goodwin (1973) followed the development of 70 adopted children who were separated from temporary foster parents between birth and the age of 16 months. The researchers found strong correlations between the age at which the children were separated and feeding and sleeping problems, decreased social responsiveness, and extremes in attachment behaviors (see ● Figure 7.6). Disturbed attachment behaviors included excessive clinging to the new mother and violent rejection of her. None of the children who were separated from the initial foster mothers before the age of 3 months showed moderate or severe disturbances. All the children who were separated at 9 months or older did show such disturbances. Forty percent to ninety percent of the children separated between the ages of 3 and 9 months showed moderate to severe disturbances. The incidence of problems increased as the age advanced.

The Yarrow studies suggest that babies in institutions, at least up to the age of 3 months or so, may require general sensory and social stimulation more than a

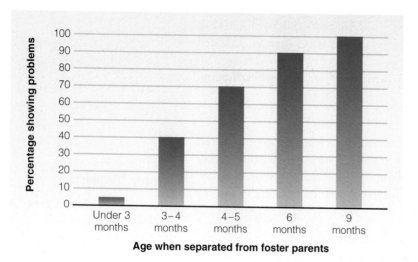

● Figure 7.6
The Development of Adopted Children Separated from Temporary Foster Parents

The older the child at the time of separation, the more likely it is that behavioral disturbances will occur.

Source: Yarrow & Goodwin (1973).

specific relationship with a primary caregiver. After the age of 3 months, some disturbance is likely if there is instability in the care-giving staff. By the ages of 6 to 9 months, disturbance seems to be guaranteed if there is instability in the position of primary caregiver. Fortunately, there is also evidence that children show some capacity to recover from early social deprivation.

The Capacity to Recover from Social Deprivation

Studies with animals and children show that early social deprivation is linked to developmental deficits. But the research also suggests that infants also have powerful capacities to recover from deprivation.

One study showed how many children may be able to recover fully from 13 or 14 months of deprivation (Kagan & Klein, 1973). The natives in an isolated Guatemalan village believe that fresh air and sunshine will make children ill. Thus, children are kept in windowless huts until they can walk. They are played with infrequently. During their isolation, the infants behave apathetically; they are physically and socially retarded when they start to walk. But by 11 years of age they are alert, active, and as intellectually able as American children of the same age.

A classic longitudinal study of orphanage children also offers evidence of the ability of children to recover from social deprivation (Skeels, 1966). In this study, a group of 19-month-old apparently retarded children were placed in the care of older institutionalized girls. The girls spent a great deal of time playing with, talking to, and nurturing them. Four years after being placed with the girls, the "retarded" children made dramatic gains in intelligence test scores, whereas children remaining in the orphanage showed declines in IQ.

The children placed in the care of the older girls also appeared to be generally well adjusted. By the time Skeels reported on their progress in 1966, most were married and were rearing children of their own who showed no intellectual or social deficits. Unfortunately, many of the children who had been left in the orphanage were still in some type of institutional setting. Few of them showed normal social and emotional development. Few were functioning as independent adults.

The good news is that many children who have been exposed to early social deprivation can catch up in their social and emotional development and lead normal adult lives if they receive individual attention and environmental stimulation (Rutter, 2006a). The bad news is that society has not yet allocated the resources to give all children the opportunity to do so.

Child Abuse and Neglect

We have considered the results of rearing children in settings in which contact with parents is reduced or absent. Yet living with one's parents does not guarantee that a child will receive tender loving care. Sadly, sometimes there's no place like home—for violence. *Questions: What are the incidences of child abuse and neglect? What are their effects?* Consider the following statistics from national surveys by Straus and his colleagues (Straus & Field, 2003; Straus & Stewart, 1999):

- By the time a child is 2 years of age, 90% of parents have engaged in some sort of psychological or emotional abuse.
- 55% of parents have slapped or spanked their children.
- 31% of parents have pushed, grabbed, or shoved their children.
- 10% have hit their children with an object.
- 3% have thrown something at their children.
- 1% or less of parents have kicked or bitten their children or hit them with their fists, threatened their children with a knife or a gun, or actually used a knife or a gun on their children.

Mexican University Students Protest against Child Abuse

Nearly 3 million American children are neglected or abused each year by their parents or caregivers (U.S. Department of Health and Human Services, 2004). About one in six of these children experiences serious injury. Thousands die. Physical abuse is more prevalent among poor and among southern parents (Straus & Stewart, 1999). Boys are more likely than girls to be hit, and the mother is more likely than the father to be the aggressor, perhaps because she spends more time than the father with the children (Straus & Stewart, 1999). More than 150,000 of the 3 million are sexually abused (Letourneau et al., 2004; U.S. Department of Health and Human Services, 2004). But researchers believe that 50–60% of cases of child abuse and neglect go unreported, so the actual incidences are higher (U.S. Department of Health and Human Services, 2004).

The U.S. Department of Health and Human Services recognizes six types of maltreatment of children:

- Physical abuse: actions causing pain and physical injury
- Sexual abuse: sexual molestation, exploitation, and intercourse
- Emotional abuse: actions impairing the child's emotional, social, or intellectual functioning
- Physical neglect: failure to provide adequate food, shelter, clothing, or medical care
- Emotional neglect: failure to provide adequate nurturance and emotional support
- Educational neglect: permitting or forcing the child to be truant

Physical neglect is more common (38%) than active physical abuse (30%) (U.S. Department of Health and Human Services, 2004). Although blatant abuse is more horrifying, more injuries, illnesses, and deaths result from neglect (U.S. Department of Health and Human Services, 2004).

Sexual Abuse of Children

No one knows how many children are sexually abused (Hines & Finkelhor, 2007; Finkelhor et al., 2005a, 2005b). Although most sexually abused children are girls, one quarter to one third are boys (Edwards et al., 2003). Interviews with 8,667 adult members of an HMO suggest that the prevalence of sexual abuse among boys is about 18% and among girls it is 25% (Edwards et al., 2003). These estimates may underrepresent the actual prevalence because people may fail to report incidents due to faulty memory, shame, or embarrassment.

Sexual abuse of children ranges from exhibitionism, kissing, fondling, and sexual touching to oral sex and anal intercourse and, with girls, vaginal intercourse. Acts such as touching children's sexual organs while changing or bathing them, sleeping with children, or appearing nude before them are open to interpretation and are often innocent (Haugaard, 2000).

Effects of Child Abuse

Abused children show a high incidence of personal and social problems and psychological disorders (Letourneau et al., 2004). In general, abused children are less securely attached to their parents. They are less intimate with their peers and are more aggressive, angry, and noncompliant than other children (Joshi et al., 2006). They rarely express positive emotions, have lower self-esteem, and show impaired cognitive functioning, leading to poorer performance in school (Shonk & Cicchetti, 2001). When they reach adulthood, they are more likely to act aggressively toward their intimate partners (Malinosky-Rummell & Hansen, 1993). As they mature, maltreated children are at greater risk for delinquency, academic failure, and substance abuse (Eckenrode et al., 1993; Haapasalo & Moilanen, 2004).

There is no single concrete identifiable syndrome—cluster of symptoms—that indicates a history of physical abuse or neglect or sexual abuse (Saywitz et al., 2000). More generally, however, there seems to be little doubt that victims of child sexual abuse develop a higher incidence of psychological and physical health problems than other children (Saywitz et al., 2000). Child sexual abuse, as with physical abuse, also appears to have lingering effects on children's relationships in adulthood. For one thing, sexually abused children are more likely to engage in risky sexual behavior later in life (Letourneau et al., 2004; Noll et al., 2000). Abusive experiences at the hands of adults also color children's expectation of other adults.

Causes of Child Abuse

A number of factors contribute to the probability that parents will abuse their children. These factors include situational stress, a history of child abuse in at least one of the parents' families of origin, lack of adequate coping and problem-solving skills, de-

A Closer Look

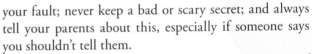

Prevention of Sexual Abuse of Children

Many of us were taught by our parents never to accept a ride or an offer of candy from a stranger. Unfortunately, many instances of sexual abuse are perpetrated by familiar adults, often a family member or friend (Ullman, 2007). Prevention programs help children understand what sexual abuse is and how they can avoid it. In addition to learning to avoid strangers, children need to recognize the differences between acceptable touching, as in an affectionate embrace or pat on the head, and unacceptable or "bad" touching. Even elementary-school-age children can learn the distinction between good touching and bad touching. School-based programs can help prepare children handle an actual encounter with a molester. Children who receive training are more likely to use strategies such as running away, yelling, or saying no if they are threatened by an abuser. They are also more likely to report incidents to adults.

Researchers recognize that children can easily be intimidated or overpowered by adults or older children (Miller, 2005). Children may be unable to say no in a sexually abusive situation, even though they want to and know it is the right thing to do. Although children may not always be able to prevent abuse, they can be encouraged to tell someone about it. Most prevention programs emphasize teaching children messages such as: it's not

your fault; never keep a bad or scary secret; and always tell your parents about this, especially if someone says you shouldn't tell them.

Children also need to be alerted to the types of threats they might receive for disclosing the abuse. They are more likely to resist threats if they are reassured that they will be believed if they disclose the abuse, that their parents will continue to love them, and that they and their families will be protected from the molester.

School-based prevention programs focus on protecting the child. In most states, teachers and helping professionals are required to report suspected abuse to authorities. Tighter controls and better screening are needed to monitor the hiring of day-care employees. Administrators and teachers in preschool and day-care facilities also need to be educated to recognize the signs of sexual abuse and to report suspected cases. Treatment programs to help people who are sexually attracted to children *before* they commit abusive acts would also be of use.

Reflect: How would you attempt to teach a child the difference between good touching and bad touching?

■ **Table 7.1** Responses of Women With or Without a History of Child Abuse to a Stressor

History of Child Abuse	Women Who Are Not Experiencing a Major Depressive Episode	Women Who Are Experiencing a Major Depressive Episode
Women with no history of child abuse	*Group A: 12 Women* Endocrine system • ACTH peak: 4.7 parts/liter • Cortisol peak: 339 parts/liter Autonomic nervous system • Heart rate: 78.4/minute	*Group B: 10 Women* Endocrine system • ACTH peak: 5.3 parts/liter • Cortisol peak: 337 parts/liter Autonomic nervous system • Heart rate: 83.8/minute
Women with a history of child abuse	*Group C: 14 Women* Endocrine system • ACTH peak: 9.3 parts/liter • Cortisol peak: 359 parts/liter Autonomic nervous system • Heart rate: 82.2/minute	*Group D: 13 Women* Endocrine system • ACTH peak: 12.1 parts/liter • Cortisol peak: 527 parts/liter Autonomic nervous system • Heart rate: 89.7/minute

The patterns of attachment of the perpetrators of child abuse have also been studied. One study, for example, found that nonfamilial perpetrators of sexual child abuse were significantly less likely to have a secure attachment style in their relationships (Jamieson & Marshall, 2000).

In any event, child abuse must be conceptualized and dealt with as a crime of violence. Whether or not child abusers happen to be victims of abuse themselves, child abusers are criminals and children must be protected from them.

What to Do

Dealing with child abuse is a frustrating task. Social agencies and the courts can find it as difficult to distinguish between spanking and abuse, as many abusers do. Because of the belief in the United States that parents have the right to rear their children as they wish, police and the courts have also historically tried to avoid involvement in domestic quarrels and family disputes. However, the alarming incidence of child abuse has spawned new efforts at detection and prevention. Many states require helping professionals such as psychologists and physicians to report any suspicion of child abuse. Many states legally require *anyone* who suspects child abuse to report it to authorities.

A number of techniques have been developed to help prevent child abuse. One approach focuses on strengthening parenting skills among the general population (Joshi et al., 2006). Parent-education classes in high school are an example of this approach.

Another approach targets groups at high risk for abuse, such as poor, single teen mothers (Joshi et al., 2006). In some programs, for example, home visitors help new parents develop skills in caregiving and home management (Duggan et al., 2004).

A third technique focuses on presenting information about abuse and providing support to families. For instance, many locales have child abuse hotlines. Private citizens who suspect child abuse may call for advice. Parents who are having difficulty controlling aggressive impulses toward their children are encouraged to call. Some hotlines are serviced by groups such as Parents Anonymous, whose members have had similar difficulties and can help callers diffuse feelings of anger in less harmful ways.

Another helpful measure is increased publicity on the dimensions of the child abuse problem. The public may also need more education about where an occasional swat on the behind ends and child abuse begins. Perhaps the format for such education could be something like, "If you are doing such and such, make no mistake about it: You are abusing your child."

A CLOSER LOOK

What to Do If You Think a Child Has Been the Victim of Sexual Abuse

What can you do if you suspect that a child has been victimized by sexual abuse? The American Psychological Association (APA) suggests the following guidelines:

- Give the child a safe environment in which to talk to you or another trusted adult. Encourage the child to talk about what he or she has experienced, but be careful to not suggest events to him or her that may not have happened. Guard against displaying emotions that would influence the child's telling of the information.
- Reassure the child that he or she did nothing wrong.
- Seek mental health assistance for the child.
- Arrange for a medical examination for the child. Select a medical provider who has experience in examining children and identifying sexual and physical trauma. It may be necessary to explain to the child the difference between a medical examination and the abuse incident.
- Be aware that many states have laws requiring that persons who know or have a reason to suspect that a child has been sexually abused must report that abuse to either local law enforcement officials or child protection officials. In all 50 states, medical personnel, mental health professionals, teachers, and law enforcement personnel are required by law to report suspected abuse.

The American Psychological Association also lists the following resources:

American Professional Society on the Abuse of Children, 407 South Dearborn, Suite 1300, Chicago, IL 60605 (312) 554-0166
www.apsac.org

National Center for Missing and Exploited Children, Charles B. Wang International Children's Building, 699 Prince Street, Alexandria, VA 22314-3175
24-hour hotline: 1-800-THE-LOST
www.missingkids.com

Child Help USA, 15757 North 78th Street, Scottsdale, AZ 85260
1-800-4-A-CHILD
www.childhelpusa.org

National Clearinghouse on Child Abuse and Neglect Information, U.S. Department of Health and Human Services, P.O. Box 1182, Washington, DC 20013
1-800-FYI-3366
www.calib.com/nccanch

Prevent Child Abuse America, 332 S. Michigan Ave., Suite 1600, Chicago, IL 60604-4357
1-800-CHILDREN
www.preventchildabuse.org

Reflect: In most states, helping professionals are required by law to report suspected cases of child abuse to authorities. Do you think that all adults should be required by law to reported suspected cases of child abuse to authorities? Why or why not?

Guidelines from Office of Public Communications, American Psychological Association, 750 First Street, NE, Washington DC 20002-4242.
(202) 336-5700. www.apa.org/releases/sexabuse/todo.html.
Copyright © American Psychological Association.
Reprinted by permission.

Autism Spectrum Disorders: Alone among the Crowd

Question: What are autism spectrum disorders? **Autism spectrum disorders (ASDs)** are characterized by impairment in communication skills, social interactions, and repetitive, stereotyped behavior (Strock, 2004) (■ Table 7.2). They tend to become evident by the age of 3 years and sometimes before the end of the first year. A CDC study of 407,578 children from 14 different areas in the United States found that about one in every 152 children was identified as having an ASD (Rice et al., 2007). There are several variations of ASDs, but autism is the major type and is the focus here. Other forms of ASDs include the following:

- *Asperger's disorder.* An ASD characterized by social deficits and stereotyped behavior but without the significant cognitive or language delays associated with autism.
- *Rett's disorder.* An ASD characterized by a range of physical, behavioral, motor, and cognitive abnormalities that begins after a few months of apparently normal development.
- *Childhood disintegrative disorder.* An ASD involving abnormal functioning and loss of previously acquired skills that begins after about 2 years of apparently normal development.

autism spectrum disorders (ASDs) Developmental disorders—including autism, Asperger's syndrome, Rett's disorder, and childhood disintegrative disorder—that are characterized by impairment in communication skills, social interactions, and repetitive, stereotyped behavior. Also referred to as pervasive developmental disorders.

Autism

Peter nursed eagerly, sat and walked at the expected ages. Yet some of his behavior made us vaguely uneasy. He never put anything in his mouth. Not his fingers nor his toys—nothing. . . .

More troubling was the fact that Peter didn't look at us, or smile, and wouldn't play the games that seemed as much a part of babyhood as diapers. He rarely laughed, and when he did, it was at things that didn't seem funny to us. He didn't cuddle, but sat upright in my lap, even when I rocked him. But children differ and we were content to let Peter be himself. We thought it hilarious when my brother, visiting us when Peter was 8 months old, observed, "That kid has no social instincts, whatsoever." Although Peter was a

■ **Table 7.2** Characteristics of Autism Spectrum Disorders (ASDs)

Key Indicators
• Does not babble, point, or make meaningful gestures by 1 year of age
• Does not speak one word by 16 months
• Does not combine two words by 2 years
• Does not respond to name
• Loses language or social skills

Other Indicators
• Poor eye contact
• Doesn't seem to know how to play with toys
• Excessively lines up toys or other objects
• Is attached to one particular toy or object
• Doesn't smile
• At times seems to be hearing impaired

Source: Adapted from Strock (2004).

first child, he was not isolated. I frequently put him in his playpen in front of the house, where the schoolchildren stopped to play with him as they passed. He ignored them, too.

It was Kitty, a personality kid, born two years later, whose responsiveness emphasized the degree of Peter's difference. When I went into her room for the late feeding, her little head bobbed up and she greeted me with a smile that reached from her head to her toes. And the realization of that difference chilled me more than the wintry bedroom.

Peter's babbling had not turned into speech by the time he was 3. His play was solitary and repetitive. He tore paper into long thin strips, bushel baskets of it every day. He spun the lids from my canning jars and became upset if we tried to divert him. Only rarely could I catch his eye, and then saw his focus change from me to the reflection in my glasses. . . .

[Peter's] adventures into our suburban neighborhood had been unhappy. He had disregarded the universal rule that sand is to be kept in sandboxes, and the children themselves had punished him. He walked around a sad and solitary figure, always carrying a toy airplane, a toy he never played with. At that time, I had not heard the word that was to dominate our lives, to hover over every conversation, to sit through every meal beside us. That word was autism.

—Adapted from Eberhardy (1967)

Peter, the boy with "no social instincts," was autistic. ***Question: What is autism?*** The word *autism* derives from the Greek *autos*, meaning "self." (An automobile is a self-driven method of moving from place to place.) **Autism** is four to five times more common among boys than girls. Perhaps the most poignant feature of autism is the child's utter aloneness (Constantino et al., 2006). Autistic children do not show interest in social interaction and may avoid eye contact. Attachment to others is weak or absent.

Other features of autism include communication problems, intolerance of change, and ritualistic or stereotypical behavior (Georgiades et al., 2007). Parents of autistic children frequently report that they were "good babies," which usually means that they made few demands. But as autistic children develop, they tend to shun affectionate contacts such as hugging, cuddling, and kissing.

Development of speech lags in autistic children (Mackic-Magyar & McCracken, 2004). There is little babbling and communicative gesturing during the first year. Autistic children may show **mutism, echolalia,** and pronoun reversal, referring to themselves as "you" or "he." About half use language by middle childhood, but their speech is unusual and troubled (Dobbinson et al., 2003).

Autistic children become bound by ritual (Georgiades et al., 2007). Even slight changes in routines or the environment may cause distress. The teacher of a 5-year-old autistic girl would greet her each morning with, "Good morning, Lily, I am very, very glad to see you." Lily would ignore the greeting, but she would shriek if the teacher omitted even one of the *very*s. This feature of autism is termed "preservation of sameness." When familiar objects are moved from their usual places, children with autism may throw tantrums or cry until they are restored. They may insist on eating the same food every day. Autistic children show deficits in peer play, imaginative play, imitation, and emotional expression. Many sleep less than their age-mates (Georgiades et al., 2007).

Some autistic children mutilate themselves, even as they cry out in pain. They may bang their heads, slap their faces, bite their hands and shoulders, or pull out their hair. ***Question: What are the origins of autism spectrum disorders?***

Permission by Lori Furton, China Township, Michigan; photo by Melissa Wawzysko/Times Herald-Port Huron, MI

Autism
The most poignant feature of autism is the child's utter aloneness. Autism is rather rare, but it is more common in boys than in girls. Symptoms include communication problems, intolerance of any change, and ritualistic or stereotypical behavior.

autism An autism spectrum disorder characterized by extreme aloneness, communication problems, intolerance of change, and ritualistic behavior.

mutism Inability or refusal to speak.

echolalia The automatic repetition of sounds or words.

Causes of Autism Spectrum Disorders

Some theorists argue that children develop ASDs in response to parental rejection. From this viewpoint, autistic behavior shuts out the cold outside world. But research evidence shows that the parents of autistic children are not deficient in child rearing (Mackie-Magyar & McCracken, 2004).

Various lines of evidence suggest a key role for biological factors in autism. For example, very low birth weight and advanced maternal age may heighten the risk of autism (Maimburg & Væth, 2006). A role for genetic mechanisms is suggested by kinship studies (Constantino et al., 2006; Gutknecht, 2001; Plomin, 2001). For example, the concordance (agreement) rates for ASDs are about 60% among pairs of identical (monozygotic) twins, who fully share their genetic heritage, compared with about 10% for pairs of fraternal (dizygotic) twins, whose genetic codes overlap by only 50% (Plomin et al., 1994). Twin status appears to increase susceptibility to the symptoms of autism, especially among males (Ho et al., 2005). Researchers suspect that multiple genes are involved in ASDs and interact with other factors, environmental, biological, or a combination of the two.

Biological factors focus on neurological involvement. Many children with ASDs have abnormal brain wave patterns or seizures (Canitano, 2007; Roulet-Perez & Deonna; 2006). Other researchers have found that, compared with others, the brains of children with ASDs have abnormal sensitivities to neurotransmitters such as serotonin, dopamine, acetylcholine, and norepinephrine (Bauman et al., 2006). Other researchers note unusual activity in the motor region of the cerebral cortex (R. Mueller et al., 2001) and less activity in some other areas of the brain, including the frontal and temporal lobes and the limbic system (Lam et al., 2006; Penn, 2006). Still other researchers link autism to disorders of the immune system that they believe originate during prenatal development (Zimmerman et al., 2006).

Truth or Fiction Revisited: While we are discussing biological factors in causation, let us delete one. It has been widely believed—it is almost something of a myth—that vaccines or the mercury preservative used in a number of vaccines is a cause of autism. But let us note, rather strongly, that there is *no* scientific evidence for this view, regardless of whether or not it is widely held (Richler et al., 2006; Taylor, 2006).

All in all, it seems rather clear that we can consider autism to be a disease of the brain and that parents of children with autism should not be blaming themselves. Moreover, although researchers have found many biological abnormalities among children with autism, not every child has every abnormality. Although it appears that heredity creates a vulnerability to autism, the other conditions that interact with heredity to produce autistic behavior and various neurobiological signs of autism remain unknown.

Treatment of Autism Spectrum Disorders

Question: What can be done to help children with autism spectrum disorders?
Treatment for ASDs is mainly based on principles of learning, although investigation of biological approaches is also under way (Strock, 2004). Behavior modification has been used to increase the child's ability to attend to others, to play with other children, and to discourage self-mutilation. Brief bursts of mild, harmless electric shock rapidly eliminate self-mutilation (Lovaas, 1977). The use of electric shock raises serious moral, ethical, and legal concerns, but O. Ivar Lovaas has countered that failure to eliminate self-injurious behavior places the child at yet greater risk.

Because children with ASDs show behavioral deficits, behavior modification is used to help them develop new behavior. **Truth or Fiction Revisited:** For example, many autistic children do respond to people as though they were furniture. They run around them rather than relate to them as people. But many autistic children can be taught to accept people as reinforcers, for example, by pairing praise with food treats (Drasgow et al., 2001). Praise can then be used to encourage speech and social play.

The most effective treatment programs focus on individualized instruction to correct behavioral, educational, and communication deficits (Rapin, 1997). In a classic study conducted by Lovaas at UCLA (Lovaas et al., 1989), autistic children received more than 40 hours of one-to-one behavior modification a week for at least 2 years. Significant intellectual and educational gains were reported for 9 of the 19 children (47%) in the program. The children who improved achieved normal scores on intelligence tests and succeeded in first grade. Only 2% of an untreated control group achieved similar gains. Treatment gains were maintained at a follow-up at the age of 11 (McEachin et al., 1993). Somewhat less intensive educational programs have also yielded positive results with many autistic toddlers (Stahmer et al., 2004).

Biological approaches for the treatment of ASDs are under study. Drugs that enhance serotonin activity (selective serotonin reuptake inhibitors, or SSRIs, such as those used to treat depression) can help prevent self-injury, aggressive outbursts, depression and anxiety, and repetitive behavior (Kwok, 2003). Drugs that are usually used to treat schizophrenia—the "major tranquilizers"—are helpful with stereotyped behavior, hyperactivity, and self-injury but not with cognitive and language problems (Kwok, 2003; McClellan & Werry, 2003; Volkmar, 2001).

Autistic behavior generally continues into adulthood to one degree or another. Nevertheless, some autistic children go on to achieve college degrees and function independently (Rapin, 1997). Others need continuous treatment, which may include institutionalized care.

We have been examining the development of attachment and some of the circumstances that may interfere with its development. In recent years, a lively debate has sprung up concerning the effects of day care on children's attachment and on their social and cognitive development. Let us turn now to a consideration of these issues.

Active Review

9. The Harlows found that rhesus infants reared in isolation later (Sought or Avoided?) contact with other monkeys.
10. Spitz noted that many institutionalized children appear to develop a syndrome characterized by _____ and depression.
11. Relatively more deaths occur from (Physical abuse or Neglect?).
12. Children with _____ do not show interest in social interaction, have communication problems, are intolerant of change, and display repetitive behavior.

Reflect & Relate: What would you do if you learned that the child of a neighbor was being abused? What would you do if you were a teacher and learned that a child in your class was being abused?

Go to

http://www.thomsonedu.com/psychology/rathus

for an interactive version of this review.

© AP

Children in Day Care
High-quality day care often has a positive influence on children's cognitive development.

Yet the findings of the National Institute on Child Health and Human Development study also reveal that children placed in day care may be less cooperative and more aggressive toward peers and adults than children who are reared in the home. For example, the more time preschoolers spent in child care, the more likely they were to display behavioral problems in kindergarten (Belsky et al., 2001). The more time spent away from their mothers, the more likely these children were to be rated as defiant, aggressive, and disobedient once they got to kindergarten. **Truth or Fiction Revisited:** It therefore appears to be true that children who attend day-care programs behave more aggressively than children who do not.

Seventeen percent of children who were in child care for more than 30 hours a week received higher scores on rating items such as "gets in lots of fights," "cruelty," "talking too much," "explosive behavior," "argues a lot," and "demands a lot of attention." Only 6% of children who were in child care for fewer than 10 hours a week had these problems. Children who were cared for in traditional day-care settings—by a grandmother, by a nanny, even by their fathers—received the troublesome ratings. Was Mom the only answer?

The study also held some good news. For example, it found that children who are enrolled in high-quality day care show cognitive benefits compared with children who are in lower-quality day care or who spend more time in the home with their mothers.

Although the study found a connection between time spent away from mothers and aggression, disobedience, and defiance in kindergarten, the reasons for these problems were not clear. For example, was it the time spent away from mothers that brought on the problems, or did the problems stem from other factors, such as the stresses encountered by families who need two incomes?

A number of the researchers on the team added that if other information yielded by the study had been presented, the reaction might have been different. Note the following:

- Although 17% of kindergartners who had been in child care acted more assertively and aggressively, that percentage is actually the norm for the general population of children. (In addition, 9% of the children who spent most of their time with their mothers were also rated by teachers as showing the more troubling behaviors.)
- The nature of family–child interactions had a greater effect on children's behavior than the number of hours spent in child care.
- Some aspects of aggressiveness—and the fact that infants in day care may demand more attention as kindergartners—may be adaptive responses to being placed in a situation where many children are competing for limited resources.

In addition, the researchers admitted that the statistics are modest: Yes, 17% of the children in day care acted aggressively and assertively, but only a few of them exhibited above-average behavior problems. Moreover, the problems were not that serious.

In any case, millions of parents do not have the option of deciding whether to place their children in day care; their only choice is where to do so. (Some parents, given their financial and geographic circumstances, might not even have such a choice.) The "A Closer Look" feature on page 247 may help you make the choice that is right for you.

A Closer Look

*Finding Child Care You
(and Your Child) Can Live With*

It is normal to be anxious. You are thinking about selecting a day-care center or a private home for your precious child, and there are risks. So be a little anxious, but it may not be necessary to be overwhelmed. You can go about the task with a checklist that can guide your considerations. Above all, don't be afraid to open your mouth and ask questions, even pointed, challenging questions. If the day-care provider does not like questions or if the provider does not answer them satisfactorily, you want your child someplace else. So much for the preamble. Here's the checklist.

1. Does the day-care center have a license? Who issued the license? What did the day-care center have to do to acquire the license? (You can also call the licensing agency to obtain the answer to the last question.)

2. How many children are cared for by the center? How many caregivers are there? Remember this nursery rhyme: There was an old woman who lived in a shoe. She had so many children she didn't know what to do. All right, the rhyme is sexist and ageist and maybe even shoe-ist, but it suggests that it is important for caregivers not to be overburdened by too many children, especially infants. It is desirable to have at least one caregiver for every four infants, although fewer workers are required for older children.

3. How were the caregivers hired? How were they trained? Did the center check references? What were the minimum educational credentials? Did the center check the references and credentials? Do the caregivers have any education or training in the behavior and needs of children? Do the caregivers seem to be proactive and attempt to engage the children in activities and educational experiences, or are they inactive unless a child cries or screams? Sometimes it is impossible to find qualified day-care workers, because they tend to be paid poorly (often the minimum wage, and sometimes less).

4. Is the environment child-proofed and secure? Can children stick their fingers in electric sockets? Are toys and outdoor equipment in good condition? Are sharp objects within children's reach? Can anybody walk in off the street? What is the history of children being injured or otherwise victimized in this day-care center? Is the day-care provider hesitant about answering any of these questions? When are meals served? Snacks? What do they consist of? Will your child find them appetizing or go hungry? Some babies are placed in day care at 6 months or younger, and parents will need to know what formulas are used.

5. Is it possible for you to meet the caregivers who will be taking care of your child? If not, why not?

6. With what children will your child interact and play?

7. Does the center seem to have an enriching environment? Do you see books, toys, games, and educational objects strewn about?

8. Are there facilities and objects such as swings and tricycles that will enhance your child's physical and motor development? Are children supervised when they play with these things, or are they often left on their own?

9. Does the center's schedule coincide with your needs?

10. Is the center located conveniently for you? Does it appear to be in a safe location or to have adequate security arrangements? (Let me emphasize that you have a right to ask whether neighborhood or other people can walk in unannounced to where the children are. It's a fair question. You can also ask what they would do if a stranger broke into the place.)

11. Are parents permitted to visit unannounced?

12. Do you like the overall environment and feel of the center or home? Listen to your "gut."

Reflect: Which of the considerations in selecting a day-care center are most important to you? Why?

Active Review

13. The (Minority or Majority?) of mothers in the United States work outside the home.
14. Infants with day-care experience play at (Higher or Lower?) developmental levels than do home-reared babies.
15. Belsky and his colleagues found that once children are in school, those who had spent more time in day care were rated by teachers, caregivers, and mothers as being (More or Less?) aggressive toward other children.

Reflect & Relate: What are your concerns about placing children in day care? How do your concerns fit with the evidence on the effects of day care?

Go to

http://www.thomsonedu.com/psychology/rathus
for an interactive version of this review.

Emotional Development

Emotions color our lives. We are green with envy, red with anger, blue with sorrow. Positive emotions such as love can fill our days with pleasure. Negative emotions such as fear, depression, and anger can fill us with dread and make each day a chore.

Question: What are emotions? An **emotion** is a state of feeling that has physiological, situational, and cognitive components. Physiologically, when emotions are strong, our hearts may beat more rapidly and our muscles may tense. Situationally, we may feel fear in the presence of a threat and joy or relief in the presence of a loved one. Cognitively, fear is accompanied by the idea that we are in danger.

Theories of the Development of Emotions

Question: How do emotions develop? A number of theories concerning the development of emotions have been offered. They break down into two basic camps. The first, proposed originally by Katherine Bridges (1932), holds that we are born with a single emotion and that other emotions become differentiated as time passes. The second, Carroll Izard's **differential emotions theory** (2004), holds that the major emotions are present and differentiated at birth. But they are not shown all at once. Instead, they emerge in response to the child's developing needs and maturational sequences.

Bridges's and Sroufe's Theory

On the basis of her observations of babies, Bridges proposed that newborns experience one emotion—diffuse excitement. By the age of 3 months, two other emotions have differentiated from this general state of excitement—a negative emotion, distress, and a positive emotion, delight. By 6 months of age, fear, disgust, and anger will have developed from distress. By 12 months, elation and affection will have differentiated from delight. Jealousy develops from distress, and joy develops from delight—both during the second year.

Alan Sroufe (1979, 2005) has advanced Bridges's theory by focusing on the ways in which cognitive development provides a basis for emotional development. Jealousy, for example, could not become differentiated without some understanding of object

emotion A state of feeling that has physiological, situational, and cognitive components.

differential emotions theory Izard's view that the major emotions are distinct at birth but emerge gradually in accord with maturation and the child's developing needs

permanence (the continuing existence of people and objects) and possession. Similarly, infants usually show distress at the mother's departure after they have developed object permanence. Fear of strangers cannot occur without the perceptual ability to discriminate familiar people from others.

Izard's Theory

Carroll Izard's (2004; Izard et al., 2006) differential emotions theory proposes that infants are born with discrete emotional states, but the timing of their appearance is linked to the child's cognitive development and social experiences. For example, Izard and his colleagues (1987) reported that 2-month-old babies receiving inoculations showed distress, whereas older infants showed anger.

Izard's view may sound similar to Sroufe's. Both suggest an orderly unfolding of emotions such that they become more specific as time passes. But in keeping with Izard's view, researchers have found that a number of different emotions appear to be shown by infants at ages earlier than those suggested by Bridges and Sroufe (Bennett et al., 2004). In one study of emotions shown by babies during the first 3 months, 95% of the mothers interviewed reported observing joy; 84%, anger; 74%, surprise; and 58%, fear (Johnson et al., 1982).

Izard claimed to have found many discrete emotions at the age of 1 month by using his Maximally Discriminative Facial Movement Scoring System. ● Figure 7.7 shows some infant facial expressions that Izard believes are associated with the basic emotions of anger/rage, enjoyment/joy, fear/terror, and interest/excitement. Izard and his colleagues reported that facial expressions indicating interest, disgust, and pain are present at birth. They and others have observed expressions of anger and sadness at 2 months of age, expressions of surprise at 4 months, and expressions of fear at 7 months (Izard & Malatesta, 1987). However, some researchers believe that this type of research has many problems. First, observers cannot always accurately identify the emotions shown in slides or drawings of infant facial expressions. Second, we cannot know the exact relationship between a facial expression and an infant's inner feelings, which, of course, are private events. Even if the drawings accurately represent young infants' facial expressions, we cannot be certain that they express the specific emotions they would suggest if they were exhibited by older children and adults.

In sum, researchers agree that infants show only a few emotions during the first few months. They agree that other emotions develop in an orderly manner. They agree that emotional development is linked to cognitive development and social experience. They do not agree on exactly when specific emotions are first shown or whether discrete emotions are present at birth.

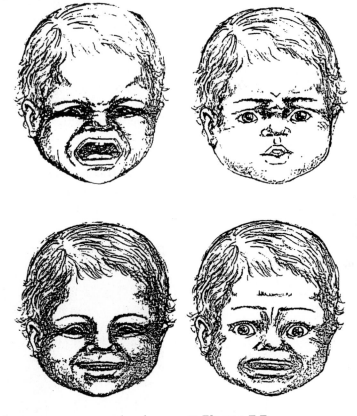

● **Figure 7.7**
Illustrations from Izard's Maximally Discriminative Facial Movement Scoring System

What emotion do you think is being experienced by each of these infants?

Source: Izard (1983).

Emotional Development and Patterns of Attachment

Emotional development has been linked with various histories of attachment. In a longitudinal study of 112 children at ages 9, 14, 22, and 33 months, Kochanska (2001) studied the development of fear, anger, and joy using laboratory situations designed to evoke these emotions. Patterns of attachment were assessed using the strange-situation method. Differences in emotional development could first be related to attachment at the age of 14 months. Resistant children were most fearful and least joyful. Fear was their most powerful emotion. They frequently responded with distress even in episodes designed to evoke joy. When they were assessed repeatedly over time, it became apparent that securely attached children were becoming significantly less angry. By contrast, the negative emotions of insecurely attached children rose: Avoidant children grew more fearful, and resistant children became less joyful. At 33 months of age, securely attached children were less likely to show fear and anger, even when they were exposed to situations designed to elicit these emotions.

Enough disagreement. Let us focus on an emotion that we can all agree is little fun: fear. We focus on a common fear of infants: the fear of strangers.

Fear of Strangers

When my daughter Jordan was 1 year old, her mother and I decided that we had to get a nanny for a few hours a day so that we could teach, write, breathe, and engage in other life activities. We hired a graduate student in social work who had a mild, engaging way about her. She nurtured Jordan and played with her for about 4 months, during which time Jordan came to somewhat grudgingly accept her, most of the time. Even so, Jordan was never completely comfortable with her. Jordan frequently let out a yowl as if buildings were collapsing around her, although the nanny did nothing except attempt to soothe her in a calm, consistent manner.

Jordan had a nanny and she had fear of strangers. Unfortunately, she met the nanny during the period when she had developed fear of strangers. The fear was eventually to subside, as these fears do, but during her entire encounter with the nanny, the nanny wondered what she was doing wrong. The answer, of course, was simple: She was existing, within sight of Jordan. Worse yet, Jordan's parents were not there to protect her from this vicious foe.

stranger anxiety A fear of unfamiliar people that emerges between 6 and 9 months of age. Also called fear of strangers.

Was Jordan's response to her nanny "normal"? ***Question: Is fear of strangers normal?*** **Truth or Fiction Revisited:** Development of fear of strangers—sometimes termed **stranger anxiety**—is normal. Most infants develop it. Stranger anxiety appears at about 6 to 9 months of age in many different cultures, including those of the United States, Great Britain, Guatemala, and Zambia (Smith, 1979). By 4 or 5

Stranger Anxiety

Infants in many cultures develop a fear of strangers, known as stranger anxiety, at about 6 to 9 months of age. This infant shows clear signs of distress when held by a stranger even though mother is close by. How would you behave around an infant who does not know you to try to minimize her or his stranger anxiety?

months of age, infants smile more in response to their mothers than to strangers. At this age, infants may compare the faces of strangers and their mothers, looking back and forth. Somewhat older infants show marked distress by crying, whimpering, gazing fearfully, and crawling away. Fear of strangers may peak between 9 and 12 months of age and decline in the second year or reach a second peak between the ages of 18 and 24 months and then decline in the third year (Thompson & Limber, 1990).

Children who have developed fear of strangers show less distress in response to strangers when their mothers are present. Babies are less likely to show fear of strangers when they are held by their mothers than when they are placed a few feet away (Thompson & Limber, 1990). Children also are less likely to show fear of strangers when they are in familiar surroundings, such as their homes, than when they are in the laboratory (Sroufe et al., 1974).

In terms of proximity, the fear response to strangers is the mirror image of attachment. Children attempt to remain near people to whom they are attached. But the closer they are to strangers, the greater their signs of distress (Boccia & Campos, 1989). They are most distressed when the strangers touch them. For this reason, if you find yourself in a situation in which you are trying to comfort an infant who does not know you, it may be more effective to talk in a friendly and soothing manner from a distance. Reconsider rushing in and picking up the child. Your behavior with an unfamiliar child also can make a difference. Studies have found that adults who are active and friendly—who gesture, smile, and offer toys—receive more positive response from 6- to 18-month-olds than do strangers who are quiet and passive (Bretherton et al., 1981; Mangelsdorf, 1992).

Social Referencing: What Should I Do Now?

Social referencing is the seeking out of another person's perception of a situation to help us form our own view of it (Hertenstein & Campos, 2004). In novel situations, adolescents and adults frequently observe how others behave and pattern their behavior after them. For example, people who are not afraid may help children reduce their fears. Essentially, the models provide information about how to act in a frightening situation.

Question: When does social referencing develop? Infants also display social referencing, as early as 6 months of age. They use caregivers' facial expressions or tone of voice to provide clues on how to respond (Hertenstein & Campos, 2004). In one study, for example, 8-month-old infants were friendlier to a stranger when their mothers exhibited a friendly facial expression in the stranger's presence than when she displayed a worried expression (Boccia & Campos, 1989).

Leslie Carver and Brenda Vaccaro (2007) suggest that social referencing requires three components: (1) looking at another, usually older individual in a novel, ambiguous situation; (2) associating that individual's emotional response with the unfamiliar situation; and (3) regulating their own emotional response in accord with the response of the older individual. In an experiment, Carver and Vaccaro (2007) found that 12-month-old infants were quicker to mold their responses to those of an adult who displayed a negative emotion rather than a neutral or a positive emotion. Perhaps we are wired to respond to danger first and pleasure later.

Emotional Regulation: Keeping on an Even Keel

Infants use emotional signals from an adult to help them cope with uncertainty. Another important feature of early emotional development is emotional regulation (Rothbart & Sheese, 2007). *Question: What is emotional regulation?* **Emotional regulation** refers to the ways in which young children control their own emotions. Even young infants display certain behaviors to control unpleasant emotional states.

social referencing Using another person's reaction to a situation to form one's own assessment of it.

emotional regulation Techniques for controlling one's emotional states.

They may look away from a disturbing event or suck their thumbs (Rothbart & Sheese, 2007). Caregivers play an important role in helping infants learn to regulate their emotions. Early in life, a two-way communication system develops in which the infant signals the caregiver that help is needed and the caregiver responds. Claire Kopp (1989, p. 347) gave an example of how this system works:

> A 13-month-old, playing with a large plastic bottle, attempted to unscrew the cover, but could not. Fretting for a short time, she initiated eye contact with her mother and held out the jar. As her mother took it to unscrew the cover, the infant ceased fretting.

Research evidence suggests that the children of secure mothers are not only likely to be securely attached themselves but also are likely to regulate their own emotions in a positive manner (Grolnick et al., 2006; Thompson & Meyer, 2007). A German longitudinal study (Zimmermann et al., 2001) related emotional regulation in adolescence with patterns of attachment during infancy, as assessed using the strange-situation method. Forty-one adolescents, age 16 and 17 years, were placed in complex problem-solving situations with friends. It turned out that those adolescents who were secure as infants were most capable of regulating their emotions to interact cooperatively with their friends. Another study (Volling, 2001) addressed the relationship between attachment in infancy and emotional regulation in an interaction with a distressed sibling at the age of 4. Of 45 preschoolers in the study, those who had an insecure-resistant infant–mother attachment at the age of 1 year engaged in more conflict with their siblings and showed greater hostility at the age of 4.

Active Review

16. Bridges proposed that we are born with a single emotion: diffuse _____.
17. The (Majority or Minority?) of infants develop fear of strangers.
18. Social _____ is the seeking out of another person's perception of a situation to help us form our own view of it.
19. Emotional _____ refers to the ways in which young children control their own emotions.

Reflect & Relate: Have you ever been in a novel situation and been uncertain about what to do? How about when you entered adolescence or began your first college class? Did you observe other people's reactions to the situation in an effort to determine what to do? This behavior is called *social referencing*. At what age do humans begin to use social referencing?

Go to

http://www.thomsonedu.com/psychology/rathus

for an interactive version of this review.

Personality Development

personality An individual's distinctive ways of responding to people and events.

An individual's **personality** refers to his or her distinctive ways of responding to people and events. In this section, we examine important aspects of personality development in the infant years. First, we look at the emergence of the self-concept. We then turn to a discussion of temperament. Finally, we consider sex differences in behavior.

The Self-Concept

At birth, we may find the world to be a confusing blur of sights, sounds, and inner sensations—yet the "we" may be missing, at least for a while. When our hands first come into view, there is little evidence we realize that the hands "belong" to us and that we are somehow separate and distinct from the world outside.

Questions: What is the self-concept? How does it develop? The **self-concept** is the sense of self. It appears to emerge gradually during infancy. At some point, infants understand that the hand they are moving in and out of sight is "their" hand. At some point, they understand that their own bodies extend only so far and that at a certain point, external objects and the bodies of others begin.

Development of the Self-Concept

Psychologists have devised ingenious methods to assess the development of the self-concept among infants. One of these is the mirror technique, which involves the use of a mirror and a dot of rouge. Before the experiment begins, the researcher observes the infant for baseline data on how frequently the infant touches his or her nose. Then the mother places rouge on the infant's nose, and the infant is placed before a mirror. Not until about the age of 18 months do infants begin to touch their own noses upon looking in the mirror (Campbell et al., 2000; Keller et al., 2005).

Nose touching suggests that children recognize themselves and that they have a mental picture of themselves that allows them to perceive that the dot of rouge is an abnormality. Most 2-year-olds can point to pictures of themselves, and they begin to use "I" or their own name spontaneously (Smiley & Johnson, 2006).

Self-awareness affects the infant's social and emotional development (Foley, 2006). Knowledge of the self permits the infant and child to develop notions of sharing and cooperation. In one study, for example, 2-year-olds who had a better developed sense of self were more likely to cooperate with other children (Brownell & Carriger, 1990).

Self-awareness also makes possible the development of "self-conscious" emotions such as embarrassment, envy, empathy, pride, guilt, and shame (Foley, 2006). One illustration of the development of these "self-conscious" emotions comes from a study by Deborah Stipek and her colleagues (1992). They found that children older than 21 months often seek their mother's attention and approval when they have successfully completed a task, whereas younger toddlers do not.

Self-Awareness
In the middle of the second year, infants begin to develop self-awareness, which has a powerful effect on social and emotional development.

Psychoanalytic Views of the Self-Concept

Margaret Mahler, a psychoanalyst, has proposed that development of self-concept comes about through a process of **separation–individuation**, which lasts from about 5 months until 3 years of age (Mahler et al., 1975). Separation involves the child's growing perception that her mother is separate from herself. Individuation refers to the child's increasing sense of independence and autonomy.

The word *autonomy* may remind you of a similar view proposed by Erik Erikson that was discussed in Chapter 1. Erikson states that the major developmental task of the child from ages 2 to 3 is acquiring a sense of autonomy and independence from parents. Remember that Freud, too, believed that children of this age are gaining greater independence and control. His focus, however, was primarily on such bodily functions as toileting behavior.

One of the ways toddlers demonstrate their growing autonomy, much to the dismay of their parents, is by refusing to comply with parental requests or commands. Studies of toddlers and preschoolers between the ages of 1½ and 5 years have found that as children grow older, they adopt more skillful ways of expressing resistance to

self-concept One's impression of oneself; self-awareness.

separation–individuation The child's increasing sense of becoming separate from and independent of the mother.

parental requests (Smith et al., 2004; Stifter & Wiggins, 2004). For example, young toddlers are more likely to ignore a parent's request or defy it ("No, I won't," accompanied by foot stamping). Older toddlers and preschoolers are more likely to make excuses ("I'm not hungry") or engage in negotiations ("Can I just eat some of my vegetables?").

Temperament: Easy, Difficult, or Slow to Warm Up?

Question: What is meant by the temperament of a child? Each child has a characteristic way of reacting and adapting to the world. The term **temperament** refers to stable individual differences in styles of reaction that are present early in life (Wachs, 2006). Many researchers believe that temperament forms the basic core of personality and that there is a strong genetic component to temperament (e.g., Goldsmith et al., 2003; Plomin, 2000; Wachs, 2006).

The child's temperament includes many aspects of behavior. Alexander Thomas and Stella Chess, in their well-known New York Longitudinal Study, followed the development of temperament in 133 girls and boys from birth to young adulthood (Chess & Thomas, 1991; Thomas & Chess, 1989) and identified nine characteristics of temperament. Other researchers have identified other characteristics (e.g., Gartstein et al., 2003). They include the following:

1. Activity level
2. Smiling/laughter
3. Regularity in child's biological functions, such as eating and sleeping
4. Approach or withdrawal from new situations and people
5. Adaptability to new situations
6. Sensitivity to sensory stimulation
7. Intensity of responsiveness
8. Quality of mood—generally cheerful or unpleasant
9. Distractibility
10. Attention span and persistence
11. Soothability
12. Distress at limitations

Questions: What types of temperament do we find among children? How do they develop?

Types of Temperament

Thomas and Chess (1989) found that from the first days of life, many of the children in their study could be classified into one of three types of temperament: "easy" (40% of their sample), "difficult" (10%), and "slow to warm up" (15%). Only 65% of the children studied by Chess and Thomas fit into one of the three types of temperament. Some of the differences among these three types of children are shown in ■ Table 7.3. As you can see, the easy child has regular sleep and feeding schedules, approaches new situations (such as a new food, a new school, or a stranger) with enthusiasm and adapts easily to them, and is generally cheerful. It is obvious why such a child would be relatively easy for parents to raise. Some children are more inconsistent and show a mixture of temperament traits. For example, a toddler may have a pleasant disposition but be frightened of new situations.

The difficult child, on the other hand, has irregular sleep and feeding schedules, is slow to accept new people and situations, takes a long time to adjust to new routines, and responds to frustrations with tantrums and loud crying. Parents find this type of child more difficult to deal with. The slow-to-warm-up child falls somewhere between the other two. These children have somewhat irregular feeding and sleeping

temperament Individual differences in styles of reaction that are present early in life.

■ **Table 7.3** Types of Temperament

Temperament Category	Easy	Difficult	Slow to warm up
• Regularity of biological functioning	Regular	Irregular	Somewhat irregular
• Response to new stimuli	Positive approach	Negative withdrawal	Negative withdrawal
• Adaptability to new situations	Adapts readily	Adapts slowly or not at all	Adapts slowly
• Intensity of reaction	Mild or moderate	Intense	Mild
• Quality of mood	Positive	Negative	Initially negative; gradually more positive

Sources: Chess & Thomas (1991) and Thomas & Chess (1989).

patterns and do not react as strongly as difficult children. They initially respond negatively to new experiences and adapt slowly only after repeated exposure.

Stability of Temperament

How stable is temperament? **Truth or Fiction Revisited:** Children are not all "born" with the same temperament. Thomas and Chess found that many children have one of three kinds of temperament from the first days of life. Evidence also indicates that there is at least moderate consistency in the development of temperament from infancy onward (Wachs, 2006). The infant who is highly active and cries in novel situations often becomes a fearful toddler. An anxious, unhappy toddler tends to become an anxious, unhappy adolescent. The child who refuses to accept new foods during infancy may scream when getting the first haircut, refuse to leave a parent's side during the first day of kindergarten, and have difficulty adjusting to college as a young adult. Difficult children in general are at greater risk for developing psychological disorders and adjustment problems later in life (Pauli-Pott et al., 2003; Rothbart et al., 2004). A longitudinal study tracked the progress of infants with a difficult temperament from 1½ through 12 years of age (Guerin et al., 1997). Temperament during infancy was assessed by the mother. Behavior patterns were assessed both by parents during the third year through the age of 12 and by teachers from the ages of 6 to 11. A difficult temperament correlated significantly with parental reports of behavioral problems from ages 3 to 12, including problems with attention span and aggression. Teachers concurred that children who had shown difficult temperaments during infancy were more likely to be aggressive later on and to have shorter attention spans.

Goodness of Fit: The Role of the Environment

The environment also affects the development of temperament. An initial biological predisposition to a certain temperament may be strengthened or weakened by the parents' reaction to the child. Consider the following: Parents may react to a difficult child by becoming less available and less responsive (Schoppe-Sullivan et al., 2007). They may insist on imposing rigid care-giving schedules, which in turn can cause the child to become even more difficult to handle (Schoppe-Sullivan et al., 2007). This example illustrates a discrepancy, or poor fit, between the child's behavior style and the parents' expectations and behaviors.

Differences in Temperament

Differences in temperament emerge in early infancy. The photo on the left shows the positive reactions of a 5-month-old girl being fed a new food for the first time. The photo on the right shows the very different response of another girl of about the same age when she is introduced to a new food.

© Elizabeth Crews

On the other hand, parents may respond in such a way as to modify a child's initial temperament in a more positive direction. Take the case of Carl, who in early life was one of the most difficult children in the New York Longitudinal Study:

> Whether it was the first solid foods in infancy, the beginning of nursery and elementary school, first birthday parties, or the first shopping trip, each experience evoked stormy responses, with loud crying and struggling to get away. However, his parents learned to anticipate Carl's reactions, knew that if they were patient, presented only one or a few new situations at a time, and gave him the opportunity for repeated exposure, Carl would finally adapt positively. Furthermore, once he adapted, his intensity of responses gave him a zestful enthusiastic involvement, just as it gave his initial negative reactions a loud and stormy character. His parents became fully aware that the difficulties in raising Carl were due to his temperament and not to their being "bad parents." The father even looked on his son's shrieking and turmoil as a sign of lustiness. As a result of this positive parent–child interaction, Carl never became a behavior problem.
>
> —Chess & Thomas (1984, p. 263)

This example demonstrates **goodness of fit** between the behaviors of child and parent. A key factor is the parents' realization that their youngster's behavior does not mean that the child is weak or deliberately disobedient, or that they are bad parents. This realization helps parents modify their attitudes and behaviors toward the child, whose behavior may in turn change in the desired direction (Bird et al., 2006; Schoppe-Sullivan et al., 2007).

Sex Differences

All cultures make a distinction between females and males and have beliefs and expectations about how they ought to behave. For this reason, a child's sex is a key factor in shaping its personality and other aspects of development. *Questions: How do girls and boys differ in their social, emotional, and other behaviors?*

goodness of fit Agreement between the parents' expectations of or demands on the child and the child's temperamental characteristics.

Behaviors of Infant Girls and Boys

Girls tend to advance more rapidly in their motor development in infancy: They sit, crawl, and walk earlier than boys do (Matlin, 2008). Female and male infants are quite similar in their responses to sights, sounds, tastes, smells, and touch. Although a few studies have found that infant boys are more active and irritable than girls, others have not (Matlin, 2008). Girls and boys also are similar in their social behaviors. They are equally likely to smile at people's faces, for example, and do not differ in their dependency on adults (Maccoby & Jacklin, 1974; Matlin, 2008). One area in which girls and boys begin to differ early in life is their preference for certain toys and play activities. By 12 to 18 months of age, girls prefer to play with dolls, doll furniture, dishes, and toy animals, whereas boys prefer transportation toys (trucks, cars, airplanes, and the like), tools, and sports equipment as early as 9 to 18 months of age (Campbell et al., 2000; Serbin et al., 2001). On the other hand, sex differences that appear to show up later, such as differences in spatial relations skills, are not necessarily evident in infancy (Örnk-loo & von Hofsten, 2007). By 24 months, both girls and boys appear to be quite aware of which behaviors are considered gender-consistent and gender-inconsistent, as measured in terms of time spent looking at the "novel" (in this case, "gender-inconsistent," as dictated by cultural stereotypes) behavior (Hill & Flom, 2007).

   Truth or Fiction Revisited: Thus, it appears to be fiction that children play with gender-typed toys only after they have become aware of the gender roles assigned to them by society. It may well be the case that (most) girls prefer dolls and toy animals and that (most) boys prefer toy trucks and sports equipment before they have been socialized, even before they fully understand whether they themselves are female or

Lessons in Observation
Gender

 To watch this video, visit the book companion website. You can also answer the questions and e-mail your responses to your professor.

Learning Objectives

- What are gender roles?
- Why do children seem to engage in gender-typed behavior?
- How do adults encourage gender-typed behavior through expectations and gifts?
- Do children show preference for same-sex playmates, or do they play with others regardless of sex?

Applied Lesson

Describe how parental expectations and gifts can influence gender-typed behavior in children.

Critical Thinking

How might parents try to raise their children in a more "gender-free" environment? Do you think a child raised in a relatively gender-free environment will develop differently from other children?

Researchers believe that children may be born with gender-typed preferences but that peers and adults also encourage these behaviors. Does this toddler girl's desire to feed her doll reflect her genetic code, learning from peers or adults, or all three?

© Graham Light/Alamy

Adults Treat Infant Girls and Boys Differently

Perhaps the most obvious way in which parents treat their baby girls and boys differently is in their choice of clothing, toys, and room furnishings. If you were to meet this infant, would you have any doubt as to his or her sex?

male. Researchers continue to try to sort out the effects of nature and nurture in children's gender-related preferences.

Adults' Behaviors toward Infant Girls and Boys

Adults respond differently to girls and boys. For example, in some studies adults are presented with an unfamiliar infant who is dressed in boy's clothes and has a boy's name, whereas other adults are introduced to a baby who is dressed in girl's clothing and has a girl's name. (In reality, it is the same baby who simply is given different names and clothing.) When adults believe they are playing with a girl, they are more likely to offer "her" a doll; when they think the child is a boy, they are more likely to offer a football or a hammer. "Boys" also are encouraged to engage in more physical activity than are "girls" (Worell & Goodheart, 2006). Perhaps it is no wonder that infants labeled as "girls" are perceived as littler and softer (as well as nicer and more beautiful) than infants labeled as "boys."

Parents' Behaviors toward Sons and Daughters

Do parents treat infant sons and daughters differently? Yes, as did the adults with the unfamiliar babies, parents are more likely to encourage rough-and-tumble play in their sons than in their daughters. Fathers are especially likely to do so (Eccles et al., 2000; Fagot et al., 2000). On the other hand, parents talk more to infant daughters than to infant sons. They smile more at daughters, are more emotionally expressive toward them, and focus more on feelings when talking to them (Matlin, 2008; Powlishta et al., 2001).

Perhaps the most obvious way in which parents treat their baby girls and boys differently is in their choice of clothing, room furnishings, and toys. Infant girls are likely to be decked out in a pink or yellow dress, embellished with ruffles and lace, whereas infant boys wear blue or red (Eccles et al., 2000; Powlishta et al., 2001). Parents provide baby girls and boys with different bedroom decorations and toys. Examination of the contents of rooms of children from 5 months to 6 years of age found that boys' rooms were often decorated with animal themes and with blue bedding and curtains. Girls' rooms featured flowers, lace, ruffles, and pastels. Girls owned more dolls; boys had more vehicles, military toys, and sports equipment.

Other studies find that parents react favorably when their preschool daughters play with "toys for girls" and their sons play with "toys for boys." Parents and other adults show more negative reactions when girls play with toys for boys and boys play with toys for girls (Martin et al., 2002; Worell & Goodheart, 2006). In general, fathers are more concerned than mothers that their children engage in activities viewed as "appropriate" for their sex.

Parents thus attempt to influence their children's behavior during infancy and lay the foundation for development in early childhood. It is to that period of life that we turn next, in Chapter 8.

Active Review

20. Psychologists devised the mirror technique to assess development of the self-_____.
21. The child's _____ refers to the stable individual differences in styles of reaction that are present very early in life.
22. The three basic types of temperament are easy, difficult, and _____ to warm up.
23. Girls prefer to play with dolls, whereas boys show a preference to play with transportation toys as early as _____ months of age.

Reflect & Relate: Have you known infants who were easygoing or difficult? How did their temperaments affect their relationships with their parents?

Go to

http://www.thomsonedu.com/psychology/rathus

for an interactive version of this review.

R E C I T E : *An Active Summary*

1. What is meant by "attachment"?

An attachment is an enduring emotional tie between one animal or person and another specific individual. Children try to maintain contact with persons to whom they are attached.

2. What does it mean for a child to be "secure"?

Most infants in the United States are securely attached. In the strange situation, securely attached infants mildly protest mother's departure and are readily comforted by her.

3. What, then, is "insecurity"?

The two major types of insecure attachment are avoidant attachment and ambivalent/resistant attachment. Infants with avoidant attachment are least distressed by their mothers' departure. Infants with ambivalent/resistant attachment show severe distress when their mothers leave but are ambivalent upon reunion.

4. Is it better for an infant to be securely attached to its caregivers?

Yes, securely attached infants are happier, more sociable, and more cooperative. They use the mother as a secure base from which to explore the environment. At ages 5 and 6, securely attached children are preferred by peers and teachers and more competent.

5. What are the roles of the parents in the formation of bonds of attachment?

High-quality care contributes to security. Parents of securely attached infants are more likely to be affectionate and sensitive to their needs. Security of attachment is related to the infant's temperament as well as to caregivers' behavior.

Key Terms

Active Learning Resources

Childhood & Adolescence Book Companion Website
http://www.thomsonedu.com/psychology/rathus

Visit your book companion website where you will find more resources to help you study. There you will find interactive versions of your book features, including the Lessons in Observation video, Active Review sections, and the Truth or Fiction feature. In addition, the companion website contains quizzing, flash cards, and a pronunciation glossary.

 is an easy-to-use online resource that helps you study in less time to get the grade you want—NOW.

http://www.thomsonedu.com/login

Need help studying? This site is your one-stop study shop. Take a Pre-Test and ThomsonNOW will generate a Personalized Study Plan based on your test results. The Study Plan will identify the topics you need to review and direct you to online resources to help you master those topics. You can then take a Post-Test to determine the concepts you have mastered and what you still need to work on.

ark is a 2-year-old boy having lunch in his high chair. He is not without ambition. He begins by shoving fistfuls of hamburger into his mouth. He picks up his cup with both hands and drinks milk. Then he starts banging his spoon on his tray and his cup. He kicks his feet against the chair. He throws hamburger on the floor. Compare Mark's behavior with that of Larry, age 3½, who is getting ready for bed. Larry carefully pulls his plastic train track apart and places each piece in the box. Then he walks to the bathroom, brings his stool over to the sink, and stands on it. He takes down his toothbrush and toothpaste, opens the cap, squeezes toothpaste on the brush, and begins to brush his teeth (Rowen, 1973).

Mark and Larry are in early childhood, the years from 2 to 6, which are also known as the preschool period. During early childhood, physical growth is slower than it was in infancy. Children become taller and leaner, and by the end of early childhood they look more like adults than infants. An explosion of motor skills occurs as children become stronger, faster, and better coordinated.

Language improves enormously, and children can carry on conversations with others. As cognitive skills develop, a new world of make believe or "pretend" play emerges. Curiosity and eagerness to learn are hallmarks of the preschool years.

Increased physical and cognitive capabilities enable the child to emerge from total dependence on parents and caregivers to become part of the broader world outside the family. Peers take on an increasingly important role in the life of the preschooler. Children begin to acquire a sense of their own abilities and shortcomings.

We learn about all these developments of early childhood—physical, cognitive, social, and emotional—in Chapters 8, 9, and 10.

Growth Patterns

During the preschool years, physical and motor development proceeds, literally, by leaps and bounds. While toddlers like Mark are occupied with grasping, banging, and throwing things, 3-year-olds like Larry are busy manipulating objects and exercising their newly developing fine motor skills. *Question: What changes occur in height and weight during early childhood?*

Height and Weight

Following the dramatic gains in height in a child's first 2 years, the growth rate slows down during the preschool years (Kuczmarski et al., 2000). Girls and boys tend to gain about 2 to 3 inches in height per year throughout early childhood. Weight gains also remain fairly even, at about 4 to 6 pounds per year (see Figure 8.1). Children become increasingly slender during early childhood, as they gain in height and lose some of their "baby fat." Boys as a group are only slightly taller and heavier than girls in early childhood (■ Figure 8.1). Noticeable variations in growth patterns also occur from child to child.

Development of the Brain

Question: How does the brain develop during early childhood? The brain develops more quickly than any other organ in early childhood. At 2 years of age, for example, the brain already has attained 75% of its adult weight. By the age of 5, the brain has reached 90% of its adult weight, even though the total body weight of the 5-year-old is barely one-third of what it will be as an adult (Tanner, 1989).

The increase in brain size is due in part to the continuing process of myelination of nerve fibers (see Chapter 5). Completion of the myelination of the neural path-

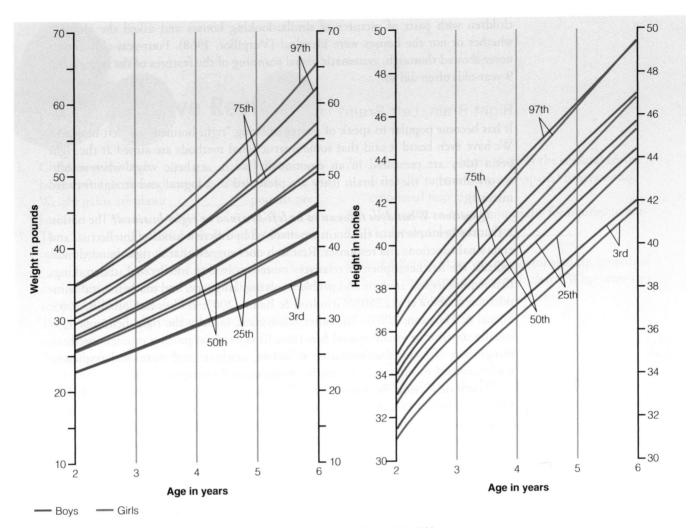

● **Figure 8.1**   Growth Curves for Height and Weight, Ages 2 to 6 Years

The numbers on the curves indicate the percentiles for height and weight at different ages. The growth rate slows down during early childhood. As in infancy, boys are only slightly taller and heavier than girls. Variations in growth patterns from child to child are evident.

Source: Kuczmarski et al. (2000, Figures 9–12).

ways that link the cerebellum to the cerebral cortex facilitates the development of fine motor skills (Nelson & Luciana, 2001; Paus et al., 1999). The cerebellum is involved in balance and coordination, and the young child's balancing abilities increase dramatically as myelination of these pathways nears completion.

Brain Development and Visual Skills

Brain development is also linked to improvements in the ability to attend to and process visual information (Yamada et al., 2000). These skills are critical in learning to read. The parts of the brain that enable the child to sustain attention and screen out distractions become increasingly myelinated between the ages of about 4 and 7 (Nelson & Luciana, 2001). As a result, most children are ready to focus on schoolwork between these ages.

The speed with which children process visual information improves throughout childhood, reaching adult levels at the beginning of adolescence (Chou et al., 2006; Paus et al., 1999). The child's ability to systematically scan visual material also improves in early childhood. For example, researchers in one classic study presented

■ **Table 8.1** Development of Gross Motor Skills in Early Childhood

2 Years (24–35 Months)	3 Years (36–47 Months)	4 Years (48–59 Months)	5 Years (60–71 Months)
• Runs well straight ahead	• Goes around obstacles while running	• Turns sharp corners while running	• Runs lightly on toes
• Walks up stairs, two feet to a step	• Walks up stairs, one foot to a step	• Walks down stairs, one foot to a step	• Jumps a distance of 3 feet
• Kicks a large ball	• Kicks a large ball easily	• Jumps from a height of 12 inches	• Catches a small ball, using hands only
• Jumps a distance of 4–14 inches	• Jumps from the bottom step	• Throws a ball overhand	• Hops 2 to 3 yards forward on each foot
• Throws a small ball without falling	• Catches a bounced ball, using torso and arms to form a basket	• Turns sharp corners while pushing and pulling toys	• Stands on one foot for 8–10 seconds
• Pushes and pulls large toys	• Goes around obstacles while pushing and pulling toys	• Hops on one foot, four to six hops	• Climbs actively and skillfully
• Hops on one foot, two or more hops	• Hops on one foot, up to three hops	• Stands on one foot for 3–8 seconds	• Skips on alternate feet
• Tries to stand on one foot	• Stands on one foot	• Climbs ladders	• Rides a bicycle with training wheels
• Climbs on furniture to look out of window	• Climbs nursery-school apparatus	• Skips on one foot	
		• Rides a tricycle well	

Note: The ages are averages; there are individual variations.

early childhood. For example, children with early crawling experience perform better than those who do not on tests of motor skills in the preschool years (McEwan et al., 1991).

Physical Activity

Preschool children spend quite a bit of time in physical activity. One study found that preschoolers spend an average of more than 25 hours a week in large muscle activity (D. W. Campbell et al., 2002). Younger preschoolers are more likely than older preschoolers to engage in physically oriented play, such as grasping, banging, and mouthing objects (D. W. Campbell et al., 2002). Consequently, they need more space and less furniture in a preschool or day-care setting.

Truth or Fiction Revisited: It is not true that motor activity increases during the preschool years. Motor activity level begins to decline after 2 or 3 years of age. Children become less restless and are able to sit still longer (D. W. Campbell et al., 2002; Eaton et al., 2001). Between the ages of 2 and 4, children in free play show an increase in sustained, focused attention.

Gross Motor Skills

During the preschool years, children make great strides in the development of gross motor skills. By age 4 or 5, they can pedal a tricycle quite skillfully.

Rough-and-Tumble Play

One form of physical and social activity often observed in young children is known as **rough-and-tumble play**. Rough-and-tumble play consists of running, chasing, fleeing, wrestling, hitting with an open hand, laughing, and making faces. Rough-and-tumble play is not the same as aggressive behavior. Aggression involves hitting with fists, pushing, taking, grabbing, and angry looks. Unlike aggression, rough-and-tumble play helps develop both physical and social skills in children (Fry, 2005; Colwell & Lindsey, 2005; Smith, 2005).

Play fighting and chasing activities are found among young children in societies around the world (Whiting & Edwards, 1988). But the particular form that rough-and-tumble play takes is influenced by culture and environment. For example, rough-and-tumble play among girls is quite common among the Pilaga Indians and the !Kung of Botswana but less common among girls in the United States. In the United States, rough-and-tumble play usually occurs in groups made up of the same sex. However, !Kung girls and boys engage in rough-and-tumble play together, and among the Pilaga, girls often are matched against the boys.

Individual Differences in Activity Level

Children differ widely in their activity levels. Some children are much more active than others.

Truth or Fiction Revisited: It is true that sedentary parents are more likely to have "couch potatoes" for children. Physically active children are more likely to have physically active parents. In a study of 4- to 7-year-olds (Moore et al., 1991), children of active mothers were twice as likely to be active as children of inactive mothers. Children of active fathers were 3.5 times as likely to be active as children of inactive fathers.

Several reasons may explain this relationship. First, active parents may serve as role models for activity. Second, sharing of activities by family members may be responsible. Parents who are avid tennis players may involve their children in games of tennis from an early age. By the same token, couch-potato parents who prefer to view tennis on television rather than play it may be more likely to share this sedentary activity with their children. A third factor is that active parents may encourage and

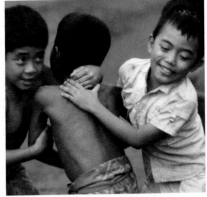

Rough-and-Tumble Play

Play fighting and chasing activities—known as rough-and-tumble play—are found among young children in societies around the world.

rough-and-tumble play Play fighting and chasing.

■ **Table 8.2** Development of Fine Motor Skills in Early Childhood

2 Years (24–35 Months)	3 Years (36–47 Months)	4 Years (48–59 Months)	5 Years (60–71 Months)
• Builds tower of 6 cubes • Copies vertical and horizontal lines • Imitates folding of paper • Prints on easel with a brush • Places simple shapes in correct holes	• Builds tower of 9 cubes • Copies circle and cross • Copies letters • Holds crayons with fingers, not fist • Strings 4 beads using a large needle	• Builds tower of 10 or more cubes • Copies square • Prints simple words • Imitates folding paper three times • Uses pencil with correct hand grip • Strings 10 beads	• Builds 3 steps from 6 blocks, using a model • Copies triangle and star • Prints first name and numbers • Imitates folding of piece of square paper into a triangle • Traces around a diamond drawn on paper • Laces shoes

Note: The ages are averages; there are individual variations.

fine motor skills Skills employing the small muscles used in manipulation, such as those in the fingers.

placement stage An early stage in drawing, usually found among 2-year-olds, in which children place their scribbles in various locations on the page (such as in the middle or near a border).

support their child's participation in physical activity. Finally, a tendency to be active or inactive may be transmitted genetically, as shown by evidence from twin studies (see Chapter 2) (Saudino & Eaton, 1993; Stevenson, 1992). Genetic and environmental factors apparently interact to determine a child's activity level.

Fine Motor Skills

In yet another example of the proximodistal trend in development, (see Chapters 3 and 5) **fine motor skills** develop gradually and lag gross motor skills. Fine motor skills involve the small muscles used in manipulation and coordination. Control over the wrists and fingers enables children to hold a pencil properly, dress themselves, and stack blocks (see ■ Table 8.2). Preschoolers can labor endlessly in attempting to tie their shoelaces and get their jackets zipped. There are terribly frustrating (and funny)

Developing in a World of Diversity

Sex Differences in Motor Activity

Question: *Do girls and boys differ in their activity levels during early childhood?* During early childhood, boys tend to be more active than girls, at least in some settings (Campbell & Eaton, 1999; D. W. Campbell et al., 2002). Boys spend more time than girls in large muscle activities. Boys tend to be more fidgety and distractible than girls and to spend less time focusing on tasks (McGuinness, 1990).

Why are boys more active and restless than girls? One theory is that boys of a given age are less mature physically than girls of the same age. Children tend to become less active as they develop (Eaton & Yu, 1989).

Boys also are more likely than girls to engage in rough-and-tumble play (Moller et al., 1992; Pellegrini, 1990). What might account for this sex difference? Some psychologists suggest that the reasons might be

partly based in biology (Maccoby, 1990a, 1991). Others argue that the socializing influences of the family and culture at large promote play differences among girls and boys (Caplan & Larkin, 1991; Meyer et al., 1991).

Reflect: *Why is it useful to know about sex differences in motor activity?*

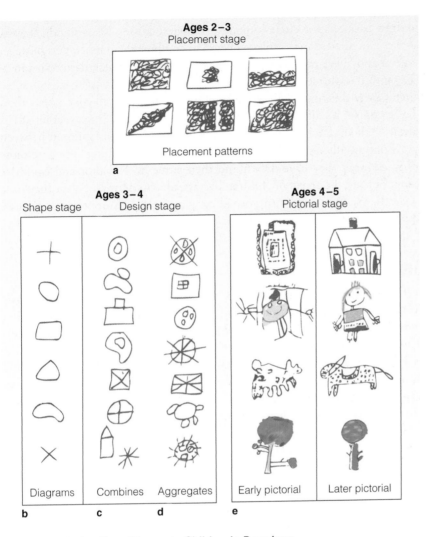

Figure 8.3 Four Stages in Children's Drawings

Children go through four stages in drawing pictures. (a) They first place their scribbles in various locations on the page. They then (b) draw basic shapes and (c, d) combine shapes into designs. Finally, (e) they draw recognizable objects.

Source: Kellogg (1970).

● **Figure 8.2**
The Twenty Basic Scribbles (Really)

By the age of 2, children can scribble. Rhoda Kellogg has identified these 20 basic scribbles as the building blocks of the young child's drawings.

Source: Kellogg (1970).

Fine Motor Skills
Control over the wrists and fingers enables children to hold a pencil, play a musical instrument, and, as shown in this photograph, play with clay.

scenes of children alternating between steadfastly refusing to allow a parent to intervene and requesting the parent's help.

Children's Drawings

The development of drawing in young children is closely linked to the development of both motor and cognitive skills. Children first begin to scribble during the second year of life. Initially, they seem to make marks for the sheer joy of it (Eisner, 1990).

Question: Are children's scribbles the result of random motor activity? Rhoda Kellogg (1959, 1970) studied more than 1 million drawings made by children. She found a meaningful pattern in the scribbles. She identified 20 basic scribbles that she considered the building blocks of all art including vertical, horizontal, diagonal, circular, curving, waving or zigzagging lines, and dots (see ● Figure 8.2).

Children go through four stages as they progress from making scribbles to drawing pictures. These are the **placement, shape, design**, and **pictorial stages** (see ● Figure 8.3). Two-year-olds place their scribbles in various locations on the page

shape stage A stage in drawing, attained by age 3, in which children draw basic shapes such as circles, squares, triangles, crosses, X's and odd shapes.

design stage A stage in drawing in which children begin to combine shapes.

(e.g., in the middle of the page or near one of the borders). By age 3, children are starting to draw basic shapes: circles, squares, triangles, crosses, X's, and odd shapes. As soon as they can draw shapes, children begin to combine them in the design stage. Between ages 4 and 5, the child reaches the pictorial stage, in which designs begin to resemble recognizable objects.

Children's early drawings tend to be symbolic of a broad category rather than specific. For example, a child might draw the same simple building whether she is asked to draw a school or a house (Tallandini & Valentini, 1991). Children between 3 and 5 years old usually do not start out to draw a particular thing. They are more likely to first see what they have drawn and then name it. As motor and cognitive skills improve beyond the age of 5, children become able to draw an object they have in mind (Matthews, 1990). They improve at copying figures (Karapetsas & Kantas, 1991; Pemberton, 1990).

Handedness

Truth or Fiction Revisited: Yes, Julius Caesar, Michelangelo, Tom Cruise, and Oprah do have something in common. They are all left-handed. *Questions: When does handedness emerge? How many children are left-handed?* **Handedness** emerges during infancy. By the age of 2 to 3 months, a rattle placed in an infant's hand is held longer with the right hand than with the left (Fitzgerald et al., 1991). By 4 months of age, most infants show a clear-cut right-hand preference in exploring objects using the sense of touch (Streri, 2002). Preference for grasping with one hand or the other increases markedly between the ages of 7 and 11 months (Hinojosa et al., 2003). Handedness becomes more strongly established during the early childhood years (McManus et al., 1988). Most people are right-handed, although studies vary as to how many are left-handed.

Left-Handedness: Is It Gauche To Be Left-Handed? Myths and Realities

Question: Are there problems connected with being left-handed? Being a "lefty" was once regarded as a deficiency. The language still swarms with slurs on lefties. We speak of "left-handed compliments," of having "two left feet," of strange events as "coming out of left field." The word *sinister* means "left-hand or unlucky side" in Latin. *Gauche* is a French word that literally means "left," although in English it is used to mean awkward or ill-mannered. The English word *adroit*, meaning "skillful," derives from the French *à droit*, literally translated as "to the right." Also consider positive usages such as "being righteous" or "being on one's right side."

Being left-handed is not gauche or sinister, but left-handedness may matter because it appears to be connected with language problems, such as dyslexia and stuttering, and with health problems, such as high blood pressure and epilepsy (Andreou et al., 2002; Bryden et al., 2005; Ostatnikova et al., 2002). Left-handedness is also apparently connected with psychological disorders, including schizophrenia and depression (Annett & Moran, 2006; Dollfus et al., 2005).

There may be advantages to being left-handed. **Truth or Fiction Revisited:** A disproportionately high percentage of math whizzes are in fact left-handed. In a series of studies, Camilla Benbow (O'Boyle & Benbow, 1990) related handedness to scores on the math part of the Scholastic Assessment Test (SAT) among 12- and 13-year-olds. Twenty percent of the highest-scoring group was left-handed. Only 10% of the general population is left-handed, so it appears that left-handed children are more than adequately represented among the most academically gifted in mathematics.

pictorial stage A stage in drawing attained between ages 4 and 5 in which designs begin to resemble recognizable objects.

handedness The tendency to prefer using the left or right hand in writing and other activities.

Left-handedness (or use of both hands) also has been associated with success in athletic activities such as handball, fencing, boxing, basketball, and baseball (Coren, 1992; Dane & Erzurumluoglu, 2003). Higher frequencies of left-handedness also are found among musicians, architects, and artists (Natsopoulos et al., 1992; O'Boyle & Benbow, 1990). Two of the greatest artists in history—Leonardo da Vinci and Michelangelo—were left-handed.

In the next section, we consider how it can be that left-handedness is associated with both talent and giftedness on the one hand (excuse the pun!) and with problems and deficits on the other. What are the origins of handedness?

Theories of Handedness

The origins of handedness apparently have a genetic component (Geschwind, 2000; McManus, 2003). Left-handedness runs in families. In the English royal family, the Queen Mother was left-handed as are Queen Elizabeth II, Prince Charles, and Prince William (Rosenbaum, 2000). If both of your parents are right-handed, your chances of being right-handed are about 92%. If one of your parents is left-handed, your chances of being right-handed drop to about 80%. And if both of your parents are left-handed, your chances of also being left-handed are about 50% (Annett, 1999; Clode, 2006).

Lessons in Observation
Gross and Fine Motor Skills

To watch this video, visit the book companion website. You can also answer the questions and e-mail your responses to your professor.

Although 3-year-old Olivia can kick a ball, she has to use her torso and arms formed into a basket to catch a ball.

Fine motor activities, such as building things with blocks, help children improve their skills and prepare them for drawing and writing.

Learning Objectives

- What is the difference between gross motor skills and fine motor skills?
- How do gross motor skills improve as children age?
- How does Olivia's attempt to catch a ball illustrate the proximodistal trend in motor development?
- What activities help prepare children for writing and drawing?

Applied Lesson

Describe the different stages of climbing and how each stage represents an advancement in gross motor skills.

Critical Thinking

How might parents help their child improve fine motor development? At what stage(s) should a parent introduce new toys and activities?

On the other hand, identical (monozygotic) twins frequently are different in handedness (Sommer et al., 2002). One explanation is that monozygotic twins are sometimes mirror opposites (Sommer et al., 2002). If that were so, the disagreement on handedness among monozygotic twins would not contradict a role for genetics in handedness.

In any case, handedness develops early. An ultrasound study found that about 95% of fetuses suck their right thumbs rather than their left (Hepper et al., 1990).

Interestingly, handedness is also found in species other than humans, for example, chimpanzees and parrots (yes, parrots). It appears that hand preferences in chimpanzees are heritable, as they are in humans, but that environmental factors can modify inborn preferences, in chimps as well as in humans (Hopkins et al., 2001).

In sum, left-handed children are not necessarily clumsier than right-handed children. They are somewhat more prone to allergies. Academically, left-handedness is associated with positive as well as negative outcomes. Because handedness may reflect the differential development of the hemispheres of the cortex, there is no point in struggling to write with the nondominant hand. After all, would training right-handed children to write with their left hands help them in math?

Active Review

9. (Girls or Boys?) are somewhat better at tasks requiring balance and precision of movement.
10. (Girls or Boys?) show some advantage in throwing and kicking.
11. Motor activity begins to (Increase or Decrease?) after 2 or 3 years of age.
12. During early childhood, (Girls or Boys?) tend to be more active.
13. Left-handed people have a (Higher or Lower?) incidence of language problems and psychological disorders compared with right-handed people.

Reflect & Relate: Think of left-handed people you know (perhaps including yourself). Do they seem to be awkward in any activities? Explain. Do you know anyone who was "changed" from a lefty to a righty? Why was the change made? How was it done? Was it successful? Explain.

Go to

http://www.thomsonedu.com/psychology/rathus

for an interactive version of this review.

Nutrition

Nutrition affects both physical and behavioral development. *Question: What are children's nutritional needs and their eating behavior like in early childhood?*

Nutritional Needs

As children move from infancy into the preschool years, their nutritional needs change. True, they still need to consume the basic foodstuffs—proteins, fats, carbohydrates, minerals, and vitamins—but more calories are required as children get older. For example, the average 4- to 6-year-old needs about 1,400 calories, compared with about 1,000 to 1,300 calories for the average 1- to 3-year-old (American Academy of Family Physicians, 2006). However, preschoolers grow at a slower rate than infants, so preschoolers need fewer calories per pound of body weight.

Patterns of Eating

During the second and third years, a child's appetite typically decreases and becomes erratic, often causing parents great worry. But it must be remembered that because the child is growing more slowly now, he or she needs fewer calories than before. Also, young children who eat less at one meal typically compensate by eating more at another. Children may develop strong (and strange) preferences for certain foods (Cooke et al., 2003). At one time during her third year, my daughter Allyn wanted to eat nothing but Spaghetti-O's.

Many children (and adults) consume excessive amounts of sugar and salt, which can be harmful to their health. Infants seem to be born liking the taste of sugar, although they are fairly indifferent to salty tastes. But preference for both sweet and salty foods increases if children are repeatedly exposed to them during childhood. Parents also serve as role models in the development of food preferences. If a parent—especially the parent who usually prepares meals—displays an obvious dislike for vegetables, children may develop a similar dislike (Hannon et al., 2003). The message to parents is clear: The eating habits you help create will probably last.

What is the best way to get children to eat their green peas or spinach or other healthful foods they may dislike? (Notice that it is rarely dessert that the child refuses to eat.) One method is to encourage the child to taste tiny amounts of the food 8 or 10 times within a period of a few weeks so that it becomes more familiar. Perhaps familiarity with food becomes content and not contempt.

■ Table 8.3 shows a healthful 1-day diet for a 4-year-old girl, a diet too high in sugar, and another too high in fat. Both the unhealthful diets are excessively high in calories, which can lead to the child's being overweight. Overweight children have a way of becoming overweight adults (American Academy of Family Physicians, 2006).

"He just learned in school that potato chips are vegetables."

Food Aversions
Strong preferences—and aversions—for certain foods may develop in early childhood.

■ **Table 8.3** Sample Meal Patterns for a Four-Year-Old Girl

Meal	Recommended	Excessive sugar	Excessive fat*
Breakfast	1/2 cup oatmeal 4 oz of 2 percent milk 1 orange	1 package of oatmeal with "dinosaur bones" 4 oz of 2 percent milk 4 oz orange juice	1 store-bought blueberry muffin with 1/2 Tbsp butter 4 oz of 2 percent milk 1 orange
Snack	1 apple, quartered 1 oz cheese	8 oz fruit punch drink 10 animal crackers	1 peanut butter granola bar with chocolate coating
Lunch	1/2 egg salad sandwich (1 boiled egg, 1 Tbsp mayonnaise, 1 slice wheat bread) 4 oz of 2 percent milk 10 baby carrots 1/2 banana	1/2 egg salad sandwich (1 boiled egg, 1 Tbsp mayonnaise, 2 slices wheat bread) 4 oz orange juice 10 baby carrots	1/2 egg salad sandwich (1 boiled egg, 2 Tbsp mayonnaise, 1/2 Tbsp butter, 1 slice wheat bread) 1/2 cup chocolate pudding 1/2 banana
Snack	1/2 raisin bagel 1 Tbsp peanut butter	1/2 plain bagel 1 Tbsp strawberry jam	1/4 bag (8 oz) plain potato chips *(continued)*

■ **Table 8.3** Sample Meal Patterns for a Four-Year-Old Girl (*continued*)

Meal	Recommended	Excessive sugar	Excessive fat*
Supper	1/2 chicken breast, grilled 1/2 cup cooked peas 1/2 cup cauliflower 1/2 cup cooked long-grain rice 4 oz of 2 percent milk 1/4 cantaloupe, cubed	1/2 chicken breast, grilled 1/2 cup cooked peas 1/2 cup cauliflower 1/2 cup cooked long-grain rice 4 oz apple juice 2 fruit-flavored wraps	6 chicken nuggets Medium order of French fries 4 oz of 2 percent milk Chocolate-covered ice cream bar
Snack	2 slices Black Forest ham 6 saltine crackers	1 store-bought blueberry muffin 1 Tbsp raspberry jam	2 slices Black Forest ham 6 saltine crackers
Nutritional information			
Calories	1,393	1,945	2,526
Fat (% calories)	43 g (28%)	39 g (18%)	130.6 g (47%)
Protein (g per kg)	70.2 g (4.4)	59.4 g (3.7)	65.7 g (4.1)
Fiber	25 g	21.8 g	18.9 g

Source: American Academy of Family Physicians (2006).

Note: Child's length is 39.5 inches (100 cm), and weight is 16 kg (35 lb, 3 oz).

*The high-fat meal pattern has adequate protein intake but almost no fruits or vegetables.

Active Review

14. During the second and third years, a child's appetite typically (Increases or Decreases?).

Reflect & Relate: Did you ever try to convince a 2- or 3-year-old to eat something? What did you do? What were the consequences?

Go to

http://www.thomsonedu.com/psychology/rathus

for an interactive version of this review.

Health and Illness

Almost all children get ill now and then. Some seem to be ill every other week or so. Most of these illnesses are minor, and children seem to eventually outgrow many of them, including ear infections. However, some illnesses are more serious. Fortunately, we have ways of preventing or curing a great many of them.

Questions: How healthy are children in the United States and in other countries? What are some of the illnesses and environmental hazards encountered during early childhood?

A Closer Look

Ten Things You Need to Know about Immunizations

1. **Why your child should be immunized.** Children need immunizations (shots) to protect them from dangerous childhood diseases. These diseases can have serious complications and even kill children.

2. **Diseases that childhood vaccines prevent:**
   • Diphtheria
   • *Haemophilus influenzae* type b (Hib disease, a major cause of bacterial meningitis)
   • Hepatitis A
   • Hepatitis B
   • Measles
   • Meningococcal
   • Mumps
   • Pertussis (whooping cough)
   • Pneumococcal (causes bacterial meningitis and blood infections)
   • Polio
   • Rotavirus
   • Rubella (German measles)
   • Tetanus (lockjaw)
   • Varicella (chickenpox)

   Audio, text-only, and other language versions of the Vaccine Information Sheets are available on the Centers for Disease Control website.

3. **Number of doses your child needs:** The following vaccinations are recommended by age two and can be given over five visits to a doctor or clinic:
   • 4 doses of diphtheria, tetanus & pertussis vaccine (DTaP)
   • 3–4 doses of Hib vaccine (depending on the brand used)
   • 4 doses of pneumococcal vaccine
   • 3 doses of polio vaccine
   • 2 doses of hepatitis A vaccine
   • 3 doses of hepatitis B vaccine
   • 1 dose of measles, mumps, and rubella vaccine (MMR)
   • 3 doses of rotavirus vaccine
   • 1 dose of varicella vaccine
   • 2–3 doses of influenza vaccine (6 months and older) (number of doses depends on child's birthday)

4. **Like any medicine, there may be minor side effects.** Side effects can occur with any medicine, including vaccines. Depending on the vaccine, the side effects can include slight fever, rash, and soreness at the site of injection. Slight discomfort is normal and should not be a cause for alarm. Your health-care provider can give you additional information.

5. **It's extremely rare, but vaccines can cause serious reactions, so weigh the risks!** Serious reactions to vaccines are extremely rare. The risks of serious disease from not vaccinating are far greater than the risks of serious reaction to a vaccination.

6. **What to do if your child has a serious reaction.** If you think your child is experiencing a persistent or severe reaction, call your doctor or get the child to a doctor right away. Write down what happened and the date and time it happened. Ask your doctor, nurse, or health department to file a Vaccine Adverse Event Report form or call 1-800-338-2382 to file this form yourself.

7. **Why you should not wait to vaccinate.** Children under 5 are especially susceptible to disease because their immune systems have not built up the necessary defenses to fight infection. By immunizing on time (by age 2), you can protect your child from disease and also protect others at school or in day care.

8. **Be sure to track your shots via a health record.** A vaccination health record helps you and your health-care provider keep your child's vaccinations on schedule. If you move or change providers, having an accurate record might prevent your child from repeating vaccinations he or she has already had. A shot record should be started when your child receives his or her first vaccination and updated with each vaccination visit.

9. **Some are eligible for free vaccinations.** A federal program called Vaccines for Children provides free vaccines to eligible children, including those without health insurance coverage, all those who are enrolled in Medicaid, American Indians, and Alaskan Natives.

10. **More information is available.** General immunization questions can be answered by the CDC Contact Center at 1-800-CDC-INFO (1-800-232-4636); English and Español.

Source: Centers for Disease Control and Prevention (2007b).

Reflect:
• Are you unclear about the meaning of any of the diseases these vaccinations protect against?
• Do you know whether or not the children in your life have gotten every recommended vaccine?
• Do you know what to do if a child has missed a vaccination?
• Do you know what to do if you are unsure of the answer to any of these questions?

■ **Table 8.5** Ten Leading Causes of Death in Early Childhood, United States, 2004, All Races, Both Sexes

Rank	Age Group 2–6
1	Unintentional Injury
2	Malignant neoplasms (cancer)
3	Congenital anomalies (malformations, deformations, and chromosomal abnormalities with which the child is born)
4	Homicide
5	Heart disease
6	Influenza and pneumonia
7	Benign neoplasms (usually nonfatal cancers)
8	Septicemia (blood poisoning)
9	Chronic respiratory disease
10	Cerebrovascular problems (e.g., stroke)

Source: Adapted from National Center for Injury Prevention and Control, Centers for Disease Control and Prevention (2007).

A CLOSER LOOK

Assessing and Minimizing the Risk of Lead Poisoning

People can get lead in their body if they put their hands or other objects covered with lead dust in their mouths, eat paint chips or soil that contains lead, or breathe in lead dust (especially during renovations that disturb painted surfaces). If not detected early, children with high levels of lead in their bodies can suffer from damage to the brain and nervous system, behavior and learning problems (such as hyperactivity), slowed growth, hearing problems, and headaches.

Lead is found mainly in paint. Many homes built before 1978 have lead-based paint. The federal government banned lead-based paint from housing in 1978. Some states stopped its use even earlier. Lead can also be found in homes in the city, country, or suburbs; in apartments, single-family homes, and both private and public housing; in soil inside and outside of a house; in household dust; and in drinking water. Your home might have plumbing with lead or lead solder. Call your local health department or water supplier to find out about testing your water. Use only cold water for drinking and cooking, and run water for 15 to 30 seconds before drinking it, especially if you have not used your water for a few hours. Lead is also found on some jobs, on old painted toys and furniture, on food and liquids stored in lead crystal or lead-glazed pottery or porcelain, and near lead smelters or other industries that release lead into the air.

Peeling, chipping, chalking, or cracking lead-based paint is a hazard and needs immediate attention. Lead-based paint may also be a hazard when found on surfaces that children can chew or that get a lot of wear-and-tear. Lead-based paint that is in good condition is usually not a hazard.

Consult your doctor for advice on testing your children. A simple blood test can detect high levels of lead. You can get your home checked in one of two ways, or both: A paint inspection tells you the lead content of every different type of painted surface in your home. A risk assessment tells you if there are any sources of serious lead exposure (such as peeling paint and lead dust). It also tells you what actions to take to address these hazards. Have qualified professionals do the work.

Contact the National Lead Information Center for more information:

By phone: 1-800-424-LEAD [5323].
By e-mail: http://www.epa.gov/lead/pubs/nlic.htm

Reflect: Have you checked your residence for the risk of lead poisoning? If not, why not? (Will you? When?)

Source: Abridged from the Environmental Protection Agency (2007).

(National Center for Injury Prevention and Control, 2007). The single most common cause of death in early childhood is motor vehicle accidents, followed by drowning and fires.

Accidents also are the major killer of children in most countries of the world, except for those developing nations still racked by high rates of malnutrition and disease. Injuries are responsible for nearly half the deaths of children 2 to 6 years of age and for more than half the deaths of children through the age of 14. Boys are more likely than girls to incur accidental injuries at all ages and in all socioeconomic groups.

Accidental injuries occur most often among low-income children. Poor children are five times as likely to die from fires and more than twice as likely to die in motor vehicle accidents than are children who are not poor (National Center for Injury Prevention and Control, 2007). The high accident rate of low-income children may result partly from living in dangerous housing and neighborhoods. Poor parents also are less likely than higher-income parents to take such preventive measures as using infant safety seats, fastening children's seat belts, installing smoke detectors, or having the telephone number of a poison control center. The families of children who are injured frequently may be more disorganized and under more stress than other families. Injuries often occur when family members are distracted and children are under minimal supervision.

Prevention of Accidental Injury

Legislation has helped reduce certain injuries in children (National Center for Injury Prevention and Control, 2007). All 50 states and the District of Columbia now require child safety seats in automobiles, and their use has decreased deaths resulting from automobile injuries. Most large cities in the United States also now have laws requiring installation of window guards in high-rise apartment buildings. In a number of countries, the risks of injury to children have been reduced because of legislation requiring manufacturers to meet safety standards for such items as toys and flammable clothing.

© Robert Glenn/Getty Images

Automobile Safety
Automobile accidents are the most common cause of death in young children in the United States. All 50 states and the District of Columbia now require child-restraint seats in automobiles. These laws have contributed to a reduction in child deaths and injuries.

Active Review

15. The most frequent cause of death of children in the United States is _____.
16. Many children are exposed to the poisonous metal _____ by eating chips of paint.

Reflect & Relate: What pollutants in your area are harmful to children? What can you do about them?

Go to

http://www.thomsonedu.com/psychology/rathus
for an interactive version of this review.

Sleep

Question: How much sleep is needed in early childhood? Children in the early years do not need as much sleep as infants. Most preschoolers sleep 10 to 11 hours in a 24-hour period (National Sleep Foundation, 2007) (see ■ Table 8.6). A common pattern includes 9 to 10 hours at night and a nap of 1 to 2 hours. In the United States,

■ **Table 8.6** Sleep Obtained by Children during a 24-Hour Period

	Infancy	Preschoolers	Younger School-Age Children	Older School-Age Children
Bottom 25%	11 hours or less	9.9 hours or less	9 hours or less	8.9 hours or less
Middle 50%	11.1–14.9 hours	10–11 hours	9.1–10 hours	9–9.9 hours
Upper 25%	15 hours or more	11.1 hours or more	10.1 hours or more	10 hours or more

Source: National Sleep Foundation (2007).

the young child's bedtime routine typically includes putting on pajamas, brushing teeth, and being read a story. Many young children also take a so-called **transitional object**—such as a favored blanket or a stuffed animal—to bed with them (Morelli et al., 1992). Such objects apparently help children make the transition to greater independence and separation from their parents.

But we're not ending the topic here, because it sounds much too easy. As too many parents know, getting children to sleep can be a major challenge of parenthood. Many children resist going to bed or going to sleep (Christophersen & Mortweet, 2003). A Japanese study suggests that getting to sleep late can be a problem, because preschoolers tend not to make up fully for lost sleep (Kohyama et al., 2002). But resisting sleep is a run-of-the-mill problem. In the next section we focus on more serious problems, called sleep disorders.

Sleep Disorders

Question: What kinds of problems or disorders disrupt sleep during early childhood? In this section, we focus on the sleep disorders of sleep terrors, nightmares, and sleep walking.

Sleep Terrors and Nightmares

First, a few words about terms. **Sleep terrors** are more severe than the anxiety dreams we refer to as nightmares. For one thing, sleep terrors usually occur during deep sleep. **Nightmares** take place during lighter rapid-eye-movement (REM) sleep, when about 80% of normal dreams occur. In fact, nightmares sort of qualify as "normal" dreams because of their frequency, not because of their desirability!

Deep sleep alternates with lighter REM sleep. Sleep terrors tend to occur early during the night, when periods of deep sleep are longest. Nightmares tend to occur more often in the morning hours, when periods of REM sleep tend to lengthen (National Sleep Foundation, 2007). Children have several periods of REM sleep a night and may dream in each one of them. Don't be confused by the fact that sleep terrors are sometimes referred to as *night terrors*. "Night terrors" always refer to sleep terrors and never to nightmares.

Sleep terrors usually begin in childhood or early adolescence and are outgrown by late adolescence. They are often but not always associated with stress, such as moving to a new neighborhood, attending school for the first time, adjusting to parental divorce, or being caught up in a war zone (Krippner & McIntyre, 2003). (Children are also more likely to experience nightmares during stressful periods.) Children with sleep terrors may wake up suddenly with a surge in heart and respiration rates, talk incoherently, and thrash about. Children are not completely awake during sleep terrors and may fall back into more restful sleep. Fortunately, the incidence of sleep terrors wanes as children develop and spend less time in deep sleep. Sleep terrors are all but absent among adults.

transitional object A soft, cuddly object often carried to bed by a child to ease the separation from parents.

sleep terrors Frightening dreamlike experiences that occur during the deepest stage of non-REM sleep, shortly after the child has gone to sleep.

nightmares Frightening dreams that occur during REM sleep, often in the morning hours.

Developing in a World of Diversity

Cross-Cultural Differences in Sleeping Arrangements

The commonly accepted practice in middle-class American families is for infants and children to sleep in separate beds and, when finances permit, in separate rooms from their parents. Child-care experts in the United States have generally endorsed this practice. Sleeping in the same room, they have sometimes warned, can lead to problems such as the development of overdependence, the difficulty of breaking the habit when the child gets older, and even accidental sexual stimulation of the child (Morelli et al., 1992).

Nevertheless, bed-sharing has more recently been promoted as a means for facilitating breast feeding (McCoy et al., 2004). In fact, co-sleeping or bed-sharing is the most common sleeping arrangement throughout the world for mothers who are breast feeding (Young, 2006). Although some are concerned that bed-sharing can be dangerous for an infant, with parents rolling onto them and crushing or suffocating them (Mesich, 2005), observational evidence suggests that such dangers are more likely to emanate from fathers than mothers and are least likely to derive from mothers who are breast feeding (Ball, 2006).

In many other cultures, as noted, children sleep with their mothers for the first few years of life, often in the same bed (Javo et al., 2004; Young, 2006). Co-sleeping occurs in cultures that are technologically advanced, such as Austria (Rothrauff et al., 2004) and Japan (Takahashi, 1990), as well as in those that are less technologically sophisticated, such as among the indigenous Sami people of Norway (Javo et al., 2004).

Resistance to going to bed occurs regularly in 20% to 40% of American infants and preschoolers

Getting Their Z's

In the United States, most parents believe that it is harmful or at least inappropriate for parents to sleep with their children. Parents in many other cultures are more relaxed about sleeping arrangements.

(Johnson, 1991), but it seldom occurs in cultures that practice co-sleeping. Some psychologists believe that the resistance shown by some young American children at bedtime is caused by the stress of separating from parents. This view is supported by the finding that young children who sleep with or near their parents are less likely to use transitional objects or to suck their thumbs at night than are children who sleep alone (Morelli et al., 1992; Wolf & Lozoff, 1989). Bed-sharing has also been shown to help children settle down and sleep better through the night especially children with developmental disabilities (Cotton & Richdale, 2006).

Research does not reveal harmful effects for co-sleeping. For example, an Austrian study found no significant differences between children's sleeping arrangements and their subsequent social development (Rothrauff et al., 2004). Among the Norwegian Sami, children not only slept with their parents but—also unlike other Norwegians—regulated their own sleeping and eating schedules. Sami parents were less tolerant of aggressive behavior in their children than Norwegian parents were. The outcome of all these cultural approaches was connected with relatively greater social independence among Sami children.

Reflect: *Would you (do you) allow your child to share your bed with you? Why or why not? Is your decision based on the scientific literature related to bed-sharing? (Should it be?)*

Children who have frequent nightmares or sleep terrors may come to fear going to sleep. They may show distress at bedtime, refuse to get into their pajamas, and insist that the lights be kept on during the night. As a result, they can develop **insomnia**. Children with frequent nightmares or sleep terrors need their parents' understanding and affection. They also profit from a regular routine in which they are expected to get to sleep at the same time each night (Christophersen & Mortweet, 2003). Yelling at them over their "immature" refusal to have the lights out and return to sleep will not alleviate their anxieties.

Sleep Walking

Sleep walking, or **somnambulism**, is much more common among children than adults. As with sleep terrors, sleep walking tends to occur during deep sleep (Stores & Wiggs, 2001). Onset is usually between the ages of 3 and 8.

During medieval times, people believed that sleep walking was a sign of possession by evil spirits. Psychoanalytic theory suggests that sleep walking allows people the chance to express feelings and impulses they would inhibit while awake. But children who sleepwalk have not been shown to have any more trouble controlling impulses than other children do. Moreover, what children do when they sleepwalk is usually too boring to suggest exotic motivation. They may rearrange toys, go to the bathroom, or go to the refrigerator and have a glass of milk. Then they return to their rooms and go back to bed. Their lack of recall in the morning is consistent with sleep terrors, which also occur during deep sleep. Sleep-walking episodes are brief; most tend to last no longer than half an hour.

There are some myths about sleep walking, such as that sleepwalkers' eyes are closed, that they will avoid harm, and that they will become violently agitated if they are awakened during an episode. All these notions are false. Sleepwalkers' eyes are usually open, although they may respond to onlooking parents as furniture to be walked around and not as people. Children may incur injury when sleep walking, just as they may when awake. **Truth or Fiction Revisited:** It is also not true that it is dangerous to awaken a sleepwalker. Children may be difficult to rouse when they are sleep walking, just as during sleep terrors, but if they are awakened, they are more likely to show confusion and disorientation (again, as during sleep terrors) than violence.

Today, sleep walking in children is assumed to reflect immaturity of the nervous system, not acting out of dreams or psychological conflicts. As with sleep terrors, the incidence of sleep walking drops as children develop. It may help to discuss a child's persistent sleep terrors or sleep walking with a health professional.

insomnia One or more sleep problems including falling asleep, difficulty remaining asleep during the night, and waking early.

somnambulism Sleep walking (from the Latin *somnus*, meaning "sleep," and *ambulare*, meaning "to walk").

Active Review

17. Most 2–3-year-olds sleep about _____ hours at night and also have one nap during the day.
18. (Nightmares or Sleep terrors?) usually occur during deep sleep.
19. _____ is also referred to as somnambulism.

Reflect & Relate: Critical thinkers insist on evidence before they will accept beliefs, even widely held cultural beliefs. What are your attitudes toward children sleeping with their parents? Are your attitudes supported by research evidence? Explain.

Go to

http://www.thomsonedu.com/psychology/rathus

for an interactive version of this review.

Elimination Disorders

The elimination of waste products occurs reflexively in neonates. As children develop, their task is to learn to inhibit the reflexes that govern urination and bowel movements. The process by which parents teach their children to inhibit these reflexes is referred to as toilet training. The inhibition of eliminatory reflexes makes polite conversation possible. *Questions: When are children considered to be gaining control over elimination too slowly? What can be done to help them gain control?*

Truth or Fiction Revisited: It is not true that more competent parents toilet train their children by the child's second birthday. Most American children are toilet trained between the ages of 3 and 4 (Scheres & Castellanos, 2003). They may have accidents at night for another year or so.

In toilet training, as in so many other areas of physical growth and development, maturation plays a crucial role. During the first year, only an exceptional child can be toilet trained, even when parents devote a great deal of time and energy to the task. If parents wait until the third year to begin toilet training, the process usually runs smoothly.

An end to diaper changing is not the only reason parents are motivated to toilet train their children. Parents often experience pressure from grandparents, other relatives, and friends who point out that so-and-so's children were all toilet trained before the age of _____. (You fill it in. Choose a number that will make most of us feel like inadequate parents.) Parents, in turn, may pressure their children to become toilet trained, and toilet training can become a major arena for parent–child conflict. Children who do not become toilet trained within reasonable time frames are said to have enuresis, encopresis, or both.

Toilet Training
If parents wait until the third year to begin toilet training, the process usually goes relatively rapidly and smoothly.

Enuresis

Give it a name like **enuresis** (en-you-REE-sis), and suddenly it looms like a serious medical problem rather than a bit of an annoyance. Enuresis is the failure to control the bladder (urination) once the "normal" age for achieving control of the bladder has been reached. Conceptions as to the normal age vary. The American Psychiatric Association (2000) is reasonably lenient on the issue and places the cutoff age at 5 years. The frequency of "accidents" is also an issue. The American Psychiatric Association does not consider such accidents enuresis unless the incidents occur at least twice a month for 5- and 6-year-olds or once a month for children who are older.

A nighttime accident is referred to as **bed-wetting**. Nighttime control is more difficult to achieve than daytime control. At night, children must first wake up when their bladders are full. Only then can they go to the bathroom.

Overall, 8% to 10% of American children wet their beds (Mellon & Houts, 2006), with the problem about twice as common among boys as girls. The incidence drops as age increases. A study of 3,344 Chinese children found that these children appeared to attain control a bit earlier: 7.7% obtained nocturnal urinary control by the age of 2, 53% by the age of 3, and 93% by the age of 5 (Liu et al., 2000b). As with American studies, girls achieved control earlier than boys.

Causes of Enuresis

It is believed that enuresis might have organic causes, such as infections of the urinary tract or kidney problems, or immaturity in development of the motor cortex of the brain (von Gontard, 2006; von Gontard et al., 2006). If so, cases with different causes might clear up at different rates or profit from different kinds of treatment. In the case of immaturity of parts of the brain, no treatment at all might be in order.

Numerous psychological explanations of enuresis have also been advanced. Psychoanalytic theory suggests that enuresis is a way of expressing hostility toward

enuresis (en-you-REE-sis) Failure to control the bladder (urination) once the normal age for control has been reached.

bed-wetting Failure to control the bladder during the night. (Frequently used interchangeably with enuresis, although bed-wetting refers to the behavior itself and enuresis is a diagnostic category, related to the age of the child.)

A CLOSER LOOK

What to Do about Bed-Wetting

Parents are understandably disturbed when their children continue to wet their beds long after most children are dry through the night. Cleaning up is a hassle, and parents also often wonder what their child's bed-wetting "means," about the child and about their own adequacy as parents.

Bed-wetting may only "mean" that the child is slower than most children to keep his or her bed dry through the night. Bed-wetting may mean nothing at all about the child's intelligence or personality or about the parents' capabilities (von Gontard et al., 2006). Certainly a number of devices (alarms) can be used to teach the child to awaken in response to bladder pressure (Ikeda et al., 2006). Medications also can be used to help the child retain fluids through the night (Sumner et al., 2006). Before turning to these methods, however, methods such as the following may be of help.

- **Limit fluid intake late in the day.** Less pressure on the bladder makes it easier to control urinating, but do not risk depriving the child of liquids. On the other hand, it makes sense to limit fluid intake in the evening, especially at bedtime. Because drinks with caffeine, such as colas, coffee, and tea, act as diuretics, making it more difficult to control urination, it is helpful to cut down on them after lunch.

- **Wake the child during the night.** Waking the child at midnight or 1:00 in the morning may make it possible for him or her to go to the bathroom and urinate. Children may complain and say that they don't have to go, but often they will. Praise the child for making the effort.

- **Try a night-light.** Many children fear getting up in the dark and trying to find their way to the bathroom. A night-light can make the difference. If the bathroom is far from the child's bedroom, it may be helpful to place a chamber pot in the bedroom. The child can empty the pot in the morning.

- **Maintain a consistent schedule so that the child can form helpful bedtime and nighttime habits.** Having a regular bedtime not only helps ensure that your child gets enough sleep but also enables the child to get into a routine of urinating before going to bed and keeps the child's internal clock in sync with the clock on the wall. Habits can be made to work for the child rather than against the child.

- **Use a "sandwich" bed.** A sandwich bed is simply a plastic sheet, covered with a cloth sheet, covered with yet another plastic sheet, and then still another cloth sheet. If the child wets his or her bed, the top wet sheet and plastic sheet can be pulled off, and the child can get back into a comfortable dry bed. In this way, the child develops the habit of sleeping in a dry bed. Moreover, the child learns how to handle his or her "own mess" by removing the wet sheets.

- **Have the child help clean up.** The child can throw the sheets into the wash and, perhaps, operate the washing machine. The child can make the bed or at least participate. These behaviors are not punishments; they help connect the child to the reality of what is going on and what needs to be done to clean things up.

- **Reward the child's successes.** Parents risk becoming overly punitive when they pay attention only to the child's failures. Ignoring successes also allows them to go unreinforced. When the child has a dry night, or half of a dry night, make a note of it. Track successes on a calendar. Connect them with small treats, such as more TV time or time with you. Make a "fuss," that is, a positive fuss. Also consider rewarding partial successes, such as the child getting up after beginning to urinate so that there is less urine in the bed.

- **Show a positive attitude.** ("Accentuate the positive.") Talk with your child about "staying dry" rather than "not wetting." Communicate the idea that you have confidence that things will get better. (They almost always do.)

Reflect:

- Why do so many parents "take it personally" when their children wet their beds?
- What do we mean when we say that children "outgrow" bed-wetting?
- How do you feel about giving a preschool child medicine to help curb bed-wetting? Explain.

parents (because of their harshness in toilet training) or a form of symbolic masturbation. These views are largely unsubstantiated. Learning theorists point out that enuresis is most common among children whose parents attempted to train them early. Early failures might have conditioned anxiety over attempts to control the bladder. Conditioned anxiety, then, prompts rather than inhibits urination.

Situational stresses seem to play a role. Children are more likely to wet their beds when they are entering school for the first time, when a sibling is born, or when they are ill. There may also be a genetic component in that there is a strong family history in the majority of cases (Bayoumi et al., 2006).

It has also been noted that bed-wetting tends to occur during the deepest stage of sleep. That is also the stage when sleep terrors and sleep walking take place. For this reason, bed-wetting could be considered a sleep disorder. Like sleep walking, bedwetting could reflect immaturity of certain parts of the nervous system (von Gontard, 2006). Just as children outgrow sleep terrors and sleep walking, they tend to outgrow bed-wetting (Mellon & Houts, 2006). In most cases, bed-wetting resolves itself by adolescence, and usually by the age of 8.

Encopresis

Soiling, or **encopresis**, is lack of control over the bowels. Soiling, like enuresis, is more common among boys than among girls, but the overall incidence of soiling is lower than that of enuresis. About 1% to 2% of children at the ages of 7 and 8 have continuing problems controlling their bowels (Mellon, 2006; von Gontard, 2006).

Soiling, in contrast to enuresis, is more likely to occur during the day. Thus, it can be acutely embarrassing to the child, especially in school.

Encopresis stems from both physical causes, such as chronic constipation, and psychological factors (Mellon, 2006; Needlman, 2001; von Gontard, 2006). Soiling may follow harsh punishment of toileting accidents, especially in children who are already anxious or under stress. Punishment may cause the child to tense up on the toilet, when moving one's bowels requires that one relax the anal sphincter muscles. Harsh punishment also focuses the child's attention on soiling. The child then begins to ruminate about soiling so that soiling, punishment, and worrying about future soiling become a vicious cycle.

We now leave our exploration of physical development in early childhood and begin an examination of cognitive development.

encopresis Failure to control the bowels once the normal age for bowel control has been reached. Also called soiling.

Active Review

20. In toilet training, maturation (Does or Does not?) play a crucial role.
21. Bed-wetting is more common among (Girls or Boys?).
22. A common physical cause of encopresis is _____.

Reflect & Relate: Why do you think so many parents become upset when their children are a bit behind others in toilet training? Do you think it is bad if it takes 3 or 4 years for a child to learn to use the toilet reliably? If so, why?

Go to

http://www.thomsonedu.com/psychology/rathus

for an interactive version of this review.

Active Learning Resources

Childhood & Adolescence Book Companion Website
http://www.thomsonedu.com/psychology/rathus

Visit your book companion website where you will find more resources to help you study. There you will find interactive versions of your book features, including the Lessons in Observation video, Active Review sections, and the Truth or Fiction feature. In addition, the companion website contains quizzing, flash cards, and a pronunciation glossary.

 is an easy-to-use online resource that helps you study in less time to get the grade you want—NOW.
http://www.thomsonedu.com/login

Need help studying? This site is your one-stop study shop. Take a Pre-Test and ThomsonNOW will generate a Personalized Study Plan based on your test results. The Study Plan will identify the topics you need to review and direct you to online resources to help you master those topics. You can then take a Post-Test to determine the concepts you have mastered and what you still need to work on.

Early Childhood:
Cognitive Development

was confused when my daughter Allyn, at the age of 2½, insisted that I continue to play "Billy Joel" on the stereo. Put aside the question of her taste in music. My problem was that when Allyn asked for Billy Joel, the name of the singer, she could be satisfied only by my playing the song "Moving Out." When "Moving Out" had ended and the next song, "The Stranger," had begun to play, she would insist that I play "Billy Joel" again. "That is Billy Joel," I would protest. "No, no," she would insist, "I want Billy Joel!"

Finally, it dawned on me that, for her, "Billy Joel" symbolized the song "Moving Out," not the name of the singer. Of course my insistence that the second song was also "Billy Joel" could not satisfy her! She was conceptualizing Billy Joel as a property of a particular song, not as the name of a person who could sing many songs.

Children between the ages of 2 and 4 tend to show confusion between symbols and the objects they represent. They do not yet recognize that words are arbitrary symbols for objects and events and that people can use different words. They tend to think of words as inherent properties of objects and events.

In this chapter, we discuss cognitive development during early childhood. First, we examine Jean Piaget's preoperational stage of cognitive development. Piaget largely viewed cognitive development in terms of maturation; however, in the section on factors in cognitive development, we will see that social and other factors foster cognitive development by placing children in "the zone," as Lev Vygotsky might have put it. Next, we consider other aspects of cognitive development, such as how children acquire a "theory of mind" and develop memory. Finally, we continue our exploration of language development.

Jean Piaget's Preoperational Stage

According to Piaget, the **preoperational stage** of cognitive development lasts from about age 2 to age 7. Be warned: Any resemblance between the logic of a preschooler and your own may be purely coincidental.

Symbolic Thought

Question: How do children in the preoperational stage think and behave? Preoperational thought is characterized by the use of symbols to represent objects and relationships among them. Perhaps the most important kind of symbolic activity of young children is language, but we will see that children's early use of language leaves something to be desired in the realm of logic.

Children begin to scribble and draw pictures in their early years. These drawings are symbols of objects, people, and events in children's lives. Symbolism is also expressed as symbolic or pretend play, which emerges during these years.

Symbolic or Pretend Play: "We Could Make Believe"

Children's **symbolic play**—the "let's pretend" type of play—may seem immature to busy adults meeting the realistic demands of the business world, but it requires cognitive sophistication (Feldman & Masalha, 2007; Keen et al., 2007; Lytle, 2003).

Piaget (1962 [1946]) wrote that pretend play usually begins in the second year, when the child begins to symbolize objects. The ability to engage in pretend play is based on the use and recollection of symbols, that is, on mental representations of things children have experienced or heard about. At 19 months, Allyn picked up a pinecone and looked it over. Her babysitter said, "That's a pinecone." Allyn pretended to lick it, as if it were an ice-cream cone.

preoperational stage
The second stage in Piaget's scheme, characterized by inflexible and irreversible mental manipulation of symbols.

symbolic play Play in which children make believe that objects and toys are other than what they are. Also called pretend play.

Children first engage in pretend play at about 12 or 13 months of age. They make believe that they are performing familiar activities, such as sleeping or feeding themselves. By age 15 to 20 months, they can shift their focus from themselves to others. A child may thus pretend to feed her doll. By 30 months, she or he can make believe that the other object takes an active role. The child may now pretend that the doll is feeding itself (McCune, 1993; Paavola et al., 2006; Thyssen, 2003).

© Elizabeth Crews

Symbolic Play
Symbolic play—also called pretend play—usually begins in the second year, when the child begins to form mental representations of objects. This 2½-year-old may engage in a sequence of play acts such as making a doll sit down at the table and offering it a make-believe cup of tea.

The quality of preschoolers' pretend play has implications for subsequent development. For example, preschoolers who engage in violent pretend play are less empathic, less likely to help other children, and more likely to engage in antisocial behavior later on (Dunn & Hughes, 2001). Preschoolers who engage in more elaborate pretend play are also more likely to do well in school later on (Stagnitti et al., 2000). The quality of pretend play is also connected with preschoolers' creativity and their ability to relate to peers (Russ, 2006).

Imaginary friends are one example of pretend play. At age 2, Allyn acquired an imaginary playmate named Loveliness. He told Allyn to do lots of things, such as move things from here to there and get food for him. At times, Allyn was overheard talking to Loveliness in her room. As many as 65% of preschoolers have such friends; they are more common among firstborn and only children than among children with siblings (Gleason et al., 2003).

Truth or Fiction Revisited: It is not true that having imaginary playmates is a sign of loneliness or psychological problems. Having an imaginary playmate does not mean that the child is having difficulty in real relationships (Gleason, 2004; Hoff, 2005). In fact, children with imaginary companions are less aggressive, more cooperative—they often nurture the imaginary friend (Gleason, 2002)—and more creative than children without such companions. They have more real friends, show greater ability to concentrate, and are more advanced in language development (Taylor, 1999).

As long as we are talking about play, let's note that some toys are called Transformers. In the following section, we see that the mental processes of children are also "transformers." (Clever transition from one section to another?)

Operations: "Transformers" of the Mind

Any resemblance between the logic of children ages 2 to 7 and your own may be purely coincidental. *Question: How do we characterize the logic of the preoperational child?* **Operations** are mental acts (or schemes) in which objects are changed or transformed and then can be returned to their original states. Mental operations are flexible and reversible.

Consider the example of planning a move in checkers. A move requires knowledge of the rules of the game. The child who plays the game well (as opposed to simply making moves) is able to picture the results of the move: how, in its new position, the piece will support or be threatened by other pieces and how other pieces might

operations Flexible, reversible mental manipulations of objects, in which objects can be mentally transformed and then returned to their original states.

be left undefended by the move. Playing checkers well requires that the child be able to picture, or focus on, different parts of the board and on relationships between pieces at the same time. By considering several moves, the child shows flexibility. By picturing the board as it would be after a move and then as it is, the child shows reversibility.

Having said all that, let us return to preoperational children, children who cannot yet engage in flexible and reversible mental operations. Young children's logic reflects that their ability to perform operations is "under construction." The preoperational stage is thus characterized by features such as egocentrism, immature notions about what causes what, confusion between mental and physical events, and the ability to focus on only one dimension at a time.

Egocentrism: It's All About Me

Sometimes the attitude "It's all about me" is a sign of early childhood, not of selfishness. One consequence of one-dimensional thinking is **egocentrism.** *Question: What is egocentrism?* Egocentrism, in Piaget's use of the term, does not mean that preoperational children are selfish (although, of course, they may be). Rather, it means that they do not understand that other people may have different perspectives on the world.

Truth or Fiction Revisited: Two-year-olds may, in fact, assume that their parents are aware of everything that is happening to them, even when their parents are not present. They may view the world as a stage that has been erected to meet their needs and amuse them. When I asked Allyn—still at the age of 2½—to tell me about a trip to the store with her mother, she answered, "You tell me." It did not occur to her that I could not see the world through her eyes.

Piaget used the "three-mountains test" (see ● Figure 9.1) to show that egocentrism literally prevents young children from taking the viewpoints of others. In this demonstration, the child sits at a table before a model of three mountains, which differ in color. One has a house on it, and another has a cross at the summit.

Piaget then placed a doll elsewhere on the table and asked the child what the doll sees. The language abilities of very young children do not permit them to provide verbal descriptions of what can be seen from where the doll is situated, so they can answer in one of two ways. They can either select a photograph taken from the proper vantage point, or they can construct another model of the mountains as they would be seen by the doll. The results of a classic experiment with the three-mountains test suggest that 5- and 6-year-olds usually select photos or build models that correspond to their own viewpoints (Laurendeau & Pinard, 1970).

Causality: Why? Because.

Preoperational children's responses to questions such as "Why does the sun shine?" show other facets of egocentrism. At the age of 2 or so, they may answer that they do not know or change the subject. **Truth or Fiction Revisited:** Three-year-olds may report themselves as doing things because they want to do them or "Because Mommy wants me to." In egocentric fashion, this explanation of behavior is extended to inanimate objects. The sun may thus be thought of as shining because it wants to shine or because someone (or something) else wants it to shine. In this case, the sun's behavior is thought of as being caused by will, perhaps the sun's wish to bathe the child in its rays or the child's wish to remain warm. In either case, the answer puts the child at the center of the conceptual universe. The sun becomes an instrument similar to a lightbulb.

Piaget labels this type of structuring of cause and effect **precausal.** *Question: What is precausal thinking?* Preoperational children believe that things happen for reasons and not by accident. However, unless preoperational children know the

egocentrism Putting oneself at the center of things such that one is unable to perceive the world from another person's point of view. Egocentrism is normal in early childhood but is a matter of choice, and rather intolerable, in adults. (Okay, I sneaked an editorial comment into a definition. Dr. Samuel Johnson also did that.)

precausal A type of thought in which natural cause-and-effect relationships are attributed to will and other preoperational concepts. (For example, the sun sets because it is tired.)

natural causes of an event, their reasons are likely to have an egocentric flavor and not be based on science. Consider the question, "Why does it get dark outside?" The preoperational child usually does not have knowledge of Earth's rotation and is likely to answer something like, "So I can go to sleep."

Another example of precausal thinking is **transductive reasoning.** In transductive reasoning, children reason by going from one specific isolated event to another. For example, a 3-year-old may argue that she should go on her swings in the backyard because it is light outside or that she should go to sleep because it is dark outside. That is, separate specific events, daylight and going on the swings (or being awake), are thought of as having cause-and-effect relationships.

Piaget used the three-mountains test to learn whether children at certain ages are egocentric or can take the viewpoints of others.

Preoperational children also show **animism** and **artificialism** in their attributions of causality. In animistic thinking, they attribute life and intentions to inanimate objects, such as the sun and the moon. ("Why is the moon gone during the day?" "It is afraid of the sun.") Artificialism assumes that environmental features such as rain and thunder have been designed and made by people. In *Six Psychological Studies,* Piaget (1967 [1964], p. 28) wrote: "Mountains 'grow' because stones have been manufactured and then planted. Lakes have been hollowed out, and for a long time the child believes that cities are built [before] the lakes adjacent to them."

■ Table 9.1 shows other examples of egocentrism, animism, and artificialism.

Confusion of Mental and Physical Events: On "Galaprocks" and Dreams That Are Real

What would you do if someone asked you to pretend you were a galaprock? Chances are, you might inquire what a galaprock is and how it behaves. So might a 5-year-old child. But a 3-year-old might not think that such information is necessary (Gottfried et al., 2003). Have you seen horror movies in which people's dreams become real? It could be said that preoperational children tend to live in such worlds, although, for them, that world is normal and not horrible.

Question: Why do young children think that they can pretend to be galaprocks without knowing what galaprocks are? According to Piaget, the preoperational child has difficulty making distinctions between mental and physical phenomena. Children between the ages of 2 and 4 show confusion between symbols and the things that they represent. Egocentrism contributes to the assumption that their thoughts exactly reflect external reality. They do not recognize that words are arbitrary and that people can use different words to refer to things. In *Play, Dreams, and Imitation in Childhood,* Piaget (1962 [1946]) asked a 4-year-old child, "Could you call this table a cup and that cup a table?" "No," the child responded. "Why not?" "Because," explained the child, "you can't drink out of a table!"

Another example of the preoperational child's confusion of the mental and the physical is the tendency to believe that dreams are real. Dreams are cognitive events that originate within the dreamer but seem to be perceived through the dreamer's senses. These facts are understood by 7-year-olds, but many 4-year-olds believe that dreams are real (Meyer & Shore, 2001). They think that their dreams are visible to others and that dreams come from the outside. It is as though they were watching a movie (Crain, 2000).

transductive reasoning Reasoning from the specific to the specific. (In deductive reasoning, one reasons from the general to the specific; in inductive reasoning, one reasons from the specific to the general.)

animism The attribution of life and intentionality to inanimate objects.

artificialism The belief that environmental features were made by people.

● **Figure 9.4**
Class Inclusion

A typical 4-year-old child will say that there are more dogs than animals in the example.

In one of Piaget's class-inclusion tasks, the child is shown several objects from two subclasses of a larger class (see ● Figure 9.4). For example, a 4-year-old child is shown pictures of four cats and six dogs. She is asked whether there are more dogs or more animals. Now, she knows what dogs and cats are. She also knows that they are both animals. What do you think she will say? Pre-operational children typically answer that there are more dogs than animals (Piaget, 1963 [1936]). That is, they do not show class inclusion.

Why do children make this error? According to Piaget, the preoperational child cannot think about the two subclasses and the larger class at the same time. Therefore, he or she cannot easily compare them. The child views dogs as dogs, or as animals, but finds it difficult to see them as both dogs and animals at once (Branco & Lourenço, 2004; Rabinowitz et al., 2002).

Evaluation of Piaget

Piaget was an astute observer of the cognitive processes of young children. But more recent research questions the accuracy of his age estimates concerning children's failures (or apparent failures) to display certain cognitive skills. For example, Donaldson (1979) argues that the difficulty young children have with the three-mountains test may not be due to egocentrism. Instead, she attributes much of the problem to the demands that this method makes on the child. The three-mountains test presents a

Lessons in Observation
Piaget's Preoperational Stage

To watch this video, visit the book companion website. You can also answer the questions and e-mail your responses to your professor.

Preoperational children, such as this young girl, fail to conserve volume. She believes that there is more liquid in the taller glass because she is focusing on height alone.

Learning Objectives

■ How do pretend play and symbolic representation illustrate Piaget's preoperational stage of development?
■ How do children show egocentrism?
■ What is the meaning of conservation in Piaget's theory?
■ How do children show failure to conserve?

Applied Lesson

How do preoperational inflexibility and irreversibility affect the children's failure to conserve in this video?

Critical Thinking

How did Piaget's experimental procedures and task demands influence the responses of children in conservation tasks?

Developing in a World of Diversity

Development of Concepts of Ethnicity and Race

Americans are encouraged to be "colorblind" in matters of employment, housing, and other areas in which discrimination has historically occurred (Quintana et al., 2006). However, children, like adults, are not literally colorblind. Therefore, it is fascinating to see how children's concepts of race and ethnicity develop. Knowledge of the connection between cognitive development and the development of concepts about people from different ethnic and racial backgrounds suggests when it might be most useful to intervene to help children develop open attitudes toward people from different backgrounds.

From interviews of 500 African American, Asian American, Latino and Latina American, and Native American children, psychologist Stephen Quintana (1998) concluded that children undergo four levels of understanding of ethnicity and race. Between the ages of 3 and 6, children generally think about racial differences in physical terms. They do not necessarily see race as a fixed or stable attribute. They may think that a person could change his or her race by means of surgery or tanning in the sun.

From age 6 to age 10, children generally understand that race is a matter of ancestry that affects not only physical appearance but also one's language, diet, and leisure activities. But understanding at this stage is literal, or concrete. For example, children believe that being Mexican American means that one speaks Spanish and eats Mexican-style food. Interethnic friendships are likely to develop among children of this age group.

From the age of about 10 to age 14, children tend to link ethnicity with social class. They become aware of connections between race and income, race and neighborhood, and race and affirmative action. During adolescence, many individuals begin to take pride in their ethnic heritage and experience a sense of belonging to their ethnic group. They are less open to intergroup relationships than younger children are.

Quintana's research found that middle childhood and early adolescence (ages 6 to 14) are probably the best times to fend off the development of prejudice by teaching children about people from different cultural backgrounds. "That's when [children are] able to go beyond the literal meaning of the words and address their own observations about race and ethnicity," he noted (cited in Rabasca, 2000). Children at these ages also tend to be more open to forming relationships with children from different backgrounds than they are during adolescence.

Reflect: *Why does Quintana suggest that early childhood might be too soon to try to prevent the development of prejudice? Do you agree? Explain.*

© Bonnie Kamin/PhotoEdit

If You Are Born White, Do You Remain White? If You Are Born Asian, Do You Remain Asian? If You Are Born . . .
According to research by Quintana, children between the ages of 3 and 6 tend to think about racial differences in physical terms. They do not necessarily see race as a fixed or stable attribute. They may think that people can change their race by means of surgery or sun tanning.

Factors in Cognitive Development

Question: What are some of the factors that influence cognitive development in early childhood? Two factors are Vygotsky's concepts of scaffolding and the zone of proximal development. Other factors include social and family factors: family income, parents' educational level, family size, parents' mental health, and stressful family events such as divorce, job loss, and illness (Bradley, 2006). In this section, we consider Vygotsky's theory, the home environment, preschool education, and television.

Scaffolding and the Zone of Proximal Development

Parental responsiveness and interaction with the child are key ingredients in the child's cognitive development. One component of this social interaction is **scaffolding** (see Chapter 1). A scaffold is a temporary structure used for holding workers during building construction. Similarly, cognitive scaffolding refers to temporary support provided by a parent or teacher to a learning child. The guidance provided by the adult decreases as the child gains skill and becomes capable of carrying out the task on her or his own (Lengua et al., 2007; Sylva et al., 2007).

A related concept is Vygotsky's **zone of proximal development (ZPD)**. The zone refers to the gap between what the child is capable of doing now and what she or he could do with help from others. Adults or older children can best guide the child through this zone by gearing their assistance to the child's capabilities (Lantolf & Thorne, 2007; Wennergren & Rönnerman, 2006). These researchers recognize that human neurobiology underlies cognitive development in early childhood. However, they argue that the key forms of children's cognitive activities develop through interaction with older, more experienced individuals who teach and guide them within appropriate learning environments such as schools and shops.

In a related study, K. Alison Clarke-Stewart and Robert Beck (1999) had 31 children, all 5-year-olds, observe a videotaped film segment with their mothers, talk about it with their mothers, and then retell the story to an experimenter. The researchers found that the quality of the stories, as retold by the children, was related to the scaffolding strategies the mothers had used with them. Children whose mothers focused the children's attention on the tape, asked their children to talk about it, and discussed the feelings of the characters told better stories than children whose mothers did not use such scaffolding strategies and children in a control group who did not discuss the story at all. Children's understanding of the characters' emotional states was most strongly connected with the number of questions the mother asked and her correction of the child's misunderstandings of what he or she saw.

Researchers observed 21 mother–child pairs as they engaged in specially constructed tasks when the children were 30, 36, and 42 months of age (Haden et al., 2001). They analyzed the children's recall of their performance 1 and 3 days afterward at all three ages. It turned out that the children best recalled those aspects of the tasks they had both worked on and discussed with their mothers. Recall under these circumstances exceeded recall when the activities were (1) handled jointly but talked about only by the mother or (2) handled jointly but not discussed.

In sum, scaffolding within a zone of proximal development helps children learn.

Being at HOME: The Effect of the Home Environment

Bettye Caldwell and her colleagues (e.g., Bradley, Caldwell, & Corwyn, 2003) developed a measure for evaluating children's home environments labeled, appropriately enough, HOME, an acronym for Home Observation for the Measurement of the Environment. With this method, researchers directly observe parent–child interaction

scaffolding Vygotsky's term for temporary cognitive structures or methods of solving problems that help the child as he or she learns to function independently.

zone of proximal development (ZPD) Vygotsky's term for the situation in which a child carries out tasks with the help of someone who is more skilled, frequently an adult who represents the culture in which the child develops.

■ Table 9.2 Scales of the HOME Inventory

Scale	Sample Items
Parental emotional and verbal responsiveness	• The parent spontaneously vocalizes to the child during the visit. • The parent responds to the child's vocalizations with vocal or other verbal responses.
Avoidance of restriction and punishment	• The parent does not shout at the child. • The parent does not interfere with the child's actions or restrict the child's movements more than three times during the visit.
Organization of the physical environment	• The child's play environment seems to be safe and free from hazards.
Provision of appropriate play materials	• The child has a push or a pull toy. • The child has one or more toys or pieces of equipment that promote muscle activity. • The family provides appropriate equipment to foster learning.
Parental involvement with child	• The parent structures the child's play periods. • The parent tends to keep the child within her or his visual range and looks at the child frequently.
Opportunities for variety in daily stimulation	• The child gets out of the house at least four times a week. • The parent reads stories to the child at least three times a week.

in the home. The HOME inventory contains six subscales, as shown in ■ Table 9.2. The HOME inventory items are better predictors of young children's later IQ scores than social class, mother's IQ, or infant IQ scores (Bradley, 2006; Luster & Dubow, 1992). Longitudinal research also shows that the home environment is connected with occupational success as an adult (Huesmann et al., 2006).

Truth or Fiction Revisited: It is true that early learning experiences affect children's levels of intellectual functioning. In a longitudinal study, Caldwell and her colleagues observed children from poor and working-class families over a period of years, starting at 6 months of age. The HOME inventory was used at the early ages, and standard IQ tests were given at ages 3 and 4. The children of mothers who were emotionally and verbally responsive, who were involved with their children, and who provided appropriate play materials and a variety of daily experiences during the early years showed advanced social and language development even at 6 months of age (Parks & Bradley, 1991). These children also attained higher IQ scores at ages 3 and 4 and higher achievement test scores at age 7. Other studies support the view that being responsive to preschoolers, stimulating them, and encouraging independence is connected with higher IQ scores and greater school achievement later on (Bradley, 2006; Bradley & Corwyn, 2006; Molfese et al., 1997). Victoria Molfese and her colleagues (1997) found that the home environment was the single most important predictor of scores on IQ tests among children aged 3 to 8.

© Jonathan Nourok/PhotoEdit

Sesame Street

Sesame Street is viewed regularly by an estimated 50% to 60% of children in the United States between the ages of 2 and 3 years. Research shows that regular viewing of the program improves children's cognitive and language skills.

increases children's learning of numbers, letters, and cognitive skills such as sorting and classification (Fisch, 2004). These effects are found for African American and European American children, girls and boys, and urban, suburban, and rural children.

Other researchers (e.g., Linebarger & Walker, 2005) reviewed the effects of watching a potpourri of children's TV shows, including *Sesame Street, Dora the Explorer, Blue's Clues, Arthur, Barney & Friends, Clifford, Teletubbies,* and *Dragon Tales.* Of these shows, watching *Dora the Explorer, Blue's Clues, Arthur, Clifford,* or *Dragon Tales* was associated with better vocabulary and expressive language scores on standardized tests for 30-month-old children. *Teletubbies* was associated with poorer vocabularies. *Sesame Street* yielded only a slight positive effect on expressive language. *Barney & Friends* had mixed effects, if any.

What about the effects of television on other aspects of cognitive behavior in the young child? Characters on *Sesame Street* talk out differences and do not fight with one another. Therefore, it is not surprising that most research indicates that exposure to such educational programs as *Sesame Street* may increase impulse control and concentration among preschoolers (Cole et al., 2003). In fact, a joint project by Israelis and Palestinians is under way to bring a Middle Eastern version of *Sesame Street* to the region in the hope that it may contribute to a more peaceful interaction between the groups (Lampel & Honig, 2006).

We can argue about just how much good a program like *Sesame Street* does, but few would argue that it does any harm. However, television programs—even those that target children—differ widely. Readers may profit from reviewing the suggested guidelines for helping children use television wisely in the nearby "A Closer Look" feature.

Commercials

Critics are concerned that the cognitive limitations of young children make them particularly susceptible to commercial messages, which can be potentially misleading and even harmful. Preschoolers do not understand the selling intent of advertising, and they often are unable to tell the difference between commercials and program content (Kundanis & Massaro, 2004; Palmer, 2003). Exposure to commercials does not make the child a sophisticated consumer. In fact, children who are heavy TV viewers are more likely than light viewers to believe commercial claims.

Commercials that encourage children to choose nutritionally inadequate foods—such as sugared breakfast cereals, candy, and fast foods—are harmful to children's nutritional beliefs and diets. Young children do not understand that sugary foods are detrimental to health, nor do they understand disclaimers in ads that, for example, state that sugared cereals should be part of a balanced breakfast (Palmer, 2003; Pine & Nash, 2002).

The Couch-Potato Effect

Watching television, of course, is also a sedentary activity. Parents might prefer that children spend more time exercising, but television also functions as an engrossing babysitter. However, research in the United States, England, and even China shows that preschool children who watch more television are more likely to be overweight than peers who watch less television (Hawkins & Law, 2006; Jago et al., 2006; Jiang et al., 2006). The American study in this case (Jago et al., 2006) found that the number of hours watching television was a stronger predictor of being overweight than diet!

A Closer Look

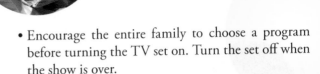

Helping Children Use Television Wisely

Overall, television appears to have some positive effects on cognitive development. But there is more to life than television. Let me share some ideas on how parents can help their children reap the benefits of television without allowing it to take over their lives.

General Suggestions

- Encourage children to watch educational programming.
- Help them choose among cartoon shows. Not all are filled with violence. *It's a Big, Big World* and *Rugrats* may help foster intellectual and social development.
- Encourage your children to sit with you when you are watching educational programming.
- If your child is spending too much time in front of the tube, keep a chart with the child of his or her total activities, including TV, homework, and play with friends. Discuss what to eliminate and what to substitute.
- Set a weekly viewing limit.
- Rule out TV at certain times, such as before breakfast or on school nights.
- Make a list of alternative activities, such as riding a bicycle, reading a book, working on a hobby.

© David Young-Wolff/PhotoEdit

TV, TV Everywhere: How Do We Teach Children to Stop to Think?
Parents can have a positive effect on children's cognitive processing of the information they glean from TV programs and commercials.

- Encourage the entire family to choose a program before turning the TV set on. Turn the set off when the show is over.

Coping with Violence

- Watch at least one episode of programs the child watches to see how violent they are.
- When viewing TV together, discuss the violence with the child. Talk about why the violence happened and how painful it is. Discuss how conflict can be resolved without violence.
- Explain to the child how violence on TV shows is faked.
- Encourage children to watch programs with characters who cooperate, help, and care for one another. Such programs can influence children in a positive way.

Applying TV to Real Life

- Ask children to compare what they see on the screen with people, places, and events they know firsthand, have read about, or have studied in school.
- Tell children what is real and what is make-believe on TV, such as the use of stunt people, dream sequences, and animation.
- Explain to the child your values with regard to sex, alcohol, and drugs.

Understanding Advertising

- Explain to children that the purpose of advertising is to sell products.
- On shopping trips, let children see that toys that look big, fast, and exciting on the screen are disappointingly small and slow close up.
- Talk to the child about nutrition. If the child can read package labels, allow her or him to choose a breakfast cereal from those in which sugar levels are low.

Reflect: Do you know parents who use television as a babysitter? What risks do they run?

The ability to understand false beliefs is related to the development of executive functioning, including working memory, ability to pay sustained attention to problems, and self-control (Flynn et al., 2004; Hala et al., 2003; Ziv & Frye, 2003).

Origins of Knowledge: Where Does It Come From?

Another aspect of theory of mind is how we acquire knowledge. *Questions: Do children understand where their knowledge comes from? If so, how early do they show this ability?*

By age 3, most children begin to realize that people gain knowledge about something by looking at it (Pratt & Bryant, 1990). By age 4, children understand that particular senses provide information about only certain qualities of an object; for example, we come to know an object's color through our eyes, but we learn about its weight by feeling it (O'Neill & Chong, 2001). In a study by Daniela O'Neill and Alison Gopnik (1991), 3-, 4-, and 5-year-olds learned about the contents of a toy tunnel in three different ways: They saw the contents, were told about them, or felt them. The children were then asked to state what was in the tunnel and also how they knew what was in the tunnel. Although 4- and 5-year-olds had no trouble identifying the sources of their knowledge, the 3-year-olds did. For example, after feeling but not seeing a ball in the tunnel, a number of 3-year-olds told the experimenter that they could tell it was a blue ball. The children apparently did not realize that it was impossible to discover the ball's color simply by feeling it.

The Appearance–Reality Distinction: Appearances Are More Deceiving at Some Ages than at Others

Questions: Is seeing believing? What do preoperational children have to say about that? One of the most important things children must acquire in developing a theory of mind is a clear understanding of the difference between real events, on the one hand, and mental events, fantasies, and misleading appearances, on the other hand (Bialystock & Senman, 2004; Flavell et al., 2002). This understanding is known as the **appearance–reality distinction.**

Piaget's view was that children do not differentiate reality from appearances or mental events until the age of 7 or 8. But more recent studies have found that children's ability to distinguish between the two emerges in the preschool years. Children as young as age 3 can distinguish between pretend actions and real actions, between pictures of objects and the actual objects, and between toy versions of an object and the real object (Cohen, 2006; Wellman, 2002). By the age of 4, children make a clear distinction between real items (such as a cup) and imagined items (such as an imagined cup or an imagined monster) (Harris et al., 1991).

Despite these accomplishments, preoperational children still show some difficulties in recognizing the difference between reality and appearances, perhaps because children of this age still have only a limited understanding of **mental representations.** They have trouble understanding that a real object or event can take many forms in our minds (Abelev & Markman, 2006). In a study by Marjorie Taylor and Barbara Hort (1990), children aged 3 to 5 were shown a variety of objects that had misleading appearances, such as an eraser that looked like a cookie. The children initially reported that the eraser looked like a cookie. However, once they learned that it was actually an eraser, they tended to report that it looked like an eraser, ignoring its cookie-like appearance. Apparently, the children could not mentally represent the eraser as both being an eraser and looking like a cookie.

Three-year-olds also apparently cannot understand changes in their mental states. In one study (Gopnik & Slaughter, 1991), 3-year-olds were shown a crayon box. They

appearance–reality distinction The difference between real events on the one hand and mental events, fantasies, and misleading appearances on the other hand.

mental representations The mental forms that a real object or event can take, which may differ from one another. (Successful problem solving is aided by accurate mental representation of the elements of the problem.)

consistently said they thought crayons were inside. The box was opened, revealing birthday candles, not crayons. When the children were asked what they had thought was in the box before it was opened, they now said "candles."

Two-and-a-half- to 3-year-olds also find it difficult to understand the relationship between a scale model and the larger object or space that it represents (Sharon & DeLoache, 2002; Ware et al., 2006). Perhaps it is because the child cannot conceive that the model can be two things at once: both a representation of something else and an object in its own right.

Active Review

14. Moses and Flavell used crayons and a clown to learn whether preschoolers can understand _____ beliefs.

15. By age 3, most children begin to realize that people gain knowledge about things through the _____.

Reflect & Relate: Think of research on the origins of knowledge, on where knowledge comes from. Can you relate this area of research to arguments we might find among adults about sources of knowledge such as experience versus revelation?

Go to

http://www.thomsonedu.com/psychology/rathus

for an interactive version of this review.

Development of Memory: Creating "Documents," Storing Them, Retrieving Them

Even newborns have some memory skills, and memory improves substantially throughout the first 2 years of life. *Question: What sorts of memory skills do children possess in early childhood?*

Memory Tasks: Recognition and Recall

Two of the basic tasks used in the study of memory are recognition and recall. Recognition is the easiest type of memory task. For this reason, multiple-choice tests are easier than fill-in-the-blank or essay tests. In a **recognition** test, one simply indicates whether a presented item has been seen before or which of a number of items is paired with a stimulus (as in a multiple-choice test). Children are capable of simple recognition during early infancy; they recognize their mother's nursing pads, her voice, and her face. To test recognition memory in a preschooler, you might show the child some objects and then present those objects along with some new ones. The child is then asked which objects you showed her the first time.

Recall is more difficult than recognition. In a **recall** task, children must reproduce material from memory without any cues. If I ask you to name the capital of Wyoming, that is a test of recall. A recall task for a preschooler might consist of showing her some objects, taking them away, and asking her to name the objects from memory.

recognition A memory task in which the individual indicates whether presented information has been experienced previously.

recall A memory task in which the individual must reproduce material from memory without any cues.

● **Figure 9.6** Recognition
and Recall Memory

Preschoolers can recognize previously seen objects (a) better than
they can recall them (b). They
also are better at recalling their
activities (c) than at recalling
objects (b). Older preschoolers
(green bars) have better memories
than younger ones (gold bars).

Source: Jones et al. (1988).

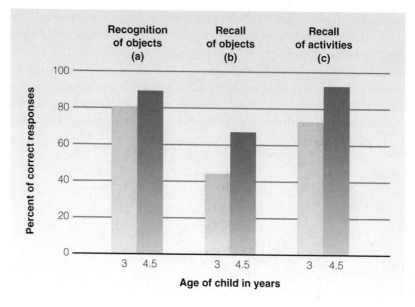

When preschoolers are presented with objects, words, or TV shows, they typically recognize more later on than they can recall (Holliday, 2003; Valkenburg &
Buijzen, 2005). In fact, younger preschoolers are almost as good as older ones in recognizing objects they have seen, but they are not nearly as good at recall (Holliday,
2003). In ● Figure 9.6, compare the ability of 3- and 4-year-olds to recognize and
recall various objects from a life-size playhouse (Jones et al., 1988). (We discuss the
"activities" part of this figure later.)

Competence of Memory in Early Childhood

Until recently, most studies of children's memory were conducted in laboratory settings. The tasks had little meaning for the children. The results appeared to show that
the memories of young children are deficient relative to those of older children. But
parents often tell you that their children have excellent memories for events. It turns
out that they are correct. Children, like adults, frequently remember what they *want*
to remember. More recently, psychologists have focused their research on children's
memory for meaningful events and activities.

Truth or Fiction Revisited: It is not true that 1- and 2-year-olds are too young
to remember past events. Children as young as 11½ months of age can remember
organized sequences of events they have just experienced (Bauer & Mandler, 1992).
Even after a delay of 6 weeks, 16-month-old children can reenact a sequence of events
they experienced only one time, such as placing a ball in a cup, covering it with
another cup, and shaking the resulting "rattle" (Bauer & Mandler, 1990). By the
age of 4 years, children can remember events that occurred at least 1½ years earlier
(Fivush & Hammond, 1990).

Katherine Nelson (1990, 1993) interviewed children aged 2 to 5 to study their
memory for recurring events in their lives, such as having dinner, playing with friends,
and going to birthday parties. She found that even 3-year-olds can present coher-
ent, orderly accounts of familiar events. Furthermore, young children seem to form
scripts, which are abstract, generalized accounts of these repeated events. For example, in describing what happens during a birthday party, a child might say, "You play
games, open presents, and eat cake" (Fivush, 2002). Details of particular events often
are omitted. However, an unusual experience, such as a devastating hurricane, may
be remembered in detail for many years (Fivush et al., 2004).

scripts Abstract generalized
accounts of familiar repeated
events.

Young children begin forming scripts after experiencing an event only once. The script becomes more elaborate with repeated experiences. As might be expected, older preschoolers form detailed scripts more quickly than younger preschoolers (Fivush, 2002).

Even though children as young as 1 and 2 years of age clearly can remember events, these memories seldom last into adulthood. This memory of specific events—known as **autobiographical memory** or *episodic memory*—appears to be linked to the development of language skills. It is facilitated by children talking with their parents and others about past events (Nelson & Fivush, 2004).

Factors Influencing Memory

Question: What factors affect memory in early childhood? The factors that affect memory include what the child is asked to remember, the interest level of the child, the availability of retrieval cues or reminders, and what memory measure we are using. Let us discuss each factor in turn.

Types of Memory

Preschoolers' memories for activities are better than their memories for objects. Return to Figure 9.6. Compare children's accuracy in recalling the activities they engaged in while in the playhouse with their accuracy in recalling the objects they used. You will see that children were much better at recalling their activities (e.g., washing a shirt, chopping ice) than they were at recalling specific objects, such as shirts and ice picks (Jones et al., 1988).

Children also find it easier to remember events that follow a logical order than events that do not occur in a particular order. For instance, 3- and 5-year-olds have a better memory for the activities involved in making pretend cookies out of Play-Doh (you put the ingredients in the bowl, then mix the ingredients, then roll out the dough, and so on) than they do for the activities involved in sand play, which can occur in any order (Fivush et al., 1992).

Interest Level

There is nothing new about the idea that we pay more attention to the things that interest us. The world is abuzz with signals, and we tend to remember those to which we pay attention. Attention opens the door to memory.

Childhood Memory
Despite his youth, this boy will most likely remember traumatic experiences in detail for years to come.

Interest level and motivation also contribute to memory among young children (Ghetti & Alexander, 2004; Sales et al., 2003). Research consistently shows that (most) preschool boys are more interested in playing with toys such as cars and weapons, whereas (most) preschool girls are more interested in playing with dolls, dishes, and teddy bears. Later, the children typically show better recognition and recall for the toys in which they were interested (Martin & Ruble, 2004).

Retrieval Cues

To retrieve information (a file) from your computer's storage, you have to remember its name or some part of it. Then you can use a Find routine. The name is the retrieval cue. In the same way, we need retrieval cues to find things in our own memories.

Although young children can remember a great deal, they depend more than older children do on cues provided by adults to help them retrieve their memories.

autobiographical memory
The memory of specific episodes or events.

Consider the following interchange between a mother and her 2-year-old child (Hudson, 1990, p. 186):

> Mother: What did we look for in the grass and in the bushes?
> Child: Easter bunny.
> Mother: Did we hide candy eggs outside in the grass?
> Child: (nods)
> Mother: Remember looking for them? Who found two? Your brother?
> Child: Yes, brother.

Preschoolers whose parents elaborate on the child's experiences and ask questions that encourage the child to contribute information to the narrative remember an episode better than children whose parents simply provide reminders (Nelson & Fivush, 2004). Parental assistance is more important under some conditions than others. For example, when 4-year-olds were internally motivated to remember items needed to prepare their own sack lunches, they did equally well with or without parental coaching. But when the task was simply to recall a series of items, they did better with parental assistance (Rogoff & Mistry, 1990).

Types of Measurement

What we find is in part determined by how we measure it. Children's memory is often measured or assessed by asking them to say what they remember. But verbal reports, especially from preschoolers, appear to underestimate children's memory (Mandler, 1990). In one longitudinal study, children's memory for certain events was tested at age 2½ and again at age 4. Most of the information recalled at age 4 had not been mentioned at age 2½, indicating that when they were younger, the children remembered much more than they reported (Fivush & Hammond, 1990).

What measures might be more accurate than verbal report? One study found that when young children were allowed to use dolls to reenact an event, their recall was much better than when they gave a verbal report of the event (Goodman et al., 1990).

Memory Strategies: Remembering to Remember

Question: How do we remember to remember? When adults and older children are trying to remember things, they use strategies to help their memory. One common strategy is mental repetition, or **rehearsal**. If you are trying to remember a new friend's phone number, for example, you might repeat it several times. Another strategy is to organize things to be remembered into categories. Many students outline textbook chapters to prepare for an exam. Organizing information in a meaningful way makes it easier to learn and remember. Similarly, if you are going to buy some things at the grocery store, you might mentally group together items that belong to the same category: dairy items, produce, household cleaners, and so on.

Preschool children, though, generally do not appear to use memory strategies on their own initiative. Most young children do not spontaneously engage in rehearsal until about 5 years of age (Labrell & Ubersfeld, 2004). They also rarely group objects into related categories to help them remember. By about age 5, many children have learned to verbalize information silently to themselves by counting mentally, for example, rather than aloud.

Even very young children are capable of using some simple and concrete memory aids to help them remember. They engage in behaviors such as looking, pointing, and touching when trying to remember. For example, in a study by Judith DeLoache and her colleagues (1985), 18- to 24-month-old children observed as the experimenter hid a Big Bird doll under a pillow. Then they were given attractive toys to play with and, after a short period of time, were asked to find the hidden object. During the play

rehearsal Repetition.

interval, the children frequently looked or pointed at the hiding place or repeated the name of the hidden object. These behaviors suggest the beginning of the use of strategies to prompt the memory.

Young children also can be taught to successfully use strategies they might not use on their own. For example, 6-year-old children who are trained to rehearse show improvement in their ability to recall items on a memory test (Small, 1990). Similarly, having preschoolers sort objects into categories enhances memory (Howe, 2006; Lange & Pierce, 1992). Even 3- and 4-year-olds will use rehearsal and labeling if they are instructed to try to remember something (DeMarie et al., 2004; Fabricius & Cavalier, 1989).

The preschooler's use of memory strategies is not nearly as sophisticated as that of the school-age child. Children's use of memory strategies and understanding of how memory works advance greatly in middle childhood.

© Brad Wrobleski/Masterfile

Helping Young Children Remember
Memory functioning in early childhood—and at other ages—is aided when adults provide cues to help children remember. Adults can help by elaborating on the child's experiences and asking questions that encourage the child to contribute information.

Active Review

16. Children are capable of simple (Recognition or Recall?) during infancy.
17. Memory for events in one's life is referred to as _____ memory.
18. Preschoolers' memories for activities are (Better or Worse?) than their memories for objects.
19. Interest level is (Positively or Negatively?) connected with ability to remember.
20. Using mental repetition to remember is termed _____.

Reflect & Relate: How do you prepare for a test? How do you remember lists of new vocabulary words, for example? What strategies does your textbook author (that's me!) use to help you remember the subject matter in this course?

Go to
http://www.thomsonedu.com/psychology/rathus
for an interactive version of this review.

Language Development: Why "Daddy Goed Away"

Children's language skills grow dramatically during the preschool years. By the fourth year, children are asking adults and each other questions, taking turns talking, and engaging in lengthy conversations. *Question: What language developments occur during early childhood?* Some milestones of language development that occur during early childhood are shown in ■ Table 9.3. Let us consider a number of them.

Development of Vocabulary: Words, Words, and More Words

The development of vocabulary proceeds at an extraordinary pace during early childhood. Preschoolers learn an average of nine new words per day (Tamis-LaMonda et al., 2006). But how can that be possible when each new word has so many potential meanings? Consider the following example. A toddler observes a small, black dog

Active Learning Resources

Childhood & Adolescence Book Companion Website
http://www.thomsonedu.com/psychology/rathus

Visit your book companion website where you will find more resources to help you study. There you will find interactive versions of your book features, including the Lessons in Observation video, Active Review sections, and the Truth or Fiction feature. In addition, the companion website contains quizzing, flash cards, and a pronunciation glossary.

 is an easy-to-use online resource that helps you study in less time to get the grade you want—NOW.

http://www.thomsonedu.com/login

Need help studying? This site is your one-stop study shop. Take a Pre-Test and ThomsonNOW will generate a Personalized Study Plan based on your test results. The Study Plan will identify the topics you need to review and direct you to online resources to help you master those topics. You can then take a Post-Test to determine the concepts you have mastered and what you still need to work on.

Inductive Reasoning
Inductive methods for enforcing restrictions attempt to teach children the principles they should use in guiding their own behavior. This mother is using the inductive technique of reasoning.

with toddlers. "It hurts!" is an explanation, although a brief one. **Truth or Fiction Revisited:** Thus, there is a point in trying to reason with a 4-year-old. The inductive approach helps the child understand moral behavior and fosters prosocial behavior such as helping and sharing (Paulussen-Hoogeboom et al., 2007).

Power-Assertive Methods

Power-assertive methods include physical punishment and denial of privileges. Parents often justify physical punishment with sayings such as "Spare the rod, spoil the child." Parents may insist that power assertion is necessary because their children are noncompliant. However, the use of power-assertive methods is related to parental authoritarianism as well as to children's behavior (Roopnarine et al., 2006; Rudy & Grusec, 2006). Parental power assertion is associated with lower acceptance by peers, poorer grades, and higher rates of antisocial behavior in children (Roopnarine et al., 2006). The more parents use power-assertive techniques, the less children appear to develop internal standards of moral conduct. Parental punishment and rejection are often linked with aggression and delinquency (Rudy & Grusec, 2006).

Withdrawal of Love

Some parents control children by threatening them with withdrawal of love. They isolate or ignore misbehaving children. Because most children need parental approval and contact, loss of love can be more threatening to a child than physical punishment. Withdrawal of love may foster compliance, but it may also instill guilt and anxiety (Grusec, 2002).

Preschoolers more readily comply when asked to do something than when asked to stop doing something (Kochanska et al., 2001). One way to manage children who are doing something wrong or bad is to involve them in something else.

Parenting Styles: How Parents Transmit Values and Standards

Traditional views of the ways in which children acquire values and standards for behavior focus on parenting styles (Grusec, 2006). However, many other factors are involved, including the characteristics of a particular child, the child's situation, and other aspects of parental behavior.

Psychologist Diana Baumrind (1989, 1991b) focused on the relationship between parenting styles and the development of competent behavior in young children. She used the dimensions of warmth–coldness and restrictiveness–permissiveness to develop a grid of four parenting styles based on whether parents are high or low on each of the two dimensions, as seen in ■ Table 10.1. *Question: What are the parenting styles involved in the transmission of values and standards?*

Authoritative Parents

The parents of the most capable children are rated as high on both dimensions of behavior (see Table 10.1). They make strong efforts to control their children (i.e., they are highly restrictive), and they make strong demands for maturity. However, they also reason with their children and show them strong support and feelings of love. Baumrind applies the label **authoritative** to these parents not only to suggest that they have a clear vision of what they want their children to do, but also to suggest that they respect their children and provide them with warmth.

Compared with other children, the children of authoritative parents tend to show self-reliance and independence, high self-esteem, high levels of activity and exploratory behavior, and social competence. They are highly motivated to achieve and do well in school (Baumrind, 1989, 1991b; Grusec, 2006).

authoritative A child-rearing style in which parents are restrictive and demanding yet communicative and warm.

■ **Table 10.1** Baumrind's Patterns of Parenting

Parental Style	Parental Behavior Patterns	
	Restrictiveness and Control	Warmth and Responsiveness
Authoritative	High	High
Authoritarian	High	Low
Permissive–indulgent	Low	High
Rejecting–neglecting	Low	Low

© Masterfile

Permissive Parents
Some parents are considered permissive and demand little of their children in terms of mature behavior or control. Permissive–indulgent parents still provide plenty of warmth and support for their children, whereas rejecting–neglecting parents tend to neglect or ignore their children.

Authoritarian Parents

"Because I say so" could be the motto of parents that Baumrind labels **authoritarian.** These parents tend to value obedience regardless of the situation. Authoritarian parents have strict guidelines for right and wrong. They demand that their children accept these guidelines without question. Like authoritative parents, they are controlling. But unlike authoritative parents, their enforcement methods rely on force. Moreover, authoritarian parents do not communicate well with their children. They do not show respect for their children's viewpoints, and most researchers find them to be generally cold and rejecting. But among some ethnic groups—such as Egyptians—authoritarianism reflects cultural values, and these authoritarian parents may also be warm and reasonably flexible (Grusec, 2002; Rudy & Grusec, 2006).

In Baumrind's research, the sons of authoritarian parents were relatively hostile and defiant and the daughters were low in independence and dominance (Baumrind, 1989). Other researchers have found that children of authoritarian parents are less competent socially and academically than children of authoritative parents. Children of authoritarian parents also tend to be conflicted, anxious, and irritable. They are less friendly and spontaneous in their social interactions (Grusec, 2002). As adolescents, they may be conforming and obedient but have lower self-reliance and self-esteem.

Permissive Parents

Baumrind found two types of parents who are permissive as opposed to restrictive. One type is labeled permissive–indulgent and the other rejecting–neglecting. **Permissive–indulgent** parents are rated low in their attempts to control their children and in their demands for mature behavior. They are easygoing and unconventional. Their brand of permissiveness is accompanied by high nurturance (warmth and support).

Rejecting–neglecting parents also are rated low in their demands for mature behavior and their attempts to control their children. But unlike indulgent parents, they are low in support and responsiveness.

The neglectful parenting style is associated with poor outcomes for children. By and large, the children of neglectful parents are the least competent, responsible, and mature and the most prone to problem behaviors. Children of permissive–indulgent parents, like those of neglectful parents, show less competence in school and more deviant behavior (e.g., misconduct and substance abuse) than children of more restrictive, controlling parents. But children from permissive–indulgent homes, unlike those from neglectful homes, are fairly high in social competence and self-confidence (Baumrind, 1991a).

authoritarian A child-rearing style in which parents demand submission and obedience from their children but are not very communicative and warm.

permissive–indulgent A child-rearing style in which parents are not controlling and restrictive but are warm.

rejecting–neglecting A child-rearing style in which parents are neither restrictive and controlling nor supportive and responsive.

Birth Order: Not Just Where in the World but Also Where in the Family

Let me confess at the beginning of this section that I am an only child. As I was developing, I experienced what I imagine are most of the rewards and, yes, punishments of being an only child. First and perhaps foremost, I was the little king in my household in the Bronx. A petty tyrant at best, and at worst. I enjoyed all the resources my family had to offer: a relatively good allowance (with which I bought a comic book a day; Superman did nothing that escaped my young attention) and lots of parental attention. Because I got most of what I wanted, I never knew that we were poor.

On the other hand, for many years I was more comfortable relating to adults than to other children. And many times I was lonely in the home and wished that I had a sister or a brother. But these are the experiences of one person, and it is difficult to know how accurately they are recalled. So let's be more scientific about it. *Question: What does the research say about the effects of being a firstborn or an only child?*

Many differences in personality and achievement have been observed among firstborn and only children compared with later-born children. **Truth or Fiction Revisited:** It is true that firstborn children, as a group, are more highly motivated to achieve than later-born children (Latham & Budworth, 2007). As a group, firstborn and only children perform better academically (that's me) and are more cooperative (not so sure that was me) (Healy & Ellis, 2007). They are also helpful (not so sure), are adult-oriented (that's me), and are less aggressive than later-born children (I guess that was me; not easy to recall) (Beck et al., 2006; Braza et al., 2000; Zajonc, 2001). They also obtain higher standardized test scores, including intelligence and SAT scores (Kristensen & Bjerkedal, 2007; Sulloway, 2007; Zajonc & Mullally, 1997). An adoptee study found that first-reared children, regardless of their biological birth order, were more conscientious than later-reared children (Beer & Horn, 2000). As part of their achievement orientation, firstborn children also see themselves as being more in control of their successes (Phillips & Phillips, 2000). On the negative side, firstborn and only children show greater anxiety (that's me) and are less self-reliant (hmmm . . . I wonder) than later-born children.

Interviews with the parents of 478 children ranging in age from 3 to 9 years found that firstborn children are more likely than later-born children to have imaginary playmates (Bouldin & Pratt, 1999). It is Allyn, our firstborn, who had the imaginary playmate Loveliness. Our second-born (Jordan) and our third-born (Taylor) may have been too busy coping with older siblings to have imaginary playmates.

Later-born children may learn to act aggressively to compete for the attention of their parents and older siblings (Carey, 2007b). They must also deal with the fact that they do not come first (Downey, 2001). Perhaps for that reason, their self-concepts tend to be lower than those of firstborn or only children. But the social skills later-born children acquire from dealing with their family position seem to translate into greater popularity with peers (Carey, 2007). They tend to be more rebellious, liberal, and agreeable than firstborn children, factors that are connected with their popularity (Beck et al., 2006; Zweigenhaft & Von Ammon, 2000).

Differences in personality and achievement among firstborn and later-born children may be linked to contrasting styles in parenting (Carey, 2007). Firstborn children start life as only children. For a year or more, they receive the full attention of parents. Even after other children come along, parents still tend to relate more often to the first child. Parents continue to speak at levels appropriate for the firstborn. Parents impose tougher restrictions on firstborn children and make greater demands of them. Parents are more highly involved in the activities of their firstborn child. Firstborn children are often recruited to help teach younger siblings (Zajonc, 2001). As

I can testify, being asked to teach something (often) prompts one to learn something about it.

By and large, parents are more relaxed and flexible with later-born children. A firstborn child is aware of the greater permissiveness often given to later-born children and may complain about it. (Endlessly). Why are parents more indulgent with later-born children? They have probably gained some self-confidence in child rearing. They see that the firstborn child is turning out just fine. (All right, the firstborn child usually turns out to be just fine, and sometimes "just fine" needs to be qualified as "just fine much of the time.") Parents may therefore assume that later-born children will also turn out, well, just fine. In any event, my wife and I were more relaxed with Jordan and with Taylor than we were with Allyn.

There is a more negative interpretation of parents' relative "relaxation" in rearing later-born children. Parents have only so many resources, in terms of time, energy, and, yes, money. As new children come along, they dilute the resources so that not as much can be devoted to each child (Downey, 2001).

All right, then, siblings hold key places in child development. *Question: How do peers influence social and emotional development in early childhood?*

Tom Prettyman/PhotoEdit

Friendship

Friendship takes on different meanings as children develop. Preschoolers focus on sharing toys and activities. Five- to 7-year-olds report that friends are children with whom they have "fun." Sharing confidences becomes important in late childhood and in adolescence.

Peer Relationships

The importance of **peers** in the development of the young child is widely recognized. As children move into the preschool years, they spend more time in the company of other children. Peer interactions serve many functions. Children develop social skills—sharing, helping, taking turns, dealing with conflict—in the peer group. They learn how to lead and how to follow. Physical and cognitive skills develop through peer interactions. Peers also provide emotional support (Dishion & Stormshak, 2007; Grusec, 2006).

Infants first show positive interest in one another at about 6 months. If they are placed on the floor facing one another, they will smile, occasionally imitate one another, and often touch one another. Social interaction increases over the next few months, but during the first year, contacts between infants tend to be brief. In the second year, children show more interest in other children and interact by playing with one another's toys. But they still show relatively little social interaction (Gevers Deynoot-Schaub & Riksen-Walraven, 2006; Valentino et al., 2006). But by about 2 years of age, children imitate one another's play and engage in social games such as follow the leader (Fontaine, 2005; Kavanaugh, 2006). By the age of 2, children show preferences for a few particular playmates.

The preference of a toddler for certain other children is an early sign of friendship (Gleason & Hohmann, 2006; Sherwin-White, 2005). Friendship extends beyond casual interactions. It is characterized by shared positive experiences and feelings of attachment (Grusec, 2002; Park et al., 1993). Even early friendships can be fairly stable. One- to 6-year-olds tend to maintain their friendships from one year to the next, some for as long as 3 years (Rubin et al., 2006). On the other hand, parental conflict can spill over into peer conflict. Children of fighting parents are less tolerant of the bumps and bruises of peer relationships than children of more agreeable parents (Du Rocher Schudlich et al., 2004).

peers Children of the same age. (More generally, people of similar background and social standing.)

Social Behaviors: In the World, among Others

During the early childhood years, children make tremendous strides in the development of social skills and behavior. Their play activities increasingly involve other children. They learn how to share, cooperate, and comfort others. But young children, like adults, are complex beings. They can be aggressive at times as well as loving and helpful. We turn now to the development of social behaviors in the early years.

Play—Child's Play, That Is

*Question: **What do developmentalists know about child's play?*** While children play, developmentalists work to understand just how they do so. Researchers have found that play has many characteristics. It is meaningful, pleasurable, voluntary, and internally motivated (Elkind, 2007). Play is fun! But play also serves many important functions in the life of the young child (Elkind, 2007). Play helps children develop motor skills and coordination. It contributes to social development, because children learn to share play materials, take turns, and try on new roles through **dramatic play.** It supports the development of such cognitive qualities as curiosity, exploration, symbolic thinking, and problem solving. Play may even help children learn to control impulses (Elkind, 2007).

Play and Cognitive Development

Play contributes to and expresses milestones in cognitive development. Jean Piaget (1962 [1946]) identified kinds of play, each characterized by increasing cognitive complexity:

- *Functional play.* Beginning in the sensorimotor stage, the first kind of play involves repetitive motor activity, such as rolling a ball or running and laughing.
- *Symbolic play.* Also called pretend play, imaginative play, or dramatic play, symbolic play emerges toward the end of the sensorimotor stage and increases during early childhood. In symbolic play, children create settings and characters and scripts (Kavanaugh, 2006).
- *Constructive play.* Constructive play is common in early childhood. Children use objects or materials to draw something or make something, such as a tower of blocks.
- *Formal games.* The most complex form of play, according to Piaget, involves formal games with rules. Formal games include board games, which are sometimes enhanced or invented by children, and games involving motor skills, such as marbles and hopscotch, ball games involving sides or teams, and video games. Such games may involve social interaction as well as physical activity and rules. People play such games for a lifetime.

Mildred Parten, whom we discuss next, focused on the social dimensions of play.

Parten's Types of Play

In classic research on children's play, Mildred Parten (1932) observed the development of six types of play among 2- to 5-year-old nursery school children: unoccupied play, solitary play, onlooker play, parallel play, associative play, and cooperative play (see ■ Table 10.5). Solitary play and onlooker play are considered types of **nonsocial play,** that is, play in which children do not interact socially. Nonsocial play occurs more often in 2- and 3-year-olds than in older preschoolers. Parallel play, associative play,

dramatic play   Play in which children enact social roles; made possible by the attainment of symbolic thought. A form of pretend play.

nonsocial play   Forms of play (solitary play or onlooker play) in which play is not influenced by the play of nearby children.

■ **Table 10.5** Parten's Categories of Play

Category	Nonsocial or Social?	Description
Unoccupied play	Nonsocial	Children do not appear to be playing. They may engage in random movements that seem to be without a goal. Unoccupied play appears to be the least frequent kind of play in nursery schools.
Solitary play	Nonsocial	Children play with toys by themselves, independently of the children around them. Solitary players do not appear to be influenced by children around them. They make no effort to approach them.
Onlooker play	Nonsocial	Children observe other children who are at play. Onlookers frequently talk to the children they are observing and may make suggestions, but they do not overtly join in.
Parallel play	Social	Children play with toys similar to those of surrounding children. However, they treat the toys as they choose and do not directly interact with other children.
Associative play	Social	Children interact and share toys. However, they do not seem to share group goals. Although they interact, individuals still treat toys as they choose. The association with the other children appears to be more important than the nature of the activity. They seem to enjoy each other's company.
Cooperative play	Social	Children interact to achieve common, group goals. The play of each child is subordinated to the purposes of the group. One or two group members direct the activities of others. There is also a division of labor, with different children taking different roles. Children may pretend to be members of a family, animals, space monsters, and all sorts of creatures.

and cooperative play are considered **social play.** In each case, children are influenced by other children as they play. Parten found that associative play and cooperative play become common by age 5. They are more likely to be found among older and more experienced preschoolers (Dyer & Moneta, 2006). Girls are somewhat more likely than boys to engage in social play (Zheng & Colombo, 1989).

But there are exceptions to these age trends in social play. Nonsocial play can involve educational activities that foster cognitive development. In fact, many 4- and

social play Play in which children interact with and are influenced by the play of others. Examples are parallel play, associative play, and cooperative play.

Associative Play
Associative play is a form of social play in which children interact and share toys.

© Michael Newman / PhotoEdit

5-year-olds spend a good deal of time in parallel constructive play. For instance, they may work on puzzles or build with blocks near other children. Parallel constructive players are frequently perceived by teachers to be socially skillful and are popular with their peers (Coplan et al., 1994). Some toddlers are also more capable of social play than one might expect, given their age. Two-year-olds with older siblings or with a great deal of group experience may engage in advanced forms of social play.

Lisa Serbin and her colleagues (2001) explored infants' visual preferences for gender-stereotyped toys using the time-honored assumption that infants spend more time looking at objects that are of greater interest to them. They found that both girls and boys showed significant preferences for gender-stereotyped toys by 18 months of age. Although preferences for gender-typed toys are well developed by the ages of 15 to 36 months, girls are more likely to stray from the stereotypes (Bussey & Bandura, 1999). Girls ask for and play with "boys' toys" such as cars and trucks more often than boys choose dolls and other "girls' toys." "Cross-role" activities may reflect the greater prestige of "masculine" activities and traits in American culture. Therefore, a boy's playing with "girls' toys" might be seen as taking on an inferior role. A girl's playing with "boys' toys" might be interpreted as having an understandable desire for power or esteem.

Sex Differences in Play

Question: Are there boys' toys and girls' toys? It appears that there are. The reasons are a bit harder to pin down.

Girls and boys differ not only in toy preferences but also in their choice of play environments and activities. During the preschool and early elementary school years, boys prefer vigorous physical outdoor activities such as climbing, playing with large vehicles, and rough-and-tumble play (Else-Quest et al., 2006). In middle childhood, boys spend more time than girls in large play groups of five or more children and spend more time in competitive play (Crombie & Desjardins, 1993; Else-Quest et al., 2006). Girls are more likely than boys to engage in arts and crafts and domestic play. Girls' activities are more closely directed and more structured by adults than are boys' activities (A. Campbell et al., 2002). Girls spend more time than boys playing with only one other child or with a small group of children (Crombie & Desjardins, 1993).

Why do children show these early preferences for gender-stereotyped toys and activities? Although one cannot rule out the possibility of biological factors, such as boys' slightly greater strength and activity levels and girls' slightly greater physical maturity and coordination, note that these differences are simply that—slight. On the other hand, parents and other adults treat girls and boys differently from birth onward. They consistently provide gender-stereotyped toys and room furnishings and encourage gender typing in children's play activities and even household chores (Leaper, 2002). Children, moreover, tend to seek out information on which kinds of toys and play are "masculine" or "feminine" and then conform to the label (Martin & Ruble, 2004).

A Girl Enjoying a Game of Baseball
Although preferences for gender-typed toys are well established by the age of 3, girls are more likely to stray from the stereotypes, as in this photograph of a girl playing the masculine-typed game of baseball.

Whom Do You Want to Play With?
During early and middle childhood, children tend to prefer the company of children of their own sex. Why?

Some studies find that children who "cross the line" by exhibiting an interest in toys or activities considered appropriate for the other sex are often teased, ridiculed, rejected, or ignored by their parents, teachers, other adults, and peers. Boys are more likely to be criticized than girls (Fagot & Hagan, 1991; Garvey, 1990). On the other hand, one study of 50 preschoolers—25 girls and 25 boys—found that most children believed that their peers should not be excluded from gender-typed play on the basis of sex (Theimer et al., 2001). That is, most believed that it was unfair to prevent girls from playing with trucks and boys from playing with dolls. Perhaps the inconsistency in research findings has something to do with the difference between what preschoolers are observed to do and what they say. (Why should children be more consistent than the rest of us?)

Another well-documented fact involving sex and play is that girls prefer the company of girls, whereas boys prefer to play with boys. This phenomenon is found in a wide variety of cultures and ethnic groups, and it appears early in life. Children begin to prefer playmates of the same sex by the age of 2, with girls developing this preference somewhat earlier than boys (Fagot, 1990; Hay et al., 2004; Strayer, 1990). The tendency to associate with peers of the same sex becomes stronger during middle childhood (Bukowski et al., 1993a; Crombie & Desjardins, 1993). Do you remember a period during your childhood when you and your friends found members of the other sex to be loathsome and wanted nothing to do with them?

Question: Why do children choose to associate with peers of their own sex? Eleanor Maccoby (1990b) believed that two factors are involved. One is that boys' play is more oriented toward dominance, aggression, and rough play than girls' play is. The second is that boys are not very responsive to girls' polite suggestions. Maccoby suggested that girls avoid boys because they want to protect themselves from boys' aggression and because they find it unpleasant to interact with unresponsive people. Boys may avoid the company of girls because they see girls as inferior (Caplan & Larkin, 1991).

Another view is that children "like" peers of their own sex more than peers of the other sex (Bukowski et al., 1993a). But "liking" is usually based on similarity in interests. Children who prefer dolls to transportation toys may prefer to associate with children who share their preference.

Prosocial Behavior: It Could Happen, and Does

My wife recalls always trying to help others in early childhood. She remembers sharing her toys, often at her own expense. She had many sad times when toys or favors she gave were not returned or when toys were broken by others.

Prosocial behavior, sometimes known as *altruism,* is behavior intended to benefit another without expectation of reward. Prosocial behavior includes helping and

prosocial behavior Behavior intended to benefit another without expectation of reward.

Theories of Aggression

Question: What causes aggression in children? What causes some children to be more aggressive than others? Aggression in childhood appears to result from a complex interplay of biological factors and environmental factors such as reinforcement and modeling.

Evolutionary Theory

Is aggression "natural"? According to evolutionary theory, more individuals are produced than can find food and survive into adulthood. Therefore, there is a struggle for survival. Individuals who possess characteristics that give them an advantage in this struggle are more likely to reach reproductive maturity and contribute their genes to the next generation. In many species, then, whatever genes are linked to aggressive behavior are more likely to be transmitted to new generations (Buss & Duntley, 2006; Vitaro et al., 2006).

Biological Factors

Evidence suggests that genetic factors may be involved in aggressive behavior, including criminal and antisocial behavior (Hicks et al., 2007; Lykken, 2006a; E. O. Wilson, 2004). Jasmine Tehrani and Sarnoff Mednick (2000) report that there is a greater concordance (agreement) rate for criminal behavior between monozygotic (MZ) twins, who fully share their genetic code, than dizygotic (DZ) twins, who, like other brothers and sisters, share only half of their genetic code.

If genetics is involved in aggression, genes may do their work at least in part through the male sex hormone testosterone. Testosterone is apparently connected with feelings of self-confidence, high activity levels, and—the negative side—aggressiveness (Archer, 2006; Cunningham & McGinnis, 2007; Popma et al., 2007). Males are more aggressive than females, and males have higher levels of testosterone than females (Pope et al., 2000). Studies show, for example, that 9- to 11-year-old boys with conduct disorders are likely to have higher testosterone levels than their less aggressive peers (A. Booth et al., 2003; Chance et al., 2000). Research with same-sex female DZ twins and opposite-sex female DZ twins suggests that fetal exposure to male sex hormones (in this case from a male fraternal twin) may heighten aggressiveness (Cohen-Bendahan et al., 2005).

Cognitive Factors

Aggressive boys are more likely than nonaggressive boys to incorrectly interpret the behavior of other children as potentially harmful (Dodge et al., 2002). This bias may make the aggressive child quick to respond aggressively in social situations. Research with primary schoolchildren finds that children who believe in the legitimacy of aggression are more likely to behave aggressively when they are presented with social provocations (Tapper & Boulton, 2004).

Aggressive children are also often found to be lacking in empathy and the ability to see things from the perspective of other people (Hastings et al., 2000). They fail to conceptualize the experiences of their victims, and so they are less likely to inhibit their aggressive impulses.

Social Learning

Social-cognitive explanations of aggression focus on the role of environmental factors such as reinforcement and observational learning. Children, like adults, are most likely to be aggressive when they are frustrated in attempts to gain something they want, such as attention or a toy. When children repeatedly push, shove, and hit to grab toys or break into line, other children usually let them have their way (Kempes et al., 2005). Children who are thus rewarded for acting aggressively are likely to continue to use aggressive means, especially if they do not have alternative means to achieving their ends.

Aggressive children may associate with peers who value their aggression and encourage it (Cairns & Cairns, 1991; Stauffacher & DeHart; 2006). Aggressive children have often been rejected by less aggressive peers, which decreases their motivation to please less aggressive children and reduces their opportunity to learn social skills (Henry et al., 2000; Walter & LaFreniere, 2000).

Parents may also encourage aggressive behavior, sometimes inadvertently. Gerald Patterson (2005) studied families in which parents use coercion as the primary means for controlling children's behavior. In a typical pattern, parents threaten, criticize, and punish a "difficult" or "impossible" child. The child then responds by whining, yelling, and refusing to comply until the parents give in. Both parents and child are relieved when the cycle ends. Thus, when the child misbehaves again, the parents become yet more coercive and the child yet more defiant, until parents or child gives in. A study with 407 children, all 5-year-olds, found that the Patterson model predicts aggressive behavior in both sexes (Eddy et al., 2001).

Children learn not only from the effects of their own behavior but also from observing the behavior of others. They may model the aggressive behavior of their peers, their parents, or their communities at large (Thomas et al., 2006). Children are more apt to imitate what their parents do than to heed what they say. If adults say they disapprove of aggression but smash furniture or hit each other when frustrated, children are likely to develop the notion that aggression is the way to handle frustration.

Truth or Fiction Revisited: It is true that children who are physically punished are more likely to be aggressive themselves than children who are not physically punished (Patterson, 2005). Physically aggressive parents serve as models for aggression and also stoke their children's anger.

Media Influences

Real people are not the only models of aggressive behavior in children's lives. A classic study by Albert Bandura and his colleagues (1963) suggested that televised models had a powerful influence on children's aggressive behavior. One group of preschool children observed a film of an adult model hitting and kicking an inflated Bobo doll, whereas a control group saw an aggression-free film. The experimental and control children were then left alone in a room with the same doll as hidden observers recorded their behavior. The children who had observed the aggressive model showed significantly more aggressive behavior toward the doll themselves (see ● Figure 10.2). Many children imitated bizarre attack behaviors devised for the model in this experiment, behaviors that they would not have thought up themselves.

The children exposed to the aggressive model also showed aggressive behavior patterns that had not been modeled. Therefore, observing the model not only led to imitation of modeled behavior patterns but also apparently **disinhibited** previously learned aggressive responses. The results were similar whether children observed human or cartoon models on film.

The Bandura study was a setup; it was an experimental setup, to be sure, but still a setup. It turns out that television is one of children's major sources of informal observational learning. It also turns out that television is a fertile source of aggressive models throughout much of the world (Villani, 2001). Children are routinely exposed to scenes of murder, beating, and sexual assault simply by turning on the TV set. **Truth or Fiction Revisited:** It is true that children who watch 2 to 4 hours of TV a day will see 8,000 murders and another 100,000 acts of violence by the time they have finished elementary school (Eron, 1993). Are children less likely to be exposed to violence by watching only G-rated movies? No. One study found that virtually all

disinhibit To stimulate a response that has been suppressed (inhibited) by showing a model engaging in that response without aversive consequences.

Albert Bandura / Dept. of Psychology, Stanford University

● **Figure 10.2**   Photos from Albert Bandura's Classic Experiment in the Imitation of Aggressive Models

Research by Albert Bandura and his colleagues has shown that children frequently imitate the aggressive behavior they observe. In the top row, an adult model strikes a clown doll. The second and third rows show a boy and a girl imitating the aggressive behavior.

G-rated animated films have scenes of violence, with a mean duration of 9 to 10 minutes per film (Yokota & Thompson, 2000). Other media that contain violence include movies, rock music and music videos, advertising, video games, and the Internet (Villani, 2001).

In any event, most organizations of health professionals agree that media violence does contribute to aggression (Holland, 2000; Villani, 2001). This relationship has been found for girls and boys of different ages, social classes, ethnic groups, and cultures. Consider a number of ways in which depictions of violence make such a contribution:

- *Observational learning.* Children learn from observation (Holland, 2000). TV violence supplies models of aggressive "skills," which children may acquire. Classic experiments show that children tend to imitate the aggressive behavior they see in the media (Bandura et al., 1963) (see Figure 10.2).
- *Disinhibition.* Punishment inhibits behavior. Conversely, media violence may disinhibit aggressive behavior, especially when media characters "get away" with violence or are rewarded for it.
- *Increased arousal.* Media violence and aggressive video games increase viewers' level of arousal. That is, television "works them up." We are more likely to be aggressive under high levels of arousal.
- *Priming of aggressive thoughts and memories.* Media violence "primes" or arouses aggressive ideas and memories (Bushman, 1998; Meier et al., 2006).

A CLOSER LOOK

When Doom *Leads to . . .* Doom: *What Children Learn from Violent Video Games*

Dylan Klebold and Eric Harris were engrossed in violent video games for hours at a time. They were particularly keen on a game named *Doom*. Harris had managed to reprogram *Doom* so that he, the player, became invulnerable and had an endless supply of weapons. He would "mow down" all the other characters in the game. His program caused some of the characters to ask God why they had been shot as they lay dying. Later on, Klebold and Harris asked some of their shooting victims at Columbine High School in Colorado whether they believed in God. One of the killers also referred to his shotgun as Arlene, the name of a character in *Doom* (Saunders, 2003).

In the small rural town of Bethel, Alaska, Evan Ramsey would play *Doom, Die Hard,* and *Resident Evil* for endless hours. Ramsey shot four people, killing two and wounding two. Afterward, he said the video games taught him that being shot would reduce a player's "health factor," but probably would not be lethal.

Michael Carneal was also a fan of *Doom* and another video game, *Redneck Revenge*. He showed up at school one morning with a semiautomatic pistol, two shotguns, and two rifles. He aimed them at people in a prayer group. Before he was finished, three people lay dead and five were wounded. Although Carneal had had no ap-

preciable experience with firearms, authorities noted that his aim was uncannily accurate. He fired just once at each person's head, as one would do to rack up points in a video game, especially a game that offers extra points for head shots.

The debate as to whether violence in media such as films, television, and video games fuel violence in the real world has been going on for many years. However, research strongly suggests that media violence is a risk factor for increasing emotional arousal, aggressive behavior, and violent thoughts (Arriaga et al., 2006; Buckley & Anderson, 2006; Sherry et al., 2006; Weber et al., 2006).

One reason to be particularly concerned about violent video games is that they require audience participation (Buckley & Anderson, 2006). Players don't just watch; they *participate*. Violent games like *Grand Theft Auto* have grown increasingly popular. Some games reward players for killing police, prostitutes, and bystanders. Virtual weapons include guns, knives, flamethrowers, swords, clubs, cars, hands, and feet. Sometimes the player assumes the role of a hero, but it is also common for the player to assume the role of a criminal.

What do we *learn* from violent video games and violence in other media, such as television, films, and books? The research suggests that we learn a great deal, not only aggressive skills, but also the idea that violence is the normal state of affairs.

© David Young-Wolff/Photo Edit

Reflect:

- Why is it that some, but not all, children react violently to violent video games?
- For debate: Should violent video games be censored?
- Have you ever played a violent video game? What were its effects on you?
- Why do you think that violent video games are more appealing to boys than girls?

- *Habituation.* We become "habituated to," or used to, repeated stimuli. Repeated exposure to TV violence may decrease viewers' sensitivity to real violence (Holland, 2000).

A joint statement issued by the American Medical Association, the American Academy of Pediatrics, the American Psychological Association, and the American Academy of Child and Adolescent Psychiatry (Holland, 2000) made some additional points:

- Children who see a lot of violence are more likely to view violence as an effective way of settling conflicts. Children exposed to violence are more likely to assume that violence is acceptable.
- Viewing violence can decrease the likelihood that one will take action on behalf of a victim when violence occurs.
- Viewing violence may lead to real-life violence. Children exposed to violent programming at a young age are more likely to be violent themselves later on in life.

There is no simple one-to-one connection between media violence and violence in real life. **Truth or Fiction Revisited:** Therefore, it is not true that children mechanically imitate the aggressive behavior they view in the media. But exposure to violence in the media increases the probability of violence in viewers in several ways.

There is apparently a circular relationship between exposure to media violence and aggressive behavior (Anderson & Dill, 2000; Eron, 1982; Funk et al., 2000). Yes, media violence contributes to aggressive behavior, but aggressive youngsters are also more likely to seek out this kind of "entertainment."

The family constellation also affects the likelihood that children will imitate the violence they see on TV. Studies find that parental substance abuse, physical punishments, and father absence contribute to the likelihood of aggression in early childhood (Bendersky et al., 2006; Chang et al., 2003; Roelofs et al., 2006). Parental rejection further increases the likelihood of aggression in children (Eron, 1982). These family factors suggest that the parents of aggressive children are absent or unlikely to help young children understand that the kinds of socially inappropriate behaviors they see in the media are not for them. A harsh home life may also confirm the TV viewer's vision of the world as a violent place and further encourage reliance on television for companionship. In Chapter 9, we saw how parents can help children understand that the violence they view in the media is not real and not to be imitated.

Active Review

6. In _____ play, children play with toys by themselves.

7. In _____ play, children interact and share toys.

8. Preschoolers tend to prefer to play with children of the (Other or Same?) sex.

9. _____ is another term for prosocial behavior.

10. Preschoolers tend to (Admire or Reject?) aggressive peers.

11. Aggressive behavior is linked with the hormone _____.

12. _____ theorists explain aggressive behavior in terms of reinforcement and observational learning.

13. The observation of aggression in the media tends to (Inhibit or Disinhibit?) aggressive behavior in children.

Reflect & Relate: Do you believe that violence in the media causes aggression? (What does the word *cause* mean?) Media violence is everywhere, not only in R-rated films but also in G-rated films and in video games. There are connections between media violence and aggression,

but not everyone who witnesses media violence behaves aggressively. So, how do we explain the connections between violence in the media and aggression?

Go to

http://www.thomsonedu.com/psychology/rathus

for an interactive version of this review.

Personality and Emotional Development

In the early childhood years, children's personalities start becoming more defined. Their sense of self—who they are and how they feel about themselves—continues to develop and becomes more complex. They begin to acquire a sense of their own abilities and their increasing mastery of the environment. As they move out into the world, they also face new experiences that may cause them to feel fearful and anxious. Let's explore some of these facets of personality and emotional development.

The Self

The sense of self, or the **self-concept,** emerges gradually during infancy. Infants and toddlers visually begin to recognize themselves and differentiate from other individuals such as their parents.

   Question: How does the self develop during early childhood? In the preschool years, children continue to develop their sense of self. Almost as soon as they begin to speak, they describe themselves in terms of certain categories, such as age groupings (baby, child, adult) and sex (girl, boy). These self-definitions that refer to concrete external traits have been called the **categorical self.**

   Children as young as 3 years are able to describe themselves in terms of behaviors and internal states that appear to occur frequently and are fairly stable over time (Eder, 1989, 1990). For example, in response to the question "How do you feel when you're scared?" young children frequently respond, "Usually like running away" (Eder, 1989). Or, in answer to the question "How do you usually act around grown-ups?" a typical response might be, "I mostly been good with grown-ups." Thus, even preschoolers seem to understand that they have stable characteristics that endure over time.

   One aspect of the self-concept is **self-esteem,** the value or worth that people attach to themselves. Children who have a good opinion of themselves during the preschool years are more likely to show secure attachment and have parents who are attentive to their needs (Booth-LaForce et al., 2006; Patterson & Bigler, 2006). They also are more likely to engage in prosocial behavior (Salmivalli et al., 2005).

   Preschool children begin to make evaluative judgments about two different aspects of themselves by the age of 4 (Harter & Pike, 1984). One is their cognitive and physical competence (e.g., being good at puzzles, counting, swinging, tying shoes), and the second is their social acceptance by peers and parents (e.g., having lots of friends, being read to by Mom) (Clark & Symons, 2004; Piek et al., 2006). But preschoolers do not yet make a clear distinction between different areas of competence. For example, a child of this age is not likely to report being good in school but poor in physical skills. One is either "good at doing things" or one is not (Harter & Pike, 1984).

self-concept One's impression of oneself; self-awareness.

categorical self Definitions of the self that refer to concrete external traits.

self-esteem The sense of value, or worth, that people attach to themselves.

Active Review

14. Self-definitions that refer to concrete external traits are called the _____ self.

15. Self-_____ is the value or worth that people attach to themselves.

16. Children who are _____ attached tend to have high self-esteem.

17. Erikson referred to early childhood as the stage of _____ versus guilt.

18. Early childhood fears tend to revolve around personal _____.

19. (Boys or Girls?) report more fears and higher levels of anxiety.

Reflect & Relate: Do you remember any fears from early childhood? Have they faded over the years?

Go to

http://www.thomsonedu.com/psychology/rathus
for an interactive version of this review.

Development of Gender Roles and Sex Differences

> I am woman, hear me roar . . . I am strong
> I am invincible
> I am woman

These lyrics are from the song "I Am Woman" by Helen Reddy and Ray Burton. They capture the attention because they run counter to the **stereotype** of the woman as vulnerable and in need of the protection of a man. The stereotype of the vulnerable woman, as with all stereotypes, is a fixed, oversimplified, and often distorted idea about a group of people, in this case, women. The stereotype of the chivalrous, protective man is also a stereotype. *Questions: What are stereotypes and gender roles? How do they develop?*

Cultural stereotypes of males and females involve broad expectations of behavior that we call **gender roles.** In our culture, the feminine gender-role stereotype includes such traits as dependence, gentleness, helpfulness, warmth, emotionality, submissiveness, and home orientation. The masculine gender-role stereotype includes aggressiveness, self-confidence, independence, competitiveness, and competence in business, math, and science (Miller et al., 2006).

Gender-role stereotypes appear to develop through a series of stages. First, children learn to label the sexes. At about 2 to 2½ years of age, they become quite accurate in identifying pictures of girls and boys (Fagot & Leinbach, 1993). By age 3, they display knowledge of gender stereotypes for toys, clothing, work, and activities (Campbell et al., 2004). For example, children of this age generally agree that boys play with cars and trucks, help their fathers, and tend to hit others. They also agree that girls play with dolls, help their mothers, and do not hit others (Cherney et al., 2006).

Showing distress apparently becomes gender typed so that preschoolers judge it to be acceptable for girls. One study found that preschool boys but not girls were rejected by their peers when they showed distress (Walter & LaFreniere, 2000). The

stereotype A fixed, conventional idea about a group.

gender role A complex cluster of traits and behaviors that are considered stereotypical of females and males.

same study found that peers rejected preschoolers of both sexes when they displayed too much anger.

Children become increasingly traditional in their stereotyping of activities, occupational roles, and personality traits between the ages of 3 and 9 or 10 (Miller et al., 2006). For example, traits such as "cruel" and "repairs broken things" are viewed as masculine, and traits such as "often is afraid" and "cooks and bakes" are seen as feminine. A study of 55 middle-class, primarily European American children, age 39–84 months, found that they considered men to be more competent in traditionally masculine-typed occupations (such as occupations in science and transportation) and women to be more competent in traditionally feminine-typed occupations (such as nursing and teaching) (Levy et al., 2000). The children equated competence with income: They believed that men earned more money in the masculine-typed jobs but that women earned more in the feminine-typed jobs.

Stereotyping levels off or declines beyond the preschool years (Martin & Ruble, 2004). Older children and adolescents apparently become somewhat more flexible in their perceptions of males and females. They retain the broad stereotypes but also perceive similarities between the sexes and recognize that there are individual differences. They are more capable of recognizing the arbitrary aspects of gender categories and more willing to try behaviors that typify the other sex.

Children and adolescents show some chauvinism by perceiving their own sex in a somewhat better light. For example, girls perceive other girls as nicer, more hardworking, and less selfish than boys. Boys, on the other hand, think that they are nicer, more hardworking, and less selfish than girls (Matlin, 2008; Miller et al., 2006).

Sex Differences

Clearly, females and males are anatomically different. And according to the gender-role stereotypes we have just examined, people believe that females and males also differ in their behaviors, personality characteristics, and abilities. *Question: How different are females and males in terms of cognitive and social and emotional development?*

Sex differences in infancy are small and rather inconsistent. In this chapter, we have reviewed sex differences during early childhood. Young girls and boys display some differences in their choices of toys and play activities. Boys engage in more rough-and-tumble play and also are more aggressive. Girls tend to show more empathy and to report more fears. Girls show greater verbal ability than boys, whereas boys show greater visual–spatial ability than girls. *Question: What are the origins of sex differences in behavior?* Different views have been proposed.

Theories of the Development of Sex Differences

Like mother, like daughter; like father, like son—at least often, if not always. Why is it that little girls (often) grow up to behave according to the cultural stereotypes of what it means to be female? Why is it that little boys (often) grow up to behave like male stereotypes? Let's have a look at various explanations of the development of sex differences.

The Roles of Evolution and Heredity

According to evolutionary psychologists, sex differences were fashioned by natural selection in response to problems in adaptation that were repeatedly encountered by humans over thousands of generations (Buss & Duntley, 2006; Geary, 2006). The story of the survival of our ancient ancestors is now etched in our genes. Genes that bestow attributes that increase an organism's chances of surviving to produce viable offspring are most likely to be transmitted to future generations. We thus possess the genetic codes for traits that helped our ancestors survive and reproduce. These traits include structural sex differences, such as those found in the brain, and differences in body chemistry, such as hormones.

Consider a sex difference. Males tend to place relatively more emphasis on physical appearance in mate selection than females do, whereas females tend to place relatively more emphasis on personal factors such as financial status and reliability (Buss, 2000; Schmitt, 2003). Why? Evolutionary psychologists believe that evolutionary forces favor the survival of women who seek status in their mates and men who seek physical allure because these preferences provide reproductive advantages. Some physical features such as cleanliness, good complexion, clear eyes, strong teeth and healthy hair, firm muscle tone, and a steady gait are found to be universally appealing to both males and females (Buss, 1999). Perhaps such traits have value as markers of better reproductive potential in prospective mates. According to the "parental investment model," a woman's appeal is more strongly connected with her age and health, both of which are markers of reproductive capacity. The value of men as reproducers, however, is more intertwined with factors that contribute to a stable environment for child rearing, such as social standing and reliability. For such reasons, these qualities may have grown relatively more alluring to women over the millennia (Brase, 2006).

This theory is largely speculative, however, and not fully consistent with all the evidence. Women, like men, are attracted to physically appealing partners, and women tend to marry men similar to them in physical attractiveness and socioeconomic standing.

But evolution has also led to the development of the human brain. As we see in the next section, the organization of the brain apparently plays a role in gender typing.

Organization of the Brain

The organization of the brain is largely genetically determined, and it at least in part involves prenatal exposure to sex hormones (Collins et al., 2000; Maccoby, 2000). The hemispheres of the brain are specialized to perform certain functions. In most people, the left hemisphere is more involved in language skills, whereas the right hemisphere is specialized to carry out visual–spatial tasks.

Both males and females have a left hemisphere and a right hemisphere. They also share other structures in the brain, but the question is whether they use them in quite the same way. Consider the hippocampus, a brain structure that is involved in the formation of memories and the relay of incoming sensory information to other parts of the brain (Ohnishi et al., 2006). Matthias Riepe and his colleagues (Grön et al., 2000) have studied the ways in which humans and rats use the hippocampus when they are navigating mazes. Males use the hippocampus in both hemispheres when they are navigating (Grön et al., 2000). Women, however, rely on the hippocampus in the right hemisphere in concert with the right prefrontal cortex, an area of the brain that evaluates information and makes plans. Researchers have also found that females tend to rely on landmarks when they are finding their way ("Go a block past Ollie's Noodle Shop, turn left, and go to the corner past Café Lalo"). Men rely more on geometry, as in finding one's position in terms of coordinates or on a map ("You're on the corner of Eleventh Avenue and 57th Street, and you want to get to Seventh Avenue and 55th Street,[2] so . . .) (Grön et al., 2000). Riepe and colleagues (Grön et al., 2000) speculated that a female's prefrontal activity represents the conscious effort to keep landmarks in mind. The "purer" hippocampal activity in males might represent a more geometric approach.

Some psychological activities, such as the understanding and production of language, are regulated by structures in the left hemisphere, particularly in Broca's area

---

[2]This is the location of the Carnegie Deli in New York. Cholesterol shmolesterol. You live just once. Go. Enjoy.

and Wernicke's area. But emotional and aesthetic responses, along with some other psychological activities, are more or less regulated in the right hemisphere. Brain-imaging research suggests that the left and right hemispheres of males may be more specialized than those of females (Shaywitz & Shaywitz, 2003). For example, if you damage the left hemisphere of a man's brain, you may cause greater language difficulties than if you cause similar damage in a woman. The right hemisphere is thought to be relatively more involved in spatial relations tasks, and damage in this hemisphere is more costly to a male's spatial-relations skills than to a female's.

If the brain hemispheres of women "get along better" than those of men—that is, if they better share the regulation of various cognitive activities—we may have an explanation of why women frequently outperform men in language tasks that involve some spatial organization, such as spelling, reading, and enunciation. Yet men, with more specialized spatial-relations skills, could be expected to generally outperform women at visualizing objects in space and reading maps.

Sex Hormones

Sex hormones and other chemical substances stoke the prenatal differentiation of sex organs. Toward the end of the embryonic stage, androgens—male sex hormones—are sculpting male genital organs. These chemicals may also "masculinize" or "feminize" the brain; in other words, they may give rise to behavioral tendencies that are consistent with gender-role stereotypes (Cohen-Bendahan et al., 2004; Pei et al., 2006).

Let us also consider psychological views of the development of sex differences.

Lessons in Observation
Gender

 To watch this video, visit the book companion website. You can also answer the questions and e-mail your responses to your professor.

When asked "What doll takes care of the babies?" children typically respond in a stereotypical manner by pointing to the female doll.

Learning Objectives

- At what age do children begin expressing stereotypical ideas about gender?
- What is the difference between gender identity and gender role?
- At what age do children seem to first understand that their own sex will remain stable?
- Are preschool children flexible or inflexible when it comes to their ideas concerning gender-typed behavior?

Applied Lesson

Describe the concepts of gender identity, gender stability, and gender constancy. How do they develop, according to Kohlberg? Does research support Kohlberg's view of when children should show preferences for gender-typed toys and activities?

Critical Thinking

If a child is reared without gender-typed toys in the household or if the child's parents avoid giving the child gender-typed messages about what kinds of behaviors are appropriate, how might that child's views on gender differ from those of his or her classmates? Are classmates likely to respond flexibly to that child's views of gender?

Social Cognitive Theory

Social cognitive theorists attempt to straddle the gulf between behaviorism and cognitive perspectives on human development. As such, they pay attention both to the roles of rewards and punishments (reinforcement) in gender typing and to the ways in which children learn from observing others and then decide what behaviors are appropriate for them. Children learn much about what society considers "masculine" or "feminine" by observing and imitating models of the same sex. These models may be their parents, other adults, other children, even characters in electronic media such as TV and video games.

The importance of observational learning was shown in a classic experiment conducted by Kay Bussey and Albert Bandura (1984). In this study, children obtained information on how society categorizes behavior patterns by observing how often they were performed either by men or by women. While children of ages 2 to 5 observed them, female and male adult role models exhibited different behavior patterns, such as choosing a blue or a green hat, marching or walking across a room, and repeating different words. Then the children were given a chance to imitate the models. Girls were twice as likely to imitate the woman's behavior as the man's, and boys were twice as likely to imitate the man's behaviors as the woman's.

Socialization also plays a role in gender typing. Parents, teachers, other adults—even other children—provide children with information about the gender-typed behaviors they are expected to display (Sabattini & Leaper, 2004). Children are rewarded with smiles and respect and companionship when they display "gender-appropriate" behavior. Children are punished (with frowns and "yucks" and loss of friends) when they display behavior considered inappropriate for their sex.

Boys are encouraged to be independent, whereas girls are more likely to be restricted and given help. Boys are allowed to roam farther from home at an earlier age and are more likely to be left unsupervised after school (Miller et al., 2006).

Fathers are more likely than mothers to communicate norms for gender-typed behaviors to their children (Miller et al., 2006). Mothers are usually less demanding. Fathers tend to encourage their sons to develop instrumental behavior (i.e., behavior that gets things done or accomplishes something) and their daughters to develop warm, nurturant behavior. Fathers are likely to cuddle daughters. By contrast, they are likely to toss their sons into the air and use hearty language with them, such as "How're yuh doin', Tiger?" and "Hey you, get your keister over here." Being a nontraditionalist, I would toss my young daughters into the air, which raised objections from relatives who criticized me for being too rough. This criticism, of course, led me to modify my behavior. I learned to toss my daughters into the air when the relatives were not around.

Acquiring Gender Roles

What psychological factors contribute to the acquisition of gender roles? Psychoanalytic theory focuses on the concept of identification. Social cognitive theory focuses on imitation of the behavior patterns of same-sex adults and reinforcement by parents and peers.

© Sylvie Villeger/Photo Researchers, Inc.

© Kathy Sloane/Photo Researchers, Inc.

Nature and Gender Typing

Deals with the roles of evolution, heredity, and biology in gender typing.

Perspective	Key Points	Comments
Evolution and heredity	Psychological sex differences were fashioned by natural selection in response to challenges that humans faced repeatedly over thousands of generations.	Evolutionary theorists believe that sex differences in aggression are natural. They suggest that a woman's allure is strongly connected with her age and health, which are markers of reproductive capacity, but the value of men as reproducers is also connected with factors that create a stable environment for child rearing.
Organization of the brain	The hemispheres of the brain are more specialized in males than in females.	Sex differences in brain organization might explain why women tend to excel in language skills and men in visual–spatial tasks.
Sex hormones	Sex hormones may prenatally "masculinize" or "feminize" the brain by creating predispositions consistent with gender roles.	Male rats are generally superior to females in maze-learning ability, a task that requires spatial skills. Aggressiveness appears to be connected with testosterone.

© Sylvie Villeger/Photo Researchers, Inc.

© Kathy Sloane/Photo Researchers, Inc.

Nurture and Gender Typing

Deals with theories in psychology—for example, learning theory, and cognitive theory—and related research.

Perspective	Key Points	Comments
Social cognitive theory	Children learn what is masculine or feminine by observational learning.	Parents and others tend to reinforce children for gender-appropriate behavior.
Cognitive-developmental theory	Gender typing is connected with the development of the concepts of gender identity, gender stability, and gender constancy.	Research evidence shows that children develop gender-typed preferences and behaviors before development of gender stability and gender constancy.
Gender-schema theory	Cultures tend to organize social life around polarized gender roles. Children accept these scripts and try to behave in accord with them.	Research evidence suggests that polarized female–male scripts pervade our culture. For example, children tend to distort their memories to conform to the gender schema.

Primary schoolchildren show less stereotyping if their mothers frequently engage in traditionally "masculine" household and child-care tasks such as yard work, washing the car, taking children to ball games, or assembling toys (Powlishta, 2004). Many daughters have mothers who serve as career-minded role models. Maternal employment is associated with less polarized gender-role concepts for girls and boys (Sabattini & Leaper, 2004; Powlishta, 2004). The daughters of employed women also have higher educational and career aspirations than daughters of unemployed women, and they are more likely to choose careers that are nontraditional for women.

Social cognitive theory has helped outline the ways in which rewards, punishments, and modeling foster gender-typed behavior. But how do rewards and punishment influence behavior? Do reinforcers mechanically increase the frequency of behavior, or, as suggested by cognitive theories, do they provide us with concepts that in turn guide our behavior? Let's consider two cognitive approaches to gender typing that address these matters: cognitive-developmental theory and gender-schema theory.

Cognitive-Developmental Theory

Lawrence Kohlberg (1966) proposed a cognitive-developmental view of gender typing. According to this perspective, children play an active role in gender typing (Martin & Ruble, 2004). They form concepts about gender and then fit their behavior to the concepts. These developments occur in stages and are entwined with general cognitive development.

According to Kohlberg, gender typing involves the emergence of three concepts: gender identity, gender stability, and gender constancy. The first step in gender typing is attaining **gender identity.** Gender identity is the knowledge that one is male or female. At 2 years, most children can say whether they are boys or girls. By the age of 3, many children can discriminate anatomic sex differences (Campbell et al., 2004; Ruble et al., 2006).

At around age 4 or 5, most children develop the concept of **gender stability,** according to Kohlberg. They recognize that people retain their sexes for a lifetime. Girls no longer believe that they can grow up to be daddies, and boys no longer think that they can become mommies. **Truth or Fiction Revisited:** Because most 2½-year-olds have not developed gender stability, a girl of this age may know that she is a girl but think that she can grow up to be a daddy.

By the age of 5 to 7 years, Kohlberg believes that most children develop the more sophisticated concept of **gender constancy.** Children with gender constancy recognize that sex does not change, even if people modify their dress or behavior. A woman who cuts her hair short remains a woman. A man who dons an apron and cooks dinner remains a man.

We could relabel gender constancy "conservation of gender," highlighting the theoretical debt to Jean Piaget. Indeed, researchers have found that the development of gender constancy is related to the development of conservation (de Lisi & Gallagher, 1991). According to cognitive-developmental theory, once children have established concepts of gender stability and constancy, they seek to behave in ways that are consistent with their sex (Martin & Ruble, 2004).

Cross-cultural studies in the United States, Samoa, Nepal, Belize, and Kenya (Munroe et al., 1984) have found that the concepts of gender identity, gender stability, and gender constancy emerge in the order predicted by Kohlberg (Leonard & Archer, 1989). Nevertheless, children may achieve gender constancy earlier than Kohlberg stated. Many 3- and 4-year-olds show some understanding of the concept (Leonard & Archer, 1989).

Kohlberg's theory also has difficulty accounting for the age at which gender-typed play emerges. Girls show preferences for dolls and soft toys and boys for hard

gender identity Knowledge that one is female or male. Also, the name of the first stage in Kohlberg's cognitive-developmental theory of the assumption of gender roles.

gender stability The concept that one's sex is a permanent feature.

gender constancy The concept that one's sex remains the same despite superficial changes in appearance or behavior.

transportation toys by the age of 1½ to 3 (Alexander, 2003; Campbell et al., 2004; Powlishta, 2004). At this age, children are likely to have a sense of gender identity, but gender stability and gender constancy remain a year or two away.

Gender-Schema Theory

Gender-schema theory proposes that children use sex as one way of organizing their perceptions of the world (Campbell et al., 2004; Martin & Ruble, 2004). A gender schema is a cluster of concepts about male and female physical traits, behaviors, and personality traits. For example, consider the dimension of strength–weakness. Children learn that strength is linked to the male gender-role stereotype and weakness to the female stereotype. They also learn that some dimensions, such as strength–weakness, are more relevant to one gender than the other—in this case, to males. A boy will learn that the strength he displays in weight training or wrestling affects the way others perceive him. But most girls do not find this trait to be important to others, unless they are competing in gymnastics, tennis, swimming, or other sports. Even so, boys are expected to compete in these sports and girls are not. A girl is likely to find that her gentleness and neatness are more important in the eyes of others than her strength.

From the viewpoint of gender-schema theory, gender identity alone can inspire "gender-appropriate" behavior (Ruble et al., 2006). As soon as children understand the labels "girl" and "boy," they seek information concerning gender-typed traits and try to live up to them. A boy may fight back when provoked because boys are expected to do so. A girl may be gentle and kind because that is expected of girls. Both boys' and girls' self-esteem will depend on how they measure up to the gender schema.

Studies indicate that children do possess information according to a gender schema. For example, boys show better memory for "masculine" toys, activities, and occupations, whereas girls show better memory for "feminine" toys, activities, and occupations (Martin & Ruble, 2004). However, gender-schema theory does not answer the question of whether biological forces also play a role in gender typing.

Psychological Androgyny

Let's be aboveboard about it. I have made several subtle suggestions about being male and about being female in this chapter. I have acknowledged that there is probably something biological involved in it, including brain organization and baths in bodily fluids that are brimming with sex hormones. But I have probably also suggested that we may put too much stock in what is "masculine" and what is "feminine" and that we may often do boys and girls more harm than good when we urge them to adhere to strict cultural stereotypes.

Cultural stereotypes tend to polarize females and males. They tend to push females and males to the imagined far ends of a continuum of gender-role traits (Rathus et al., 2008). It is common to label people as masculine or feminine. It is also common to assume that the more feminine people are, the less masculine they are, and vice versa. That is, the female U.S. Marines helicopter pilot usually is not conceptualized as wearing lipstick or baking. The tough male business executive is not usually conceptualized as changing diapers and playing peek-a-boo. An "emotional" boy who also shows the "feminine" traits of nurturance and tenderness is probably thought of as less masculine than other boys. Outspoken, competitive girls are likely to be seen not only as masculine but also as unfeminine.

However, the traits that supposedly characterize masculinity and femininity can be found within the same individual. That is, people (male or female) who obtain high scores on measures of masculine traits on personality tests can also score high on feminine traits. **Question: What is psychological androgyny?** People with both stereotypical feminine and masculine traits are termed **psychologically androgynous**

gender-schema theory The view that one's knowledge of the gender schema in one's society (the behavior patterns that are considered appropriate for men and women) guides one's assumption of gender-typed preferences and behavior patterns.

psychological androgyny Possession of both stereotypical feminine and masculine traits.

10. Why do children choose to associate with peers of their own sex?	Preschool children generally prefer playmates of their own sex partly because of shared interest in activities. Boys' play is more oriented toward dominance, aggression, and rough play.	
11. How does prosocial behavior develop?	Prosocial behavior—altruism—begins to develop in the first year, when children begin to share. Development of prosocial behavior is linked to the development of empathy and perspective taking. Girls show more empathy than boys do.	
12. How does aggression develop?	The aggression of preschoolers is frequently instrumental or possession oriented. By age 6 or 7, aggression becomes hostile and person oriented. Aggressive behavior appears to be generally stable and predictive of problems in adulthood.	
13. What causes aggression in children?	Genetic factors may be involved in aggressive behavior. Genes may be expressed in part through the male sex hormone testosterone. Impulsive and relatively fearless children are more likely to be aggressive. Aggressive boys are more likely than nonaggressive boys to incorrectly assume that other children mean them ill. Social cognitive theory suggests that children become aggressive as a result of frustration, reinforcement, and observational learning. Aggressive children are often rejected by less aggressive peers. Children who are physically punished are more likely to behave aggressively. Observing aggressive behavior teaches aggressive skills, disinhibits the child, and habituates children to violence.	
14. How does the self develop during early childhood?	Self-definitions that refer to concrete external traits are called the categorical self. Children as young as 3 years can describe themselves in terms of characteristic behaviors and internal states. Secure attachment and competence contribute to the development of self-esteem.	
15. What sorts of fears do children have in the early years?	Preschoolers are most likely to fear animals, imaginary creatures, and the dark; the theme involves threats to personal safety. Girls report more fears than boys do.	
16. What are stereotypes and gender roles? How do they develop?	A stereotype is a fixed conventional idea about a group. Females are stereotyped as dependent, gentle, and home oriented. Males are stereotyped as aggressive, self-confident, and independent. Cultural expectations of females and males are called gender roles.	
17. How different are females and males in terms of cognitive and social and emotional development?	Males tend to excel in math and spatial-relations skills, whereas girls tend to excel in verbal skills. Stereotypical gender preferences for toys and play activities are in evidence at an early age. Males are more aggressive and more interested in sex than females. The size and origins of all these sex differences is under debate.	
18. What are the origins of sex differences in behavior?	Testosterone may specialize the hemispheres of the brain, more so in males than in females, explaining why females excel in verbal skills that require some spatial organization, such as reading. Males might be better at specialized spatial-relations tasks. Male sex hormones are connected with greater maze-learning ability in rats and with aggressiveness. Social cognitive theorists explain the development of gender-typed behavior in terms of observational learning and socialization. According to Kohlberg's	

cognitive-developmental theory, gender-typing involves the emergence of three concepts: gender identity, gender stability, and gender constancy. According to gender-schema theory, preschoolers attempt to conform to the cultural gender schema.

19. **What is psychological androgyny?**

People with both stereotypical feminine and masculine traits are said to be psychologically androgynous. Theorists differ as to whether it is beneficial to promote psychological androgyny.

Key Terms

inductive, 333
authoritative, 334
authoritarian, 335
permissive–indulgent, 335
rejecting–neglecting, 335
individualist, 339
collectivist, 339
regression, 339
sibling rivalry, 339

peers, 341
dramatic play, 344
nonsocial play, 344
social play, 345
prosocial behavior, 347
empathy, 348
disinhibit, 351
self-concept, 355
categorical self, 355

self-esteem, 355
stereotype, 358
gender role, 358
gender identity, 364
gender stability, 364
gender constancy, 364
gender-schema theory, 365
psychological androgyny, 365

Active Learning Resources

Childhood & Adolescence Book Companion Website

http://www.thomsonedu.com/psychology/rathus

Visit your book companion website where you will find more resources to help you study. There you will find interactive versions of your book features, including the Lessons in Observation video, Active Review sections, and the Truth or Fiction feature. In addition, the companion website contains quizzing, flash cards, and a pronunciation glossary.

 is an easy-to-use online resource that helps you study in less time to get the grade you want—NOW.

http://www.thomsonedu.com/login

Need help studying? This site is your one-stop study shop. Take a Pre-Test and ThomsonNOW will generate a Personalized Study Plan based on your test results. The Study Plan will identify the topics you need to review and direct you to online resources to help you master those topics. You can then take a Post-Test to determine the concepts you have mastered and what you still need to work on.

t is 6-year old Jessica's first day of school. During recess, she runs to the climbing apparatus in the schoolyard and climbs to the top. As she reaches the top, she announces to the other children, "I'm coming down." She then walks to the parallel bars, goes halfway across, lets go, and tries again.

Steve and Mike are 8-year-olds. They are riding their bikes up and down the street. Steve tries riding with no hands on the handlebars. Mike starts riding fast, standing up on the pedals. Steve shouts, "Boy, you're going to break your neck!" (adapted from Rowen, 1973).

Middle childhood is a time for learning many new motor skills. Success in both gross and fine motor skills reflects children's increasing physical maturity, their opportunities to learn, and personality factors such as their persistence and self-confidence. Competence in motor skills enhances children's self-esteem and their acceptance by their peers.

In this chapter, we examine physical and motor development during middle childhood. We also discuss children with certain disabilities.

Growth Patterns

Question: What patterns of growth occur in middle childhood? Gains in height and weight are fairly steady throughout middle childhood. But notable variations in growth patterns also occur from child to child.

Height and Weight

Following the growth trends begun in early childhood, boys and girls continue to gain a little over 2 inches in height per year during the middle childhood years. This pattern of gradual gains does not vary significantly until children reach the adolescent **growth spurt** (see ● Figure 11.1). The average gain in weight between the ages of 6 and 12 is about 5 to 7 pounds a year. During these years, children continue to become less stocky and more slender (Kuczmarski et al., 2000).

Most deviations from these average height and weight figures are quite normal. Individual differences are more marked in middle childhood than they were earlier. For example, most 3-year-olds are within 8 to 10 pounds and 4 inches of one another. But by the age of 10, children's weights may vary by as much as 30 to 35 pounds, and their heights may vary by as much as 6 inches.

Nutrition and Growth

In middle childhood, average body weight doubles. Children also expend a good deal of energy as they engage in physical activity and play. To fuel this growth and activity, children need to eat more than they did in the preschool years. The average 4- to 6-year-old needs 1,400 to 1,800 calories per day. But the average 7- to 10-year-old requires 2,000 calories a day (Ekvall, 1993a).

Nutrition involves much more than calories, as we will see in the section on childhood obesity. The U.S. government has a food pyramid that suggests that it is healthful to eat fruits and vegetables, fish, poultry (without skin), and whole grains and to limit intake of fats, sugar, and starches. However, the food offered to children in school and elsewhere tends to be heavy on sugar, animal fats, and salt (Bauer et al., 2004). In addition, food portions have grown over the past couple of decades, particularly for salty snacks, desserts, soft drinks, fruit drinks, french fries, hamburgers, cheeseburgers, and Mexican food (Nielsen & Popkin, 2003). The largest portions are eaten at fast-food restaurants.

growth spurt A period during which growth advances at a dramatically rapid rate compared with other periods.

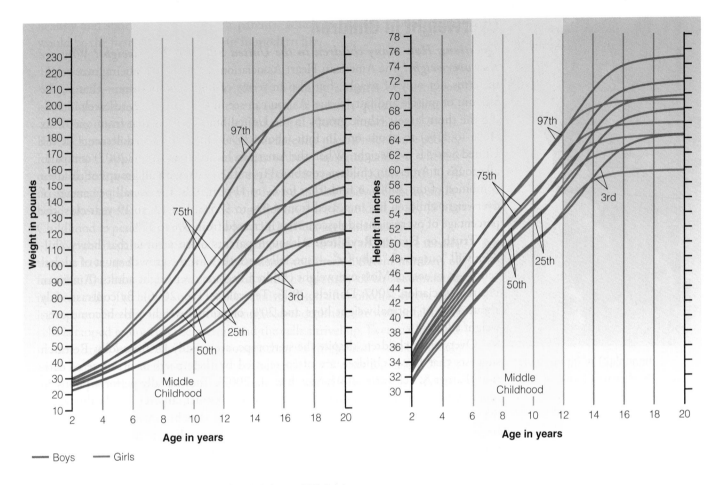

● **Figure 11.1** Growth Curves for Height and Weight

Gains in height and weight are fairly steady during middle childhood. Boys continue to be slightly heavier and taller than girls through 9 or 10 years of age. Girls then begin their adolescent growth spurt and surpass boys in height and weight until about age 13 or 14.

Source: Kuczmarski et al. (2000, Figures 9–12).

Nutrition and social class are also connected. Consider two studies with African American mothers and daughters. Daughters living at the poverty line were likely to be fed diets high in fats and fast foods (Miklos et al., 2004). Middle-class mothers, however, were concerned about the weight of their daughters and encouraged physical activity as a means of weight control. The mothers also tended to limit consumption of snack foods and sugar-laden carbonated beverages. Instead, they encouraged their daughters to drink water (V. J. Thompson et al., 2003).

Sex Similarities and Differences in Physical Growth

Figure 11.1 also reveals that boys continue to be slightly heavier and taller than girls through the age of 9 or 10. Girls then begin their adolescent growth spurt and surpass boys in height and weight until about age 13 or 14. At that time, boys are approaching the peak of their adolescent growth spurt, and they become taller and heavier than girls (Malina & Bouchard, 1991).

The steady gain in height and weight during middle childhood is paralleled by an increase in muscular strength for both girls and boys (Malina & Bouchard, 1991). The relative proportion of muscle and fatty tissue is about the same for boys and girls in early middle childhood. But this begins to change at about age 11, as males develop relatively more muscle tissue and females develop more fatty tissue (Michael, 1990).

Active Review

1. Gains in height and weight are generally (Abrupt or Steady?) throughout middle childhood.
2. Children gain a little over _____ inches in height per year during middle childhood.
3. They gain about _____ pounds a year.
4. (Boys or Girls?) are slightly heavier and taller through the age of 9 or 10.
5. Boys begin to become more muscular than girls at about the age of _____ .
6. About _____% of American children are overweight.
7. Children (Do or Do not?) tend to outgrow "baby fat."

8. Being overweight (Does or Does not?) run in families.

Reflect & Relate: How were overweight children treated by their peers in your elementary school? Were you sensitive to these children's feelings, or were you part of the problem?

Go to

http://www.thomsonedu.com/psychology/rathus

for an interactive version of this review.

Motor Development

Question: What changes in motor development occur in middle childhood? The school years are marked by increases in the child's speed, strength, agility, and balance (Abdelaziz et al., 2001; Loovis & Butterfield, 2000). These developments, in turn, lead to more skillful performance of motor activities, such as skipping.

Gross Motor Skills

Throughout middle childhood, children show steady improvement in their ability to perform various gross motor skills (Abdelaziz et al., 2001). School-age children are usually eager to participate in group games and athletic activities that require the movement of large muscles, such as catching and throwing balls. As seen in Concept Review 11.1, children are hopping, jumping, and climbing by age 6 or so; by age 6 or 7, they are usually capable of pedaling and balancing on a bicycle. By the ages of 8 to 10, children are showing the balance, coordination, and strength that allow them to engage in gymnastics and team sports.

During these years, the muscles are growing stronger, and the pathways that connect the cerebellum to the cortex are becoming increasingly myelinated. Experience also plays an indispensable role in refining many sensorimotor abilities, especially at championship levels, but individual differences that seem inborn are also present. Some people, for example, have better visual acuity or better depth perception than others. For such reasons, they will have an edge in playing the outfield or hitting a golf ball.

One of the most important factors in athletic performance is **reaction time,** or the amount of time required to respond to a stimulus. Reaction time is basic to the child's timing of a swing of the bat to meet the ball. Reaction time is also basic to

reaction time The amount of time required to respond to a stimulus.

adjusting to a fly ball or hitting a tennis ball. It is also involved in children's responses to cars and other (sometimes deadly) obstacles when they are riding their bicycles or running down the street.

Reaction time gradually improves (i.e., decreases) from early childhood to about age 18 (Abdelaziz et al., 2001; Karatekin et al., 2007). However, individual differences can be large (Largo et al., 2001). Reaction time begins to increase again in the adult years. Even so, 75-year-olds still outperform children. Baseball and volleyball may be "child's play," but, everything else being equal, adults will respond to the ball more quickly.

Fine Motor Skills

By the age of 6 to 7 years, children can usually tie their shoelaces and hold their pencils as adults do (see Concept Review 11.1). Their abilities to fasten buttons, zip zippers, brush teeth, wash themselves, coordinate a knife and fork, and use chopsticks all develop during the early school years and improve during childhood (Abdelaziz et al., 2001; Beilei et al., 2002).

Concept Review 11.1 — Development of Motor Skills during Middle Childhood

Age	Skills
Gross Motor Skills	
6 years	• Hops, jumps, climbs
7 years	• Balances on and pedals a bicycle
8 years	• Has good body balance
9 years	• Engages in vigorous bodily activities, especially team sports such as baseball, football, volleyball, and basketball
10 years	• Balances on one foot for 15 seconds; catches a fly ball
12 years	• Displays some awkwardness as a result of asynchronous bone and muscle development
Fine Motor Skills	
6–7 years	• Ties shoelaces • Throws ball by using wrist and finger release • Holds pencil with fingertips • Follows simple mazes • May be able to hit a ball with a bat
8–9 years	• Spaces words when writing • Writes and prints accurately and neatly • Copies a diamond shape correctly • Swings a hammer well • Sews and knits • Shows good hand–eye coordination

© David Fischer/Getty Images

© Monika Graff/The Image Works

Children with Disabilities

Certain disabilities of childhood are most apt to be noticed in the middle childhood years, when the child enters school. The school setting requires that a child sit still, pay attention, and master a number of academic skills. But some children have difficulty with one or more of these demands. In this section, we focus on children with various disabilities. ■ Table 11.1 highlights the types of disabilities that can affect a child's functioning, especially in school. Let us consider attention-deficit/hyperactivity disorder and learning disabilities in greater depth.

Attention-Deficit/Hyperactivity Disorder (ADHD)

Nine-year-old Eddie is a problem in class. His teacher complains that he is so restless and fidgety that the rest of the class cannot concentrate on their work. He hardly ever sits still. He is in constant motion, roaming the classroom, talking to other children while they are working. He has been suspended repeatedly for outrageous behavior, most recently swinging from a fluorescent light fixture and unable to get himself down. His mother reports that Eddie has been a problem since he was a toddler. By the age of 3, he had become unbearably restless and demanding. He has never needed much sleep and always awakened before anyone else in the family, making his way downstairs and wrecking things in the living room and kitchen. Once, at the age of 4, he unlocked the front door and wandered into traffic, but was rescued by a passerby.

Psychological testing shows Eddie to be average in academic ability but to have a "virtually nonexistent" attention span. He shows no interest in television or in games or toys that require some concentration. He is unpopular

■ Table 11.1 Types of Disabilities

Overall intellectual functioning	• Mental retardation (Chapter 12)
Learning disabilities*	• Reading disability (dyslexia) (this chapter)
	• Mathematics disability (dyscalculia) (this chapter)
	• Disorder of written expression
Speech disorders	• Articulation disorder
	• Voice disorders
	• Fluency disorders
Physical disabilities	• Visual impairment
	• Hearing impairment
	• Paralysis
Social and emotional disorders	• Attention-deficit/hyperactivity disorder (this chapter)
	• Autism spectrum disorders (Chapter 7)
	• Conduct disorders (Chapter 13)
	• Childhood depression (Chapter 13)
	• Childhood anxiety (Chapter 13)

* The American Psychiatric Association (2000) uses the term *learning disorder* rather than *learning disability*. Most educators appear to prefer the term *learning disability*.

with peers and prefers to ride his bike alone or to play with his dog. He has become disobedient at home and at school and has stolen small amounts of money from his parents and classmates.

Eddie has been treated with methylphenidate (Ritalin), but it was discontinued because it had no effect on his disobedience and stealing. However, it did seem to reduce his restlessness and increase his attention span at school.

—Adapted from Spitzer et al., 2002

Many parents think that their children do not pay enough attention to them, that they tend to run around as the whim strikes and to do things in their own way. Some inattention, especially at early ages, is to be expected. *Question: How does run-of-the-mill failure to "listen" to adults differ from attention-deficit/hyperactivity disorder?* In **attention-deficit/hyperactivity disorder (ADHD),** the child shows developmentally inappropriate or excessive inattention, impulsivity, and **hyperactivity** (Nigg et al., 2006; Weisler & Sussman, 2007). A more complete list of problems is shown in ■ Table 11.2. The degree of hyperactive behavior is crucial, because many normal children are labeled overactive and fidgety from time to time. In fact,

attention-deficit/hyperactivity disorder (ADHD) A behavior disorder characterized by excessive inattention, impulsiveness, and hyperactivity.

hyperactivity Excessive restlessness and overactivity; one of the primary characteristics of attention-deficit/hyperactivity disorder (ADHD). Not to be confused with misbehavior or with normal high-activity levels that occur during childhood.

■ **Table 11.2** Symptoms of Attention-Deficit/Hyperactivity Disorder (ADHD)

Kind of Problem	Specific Patterns of Behavior
Lack of attention	• Fails to attend to details or makes careless errors in schoolwork, and so on
	• Has difficulty sustaining attention in schoolwork or play activities
	• Does not appear to pay attention to what is being said
	• Fails to follow through on instructions or to finish work
	• Has trouble organizing work and other activities
	• Avoids work or activities that require sustained attention
	• Loses work tools (e.g., pencils, books, assignments, toys)
	• Becomes readily distracted
	• Is forgetful in daily activities
Hyperactivity	• Fidgets with hands or feet or squirms in his or her seat
	• Leaves seat in situations such as the classroom in which remaining seated is required
	• Constantly runs around or climbs on things; "running like a motor"
	• Has difficulty playing quietly
	• Shows excessive motor activity when asleep
	• Talks excessively
Impulsivity	• Often acts without thinking
	• Shifts from activity to activity
	• Cannot organize tasks or work
	• Requires constant supervision
	• Often "calls out" in class
	• Does not wait his or her turn in line, games, and so on

Source: Adapted from American Psychiatric Association (2000).

© Al Cook Photography

A Boy with Attention-Deficit/ Hyperactivity Disorder
Hyperactive children are continually on the go, as if their "motors" are constantly running. The psychological disorder we refer to as hyperactivity is not to be confused with the normal high energy levels of children. However, it is sometimes—*sometimes*—difficult to tell where one ends and the other begins.

if talking too much were the sole criterion for ADHD, the label would have applied to many of us.

The onset of ADHD occurs by age 7. According to the American Psychiatric Association (2000), the behavior pattern must have persisted for at least 6 months for the diagnosis to be made. The hyperactivity and restlessness of children with ADHD impair their ability to function in school. They simply cannot sit still. They also have difficulty getting along with others. Their disruptive and noncompliant behavior often elicits punishment from parents. ADHD is quite common. It is diagnosed in about 1% to 5% of school-age children and is one of the most common causes of childhood referrals to mental health clinics. ADHD is many times more common in boys than in girls.

Some psychologists and educators argue that ADHD is often "overdiagnosed" (Weisler & Sussman, 2007). That is, many children who do not toe the line in school tend to be diagnosed with ADHD and are medicated to encourage more acceptable behavior. Research also suggests that professionals who diagnose children with ADHD tend to be "suggestible." That is, they are more likely to diagnose children with the disorder when other sources of information—for example, from teachers and parents—say the children do not adequately control their behavior (Reddy & De Thomas, 2007; Wiesler & Sussman, 2007).

Causes of ADHD

Question: What are the causes of ADHD? Because ADHD is in part characterized by excessive motor activity, many theorists focus on possible physical causes. For one thing, ADHD tends to run in families, for both girls and boys (Faraone et al., 2000). Therefore, some researchers suggest there may be a genetic component to the disorder (Thapar et al., 2007; Walitza et al., 2006). If so, that genetic component might involve the brain messenger dopamine (Mazei-Robison et al., 2005; Walitza et al., 2006). Brain-imaging studies support the probability that many genes are involved and that they affect the brain's use of dopamine (Walitza et al., 2006).

ADHD is also found to coexist with other psychological disorders and problems, ranging from oppositional defiant disorder and anxiety disorders to mood disorders and even tics (Biederman et al., 2007; Hasler et al., 2007). Studies in brain imaging have found differences in the brain chemistry of children with ADHD and ADHD plus other disorders such as serious mood disorders, leading to the prospect that different causes and treatments will be discovered for various groups of children with ADHD.

In the 1970s, it was widely believed—because of anecdotal evidence presented by Benjamin Feingold—that artificial food colorings and (benzoate) food preservatives were largely responsible for hyperactivity. Feingold then introduced what became dubbed the "Feingold diet," which removed such chemicals from foods and, according to Feingold and a few researchers, reduced hyperactivity in children who used the diet. **Truth or Fiction Revisited:** However, over the years, studies in the use of the Feingold diet have yielded conflicting results, and researchers now generally agree that food coloring and preservatives have not been shown to cause the ADHD epidemic (Cruz & Bahna, 2006; Eigenmann & Haenggeli, 2004).

Joel T. Nigg (2001; Nigg et al., 2006) notes that children with ADHD do not *inhibit,* or control, impulses that most children can control. But Nigg argues that "inhibition" is defined differently by different theorists. Nigg (2001, Nigg et al., 2006) distinguishes between inhibition that is under the executive control of the brain—a sort of cognitive–neurological inhibition—and inhibition that is normally motivated by emotions such as anxiety and fear (e.g., anxiety about disappointing a teacher or fear of earning poor grades). Nigg argues that ADHD is unlikely to reflect failure to respond to feelings of anxiety or fear. He believes that the disorder is more

Developing in a World of Diversity

African American Youth and ADHD

The diagnosis and treatment of attention-deficit/hyperactivity disorder (ADHD) have come under scrutiny in the media and in medical circles, but as is often the case with medical concerns that become public issues, the focus has been almost exclusively on European American middle-class children (Hervey-Jumper et al., 2006).

African American children also suffer from ADHD, but cultural issues make diagnosis and treatment of the disorder challenging in these children, according to psychiatrist Gail Mattox (American Psychiatric Association, 2001). Although African American children respond to treatment as well as European American children do (Hervey-Jumper et al., 2006), European American children displaying comparable symptoms receive medications for ADHD at twice the rate of African American children.

Speaking at the 30th anniversary conference of the Black Psychiatrists of America, Mattox emphasized that a lack of "culturally competent providers" is one obstacle preventing African American children from getting optimal care for ADHD. Another challenge is poverty. Moreover, a substantial number are in the juvenile justice or child welfare systems, where the personnel change often and "inadequate medical care and diagnoses" are a fact of life.

Clinicians assessing or treating these youngsters must be aware of cultural considerations if their services are to be effective. For one thing, teachers are more likely to diagnose African American children as hyperactive than European American children when the children display essentially the same behavior (Epstein et al., 2005). For another, African American parents may be less informed about ADHD than their European American counterparts and are more likely to attribute ADHD symptoms to other causes such as sugar intake. In addition, school officials are more likely to assign African American children to special-education classes than they are European American children, and class placement is "the only educational resource used" to address many African American children's ADHD (Bailey & Owens, 2005). But proper treatment might allow them to remain in their regular classes. Special-education placements often go unchallenged by African American parents because they may be less aware of their rights regarding school decisions and because they face limited access to other potentially useful services in their communities.

■ Table 11.3 reveals the results of a Harris Poll on barriers that prevent African American, European American, and Latino and Latina American children from getting treatment for ADHD.

Reflect: *Check out Table 11.3. How would you say the three groups are alike in the barriers they perceive? How do they seem to differ?*

■ **Table 11.3** Barriers That Prevent Parents from Obtaining Treatment for ADHD for Their Children

Barrier	Latino and Latina Americans (%)	African Americans (%)	European Americans (%)
Concern that the child will be "labeled"	51	57	52
Lack of information about ADHD	57	58	51
Concern that treatment will be based on the child's racial or ethnic background	19	36	13
Language barriers between parent or child and health care professional	32	28	23
Cost of treatment	53	52	47

Source: Adapted from Taylor & Leitman (2003).

likely due to a lack of executive control of the brain but admits that the precise nature of this control—its exact neurological aspects—remains poorly understood.

Treatment and Outcome

Truth or Fiction Revisited: Stimulants such as Ritalin are often used to treat hyperactive children. In fact, they are the most widespread treatment for ADHD. *Question: Why are children with ADHD treated with stimulants?* It may seem ironic that stimulants are used with children who are already overly active. The rationale is that the activity of the hyperactive child stems from inability of the cerebral cortex to inhibit more primitive areas of the brain (Hazell, 2007; Reiff & Mansoor, 2007).

The stimulants that are used block the "reuptake"—that is, the reabsorption—of two brain chemicals: dopamine and noradrenaline. Keeping more of these brain chemicals active stimulates the cerebral cortex. Because the cerebral cortext contains the "executive center" of the brain—the part of the brain that makes decisions and plans—the chemicals also have the effect of helping the cerebral cortex control more primitive areas of the brain. It is of interest that another stimulant, caffeine, the stimulant found in coffee, tea, colas, and chocolate (yes, chocolate), also helps children control hyperactivity (Leon, 2000; Rezvani & Levin, 2001).

Stimulants help children with ADHD increase their attention span, improve their cognitive and academic performance, and reduce their disruptive, annoying, and aggressive behavior (Posey et al., 2007). But the use of stimulants is controversial. Some critics argue that stimulants suppress gains in height and weight, do not contribute to academic gains, and lose effectiveness over time. Another concern is that stimulants are overused or misused in an attempt to control normal high-activity levels of children—especially boys in middle childhood—at home or in the classroom. Supporters of stimulant treatment argue that many ADHD children are helped by medication. They counter that the suppression of growth appears to be related to the dosage of the drug and that low doses seem to be about as effective as large doses (Evans et al., 2001).

Cognitive behavioral therapy (CBT) also shows some promise in treating children with ADHD. CBT attempts to increase the child's self-control and problem-solving abilities through modeling, role playing, and self-instruction. A Spanish study taught many children with ADHD to "stop and think" before giving in to angry impulses and behaving aggressively (Miranda & Presentacion, 2000). However, the Multimodal Treatment Study sponsored by the National Institute of Mental Health found that stimulant medication was more effective than cognitive behavioral therapy (Greene & Ablon, 2001; Whalen, 2001). Stephen Hinshaw (2006) argues that CBT for children should use clear rewards and punishments, and they should involve parents and teachers. James Waxmonsky (2005) suggests that children may fare better with medication, whereas adolescents and adults with ADHD may profit more from CBT.

Many but not all children "outgrow" ADHD. Longitudinal studies have found that at least two-thirds of children with ADHD continue to have problems in attention, conduct, hyperactivity, or learning in adolescence and adulthood (Barkley, 2004; Nigg et al., 2004).

Learning Disabilities

Nelson Rockefeller served as vice president of the United States under Gerald Ford. He was intelligent and well educated. Yet despite the best of tutors, he could never master reading. Rockefeller suffered from **dyslexia. Truth or Fiction Revisited:** It is true that some children who are intelligent and who are provided with enriched home environments cannot learn how to read or do simple math problems. Many such children have learning disabilities.

stimulants Drugs that increase the activity of the nervous system.

dyslexia A reading disorder characterized by problems such as letter reversals, mirror reading, slow reading, and reduced comprehension (from the Greek roots *dys,* meaning "bad," and *lexikon,* meaning "of words").

Question: What are learning disabilities? Dyslexia is one type of **learning disability.** The term *learning disabilities* refers to a group of disorders characterized by inadequate development of specific academic, language, and speech skills (see Concept Review 11.2). Learning-disabled children may show problems in math, writing, or reading. Some have difficulties in articulating sounds of speech or in understanding spoken language. Others have problems in motor coordination. Children are usually considered to have a learning disability when they are performing below the level expected for their age and level of intelligence and when there is no evidence of other handicaps such as vision or hearing problems, mental retardation, or socioeconomic disadvantage (Joshi, 2003; Lyon et al., 2003). However, some psychologists and educators argue that too much emphasis is placed on the discrepancy between intelligence and reading achievement (Fiorello et al., 2007; Vellutino et al., 2004).

Children with learning disabilities frequently have other problems as well. They are more likely than other children to have ADHD (Schulte-Körne et al., 2006), and, as they mature, they are more likely than other adolescents or adults to develop schizophrenia (Maneschi et al., 2006). They do not communicate as well with their

learning disabilities A group of disorders characterized by inadequate development of specific academic, language, and speech skills.

Concept Review 11.2 Types of Learning Disabilities

Reading Disability (Dyslexia)	• As measured by a standardized test that is given individually, the child's ability to read (accuracy or comprehension) is substantially less than what one would expect considering his or her age, level of intelligence, and educational experiences. • The reading disorder materially interferes with the child's academic achievement or daily living. • If there is also a sensory or perceptual defect, the reading problems are worse than one would expect with it.
Mathematics Disability (Dyscalculia)	• As measured by a standardized test that is given individually, the child's mathematical ability is substantially less than what one would expect considering his or her age, level of intelligence, and educational experiences. • The mathematics disorder materially interferes with the child's academic achievement or daily living. • If there is also a sensory or perceptual defect, the problems in mathematics are worse than one would expect with it.
Disorder of Written Expression	• As measured by assessment of functioning or by a standardized test that is given individually, the child's writing ability is substantially less than what one would expect considering his or her age, level of intelligence, and educational experiences. • The problems in writing grammatically correct sentences and organized paragraphs materially interfere with the child's academic achievement or daily living. • If there is also a sensory or perceptual defect, the problems in writing are worse than one would expect with it.

Source: Adapted from American Psychiatric Association (2000).
Note: The American Psychiatric Association uses the term *learning disorder* rather than *learning disability*. However, most educators appear to prefer the term *learning disability*.

● **Figure 11.4**   Writing Sample of a Dyslexic Child

Dyslexic children have trouble perceiving letters in their correct orientation. They may perceive letters upside down (confusing *w* with *m*) or reversed (confusing *b* with *d*). This perceptual difficulty may lead to rotations or reversals in their writing, as shown here.

peers, have poorer social skills, show more behavior problems in the classroom, and are more likely to experience emotional problems (Frith, 2001; Lyon et al., 2003).

Learning disabilities most often persist through life. But with early recognition and appropriate remediation, many individuals can learn to overcome or compensate for their learning disability (Vellutino et al., 2004).

It has been estimated that dyslexia affects anywhere from 5% to 17.5% of American children (Shaywitz, 1998). Most studies show that dyslexia is much more common in boys than in girls. ● Figure 11.4 is a writing sample from a dyslexic child.

In childhood, treatment of dyslexia focuses on remediation (Bakker, 2006; Tijms, 2007). Children are given highly structured exercises to help them become aware of how to blend sounds to form words, such as identifying word pairs that rhyme and do not rhyme. Later in life, the focus tends to be on accommodation rather than on remediation. For example, college students with dyslexia may be given extra time to do the reading involved in taking tests. Interestingly, college students with dyslexia are frequently excellent at word recognition. Even so, they continue to show problems in decoding new words.

Origins of Dyslexia

Question: What are the origins of dyslexia? Current views of dyslexia focus on the ways in which sensory and neurological problems may contribute to reading problems we find in dyslexic individuals, but first let us note that genetic factors appear to be involved in dyslexia. Dyslexia runs in families. It has been estimated that 25% to 65% of children who have one dyslexic parent are dyslexic themselves (Fernandez & State, 2004; Plomin & Walker, 2003). About 40% of the siblings of children with dyslexia are also dyslexic.

Genetic factors may give rise to neurological problems. The problems can involve "faulty wiring" or circulation problems in the left hemisphere of the brain, which is usually involved in language functions (Arduini et al., 2006; Grigorenko, 2007). The circulation problems would result in less oxygen than is desirable. A part of the brain called the angular gyrus lies in the left hemisphere between the visual cortex and Wernicke's area. The angular gyrus "translates" visual information, such as written words, into auditory information (sounds) and sends it on to Wernicke's area. Problems in the angular gyrus may give rise to reading problems because it becomes difficult for the reader to associate letters with sounds (Greigorenko, 2007; Shaywitz et al., 2006b). For example, we develop habits of seeing an *f* or *aph* or *agh* and saying or hearing an *f* sound in our brains. Dyslexic individuals find it more difficult to go from the visual stimulus to the correct sound.

Some researchers report evidence that dyslexic children have difficulty controlling their eye movements (Boden & Giaschi, 2007), but most researchers today focus on dyslexic individuals' "phonological processing," that is, the ways in which they make, or do not make, sense of sounds. It was once thought that dyslexic children hear as well as other children do, but now it seems that they may not discriminate sounds as accurately as other children do (Halliday & Bishop, 2006). As a result, *b*'s and *d*'s and *p*'s, for example, may have been hard to tell apart at times, creating confusion that impaired reading ability (Boada & Pennington, 2006; Shaywitz et al., 2006a).

We also have the **double-deficit hypothesis** of dyslexia, which suggests that dyslexic children have neurologically based deficits both in *phonological processing* and in *naming speed.* (Sawyer, 2006; Vukovic & Siegel, 2006). Therefore, not only do they have difficulty sounding out a *b* as a *b;* it also takes them longer than other children to name or identify a *b* when they attempt to do so.

Educating Children with Disabilities

Special educational programs have been created to meet the needs of schoolchildren with mild to moderate disabilities. These disabilities include learning disabilities, emotional disturbance, mild mental retardation, and physical disabilities such as blindness, deafness, or paralysis. *Question: Should children with learning disabilities be placed in regular classrooms (i.e., should they be "mainstreamed")?* Evidence is mixed on whether placing disabled children in separate classes can also stigmatize them and segregate them from other children. Special-needs classes also negatively influence teacher expectations. Neither the teacher nor the students themselves come to expect very much. This negative expectation becomes a self-fulfilling prophecy, and the exceptional students' achievements suffer.

Mainstreaming is intended to counter the negative effects of special-needs classes. In mainstreaming, disabled children are placed in regular classrooms that have been adapted to their needs. Most students with mild learning disabilities spend most of their school day in regular classrooms (Soan & Tod, 2006).

Although the goals of mainstreaming are laudable, observations of the results are mixed. Some studies indicate that disabled children may achieve more when they are mainstreamed (e.g., Fergusson, 2007). But other studies suggest that many disabled children do not fare well in regular classrooms (Frostad & Pijl, 2007). Rather than inspiring them to greater achievements, regular classrooms can be overwhelming for many disabled students.

High-quality teaching methods are needed for children with learning disabilities. For example, in an experiment on instructing children with learning disabilities,

double-deficit hypothesis The theory of dyslexia which suggests that dyslexic children have biological deficits in two areas *phonological processing* (interpreting sounds) and in *naming speed* (for example, identifying letters such as *b* versus *d,* or *w* versus *m*).

mainstreaming Placing disabled children in classrooms with nondisabled children.

Mainstreaming

Today, most students with mild disabilities spend at least part of their school day in regular classrooms. The goals of mainstreaming include providing broader educational opportunities for disabled students and fostering interactions with nondisabled children.

© Tony Freeman/PhotoEdit

Alice Wilder and Joanna Williams (2001) recruited 91 students (59 boys and 32 girls) from special-education classrooms in New York City. The city Board of Education had certified the students as being learning disabled. Most children had obtained IQ scores of at least 85. The study attempted to determine whether special instruction could help the students pick out the themes in stories. A story was read aloud, and students were then asked to consider questions, such as the following:

> Who was the main character?
> What was his or her problem?
> What did he or she do?
> What happened at the end of the story?
> Was what happened good or bad?
> Why was it good or bad?

Students receiving this form of instruction were more capable of identifying the themes and applying them to everyday life than children who received more traditional instruction. The investigators concluded that this sort of "theme identification" program enables children with severe learning disabilities to profit from instruction that is geared toward abstract thinking and understanding. Perhaps we can generalize to note that these results seem to be underscoring that "good teaching helps," often, if not always. (Why isn't this kind of teaching "traditional instruction"?)

Perhaps any method that carefully assesses the child's skills, identifies deficits, and creates and follows precise plans for remediating these deficits can be of help. Having said that, it seems that no method identified to date provides children with the levels of skills that so many children apply with ease. But reading and other academic skills are important in everyday life in our society, and any advance would appear to be better than none.

Our examination of educational programs for children with disabilities leads us next into an investigation of cognitive development in middle childhood and the conditions that influence it. We address this topic in Chapter 12.

Active Review

15. Children with _____ (ADHD) show developmentally inappropriate or excessive inattention, impulsivity, and hyperactivity.
16. ADHD is more common among (Boys or Girls?).
17. ADHD (Does or Does not?) tend to run in families.
18. Children with ADHD are likely to be treated with (Stimulants or Tranquilizers?).
19. Learning _____ are a group of disorders characterized by inadequate development of specific academic, language, and speech skills.
20. Difficulty learning to read is called _____.
21. Current views of dyslexia focus on the ways that _____ problems contribute to the perceptual problems we find in dyslexic children.

22. Dyslexia (Does or Does not?) tend to run in families.

Reflect & Relate: Did you know any children with disabilities who were "mainstreamed" in your classes? How were they treated by other students? How were they treated by teachers? Do you believe that mainstreaming was helpful for them?

Go to

http://www.thomsonedu.com/psychology/rathus

for an interactive version of this review.

1. **What patterns of growth occur in middle childhood?**

Children tend to gain a little over 2 inches in height and 5 to 7 pounds in weight per year during middle childhood. Children become more slender. Boys are slightly heavier and taller than girls through the ages of 9 or 10, when girls begin the adolescent growth spurt. At around age 11, boys develop relatively more muscle tissue and females develop more fatty tissue.

2. **How many children in the United States are overweight? Why are they overweight?**

About one-sixth of American children are overweight, and the prevalence of being overweight has been increasing. Overweight children usually do not "outgrow" "baby fat." During childhood, heavy children are often rejected by their peers. Heredity plays a role in being overweight. Children with high numbers of fat cells feel food deprived sooner than other children. Overweight parents may encourage overeating by keeping fattening foods in the home. Sedentary habits also foster being overweight.

3. **What changes in motor development occur in middle childhood?**

Middle childhood is marked by increases in speed, strength, agility, and balance. Children show regular improvement in gross motor skills and are often eager to participate in athletic activities, such as ball games that require movement of large muscles. Muscles grow stronger and pathways that connect the cerebellum to the cortex become more myelinated. Reaction time gradually decreases. Fine motor skills also improve, with 6- to 7-year-olds tying shoelaces and holding pencils as adults do.

4. **Are there sex differences in motor skills?**

Boys have slightly greater overall strength, whereas girls have better coordination and flexibility, which is valuable in dancing, balancing, and gymnastics. Boys generally receive more encouragement than girls to excel in athletics.

5. **Are children in the United States physically fit? If not, why not?**

Most children in the United States are not physically fit. One reason is the amount of time spent watching television.

6. **How does run-of-the-mill failure to "listen" to adults differ from attention-deficit/hyperactivity disorder?**

Attention-deficit/hyperactivity disorder (ADHD) involves lack of attention, impulsivity, and hyperactivity. ADHD impairs children's ability to function in school. ADHD tends to be overdiagnosed and overmedicated.

7. **What are the causes of ADHD?**

ADHD runs in families and coexists with other problems. Abnormalities may suggest brain damage. Children with ADHD do not inhibit impulses that most children control, suggesting poor executive control in the brain.

8. **Why are children with ADHD treated with stimulants?**

Stimulants are used to stimulate the cerebral cortex to inhibit more primitive areas of the brain. Stimulants increase the attention span and academic performance of children with ADHD, but there are side effects and the medications may be used too often. Cognitive behavioral therapy can also help teach children self-control.

9. **What are learning disabilities?**

Learning disabilities are characterized by inadequate development of specific academic, language, and speech skills. Children may be diagnosed with a learning disability when their performance is below that expected for their age and level of intelligence. Learning disabilities tend to persist.

1. What are the origins of dyslexia?	Current views of dyslexia focus on the ways that neurological problems may contribute to perceptual problems. Genetic factors appear to be involved, because dyslexia runs in families. The double-deficit hypothesis suggests that dyslexic children have neurologically based deficits in phonological processing and in naming speed.
11. Should children with learning disabilities be placed in regular classrooms (i.e., should they be "mainstreamed")?	Research evidence on this question is mixed. Some studies suggest that disabled children achieve more when they are mainstreamed. Other studies suggest that many disabled children find regular classrooms overwhelming.

Key Terms

growth spurt, 372
adipose tissue, 375
reaction time, 378
attention-deficit/hyperactivity
   disorder (ADHD), 383

hyperactivity, 383
stimulants, 386
dyslexia, 386
learning disabilities, 387

double-deficit hypothesis, 389
mainstreaming, 389

Active Learning Resources

Childhood & Adolescence Book Companion Website

http://www.thomsonedu.com/psychology/rathus

Visit your book companion website where you will find more resources to help you study. There you will find interactive versions of your book features, including the Lessons in Observation video, Active Review sections, and the Truth or Fiction feature. In addition, the companion website contains quizzing, flash cards, and a pronunciation glossary.

 is an easy-to-use online resource that helps you study in less time to get the grade you want—NOW.

http://www.thomsonedu.com/login

Need help studying? This site is your one-stop study shop. Take a Pre-Test and ThomsonNOW will generate a Personalized Study Plan based on your test results. The Study Plan will identify the topics you need to review and direct you to online resources to help you master those topics. You can then take a Post-Test to determine the concepts you have mastered and what you still need to work on.

12

Middle Childhood:
Cognitive Development

Truth or Fiction?

 Don't try the "Yes, but" defense with a 5-year-old. If you did it, you're guilty, even if it was an accident. p. 402

 Memorizing the alphabet requires that children keep 26 chunks of information in mind at once. p. 409

An IQ is a score on a test. p. 416

 Two children can answer exactly the same items on an intelligence test correctly, yet one can be above average in intelligence and the other below average. p. 419

Highly intelligent children are creative. p. 426

Adopted children are more similar in intelligence to their adoptive parents than to their biological parents. p. 428

Bilingual children encounter more academic problems than children who speak only one language. p. 434

© Howard Kingsnorth/Getty Images

Preview

 Go to

http://www.thomsonedu.com/psychology/rathus
for an interactive version of this "Truth or Fiction" feature.

id you hear the one about the judge who pounded her gavel and yelled, "Order! Order in the court!"? "A hamburger and French fries, Your Honor," responded the defendant. Or how about this one? "I saw a man-eating lion at the zoo." "Big deal! I saw a man eating snails at a restaurant." Or how about, "Make me a glass of chocolate milk!"? "Poof! You're a glass of chocolate milk." These children's jokes are based on ambiguities in the meanings of words and phrases. Most 7-year-olds will find the joke about order in the court funny and can recognize that the word *order* has more than one meaning. The jokes about the man-eating lion and chocolate milk will strike most children as funny at about the age of 11, when they can understand ambiguities in grammatical structure.

Children make enormous strides in their cognitive development during the middle childhood years. Their thought processes and language become more logical and more complex. In this chapter, we follow the course of cognitive development in middle childhood. First, we continue our discussion of Piaget's cognitive-developmental view from Chapter 9. We then consider the information-processing approach that has been stimulated by our experience with the computer. We next explore the development of intelligence, ways of measuring it, and the roles of heredity and environment in shaping it. Finally, we turn to the development of language.

Piaget: The Concrete-Operational Stage

According to Jean Piaget, the typical child is entering the stage of **concrete operations** by the age of 7. *Question: What is meant by the stage of concrete operations?* In the stage of concrete operations, which lasts until about the age of 12, children show the beginnings of the capacity for adult logic. However, their thought processes, or operations, generally involve tangible objects rather than abstract ideas, which is why we refer to their thinking as "concrete."

The thinking of the concrete-operational child is characterized by **reversibility** and flexibility. Consider adding the numbers 2 and 3 to get 5. Adding is an operation. The operation is reversible in that the child can then subtract 2 from 5 to get 3. There is flexibility in that the child can also subtract 3 from 5 to get the number 2. To the concrete-operational child, adding and subtracting are not simply rote activities. The concrete-operational child recognizes that there are relationships among numbers, that operations can be carried out according to rules. This understanding lends concrete-operational thought flexibility and reversibility.

Concrete-operational children are less egocentric than other children. Their abilities to take on the roles of others and to view the world and themselves from other peoples' perspectives are greatly expanded. They recognize that people see things in different ways because of different situations and different sets of values.

Compared with preoperational children, who can focus on only one dimension of a problem at a time, concrete-operational children can engage in **decentration.** That is, they can focus on multiple parts of a problem at once. Decentration has implications for conservation and other intellectual undertakings.

Conservation

Concrete-operational children show understanding of the laws of conservation. The 7-year-old girl in ● Figure 12.1 would say that the flattened ball still has the same amount of clay. If asked why, she might reply, "Because you can roll it up again like the other one." This answer shows reversibility.

concrete operations The third stage in Piaget's scheme, characterized by flexible, reversible thought concerning tangible objects and events.

reversibility According to Piaget, recognition that processes can be undone, leaving things as they were before. Reversibility is a factor in conservation of the properties of substances.

decentration Simultaneous focusing (centering) on more than one aspect or dimension of a problem or situation.

Judy Allen-Newberry

● **Figure 12.1**
Conservation of Mass

This girl is in the concrete-operational stage of cognitive development. She has rolled two clay balls. In the photo on the left, she agrees that both have the same amount (mass) of clay. In the photo on the right, she (gleefully) flattens one clay ball. When asked whether the two pieces still have the same amount of clay, she says yes.

Lessons in Observation
Piaget's Concrete-Operational Stage

 To watch this video, visit the book companion website. You can also answer the questions and e-mail your responses to your professor.

Children in Piaget's concrete-operational stage can not only understand that both glasses contain the same amount of water no matter what the shape of the glass is but can also explain why.

Learning Objectives

■ What is the concrete-operational stage of cognitive development?
■ How do conservation tasks help illustrate whether or not a child has reached the concrete-operational stage?
■ What is the difference between logical and intuitive approaches to problem solving?
■ How is reversibility related to ability to engage in concrete operations?

Applied Lesson

Imagine that you are showing a preoperational child 100 rolls of 100 pennies each and a $100 bill. You ask the child which is more money. What do you think the child will say? Why? Now imagine that you ask the same question of a concrete-operational child. Would you expect the same answer? Why or why not? Now do some thinking of your own. Which is less expensive: a $3,000 computer or a $12,000 car? Explain your answer in as much detail as you like.

Critical Thinking

Recall the video you watched in Chapter 9, "Piaget's Preoperational Stage." Describe the differences in reasoning between the younger children in Chapter 9 and the children in this chapter. How has the reasoning of the children in this chapter advanced over that of the children shown in the video that accompanies Chapter 9?

The concrete-operational girl knows that objects can have several properties or dimensions. Things that are tall can also be heavy or light. Things that are red can also be round or square, or thick or thin. Knowledge of this principle allows the girl to decenter and to avoid focusing on only the diameter of the clay pancake. By attending to both the height and the width of the clay, she recognizes that the loss in height compensates for the gain in width.

Children do not necessarily develop conservation in all kinds of tasks simultaneously. Conservation of mass usually develops first, followed by conservation of weight and conservation of volume. Piaget theorized that the gains of the concrete-operational stage are so tied to specific events that achievement in one area does not necessarily transfer to achievement in another.

Transitivity

Question of the day: If your parents are older than you are and you are older than your children, are your parents older than your children? (How do you know?)

We have posed some tough questions in this book, but the one about your parents is a real ogre. The answer, of course, is yes. But how did you arrive at this answer? If you said yes simply on the basis of knowing that your parents are older than your children (e.g., 58 and 56 compared with 5 and 3), your answer did not require concrete-operational thought. One aspect of concrete-operational is the principle of **transitivity:** If A exceeds B in some property (say, age or height) and if B exceeds C, then A must also exceed C.

Researchers can assess whether or not children understand the principle of transitivity by asking them to place objects in a series, or order, according to some property or trait, such as lining up one's family members according to age, height, or weight. Placing objects in a series is termed **seriation.** Let's consider some examples with preoperational and concrete-operational children.

Piaget frequently assessed children's abilities at seriation by asking them to place 10 sticks in order of size. Children who are 4 to 5 years of age usually place the sticks in a random sequence, or in small groups, as in small, medium, or large. Six- to 7-year-old children, who are in transition between the preoperational and concrete-operational stages, may arrive at proper sequences. However, they usually do so by trial and error, rearranging their series a number of times. In other words, they are capable of comparing two sticks and deciding that one is longer than the other, but their overall perspective seems limited to the pair they are comparing at the time and does not seem to encompass the entire array.

But consider the approach of 7- and 8-year-olds who are capable of concrete operations. They go about the task systematically, usually without error. For the 10 sticks, they look over the array, then select either the longest or shortest and place it at the point from which they will build their series. Then they select the next longest (or shortest) and continue in this fashion until the task is complete.

Knowledge of the principle of transitivity allows concrete-operational children to go about their task unerringly. They realize that if stick A is longer than stick B and stick B is longer than stick C, then stick A is also longer than stick C. After putting stick C in place, they need not double-check in hope that it will be shorter than stick A; they know it will be.

Concrete-operational children also have the decentration capacity to allow them to seriate in two dimensions at once. Consider a seriation task used by Piaget and his longtime colleague Barbel Inhelder. In this test, children are given 49 leaves and asked to classify them according to size and brightness (from small to large and from dark to light) (see ● Figure 12.2). As the grid is completed from left to right, the leaves become lighter. As it is filled in from top to bottom, the leaves become larger.

transitivity The principle that if A is greater than B in a property and B is greater than C, then A is greater than C.

seriation Placing objects in an order or series according to a property or trait.

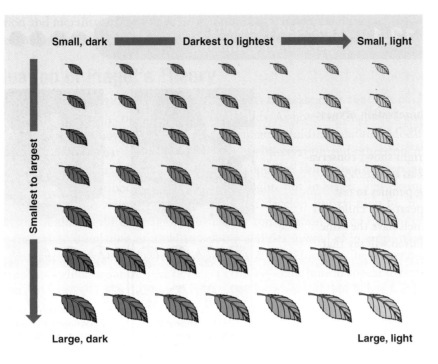

● **Figure 12.2** A Grid for Demonstrating the Development of Seriation

To classify these 49 leaves, children must be able to focus on two dimensions at once: size and lightness. They must also recognize that if quantity A exceeds quantity B and quantity B exceeds quantity C, then quantity A must also exceed quantity C. This relationship is called the *principle of transitivity.*

Preoperational 6-year-olds can usually order the leaves according to size or brightness, but not both simultaneously. But concrete-operational children of age 7 or 8 can work with both dimensions at once and fill in the grid properly.

A number of researchers have argued that children can seriate earlier than Piaget believed and that Piaget's results reflected the demand characteristics of his experiments (Blevins-Knabe, 1987; Siegler & Alibali, 2005). This may be so, but the sequence of developments in seriation and transitivity seems to have been captured fairly well by Piaget.

Class Inclusion

Another example of an operation is **class inclusion,** which we learned about in Chapter 9. In the example in Chapter 9 (see page 302), a 4-year-old was shown pictures of four cats and six dogs. When asked whether there were more dogs or more animals, she said more dogs. This preoperational child apparently could not focus on the two subclasses (dogs, cats) and the larger subclass (animals) at the same time. But concrete-operational children can focus on two dimensions (in this case, classes and subclasses) at the same time. Therefore, they are more likely to answer the question about the dogs and the animals correctly (Chapman & McBride, 1992). But their thought remains concrete in that they will give you the correct answer if you ask them about dogs and animals (or daffodils and flowers) but not if you attempt to phrase the question in terms of abstract symbols, such as A, B_1, and B_2. As with other areas of cognitive development, researchers have taken issue with Piaget's views of the ages at which class-inclusion skills develop. They have argued that language continues to pose hazards for the children being tested. Aspects of concrete-operational thinking are summarized in Concept Review 12.1.

Applications of Piaget's Theory to Education

Question: Can we apply Piaget's theory of cognitive development to educational practices? It seems that we can (Crain, 2000). Piaget pointed out some applications himself. First, Piaget believed that learning involves active discovery. Therefore,

class inclusion The principle that one category or class of things includes several subclasses.

Piaget and Kohlberg argued that moral reasoning undergoes the same cognitive-developmental pattern around the world. The moral considerations that children weigh at a given age are likely to reflect the values of the social and cultural settings in which they are being reared. However, moral reasoning is also theorized to reflect the orderly unfolding of cognitive processes (Krebs & Denton, 2006; Lapsley, 2006). Moral reasoning is related to the child's overall cognitive development. *Question: How does Piaget view the development of moral reasoning?*

Piaget's Theory of Moral Development

For years, Piaget observed children playing games such as marbles and making judgments on the seriousness of the wrongdoing of characters in stories. On the basis of these observations, he concluded that children's moral judgments develop in two major overlapping stages: moral realism and autonomous morality (Piaget, 1932).

The Stage of Moral Realism

The first stage is usually referred to as the stage of **moral realism,** or of **objective morality.** During this stage, which emerges at about the age of 5, children consider behavior to be correct when it conforms to authority or to the rules of the game. When asked why something should be done in a certain way, the 5-year-old may answer "Because that's the way to do it" or "Because my Mommy says so."

At about the age of 5, children perceive rules as embedded in the structure of things. Rules, to them, reflect ultimate reality, hence the term *moral realism*. Rules and right and wrong are seen as absolute. They are not seen as deriving from people to meet social needs.

Another consequence of viewing rules as embedded in the fabric of the world is **immanent justice,** or automatic retribution. Thinking that negative experiences are punishment for prior misdeeds, even when realistic causal links are absent, is what is meant by immanent justice reasoning (Callan et al., 2006). Five- or 6-year-old children who lie or steal usually believe that they will be found out or at least punished for their acts. If they trip and scrape their knees, they may assume that this accident represents punishment for a transgression.

Truth or Fiction Revisited: It is true that you are guilty in the eyes of a 5-year-old even if your behavior was an accident. Preoperational children tend to focus on only one dimension at a time. Therefore, they judge the wrongness of an act only in terms of the amount of damage done, not in terms of the intentions of the wrongdoer. Children in the stage of moral realism are tough jurors indeed. They do not excuse the person who harms by accident. As an illustration, consider children's response to Piaget's story about the broken cups. Piaget told children a story in which one child breaks 15 cups accidentally and another child breaks one cup deliberately. Which child is naughtiest? Which should be punished most? Children in the stage of moral realism typically say that the child who did the most damage is the naughtiest and should be punished most. The amount of damage is more important than the child's intentions (Piaget, 1932).

The Stage of Autonomous Morality

Piaget found that when children reach the ages of 9 to 11, they begin to show **autonomous morality.** Their moral judgments tend to become more autonomous, or self-governed. Children come to view social rules as arbitrary agreements that can be changed. Children no longer automatically view obedience to authority figures as right. They realize that circumstances can require breaking rules.

Children who show autonomous morality are capable of flexible operational thought. They can focus simultaneously on multiple dimensions, so they consider not only social rules but also the motives of the wrongdoer.

moral realism According to Piaget, the stage during which children judge acts as moral when they conform to authority or to the rules of the game. Morality at this stage is perceived as embedded in the structure of the universe.

objective morality The perception of morality as objective, that is, as existing outside the cognitive functioning of people; a characteristic of Piaget's stage of moral realism.

immanent justice The view that retribution for wrongdoing is a direct consequence of the wrongdoing, reflective of the belief that morality is embedded within the structure of the universe.

autonomous morality The second stage in Piaget's cognitive-developmental theory of moral development. In this stage, children base moral judgments on the intentions of the wrongdoer and on the amount of damage done. Social rules are viewed as agreements that can be changed.

Children in this stage also show a greater capacity to take the point of view of others, to empathize with them. Decentration and increased empathy prompt children to weigh the intentions of the wrongdoer more heavily than the amount of damage done. The child who broke one cup deliberately may be seen as deserving of more punishment than the child who broke 15 cups accidentally. Children become capable of considering mitigating circumstances. Accidents are less likely to be considered crimes.

Piaget assumed that autonomous morality usually develops as a result of cooperative peer relationships. But he also believed that parents could help foster autonomous morality by creating egalitarian relationships with their children and explaining the reasons for social rules. As we see in the next section, knowledge of social rules is also a key factor in Kohlberg's theory of moral development.

Corbis Premium RF/Alamy

Moral Realism
It looks bad, but Mom asked her to find the car keys. Mom wasn't thinking of having her go through her purse, however. If she breaks things or drops them on the floor in the effort, is she being "bad"? Children in the stage of moral realism might well say yes because they focus on the damage done, not on the intentions of the wrongdoer.

Kohlberg's Theory of Moral Development

Question: What is Kohlberg's theory of moral development? Kohlberg (1981, 1985) advanced the cognitive-developmental theory of moral development by elaborating on the kinds of information children use and on the complexities of moral reasoning. Before we discuss Kohlberg's views, read the tale that Kohlberg used in his research and answer the questions that follow.

> In Europe, a woman was near death from a special kind of cancer. There was one drug that the doctors thought might save her. It was a form of radium that a druggist in the same town had recently discovered. The drug was expensive to make, but the druggist was charging 10 times what the drug cost him to make. He paid $200 for the radium and charged $2,000 for a small dose of the drug. The sick woman's husband, Heinz, went to everyone he knew to borrow the money, but he could only get together about $1,000 which was half of what it cost. He told the druggist that his wife was dying and asked him to sell it cheaper or let him pay later. But the druggist said: "No, I discovered the drug and I'm going to make money from it." So Heinz got desperate and broke into the man's store to steal the drug for his wife.
>
> —Kohlberg (1969)

Kohlberg emphasized the importance of being able to view the moral world from the perspective of another person (Krebs & Denton, 2005). Look at this situation from Heinz's perspective. What do you think? Should Heinz have tried to steal the drug? Was he right or wrong? As you can see from ■ Table 12.1, the issue is more complicated than a simple yes or no. Heinz is caught in a moral dilemma in which legal or social rules (in this case, laws against stealing) are pitted against a strong human need (Heinz's desire to save his wife). According to Kohlberg's theory, children

■ **Table 12.1** Kohlberg's Levels and Stages of Moral Development

Stage of Development	Examples of Moral Reasoning That Support Heinz's Stealing the Drug	Examples of Moral Reasoning That Oppose Heinz's Stealing the Drug
Level I: Preconventional—Typically Begins in Early Childhood[a]		
Stage 1: Judgments guided by obedience and the prospect of punishment (the consequences of the behavior)	It is not wrong to take the drug. Heinz did try to pay the druggist for it, and it is only worth $200, not $2,000.	Taking things without paying is wrong because it is against the law. Heinz will get caught and go to jail.
Stage 2: Naively egoistic, instrumental orientation (things are right when they satisfy people's needs)	Heinz ought to take the drug because his wife really needs it. He can always pay the druggist back.	Heinz should not take the drug. If he gets caught and winds up in jail, it won't do his wife any good.
Level II: Conventional—Typically Begins in Middle Childhood		
Stage 3: Good-boy/good-girl orientation (moral behavior helps others and is socially approved)	Stealing is a crime, so it is bad, but Heinz should take the drug to save his wife or else people would blame him for letting her die.	Stealing is a crime. Heinz should not just take the drug because his family will be dishonored and they will blame him.
Stage 4: Law-and-order orientation (moral behavior is doing one's duty and showing respect for authority)	Heinz must take the drug to do his duty to save his wife. Eventually, he has to pay the druggist for it, however.	If we all took the law into our own hands, civilization would fall apart, so Heinz should not steal the drug.
Level III: Postconventional—Typically Begins in Adolescence[b]		
Stage 5: Contractual, legalistic orientation (one must weigh pressing human needs against society's need to maintain social order)	This thing is complicated because society has a right to maintain law and order, but Heinz has to take the drug to save his wife.	I can see why Heinz feels he has to take the drug, but laws exist for the benefit of society as a whole and cannot simply be cast aside.
Stage 6: Universal ethical principles orientation (people must follow universal ethical principles and their own conscience, even if it means breaking the law)	In this case, the law comes into conflict with the principle of the sanctity of human life. Heinz must take the drug because his wife's life is more important than the law.	If Heinz truly believes that stealing the drug is worse than letting his wife die, he should not take it. People have to make sacrifices to do what they think is right.

[a] Tends to be used less often in middle childhood.

[b] May not develop at all.

and adults arrive at yes or no answers for different reasons. These reasons can be classified according to the level of moral development they reflect.

Children (and adults) are faced with many moral dilemmas. Consider cheating in school. When children fear failing a test, they may be tempted to cheat. Different children may decide not to cheat for different reasons. One child may simply fear getting caught. A second child may decide that it is more important to live up to her moral principles than to get the highest possible grade. In each case, the child's decision is not to cheat. However, the cognitive processes behind each decision reflect different levels of reasoning.

As a stage theorist, Kohlberg argued that the developmental stages of moral reasoning follow the same sequence in all children. Children progress at different rates, and not all children (or adults) reach the highest stage. But children must experience Stage 1 before they enter Stage 2, and so on. According to Kohlberg, there are three levels of moral development and two stages within each level.

Let us return to Heinz and see how responses to the questions we have posed can reflect different levels and stages of moral development.

The Preconventional Level

In the **preconventional level,** children base their moral judgments on the consequences of their behavior. For instance, Stage 1 is oriented toward obedience and punishment. Good behavior means being obedient, which allows one to avoid punishment. According to Stage 1 reasoning, Heinz could be urged to steal the drug because he did ask to pay for it first. But he could also be urged not to steal the drug so that he will not be sent to jail (see Table 12.1).

In Stage 2, good behavior allows people to satisfy their own needs and, perhaps, the needs of others. A Stage 2 reason for stealing the drug is that Heinz's wife needs it. Therefore, stealing the drug—the only way of attaining it—is not wrong. A Stage 2 reason for not stealing the drug would be that Heinz's wife might die even if he does so. Thus, he might wind up in jail needlessly.

In a study of American children age 7 through 16, Kohlberg (1963) found that Stage 1 and 2 types of moral judgments were offered most frequently by 7- and 10-year-olds. There was a steep falling off of Stage 1 and 2 judgments after age 10.

The Conventional Level

In the **conventional level** of moral reasoning, right and wrong are judged by conformity to conventional (family, religious, societal) standards of right and wrong. According to the Stage 3 "good-boy/good-girl orientation," it is good to meet the needs and expectations of others. Moral behavior is what is "normal," what the majority does. From the Stage 3 perspective, Heinz should steal the drug because that is what a "good husband" would do. It is "natural" or "normal" to try to help one's wife. Or Heinz should not steal the drug because "good people do not steal." Stage 3 judgments also focus on the role of sympathy, the importance of doing what will make someone else feel good or better.

In Stage 4, moral judgments are based on rules that maintain the social order. Showing respect for authority and duty is valued highly. From this perspective, one could argue that Heinz must steal the drug, because it is his duty to save his wife. He would pay the druggist when he could. Or one could argue that Heinz should not steal the drug, because he would be breaking the law. He might also be contributing to the breakdown of the social order. Many people do not develop beyond the conventional level.

Kohlberg (1963) found that Stage 3 and 4 types of judgments emerge during middle childhood. They are all but absent among 7-year-olds. However, they are reported by about 20% of 10-year-olds (and by higher percentages of adolescents).

preconventional level According to Kohlberg, a period during which moral judgments are based largely on expectations of rewards or punishments.

conventional level According to Kohlberg, a period during which moral judgments largely reflect social rules and conventions.

The Postconventional Level

In the **postconventional level,** moral reasoning is based on the person's own moral standards. If this level of reasoning develops at all, it is found among adolescents and adults (see Table 12.1).

Active Review

4. Piaget believed that children's moral judgments develop in two stages: moral realism and _____ morality.
5. Preoperational children judge the wrongness of an act in terms of (The amount of damage done or The intentions of the wrongdoer?).
6. In Kohlberg's _____ level, children base their moral judgments on the consequences of their behavior.
7. In the _____ level, right and wrong are judged by conformity to conventional (family, religious, societal) standards of right and wrong.

Reflect & Relate: Do you believe that Heinz should have taken the drug without paying? Why or why not? What does your reasoning suggest about your level of moral development?

Go to

http://www.thomsonedu.com/psychology/rathus

for an interactive version of this review.

Information Processing: Learning, Remembering, Problem Solving

Question: What is the difference between Piaget's view of cognitive development and the information-processing approach? Whereas Piaget looked on children as budding scientists, psychologists who view cognitive development in terms of **information processing** see children (and adults) as somewhat akin to computers. Children, like computers, attain information (input) from the environment, store it, retrieve it, manipulate it, and then respond to it overtly (output). One goal of the information-processing approach is to learn how children store, retrieve, and manipulate information, how their "mental programs" develop. Information-processing theorists also study the development of children's strategies for processing information (Bjorklund & Rosenblum, 2001; Pressley & Hilden, 2006).

Although something may be gained from thinking of children in terms of computers, children, of course, are not computers. Children are self-aware and capable of creativity and intuition.

Key elements in information processing include the following:

- Development of selective attention: development of children's abilities to focus on the elements of a problem and find solutions
- Development of capacity for storage and retrieval of information: development of the capacity of memory and of children's understanding of the processes of memory and how to strengthen and use memory
- Development of strategies for processing information: development of ability to solve problems as, for example, by finding the correct formula and applying it

postconventional level
According to Kohlberg, a period during which moral judgments are derived from moral principles and people look to themselves to set moral standards.

information processing
The view in which cognitive processes are compared to the functions of computers. The theory deals with the input, storage, retrieval, manipulation, and output of information. The focus is on the development of children's strategies for solving problems, or their "mental programs."

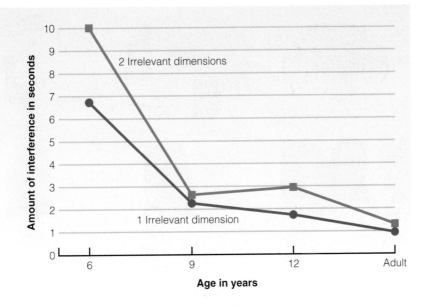

● **Figure 12.3**
Development of the Ability to
Ignore Distractions

Strutt and his colleagues demonstrated how the ability to ignore
distractions develops during
middle childhood. The effect of
irrelevant dimensions on sorting
speed was determined by subtracting the speed of the sort in
the no-irrelevant-dimension condition from the speed of the other
two conditions. As shown here,
irrelevant information interfered
with sorting ability for all age
groups, but older children were
less affected than younger ones.
Strutt et al. (1975).

Development of Selective Attention

A key cognitive process is the ability to pay attention to relevant features of a task. The ability to focus one's attention and screen out distractions advances steadily through middle childhood (Rubia et al., 2006). Preoperational children engaged in problem solving tend to focus (or center) their attention on one element of the problem at a time, which is a major reason that they lack conservation. Concrete-operational children, by contrast, can attend to multiple aspects of the problem at once, permitting them to conserve number, volume, and so on.

An experiment illustrates how selective attention and the ability to ignore distractions develop during middle childhood. The researchers (Strutt et al., 1975) asked children between 6 and 12 years of age to sort a deck of cards as quickly as possible on the basis of the figures depicted on each card (e.g., circle versus square). In one condition, only the relevant dimension (i.e., form) was shown on each card. In another condition, a dimension not relevant to the sorting also was present (e.g., a horizontal or vertical line in the figure). In a third condition, two irrelevant dimensions were present (e.g., a star above or below the figure, in addition to a horizontal or vertical line in the figure). As seen in ● Figure 12.3, the irrelevant information interfered with sorting ability for all age groups, but older children were much less affected than younger children. In the next section, we learn more about how children gain the ability to store and retrieve information.

Developments in the Storage and Retrieval of Information

Question: What is meant by the term memory? Keep in mind that the word **memory** is not a scientific term, even though psychologists and other scientists may use it for the sake of convenience. Psychologists usually use the term to refer to the processes of storing and retrieving information. Many but not all psychologists divide memory functioning into three major processes or structures: sensory memory, working memory (short-term memory), and long-term memory (● Figure 12.4).

Sensory Memory

When we look at an object and then blink our eyes, the visual impression of the object lasts for a fraction of a second in what is called **sensory memory,** or the **sensory register.** Then the "trace" of the stimulus decays. The concept of sensory memory applies

memory The processes by which we store and retrieve information.

sensory memory The structure of memory first encountered by sensory input. Information is maintained in sensory memory for only a fraction of a second.

sensory register Another term for sensory memory.

● **Figure 12.4**

The Structure of Memory

Many psychologists divide memory into three processes or "structures." Sensory information enters the registers of sensory memory, where memory traces are held briefly before decaying. If we attend to the information, much of it is transferred to working memory (also called short-term memory), where it may decay or be displaced if it is not transferred to long-term memory. We usually use rehearsal (repetition) or elaborative strategies to transfer memories to long-term memory. Once in long-term memory, memories can be retrieved through appropriate search strategies. But if information is organized poorly or if we cannot find cues to retrieve it, it may be "lost" for all practical purposes.

See your student companion website for an interactive version of Figure 12.4.

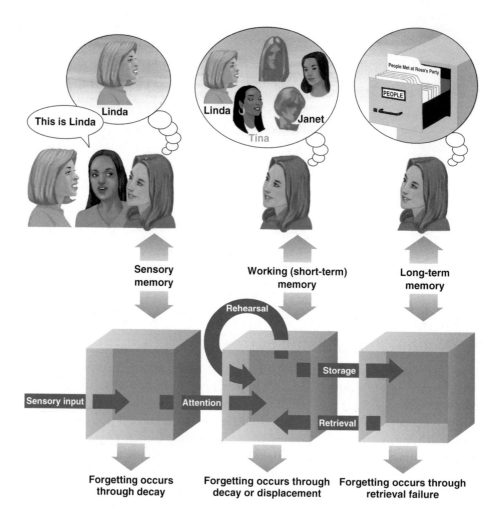

to all the senses. For example, when we are introduced to somebody, the trace of the sound of the name also decays, but as we see in the next section, we can maintain the name in memory by focusing on it.

Working Memory (Short-Term Memory)

When children focus their attention on a stimulus in the sensory register, it tends to be retained in **working memory** (also called *short-term memory*) for up to 30 seconds after the trace of the stimulus decays. Ability to maintain information in short-term memory depends on cognitive strategies and on basic capacity to continue to perceive a vanished stimulus. Memory function in middle childhood seems largely adult-like in organization and strategies and shows only gradual improvement in a quantitative sense through early adolescence (Alloway et al., 2004; Archibald & Gathercole, 2006).

Auditory stimuli can be maintained longer in short-term memory than can visual stimuli. For this reason, one strategy for promoting memory is to **encode** visual stimuli as sounds, or auditory stimulation. Then the sounds can be repeated out loud or mentally. For example, in Figure 12.4, mentally repeating the sound of Linda's name helps the other girl remember it. That is, the sounds can be **rehearsed**.

Capacity of Short-Term Memory

The basic capacity of the short-term memory can be described in terms of the number of "bits" or chunks of information that can be kept in memory at once. To remember a new phone number, for example, one must keep seven chunks of information in short-term memory simultaneously; that is, one must rehearse them consecutively.

Classic research shows that the typical adult can keep about seven chunks of information—plus or minus two—in short-term memory at a time (Miller, 1956).

working memory The structure of memory that can hold a sensory stimulus for up to 30 seconds after the trace decays. Also called *short-term memory*.

encode To transform sensory input into a form that is more readily processed.

rehearse Repeat.

As measured by the ability to recall digits, the typical 5- to 6-year-old can work on two chunks of information at a time. The ability to recall a series of digits improves throughout middle childhood, and adolescents can keep about seven chunks of information in short-term memory at the same time (Chen & Cowan, 2005; Towse & Cowan, 2005; Gathercole et al., 2004b).

The information-processing view focuses on children's capacity for memory and their use of cognitive strategies, such as the way in which they focus their attention (Gathercole et al., 2004a, 2004b). Certain Piagetian tasks require several cognitive strategies instead of one. Young children frequently fail at such tasks because they cannot simultaneously hold many pieces of information in their short-term memories. Put another way, preschoolers can solve problems that have only one or two steps, whereas older children can retain information from earlier steps as they proceed to subsequent steps.

But how do young children remember the alphabet, which is 26 chunks of information? **Truth or Fiction Revisited:** It is not true that learning the alphabet requires keeping 26 chunks of information in mind at once. Children usually learn the alphabet by **rote learning**, simple associative learning based on repetition. After the alphabet is repeated many, many times, M triggers the letter N, N triggers O, and so on. The typical 3-year-old who has learned the alphabet by rote will not be able to answer the question "What letter comes after N?" However, if you recite "H, I, J, K, L, M, N" with the child and then pause, the child is likely to say, "O, P." The 3-year-old probably will not realize that he or she can find the answer by using the cognitive strategy of reciting the alphabet, but many 5- or 6-year-olds will.

Long-Term Memory

Think of **long-term memory** as a vast storehouse of information containing names, dates, places, what Johnny did to you in second grade, what Alyssa said about you when you were 12. Long-term memories may last days, years, or, for practical purposes, a lifetime.

Questions: How much information can be stored in long-term memory? How is it "filed"? There is no known limit to the amount of information that can be stored in long-term memory. From time to time, it may seem that we have forgotten, or lost, a long-term memory, such as the names of elementary or high school classmates. But it is more likely that we simply cannot find the proper cues to help us retrieve the information. It is "lost" in the same way as when we misplace an object but know that it is still in the house. It remains there somewhere for the finding.

How is information transferred from short-term memory to long-term memory? Rehearsal is one method. Older children are more likely than younger children to use rehearsal (Cowan et al., 2003; Saito & Miyake, 2004; Towse & Cowan, 2005). But pure rehearsal, with no attempt to make information meaningful by linking it to past learning, is no guarantee that the information will be stored permanently.

A more effective method than simple rehearsal is to purposefully relate new material to well-known information. Relating new material to well-known material is known as an **elaborative strategy** (Siegler & Alibali, 2005). English teachers encourage children to use new vocabulary words in sentences to help them remember them. This is an example of an elaborative strategy. In this way, children are building extended **semantic codes** that will help them retrieve the words' meanings in the future.

Before we proceed to the next section, here's a question for you. Which of the following words is spelled correctly: *retreival* or *retrieval*? The spellings sound alike, so an acoustic code for reconstructing the correct spelling would not be of help. But a semantic code, such as the spelling rule "*i* before *e* except after *c*," would allow you to reconstruct the correct spelling: retrieval. That is why children are taught rules and principles. Of course, whether these rules are retrieved in the appropriate situation is another issue.

rote learning Learning by repetition.

long-term memory The memory structure capable of relatively permanent storage of information.

elaborative strategy A method for increasing retention of new information by relating it to well-known information.

semantic code A code based on the meaning of information.

Organization in Long-Term Memory

As children's knowledge of concepts advances, the storehouse of their long-term memory becomes gradually organized according to categories. Preschoolers tend to organize their memories by grouping objects that share the same function (Lucariello et al., 2004; Towse, 2003). "Toast" may be grouped with "peanut butter sandwich," because both are edible. Only during the early elementary school years are toast and peanut butter likely to be joined under the concept of food.

When items are correctly categorized in long-term memory, children are more likely to recall accurate information about them. For instance, do you "remember" whether whales breathe underwater? If you did not know that whales are mammals or if you knew nothing about mammals, a correct answer might depend on some remote instance of rote learning. If children have incorrectly classified whales as fish, they might search their "memories" and construct the incorrect answer that whales breathe underwater. Correct categorization, in sum, expands children's knowledge and allows them to retrieve information more readily.

But it has also been shown that when the knowledge of children in a particular area surpasses that of adults, the children show superior capacity to store and retrieve related information. For example, chess experts are superior to amateurs at remembering where chess pieces had been placed on the board (Gobet & Simon, 2000; Saariluoma, 2001). This finding may not surprise you, until you learn that in these studies, the experts were 8- to 12-year-old children and the amateurs were adults.

Development of Recall Memory

Recall memory involves retrieval of information from memory. As children develop, their capacity for recalling information increases (Gathercole et al., 2004a, 2004b). Improvement in memory is linked to their ability to quickly process (i.e., scan and categorize) information. Children's memory is a good overall indicator of their cognitive ability (Towse & Cowan, 2005).

In an experiment on categorization and memory, researchers placed objects that fell into four categories (furniture, clothing, tools, fruit) on a table before second- and fourth-graders (Hasselhorn, 1992). The children were allowed 3 minutes to arrange the pictures as they wished and to remember as many as they could. Fourth-graders were more likely to categorize, and recall, the pictures than second-graders.

Research also reveals that children are more likely to accurately recall information when they are strongly motivated to do so (Roebers et al., 2001). Fear of poor grades can encourage recall even in middle childhood. The promise of rewards also helps.

Development of Metacognition and Metamemory

Question: What do children understand about the functioning of their cognitive processes and, more particularly, their memory? Children's knowledge and control of their cognitive abilities is termed **metacognition**. The development of metacognition is shown by the ability to formulate problems, awareness of the processes required to solve a problem, activation of cognitive strategies, maintaining focus on the problem, and checking answers.

When a sixth-grader decides which homework assignments to do first, memorizes the state capitals for tomorrow's test, and then tests herself to see which ones she needs to study more, she is displaying metacognition. Teaching students metacognitive skills improves their performance in reading and other areas of education (Flavell et al., 2002; Stright et al., 2001).

Metamemory is one aspect of metacognition. It more specifically refers to children's awareness of the functioning of their memory. Older children show greater

metacognition Awareness of and control of one's cognitive abilities, as shown by the intentional use of cognitive strategies in solving problems.

metamemory Knowledge of the functions and processes involved in one's storage and retrieval of information (memory), as shown by use of cognitive strategies to retain information.

insight into how memory works (Towse & Cowan, 2005). For example, young elementary school students frequently announce that they have memorized educational materials before they have actually done so. Older students are more likely to accurately assess their knowledge (Paris & Winograd, 1990). As a result, older children store and retrieve information more effectively than younger children (Siegler & Alibali, 2005).

Older children also show more knowledge of strategies that can be used to facilitate memory. Preschoolers will usually use rehearsal if someone else suggests that they do, but not until about the age of 6 or 7 do children use rehearsal on their own (Flavell et al., 2002). Older elementary school children also become better at adapting their memory strategies to fit the characteristics of the task at hand (Siegler & Alibali, 2005; Towse et al., 2002).

As children develop, they also are more likely to use selective rehearsal to remember important information. That is, they exclude the meaningless mass of perceptions milling about them by confining rehearsal to what they are trying to remember. Selectivity in rehearsal is found more often among adults than among 10-year-olds (Karatekin, 2004).

If you are trying to remember a new phone number, you would know to rehearse it several times or to write it down before setting out to do math problems. However, 5-year-olds, asked whether it would make a difference if they jotted the number down before or after doing the math problems, do not reliably report that doing the problems first would matter. Ten-year-olds, however, are aware that new mental activities (the math problems) can interfere with old ones (memorizing the telephone number) and usually suggest jotting the number down before doing the math problems.

Your metamemory is advanced to the point, of course, where you recognize that it would be poor judgment to read this book while watching *General Hospital* or fantasizing about your next vacation, isn't it?

We have seen that children's memory improves throughout middle childhood. But how good is the memory of children for observed or experienced events? For a discussion of this controversial issue, turn to the nearby "A Closer Look" feature.

Active Review

8. Ability to screen out distractions (Increases or Decreases?) through middle childhood.

9. When children focus on stimuli, they can keep them in _____ memory for about 30 seconds.

10. Children can remember visual stimuli longer when they _____ it as sounds.

11. Repetition of sounds or other stimuli is known as _____ learning.

12. _____ rehearsal is relation of new information to things that are already known.

13. _____ refers to children's awareness of the functioning of their memory processes.

Reflect & Relate: How is information transferred from short-term memory to long-term memory? How is the process analogous to placing information in a computer's "memory" into a computer's "storage" device? What happens if you forget to "save" information in the computer's memory?

Go to

http://www.thomsonedu.com/psychology/rathus
for an interactive version of this review.

A CLOSER LOOK

Children's Eyewitness Testimony

Jean Piaget distinctly "remembered" an attempt to kidnap him from his baby carriage as he was being wheeled along the Champs Élysées. He recalled the excited throng, the abrasions on the face of the nurse who rescued him, the police officer's white baton, and the flight of the assailant. Although they were graphic, Piaget's memories were false. Years later, the nurse admitted that she had made up the tale.

Children are often called on to testify about events they have seen or experienced, often involving child abuse (Koriat et al., 2001). But how reliable is children's testimony?

Even preschoolers can recall and describe personally experienced events, although the accounts may be sketchy (Bruck et al., 2006; Roebers & Schneider, 2002). However, there are many individual differences. Consequently, the child witness is typically asked questions to prompt information. But such questions may be "leading," that is, they may suggest an answer. For example, "What happened at school?" is not a leading question, but "Did your teacher touch you?" is.

Can children's testimony be distorted by leading questions? It appears that by the age of 10 or 11, children are no more suggestible than adults, but younger children are more likely to be misled (Bruck et al., 2006; Krackow & Lynn, 2003).

One hotly debated question is whether children can be led into making false reports of abuse (Krackow & Lynn, 2003). There is no simple answer to this question, as illustrated by a study carried out by Gail Goodman and her colleagues (Goodman & Clarke-Stewart, 1991). They interviewed 5- and 7-year-old girls following a routine medical checkup that included genital and anal exams for half the girls. Most of the children who experienced genital and anal touching failed to mention it

How Reliable Is Children's Eyewitness Testimony?
This question remains hotly debated. By age 10 or 11, children may be no more suggestible than adults. The findings for younger children are inconsistent, however.

when simply asked what happened during the exam. But when asked specific leading questions ("Did the doctor touch you there?"), 31 of 36 girls mentioned the experience. Of the 36 girls who did not have genital and anal exams, none reported any such experience when asked what happened during the exam. When asked the leading questions, three falsely reported being touched in these areas, illustrating the dilemma faced by investigators of sexual abuse. Although children may not reveal genital contact until specifically asked, asking may influence some children to give a false report.

Research indicates that repeated questioning may lead children to make up events that never happened to them (Roebers & Schneider, 2002). In one study, preschoolers were questioned each week for 11 weeks about events that either had or had not happened to them (Ceci, 1993). By the 11th week, 58% of the children reported at least one false event as true.

What, then, are investigators to do when the only witnesses to criminal events are children? Maggie Bruck and her colleagues (2006) recommended that interviewers avoid leading or suggestive questions to minimize influencing the child's response. It might also be useful to ask the child whether he or she actually saw what happened or merely heard about it. Young children do not always make this distinction by themselves.

Reflect:

• There are problems in children's eyewitness testimony. What would be lost if we did not allow children's eyewitness testimony? Give examples.

Intellectual Development, Creativity, and Achievement

At an early age, we gain impressions of how intelligent we are compared with other family members and schoolmates. We think of some people as having more **intelligence** than others. We associate intelligence with academic success, advancement on the job, and appropriate social behavior.

Question: What is intelligence? Despite our sense of familiarity with the concept of intelligence, intelligence cannot be seen, touched, or measured physically. For this reason, intelligence is subject to various interpretations. Theories about intelligence are some of the most controversial issues in psychology today.

Psychologists generally distinguish between **achievement** and intelligence. Achievement is what a child has learned, the knowledge and skills that have been gained by experience. Achievement involves specific content areas such as English, history, and math. Educators and psychologists use achievement tests to measure what children have learned in academic areas. The strong relationship between achievement and experience seems obvious. We are not surprised to find that a student who has taken Spanish but not French does better on a Spanish achievement test than on a French achievement test.

The meaning of *intelligence* is more difficult to pin down (Cornoldi, 2006; Fuster, 2005; Sternberg et al., 2005). Most psychologists would agree that intelligence provides the cognitive basis for academic achievement. Intelligence is usually perceived as a child's underlying competence or *learning ability,* whereas achievement involves a child's acquired competencies or *performance.* Most psychologists also would agree that many of the competencies underlying intelligence manifest themselves during middle childhood, when most children are first exposed to formal schooling. Psychologists disagree, however, about the nature and origins of a child's underlying competence or learning ability.

Theories of Intelligence

Let's consider some theoretical approaches to intelligence. Then we see how researchers and practitioners actually assess intellectual functioning.

Factor Theories

Many investigators have viewed intelligence as consisting of one or more major mental abilities, or **factors.** *Question: What are "factor theories" of intelligence?* In 1904, British psychologist Charles Spearman suggested that the various behaviors we consider intelligent have a common, underlying factor: *g,* or "general intelligence." He thought that *g* represented broad reasoning and problem-solving abilities. He supported this view by noting that people who excel in one area generally show the capacity to excel in others. But he also noted that even the most capable people seem more capable in some areas—perhaps in music or business or poetry—than in others. For this reason, he also suggested that *s,* or specific capacities, accounts for a number of individual abilities (Lubinski, 2004).

This view seems to make sense. Most of us know children who are good at math but poor in English and vice versa. Nonetheless, some link—*g*—seems to connect different mental abilities. Few if any people surpass 99% of the population in one mental ability, yet are surpassed by 80% to 90% of the population in other abilities.

To test his views, Spearman developed **factor analysis**, a statistical technique that allows researchers to determine which items on tests seem to be measuring the same things. Researchers continue to find a key role for *g* in performance on many intelligence tests. Some (e.g., Jackson & Rushton, 2006) claim that *g* underlies scores

intelligence A complex and controversial concept, defined by David Wechsler as the "capacity . . . to understand the world [and the] resourcefulness to cope with its challenges." Intelligence implies the capacity to make adaptive choices (from the Latin *inter*, meaning "among," and *legere*, meaning "to choose").

achievement That which is attained by one's efforts and presumed to be made possible by one's abilities.

factor A condition or quality that brings about a result; in this case, "intelligent" behavior. A cluster of related items, such as those found on an intelligence or personality test.

factor analysis A statistical technique that allows researchers to determine the relationships among a large number of items, such as test items.

● **Figure 12.5**
Sternberg's Triarchic Theory
of Intelligence

Robert Sternberg views intelligence as three-pronged: as having
analytical, creative, and practical
aspects.

Analytical intelligence
(academic ability)
Abilities to solve problems,
compare and contrast, judge,
evaluate, and criticize

Creative intelligence
(creativity and insight)
Abilities to invent, discover,
suppose, and theorize

Practical intelligence
("street smarts")
Abilities to adapt to the demands
of one's environment and apply
knowledge in practical situations

on the verbal and quantitative Scholastic Achievement Tests (SATs), although we can
also note that it would be absurd to argue that education has nothing to do with SAT
scores. A number of researchers (e.g., Colom et al., 2003; Saggino et al., 2006) claim
to have found evidence that connects *g* with *working memory,* that is, the ability to
keep various elements of a problem in mind at once. Contemporary psychologists
continue to speak of the extent to which a particular test of intellectual ability measures *g* (Lubinski, 2006).

American psychologist Louis Thurstone (1938) used factor analysis and concluded that intelligence consists of several specific factors, which he termed *primary
mental abilities,* including visual–spatial abilities, perceptual speed, numerical ability,
the ability to learn the meanings of words, ability to bring to mind the right word
rapidly, and ability to reason. Thurstone believed that these factors were somewhat
independent; therefore, we might be able to rapidly develop lists of words that rhyme
but might not be particularly able to solve math problems.

The Triarchic Theory of Intelligence

Psychologist Robert Sternberg (Sternberg, 2000; Sternberg & The Rainbow Project,
2006) constructed a three-pronged, or **triarchic,** theory of intelligence, which is similar to a view proposed by the Greek philosopher Aristotle (Tigner & Tigner, 2000).
Question: What is Sternberg's triarchic model of intelligence? The three prongs
of Sternberg's theory are *analytical intelligence, creative intelligence,* and *practical intelligence* (see ● Figure 12.5).

Analytical intelligence is academic ability. It enables us to solve problems and
acquire new knowledge. Creative intelligence is defined by the abilities to cope with
novel situations and to profit from experience. Creativity allows us to relate novel situations to familiar situations (i.e., to perceive similarities and differences) and fosters
adaptation. Both Aristotle and Sternberg speak of practical intelligence, or "street
smarts." Practical intelligence enables people to adapt to the demands of their environment, including the social environment. Psychologists who believe that creativity
is separate from analytical intelligence (academic ability) find only small to moderate relationships between academic ability and creativity (Kim, 2005). However, to
Sternberg, creativity is a basic facet of intelligence.

The Theory of Multiple Intelligences

Psychologist Howard Gardner (1983, 2006), like Sternberg, believes that intelligence—or intelligences—reflects more than academic ability. ***Question: What is
meant by multiple intelligences?*** Gardner refers to each kind of intelligence in his
theory as "an intelligence" because the kinds differ in quality (see ● Figure 12.6). He
also believes that each intelligence is based in a different part of the brain.

triarchic Governed by three.
Descriptive of Sternberg's
view that intellectual functioning has three aspects:
analytical intelligence, creative
intelligence, and practical
intelligence.

● **Figure 12.6**
Gardner's Theory
of Multiple Intelligences

Howard Gardner argued that there are many intelligences, not just one, including bodily talents as expressed through dancing or gymnastics. Each "intelligence" is presumed to have its neurological base in a different part of the brain. Each is an inborn talent that must be developed through educational experiences if it is to be expressed.

Three of Gardner's intelligences are familiar enough: verbal ability, logical–mathematical reasoning, and spatial intelligence (visual–spatial skills). But Gardner also includes bodily–kinesthetic intelligence (as shown by dancers and gymnasts), musical intelligence, interpersonal intelligence (as shown by empathy and ability to relate to others), and personal knowledge (self-insight). Occasionally, individuals show great "intelligence" in one area, such as the genius of the young Mozart with the piano or the island girl who can navigate her small boat to hundreds of islands by observing the changing patterns of the stars, without notable abilities in others. Gardner (2001) recently added "naturalist intelligence" and "existential intelligence." Naturalist intelligence refers to the ability to look at natural events, such as various kinds of animals and plants or the stars above, and develop insights into their nature and the laws that govern their behavior. Existential intelligence involves dealing with the larger philosophical issues of life. According to Gardner, one can compose symphonies or advance mathematical theory yet be average in, say, language and personal skills. (Are not some academic "geniuses" foolish in their personal lives?)

Critics of Gardner's view agree that people function more intelligently in some areas of life than others. They also agree that many people have special talents, such as bodily–kinesthetic talents, even if their overall intelligence is average. But they question whether such special talents are "intelligences" (Neisser et al., 1996). Language skills, reasoning ability, and ability to solve math problems seem to be more closely related than musical or gymnastic talent to what most people mean by intelligence.

The various theories of intelligence are reviewed in Concept Review 12.2. We do not yet have the final word on the nature of intelligence, but I would like to share with you David Wechsler's definition of intelligence. Wechsler is the originator of the most widely used series of contemporary intelligence tests, and he defined intelligence as the "capacity of an individual to understand the world [and the] resourcefulness to cope with its challenges" (Wechsler, 1975, p. 139). To Wechsler, intelligence involves accurate representation of the world and effective problem solving (adapting to one's

Concept Review 12.2   Theories of Intelligence

Theory	Basic Information	Comments
General versus specific factors (main proponent: Charles Spearman)  *Archives of the History of American Psychology—The University of Akron*	• Spearman created factor analysis to study intelligence • Strong evidence for general factor (*g*) in intelligence • s factors are specific abilities, skills, talents	• Concept of *g* remains in use to-day—a century later
Primary mental abilities (proponent: Louis Thurstone)  *© George Skadding/ Getty Images*	• Used factor analysis • Found many "primary" abilities • All abilities/factors academically oriented	• Other researchers (e.g., Guilford) claim to have found hundreds of factors • The more factors claimed, the more they overlap
Triarchic theory (proponent: Robert Sternberg)  *Courtesy of Robert Sternberg*	• Intelligence as three-pronged—with analytical, creative, and practical components • Analytical intelligence analogous to academic ability	• Coincides with views of Aristotle • Critics do not view creativity as a component of intelligence
Multiple intelligences (proponent: Howard Gardner) *© 2003 J. Gardner*	• Theorized distinct "intelligences" • Includes academic intelligences, personal and social intelligences, talents, and philosophical intelligences • Theorizes different bases in brain for different intelligences	• Continues to expand number of "intelligences" • Critics see little value to theorizing "intelligences" rather than aspects of intelligence • Most critics consider musical and bodily skills to be special talents, not "intelligences"

environment, profiting from experience, selecting the appropriate formulas and strategies, and so on).

Measurement of Intellectual Development

There may be disagreements about the nature of intelligence, but thousands of intelligence tests are administered by psychologists and educators every day.

The Stanford–Binet Intelligence Scale (SBIS) and the Wechsler scales for preschool children, school-age children, and adults are the most widely used and well-respected intelligence tests. The SBIS and Wechsler scales yield scores called **intelligence quotients (IQs)**. **Truth or Fiction Revisited:** An IQ is in fact a score on a test.

intelligence quotient (IQ)
(1) Originally, a ratio obtained by dividing a child's score (or "mental age") on an intelligence test by his or her chronological age. (2) In general, a score on an intelligence test.

A Closer Look

*Emotional Intelligence
and Social Intelligence?*

Psychologists Peter Salovey and John Mayer developed the theory of emotional intelligence, which was popularized by *New York Times* writer Daniel Goleman (1995). The theory holds that social and emotional skills are a form of intelligence, just as academic skills are (Barchard & Hakstian, 2004; Mayer et al., 2004; Salovey & Pizarro, 2003). Emotional intelligence bears resemblance to two of Gardner's intelligences: awareness of one's inner feelings and sensitivity to the feelings of others. It also involves recognition and control of one's feelings.

The theory suggests that self-awareness and social awareness are best learned during childhood. Failure to develop emotional intelligence is connected with childhood depression and aggression. Moreover, childhood experiences may even mold the brain's emotional responses to life's challenges. Therefore, it is useful for schools to teach skills related to emotional intelligence as well as academic ability. "I can foresee a day," wrote Goleman (1995), "when education will routinely include [teaching] essential human competencies such as self-awareness, self-control and empathy, and the arts of listening, resolving conflicts and cooperation."

No one argues that self-awareness, self-control, empathy, and cooperation are unimportant. But critics argue that schools may not have the time to teach these skills. Psychologist Robert McCall (1997) wrote, "There are so many hours in a day, and one of the characteristics of American schools is we've saddled them with teaching driver's education, sex education, drug education and other skills, to the point that we don't spend as much time on academics as other countries do. There may be consequences for that."

Is emotional intelligence a form of intelligence? Psychologist Ulric Neisser (1997) wrote, "The skills that Goleman describes . . . are certainly important for determining life outcomes, but nothing is to be gained by calling them forms of intelligence."

Ten years later, Goleman stirred the controversy anew by returning with another best-seller, *Social Intelligence* (2006). This time around, Goleman described how an American commander prevented a confrontation between his troops and an Iraqi mob by ordering the troops to point their rifles at the ground and smile. Although there was a language barrier, the aiming of the weapons downward and the smiles were a form of universal language that was understood by the Iraqis who then smiled back. Conflict was avoided. According to Goleman, the commander had shown social intelligence: the ability to read the Iraqi's social concerns and the ability to solve the social problem by coming up with a useful social response. Social intelligence, like emotional intelligence, also corresponds to Gardner's intelligences, and critics ask whether it brings anything new to the table (Landy, 2006).

Goleman (and Gardner before him) suggests that we may be genetically "prewired" to connect with other people. But some people are better at it than others. Nevertheless, we can all work at developing social intelligence by trying to understanding other people's feelings, seeing things from their points of view, and observing their facial expressions and their tones of voices. The purpose of social intelligence, as Goleman sees it, is not to manipulate other people, but rather to understand them, feel what they are feeling, and develop mutually nourishing relationships with them. Children can be encouraged to develop social intelligence by being asked what their classmates and friends might be thinking in certain situations and to interpret their facial expressions. Parents and teachers can give children practice solving social problems and conflicts in nonaggressive ways.

Reflect:

- Do you think that the concepts of emotional intelligence and social intelligence add anything to Howard Gardner's views? Explain.
- Do emotional intelligence and social intelligence seem like kinds of intelligence to you or like something else? Explain.
- You tell someone "I don't think there's any such thing as social intelligence" and the other person says, "Oh, you don't think it's important to understand how other people feel?" How do you respond?

The concept of intelligence per se is more difficult to define. The SBIS and Wechsler scales have been carefully developed and revised over the years. Each of them has been used to make vital educational decisions about children. In many cases, children whose test scores fall below or above certain scores are placed in special classes for mentally retarded or gifted children.

It must be noted just as emphatically that each test has been accused of discriminating against ethnic minorities (such as African American children and Latino and Latina American children), the foreign-born, and the children of socially and economically disadvantaged people (Harris et al., 2003; Maynard et al., 2005). Because of the controversy surrounding IQ tests, important decisions about children should not be made on the basis of a single test score. Decisions about children should be made on the basis of a battery of tests given by a qualified psychologist in the student's native language, and in consultation with the student's family, teachers, and, when appropriate, social agencies.

Question: What is the Stanford–Binet Intelligence Scale (SBIS)?

The Stanford–Binet Intelligence Scale

The SBIS originated in the work of Frenchmen Alfred Binet and Theodore Simon about a century ago. The French public school system sought an instrument to identify children who were unlikely to profit from the regular classroom so that they could receive special attention. The Binet–Simon scale came into use in 1905. Since then, it has undergone revision and refinement.

Binet assumed that intelligence increased with age. Therefore, older children should get more items right. Thus, Binet arranged a series of questions in order of difficulty, from easier to harder. Items that were answered correctly by about 60% of the children at a given age level were considered to reflect intellectual functioning at that age. It was also required that the questions be answered correctly by fewer children who were a year younger and by a greater number of children who were a year older.

The Binet–Simon scale yielded a score called a **mental age (MA)**. The MA shows the intellectual level at which a child is functioning. A child with an MA of 6 is functioning, intellectually, like the average 6-year-old child. In taking the test, children earned months of credit for each correct answer. Their MA was determined by adding the months of credit they attained.

Louis Terman adapted the Binet–Simon scale for use with American children. Because Terman carried out his work at Stanford University, he renamed the test the Stanford–Binet Intelligence Scale. The first version of the SBIS was published in 1916. The SBIS yielded an intelligence quotient, or IQ, rather than an MA. The SBIS today can be used with children from the age of 2 onward up to adults. ■ Table 12.2 shows the kinds of items that define typical performance at various ages.

The IQ states the relationship between a child's mental age and his or her actual or **chronological age (CA).** The ratio reflects that the same MA score has different meanings for children of different ages. That is, an MA of 8 is an above-average score for a 6-year-old but a below-average score for a 10-year-old.

The IQ is computed by the formula

$$\text{IQ} = \frac{\text{Mental Age (MA)}}{\text{Chronological Age (CA)}} \times 100$$

mental age (MA) The accumulated months of credit that a person earns on the Stanford–Binet Intelligence Scale.

chronological age (CA) A person's age.

According to this formula, a child with an MA of 6 and a CA of 6 would have an IQ of 100. Children who can handle intellectual problems and older children will have IQs above 100. For instance, an 8-year-old who does as well on the SBIS as the average 10-year-old will attain an IQ of 125. Children who do not answer as many items correctly as other children of their age will attain MAs that are lower than their CAs. Their IQ scores will be below 100.

■ **Table 12.2** Items Similar to Those on the Stanford–Binet Intelligence Scale

Age	Item
2 years	1. Children show knowledge of basic vocabulary words by identifying parts of a doll, such as the mouth, ears, and hair.
	2. Children show counting and spatial skills along with visual–motor coordination by building a tower of four blocks to match a model.
4 years	1. Children show word fluency and categorical thinking by filling in the missing words when they are asked questions such as "Father is a man; mother is a _____?" and "Hamburgers are hot; ice cream is _____?"
	2. Children show comprehension by answering correctly when they are asked questions such as "Why do people have automobiles?" and "Why do people have medicine?"
9 years	1. Children can point out verbal absurdities, as in this question: "In an old cemetery, scientists unearthed a skull which they think was that of George Washington when he was only 5 years of age. What is silly about that?"
	2. Children display fluency with words, as shown by answering questions such as "Can you tell me a number that rhymes with snore?" and "Can you tell me a color that rhymes with glue?"
Adult	1. Adults show knowledge of the meanings of words and conceptual thinking by correctly explaining the differences between word pairs such as "sickness and misery," "house and home," and "integrity and prestige."
	2. Adults show spatial skills by correctly answering questions such as "If a car turned to the right to head north, in what direction was it heading before it turned?"

Truth or Fiction Revisited: It is true that two children can answer exactly the same items on an intelligence test correctly, yet one can be above average in intelligence and the other below average. When we consider each child's chronological age, we see that the younger of the two children obtains a higher intelligence test score.

Today, IQ scores on the SBIS are derived by comparing children's and adults' performances with those of other people of the same age. People who get more items correct than average attain IQ scores above 100, and people who answer fewer items correctly attain scores below 100. But again, if two children answer exactly the same items correctly, the younger of the two will obtain the higher score.

Question: How do the Wechsler scales differ from the Stanford–Binet test?

The Wechsler Scales

David Wechsler (1975) developed a series of scales for use with school-age children (Wechsler Intelligence Scale for Children; WISC), younger children (Wechsler Preschool and Primary Scale of Intelligence; WPPSI), and adults (Wechsler Adult Intelligence Scale; WAIS). These tests have been repeatedly revised. For example, the current version of the WISC is the WISC–IV, and it is available both in Spanish and English.

The Wechsler scales group test questions into subtests (such as those shown in ■ Table 12.3). Each subtest measures a different intellectual task. For this reason, the test compares a person's performance on one type of task (such as defining words)

■ **Table 12.3** Kinds of Items Found on Wechsler's Intelligence Scales

Verbal Items	Nonverbal–Performance Items
Information: "What is the capital of the United States?" "Who was Shakespeare?"	Picture completion: Pointing to the missing part of a picture.
Comprehension: "Why do we have ZIP codes?" "What does 'A stitch in time saves 9' mean?"	Picture arrangement: Arranging cartoon pictures in sequence so that they tell a meaningful story.
Arithmetic: "If 3 candy bars cost 25 cents, how much will 18 candy bars cost?"	Block design: Copying pictures of geometric designs using multicolored blocks.
Similarities: "How are good and bad alike?" "How are peanut butter and jelly alike?"	Object assembly: Putting pieces of a puzzle together so that they form a meaningful object.
Vocabulary: "What does canal mean?"	Coding: Rapid scanning and drawing of symbols that are associated with numbers.
Digit span: Repeating a series of numbers, presented by the examiner, forward and backward.	Mazes: Using a pencil to trace the correct route from a starting point to home.

Note: Items for verbal subtests are similar but not identical to actual test items on the Wechsler intelligence scales.

with another (such as using blocks to construct geometric designs). The Wechsler scales thus suggest children's strengths and weaknesses and provide overall measures of intellectual functioning.

Wechsler described some subtests as measuring verbal tasks and others as assessing performance tasks. In general, verbal subtests require knowledge of verbal concepts, whereas performance subtests (see ● Figure 12.7) require familiarity with spatial-relations concepts. Wechsler's scales permit the computation of verbal and performance IQs. Nontechnically oriented college students often obtain higher verbal than performance IQs.

● Figure 12.8 indicates the labels that Wechsler assigned to various IQ scores and the approximate percentages of the population who attain IQ scores at those levels. As you can see, most children's IQ scores cluster around the average. Only about 5% of the population have IQ scores above 130 or below 70.

Question: Many psychologists and educators consider standard intelligence tests to be culturally biased. What is that controversy about?

The Testing Controversy

> I was almost one of the testing casualties. At 15 I earned an IQ test score of 82, three points above the track of the special education class. Based on this score, my counselor suggested that I take up brick-laying because I was "good with my hands." My low IQ, however, did not allow me to see that as desirable.

> —Williams (1974, p. 32)

This ironic testimony, offered by African American psychologist Robert Williams, echoes the sentiments of many psychologists. Most psychologists and educational specialists consider intelligence tests to be at least somewhat biased against African Americans and members of lower social classes (Snyderman & Rothman, 1990). To fill in a bit more historical background, let's note that during the 1920s, intel-

Picture arrangement

These pictures tell a story, but they are in the wrong order. Put them in the right order so that they tell a story.

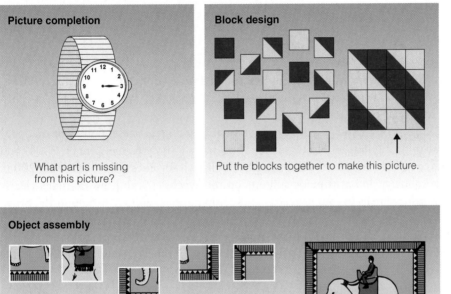

Picture completion

What part is missing from this picture?

Block design

Put the blocks together to make this picture.

Object assembly

Put the pieces together as quickly as you can.

● **Figure 12.7**
Performance Items on an Intelligence Test

This figure shows a number of items that resemble those found on the Wechsler Intelligence Scale for Children.

See your student companion website for an interactive version of Figure 12.7.

ligence tests were used to prevent many Europeans and others from immigrating to the United States. For example, testing pioneer H. H. Goddard assessed 178 newly arrived immigrants at Ellis Island and claimed that most of the Hungarians, Italians, and Russians were "feeble-minded." It was apparently of little concern to Goddard that these immigrants, by and large, did not understand English, the language in

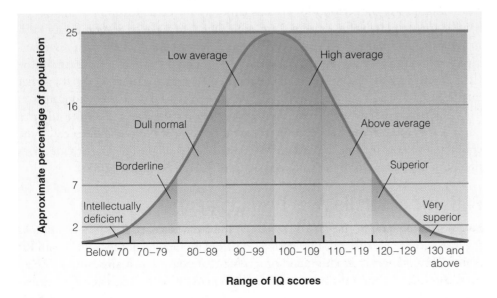

Range of IQ scores

● **Figure 12.8**
Variations in IQ Scores

IQ scores vary according to a bell-shaped, or "normal," curve. Scores tend to bunch around the central score (100) and then to decrease in frequency as they move upward and downward.

● **Figure 12.9** Sample Items from Cattell's Culture-Fair Intelligence Test

Culture-fair tests attempt to exclude items that discriminate on the basis of cultural background rather than intelligence.

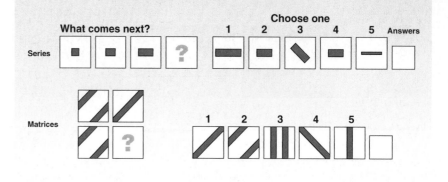

which the tests were administered! Because of a history of abuse of intelligence testing, some states have outlawed the use of IQ tests as the sole standard for placing children in special-education classes.

On the other hand, supporters of standard intelligence tests point out that they appear to do a good job of measuring Spearman's *g* (Frey & Detterman, 2004) and cognitive skills that are valued in modern high-tech societies (Maynard et al., 2005). The vocabulary and arithmetic subtests on the Wechsler scales, for example, clearly reflect achievement in language arts and computational ability. Although the broad types of achievement measured by these tests reflect intelligence, they might also reflect cultural familiarity with the concepts required to answer questions correctly. In particular, the tests seem to reflect middle-class European American culture in the United States (Maynard et al., 2005; Okazaki & Sue, 2000).

If scoring well on intelligence tests requires a certain type of cultural experience, the tests are said to have a **cultural bias.** Children reared in African American neighborhoods could be at a disadvantage, not because of differences in intelligence but because of cultural differences (Helms, 2006). Latino and Latina American children's performance might be compromised by differences in motivation and lack of self-confidence on intelligence tests (Stevens et al., 2006). For this reason, psychologists have tried to construct **culture-free** or culture-fair intelligence tests.

Some tests do not rely on expressive language at all. For example, Raymond Cattell's (1949) Culture-Fair Intelligence Test evaluates reasoning ability through the child's comprehension of the rules that govern a progression of geometric designs, as shown in ● Figure 12.9.

Unfortunately, culture-free tests have not lived up to their promise. First, middle-class children still outperform lower-class children on them (Rushton et al., 2003). Middle-class children, for example, are more likely to have basic familiarity with materials such as blocks and pencils and paper. They are more likely than disadvantaged children to have arranged blocks into various designs (a practice relevant to the Cattell test). Second, culture-free tests do not predict academic success as well as other intelligence tests, and scholastic aptitude remains the central concern of educators.

Might there be no such thing as a culture-free intelligence test? Motivation to do well, for example, might be a cultural factor. Because of lifestyle differences, some children from low-income families in the United States might not share the motivation of middle-class children to succeed on tests (Keogh & Whyte, 2006).

Patterns of Intellectual Development

Sometimes you have to run rapidly to stay in the same place, at least in terms of taking intelligence tests. That is, the "average" taker of an intelligence test obtains an IQ score of 100. However, as childhood progresses that person must answer more questions correctly to obtain the same score. Even though his or her intelligence is "devel-

cultural bias A factor hypothesized to be present in intelligence tests that provides an advantage for test takers from certain cultural or ethnic backgrounds but that does not reflect true intelligence.

culture-free Descriptive of a test in which cultural biases have been removed. On such a test, test takers from different cultural backgrounds would have an equal opportunity to earn scores that reflect their true abilities.

oping" at a typical pace, he or she continues to obtain the same score. *Question: Putting test scores aside, how does intelligence develop?*

Rapid advances in intellectual functioning occur during childhood. Within a few years, children gain the ability to symbolize experiences and manipulate symbols to solve increasingly complex problems. Their vocabularies leap, and their sentences become more complex. Their thought processes become increasingly logical and abstract, and they gain the capacity to focus on two or more aspects of a problem at once.

Intellectual growth seems to occur in at least two major spurts. The first growth spurt occurs at about the age of 6. This spurt coincides with entry into a school system and also with the shift from preoperational to concrete-operational thought. The school experience may begin to help crystallize intellectual functioning at this time. The second spurt occurs at about age 10 or 11.

Once they reach middle childhood, however, children appear to undergo relatively more stable patterns of gains in intellectual functioning, although there are still spurts (Deary et al., 2004). As a result, intelligence tests gain greater predictive power. In a classic study by Marjorie Honzik and her colleagues (1948), intelligence test scores taken at the age of 9 correlated strongly (+0.90) with scores at the age of 10 and more moderately (+0.76) with scores at the age of 18. Testing at age 11 even shows a moderate to high relationship with scores at the age of 77 (Deary et al., 2004).

Despite the increased predictive power of intelligence tests during middle childhood, individual differences exist. In the classic Fels Longitudinal Study (see ● Figure 12.10), two groups of children (Groups 1 and 3) made reasonably consistent gains in intelligence test scores between the ages of 10 and 17, whereas three groups showed declines. Group 4, children who had shown the most intellectual promise at age 10, went on to show the most precipitous decline, although they still wound up in the highest 2% to 3% of the population (McCall et al., 1973). Many factors influence changes in intelligence test scores, including changes in the child's home environment, social and economic circumstances, educational experiences, even B vitamins such as folic acid (Deary et al., 2004).

Although intelligence test scores change throughout childhood, many children show reasonably consistent patterns of below-average or above-average performance. In the next section, we discuss children who show consistent patterns of extreme scores, low and high.

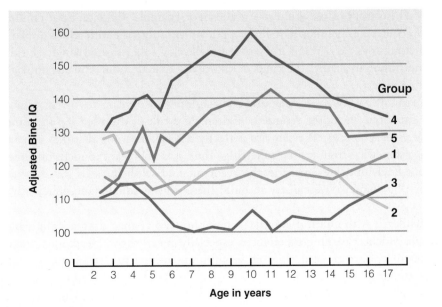

● **Figure 12.10** Five Patterns of Change in IQ Scores for Children in the Fels Longitudinal Study

In the Fels Longitudinal Study, IQ scores remained stable between the ages of 2½ and 17 for only one of five groups, Group 1.

Source: McCall et al. (1973).

Differences in Intellectual Development

The average IQ score in the United States is close to 100. About half the children in the United States attain IQ scores in the broad average range from 90 to 110 (see Figure 12.8). Nearly 95% attain scores between 70 and 130. But what of the other 5%? Children who attain IQ scores below 70 are generally labeled "intellectually deficient" or "mentally retarded." Children who attain scores of 130 or above are usually labeled "gifted." These labels—these verbal markers of extreme individual differences—lead to certain expectations of children. Ironically, the labels can place heavy burdens on children and parents.

Mental Retardation

Question: What is mental retardation? According to the American Association on Intellectual and Developmental Disabilities (AAIDD, 2007), "Mental retardation is a disability characterized by significant limitations both in intellectual functioning and in adaptive behavior as expressed in conceptual, social, and practical adaptive skills." Mental retardation involves an IQ score of no more than 70 to 75.

Most of the children (more than 80%) who are retarded are mildly retarded. Mildly retarded children, as the term implies, are the most capable of adjusting to the demands of educational institutions and, eventually, to society at large. Many mildly retarded children are mainstreamed in regular classrooms, as opposed to being placed in special-needs classes.

Children with Down syndrome are most likely to fall within the moderately retarded range. Moderately retarded children can learn to speak, dress, feed, and clean themselves, and, eventually, engage in useful work under supportive conditions, as in a sheltered workshop. However, they usually do not acquire skills in reading and arithmetic. Severely and profoundly retarded children may not acquire speech and self-help skills and may remain highly dependent on others for survival throughout their lives.

What causes retardation? Some of the causes of retardation are biological. Retardation, for example, can stem from chromosomal abnormalities, such as Down syndrome; genetic disorders, such as phenylketonuria (PKU); and brain damage (AAIDD, 2007). Brain damage can have many origins, including accidents during childhood and problems during pregnancy. For example, maternal alcohol abuse, malnutrition, or diseases during pregnancy can lead to retardation in the fetus.

There is also **cultural–familial retardation,** in which the child is biologically normal but does not develop age-appropriate behaviors at the normal pace because of social isolation of one kind or another. For example, the later-born children of impoverished families may have little opportunity to interact with adults or play with stimulating toys. As a result, they may not develop sophisticated language skills or the motivation to acquire the kinds of knowledge that are valued in a technologically oriented society.

Naturally, we wish to encourage all children to develop to the maximum of their capacities, including retarded children. As a rule of thumb, keep in mind that IQs are scores on tests. They are not perfectly reliable, meaning that they can and do change somewhat from testing to testing. Thus, it is important to focus on children's current levels of achievement in the academic and self-help skills that we wish to impart; by doing so, we can try to build these skills gradually and coherently, step by step.

Children with cultural–familial retardation can change dramatically when we provide enriched learning experiences, especially at early ages. Head Start programs, for example, have enabled children at cultural–familial risk to function at above-average levels.

cultural–familial retardation Substandard intellectual performance that is presumed to stem from lack of opportunity to acquire the knowledge and skills considered important within a cultural setting.

Giftedness

Question: What does it mean to be gifted? Giftedness involves more than excellence on the tasks provided by standard intelligence tests. In determining who is gifted, most educators include children who have outstanding abilities; are capable of high performance in a specific academic area, such as language or mathematics; or who show creativity, leadership, distinction in the visual or performing arts, or bodily talents, as in gymnastics and dancing. Sternberg (2007) presents a "WICS" model of giftedness, which is a play on the letters in the WISC–IV. Sternberg describes giftedness as involving wisdom, intelligence, and creativity synthesized (assembled together). He claims that giftedness basically involves expertise. In gifted children, it involves expertise in development.

Question: What are the socioeconomic and ethnic differences in intelligence? As you can see in the nearby "Developing in a World of Diversity" feature, there are also socioeconomic and ethnic differences in IQ.

Creativity and Intellectual Development

Question: What is creativity? To illustrate something about the nature of creativity, let me ask you a rather ordinary question: What does the word *duck* mean? Now let me ask you a somewhat more interesting question: How many meanings can you find for the word *duck*? Arriving at a single correct answer to the question might earn you points on an intelligence test. Generating many answers to the question, as we will see, may be a sign of creativity as well as of the knowledge of the meaning of words.

Creativity is the ability to do things that are novel and useful (Sternberg, 2007). Creative children and adults can solve problems to which there are no preexisting solutions, no tried and tested formulas (Mumford, 2003; Simonton, 2006). Creative children share a number of qualities (Milgram & Livne, 2006; Sternberg, 2006; Sternberg & Lubart, 1995, 1996):

- They take chances. (They may use sentence fragments in essays, and they may color outside the lines in their coloring books.)
- They refuse to accept limitations and try to do the impossible.
- They appreciate art and music (which sometimes leaves them out among their peers).
- They use the materials around them to make unique things.
- They challenge social norms. (Creative children are often independent and nonconformist, but independence and nonconformity do not necessarily make a child creative. Creative children may be at odds with their teachers because of their independent views. Faced with the task of managing large classes, teachers often fall into preferences for quiet, submissive, "good" children.)
- They take unpopular stands (which sometimes gives them the appearance of being oppositional, when they are expressing their genuine ideas and feelings).
- They examine ideas that other people accept at face value. (They come home and say, "_____ said that yada yada. What's that all about?")

A professor of mine once remarked that there is nothing new under the sun, only new combinations of existing elements. Many psychologists agree. They see creativity as the ability to make unusual, sometimes remote, associations to the elements of a problem to generate new combinations. An essential aspect of a creative response is the leap from the elements of the problem to the novel solution. A predictable solution is not creative, even if it is hard to reach.

creativity The ability to generate novel solutions to problems. A trait characterized by flexibility, ingenuity, and originality.

Question: What is the relationship between creativity and intelligence? The answer to this question depends on how one defines intelligence. If one accepts Sternberg's model, creativity is one of three aspects of intelligence (along with analytical thinking and practical intelligence). From this perspective, creativity overlaps with intelligence. **Truth or Fiction Revisited:** However, otherwise it is not necessarily true that highly intelligent children are creative.

Some scientists argue that creativity and innovation require high levels of general intelligence (Heilman et al., 2003), but the tests we use to measure intelligence and creativity tend to show only a moderate relationship between global intelligence test scores and measures of creativity (Simonton, 2006; Sternberg & Williams, 1997). In terms of Gardner's theory of multiple intelligences, we can note that some children who have only average intellectual ability in some areas, such as logical analysis, can excel in areas that are considered more creative, such as music or art.

Children mainly use convergent thinking to arrive at the correct answers on intelligence tests. In **convergent thinking,** thought is limited to present facts; the problem solver narrows his or her thinking to find the best solution. (A child uses convergent thinking to arrive at the right answer to a multiple-choice question or to a question on an intelligence test.)

convergent thinking A thought process that attempts to focus in on the single best solution to a problem.

Developing in a World of Diversity

Socioeconomic and Ethnic Differences in IQ

What is your own ethnic background? Are there any stereotypes about how people from your ethnic background perform in school or on IQ tests? If so, what is your reaction to these stereotypes? Why?

Research suggests that differences in IQ exist between socioeconomic and ethnic groups. Lower-class American children obtain IQ scores some 10 to 15 points lower than those obtained by middle- and upper-class children. African American children tend to obtain IQ scores some 15 points lower than those obtained by their European American peers (Neisser et al., 1996). Latino and Latina American and Native American children also tend to score below the norms for European Americans (Neisser et al., 1996).

Several studies of IQ have confused social class with ethnicity because larger proportions of African

Americans, Latino and Latina Americans, and Native Americans have lower socioeconomic status (Neisser et al., 1996). When we limit our observations to particular ethnic groups, we still find an effect for social class. That is, middle-class European Americans outscore lower-class

Who's Smart?

Asian children and Asian American children frequently outscore other American children on intelligence tests. Can we attribute the difference to genetic factors or to Asian parents' emphasis on acquiring cognitive skills?

European Americans. Middle-class African Americans, Latino and Latina Americans, and Native Americans also outscore their less affluent counterparts.

Research has also suggested possible cognitive differences between Asians and Caucasians. Youth of Asian descent, for example, frequently outscore youth of European backgrounds on achievement tests in math and science, including the math portion of the SAT (Dandy & Nettelbeck, 2002; Stevenson et al., 1993). Asian Americans are more likely than European Americans, African Americans, and Latino and Latina Americans to graduate from high school and complete college (Sue & Okazaki, 1990). Asian Americans are highly overrepresented in competitive U.S. colleges and universities.

Attributions for success may also be involved. Research shows that Asian students and their mothers

Flash Film/Getty Images

Creative thinking tends to be divergent rather than convergent (Vartanian et al., 2003). In **divergent thinking,** the child associates freely to the elements of the problem, allowing "leads" to run a nearly limitless course. (Children use divergent thinking when they are trying to generate ideas to answer an essay question or to find keywords to search on the Internet.) Tests of creativity determine how flexible, fluent, and original a person's thinking is. Here, for example, is an item from a test used to measure associative ability, a factor in creativity (Getzels & Jackson, 1962): "Write as many meanings as you can for each of the following words: (a) duck; (b) sack; (c) pitch; (d) fair." Those who write several meanings for each word, rather than only one, are rated as potentially more creative.

Another measure of creativity might ask children to produce as many words as possible that begin with T and end with N within a minute. Still another item might give people a minute to classify a list of names in as many ways as possible. In how many ways can you classify the following group of names?

> Martha   Paul   Jeffry   Sally   Pablo   Joan

Sometimes, arriving at the right answer involves both divergent and convergent thinking. When presented with a problem, a child may first use divergent thinking to generate many possible solutions to the problem. Convergent thinking may then be used to select likely solutions and reject others.

divergent thinking
A thought process that attempts to generate multiple solutions to problems. Free and fluent association to the elements of a problem.

(continued)

tend to attribute academic successes to hard work (Randel et al., 2000). American mothers, in contrast, are more likely to attribute children's academic successes to "natural" ability (Basic Behavioral Science Task Force, 1996). Asians are more likely to believe that they can work to make good scores happen.

Stanley Sue and Sumie Okazaki (1990) argue that because Asian Americans have been discriminated against in blue-collar careers, they have come to emphasize the value of education. This finding also holds true in Australia (Dandy & Nettelbeck, 2002). In Japan, emphasis on succeeding through hard work is illustrated by the increasing popularity of cram schools, or *juku,* which prepare Japanese children for entrance exams to private schools and colleges (Ruiz & Tanaka, 2001). More than half of all Japanese schoolchildren are enrolled in these schools, which meet after the regular school day is

over. Looking to other environmental factors, Laurence Steinberg and his colleagues (1996) claimed that parental encouragement and supervision in combination with peer support for academic achievement partially explain the superior performances of European Americans and Asian Americans compared with African Americans and Latino and Latina Americans.

Psychologist Richard Nisbett (2005) argues that continuing to believe that European Americans are superior to African Americans in intelligence ignores evidence about the alterability of African American children's IQ scores by early education programs and the results of adoptee studies. Robert Sternberg and his colleagues (2005) argue that as long as there remains a dispute as to what intelligence *is,* the attempt to relate intelligence to ethnicity makes no sense.

Reflect:
• *In my classes, many European American students are willing to believe that they are smarter than African American students for genetic reasons. However, they believe that if Asian students are smarter than they are, it is because the Asian students work harder. How would you explain that difference?*
• *If one ethnic group is smarter, on average, than another, does that make them "better"?*
• *To say that one ethnic group is genetically smarter than another, do we have to be able to point to the genes that are responsible? Explain.*
• *Do you think we should be conducting research into the relationships between ethnicity and intelligence? Explain.*

Intelligence tests such as the Stanford–Binet and Wechsler scales require children to focus in on the single right answer. On intelligence tests, ingenious responses that differ from the designated answers are marked wrong. Tests of creativity, by contrast, are oriented toward determining how flexible and fluent one's thinking can be. Such tests include items such as suggesting improvements or unusual uses for a familiar toy or object, naming things that belong in the same class, producing words similar in meaning, and writing different endings for a story.

Determinants of Intellectual Development

Questions: What are the roles of nature (heredity) and nurture (environmental influences) on the development of intelligence? No research strategy for attempting to ferret out genetic and environmental determinants of IQ is flawless (McLafferty, 2006; Moore, 2007). Still, a number of ingenious approaches have been devised. The evidence provided through these approaches is instructive.

Genetic Influences

Various strategies have been devised for research into genetic factors, including kinship studies and studies of adopted children.

If heredity is involved in human intelligence, closely related people ought to have more similar IQs than distantly related or unrelated people, even when they are reared separately. ● Figure 12.11 shows the averaged results of more than 100 studies of IQ and heredity in human beings (T. J. Bouchard et al., 1990). The IQ scores of identical (monozygotic; MZ) twins are more alike than the scores for any other pairs, even when the twins have been reared apart. The average correlation for MZ twins reared together is +0.85; for those reared apart, it is +0.67. Correlations between the IQ scores of fraternal (dizygotic; DZ) twins, siblings, and parents and children are generally comparable, as is their degree of genetic relationship. The correlations tend to vary from about +0.40 to +0.59. Correlations between the IQ scores of children and their natural parents (+0.48) are higher than those between children and adoptive parents (+0.18). **Truth or Fiction Revisited:** Actually, adopted children are more similar in intelligence to their biological parents than to their adoptive parents, which is suggestive of the role of genetic factors in intellectual functioning.

All in all, studies suggest that the **heritability** of intelligence is between 40% and 60% (T. J. Bouchard et al., 1990; Neisser et al., 1996). In other words, about

heritability The degree to which the variations in a trait from one person to another can be attributed to, or explained by, genetic factors.

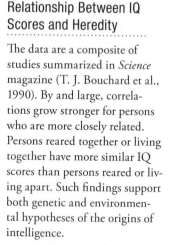

● **Figure 12.11**
Findings of Studies of the Relationship Between IQ Scores and Heredity

The data are a composite of studies summarized in *Science* magazine (T. J. Bouchard et al., 1990). By and large, correlations grow stronger for persons who are more closely related. Persons reared together or living together have more similar IQ scores than persons reared or living apart. Such findings support both genetic and environmental hypotheses of the origins of intelligence.

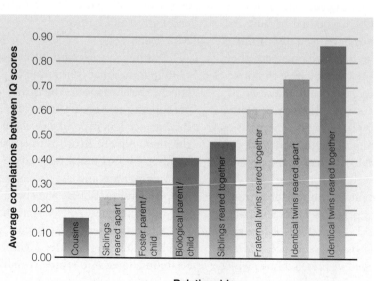

half the variations (the technical term is *variance*) in IQ scores can be accounted for by heredity. It is not the same as saying that you inherited about half of your intelligence. The implication of such a statement would be that you "got" the other half of your intelligence somewhere else. Rather, it means that about half of the difference between your IQ score and the IQ scores of other people can be explained in terms of genetic factors.

Let's return to Figure 12.11 for a moment. Note that genetic pairs (such as MZ twins) reared together show higher correlations between IQ scores than similar genetic pairs (such as other MZ twins) who were reared apart. This finding holds for MZ twins, siblings, parents, children, and unrelated people. For this reason, the same group of studies that suggests that heredity plays a role in determining IQ scores also suggests that the environment plays a role.

When children are separated from their biological parents at early ages, one can argue that strong relationships between their IQ scores and those of their natural parents reflect genetic influences. Strong relationships between their IQs and those of their adoptive parents, on the other hand, might reflect environmental influences. Classic projects involving adopted children in Colorado, Texas, and Minnesota (Coon et al., 1990; Scarr, 1993; Turkheimer, 1991) have found a stronger relationship between the IQ scores of adopted children and their biological parents than between the IQ scores of adopted children and their adoptive parents.

These studies, then, also point to a genetic influence on intelligence. Nevertheless, the environment also has an effect.

Environmental Influences

Studies of environmental influences on IQ use several research strategies, including discovering situational factors that affect IQ scores, exploring children's abilities to rebound from early deprivation, and exploring the effects of positive early environments.

In some cases, we need look no further than the testing situation to explain some of the discrepancy between the IQ scores of middle-class children and those of children from economically disadvantaged backgrounds. In one study (Zigler et al., 1982), the examiner simply made children as comfortable as possible during the test. Rather than being cold and impartial, the examiner was warm and friendly, and care was taken to see that the children understood the directions. As a result, the children's test anxiety was markedly reduced and their IQ scores were 6 points higher than those for a control group treated in a more indifferent manner. Disadvantaged children made relatively greater gains from the procedure. By doing nothing more than making testing conditions more optimal for all children, we can narrow the IQ gap between low-income and middle-class children.

Stereotype vulnerability is another aspect of the testing situation, and it also affects test scores. For example, African American and Latino and Latina American children may carry an extra burden on intelligence tests (Inzlicht & Good, 2006). They may worry that they risk confirming their group's negative stereotype by doing poorly. Their concern may create anxiety, which can distract them from the questions, hurting their scores.

In Chapter 7, we discussed a longitudinal study of retarded orphanage children that provided striking evidence that children can recover from early deprivation. In the orphanage, 19-month-old children were placed with surrogate mothers who provided a great deal of intellectual and social stimulation. Four years later, the children showed dramatic gains in IQ scores.

Children whose parents are responsive and provide appropriate play materials and varied experiences during the early years attain higher IQ and achievement test scores (Bradley, 2006). Graduates of Head Start and other preschool programs show significant gains in later educational outcomes (Phillips & Styfco, 2007).

Although kinship studies and studies of adoptees suggest that there is a genetic influence on intelligence, they also suggest a role for environmental influences. For example, an analysis of a large number of twin and kinship studies showed that the older twins and other siblings become, the less alike they are on various measures of intelligence and personality (McCartney et al., 1990). This finding appears to be due to increasing exposure to different environments and experiences outside the family.

Studies of adopted children also indicate the importance of environment. African American children who were adopted during the first year by European American parents who were above average in income and education showed IQ scores that were 15 to 25 points higher than those attained by African American children reared by their biological parents (Scarr & Weinberg, 1976). The adopted children's average IQ scores, about 106, remained somewhat below those of their adoptive parents' natural children, about 117 (Scarr & Weinberg, 1977). Even so, the adoptive early environment closed a good deal of the IQ gap. Many psychologists believe that heredity and environment interact to influence intelligence (Lubinski & Benbow, 2000; Winner, 2000). An impoverished environment may prevent some children from living up to their potential. An enriched environment may encourage others to realize their potential, minimizing possible differences in heredity.

Perhaps we need not be concerned with how much of a person's IQ is due to heredity and how much is due to environmental influences. Psychology has traditionally supported the dignity of the individual. It might be more appropriate for us to try to identify children of all races whose environments place them at high risk for failure and to do what we can to enrich them.

Active Review

14. Spearman suggested that the behaviors we consider intelligent have a common factor, which he labeled _____.

15. Gardner argues for the existence of _____ intelligences, each of which is based in a different area of the brain.

16. The IQ states the relationship between a child's _____ age and chronological age.

17. The Wechsler scales have subtests that assess _____ tasks and performance tasks.

18. If scoring well on an IQ test requires a certain type of cultural experience, the tests are said to have a cultural _____.

19. The first spurt in intellectual growth occurs at about the age of _____.

20. Lower-class children in the United States obtain IQ scores some _____ points lower than those obtained by middle- and upper-class children.

21. Children tend to use (Convergent or Divergent?) thinking when they are thinking creatively.

22. Studies find that there is a stronger relationship between the IQ scores of adopted children and their (Adoptive or Biological?) parents than between the IQ scores of adopted children and their (Adoptive or Biological?) parents.

Reflect & Relate: As you look back on your own childhood, can you point to any kinds of family or educational experiences that seem to have had an effect on your intellectual development? Would you say that your background, overall, was deprived or enriched? In what ways?

Go to

http://www.thomsonedu.com/psychology/rathus

for an interactive version of this review.

Language Development and Literacy

Question: How does language develop in middle childhood? Children's ability to understand and use language becomes increasingly sophisticated in middle childhood. Children learn to read as well. Many children are exposed to a variety of linguistic experiences other than standard English, and these experiences have important ramifications for language development. In this section, we examine each of these topics.

Vocabulary and Grammar

By the age of 6, the child's vocabulary has expanded to 10,000 words, give or take a few thousand. By 7 to 9 years of age, most children realize that words can have different meanings, and they become entertained by riddles and jokes that require semantic sophistication. (Remember the jokes at the beginning of the chapter?) By the age of 8 or 9, children are able to form "tag questions," in which the question is tagged on to the end of a declarative sentence (Weckerly et al., 2004). "You want more ice cream, don't you?" and "You're sick, aren't you?" are examples of tag questions.

Children also make subtle advances in articulation and in the capacity to use complex grammar. For example, preschool-age children have difficulty understanding passive sentences such as "The truck was hit by the car," but children in the middle years have less difficulty interpreting the meanings of passive sentences (Aschermann et al., 2004).

During these years, children develop the ability to use connectives, as illustrated by the sentence "I'll eat my spinach, but I don't want to." They also learn to form indirect object–direct object constructions (e.g., "She showed her sister the toy").

Reading Skills and Literacy

In many ways, reading is a key to unlocking the benefits society has to offer. Good readers find endless pleasure in literature, reading and rereading favorite poetic passages. Reading makes textbook learning possible. Reading also permits us to identify subway stops, to consider the contents of food packages, to assemble barbecue grills and children's swing sets, and to learn how to use a microcomputer.

As you can see in ■ Table 12.4, millions of people around the world are not literate and therefore cannot enjoy many of the benefits of contemporary knowledge

■ **Table 12.4** Literacy Rates of 15- to 24-Year-Olds, 2000–2004

Region/Nation	Total	Men	Women
Europe	99.4	99.4	99.3
Northern Africa	78.5	84.1	72.5
Sub-Saharan Africa	76.6	81.0	72.3
Latin America and the Caribbean	94.7	94.2	95.2
Eastern Asia	98.9	99.2	98.6
Southern Asia	72.3	81.5	62.5
Southeastern Asia	95.4	96.0	94.9
United States	97.0	97.0	97.0
Western Asia	85.6	84.4	78.1

Sources: Central Intelligence Agency (2004) and United Nations Statistics Division (2004).

Steve McAlister/Getty Images

Reading

Children who read at home during the school years show better reading skills in school and more positive attitudes toward reading.

and society. Even in the United States, millions of people cannot read or write even brief sentences, and the problem is most severe among recent immigrants. According to the U.S. Bureau of Labor Statistics (U.S. Department of Labor, 2004), more than 280,000 teachers are working to teach people, age 15 to 25, to read. Most Americans, fortunately, learn to read when they enter school. *Question: What cognitive skills are involved in reading?*

Integration of Auditory and Visual Information

Reading is a complex process that depends on perceptual, cognitive, and linguistic processes (Smolka & Eviatar, 2006). It relies on skills in the integration of visual and auditory information. Accurate awareness of the sounds in the child's language is an extremely important factor in subsequent reading achievement (Caravolas & Bruck, 2000; Dufva et al., 2001). Reading also requires the ability to make basic visual discriminations (Levinthal & Lleras, 2007). In reading, for example, children must "mind their *p*'s and *q*'s." That is, to recognize letters, children must be able to perceive the visual differences between letters such as *b* and *d* and *p* and *q*.

During the preschool years, neurological maturation and experience combine to allow most children to make visual discriminations between different letters with relative ease. Those children who can recognize and name the letters of the alphabet by kindergarten age are better readers in the early school grades (Siegler & Alibali, 2005).

How do children become familiar with their own written languages? More and more today, American children are being exposed to TV programs such as *Sesame Street,* but these are relatively recent educational innovations. Children are also exposed to books, street signs, names of stores and restaurants, and the writing on packages, especially at the supermarket. Some children, of course, have more books in the home than others do. Children from affluent homes where books and other sources of stimulation are plentiful learn to read more readily than children from impoverished homes. But regardless of income level, reading storybooks with parents in the preschool years helps prepare a child for reading (Dockett et al., 2006; Raikes et al., 2006). Children who read at home during the school years also show better reading skills in school and more positive attitudes toward reading.

Methods of Teaching Reading

When they read, children integrate visual and auditory information (they associate what they see with sounds), whether they are reading by the word-recognition method or the phonetic method. If they are using the **word-recognition method,** they must be able to associate visual stimuli such as *cat* and *Robert* with the sound combinations that produce the spoken words "cat" and "Robert." This capacity is usually acquired by rote learning, or extensive repetition.

In the **phonetic method,** children first learn to associate written letters and letter combinations (such as *ph* or *sh*) with the sounds they are meant to indicate. Then they sound out words from left to right, decoding them. The phonetic method has the obvious advantage of giving children skills that they can use to decode (read) new words (Bastien-Toniazzo & Jullien, 2001; Murray, 2006). However, some children learn more rapidly at early ages through the word-recognition method. The phonetic method can also slow them down when it comes to familiar words. Most children and adults, in fact, tend to read familiar words by the word-recognition method (regardless of the method of their original training) and to make some effort to sound out new words.

Which method is superior? A controversy rages over the issue, and we cannot resolve it here. But let us note that some words in English can be read only by the

word-recognition method A method for learning to read in which children come to recognize words through repeated exposure to them.

phonetic method A method for learning to read in which children decode the sounds of words based on their knowledge of the sounds of letters and letter combinations.

word-recognition method. For example, consider the words *one* and *two.* This method is useful when it comes to words such as *danger, stop, poison,* and the child's name, because it helps provide children with a basic **sight vocabulary.** But decoding skills must be acquired so that children can read new words on their own.

Diversity of Children's Linguistic Experiences in the United States: Ebonics and Bilingualism

Some children in the United States are exposed to nonstandard English. Others are exposed to English plus a second language. Let's explore their linguistic experiences.

Ebonics

Question: What is Ebonics? The term *Ebonics* is derived from the words *ebony* and *phonics.* It was coined by the African American psychologist Robert Williams. Ebonics was previously called Black Vernacular English or Black Dialect (Fasold, 2006).

Ebonics has taken hold most strongly in working-class African American neighborhoods. According to linguists, Ebonics is rooted in the remnants of the West African dialects used by slaves. It reflects attempts by the slaves, who were denied formal education, to imitate the speech of the dominant European American culture. Some observers believe that Ebonics uses verbs haphazardly, downgrading standard English. As a result, some school systems react to the concept of Ebonics with contempt, which is hurtful to the child who speaks Ebonics. Other observers say that Ebonics has different grammatical rules than standard English but that the rules are consistent and allow for complex thought (Fasold, 2006).

Ebonics in the Classroom
Ebonics is spoken by many African American children. The major differences between Ebonics and standard English lie in the use of verbs.

"To Be or Not to Be": Use of Verbs in Ebonics The use of verbs is different in Ebonics and standard English (Bohn, 2003). For example, the Ebonics usage "She-ah touch us" corresponds to the standard English "She will touch us." The Ebonics "He be gone" is the equivalent of the standard English "He has been gone for a long while." "He gone" is the same as "He is not here right now" in standard English.

Consider the rules in Ebonics that govern the use of the verb *to be.* In standard English, *be* is part of the infinitive form of the verb and is used to form the future tense, as in "I'll be angry tomorrow." Thus, "I *be* angry" is incorrect. But in Ebonics, *be* refers to a continuing state of being. The Ebonics sentence "I be angry" is the same as the standard English "I have been angry for a while" and is grammatically correct.

Ebonics leaves out forms of *to be* in cases in which standard English would use a contraction. For example, the standard "She's the one I'm talking about" could be "She the one I talking about" in Ebonics. Ebonics also often drops *-ed* from the past tense and lacks the possessive *'s.*

"Not to Be or Not to Be Nothing": Negation in Ebonics Consider the sentence "I don't want no trouble," which is, of course, commendable. Middle-class European American children would be corrected for using double negation (*don't* along with *no*) and would be encouraged to say "I don't want *any* trouble." Yet double negation is acceptable in Ebonics (Pinker, 1994).

Some African American children are bicultural and bilingual (Delpit, 2006; Rickford, 2006). They function competently within the dominant culture in the United States and among groups of people from their own ethnic background. They use standard English in a conference with their teacher or in a job interview, but switch to Ebonics with their friends.

sight vocabulary Words that are immediately recognized on the basis of familiarity with their overall shapes, rather than decoded.

© Tony Freeman/PhotoEdit

Bilingualism: Linguistic Perspectives on the World

Most people throughout the world speak two or more languages. Most countries have minority populations whose languages differ from the national tongue. Nearly all Europeans are taught English and the languages of neighboring nations. Consider the Netherlands. There, Dutch is the native tongue, but all children are also taught French, German, and English and are expected to become fluent in each of them.

In 2000, approximately 47 million Americans spoke a language other than English at home (Shin & Bruno, 2003; see ■ Table 12.5). Spanish, Chinese, Korean, or Russian is spoken in the home and, perhaps, the neighborhood. *Question: What does research reveal about the advantages and disadvantages of bilingualism?*

Truth or Fiction Revisited: It is not true that bilingual children encounter more academic problems than children who speak only one language. Nevertheless, a century ago it was widely believed that children reared in bilingual homes were retarded in their cognitive and language development. The theory was that mental capacity is limited, so people who store two linguistic systems are crowding their mental abilities. It is true that there is some "mixing" of languages by bilingual children (Gonzalez, 2005), but they can generally separate the two languages from an early age. At least half the children in the United States who speak Spanish in the home are proficient in both languages (Shin & Bruno, 2003). In fact, many children who speak Spanish in the home and English in school come to prefer to read in English because they are taught to read in English (Brenneman et al., 2007).

■ **Table 12.5** Languages Most Often Spoken at Home According to English Ability for Population 5 Years of Age and Above

Language Spoken at Home	Total	English-Speaking Ability (Percents)			
		Very Well	Well	Not Well	Not at All
Spanish	28,101,052	51.1%	20.1%	18.0%	9.9%
Chinese	2,022,143	42.3%	29.4%	20.2%	8.0%
French	1,643,838	74.8%	16.4%	8.4%	0.5%
German	1,382,613	78.1%	15.9%	5.8%	0.3%
Tagalog	1,224,241	67.6%	25.4%	6.5%	0.4%
Vietnamese	1,009,627	33.9%	33.7%	26.8%	5.5%
Italian	1,008,370	69.5%	19.4%	9.8%	1.2%
Korean	894,063	40.4%	30.0%	25.5%	4.0%
Russian	706,242	43.2%	29.6%	21.2%	6.2%
Polish	667,414	58.1%	25.1%	14.2%	2.6%
Arabic	614,582	65.6%	22.8%	9.5%	2.0%
Portuguese	564,630	56.8%	22.2%	16.0%	5.0%
Japanese	477,997	50.6%	30.7%	17.6%	1.2%
French Creole	453,368	54.2%	26.9%	15.7%	3.2%
Greek	365,436	71.9%	17.8%	9.1%	1.2%
Hindi	317,057	77.3%	16.4%	5.3%	1.0%
Persian	312,085	63.5%	22.7%	10.6%	3.3%
Urdu	262,900	68.5%	21.6%	7.9%	2.0%

Source: Adapted from U.S. Census Bureau (2007).

Moreover, analysis of older studies in bilingualism shows that the observed bilingual children often lived in poor families and received little education (Gonzalez, 2005). Yet these bilingual children were compared with middle-class monolingual children. In addition, achievement and intelligence tests were conducted in the monolingual child's language, which was the second language of the bilingual child. Lack of education and inadequate testing methods, rather than bilingualism per se, accounted for the apparent differences in achievement and intelligence.

Today most linguists consider it advantageous for children to be **bilingual**. Knowledge of more than one language expands children's awareness of different cultures and broadens their perspectives (Macrory, 2006). There is evidence that bilingualism contributes to the complexity of the child's cognitive processes (Bialystok & Craik, 2007; Gort, 2006). For example, bilingual children are more likely to understand that the symbols used in language are arbitrary. Monolingual children are more likely to think erroneously that the word *dog* is somehow intertwined with the nature of the beast. Bilingual children therefore have somewhat more cognitive flexibility.

Richard Levine/Alamy

Bilingualism

Most people throughout the world speak two or more languages. It was once thought that children reared in bilingual homes were retarded in their cognitive and language development, but today most linguists consider it advantageous for children to be bilingual.

bilingual Using or capable of using two languages with nearly equal or equal facility.

Active Review

23. Reading relies on skills in the integration of _____ and auditory information.
24. In using the _____ method of reading, children associate written letters and letter combinations (such as *ph* or *sh*) with the sounds they indicate.
25. Bilingual children generally (Can or Cannot?) separate the two languages at an early age.
26. Today most linguists consider it a(n) (Advantage or Disadvantage?) to be bilingual.

Reflect & Relate: Did you grow up speaking a language other than English in the home? If so, what special opportunities and problems were connected with the experience?

Go to

http://www.thomsonedu.com/psychology/rathus

for an interactive version of this review.

19. **What are the socio-economic and ethnic differences in intelligence?**	Lower-class children in the United States obtain lower IQ scores than more affluent children. Children from most ethnic minority groups obtain IQ scores below those obtained by European Americans. But Asian Americans tend to outscore European Americans.
20. **What is creativity?**	Creativity is the ability to do things that are novel and useful. Creative children take chances, refuse to accept limitations, and appreciate art and music.
21. **What is the relationship between creativity and intelligence?**	The relationship between intelligence test scores and measures of creativity are only moderate. Children mainly use convergent thinking to arrive at the correct answers on intelligence tests. Creative thinking tends to be divergent rather than convergent.
22. **What are the roles of nature (heredity) and nurture (environmental influences) on the development of intelligence?**	The closer the relationship between people, the more alike their IQ scores. The IQ scores of adopted children are more like those of their biological parents than those of their adoptive parents. Research also finds situational influences on IQ scores, including motivation, familiarity with testing materials, and the effects of enriched environments.
23. **How does language develop in middle childhood?**	In middle childhood, language use becomes more sophisticated, including understanding that words can have multiple meanings. There are advances in articulation and use of grammar.
24. **What cognitive skills are involved in reading?**	Reading relies on skills in the integration of visual and auditory information. During the preschool years, neurological maturation and experience combine to allow most children to make visual discriminations between letters with relative ease.
25. **What is Ebonics?**	Ebonics derives from the words ebony and phonics and refers to what was previously called Black Vernacular English. Ebonics has different grammatical rules than standard English, but the rules are consistent and allow for complex thought.
26. **What does research reveal about the advantages and disadvantages of bilingualism?**	Research shows that children can generally separate two languages from an early age and that most Americans who first spoke another language in the home also speak English well. Knowledge of more than one language expands children's knowledge of different cultures.

Key Terms

concrete operations, 396
reversibility, 396
decentration, 396
transitivity, 398
seriation, 398
class inclusion, 399
moral realism, 402

objective morality, 402
immanent justice, 402
autonomous morality, 402
preconventional level, 405
conventional level, 405
postconventional level, 406
information processing, 406

memory, 407
sensory memory, 407
sensory register, 407
working memory, 408
encode, 408
rehearse, 408
rote learning, 409

Active Learning Resources

Childhood & Adolescence Book Companion Website

http://www.thomsonedu.com/psychology/rathus

Visit your book companion website where you will find more resources to help you study. There you will find interactive versions of your book features, including the Lessons in Observation video, Active Review sections, and the Truth or Fiction feature. In addition, the companion website contains quizzing, flash cards, and a pronunciation glossary.

 Thomson™ NOW! is an easy-to-use online resource that helps you study in less time to get the grade you want—NOW.

http://www.thomsonedu.com/login

Need help studying? This site is your one-stop study shop. Take a Pre-Test and ThomsonNOW will generate a Personalized Study Plan based on your test results. The Study Plan will identify the topics you need to review and direct you to online resources to help you master those topics. You can then take a Post-Test to determine the concepts you have mastered and what you still need to work on.

13 Middle Childhood:
Social and Emotional Development

Truth or Fiction?

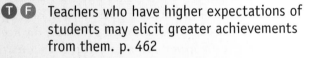

T F Children's self-esteem tends to rise in middle childhood. p. 446

T F Parents who are in conflict should stay together "for the sake of the children." p. 454

T F The daughters of employed women are more achievement oriented and set higher career goals for themselves than the daughters of unemployed women. p. 455

T F In middle childhood, popular children tend to be attractive and relatively mature for their age. p. 456

T F Teachers who have higher expectations of students may elicit greater achievements from them. p. 462

T F Some children—like some adults—blame themselves for all the problems in their lives, whether they deserve the blame or not. p. 467

T F It is better for children with school phobia to remain at home until the origins of the problem are uncovered and resolved. p. 470

Ariel Skelley/Getty Images

Preview

Go to

http://www.thomsonedu.com/psychology/rathus
for an interactive version of this "Truth or Fiction" feature.

college student taking a child development course had the following conversation with a 9-year-old girl named Karen:

Student: Karen, how was school today?
Karen: Oh, it was all right. I don't like it a lot.
Student: How come?
Karen: Sara and Becky won't talk to me. I told Sara I thought her dress was very pretty, and she pushed me out of the way. That made me so mad.
Student: That wasn't nice of them.
Karen: No one is nice except for Amy. At least she talks to me.

Here is part of a conversation between a different college student and her 9-year-old cousin Sue:

Sue: My girl friend Heather in school has the same glasses as you. My girl friend, no, not my girl friend—my friend—my friend picked them up yesterday from the doctor, and she wore them today.
Student: What do you mean—not your girl friend, but your friend? Is there a difference?
Sue: Yeah, my friend. 'Cause Wendy is my girl friend.
Student: But what's the difference between Heather, your friend, and Wendy, your girl friend?
Sue: Well, Wendy is my best friend, so she's my girl friend. Heather isn't my best friend, so she's just a friend.

—Adapted from Rowen (1973)

In the years between 6 and 12, the child's social world expands. As illustrated by the remarks of these 9-year-old girls, peers take on greater importance and friendships deepen (Hamm, 2000). Entry into school exposes the child to the influence of teachers and to a new peer group. Relationships with parents change as children develop greater independence. Some children will face adjustments resulting from the divorce and remarriage of parents. During these years, major advances occur in children's ability to understand themselves. Their knowledge of social relationships and their skill in developing such relationships increase as well (Collins, 1984; Davis, 2001). Some children, unfortunately, develop problems during these years, although some are able to cope with life's stresses better than others.

In this chapter, we discuss each of these areas. First, we examine major theories of social and emotional development in the middle years. Next we examine the development of self-concept and the development of relationships with parents and peers. Then we turn to the influences of the school. Finally, we look at some of the social and emotional problems that can arise in middle childhood.

Theories of Social and Emotional Development in Middle Childhood

Question: What are some features of social and emotional development in middle childhood? The major theories of personality have had less to say about this age group than about the other periods of childhood and adolescence. Nevertheless, common threads emerge. They include the development of skills, the importance of interpersonal relationships, and the expansion of self-understanding.

Psychoanalytic Theory

According to Sigmund Freud, children in the middle years are in the **latency stage.** Freud believed that sexual feelings remain repressed (unconscious) during this period. Children use this period to focus on developing intellectual, social, and other culturally valued skills.

Erik Erikson, like Freud, sees the major developmental task of middle childhood as the acquisition of cognitive and social skills. Erikson labels this stage **industry versus inferiority.** Children who are able to master the various tasks and challenges of the middle years develop a sense of industry or competence. Children who have difficulties in school or with peer relationships may develop a sense of inferiority.

© Joel Gordon Photography

Development of Skills
According to psychoanalytic theory, the major development task of middle childhood is to acquire cognitive, social, physical, and other culturally valued skills. Children who develop valued skills tend to have high self-esteem and to be admired by peers.

Social Cognitive Theory

Social cognitive theory focuses on the continued importance of rewards and modeling in middle childhood. During these years, children depend less on external rewards and punishments and increasingly regulate their own behavior (Crain, 2000).

How do children acquire moral and social standards for judging their own behavior? One mechanism is direct reward and punishment. For example, parents may praise a child when she shares her toys with her younger brother. In time, she incorporates the importance of sharing into her own value system.

Another mechanism for acquiring self-evaluative standards is modeling. Children in the middle years are exposed to an increasing variety of models. Not only parents but also teachers, other adults, peers, and symbolic models (such as TV characters or the heroine in a story) can serve as influential models (Anderson et al., 2007; Bandura, 2002; Oates & Messer, 2007).

Cognitive-Developmental Theory and Social Cognition

Cognitive-developmental theory stresses the importance of the child's growing cognitive capacities. According to Jean Piaget, middle childhood coincides with the stage of concrete operations and is partly characterized by a decline in egocentrism and an expansion of the capacity to view the world and oneself from other people's perspectives. This cognitive advance not only enhances the child's intellectual functioning but also has a major effect on the child's social relationships (Mischo, 2004; Zan & Hildebrandt, 2003).

Question: What is the relationship between social cognition and perspective taking? **Social cognition** refers to the development of children's knowledge about the social world. It focuses on the child's understanding of the relationship between the self and others. A key aspect of the development of social cognition is the ability to assume the role or perspective of another person. Robert Selman and his colleagues (Selman, 1980; Selman & Dray, 2006) devised a method to study the development of perspective-taking skills in childhood. Selman (1980, p. 36) presented children with a social dilemma such as the following:

> Holly is an 8-year-old girl who likes to climb trees. She is the best tree climber in the neighborhood. One day while climbing down from a tall tree, she falls off the bottom branch but does not hurt herself. Her father sees her fall. He

latency stage In psychoanalytic theory, the fourth stage of psychosexual development, characterized by repression of sexual impulses and development of skills.

industry versus inferiority The fourth stage of psychosocial development in Erikson's theory, occurring in middle childhood. Mastery of tasks leads to a sense of industry, whereas failure produces feelings of inferiority.

social cognition Development of children's understanding of the relationship between the self and others.

■ **Table 13.1** Levels of Perspective Taking

Level	Approximate Age (Years)	What Happens
0	3–6	Children are egocentric and do not realize that other people have perspectives different from their own. A child of this age will typically say that Holly will save the kitten because she likes kittens and that her father will be happy because he likes kittens too. The child assumes that everyone feels as she does.
1	5–9[a]	Children understand that people in different situations may have different perspectives. The child still assumes that only one perspective is "right." A child might say that Holly's father would be angry if he did not know why she climbed the tree. But if she told him why, he would understand. The child recognizes that the father's perspective may differ from Holly's because of lack of information. But once he has the information, he will assume the "right" (i.e., Holly's) perspective.
2	7–12[a]	The child understands that people may think or feel differently because they have different values or ideas. The child also recognizes that others are capable of understanding the child's own perspective. Therefore, the child is better able to anticipate reactions of others. The typical child of this age might say that Holly knows that her father will understand why she climbed the tree and that he therefore will not punish her.
3	10–15[a]	The child finally realizes that both she and another person can consider each other's point of view at the same time. The child may say something similar to this reasoning: Holly's father will think that Holly shouldn't have climbed the tree. But now that he has heard her side of the story, he would feel that she was doing what she thought was right. Holly realizes that her father will consider how she felt.
4	12 and above[a]	The child realizes that mutual perspective taking does not always lead to agreement. The perspectives of the larger social group also must be considered. A child of this age might say that society expects children to obey their parents and therefore that Holly should realize why her father might punish her.

Source: Selman (1976).

[a]Ages may overlap.

is upset and asks her to promise not to climb trees any more. Holly promises. Later that day, Holly and her friends meet Sean. Sean's kitten is caught up in a tree and can't get down. Something has to be done right away, or the kitten may fall. Holly is the only one who climbs trees well enough to reach the kitten and get it down, but she remembers her promise to her father.

The children then were asked a series of questions designed to test their ability to take the role of another person (e.g., "How will Holly's father feel if he finds out she climbed the tree?"). Based on the children's responses to these questions, Selman (1976) described five levels of perspective-taking skills in childhood (see ■ Table 13.1).

Research supports Selman's developmental progression in perspective taking (De Lisi, 2005; Mischo, 2005; Nakkula & Nikitopoulos, 2001). Children with better perspective-taking skills tend to be more skilled at negotiating and peer relations (Fitzgerald & White, 2003; Selman & Dray, 2006; Strough et al., 2001).

Development of the Self-Concept in Middle Childhood

Question: How does the self-concept develop during middle childhood? In early childhood, children's self-concepts, or self-definitions, focus on concrete external traits, such as appearance, activities, and living situations. But as children undergo the cognitive developments of middle childhood, their more abstract internal traits, or personality characteristics, begin to play a role in their self-definition. Social relationships and group memberships take on significance (Damon, 2000; Harter, 2006; Thompson, 2006).

An investigative method called the Twenty Statements Test bears out this progression and also highlights the relationships between the self-concept and general cognitive development. According to this method, children are given a sheet of paper with the question "Who am I?" and 20 spaces in which to write answers. Consider the answers of a 9-year-old boy and an 11-year-old girl:

The nine-year-old boy: My name is Bruce C. I have brown eyes. I have brown hair. I have brown eyebrows. I'm 9 years old. I LOVE? sports. I have 7 people in my family. I have great? eye site. I have lots! of friends. I live on 1923 Pinecrest Drive. I'm going on 10 in September. I'm a boy. I have a uncle that is almost 7 feet tall. My school is Pinecrest. My teacher is Mrs. V. I play hockey! I'm also the smartest boy in the class. I LOVE! food. I love fresh air. I LOVE school.

The eleven-year-old girl: My name is A. I'm a human being. I'm a girl. I'm a truthful person. I'm not pretty. I do so-so in my studies. I'm a very good cellist. I'm a very good pianist. I'm a little bit tall for my age. I like several boys. I like several girls. I'm old fashioned. I play tennis. I am a very good musician. I try to be helpful. I'm always ready to be friends with anybody. Mostly I'm good, but I lose my temper. I'm not well liked by some girls and boys. I don't know if boys like me or not.

—Montemayor & Eisen (1977, pp. 317–318)

Only the 9-year-old lists his age and address, discusses his family, and focuses on physical traits, such as eye color, in his self-definition. The 9-year-old mentions his likes, which can be considered rudimentary psychological traits, but they are tied to the concrete, as would be expected of a concrete-operational child.

The 9- and 11-year-olds both list their competencies. The 11-year-old's struggle to bolster her self-esteem—her insistence on her musical abilities despite her qualms about her attractiveness—shows a greater concern with internal traits, psychological characteristics, and social relationships.

Research also finds that females are somewhat more likely than males to define themselves in terms of the groups to which they belong (Madson & Trafimow, 2001). A Chinese study found that children with siblings are more likely than only children to define themselves in terms of group membership (Wang et al., 1998).

Self-Esteem

One of the most critical aspects of self-concept is **self-esteem,** the value or worth that people attach to themselves. A positive self-image is crucial to psychological adjustment in children and adults (Chen et al., 2001; Feinberg et al., 2000). *Question: How does self-esteem develop during middle childhood?*

As children enter middle childhood, their self-concepts become more differentiated and they are able to evaluate their self-worth in many different areas (Tassi et al., 2001). Preschoolers do not generally make a clear distinction between different areas of competence. They are either "good at doing things" or not. At one time, it was

self-esteem The sense of value or worth that people attach to themselves.

Zigy Kaluzny/Getty Images

Authoritative Parenting and Self-Esteem

Research suggests that parental demands for mature behavior, imposition of restrictions, and warmth help children develop behavior patterns that are connected with self-esteem.

assumed that before age 8, children could differentiate between only two broad facets of self-concept. One involved general competence and the other, social acceptance (Harter, 2006). It was also believed that an overall, or general, self-concept did not emerge until the age of 8. But research indicates that even as early as 5 to 7 years of age, children are able to make judgments about their performance in seven different areas: physical ability, physical appearance, peer relationships, parent relationships, reading, mathematics, and general school performance. They also display an overall, or general, self-concept (Harter, 2006).

Truth or Fiction Revisited: Children's self-esteem actually declines throughout middle childhood, reaching a low point at about age 12 or 13. Then it increases during adolescence (Harter, 2006). What accounts for the decline? Because young children are egocentric, their initial self-concepts may be unrealistic. As children become older, they compare themselves with other children and adjust their self-concepts. For most children, the comparison results in a more critical self-appraisal and the consequent decline in self-esteem.

Do girls or boys have a more favorable self-image? The answer depends on the area (Quatman & Watson, 2001). Girls tend to have more positive self-concepts regarding reading, general academics, and helping others than boys do, whereas boys tend to have more positive self-concepts in math, physical ability, and physical appearance (Jacobs et al., 2005; Wang, 2005). Cross-cultural studies in China (Dai, 2001), Finland (Lepola et al., 2000), and Germany (Tiedemann, 2000) also find that girls tend to have higher self-concepts in writing and that boys tend to have higher self-concepts in math.

Why do girls and boys differ in their self-concepts? Socialization and gender stereotypes appear to affect the way females and males react to their achievements. For example, girls predict that they will do better on tasks that are labeled "feminine," and boys predict better performance for themselves when tasks are labeled "masculine" (Jacobs et al., 2005; Rathus et al., 2008).

Authoritative parenting apparently contributes to children's self-esteem (Baumrind, 1991a, 1991b; Linares et al., 2002; Supple & Small, 2006). Children with a favorable self-image tend to have parents who are restrictive, involved, and loving. Children with low self-esteem are more likely to have authoritarian or rejecting–neglecting parents.

High self-esteem in children is related to their closeness to parents, especially as found in father–son and mother–daughter relationships (Fenzel, 2000). Close relationships between parents are also associated with positive self-concepts in children (DeHart et al., 2006; Maejima & Oguchi, 2001).

Peers play a role in children's self-esteem (Nesdale & Lambert, 2007). Social acceptance by peers is related to self-perceived competence in academic, social, and athletic domains (Laireiter & Lager, 2006). Parents and classmates have an equally strong effect on children's sense of self-worth in the middle years. Friends and teachers have relatively less influence in shaping self-esteem, but are also important (Harter, 2006).

Self-esteem appears to have a genetic component, which would contribute to its stability. A Japanese study found that that the concordance (agreement) rate for self-esteem is higher among identical (MZ) twins than for fraternal (DZ) twins (Kamakura et al., 2007). A longitudinal British study found that both genetic and environmental factors appeared to contribute to the stability of children's self-esteem (Neiss et al., 2006). Most children will encounter failure, but high self-esteem may contribute to the belief that they can master adversity. Low self-esteem may become a self-fulfilling prophecy: Children with low self-esteem may not carve out much to boast about.

Learned Helplessness

One outcome of low self-esteem in academics is known as **learned helplessness.** *Question: What is learned helplessness, and how does it develop in middle childhood?* Learned helplessness refers to an acquired belief that one is unable to obtain the rewards that one seeks. "Helpless" children tend to quit following failure, whereas children who believe in their own ability tend to persist in their efforts or change their strategies (Zimmerman, 2000). One reason for this difference is that helpless children believe that success is due more to ability than to effort and they have little ability in a particular area. Consequently, persisting in the face of failure seems futile (Bandura et al., 2001; Sutherland et al., 2004). "Helpless" children typically perform more poorly in school and on standardized tests of intelligence and achievement than other children (Goldstein & Brooks, 2005).

Sex Differences in Learned Helplessness

It is unclear whether girls or boys exhibit more learned helplessness in middle childhood (Boggiano & Barrett, 1991; Valas, 2001). But a sex difference does emerge in mathematics (Simpkins et al., 2006). Researchers have found that even when girls are performing as well as boys in math and science, they have less confidence in their ability (Anderman et al., 2001). Why? Parents' expectations that children will do well (or poorly) in a given area influence both the children's self-perceptions and their performance. Parents tend to hold the stereotyped view that girls have less math ability than boys. This viewpoint is true regardless of their own daughter's actual performance in math. Because of lower parental expectations, girls may shy away from math and not develop their math skills as much as boys do (Simpkins et al., 2006). Here we have an example of the self-fulfilling prophecy.

learned helplessness An acquired (hence, learned) belief that one is unable to control one's environment.

Lessons in Observation
Self-Concept

To watch this video, visit the book companion website. You can also answer the questions and e-mail your responses to your professor.

At age 4½, Christopher describes himself by listing objects and possessions in his house.

Learning Objectives

- What is a self-concept?
- How does the self-concept develop over time?
- When do children begin to incorporate personal traits into their self-descriptions?

Applied Lesson

How would you describe yourself? What information do you choose to include? Why?

Critical Thinking

You cannot see or touch a self-concept. How do researchers study the self-concept? Are you satisfied with their methods? Why or why not?

Active Review

1. Erikson labels middle childhood the stage of _____ versus inferiority.
2. According to Piaget, middle childhood coincides with the stage of _____ operations.
3. A key aspect of the development of social cognition is the ability to take the _____ of another person.
4. Children's self-esteem (Increases or Decreases?) during middle childhood.
5. (Authoritarian or Authoritative?) parenting contributes to high self-esteem in children.

Reflect & Relate: Are you "responsible" for your own self-esteem, or does your self-esteem generally vary with the opinion that others have of you? Why is this question important?

Go to

http://www.thomsonedu.com/psychology/rathus

for an interactive version of this review.

The Family

Question: What kinds of influences are exerted by the family during middle childhood? In middle childhood, the family continues to play a key role in socializing the child, even though peers, teachers, and other outsiders begin to play a greater role (Harter, 2006; Thompson, 2006). In this section, we look at developments in parent–child relationships during the middle years. We also consider the effects of different family environments: the family environment provided by lesbian and gay parents and the experience of living in families with varying marital arrangements. We also consider the effects of maternal employment.

Parent–Child Relationships

Parent–child interactions focus on some new concerns during the middle childhood years. They include school-related matters, assignment of chores, and peer activities (Collins et al., 2003).

During the middle years, parents do less monitoring of children's activities and provide less direct feedback than they did in the preschool years. In middle childhood, children do more monitoring of their own behavior. Although the parents still retain control over the child, control is gradually transferred from parent to child, a process known as **coregulation** (Maccoby, 2002; Wahler et al., 2001). Children no longer need to be constantly reminded of do's and dont's as they begin to internalize the standards of their parents.

Children and parents spend less time together in middle childhood than in the preschool years. But as in early childhood, children spend more of this time with their mothers than with their fathers (Russell & Russell, 1987). Mothers' interactions with school-age children continue to revolve around caregiving and household tasks, whereas fathers are relatively more involved in recreational activities, when they are involved, especially with sons. But here, too, mothers may actually spend more time (Wolfenden & Holt, 2005).

coregulation A gradual transferring of control from parent to child, beginning in middle childhood.

In the later years of middle childhood (ages 10 to 12), children evaluate their parents more critically than they do in the early years (Reid et al., 1990). This shift in perception may reflect the child's developing cognitive ability to view relationships in more complex ways (Selman & Dray, 2006). But throughout middle childhood, children rate their parents as their best source of emotional support, rating them more highly than friends (Cowan & Cowan, 2005; Katz et al., 2005). And emotional support is more valuable than economics in middle childhood (Santinello & Vieno, 2002).

Lesbian and Gay Parents

"Where did you get that beautiful necklace?" I asked the little girl in the pediatrician's office.

"From my Moms," she answered. It turned out that her family consisted of two women, each of whom had a biological child, one girl and one boy. *Question: What are the effects of having lesbian or gay parents?*

Research on **lesbian** and **gay** parenting has fallen into two general categories: the general adjustment of children and whether the children of lesbian and gay parents are more likely than other children to be lesbian or gay themselves. Research by Charlotte Patterson (2006) has generally found that the psychological adjustment of children of lesbian and gay parents—whether conceived by intercourse or donor insemination, or adopted—is comparable to that of children of heterosexual parents. Patterson and others (Wainright et al., 2004) have concluded that despite the stigma attached to homosexuality, lesbians and gay men frequently create and sustain positive family relationships.

Now let's consider the sexual orientation of the children of lesbian and gay parents. In doing so, we begin a generation back with the research of psychiatrist

lesbian A female who is interested romantically and sexually in other females.

gay A male who is interested romantically and sexually in other males. (Also used more broadly to refer to both lesbians and gay males.)

A Closer Look

How to Answer a 7-Year-Old's Questions about—Gulp—Sex

Daddy, where do babies come from?
Why are you asking me? Ask your mother.

Most children do not find it easy to talk to parents about sex. Only about one-quarter of the children in a national survey had done so (National Campaign to Prevent Teenage Pregnancy, 2003). Children usually find it easier to approach their mothers than their fathers (Guttmacher Institute, 2007).

Yet most children are curious about where babies come from, about how girls and boys differ, and the like. Adults who avoid these issues convey their own uneasiness about sex and may teach children that sex is something to be ashamed of.

Adults need not be sex experts to talk to their children about sex. They can surf the Internet to fill gaps in knowledge or to find books written for parents to read to children. They can admit they do not know all the answers.

Here are some pointers (Rathus et al., 2008):

- Be approachable. Be willing to discuss sex.
- Provide accurate information. The 6-year-old who wants to know where babies mature within the mother should not be told "in Mommy's tummy." It's wrong and isn't cute; the "tummy" is where food is digested. The child may worry that the baby is going to be digested. The child should be told, instead, "In Mommy's uterus" and be shown diagrams if he or she wants specifics.
- Teach children the correct names of their sex organs and that the "dirty words" others use to refer to the sex organs are not acceptable in most social settings. Avoid using silly words like "pee pee" or "private parts" to describe sex organs.

Reflect: Why do you think parents are reluctant to use anatomically correct words for sex organs when they are talking with their young children?

Richard Green. In a classic study, Green (1978) observed 37 children and young adults, age 3 to 20 years old, who were being reared—or had been reared—by lesbians or **transsexuals.** All but one of the children reported or recalled preferences for toys, clothing, and friends (male or female) that were typical for their sex and age. All the 13 older children who reported sexual fantasies or sexual behavior were heterosexually oriented. In a subsequent study, Green and his colleagues (1986) compared the children of European American mothers who were currently single, 50 of whom were lesbians and 40 of whom were heterosexual. Boys from the two groups showed no significant differences in intelligence test scores, sexual orientation, gender-role preferences, relationships with family and peer groups, and adjustment to life with a single parent. Girls showed slight differences, including somewhat more flexibility in gender roles. Green concluded that the mother's sexual orientation had no connection with parental fitness. A study by Patterson and her colleagues (Brodzinsky et al., 2002) suggested that many adoption agencies now agree with Green's conclusions.

Another review by Patterson (2003) addressed the personal and social development of children with lesbian and gay parents. Patterson found that the sexual orientation of the children was generally heterosexual. When parents had gotten divorced and created families with same-sex partners because of their sexual orientations, their children experienced a period of adjustment that entailed some difficulties, as do children when heterosexual parents get divorced. Children who are adopted by lesbian or gay parents tend to be well adjusted. The point here—reinforcing Green's findings—is that wanting the child is more important to the child's adjustment than the sexual orientation of the parents.

Generation X or Generation Ex? What Happens to Children Whose Parents Get Divorced?

To many in the United States, the 2000s are the period of "Generation X." However, it may be more accurate to think of our time as that of "Generation Ex," that is, a generation characterized by ex-wives and ex-husbands. Their children are also a part of Generation Ex, which is large and growing continuously. More than 1 million American children each year experience the divorce of their parents (U.S. Bureau of the Census, 2004). Nearly 40% of European American children and 75% of African American children in the United States who are born to married parents will spend at least part of their childhoods in single-parent families as a result of divorce (Marsiglio, 2004).

Question: What are the effects of divorce on the children? Divorce may be tough on parents; it can be even tougher on children (Amato, 2006; Rogers, 2004). The automatic aspects of family life cease being automatic. No longer do children eat with both parents. No longer do they go to ball games, the movies, or Disneyland with both of them. No longer do they curl up with them on the sofa to watch TV. No longer do they kiss both at bedtime. The parents are now often supporting two households, resulting in fewer resources for the children (Tashiro et al., 2006). Children lose other things besides family life. Sometimes the losses are minor, but many children who live with their mothers scrape by—or fail to scrape by—at the poverty level or below. Some children move from spacious houses into cramped apartments or from a desirable neighborhood to one where they are afraid to walk the streets. The mother who was once available may become an occasional visitor, spending more time at work and placing the kids in day care for extended periods.

In considering the effects of divorce on family members—both children and adults—Paul Amato (2006) suggests that researchers consider whether the effects are due to divorce or to "selection factors." For example, are the effects on children due to divorce per se, to marital conflict, to inadequate parental problem-solving ability,

transsexual A person who would prefer to be a person of the other sex and who may undergo hormone treatments, cosmetic surgery, or both to achieve the appearance of being a member of the other sex.

or to changes in financial status? Also, do children undergo a temporary crisis and gradually adjust, or do stressors persist indefinitely? For example, 3 years after the divorce, feelings of sadness, shock, disbelief, and desire for parental reunion tend to decline, but even 10 years later, children tend to retain anger toward the parent they hold responsible for the breakup.

Parents who get divorced are often in conflict about many things, and one of them typically involves how to rear the children (Amato, 2006). Because the children often hear their parents fighting over child rearing, the children may come to blame themselves for the split. Young children, who are less experienced than adolescents, are more likely to blame themselves. Young children also worry more about uncharted territory and the details of life after the breakup. Adolescents are relatively more independent and have some power to control their day-to-day lives.

Most children live with their mothers after a divorce (Amato, 2006; Ulloa & Ulibarri, 2004). Some fathers remain fully devoted to their children despite the split, but others tend to spend less time with their children as time goes on. This pattern is especially common when fathers create other families, such that the children of their new partners are competing with their biological children. Not only does the drop-off in paternal attention deprive children of activities and social interactions, but it also saps their self-esteem: "Why doesn't Daddy love me anymore? What's wrong with me?"

There is no question that divorce has challenging effects on children. The children of divorce are more likely to have conduct disorders, lower self-esteem, drug abuse, and poor grades in school (Amato, 2006; Adamsons & Pasley, 2006). Their physical health may decline, at least temporarily (Troxel & Matthews, 2004). There are individual differences, but, by and large, the fallout for children is worst during the first year after the breakup. Children tend to rebound after a couple of years or so (Malone et al., 2004).

A parental breakup is connected with a decline in the quality of parenting. A longitudinal study by E. Mavis Hetherington and her colleagues (Hetherington, 2006; Hetherington et al., 1989) tracked the adjustment of children who were 4 years old at the time of the divorce; the follow-ups occurred 2 months, 1 year, 2 years, and 6 years after the divorce. The investigators found that the organization of family life deteriorates. The family is more likely to eat meals pickup style, as opposed to sitting

© Royalty-Free/CORBIS

Generation Ex: Ex-Husband, Ex-Wife, Ex-Family, Ex-Security
Nearly half of American marriages end in divorce, and divorce turns life topsy-turvy for children. Younger children tend to erroneously blame themselves for the dissolution of the family, but children in middle childhood come to see things more accurately. Children of divorce tend to develop problems, many of which fade as time passes. Should parents in conflict stay together for the sake of the children? The answer seems to be that the children will not be better off if the parents continue to fight in front of them.

harmful family functioning (Hetherington, 1989; Wallerstein et al., 2005). **Truth or Fiction Revisited:** From a psychological perspective, when bickering parents stay together "for the sake of the children," the children encounter stress.

The Effects of Maternal Employment

Why is this section labeled "The Effects of Maternal Employment"? Why not "Parental Employment" or "Paternal Employment"? Perhaps because of the traditional role of women as homemakers.

Even so, the past half-century has witnessed one of the most dramatic social changes in the history of the United States. Mothers are entering the labor force in record numbers. A half-century ago, most women remained in the home, but today, nearly three out of four married mothers of children under age 18 are employed, as are four out of five divorced, separated, or widowed mothers (U.S. Bureau of the Census, 2007). Family lifestyles have changed as more women combine maternal and occupational roles. *Question: What are the effects of maternal employment on children?* Do problems arise when mother is not available for round-the-clock love and attention?

Many psychologists and educators—and lay commentators—have been concerned about the effects of maternal employment on children. Part of the brouhaha has been based on traditionalist, moralistic values which argue that the mother ought to remain in the home. But concern has also been based on research findings that suggest that maternal employment (and nonmaternal care) have some negative effects on children (Belsky, 2006a).

One common belief is that Mom being in the workforce rather than in the home leads to delinquency. Researchers using data on 707 adolescents, age 12 to 14, from the National Longitudinal Survey of Youth examined whether the occupational status of a mother was connected with delinquent behavior (Vander Ven et al., 2001; Vander Ven & Cullen, 2004). They found that maternal employment per se made relatively little or no difference, but there was a slight indirect effect in that deviant behavior was connected with lack of supervision. The issue, then, would seem to be for the parents to ensure that children receive adequate supervision regardless of who—Mom or Dad or both—is on the job.

We can see that this issue is gender biased in the sense that the evidence suggests that *paternal* employment is potentially as harmful as *maternal* employment. Yet, who argues that fathers rather than mothers should remain in the home to ward off problems related to poor supervision? After all, the father is the traditional breadwinner and the mother is the traditional homemaker.

Political and moral arguments aside, there is little evidence that maternal employment harms children. Elizabeth Harvey (1999) and other researchers (Han et al., 2001) have examined data from the National Longitudinal Survey of Youth on the effects of early parental employment on children. The effects were minimal. Neither the timing nor the continuity of early maternal employment was consistently related to children's development. Harvey did find that working a greater number of hours was linked with slightly lower scores on measures of cognitive development through the age of 9 and with slightly lower academic achievement scores before the age of 7. However, there was no connection between maternal employment and children's conduct disorders, compliance, or self-esteem. And now for the pluses: Harvey found that early parental employment was beneficial for single mothers and lower-income

© Ed Bock Photography, Inc./CORBIS

What Are the Effects of Maternal Employment?
Let's be honest here. Why doesn't the caption read: "What are the effects of parental employment?" The answer is that the vestiges of sexism run rampant in society. When things go wrong with children in families in which both parents must work—or choose to work—the tendency remains to blame the mother. However, research shows that maternal employment is actually connected with few problems with children; it is also connected with more egalitarian attitudes. (Go, Mom!)

families. Why? It brought in cash, and increasing family income has positive effects on children's development. (Is anyone surprised?)

There are other family benefits for maternal employment. Maternal employment appears to benefit school-age children, especially daughters, by fostering greater independence, emotional maturity, and higher achievement orientation (Hangal & Aminabhavi, 2007). **Truth or Fiction Revisited:** Daughters of employed women are more achievement oriented and do set higher career goals for themselves than daughters of nonworking women. A Canadian study found that children whose mothers were employed tended to be more prosocial and less anxious than other children (Nomaguchi, 2006). Both the sons and daughters of employed women appear to be more flexible in their gender-role stereotypes (Wright & Young, 1998). For example, sons of working women are more helpful with housework. Of course, these same findings will be considered challenging to men who wish to enforce traditional gender roles that oppress females.

There are other interesting findings on maternal employment. For example, Lois Hoffman and Lise Youngblade (1998) studied a sample of 365 mothers of third- and fourth-graders in an industrialized midwestern city. They discovered that working-class full-time homemakers were more likely to be depressed than employed mothers. Feelings of depression were related to permissive and authoritarian parenting styles, suggesting that many financially stressed homemakers do not have the emotional resources to give their children the best possible rearing. Among middle-class mothers, employment was not related to mood or style of parenting. Greater family financial resources apparently lift the mood. (Again: Is anybody surprised?)

A study of 116 urban Japanese women with children in the second grade also looked at the effects of maternal employment from the perspective of the mother. It found that the most satisfied women were those with more children but who were highly committed to their roles in the workforce, and, in case that were not enough, who felt that they were doing an excellent job as mothers (Holloway et al., 2006).

Active Review

6. During the middle years, parents do (More or Less?) monitoring of children's activities and provide less direct feedback than they did in the preschool years.

7. The children of lesbian and gay parents are most likely to be (Heterosexual or Homosexual?) in their sexual orientation.

8. Children of divorce most often experience (Upward or Downward?) movement in financial status.

9. Most children of divorce live with their (Mothers or Fathers?).

10. (Boys or Girls?) seem to have a harder time coping with divorce.

11. Research suggests that children are more likely to engage in delinquent behavior as a result of (Maternal employment or Lack of supervision?).

Reflect & Relate: Have you known children whose families have undergone divorce? What were (or *are*) the effects on the children?

Go to

http://www.thomsonedu.com/psychology/rathus

for an interactive version of this review.

■ **Table 13.2**   Stages in Children's Concepts of Friendship

Stage	Name	Approximate Age (Years)	What Happens
0	Momentary physical interaction	3–6	Children remain egocentric and unable to take one another's point of view. Thus, their concept of a friend is one who likes to play with the same things they do and who lives nearby.
1	One-way assistance	5–9[a]	Children realize that their friends may have different thoughts and feelings than they do, but they place their own desires first. They view a friend as someone who does what they want.
2	Fair-weather cooperation	7–12[a]	Friends are viewed as doing things for one another (reciprocity), but the focus remains on each individual's self-interest rather than on the relationship per se.
3	Intimate and mutual sharing	10–15[a]	The focus is on the relationship itself, rather than on the individuals separately. The function of friendship is viewed as mutual support over a long period of time, rather than concern about a given activity or self-interest.
4	Autonomous interdependence	12 and above[a]	Children (adolescents, and adults) understand that friendships grow and change as people change. They realize that they may need different friends to satisfy different personal and social needs.

Source: Selman (1980).

[a]Ages may overlap

During middle childhood, contact with members of the other sex is strongly discouraged by peers. For example, a study of European American, African American, Latino and Latina American, and Native American 10- and 11-year-olds found that those who crossed the "sex boundary" were especially unpopular with their peers (Sroufe et al., 1993).

Active Review

12. As children move into middle childhood, their activities and interests become directed (Closer to or Farther away from?) the home.
13. Popular children tend to be attractive and relatively (Mature or Immature?) for their age.
14. (Firstborn or Later-born?) children are more likely to be popular.
15. During middle childhood, contact with members of the other sex is (Encouraged or Discouraged?) by peers.

Reflect & Relate: What do you look for in a friend? What "stage" are you in, according to Table 13.2?

Go to

http://www.thomsonedu.com/psychology/rathus

for an interactive version of this review.

The School

Question: What are the effects of the school on children's social and emotional development? The school exerts a powerful influence on many aspects of the child's development. Schools, like parents, set limits on behavior, make demands for mature behavior, attempt to communicate, and are oriented toward nurturing positive physical, social, and cognitive development. The schools, like parents, have a direct influence on children's IQ scores, achievement motivation, and career aspirations (Aber et al., 2007; Woolfolk, 2008). As in the family, schools influence social and moral development (Aber et al., 2007; Killen & Smetana, 2006).

Schools are also competitive environments, and children who do too well—and students who do not do well enough—can suffer from the resentment or the low opinion of others. An Italian study placed 178 male and 182 female 8- to 9-year-old elementary school students in competitive situations (Tassi et al., 2001). It was found that when the students were given the task of trying to outperform one another, competition led to social rejection by students' peers. On the other hand, when the students were simply asked to do the best they could, high rates of success led to admiration by one's peers.

In this section, we consider children's transition to school and then examine the effects of the school environment and of teachers.

Entry into School: Getting to Know You

An increasing number of children attend preschool. About half have had some type of formal prekindergarten experience, often part-time (Slavin, 2006; Woolfolk, 2008). But most children first experience full-time schooling when they enter kindergarten or first grade. Children must master many new tasks when they start school. They will have to meet new academic challenges, learn new school and teacher expectations, and fit into a new peer group. They must learn to accept extended separation from parents and develop increased attention, self-control, and self-help skills.

What happens to children during the transition from home or preschool to elementary school may be critical for the eventual success or failure of their educational experience, particularly for low-income children. Families of children living in poverty may be less able to supply both the material and emotional supports that help the child adjust successfully to school (Slavin, 2006; Woolfolk, 2008).

How well prepared are children to enter school? Discussions of school readiness must consider at least three critical factors:

1. The diversity and inequity of children's early life experiences
2. Individual differences in young children's development and learning
3. The degree to which schools establish reasonable and appropriate expectations of children's capabilities when they enter school

Unfortunately, some children enter school less well prepared than others. In one survey, 7,000 American kindergarten teachers reported that more than one-third of their students began school unprepared to learn (Chira, 1991). Nearly half the teachers thought that children entered school less ready to learn than had children 5 years earlier. Most of the teachers said that children often lacked the language skills needed to succeed. This report and others (Slavin, 2006; Woolfolk, 2008) concluded that poor health care and nutrition and lack of adequate stimulation and support by parents place many children at risk for academic failure even before they enter school.

A study by the U.S. Department of Education concluded that schools could do a better job of easing the transition to kindergarten (Love et al., 1992). The researchers surveyed schools in 1,003 school districts and also visited 8 schools. The average school reported that between 10% and 20% of incoming kindergartners had difficulty adjusting to kindergarten. Adjusting to the academic demands of school was reported to be the area of greatest difficulty. Children whose families were low in socioeconomic status had a more difficult time adjusting than other children, particularly in academics. Children who enter school with deficits in language and math skills generally continue to show deficits in these areas during at least the first years of school (Slavin, 2006; Woolfolk, 2008).

The School Environment: Setting the Stage for Success, or . . .

Question: What are the characteristics of a good school? Research summaries (Slavin, 2006; Woolfolk, 2008) indicate that an effective school has the following characteristics:

- An active, energetic principal
- An atmosphere that is orderly but not oppressive
- Empowerment of teachers; that is, teachers participating in decision making
- Teachers who have high expectations that children will learn
- A curriculum that emphasizes academics
- Frequent assessment of student performance

A CLOSER LOOK

Bullying: An Epidemic of Misbehavior and Fear

Nine-year-old Stephanie did not want to go to school. As with many other children who refuse to go to school, she showed anxiety at the thought of leaving home. But Stephanie was not experiencing separation anxiety from her family. It turns out that she had gotten into a disagreement with Susan, and Susan had told her she would beat her mercilessly if she showed up at school again. To highlight her warning, Susan had shoved Stephanie across the hall.

Stephanie was a victim of bullying. Susan was a bully. Stephanie did not know it, but there was something of an irony. Susan was also bullied from time to time by a couple of girls at school.

Was there something unusual about all this bullying? Not really. Boys are more likely than girls to be bullies, but many girls engage in bullying (Batsche & Porter, 2006; Li, 2006, 2007; Perren & Alsaker, 2006). All in all, it is estimated that 10% of students have been exposed to extreme bullying and that 70% to 75% of students overall have been bullied (Li, 2006, 2007).

Bullying has devastating effects on the school atmosphere. It transforms the perception of school from a safe place into a violent place (Batsche & Porter, 2006; Perren & Alsaker, 2006). Bullying also impairs adjustment to middle school, where bullying is sometimes carried out by older children against younger children (Perren & Alsaker, 2006; Scheithauer, et al., 2006). It especially impairs adjustment for children who speak another language in the home, who tend to be picked on more often (Yu et al., 2003).

Many but not all bullies have some things in common. For one thing, their achievement tends to be lower than average, such that peer approval (or deference from peers) might be more important to them than academics (Batsche & Porter, 2006; Perren & Alsaker, 2006. Bullies are more likely to come from homes of lower socioeconomic status (Perren & Alsaker, 2006; Pereira et al., 2004). Many of these homes are characterized by violence between parents (Baldry, 2003; Batsche & Porter, 2006).

Numerous studies have also investigated the personalities of bullies. One study compared middle-school bullies to matched controls (Coolidge et al., 2004). Bullying was associated with more frequent diagnoses of conduct disorder, oppositional defiant disorder, attention-deficit/hyperactivity disorder, and depression. Bullies were also more likely to have personality problems, such as assuming that others were predisposed to harming them. They also showed more problems in impulse control.

Cyberbullying

Some children are bullied electronically, not in person. They receive threatening messages from fellow students by means of computers, cell phones, or personal digital assistants (PDAs) (Patchin & Hinduja, 2006). This phenomenon is referred to as *cyberbullying*. Although

• Empowerment of students; that is, students participating in setting goals, making classroom decisions, and engaging in cooperative learning activities with other students

Certain aspects of the school environment are important as well. One key factor is class size. Smaller classes permit students to receive more individual attention and to express their ideas more often (Slavin, 2006). Smaller classes lead to increased achievement in mathematics and reading in the early primary grades. Smaller classes are particularly useful in teaching the "basics"—reading, writing, and arithmetic—to elementary school students at risk for academic failure (Slavin, 2006; Woolfolk, 2008).

Teachers: Setting Limits, Making Demands, Communicating Values, and—Oh, Yes—Teaching

The influence of the schools is mainly due to teachers. Teachers, like parents, set limits, make demands, communicate values, and foster development. Teacher–student relationships are more limited than parent–child relationships, but teachers still have the opportunity to serve as powerful role models and dispensers of rein-

© Bill Bachmann/Rainbow

Bullying
For victims of bullying the school can become a violent place rather than a safe one. Although many schools and families try to control bullying, much of it goes unreported.

cyberbullying might seem to provide a "comfortable" distance between the bully and the victim, its effects can be devastating, and perhaps as devastating, as those of in-person bullying. Cases of severe anxiety, including school phobia and refusal, depression, lowered self-esteem, and even the occasional suicide, have been reported (S. P. Thomas, 2006). As with other forms of bullying, the majority of cyberbullies are male, and most victims do not report the incidents (Li, 2006, 2007).

Is there a "cure" for bullying? School systems and families have a stake in controlling bullying, and sometimes setting strict limits on bullies is of help. But, as noted, much—or most—bullying goes unreported, sometimes because children are embarrassed to admit they are being bullied, sometimes because they fear retaliation by the bully (Li, 2006, 2007). Many children simply learn to accommodate or avoid bullies until they are out of school (Hunter & Boyle, 2004). Then they go their separate ways.

Reflect:
• Were you ever bullied in school? If so, how did you handle it?
• What should teachers and school official do about bullies?
• What should parents tell their children about bullies?

forcement. After all, children spend several hours each weekday in the presence of teachers.

Teacher Influences on Student Performance

Many aspects of teacher behavior are related to student achievement (Slavin, 2006). Achievement is enhanced when teachers expect students to master the curriculum, allocate most of the available time to academic activities, and manage the classroom environment effectively. Students learn more in classes when actively instructed or supervised by teachers than when working on their own. The most effective teachers ask questions, give personalized feedback, and provide opportunities for drill and practice, as opposed to straight lecturing.

Student achievement also is linked to the emotional climate of the classroom (Slavin, 2006). Students do not do as well when teachers rely heavily on criticism, ridicule, threats, or punishment. Achievement is high in classrooms with a pleasant, friendly atmosphere but not in classrooms with extreme teacher warmth.

Teacher Expectations

There is a saying that "You find what you're looking for." Consider the so-called **Pygmalion effect** in education. In Greek mythology, the amorous sculptor Pygmalion breathed life into a beautiful statue he had carved. Similarly, in the musical *My Fair Lady,* a reworking of the Pygmalion legend, Henry Higgins fashions a great lady from the lower-class Eliza Doolittle.

Teachers also try to bring out positive traits they believe dwell within their students. **Truth or Fiction Revisited:** A classic experiment by Robert Rosenthal and Lenore Jacobson (1968) suggested that teacher expectations can become **self-fulfilling prophecies.** As reported in the classic *Pygmalion in the Classroom,* Rosenthal and Jacobson (1968) first gave students a battery of psychological tests. Then they informed teachers that a handful of the students, although average in performance to date, were about to blossom forth intellectually in the current school year.

Now, in fact, the tests had indicated nothing in particular about the "chosen" children. These children had been selected at random. The purpose of the experiment was to determine whether changing teacher expectations could affect student performance. As it happened, the identified children made significant gains in intelligence test scores.

In subsequent research, however, results have been mixed. Some studies have found support for the Pygmalion effect (Madon et al., 2001; Sarrazin et al., 2005a, 2005b). Others have not. A review of 18 such experiments found that the Pygmalion effect was most pronounced when the procedure for informing teachers of the potential in the target student had greatest credibility (Raudenbusch, 1984). A fair conclusion would seem to be that teacher expectations sometimes, but not always, affect students' motivation, self-esteem, expectations for success, and achievement.

These findings have serious implications for children from ethnic minority and low-income families. There is some indication that teachers expect less academically from children in these groups (Slavin, 2006; Woolfolk, 2008). Teachers with lower expectations for certain children may spend less time encouraging and interacting with them.

What are some of the ways that teachers can help motivate all students to do their best? Anita Woolfolk (2008) suggests the following:

- Make the classroom and the lesson interesting and inviting.
- Ensure that students can profit from social interaction.
- Make the classroom a safe and pleasant place.
- Recognize that students' backgrounds can give rise to diverse patterns of needs.

Pygmalion effect A self-fulfilling prophecy; an expectation that is confirmed because of the behavior of those who hold the expectation.

self-fulfilling prophecy An event that occurs because of the behavior of those who expect it to occur.

- Help students take appropriate responsibility for their successes and failures.
- Encourage students to perceive the links between their own efforts and their achievements.
- Help students set attainable short-term goals.

Sexism in the Classroom

Although girls were systematically excluded from formal education for centuries, today we might not expect to find **sexism** among teachers. Teachers, after all, are generally well educated. They are also trained to be fair minded and sensitive to the needs of their young charges in today's changing society.

However, we may not have heard the last of sexism in our schools. According to a classic review of more than 1,000 research publications about girls and education, girls are treated unequally by their teachers, their male peers, and the school curriculum (American Association of University Women, 1992). The reviewers concluded:

Waiting to Be Called On
Who is the teacher most likely to call on? Some studies say that teachers may favor the boy and call on him before the girl, especially in math, science, and technology classes.

- Many teachers pay less attention to girls than boys, especially in math, science, and technology classes.
- Many girls are subjected to **sexual harassment**—unwelcome verbal or physical conduct of a sexual nature—from male classmates, and many teachers minimize the harmfulness of harassment and ignore it.
- Some school textbooks still stereotype or ignore women, more often portraying males as the shakers and movers in the world.

In a widely cited study, Myra Sadker and David Sadker (1994; Sadker & Silber, 2007) observed students in fourth-, sixth-, and eighth-grade classes in four states and in the District of Columbia. Teachers and students were European American and African American, urban, suburban, and rural. In almost all cases, the findings were depressingly similar. Boys generally dominated classroom communication, whether the subject was math (a traditionally "masculine" area) or language arts (a traditionally "feminine" area). Despite the stereotype that girls are more likely to talk or even chatter, boys were eight times more likely than girls to call out answers without raising their hands. So far, it could be said, we have evidence of a sex difference, but not of sexism. However, teachers were less than impartial in responding to boys and girls when they called out. Teachers, male and female, were significantly more likely to accept calling out from boys. Girls were significantly more likely, as the song goes, to receive "teachers' dirty looks" or to be reminded that they should raise their hands and wait to be called on. Boys, it appears, are expected to be impetuous, but girls are reprimanded for "unladylike behavior." Sad to say, until they saw videotapes of themselves, the teachers generally were unaware that they were treating girls and boys differently.

Other observers note that primary and secondary teachers tend to give more attention to boys than to girls, especially in math and technology courses (Bell & Norwood, 2007; Crocco & Libresco, 2007; Koch, 2007). They call on boys more often, ask them more questions, talk to and listen to them more, give them lengthier directions, and praise and criticize them more often.

The irony is that our educational system has been responsible for lifting many generations of the downtrodden into the mainstream of American life (Sadker & Zittleman, 2007). Unfortunately, the system may be doing more to encourage development of academic skills—especially skills needed in our new technological age—in boys than in girls.

sexism Discrimination or bias against people based on their sex.

sexual harassment Unwelcome verbal or physical conduct of a sexual nature.

Childhood is the happiest time of life, correct? Not necessarily. Many children are happy enough, protected by their parents and unencumbered by adult responsibilities. From the perspective of aging adults, their bodies seem made of rubber and free of aches. Their energy is apparently boundless.

Yet many children, like Kristin, are depressed. ***Questions: What is depression? What can we do about it?*** Depressed children may feel sad, blue, down in the dumps. They may show poor appetite, insomnia, lack of energy and inactivity, loss of self-esteem, difficulty concentrating, loss of interest in people and activities they usually enjoy, crying, feelings of hopelessness and helplessness, and thoughts of suicide (American Psychiatric Association, 2000).

But many children do not recognize depression in themselves until the age of 7 or so. Part of the problem is cognitive developmental. The capacity for concrete operations apparently contributes to children's abilities to perceive internal feeling states (Glasberg & Aboud, 1982).

When children cannot report their feelings, depression is inferred from behavior. Depressed children in middle childhood engage in less social activity and have poorer social skills than peers (American Psychiatric Association, 2000). In some cases, childhood depression is "masked" by conduct disorders, physical complaints, academic problems, and anxiety.

It has been estimated that between 5% and 9% of children are seriously depressed in any given year (American Psychiatric Association, 2000). Depression occurs equally often in girls and boys during childhood but is more common among women later in life. Depressed children frequently continue to have depressive episodes as adolescents and adults.

Childhood Depression
Depressed children may complain of poor appetite, insomnia, lack of energy, difficulty concentrating, loss of interest in other people and activities they used to like, and feelings of worthlessness. But many depressed children do not recognize feelings of sadness. In some cases, childhood depression is "masked" by physical complaints, academic problems, anxiety, and even conduct disorders.

Origins of Depression

The origins of depression are complex and varied. Psychological and biological explanations have been proposed.

Some social cognitive theorists explain depression in terms of relationships between competencies (knowledge and skills) and feelings of self-esteem. Children who gain academic, social, and other competencies usually have high self-esteem. Perceived low levels of competence are linked to helplessness, low self-esteem, and depression. Longitudinal studies of primary schoolchildren have found that problems in academics, socializing, physical appearance, and sports can predict feelings of depression (Cole et al., 2001; Kistner, 2006). Conversely, self-perceived competence in these areas is negatively related to feelings of depression (Cole et al., 2001). That is, competence appears to "protect" children from depression. Children who have not developed competencies because of lack of opportunity, inconsistent parental reinforcement, and so on may develop feelings of helplessness and hopelessness. Similarly, stressful life events, daily hassles, and poor problem-solving ability can give rise to feelings of helplessness and hopelessness that trigger depression (Reinecke & DuBois, 2001).

In contrast, social support and self-confidence tend to protect children from depression. Some competent children might not credit themselves because of excessive parental expectations. Or children may be perfectionistic themselves. Perfectionistic children may be depressed because they cannot meet their own standards.

Children in elementary school are likely to be depressed because of situational stresses, such as family problems. Among middle schoolers, however, we find cognitive contributors to depression. For example, a study of 582 Chinese children from Hong Kong secondary schools found that cognitive distortions, such as minimizing accomplishments and blowing problems out of proportion, were associated with feelings of depression (Leung & Poon, 2001). A European study found that ruminating about problems (going over them again and again—and again), blaming oneself for things that are not one's fault, and blowing problems out of proportion are linked with depression (Garnefski et al., 2001).

A tendency to blame oneself (an internal attribution) or others (an external attribution) is called a child's **attributional style.** Certain attributional styles can contribute to helplessness and hopelessness and hence to depression (Kagan et al., 2004; Runyon & Kenny, 2002).

Truth or Fiction Revisited: It is true that some children blame themselves for all the problems in their lives, whether they deserve the blame or not. Research shows that children who are depressed are more likely to attribute the causes of their failures to internal, stable, and global factors, factors they are relatively helpless to change (Lewinsohn et al., 2000b). Helplessness triggers depression. Consider the case of two children who do poorly on a math test. John thinks, "I'm a jerk! I'm just no good in math! I'll never learn." Jim thinks, "That test was tougher than I thought it would be. I'll have to work harder next time." John is perceiving the problem as global (he's "a jerk") and stable (he'll "never learn"). Jim perceives the problem as specific rather than global (related to the type of math test the teacher makes up) and as unstable rather than stable (he can change the results by working harder). In effect, John thinks "It's me" (an internal attribution). By contrast, Jim thinks "It's the test" (an external attribution). Depressed children tend to explain negative events in terms of internal, stable, and global causes. As a result, they, like John, are more likely than Jim to be depressed.

There is also evidence of genetic factors in depression (Cryan & Slattery, 2007; Kendler et al., 2007; Orstavik et al., 2007). For example, the children of depressed parents are at greater risk for depression and other disorders (Jang et al., 2004; Korszun et al., 2004). A Norwegian study of 2,794 twins estimated that the heritability of depression in females was 49% and 25% in males (Orstavik et al., 2007). On a neurological level, evidence suggests that depressed children (and adults) "underutilize" the neurotransmitter **serotonin** (Vitiello, 2006). Learned helplessness is linked to lower serotonin levels in the brains of humans and rats (Joca et al., 2006; Wu et al., 1999).

Treatment of Depression

Parents and teachers can do a good deal to alleviate relatively mild feelings of depression among children. They can involve children in enjoyable activities, encourage the development of skills, offer praise when appropriate, and point out when children are being too hard on themselves. But if feelings of depression persist, treatment is called for.

Psychotherapy for depression tends to be mainly cognitive-behavioral these days, and it is often straightforward. Children (and adolescents) are encouraged to do enjoyable things and build social skills. They are made aware of their tendencies to minimize their accomplishments, catastrophize their problems, and overly blame themselves for shortcomings (e.g., Ellis & Dryden, 1996).

We noted that many depressed children underutilize the neurotransmitter serotonin. Antidepressant medication (selective serotonin reuptake inhibitors, or SSRIs), such as Luvox, Prozac, and Zoloft, increase the action of serotonin in the brain and are sometimes used to treat childhood depression. Studies of their effectiveness yield a mixed review, ranging from something like "deadly dangerous" to "often effective" (Vitiello, 2006). Although SSRIs are often effective, the Food and Drug Administration has warned that there may be a link between their use and suicidal thinking in children (Harris, 2004).

Childhood depression is frequently accompanied by anxiety (Kendler et al., 2007; Masi et al., 2004), as we see in the next section. Social and emotional problems that tend to emerge in middle childhood are summarized in Concept Review 13.1.

attributional style The way in which one is disposed toward interpreting outcomes (successes or failures), as in tending to place blame or responsibility on oneself or on external factors.

serotonin A neurotransmitter that is involved in mood disorders such as depression.

Concept Review 13.1 Social and Emotional Problems That May Emerge During Middle Childhood

Problem	Behavior Patterns	Comments
Conduct disorders 	• Precocious sexual activity, substance abuse • Truancy, stealing, lying, and aggression	• More common in boys • Child blames others for problems • Probably connected with genetic factors • Other contributors—antisocial family members, deviant peers, inconsistent discipline, physical punishment, family stress • Tends to be stable throughout adolescence and into adulthood • Frequently accompanied by ADHD
Childhood depression 	• Feelings of sadness, poor appetite, insomnia, lack of energy and inactivity, loss of self-esteem, difficulty concentrating, loss of interest in people and activities, crying, feelings of hopelessness and helplessness, and thoughts of suicide • Can be masked by conduct disorders, physical complaints, academic problems, and anxiety	• Occurs about equally in both sexes • Connected with lack of competencies (knowledge and skills) • Connected with situational stresses, such as divorce • Connected with feelings of helplessness and hopelessness • Connected with cognitive factors such as perfectionism, rumination, minimization of achievements, blowing problems out of proportion, and a negative attributional style—internal, stable, and global attributions for failures • Possibly connected with genetic factors • Connected with "underutilization" of the neurotransmitter serotonin • Frequently accompanied by anxiety
Childhood anxiety: • Phobias (e.g., separation anxiety disorder, stage fright, school phobia) • Panic disorder • Generalized anxiety disorder	• Obsessive–compulsive disorder • Stress disorders • Persistent, excessive worrying • Fear of the worst happening • Anxiety inappropriate for child's developmental level • Physical symptoms such as stomachaches, nausea, and vomiting • Nightmares • Concerns about death and dying	• More common in girls • Genetic factors implicated • Frequently develops after stressful life events, such as divorce, illness, death of relative or pet, or change of schools or homes • Often overlaps with—but not the same as—school refusal • Frequently accompanied by depression

generalized anxiety disorder (GAD) An anxiety disorder in which anxiety appears to be present continuously and is unrelated to the situation.

Childhood Anxiety

Children show many kinds of anxiety disorders, and these disorders are accompanied by depression in 50% to 60% of children (Kendler et al., 2007; Masi et al., 2004). Yet many children show anxiety disorders, such as **generalized anxiety disorder (GAD),** in the absence of depression (Kearney & Bensaheb, 2007). Other anxiety disorders shown by children include **phobias** such as **separation anxiety disorder (SAD)** and stage fright (Beidel & Turner, 2007).

A cross-cultural study compared anxiety disorders in 862 German children and 975 Japanese children between the ages of 8 and 12 (Essau et al., 2004). The German children were significantly more likely to report generalized anxiety, separation anxiety, social phobias, and **obsessive-compulsive disorder (OCD)**. The Japanese children were more likely to report physical complaints and phobias in the realm of bodily injury. In both nations, girls were more likely than boys to report anxieties.

Separation Anxiety Disorder

It is normal for children to show anxiety when they are separated from their care-givers. Separation anxiety is a normal feature of the child–caregiver relationship and begins during the first year. But the sense of security that is usually provided by bonds of attachment encourages children to explore their environments and become progressively independent of caregivers. *Question: What is separation anxiety disorder?*

Separation anxiety disorder affects an estimated 4% to 5% of children and young adolescents (American Psychiatric Association, 2000; Shear et al., 2006). The disorder occurs most often in girls and is often associated with school refusal. It also frequently occurs together with social anxiety (Ferdinand et al., 2006). The disorder may persist into adulthood, leading to an exaggerated concern about the well-being of one's children and spouse and difficulty tolerating any separation from them.

SAD is diagnosed when separation anxiety is persistent and excessive, when it is inappropriate for the child's developmental level, and when it interferes with the activities or development tasks, the most important of which is attending school. Six-year-olds ought to be able to enter first grade without anxiety-related nausea and vomiting and without dread that they or their parents will come to harm. Children with SAD tend to cling to their parents and follow them around the house. They may voice concerns about death and dying and insist that someone stay with them while they are falling asleep. They may complain of nightmares, stomachaches, and nausea and vomiting on school days. They may plead with their parents not to leave the house, or they may throw tantrums.

SAD may occur before middle childhood, preventing adjustment to day care or nursery school. In adolescence, refusal to attend school is often connected with academic and social problems, in which cases the label of SAD would not apply. SAD usually becomes a significant problem in middle childhood because that is when children are expected to adjust to school. The disorder may persist into adulthood, leading to an exaggerated concern about the well-being of one's children and spouse and difficulty tolerating any separation from them.

SAD frequently develops after a stressful life event, such as illness, the death of a relative or pet, or a change of schools or homes. Alison's problems followed the death of her grandmother:

> Alison's grandmother died when Alison was 7 years old. Her parents decided to permit her request to view her grandmother in the open coffin. Alison took a tentative glance from her father's arms across the room, then asked to be taken out of the room. Her 5-year-old sister took a leisurely close-up look, with no apparent distress.
>
> Alison had been concerned about death for two or three years by this time, but her grandmother's passing brought on a new flurry of questions: "Will I die?" "Does everybody die?" and so on. Her parents tried to reassure her by saying, "Grandma was very, very old, and she also had a heart condition. You are very young and in perfect health. You have many, many years before you have to start thinking about death."
>
> Alison also could not be alone in any room in her house. She pulled one of her parents or her sister along with her everywhere she went. She also

phobia An irrational, excessive fear that interferes with one's functioning.

separation anxiety disorder (SAD) An extreme form of otherwise normal separation anxiety that is characterized by anxiety about separating from parents; SAD often takes the form of refusal to go to school.

obsessive-compulsive disorder (OCD) An anxiety disorder characterized by obsessions (recurring thoughts or images that seem beyond control) and compulsions (irresistible urges to repeat an act, such as hand washing or checking that one has put one's homework in one's backpack).

reported nightmares about her grandmother and, within a couple of days, insisted on sleeping in the same room with her parents. Fortunately, Alison's fears did not extend to school. Her teacher reported that Alison spent some time talking about her grandmother, but her academic performance was apparently unimpaired.

Alison's parents decided to allow Alison time to "get over" the loss. Alison gradually talked less and less about death, and by the time 3 months had passed, she was able to go into any room in her house by herself. She wanted to continue to sleep in her parents' bedroom, however. So her parents "made a deal" with her. They would put off the return to her own bedroom until the school year had ended (a month away), if Alison would agree to return to her own bed at that time. As a further incentive, a parent would remain with her until she fell asleep for the first month. Alison overcame the anxiety problem in this fashion with no additional delays.

—Author's files

Separation Anxiety Disorder, School Phobia, and School Refusal

Question: ***What are the connections between separation anxiety disorder, school phobia, and school refusal?*** SAD is similar to but not the same as school phobia. SAD is an extreme form of separation anxiety. It is characterized by anxiety about separating from parents and may be expressed as **school phobia**—which means fear of school—or of refusal to go to school (which can be based on fear or other factors). Separation anxiety—fear—is not behind all instances of school refusal (Bernstein & Layne, 2006). Some children refuse school because they perceive it as unpleasant, unsatisfying, or hostile, and sometimes it is. Some children are concerned about doing poorly in school or being asked to answer questions in class (in which case, they might be suffering from the social phobia of stage fright). High parental expectations to perform may heighten concern. Other children may refuse school because of problems with classmates (Ishikawa et al., 2003).

Question: ***What can we do about school phobia or school refusal?***

Treatment of School Phobia or School Refusal

Truth or Fiction Revisited: It is usually not better for children with school phobia to remain at home until the origins of the problem are uncovered and resolved. A phobia is an irrational or overblown fear, a fear out of proportion to any danger in the situation. Therefore, one need not protect the child from school phobia. Most professionals agree that the first rule in the treatment of school phobia is: Get the child back into school. The second rule is: Get the child back into school. The third rule . . . Even without investigating the "meanings" of the child's refusal to attend school, many of the "symptoms" of the disorder disappear once the child is back in school on a regular basis.

Put it this way: There is nothing wrong with trying to understand why a child refuses to attend school. Knowledge of the reasons for refusal can help parents and educators devise strategies for assisting the child to adjust. But should such understanding precede insistence that the child return to school? Perhaps not. Here are some things parents can do to get a child back into school:

© Sean Cayton/The Image Works

Separation Anxiety

School phobia is often a form of separation anxiety. This boy is afraid to be separated from his mother. He imagines that something terrible will happen to her (or to him) when they are apart. Many mornings he complains of a tummy ache or of being too tired to go to school.

school phobia Fear of attending school, marked by extreme anxiety at leaving parents.

- Do not give in to the child's demands to stay home. If the child complains of being tired or ill, tell the child he or she may feel better at school and can rest there if necessary.
- Discuss the problem with the child's teacher, principal, and school nurse. (Gain the cooperation of school professionals.)
- If there is a specific school-related problem, such as an overly strict teacher, help the child find ways to handle the situation. (Finding ways to handle such problems can be accomplished while the child is in school. Not all such problems need be ironed out before the child returns to school.)
- Reward the child for attending school. (Yes, parents shouldn't "have to" reward children for "normal" behavior, but do you want the child in school or not?)

What if these measures don't work? How do professionals help? A variety of therapeutic approaches have been tried, and it would appear that cognitive-behavioral approaches are the most effective (Kendall et al., 2004; Turner, 2006; Valderhaug et al., 2004). One cognitive-behavioral method is counterconditioning to reduce the child's fear. (As described in Chapter 10, Mary Cover Jones used counterconditioning to reduce Peter's fear of rabbits.) Other cognitive-behavioral methods include systematic desensitization, modeling, cognitive restructuring, and the shaping and rewarding of school attendance.

When possible, the children's parents are taught to apply cognitive-behavioral methods. One study assessed the effectiveness of so-called family-based group cognitive-behavioral treatment (FGCBT) for anxious children (Shortt et al., 2001). It included 71 children between the ages of 6 and 10 who were diagnosed with SAD, generalized anxiety (anxiety that persisted throughout the day), or social phobia (e.g., stage fright). The children and their families were assigned at random to FGCBT or to a 10-week waiting list ("We'll get to you in 10 weeks"), which was the control group. The effectiveness of the treatment was evaluated after treatment and at a 12-month follow-up. The researchers found that nearly 70% of the children who had completed FGCBT were no longer diagnosable with anxiety disorders, compared with 6% of the children on the waiting list. Even at the 12-month follow-up, 68% of children remained diagnosis free.

Antidepressant medication has been used—often in conjunction with cognitive-behavioral methods—with a good deal of success (Murphy et al., 2000; Pine et al., 2001; Walkup et al., 2001). Antidepressants can have side effects, however, such as abdominal discomfort (Burke & Baker, 2001). Moreover, some professionals fear that they can trigger suicidal thoughts in children (Mosholder, 2004). However, drugs in themselves do not teach children how to cope with situations. Many health professionals suggest that the drugs—in this case, antidepressants—are best used only when psychological treatments have proven to be ineffective (Masi et al., 2001).

Daniel Pine and his colleagues (2001) reported a study on the treatment of 128 anxious children, age 6 to 17 years. Like those children in the Shortt study, they were diagnosed with a social phobia (such as stage fright), SAD, or GAD. All the children had received psychological treatment for 3 weeks without improvement. The children were assigned at random to receive an antidepressant (fluvoxamine) or a placebo (a "sugar pill") for 8 weeks. Neither the children, their parents, their teachers, nor the researchers knew which child had received which treatment. After 8 weeks, the children's anxiety was evaluated. Forty-eight of 63 children (76%) who had received the antidepressant improved significantly, compared with 19 of 65 children (29%) who had received the placebo.

It seems unfortunate to depart middle childhood following a discussion of social and emotional problems. Most children in developed nations come through middle childhood quite well, in good shape for the challenges and dramas of adolescence.

Developing in a World of Diversity

Problems? No Problem. (For Some Children)

Perhaps all children encounter some stress. But some children bear a heavy burden. The cumulative effect of stressors such as poverty, parental discord, or abuse or neglect places children at high risk of maladjustment. But some children are more resilient than others. They adapt and thrive despite stress (Haeffel & Grigorenko, 2007; Kim-Cohen, 2007). How do resilient children differ from those who are more vulnerable to stress? Two key factors appear to be the child's personality and social support.

Personality Characteristics

Genetics and temperament may play key roles in children's resilience (Bartels & Hudziak, 2007; Rutter, 2006b). At 1 year of age, resilient children are securely attached to their mothers. At age 2, they are independent and easygoing, even if they are abused or neglected. Not only is the easygoing child less likely to be the target of negative behavior from parents, but he or she is also

better able to cope with stress. By 3½ years of age, they are cheerful, persistent, flexible, and capable of seeking help from adults. In middle childhood, they distance themselves from turmoil and show independence. They believe that they can make good things happen (Griffin et al., 2001; Sandler, 2001).

Social Support

Support from others—parents, grandparents, siblings, peers, or teachers—helps children cope with stress (Davies & Windle, 2001; Greeff & Van Der Merwe, 2004; Kim-Cohen, 2007). Social support is particularly important for children who live in poverty. Children from ethnic minority groups and from families headed by single mothers are especially likely to be poor. Nearly 35 million Americans live in poverty, and most of them are children (U.S. Bureau of the Census, 2007). African Americans and Latino and Latina Americans are "overrepresented" in the statistics, with more than 20%

of each group living in poverty. By contrast, only about 7.5% of European Americans and 11% of Asian Americans live in poverty. But here's a startler: Five times as many households headed by single women live in poverty as households headed by a married couple.

Yet many poor children from ethnic minority groups have extended families that include grandparents who live with them or nearby. Extended families provide economic, social, and emotional support for children (Barrow et al., 2007; Cooper & Crosnoe, 2007). Grandmothers, in particular, play a key role. Extended families enable single mothers to attend school or work and increase the quality of child care (Barrow et al., 2007; Cooper & Crosnoe, 2007).

The message is that many, many children do well despite adversity. In fact, Ann Masten (2001) characterized such an outcome as somewhat "ordinary." Hey, kids: Just do it!

Active Review

20. Conduct disorders are more likely to be found among the (Biological or Adoptive?) parents of adopted children with conduct disorders.

21. Self-perceived competence appears to (Protect children from or Make children vulnerable to?) feelings of depression.

22. Depressed children tend to (Underutilize or Overutilize?) the neurotransmitter serotonin in the brain.

23. Separation _____ disorder is similar to but not exactly the same as school phobia.

24. Separation anxiety (Is or Is not?) behind all instances of school refusal.

Reflect & Relate: Have you known children with conduct disorders, depression, or separation anxiety disorder (or school phobia)? Do you have any thoughts about the origins of the problems? Were the problems treated? What happened to the children?

Go to

http://www.thomsonedu.com/psychology/rathus

for an interactive version of this review.

RECITE: *An Active Summary*

1. What are some features of social and emotional development in middle childhood?

Social development in middle childhood involves the development of skills, changes in interpersonal relationships, and the expansion of self-understanding. Freud viewed the period as the latency stage; Erikson saw it as the stage of industry versus inferiority. Social cognitive theorists note that children now depend less on external rewards and punishments and increasingly regulate their own behavior. Cognitive-developmental theory notes that concrete operations enhance social development.

2. What is the relationship between social cognition and perspective taking?

In middle childhood, children become more capable of taking the role or perspective of another person. Selman theorizes that children move from egocentricity to seeing the world through the eyes of others in five stages.

3. How does the self-concept develop during middle childhood?

In early childhood, children's self-concepts focus on concrete external traits. In middle childhood, children begin to include abstract internal traits. Social relationships and group membership assume importance.

4. How does self-esteem develop during middle childhood?

In middle childhood, competence and social acceptance contribute to self-esteem, but self-esteem tends to decline because the self-concept becomes more realistic. Authoritative parenting fosters self-esteem.

5. What is learned helplessness, and how does it develop in middle childhood?

Learned helplessness is the acquired belief that one cannot obtain rewards. "Helpless" children tend not to persist in the face of failure. Girls tend to feel more helpless in math than boys do, largely because of gender-role expectations.

6. What kinds of influences are exerted by the family during middle childhood?

In middle childhood, the family continues to play a key role in socialization. Parent–child interactions focus on school-related issues, chores, and peers. Parents do less monitoring of children; "coregulation" develops.

7. What are the effects of having lesbian or gay parents?

Children of lesbian and gay parents by and large develop as well as children of heterosexual parents. The sexual orientation of these children is generally heterosexual.

8. What are the effects of divorce on the children?

Divorce disrupts children's lives and usually lowers the family's financial status. Children are likely to greet divorce with sadness, shock, and disbelief. Children of divorce fare better when parents cooperate on child rearing. Children's adjustment is related to the mother's coping ability.

9. What is best for the children? Should parents who bicker remain together for their children's sake?

In terms of the child's psychological adjustment, the answer seems to be not necessarily. Children appear to suffer as much from marital conflict as from divorce per se.

10. What are the effects of maternal employment on children?

Having both parents in the workforce may be related to relative lack of supervision. However, there is little evidence that maternal employment harms children. Maternal employment fosters greater independence and flexibility in gender-role stereotypes.

11. What is the influence of peers during middle childhood?

Peers take on increasing importance and exert pressure to conform. Peer experiences also broaden children. Peers afford practice in social skills, sharing, relating to leaders, and coping with aggressive impulses. Popular children tend to be attractive and mature for their age.

12. How do children's concepts of friendship develop?

Early in middle childhood, friendships are based on proximity. Between the ages of 8 and 11, children become more aware of the value of friends as meeting each other's needs and having traits such as loyalty. At this age, peers tend to discourage contact with members of the other sex.

13. What are the effects of the school on children's social and emotional development?

Schools make demands for mature behavior and nurture positive physical, social, and cognitive development. Readiness for school is related to children's early life experiences, individual differences in development and learning, and the schools' expectations.

14. What are the characteristics of a good school?

An effective school has an energetic principal, an orderly atmosphere, empowerment of teachers and students, high expectations for children, and solid academics. Teachers' expectations can become self-fulfilling prophecies. Many girls suffer from sexism and sexual harassment in school. Math and science are generally stereotyped as masculine, and language arts as feminine.

15. What are conduct disorders? What can we do about them?

Children with conduct disorders persistently break rules or violate the rights of others. There may be a genetic component to such disorders, but sociopathic models in the family, deviant peers, and inconsistent discipline all contribute. Parental training in cognitive-behavioral methods holds promise for treating these disorders.

16. What is depression? What can we do about it?

Depressed children tend to complain of poor appetite, insomnia, lack of energy, and feelings of worthlessness. Depressed children tend to blame themselves excessively for shortcomings. Psychotherapy tends to make children aware of their tendencies to minimize their accomplishments and overly blame themselves for shortcomings. Antidepressants are sometimes helpful but controversial.

17. What is separation anxiety disorder?

Separation anxiety disorder (SAD) is diagnosed when separation anxiety is persistent and excessive and interferes with daily life. Children with SAD tend to cling to parents and may refuse to attend school.

18. What are the connections between separation anxiety disorder, school phobia, and school refusal?

SAD is an extreme form of otherwise normal separation anxiety and may take the form of school phobia. But children can refuse school for other reasons, including finding school to be unpleasant or hostile.

19. What can we do about school phobia or school refusal?

The most important aspect of treatment is to insist that the child attend school. Cognitive-behavioral therapy and medicine may also be of use.

Key Terms

latency stage, 443
industry versus inferiority, 443
social cognition, 443
self-esteem, 445
learned helplessness, 447
coregulation, 448
lesbian, 449
gay, 449

transsexual, 450
Pygmalion effect, 462
self-fulfilling prophecy, 462
sexism, 463
sexual harassment, 463
conduct disorders, 464
attributional style, 467
serotonin, 467

generalized anxiety disorder
    (GAD), 468
phobia, 469
separation anxiety disorder
    (SAD), 469
obsessive-compulsive disorder
    (OCD), 469
school phobia, 470

Active Learning Resources

Childhood & Adolescence Book Companion Website

http://www.thomsonedu.com/psychology/rathus

Visit your book companion website where you will find more resources to help you study. There you will find interactive versions of your book features, including the Lessons in Observation video, Active Review sections, and the Truth or Fiction feature. In addition, the companion website contains quizzing, flash cards, and a pronunciation glossary.

 Thomson™ NOW! is an easy-to-use online resource that helps you study in less time to get the grade you want—NOW.

http://www.thomsonedu.com/login

Need help studying? This site is your one-stop study shop. Take a Pre-Test and ThomsonNOW will generate a Personalized Study Plan based on your test results. The Study Plan will identify the topics you need to review and direct you to online resources to help you master those topics. You can then take a Post-Test to determine the concepts you have mastered and what you still need to work on.

14. False
15. Senses
16. Recognition
17. Autobiographical, episodic
18. Better
19. Positively
20. Rehearsal, rote rehearsal, rote learning
21. Mapping
22. Whole
23. One
24. Contrast
25. Inner

Chapter 10

1. Restrictiveness–permissiveness
2. Inductive
3. Authoritative
4. Authoritarian
5. Firstborn
6. Solitary
7. Associative
8. Same
9. Altruism
10. Reject
11. Testosterone
12. Social cognitive, social learning
13. Disinhibit

14. Categorical
15. Esteem
16. Securely
17. Initiative
18. Safety
19. Girls
20. Roles, role stereotypes
21. Sex
22. Males
23. Fathers
24. Constancy
25. Schema

Chapter 11

1. Steady
2. 2
3. 5 to 7
4. Boys
5. 11
6. 25
7. Do not
8. Does
9. Steady
10. 8 to 10
11. Decreases
12. Boys
13. Girls
14. Unfit
15. Attention-deficit/hyperactivity disorder
16. Boys

17. Does
18. Stimulants
19. Disabilities, disorders
20. Dyslexia
21. Neurological
22. Does

Chapter 12

1. Less
2. Transitivity
3. Inclusion
4. Autonomous
5. The amount of damage done
6. Preconventional
7. Conventional
8. Increases
9. Working, short-term
10. Encode, rehearse
11. Rote
12. Elaborative
13. Metamemory
14. *g*
15. Multiple
16. Mental
17. Verbal
18. Bias
19. 6
20. 10 to 15
21. Divergent
22. Biological, Adoptive

23. Visual
24. Phonetic
25. Can
26. Advantage

Chapter 13

1. Industry
2. Concrete
3. Perspective, viewpoint
4. Decreases
5. Authoritative
6. Less
7. Heterosexual
8. Downward
9. Mothers
10. Boys
11. Lack of supervision
12. Farther away from
13. Mature
14. Later-born
15. Discouraged
16. Low
17. Smaller
18. Self-fulfilling
19. Boys
20. Biological
21. Protect children from
22. Underutilize
23. Anxiety
24. Is not

Glossary

accommodation: According to Piaget, the modification of existing schemes so as to incorporate new events or knowledge.

achievement: That which is attained by one's efforts and presumed to be made possible by one's abilities.

adaptation: According to Piaget, the interaction between the organism and the environment. It consists of two processes: assimilation and accommodation.

adipose tissue: Fat.

adrenaline: A hormone that generally arouses the body, increasing the heart and respiration rates.

allele: A member of a pair of genes.

alpha-fetoprotein (AFP) assay: A blood test that assesses the mother's blood level of alpha-fetoprotein, a substance that is linked with fetal neural tube defects.

ambivalent/resistant attachment: A type of insecure attachment characterized by severe distress at the leave-takings of and ambivalent behavior at reunions with an attachment figure.

American Sign Language (ASL): The communication of meaning through the use of symbols that are formed by moving the hands and arms. The language used by some deaf people.

amniocentesis: (AM-nee-oh-sent-TEE-sis) A procedure for drawing and examining fetal cells sloughed off into amniotic fluid to determine the presence of various disorders.

amniotic fluid: Fluid within the amniotic sac that suspends and protects the fetus.

amniotic sac: The sac containing the fetus.

amplitude: Height. The higher the amplitude of sound waves, the louder they are.

androgens: Male sex hormones (from roots meaning "giving birth to men").

anesthetics: Agents that produce partial or total loss of the sense of pain (from Greek roots meaning "without feeling").

animism: The attribution of life and intentionality to inanimate objects.

anoxia: A condition characterized by lack of oxygen.

Apgar scale: A measure of a newborn's health that assesses appearance, pulse, grimace, activity level, and respiratory effort.

aphasia: A disruption in the ability to understand or produce language.

apnea: (AP-nee-uh) Temporary suspension of breathing (from the Greek *a-*, meaning "without," and *pnoie*, meaning "wind").

appearance–reality distinction: The difference between real events on the one hand and mental events, fantasies, and misleading appearances on the other hand.

artificial insemination: Injection of sperm into the uterus to fertilize an ovum.

artificialism: The belief that environmental features were made by people.

assimilation: According to Piaget, the incorporation of new events or knowledge into existing schemes.

attachment: An affectional bond between individuals characterized by a seeking of closeness or contact and a show of distress upon separation.

attachment-in-the-making phase: The second phase in the development of attachment, occurring at 3 or 4 months of age and characterized by preference for familiar figures.

attention-deficit/hyperactivity disorder (ADHD): A behavior disorder characterized by excessive inattention, impulsiveness, and hyperactivity.

attributional style: The way in which one is disposed toward interpreting outcomes (successes or failures), as in tending to place blame or responsibility on oneself or on external factors.

authoritarian: A child-rearing style in which parents demand submission and obedience from their children but are not very communicative and warm.

authoritative: A child-rearing style in which parents are restrictive and demanding yet communicative and warm.

autism: A developmental disorder characterized by failure to relate to others, communication problems, intolerance of change, and ritualistic behavior.

autism spectrum disorders (ASDs): Developmental disorders—including autism, Asperger's syndrome, Rett's disorder, and childhood disintegrative disorder—that are characterized by impairment in communication skills, social interactions, and repetitive, stereotyped behavior. Also referred to as pervasive developmental disorders.

autobiographical memory: The memory of specific episodes or events.

autonomous morality: The second stage in Piaget's cognitive-developmental theory of moral development. In this stage, children base moral judgments on the intentions of the wrongdoer and on the amount of damage done. Social rules are viewed as agreements that can be changed.

autosome: A member of a pair of chromosomes (with the exception of sex chromosomes).

avoidant attachment: A type of insecure attachment characterized by apparent indifference to the leave-takings of and reunions with an attachment figure.

axon: A long, thin part of a neuron that transmits impulses to other neurons through small branching structures called axon terminals.

babbling: The child's first vocalizations that have the sounds of speech.

Babinski reflex: A reflex in which infants fan their toes when the undersides of their feet are stroked.

bed-wetting: Failure to control the bladder during the night. (Frequently used interchangeably with enuresis, although bed-wetting refers to the behavior itself and enuresis is a diagnostic category, related to the age of the child.)

behavior modification: The systematic application of principles of learning to change problem behaviors or encourage desired behaviors.

behaviorism: John B. Watson's view that a science or theory of development must study observable behavior only and investigate relationships between stimuli and responses.

bilingual: Using or capable of using two languages with nearly equal or equal facility.

blastocyst: A stage within the germinal period of prenatal development in which the zygote has the form of a sphere of cells surrounding a cavity of fluid.

bonding: The process of forming bonds of attachment between parent and child.

Braxton-Hicks contractions: The first, usually painless, contractions of childbirth.

Brazelton Neonatal Behavioral Assessment Scale: A measure of a newborn's motor behavior, response to stress, adaptive behavior, and control over physiological state.

breech presentation: A position in which the fetus enters the birth canal buttocks first.

Broca's aphasia: A form of aphasia caused by damage to Broca's area and characterized by slow, laborious speech.

canalization: The tendency of growth rates to return to genetically determined patterns after undergoing environmentally induced change.

carrier: A person who carries and transmits characteristics but does not exhibit them.

case study: A carefully drawn biography of the life of an individual.

categorical self: Definitions of the self that refer to concrete external traits.

centration: Focusing on one dimension of a situation while ignoring others.

cephalocaudal: From head to tail.

cerebellum: (ser-uh-BEH-lum) The part of the hindbrain involved in muscle coordination and balance.

cerebrum: (seh-REE-brum) The large mass of the forebrain, which consists of two hemispheres.

gender identity: Knowledge that one is female or male. Also, the name of the first stage in Kohlberg's cognitive-developmental theory of the assumption of gender roles.

gender role: A complex cluster of traits and behaviors that are considered stereotypical of females and males.

gender stability: The concept that one's sex is a permanent feature.

gender-schema theory: The view that one's knowledge of the gender schema in one's society (the behavior patterns that are considered appropriate for men and women) guides one's assumption of gender-typed preferences and behavior patterns.

gene: The basic unit of heredity. Genes are composed of deoxyribonucleic acid (DNA).

general anesthesia: The process of eliminating pain by putting the person to sleep.

generalized anxiety disorder (GAD): An anxiety disorder in which anxiety appears to be present continuously and is unrelated to the situation.

genes: The basic building blocks of heredity.

genetic counseling: Advice concerning the probabilities that a couple's children will show genetic abnormalities.

genetics: The branch of biology that studies heredity.

genotype: The genetic form or constitution of a person as determined by heredity.

germinal stage: The period of development between conception and the implantation of the embryo.

goodness of fit: Agreement between the parents' expectations of or demands on the child and the child's temperamental characteristics.

grasping reflex: A reflex in which infants grasp objects that cause pressure against the palms.

gross motor skills: Skills employing the large muscles used in locomotion.

growth: The processes by which organisms increase in size, weight, strength, and other traits as they develop.

growth spur: A period during which growth advances at a dramatically rapid rate compared with other periods.

habituation: A process in which one becomes used to and therefore pays less attention to a repeated stimulus.

handedness: The tendency to prefer using the left or right hand in writing and other activities.

hemophilia: (he-moe-FEEL-yuh) A genetic disorder in which blood does not clot properly.

heredity: The transmission of traits and characteristics from parent to child by means of genes.

heritability: The degree to which the variations in a trait from one person to another can be attributed to, or explained by, genetic factors.

heterozygous: Having two different alleles.

HIV/AIDS: HIV stands for a virus, the human immunodeficiency virus, which cripples the body's immune system. AIDS stands for acquired immunodeficiency syndrome. HIV is a sexually transmitted infection that can also be transmitted in other ways, such as sharing needles when shooting up drugs. AIDS is caused by HIV and describes the body's state when the immune system is weakened to the point where it is vulnerable to a variety of diseases that would otherwise be fought off.

holophrase: A single word that is used to express complex meanings.

homozygous: Having two identical alleles.

hue: Color.

Huntington's disease: A fatal genetic neurologic disorder whose onset is in middle age.

hyaluronidase: (high-al-you-RON-uh-dace) An enzyme that briefly thins the zona pellucida, enabling a single sperm cell to penetrate. (From roots referring to a "substance that breaks down a glasslike fluid.")

hyperactivity: Excessive restlessness and overactivity; one of the primary characteristics of attention-deficit/hyperactivity disorder (ADHD). Not to be confused with misbehavior or with normal high-activity levels that occur during childhood.

hypothesis: (high-POTH-uh-sis) A Greek word meaning "groundwork" or "foundation" that has come to mean a specific statement about behavior that is tested by research.

hypoxia: A condition characterized by less oxygen than is required.

identity crisis: According to Erikson, a period of inner conflict during which one examines one's values and makes decisions about one's life roles.

immanent justice: The view that retribution for wrongdoing is a direct consequence of the wrongdoing, reflective of the belief that morality is embedded within the structure of the universe.

imprinting: The process by which some animals exhibit the fixed action pattern (FAP) of attachment in response to a releasing stimulus. The FAP occurs during a critical period and is difficult to modify.

in vitro fertilization: (VEE-tro) Fertilization of an ovum in a laboratory dish.

incubator: A heated, protective container in which premature infants are kept.

independent variable: A condition in a scientific study that is manipulated (changed) so that its effects can be observed.

indiscriminate attachment: The display of attachment behaviors toward any person.

individualist: A person who defines herself or himself in terms of personal traits and gives priority to her or his own goals.

inductive: Characteristic of disciplinary methods, such as reasoning, that attempt to foster an understanding of the principles behind parental demands.

industry versus inferiority: The fourth stage of psychosocial development in Erikson's theory, occurring in middle childhood. Mastery of tasks leads to a sense of industry, whereas failure produces feelings of inferiority.

infancy: The period of very early childhood, characterized by lack of complex speech; the first 2 years after birth.

information processing: The view in which cognitive processes are compared to the functions of computers. The theory deals with the input, storage, retrieval, manipulation, and output of information. The focus is on the development of children's strategies for solving problems, or their "mental programs."

initial-preattachment phase: The first phase in the formation of bonds of attachment, lasting from birth to about 3 months of age and characterized by indiscriminate attachment.

inner speech: Vygotsky's concept of the ultimate binding of language and thought. Inner speech originates in vocalizations that may regulate the child's behavior and become internalized by age 6 or 7.

insomnia: One or more sleep problems including falling asleep, difficulty remaining asleep during the night, and waking early.

intelligence: A complex and controversial concept, defined by David Wechsler as the "capacity . . . to understand the world [and the] resourcefulness to cope with its challenges." Intelligence implies the capacity to make adaptive choices (from the Latin *inter*, meaning "among," and *legere*, meaning "to choose").

intelligence quotient (IQ): (1) Originally, a ratio obtained by dividing a child's score (or "mental age") on an intelligence test by his or her chronological age. (2) In general, a score on an intelligence test.

intensity: Brightness.

intonation: The use of pitches of varying levels to help communicate meaning.

irreversibility: Lack of recognition that actions can be reversed.

Klinefelter syndrome: A chromosomal disorder found among males that is caused by an extra X sex chromosome and that is characterized by infertility and mild mental retardation.

Lamaze method: A childbirth method in which women are educated about childbirth, learn to relax and breathe in patterns that conserve energy and lessen pain, and have a coach (usually the father) present during childbirth. Also called prepared childbirth.

language acquisition device (LAD): In psycholinguistic theory, neural "prewiring" that facilitates the child's learning of grammar.

lanugo: (luh-NOO-go) Fine, downy hair that covers much of the body of the neonate, especially preterm babies.

latency stage: In psychoanalytic theory, the fourth stage of psychosexual development, characterized by repression of sexual impulses and development of skills.

learned helplessness: An acquired (hence, learned) belief that one is unable to control one's environment.

learning disabilities: A group of disorders characterized by inadequate development of specific academic, language, and speech skills.

lesbian: A female who is interested romantically and sexually in other females.

life crisis: An internal conflict that attends each stage of psychosocial development. Positive resolution of early life crises sets the stage for positive resolution of subsequent life crises.

local anesthetic: A method that reduces pain in an area of the body.

locomotion: Movement from one place to another.

longitudinal research: The study of developmental processes by taking repeated measures of the same group of children at various stages of development.

long-term memory: The memory structure capable of relatively permanent storage of information.

macrosystem: The basic institutions and ideologies that influence the child, such as the American ideals of freedom of expression and equality under the law (from the Greek *makros*, meaning "long" or "enlarged").

mainstreaming: Placing disabled children in classrooms with nondisabled children.

maturation: The unfolding of genetically determined traits, structures, and functions.

mean length of utterance (MLU): The average number of morphemes used in an utterance.

medulla: A part of the brain stem that regulates vital and automatic functions such as breathing and the sleep–wake cycle.

meiosis: The form of cell division in which each pair of chromosomes splits so that one member of each pair moves to the new cell. As a result, each new cell has 23 chromosomes.

memory: The processes by which we store and retrieve information.

mental age (MA): The accumulated months of credit that a person earns on the Stanford–Binet Intelligence Scale.

mental representations: The mental forms that a real object or event can take, which may differ from one another. (Successful problem solving is aided by accurate mental representation of the elements of the problem.)

mesoderm: The central layer of the embryo from which the bones and muscles develop.

mesosystem: The interlocking settings that influence the child, such as the interaction of the school and the larger community when children are taken on field trips (from the Greek *mesos*, meaning "middle").

metacognition: Awareness of and control of one's cognitive abilities, as shown by the intentional use of cognitive strategies in solving problems.

metamemory: Knowledge of the functions and processes involved in one's storage and retrieval of information (memory), as shown by use of cognitive strategies to retain information.

microsystem: The immediate settings with which the child interacts, such as the home, the school, and one's peers (from the Greek *mikros*, meaning "small").

midwife: An individual who helps women in childbirth (from Old English roots meaning "with woman").

mitosis: The form of cell division in which each chromosome splits lengthwise to double in number. Half of each chromosome combines with chemicals to retake its original form and then moves to the new cell.

models: In learning theory, those whose behaviors are imitated by others.

monozygotic (MZ) twins: Twins that derive from a single zygote that has split into two; identical twins. Each MZ twin carries the same genetic code.

moral realism: According to Piaget, the stage during which children judge acts as moral when they conform to authority or to the rules of the game. Morality at this stage is perceived as embedded in the structure of the universe.

Moro reflex: A reflex in which infants arch their back, fling out their arms and legs, and draw them back toward the chest in response to a sudden change in position.

morpheme: The smallest unit of meaning in a language.

motility: Self-propulsion.

motor development: The development of the capacity for movement, particularly that made possible by changes in the nervous system and the muscles.

multifactorial problems: Problems that stem from the interaction of heredity and environmental factors.

multiple sclerosis: A disorder in which myelin is replaced by hard fibrous tissue that impedes neural transmission.

muscular dystrophy: (DIS-truh-fee) A chronic disease characterized by a progressive wasting away of the muscles.

mutation: A sudden variation in a heritable characteristic, as by an accident that affects the composition of genes.

mutism: Inability or refusal to speak.

myelin sheath: (MY-uh-lin) A fatty, whitish substance that encases and insulates neurons, permitting more rapid transmission of neural impulses.

myelination: The process by which axons are coated with myelin.

natural childbirth: A method of childbirth in which women use no anesthesia and are educated about childbirth and strategies for coping with discomfort.

naturalistic observation: A method of scientific observation in which children (and others) are observed in their natural environments.

nature: The processes within an organism that guide that organism to develop according to its genetic code.

negative correlation: A relationship between two variables in which one variable increases as the other variable decreases.

negative reinforcer: A reinforcer that, when removed, increases the frequency of a response.

neonate: A newborn child (from the Greek *neos*, meaning "new," and the Latin *natus*, meaning "born").

nerves: Bundles of axons from many neurons.

neural: Of the nervous system.

neural tube: A hollowed-out area in the blastocyst from which the nervous system develops.

neurons: Nerve cells; cells found in the nervous system that transmit messages.

neuroticism: A personality trait characterized by anxiety and emotional instability.

neurotransmitter: A chemical substance that enables the transmission of neural impulses from one neuron to another.

nightmares: Frightening dreams that occur during REM sleep, often in the morning hours.

non-rapid-eye-movement (non-REM) sleep: Periods of sleep during which we are unlikely to dream.

nonsocial play: Forms of play (solitary play or onlooker play) in which play is not influenced by the play of nearby children.

nurture: The processes external to an organism that nourish it as it develops according to its genetic code or that cause it to swerve from its genetically programmed course. Environmental factors that influence development.

object permanence: Recognition that objects continue to exist even when they are not seen.

objective morality: The perception of morality as objective, that is, as existing outside the cognitive functioning of people; a characteristic of Piaget's stage of moral realism.

nitive assessment. *Journal of the International Neuropsychological Society, 13*(2), 209–211.

Biederman, J., et al. (2007). Effect of comorbid symptoms of oppositional defiant disorder on responses to atomoxetine in children with ADHD: A meta-analysis of controlled clinical trial data. *Psychopharmacology, 190*(1), 31–41.

Birch, L. L., Gunder, L., Grimm-Thomas, K., & Laing, D. G. (1998). Infants' consumption of a new food enhances acceptance of similar foods. *Appetite, 30*(3), 283–295.

Bird, A., Reese, E., & Tripp, G. (2006). Parent–child talk about past emotional events: Associations with child temperament and goodness-of-fit. *Journal of Cognition and Development, 7*(2), 189–210.

Bjorklund, D. F., & Rosenblum, K. E. (2001). Children's use of multiple and variable addition strategies in a game context. *Developmental Science, 4*(2), 184–194.

Black, D. W. (2007). Antisocial personality disorder, conduct disorder, and psychopathy. In J. E. Grant, & M. N. Potenza. (Eds.). *Textbook of men's mental health.* (pp. 143–170). Washington, DC: American Psychiatric Publishing, Inc.

Blanchette, N., Smith, M. L., Fernandes-Penney, A., King, S., & Read, S. (2001). Cognitive and motor development in children with vertically transmitted HIV infection. *Brain and Cognition, 46*(1–2), 50–53.

Blass, E. M., & Camp, C. A. (2003). Changing determinants in 6- to 12-week-old human infants. *Developmental Psychobiology, 42*(3), 312–316.

Blevins-Knabe, B. (1987). Development of the ability to insert into a series. *Journal of Genetic Psychology, 148,* 427–441.

Bloch, M., Rotenberg, N., Koren, D., & Ehud, K. (2006). Risk factors for early postpartum depressive symptoms. *General Hospital Psychiatry, 28*(1), 3–8.

Blom-Hoffman, J., George, J. B., & Franko, D. L. (2006). Childhood overweight. In G. G. Bear & K. M. Minke (Eds.), *Children's needs III: Development, prevention, and intervention* (pp. 989–1000). Washington, DC: National Association of School Psychologists.

Bloom, L. (1998). Language acquisition in its developmental context. In W. Damon (Ed.), *Handbook of child psychology* (5th ed.), Vol. 2. New York: Wiley.

Bloom, P. (2002). Mind reading, communication, and the learning of names for things. *Mind and Language, 17*(1–2), 37–54.

Boada, R., & Pennington, B. F. (2006). Deficient implicit phonological representations in children with dyslexia. *Journal of Experimental Child Psychology, 95*(3), 153–193.

Boccia, M., & Campos, J. J. (1989). Maternal emotional signals, social referencing, and infants' reactions to strangers. In N. Eisenberg (Ed.), *New directions for child development,* No. 44, *Empathy and related emotional responses.* San Francisco: Jossey-Bass.

Boden, C., & Giaschi, D. (2007). M-stream deficits and reading-related visual processes in developmental dyslexia. *Psychological Bulletin, 133*(2), 346–366.

Boey, C. C. M., Omar, A., & Phillips, J. A. (2003). Correlation among academic performance, recurrent abdominal pain and other factors in year-6 urban primary-school children in Malaysia. *Journal of Paediatrics and Child Health, 39*(5), 352–357.

Boggiano, A. K., & Barrett, M. (1991). Strategies to motivate helpless and mastery-oriented children: The effect of gender-based expectancies. *Sex Roles, 25,* 487–510.

Bohannon, J. N., III, & Stanowicz, L. (1988). The issue of negative evidence: Adult responses to children's language errors. *Developmental Psychology, 24,* 684–689.

Bohn, A. P. (2003). Familiar voices: Using Ebonics communication techniques in the primary classroom. *Urban Education, 38*(6), 688–707.

Boivin, M., Vitaro, F., & Poulin, F. (2005). Peer relationships and the development of aggressive behavior in early childhood. In R. E. Tremblay, W. W. Hartup, & J. Archer (Eds.), *Developmental origins of aggression* (pp. 376–397). New York: Guilford.

Boman, U. W., Hanson, C., Hjelmquist, E., & Möller, A. (2006). Personality traits in women with Turner syndrome. *Scandinavian Journal of Psychology, 47*(3), 219–223.

Bonkowski, S. (2005). Group work with children of divorce. In G. L. Greif & P. H. Ephross (Eds.), *Group work with populations at risk* (2nd ed.) (pp. 135–145). New York: Oxford University Press.

Booth, A., Johnson, D. R., Granger, D. A., Crouter, A. C., & McHale, S. (2003). Testosterone and child and adolescent adjustment: The moderating role of parent–child relationships. *Developmental Psychology, 39*(1), 85–98.

Booth-LaForce, C., et al. (2006). Attachment, self-worth, and peer-group functioning in middle childhood. *Attachment & Human Development, 8*(4), 309–325.

Bouchard, C., et al. (1990). The response to long-term overfeeding in identical twins. *New England Journal of Medicine, 322,* 1477–1482.

Bouchard, T. J., Jr., & Loehlin, J. C. (2001). Genes, evolution, and personality. *Behavior Genetics, 31*(3), 243–273.

Bouchard, T. J., Jr., Lykken, D. T., McGue, M., Segal, N. L., & Tellegen, A. (1990). Sources of human psychological differences: The Minnesota study of twins reared apart. *Science, 250,* 223–228.

Bouldin, P., & Pratt, C. (1999). Characteristics of preschool and school-age children with imaginary companions. *Journal of Genetic Psychology, 160*(4), 397–410.

Bower, T. G. R. (1974). *Development in infancy.* San Francisco: W. H. Freeman.

Bowlby, J. (1988). *A secure base.* New York: Basic Books.

Boysson-Bardies, B. de, & Halle, P. A. (1994). Speech development: Contributions of cross-linguistic studies. In A. Vyt et al. (Eds.), *Early child development in the French tradition: Contributions from current research.* Hillsdale, NJ: Erlbaum.

Bradley, R. H. (2006). The home environment. In N. F. Watt et al. (Eds.), *The crisis in youth mental health: Critical issues and effective programs,* Vol. 4, *Early intervention programs and policies, Child psychology and mental health* (pp. 89–120). Westport, CT: Praeger/Greenwood.

Bradley, R. H., Caldwell, B. M., & Corwyn, R. F. (2003). The child care HOME inventories: Assessing the quality of family child care homes. *Early Childhood Research Quarterly, 18*(3), 294–309.

Bradley, R. H., & Corwyn, R. F. (2006). The family environment. In L. Balter & C. S. Tamis-LeMonda (Eds.), *Child psychology: A handbook of contemporary issues* (2nd ed.) (pp. 493–520). New York: Psychology Press.

Bramlett, M. D., & Mosher, W. D. (2002). *Cohabitation, marriage, divorce, and remarriage.* National Center for Health Statistics, Vital Health Statistics, 23(22). Available at http://www.cdc.gov/nchs/data/series/sr_23/sr23_022.pdf.

Branco, J. C., & Lourenço, O. (2004). Cognitive and linguistic aspects in 5- to 6-year-olds' class-inclusion reasoning. *Psicologia Educação Cultura, 8*(2), 427–445.

Brandtjen, H., & Verny, T (2001). Short and long term effects on infants and toddlers in full time daycare centers. *Journal of Prenatal & Perinatal Psychology & Health, 15*(4), 239–286.

Brase, G. L. (2006). Cues of parental investment as a factor in attractiveness. *Evolution and Human Behavior, 27*(2), 145–157.

Braza, F., et al. (2000). Efecto de los hermanos en la flexibilidad de comportamiento de ninos preescolares. *Revista Mexicana de Psicologia, 17*(2), 181–190.

Brazier, A., & Rowlands, C. (2006). PKU in the family: Working together. *Clinical Child Psychology and Psychiatry, 11*(3), 483–488.

Breastfeeding. (2006). Centers for Disease Control and Prevention. Department of Health and Human Services. Available at http://www.cdc.gov/breastfeeding/faq/index.htm. Accessed July 16, 2007.

Bremner, A., & Bryant, P. (2001). The effect of spatial cues on infants' responses in the AB task, with and without a hidden object. *Developmental Science, 4*(4), 408–415.

Brenneman, M. H., Morris, R. D., & Israelian, M. (2007). Language preference and its relationship with reading skills in English and Spanish. *Psychology in the Schools, 44*(2), 171–181.

Bretherton, I., Golby, B., & Halvorsen, C. (1993, March). *Fathers as attachment and caregiving figures.* Paper presented at the meeting of the Society for Research in Child Development, New Orleans, LA.

Bridges, K. (1932). Emotional development in early infancy. *Child Development, 3,* 324–341.

Briones, T. L., Klintsova, A. Y., & Greenough, W. T. (2004). Stability of synaptic plasticity in the adult rat visual cortex induced by complex environment exposure. *Brain Research, 1018*(1), 130–135.

"British study finds leukemia risk in children of A-plant workers." (1990, February 18). *New York Times,* p. A27.

Brody, J. E. (1998, February 10). Genetic ties may be factor in violence in stepfamilies. *New York Times,* pp. F1, F4.

Brody, L. R., Zelazo, P. R., & Chaika, H. (1984). Habituation–dishabituation to speech in the neonate. *Developmental Psychology, 20,* 114–119.

Brodzinsky, D. M., Patterson, C. J., & Vaziri, M. (2002). Adoption agency perspectives on lesbian and gay prospective parents: A national study. *Adoption Quarterly, 5*(3), 5–23.

Bronfenbrenner, U. (1973). The dream of the kibbutz. In *Readings in human development.* Guilford, CT: Dushkin.

Bronfenbrenner, U., & Morris, P. A. (2006). The bioecological model of human development. In R. M. Lerner & W. Damon (Eds.), *Handbook of child psychology* (6th ed.), Vol. 1, *Theoretical models of human development* (pp. 793–828). Hoboken, NJ: Wiley.

Bronson, G. W. (1990). Changes in infants' visual scanning across the 2- to 14-week age period. *Journal of Experimental Child Psychology, 49,* 101–125.

Bronson, G. W. (1991). Infant differences in rate of visual encoding. *Child Development, 62,* 44–54.

Bronson, G. W. (1997). The growth of visual capacity: Evidence from infant scanning patterns. *Advances in Infancy Research, 11,* 109–141.

Brown, R. (1973). *A first language: The early stages.* Cambridge, MA: Harvard University Press.

Brown, R. (1977). Introduction. In C. A. Snow & C. Ferguson (Eds.), *Talking to children.* New York: Cambridge University Press.

Brownell, C. A., & Carriger, M. S. (1990). Changes in cooperation and self-other differentiation during the second year. *Child Development, 61,* 1164–1174.

Bruck, M., Ceci, S. J., & Principe, G. F. (2006). The child and the law. In K. Renninger I. E. Sigel, W. Damon, & R. M. Lerner (Eds.), *Handbook of child psychology* (6th ed.), Vol. 4,

Child psychology in practice (pp. 776–816). Hoboken, NJ: Wiley.

Bryden, P. J., Bruyn, J., & Fletcher, P. (2005). Handedness and health: An examination of the association between different handedness classifications and health disorders. *Laterality: Asymmetries of Body, Brain and Cognition, 10*(5), 429–440.

Buckley, K. E., & Anderson, C. A. (2006). A theoretical model of the effects and consequences of playing video games. In P. Vorderer & J. Bryant (Eds.), *Playing video games: Motives, responses, and consequences* (pp. 363–378). Mahwah, NJ: Erlbaum.

Bugental, D. B., & Happaney, K. (2004). Predicting infant maltreatment in low-income families: The interactive effects of maternal attributions and child status at birth. *Developmental Psychology, 40*(2), 234–243.

Bukowski, W. M., Gauze, C., Hoza, B., & Newcomb, A. F. (1993a). Differences and consistency between same-sex and other-sex peer relationships during early adolescence. *Developmental Psychology, 29,* 255–263.

Bunikowski, R., et al. (1998). Neurodevelopmental outcome after prenatal exposure to opiates. *European Journal of Pediatrics, 157*(9), 724–730.

Burke, J. M., & Baker, R. C. (2001). Is fluvoxamine safe and effective for treating anxiety disorders in children? *Journal of Family Practice, 50*(8), 719.

Bushman, B. J. (1998). Priming effects of media violence on the accessibility of aggressive constructs in memory. *Personality and Social Psychology Bulletin, 24*(5), 537–545.

Bushnell, E. W. (1993, June). *A dual-processing approach to cross-modal matching: Implications for development.* Paper presented at the Society for Research in Child Development, New Orleans, LA.

Bushnell, I. W. R. (2001). Mother's face recognition in newborn infants: Learning and memory. *Infant and Child Development, 10*(1–2), 67–74.

Buss, D., & Duntley, J. D. (2006). The evolution of aggression. In M. Schaller, J. A. Simpson, & D. T. Kenrick (Eds.), *Evolution and social psychology: Frontiers of social psychology* (pp. 263–285). Madison, CT: Psychosocial Press.

Buss, D. M. (1999). Adaptive individual differences revisited. *Journal of Personality, 67*(2), 259–264.

Buss, D. M. (2000). The evolution of happiness. *American Psychologist, 55,* 15–23.

Bussey, K., & Bandura, A. (1984). Influence of gender constancy and social power on sex-linked modeling. *Journal of Personality and Social Psychology, 47,* 1292–1302.

Butterfield, S. A., & Loovis, E. M. (1993). Influence of age, sex, balance, and sport participation on development of throwing by

children in grades K–8. *Perceptual and Motor Skills, 76,* 459–464.

Butterworth, G., Verweij, E., & Hopkins, B. (1997). The development of prehension in infants: Halverson revisited. *British Journal of Developmental Psychology, 15*(2), 223–236.

Buxhoeveden, D. P., Hasselrot, U., Buxhoeveden, N. E., Booze, R. M., & Mactutus, C. F. (2006). Microanatomy in 21 day rat brains exposed prenatally to cocaine. *International Journal of Developmental Neuroscience, 24*(5), 335–341

Cabeza, R., Locantore, J. K., & Anderson, N. D. (2003). Lateralization of prefrontal activity during episodic memory retrieval: Evidence for the production-monitoring hypothesis. *Journal of Cognitive Neuroscience, 15*(2), 249–259.

Cairns, R. B., & Cairns, B. D. (1991). Social cognition and social networks: A developmental perspective. In D. J. Pepler & K. H. Rubin (Eds.), *The development and treatment of childhood aggression.* Hillsdale, NJ: Erlbaum.

Call, J. (2001). Object permanence in orangutans (*Pongo pygmaeus*), chimpanzees (*Pan troglodytes*), and children (*Homo sapiens*). *Journal of Comparative Psychology, 115*(2), 159–171.

Callan, M. J., Ellard, J. H., & Nicol, J. E. (2006). The belief in a just world and immanent justice reasoning in adults. *Personality and Social Psychology Bulletin, 32*(12), 1646–1658.

Calvert, S. L., & Kotler, J. A. (2003). Lessons from children's television: The impact of the Children's Television Act on children's learning. *Journal of Applied Developmental Psychology, 24*(3), 275–335.

Campanella, J., & Rovee-Collier, C. (2005). Latent learning and deferred imitation at 3 months. *Infancy, 7*(3), 243–262.

Campbell, A., Shirley, L., & Caygill, L. (2002). Sex-typed preferences in three domains: Do two-year-olds need cognitive variables? *British Journal of Psychology, 93*(2), 203–217.

Campbell, A., Shirley, L., Heywood, C., & Crook, C. (2000). Infants' visual preference for sex-congruent babies, children, toys and activities: A longitudinal study. *British Journal of Developmental Psychology, 18*(4), 479–498.

Campbell, D. A., Lake, M. F. Falk, M., & Backstrand, J. R. (2006). A randomized control trial of continuous support in labor by a lay doula. *Journal of Obstetric, Gynecologic, and Neonatal Nursing, 35*(4), 456–464.

Campbell, D. W., & Eaton, W. O. (1999). Sex differences in the activity level of infants. *Infant and Child Development, 8*(1), 1–17.

Campbell, D. W., Eaton, W. O., & McKeen, N. A. (2002). Motor activity level and behavioural control in young children. *International Journal of Behavioral Development, 26*(4), 289–296.

and sex of play partner: Connections to peer competence. *Sex Roles, 52*(7–8), 497–509.

Connor, J. R. (2004). Myelin breakdown in Alzheimer's disease: A commentary. *Neurobiology of Aging, 25*(1), 45–47.

Connor, M. E. (2006). Walking the walk: Community programs that work. In M. E. Connor & J. L. White (Eds.), *Black fathers: An invisible presence in America* (pp. 257–267). Mahwah, NJ: Erlbaum.

Connor, P. D., Sampson, P. D., Streissguth, A. P., Bookstein, F. L., & Barr, H. M. (2006). Effects of prenatal alcohol exposure on fine motor coordination and balance: A study of two adult samples. *Neuropsychologia, 44*(5), 744–751.

Constantine, M. G. (2007). Racial microaggressions against African American clients in cross-racial counseling relationships. *Journal of Counseling Psychology, 54*(1), 1–16.

Constantino, J. N., et al. (2006). Autistic social impairment in the siblings of children with pervasive developmental disorders. *American Journal of Psychiatry, 163*(2), 294–296.

Coolidge, F. L., DenBoer, J. W., & Segal, D. L. (2004). Personality and neuropsychological correlates of bullying behavior. *Personality and Individual Differences, 36*(7), 1559–1569.

Coon, H., Fulker, D. W., & DeFries, J. C. (1990). Home environment and cognitive ability of 7-year-old children in the Colorado adoption project: Genetic and environmental etiologies. *Developmental Psychology, 26,* 459–468.

Cooper, C. E., & Crosnoe, R. (2007). The engagement in schooling of economically disadvantaged parents and children. *Youth & Society, 38*(3), 372–391.

Coovadia, H. (2004). Antiretroviral agents: How best to protect infants from HIV and save their mothers from AIDS. *New England Journal of Medicine, 351*(3), 289–292.

Coplan, R. J., Rubin, K. H., Fox, N. A., Calkins, S. D., & Stewart, S. L. (1994). Being alone, playing alone, and acting alone: Distinguishing among reticence, and passive-, and active-solitude in young children. *Child Development, 65,* 129–137.

Corbett, S. S., & Drewett, R. F. (2004). To what extent is failure to thrive in infancy associated with poorer cognitive development? A review and meta-analysis. *Journal of Child Psychology and Psychiatry, 45*(3), 641–654.

Coren, S. (1992). *The left-hander syndrome.* New York: Free Press.

Cornoldi, C. (2006). The contribution of cognitive psychology to the study of human intelligence. *European Journal of Cognitive Psychology, 18*(1), 1–17.

Cornwell, A. A., C., & Feigenbaum, P. (2006). Sleep biological rhythms in normal infants and those at high risk for SIDS. *Chronobiology International, 23*(5), 935–961.

Cotton, S., & Richdale, A. (2006). Brief report: Parental descriptions of sleep problems in children with autism, Down syndrome, and Prader-Willi syndrome. *Research in Developmental Disabilities, 27*(2), 151–161.

Courage, M. L., Howe, M. L., & Squires, S. E. (2004). Individual differences in 3.5-month-olds' visual attention: What do they predict at 1 year? *Infant Behavior and Development, 27*(1), 19–30.

Cowan, N., et al. (2003). Children's working-memory processes: A response-timing analysis. *Journal of Experimental Psychology: General, 132*(1), 113–132.

Cowan, P. A., & Cowan, C. P. (2005). Five-domain models: Putting it all together. In P. A. Cowan, C. P. Cowan, J. C. Ablow, V. K. Johnson, & J. R. Measelle (Eds.), *The family context of parenting in children's adaptation to elementary school, Monographs in parenting series* (pp. 315–333). Mahwah, NJ: Erlbaum.

Cratty, B. (1986). *Perceptual and motor development in infants and children* (3rd ed.). Englewood Cliffs, NJ: Prentice Hall.

Crittenden, P. M., & Ainsworth, M. D. S. (1989). Child maltreatment and attachment theory. In D. Cicchetti & V. Carlson (Eds.), *Child maltreatment: Theory and research on the causes and consequences of child abuse and neglect.* Cambridge: Cambridge University Press.

Crocco, M. S., & Libresco, A. S. (2007). Citizenship education for the 21st century—A gender inclusive approach to social studies. In D. M. Sadker & E. S. Silber (Eds.), *Gender in the classroom: Foundations, skills, methods, and strategies across the curriculum* (pp. 119–164). Mahwah, NJ: Erlbaum.

Crombie, G., & Desjardins, M. J. (1993, March). *Predictors of gender: The relative importance of children's play, games, and personality characteristics.* Paper presented at the meeting of the Society for Research in Child Development, New Orleans, LA.

Crook, C. K., & Lipsitt, L. P. (1976). Neonatal nutritive sucking: Effects of taste stimulation upon sucking rhythm and heart rate. *Child Development, 47,* 518–522.

Crowther, C., et al. (2006). Neonatal respiratory distress syndrome after repeat exposure to antenatal corticosteroids: A randomised control trial. *Lancet, 367*(9526), 1913–1919.

Cruz, N. V., & Bahna, S. L. (2006). Do foods or additives cause behavior disorders? *Psychiatric Annals, 36*(10), 724–732.

Cryan, J. F., & Slattery, D. A. (2007). Animal models of mood disorders: Recent developments. *Current Opinion in Psychiatry, 20*(1), 1–7.

Culebras, A. (2005). Sleep and neuromuscular disorders. *Neurologic Clinics, 23*(4), 1209–1223.

Cumming, S. P., Eisenmann, J. C., Smoll, F. L., Smith, R. E., & Malina, R. M. (2005). Body size and perceptions of coaching behaviors by adolescent female athletes. *Psychology of Sport and Exercise, 6*(6), 693–705.

Cunningham, R. L., & McGinnis, M. Y. (2007). Factors influencing aggression toward females by male rats exposed to anabolic androgenic steroids during puberty. *Hormones and Behavior, 51*(1), 135–141.

Curtner-Smith, M. E. (2000). Mechanisms by which family processes contribute to school-age boy's bullying. *Child Study Journal, 30*(3), 169–186.

Cystic Fibrosis Foundation. (2007). Available at www.cff.org. Accessed February 23, 2007.

Dai, D. Y. (2001). A comparison of gender differences in academic self-concept and motivation between high-ability and average Chinese adolescents. *Journal of Secondary Gifted Education, 13*(1), 22–32.

Daly, M., & Wilson, M. (2000). Genetic ties may be factor in violence in stepfamilies. *American Psychologist, 55*(6), 679–680.

Daman-Wasserman, M., Brennan, B., Radcliffe, F., Prigot, J., & Fagen, J. (2006). Auditory-visual context and memory retrieval in 3-month-old infants. *Infancy, 10*(3) 201–220.

Damon, W. (2000). Setting the stage for the development of wisdom: Self-understanding and moral identity during adolescence. In W. S. Brown (Ed.), *Understanding wisdom: Sources, science, and society* (pp. 339–360). Philadelphia: Templeton Foundation Press.

Dandy, J., & Nettelbeck, T. (2002). The relationship between IQ, homework, aspirations and academic achievement for Chinese, Vietnamese and Anglo-Celtic Australian school children. *Educational Psychology, 22*(3), 267–276.

Dane, S., & Erzurumluoglu, A. (2003). Sex and handedness differences in eye–hand visual reaction times in handball players. *International Journal of Neuroscience, 113*(7), 923–929.

Dang-Vu, T. T., Desseilles, M., Peigneux, P., & Maquet, P. (2006). A role for sleep in brain plasticity. *Pediatric Rehabilitation, 19*(2) 98–118.

Daniels, S. R. (2006). The consequences of childhood overweight and obesity. *The Future of Children, 16*(1), 47–67.

Daubenmier, J. J., et al. (2007). The contribution of changes in diet, exercise, and stress management to changes in coronary risk in women and men in the Multisite Cardiac Lifestyle Intervention Program. *Annals of Behavioral Medicine, 33*(1), 57–68.

Davies, P. T., & Windle, M. (2001). Inter-parental discord and adolescent adjustment trajectories: The potentiating and protective role of intrapersonal attributes. *Child Development, 72*(4), 1163–1178.

Davis, A. (1991). Piaget, teachers and education: Into the 1990s. In P. Light, S. Sheldon,

& M. Woodhead (Eds.), *Learning to think.* New York: Routledge.

Davis, H. A. (2001). The quality and impact of relationships between elementary school students and teachers. *Contemporary Educational Psychology, 26*(4), 431–453.

Davis, L., Edwards, H., Mohay, H., & Wollin, J. (2003). The impact of very premature birth on the psychological health of mothers. *Early Human Development, 73*(1–2), 61–70.

Davis, S. R., Davison, S. L., Donath, S., & Bell, R. J. (2005). Circulating androgen levels and self-reported sexual function in women. *Journal of the American Medical Association, 294*(1), 91–96.

Day, N. L., Goldschmidt, L., & Thomas, C. A. (2006). Prenatal marijuana exposure contributes to the prediction of marijuana use at age 14. *Addiction, 101*(9), 1313–1322.

De Haan, M., & Groen, M. (2006). Neural bases of infants' processing of social information in faces. In P. J. Marshall & N. A. Fox (Eds.), *The development of social engagement: Neurobiological perspectives. Series in affective science* (pp. 46–80). New York: Oxford University Press.

De Lisi, R. (2005). A lifetime of work using a developmental theory to enhance the lives of children and adolescents. *Journal of Applied Developmental Psychology, 26*(1), 107–110.

de Lisi, R., & Gallagher, A. M. (1991). Understanding of gender stability and constancy in Argentinean children. *Merrill-Palmer Quarterly, 37*(3), 483–502.

de Oliveira, F. S., Viana, M. R., Antoniolli, A. R., & Marchioro, M. (2001). Differential effects of lead and zinc on inhibitory avoidance learning in mice. *Brazilian Journal of Medical and Biological Research, 34*(1), 117–120.

de Villiers, J. G., & de Villiers, P. A. (1999). Language development. In M. H. Bornstein & M. E. Lamb (Eds.), *Developmental psychology: An advanced textbook* (4th ed.) (pp. 313–373). Mahwah, NJ: Erlbaum.

de Vries, J. I. P., & Hopkins, B. (2005). Fetal movements and postures: What do they mean for postnatal development? In B. Hopkins & S. P. Johnson (Eds.), *Prenatal development of postnatal functions. Advances in infancy research* (pp. 177–219). Westport, CT: Praeger Publishers/Greenwood.

Deary, I. J., Whiteman, M. C., Starr, J. M., Whalley, L. J., & Fox, H. C. (2004). The impact of childhood intelligence on later life: Following up the Scottish mental surveys of 1932 and 1947. *Journal of Personality and Social Psychology, 86*(1), 130–147.

DeCasper, A. J., & Fifer, W. P. (1980). Of human bonding: Newborns prefer their mothers' voices. *Science, 208,* 1174–1176.

DeCasper, A. J., & Prescott, P. A. (1984). Human newborns' perception of male voices: Preference, discrimination, and reinforc-

ing value. *Developmental Psychobiology, 17,* 481–491.

DeCasper, A. J., & Spence, M. J. (1986). Prenatal maternal speech influences newborns' perception of speech sounds. *Infant Behavior and Development, 9,* 133–150.

DeCasper, A. J., & Spence, M. J. (1991). Auditorially mediated behavior during the perinatal period: A cognitive view. In M. J. Weiss & P. R. Zelazo (Eds.), *Infant attention* (pp. 142–176). Norwood, NJ: Ablex.

Dehaene-Lambertz, G., Pena, M., Christophe, A., & Landrieu, P. (2004). Phoneme perception in a neonate with a left sylvian infarct. *Brain and Language, 88*(1), 26–38.

DeHart, T., Pelham, B. W., & Tennen, H. (2006). What lies beneath: Parenting style and implicit self-esteem. *Journal of Experimental Social Psychology, 42*(1), 1–17.

Delaney-Black, V., et al. (2004). Prenatal cocaine: Quantity of exposure and gender influences on school-age behavior. *Developmental and Behavioral Pediatrics, 25*(4), 254–263.

DeLoache, J. S. (2002). The symbol-mindedness of young children. In W. Hartup & R. A. Weinberg (Eds.), *Child psychology in retrospect and prospect: In celebration of the 75th anniversary of the Institute of Child Development* (pp. 73–101). Mahwah, NJ: Erlbaum.

DeLoache, J. S., Cassidy, D. J., & Brown, A. L. (1985). Precursors of mnemonic strategies in very young children's memory. *Child Development, 56,* 125–137.

Delpit, L. (2006). What should teachers do? Ebonics and culturally responsive instruction. In S. J. Nero (Ed.), *Dialects, Englishes, creoles, and education* (pp. 93–101). Mahwah, NJ: Erlbaum.

DeMarie, D., Miller, P. H., Ferron, J., & Cunningham, W. R. (2004). Path analysis tests of theoretical models of children's memory performance. *Journal of Cognition and Development, 5*(4), 461–492.

Dennis, W. (1960). Causes of retardation among institutional children: Iran. *Journal of Genetic Psychology, 96,* 47–59.

Dennis, W., & Dennis, M. G. (1940). The effect of cradling practices upon the onset of walking in Hopi children. *Journal of Genetic Psychology, 56,* 77–86.

Dezoete, J. A., MacArthur, B. A., & Tuck, B. (2003). Prediction of Bayley and Stanford–Binet scores with a group of very low birth-weight children. *Child: Care, Health and Development, 29*(5), 367–372.

Dieterich, S. E., Hebert, H. M., Landry, S. H., Swank, P. R., & Smith, K. E. (2004). Maternal and child characteristics that influence the growth of daily living skills from infancy to school age in preterm and term children. *Early Education and Development, 15*(3), 283–303.

DiLalla, D. L., Gottesman, I. I., Carey, G., & Bouchard, T. J., Jr. (1999). Heritability of

MMPI Harris–Lingoes and Subtle–Obvious subscales in twins reared apart. *Assessment, 6*(4), 353–366.

Ding, Q. J., & Hesketh, T. (2006). Family size, fertility preferences, and sex ratio in China in the era of the one child family policy: Results from National Family Planning and Reproductive Health Survey. *British Medical Journal, 333*(7564), 371–373.

Dishion, T. J., & Stormshak, E. A. (2007). Family and peer social interaction. In T. J. Dishion & E. A. Stormshak. (Eds.), *Intervening in children's lives: An ecological, family-centered approach to mental health care* (pp. 31–48). Washington, DC: American Psychological Association.

Dobbinson, S., Perkins, M., & Boucher, J. (2003). The interactional significance of formulas in autistic language. *Clinical Linguistics and Phonetics, 17*(4–5), 299–307.

Dockett, S., Perry, B., & Whitton, D. (2006). Picture storybooks and starting school. *Early Child Development and Care, 76*(8), 835–848.

Dodge, K. A., Laird, R., Lochman, J. E., Zelli, A., & Conduct Problems Prevention Research Group U.S. (2002). Multidimensional latent-construct analysis of children's social information processing patterns: Correlations with aggressive behavior problems. *Psychological Assessment, 14*(1), 60–73.

Dogil, G., et al. (2002). The speaking brain: A tutorial introduction to fMRI experiments in the production of speech, prosody, and syntax. *Journal of Neurolinguistics, 15*(1), 59–90.

Dollfus, S., et al. (2005). Atypical hemispheric specialization for language in right-handed schizophrenia patients. *Biological Psychiatry, 57*(9), 1020–1028.

Dombrowski, M. A. S., et al. (2000). Kangaroo skin-to-skin care for premature twins and their adolescent parents. *American Journal of Maternal/Child Nursing, 25*(2), 92–94.

Donaldson, M. (1979). *Children's minds.* New York: Norton.

Dorling, J., et al. (2006). Data collection from very low birthweight infants in a geographical region: Methods, costs, and trends in mortality, admission rates, and resource utilisation over a five–year period. *Early Human Development, 82*(2), 117–124.

Downey, D. B. (2001). Number of siblings and intellectual development: The resource dilution explanation. *American Psychologist, 56*(6/7), 497–504.

Drabick, D. A. G., Gadow, K. D., Carlson, G. A., & Bromet, E. J. (2004). ODD and ADHD symptoms in Ukrainian children: External validators and comorbidity. *Journal of the American Academy of Child and Adolescent Psychiatry. 43*(6), 735–743.

Dragsow, E., Halle, J. W., & Phillips, B. (2001). Effects of different social partners on the discriminated requesting of a young child with

and adults: A review of social scientific research. *Aggression and Violent Behavior, 12*(3), 300–314.

Hinojosa, T., Sheu, C., & Michel, G. F. (2003). Infant hand-use preferences for grasping objects contributes to the development of a hand-use preference for manipulating objects. *Developmental Psychobiology, 43*(4), 328–334.

Hinshaw, S. P. (2006). Treatment for children and adolescents with attention-deficit/hyperactivity disorder. In P. C. Kendall (Ed.), *Child and adolescent therapy: Cognitive-behavioral procedures* (3rd ed.) (pp. 82–113). New York: Guilford.

Ho, A., Todd, R. D., & Constantino, J. N. (2005). Autistic traits in twins vs. non-twins—A preliminary study. *Journal of Autism and Developmental Disorders, 35*(1), 129–133.

Hoegh, D. G., & Bourgeois, M. J. (2002). Prelude and postlude to the self: Correlates of achieved identity. *Youth and Society, 33*(4), 573–594.

Hoff, E. (2006). Language experience and language milestones during early childhood. In K. McCartney & D. Phillips (Eds.), *Blackwell handbook of early childhood development., Blackwell handbooks of developmental psychology* (pp. 233–251). Malden, MA: Blackwell.

Hoff, E. V. (2005). A friend living inside me—The forms and functions of imaginary companions. *Imagination, Cognition and Personality, 24*(2), 151–189.

Hoffman, L. W., & Youngblade, L. M. (1998). Maternal employment, morale, and parenting style: Social class comparisons. *Journal of Applied Developmental Psychology, 19*(3), 389–413.

Hogan, A. M., de Haan, M., Datta, A., & Kirkham, F. J. (2006). Hypoxia: An acute, intermittent and chronic challenge to cognitive development. *Developmental Science, 9*(4), 335–337.

Hogan, A. M., Kirkham, F. J., Isaacs, E. B., Wade, A. M., & Vargha-Khadem, F. (2005). Intellectual decline in children with moyamoya and sickle cell anaemia. *Developmental Medicine & Child Neurology, 47*(12), 824–829.

Holland, J. J. (2000, July 25). *Groups link media to child violence.* Available at http://www.ap.org/.

Holliday, R. E. (2003). Reducing misinformation effects in children with cognitive interviews: Dissociating recollection and familiarity. *Child Development, 74*(3), 728–751.

Holloway, S. D., Suzuki, S., Yamamoto, Y., & Mindnich, J. D. (2006). Relation of maternal role concepts to parenting, employment choices, and life satisfaction among Japanese women. *Sex Roles, 54*(3–4), 235–249.

Homer, B. D., & Nelson, K. (2005). Seeing objects as symbols and symbols as objects: Language and the development of dual representation. In B. D. Homer & C. S. Tamis-LeMonda (Eds.), *The development of social cognition and communication* (pp. 29–52). Mahwah, NJ: Erlbaum.

Honein, M. A., Paulozzi, L. J., Mathews, T. J., Erickson, J. D., & Wong, L. C. (2001). Impact of folic acid fortification of the U.S. food supply on the occurrence of neural tube defects. *Journal of the American Medical Association, 285*(23), 2981–2986.

Honzik, M. P., Macfarlane, J. W., & Allen, L. (1948). The stability of mental test performance between two and eighteen years. *Journal of Experimental Education, 17,* 309–324.

Hopkins, W. D., Dahl, J. F., & Pilcher, D. (2001). Genetic influence on the expression of hand preferences in chimpanzees (*Pan troglodytes*): Evidence in support of the right-shift theory and developmental instability. *Psychological Science, 12*(4), 299–303.

Hopkins-Golightly, T., Raz, S., & Sander, C. J. (2003). Influence of slight to moderate risk for birth hypoxia on acquisition of cognitive and language function in the preterm infant: A cross-sectional comparison with preterm-birth controls. *Neuropsychology, 17*(1), 3–13.

Hossain, M., Chetana, M., & Devi, P. U. (2005). Late effect of prenatal irradiation on the hippocampal histology and brain weight in adult mice. *International Journal of Developmental Neuroscience, 23*(4), 307–313.

Howe, M. L. (2006). Developmentally invariant dissociations in children's true and false memories: Not all relatedness is created equal. *Child Development, 77*(4), 1112–1123.

Hoy, E. A., & McClure, B. G. (2000). Preschool experience: A facilitator of very low birthweight infants' development? *Infant Mental Health Journal, 21*(6), 481–494.

Huber, J., Darling, S., Park, K., & Soliman, K. F. A. (2001). Altered responsiveness to stress and NMDA following prenatal exposure to cocaine. *Physiology and Behavior, 72*(1–2), 181–188.

Hudson, J. A. (1990). The emergence of autobiographical memory in mother–child conversation. In R. Fivush & J. A. Hudson (Eds.), *Knowing and remembering in young children.* Cambridge: Cambridge University Press.

Hudziak, J. J. (2001). Latent class analysis of ADHD and comorbid symptoms in a population sample of adolescent female twins. *Journal of Child Psychology and Psychiatry and Allied Disciplines, 42*(7), 933–942.

Huesmann, L. R., Dubow, E. F., Eron, L. D., & Boxer, P. (2006). Middle childhood family contextual factors as predictors of adult outcomes. In A. C. Huston & M. N. Ripke (Eds.), *Middle Childhood: Contexts of Development.* Cambridge, UK: Cambridge University Press.

Huestis, M. A., et al. (2002). Drug abuse's smallest victims: in utero drug exposure. *Forensic Science International, 128*(2), 20.

Huizink, A. C., & Mulder, E. J. H. (2006). Maternal smoking, drinking or cannabis use during pregnancy and neurobehavioral and cognitive functioning in human offspring. *Neuroscience & Biobehavioral Reviews, 30*(1), 24–41.

Hunt, C. E., & Hauck, F. R. (2006). Sudden infant death syndrome. *Canadian Medical Association Journal, 174*(13), 1861–1869.

Hunter, B. C., & Sahler, O. J. Z. (2006). Music for very young ears. *Birth: Issues in Perinatal Care, 33*(2), 137–138.

Hunter, S. C., & Boyle, J. M. E. (2004). Appraisal and coping strategy use in victims of school bullying. *British Journal of Educational Psychology, 74*(1), 83–107.

Hur, Y. (2005). Genetic and environmental influences on self-concept in female preadolescent twins: Comparison of Minnesota and Seoul data. *Twin Research and Human Genetics, 8*(4), 291–299.

Hurd, Y. L., et al. (2005). Marijuana impairs growth in mid–gestation fetuses. *Neurotoxicology and Teratology, 27*(2), 221–229.

Hynes, M., Sheik, M., Wilson, H. G., & Spiegel, P. (2002). Reproductive health indicators and outcomes among refugee and internally displaced persons in postemergency phase camps. *Journal of the American Medical Association, 288,* 595–603.

Hyson, M., Copple, C., & Jones, J. (2006). Early childhood development and education. In K. A. Renninger, I. E. Sigel, W. Damon, & R. M. Lerner (Eds.), *Handbook of child psychology* (6th ed.), Vol. 4, *Child psychology in practice* (pp. 3–47). Hoboken, NJ: Wiley.

IJzendoorn, M. H. van, et al. (2000). The similarity of siblings' attachments to their mother. Child *Development, 71*(4), 1086–1098.

IJzendoorn, M. H. van, & Hubbard, F. O. A. (2000). Are infant crying and maternal responsiveness during the first year related to infant–mother attachment at 15 months? *Attachment and Human Development, 2*(3), 371–391.

IJzendoorn, M. H. van, & Juffer, F. (2006). The Emanuel Miller Memorial Lecture 2006: Adoption as intervention. Meta-analytic evidence for massive catch-up and plasticity in physical, socio-emotional, and cognitive development. *Journal of Child Psychology and Psychiatry, 47*(12), 1228–1245.

Ikeda, K., Koga, A., & Minami, S. (2006). Evaluation of a cure process during alarm treatment for nocturnal enuresis. *Journal of Clinical Psychology, 62*(10), 1245–1257.

Infant and Toddler Nutrition. (2007, April 10). National Institutes of Health, Department of Health and Human Services. Available at http://www.nlm.nih.gov/medlineplus/infantandtoddlernutrition.html.

Inzlicht, M., & Good, C. (2006). How environments can threaten academic performance, self-knowledge, and sense of belonging. In S. Levin & C. van Laar (Eds.), *Stigma and group inequality: Social psychological perspectives. The Claremont symposium on Applied Social Psychology* (pp. 129–150). Mahwah, NJ: Erlbaum.

Ishikawa, S., Oota, R., & Sakano, Y. (2003). The relationship between anxiety disorders tendencies and subjective school maladjustment in childhood. *Japanese Journal of Counseling Science, 36*(3), 264–271.

Izard, C. E. (1983). *Maximally discriminative facial movement scoring system.* Newark, DE: University of Delaware Instructional Resources Center.

Izard, C. E. (2004). The generality–specificity issue in infants' emotion responses: A comment on Bennett, Bendersky, and Lewis (2002). *Infancy, 6*(3), 417–423.

Izard, C. E., Hembree, E. A., & Huebner, R. R. (1987). Infants' emotion expressions to acute pain: Developmental change and stability of individual differences. *Developmental Psychology, 23,* 105–113.

Izard, C. E., & Malatesta, C. Z. (1987). Perspectives on emotional development. I. Differential emotions theory of early emotional development. In J. D. Osofsky (Ed.), *Handbook of infant development* (2nd ed.). New York: Wiley.

Izard, C. E., Youngstrom, E. A., Fine, S. E., Mostow, A. J., & Trentacosta, C. J. (2006). Emotions and developmental psychopathology. In D. Cicchetti & D. J. Cohen (Eds.), *Developmental psychopathology,* Vol. 1, *Theory and method* (2nd ed.) (pp. 244–292). Hoboken, NJ: Wiley.

Jacklin, C. N., & McBride-Chang, C. (1991). The effects of feminist scholarship on developmental psychology. *Psychology of Women Quarterly, 15,* 549–556.

Jackson, D. N., & Rushton, J. P. (2006). Males have greater g: Sex differences in general mental ability from 100,000 17- to 18-year-olds on the Scholastic Assessment Test. *Intelligence, 34*(5), 479–486.

Jacobs, D. M., Levy, G., & Marder, K. (2006). Dementia in Parkinson's disease, Huntington's disease, and related disorders. In M. J. Farah & T. E. Feinberg (Eds.), *Patient-based approaches to cognitive neuroscience* (2nd ed.) (pp. 381–395). Cambridge, MA: MIT Press.

Jacobs, J. E., Davis-Kean, P., Bleeker, M., Eccles, J. S., & Malanchuk, O. (2005). "I can, but I don't want to": The impact of parents, interests, and activities on gender differences in math. In A. M. Gallagher & J. C. Kaufman (Eds.), *Gender differences in mathematics: An integrative psychological approach* (pp. 246–263). New York: Cambridge University Press.

Jacobson, J. L., Jacobson, S. W., Padgett, R. J., Brumitt, G. A., & Billings, R. L. (1992). Effects of prenatal PCB exposure on cognitive processing efficiency and sustained attention. *Developmental Psychology, 28,* 297–306.

Jacobson, P. F., & Schwartz, R. G. (2005). English past tense use in bilingual children with language impairment. *American Journal of Speech-Language Pathology, 14*(4), 313–323.

Jaffee, S. R., Belsky, J., Harrington, H. L., Caspi, A., & Moffitt, T. E. (2006). When parents have a history of conduct disorder: How is the caregiving environment affected? *Journal of Abnormal Psychology, 115*(2), 309–319.

Jago, R., Baranowski, T., Baranowski, J. C., Thompson, D., & Greaves, K. A. (2005). BMI from 3–6 y of age is predicted by TV viewing and physical activity, not diet. *International Journal of Obesity, 29*(6), 557–564.

James, W. 1890. *The principles of psychology.* Mineola, NY: Dover (Reprint publisher).

Jamieson, S., & Marshall, W. L. (2000). Attachment styles and violence in child molesters. *Journal of Sexual Aggression, 5*(2), 88–98.

Jang, K. L., Livesley, W. J., Taylor, S., Stein, M. B., & Moon, E. C. (2004). Heritability of individual depressive symptoms. *Journal of Affective Disorders, 80*(2–3), 125–133.

Javo, C., Ronning, J. A., & Heyerdahl, S. (2004). Child-rearing in an indigenous Sami population in Norway: A cross-cultural comparison of parental attitudes and expectations. *Scandinavian Journal of Psychology, 45*(1), 67–78.

Jeng, S.-F., Yau, K.-I. T., Liao, H.-F., Chen, L.-C., & Chen, P.-S. (2000). Prognostic factors for walking attainment in very lowbirthweight preterm infants. *Early Human Development, 59*(3), 159–173.

Jiang, J., et al. (2006). Risk factors for overweight in 2- to 6-year-old children in Beijing, China. *International Journal of Pediatric Obesity, 1*(2), 103–108.

Joca, S. R. L., Zanelati, T., & Guimaraes, F. S. (2006). Post-stress facilitation of serotonergic, but not noradrenergic, neurotransmission in the dorsal hippocampus prevents learned helplessness development in rats. *Brain Research, 1087*(1), 67–74.

Johnson, C. M. (1991). Infant and toddler sleep: A telephone survey of parents in one community. *Developmental and Behavioral Pediatrics, 12,* 108–114.

Johnson, W., Emde, R. N., Pannabecker, B., Stenberg, C., & Davis, M. (1982). Maternal perception of infant emotion from birth to 18 months. *Infant Behavior and Development, 5,* 313–322.

Johnson, W., & Krueger, R. F. (2006). How money buys happiness: Genetic and environmental processes linking finances and life satisfaction. *Journal of Personality and Social Psychology, 90*(4), 680–691.

Johnson, W., McGue, M., Krueger, R. F., & Bouchard, T. J., Jr. (2004). Marriage and personality: A genetic analysis. *Journal of Personality and Social Psychology, 86*(2), 285–294.

Johnston, C. A., & Steele, R. G. (2007). Treatment of pediatric overweight: An examination of feasibility and effectiveness in an applied clinical setting. *Journal of Pediatric Psychology, 32*(1), 106–110.

Johnston, L. D., O'Malley, P. M., Bachman, J. G. & Schulenberg, J. E. (December 21, 2006). *Teen drug use continues down in 2006, particularly among older teens; but use of prescription-type drugs remains high.* University of Michigan News and Information Services: Ann Arbor, MI. Available at www.monitoringthefuture.org. Accessed February 25, 2007.

Jones, D. C., Swift, D. J., & Johnson, M. A. (1988). Nondeliberate memory for a novel event among preschoolers. *Developmental Psychology, 24,* 641–645.

Jones, M. C. (1924). Elimination of children's fears. *Journal of Experimental Psychology, 7,* 381–390.

Jones, S. S., & Hong, H-W. (2005). How some infant smiles get made. *Infant Behavior & Development, 28*(2), 194–205.

Joshi, P. T., Salpekar, J. A., & Daniolos, P. T. (2006). Physical and sexual abuse of children. In M. K. Dulcan & J. M. Wiener (Eds.), *Essentials of child and adolescent psychiatry* (pp. 595–620). Washington, DC: American Psychiatric Publishing.

Joshi, R. M. (2003). Misconceptions about the assessment and diagnosis of reading disability. *Reading Psychology, 24*(3–4), 247–266.

Kagan, J., & Klein, R. E. (1973). Cross-cultural perspectives on early development. *American Psychologist, 28,* 947–961.

Kagan, L. J., MacLeod, A. K., & Pote, H. L. (2004). Accessibility of causal explanations for future positive and negative events in adolescents with anxiety and depression. *Clinical Psychology and Psychotherapy, 11*(3), 177–186.

Kamakura, T., Ando, J., & Ono, Y. (2007). Genetic and environmental effects of stability and change in self-esteem during adolescence. *Personality and Individual Differences, 42*(1), 181–190.

Kaminski, R. A., & Stormshak, E. A. (2007). Project STAR: Early intervention with preschool children and families for the prevention of substance abuse. In P. Tolan, J. Szapocznik, & S. Sambrano (Eds.), *Preventing youth substance abuse: Science-based programs for children and adolescents* (pp. 89–

feed their babies and factors influencing the duration of breastfeeding. *Child Care in Practice, 12*(3), 283–297.

Slobin, D. I. (2001). Form/function relations: How do children find out what they are? In M. Tomasello & E. Bates (Eds.), *Language development: The essential readings.* Malden, MA: Blackwell.

Small, M. Y. (1990). *Cognitive development.* San Diego: Harcourt Brace Jovanovich.

Smiley, P. A., & Johnson, R. S. (2006). Self-referring terms, event transitivity and development of self. *Cognitive Development, 21*(3), 266–284.

Smith, C. L., Calkins, S. D., Keane, S. P., Anastopoulos, A. D., & Shelton, T. L. (2004). Predicting stability and change in toddler behavior problems: Contributions of maternal behavior and child gender. *Developmental Psychology, 40*(1), 29–42.

Smith, P. K. (1979). The ontogeny of fear in children. In W. Sluckin (Ed.), *Fears in animals and man.* London: Van Nostrand Reinhold.

Smith, P. K. (2005). Play: Types and functions in human development. In B. J. Ellis & D. F. Bjorklund (Eds.), *Origins of the social mind: Evolutionary psychology and child development* (pp. 271–291). New York: Guilford Press.

Smolka, E., & Eviatar, Z. (2006). Phonological and orthographic visual word recognition in the two cerebral hemispheres: Evidence from Hebrew. Cognitive *Neuropsychology, 23*(6), 972–989.

Smoll, F. L., & Schultz, R. W. (1990). Quantifying gender differences in physical performance: A developmental perspective. *Developmental Psychology, 26,* 360–369.

Snedeker, J., Geren, J., & Shafto, C. L. (2007). Starting over: International adoption as a natural experiment in language development. *Psychological Science, 18*(1), 79–87.

Snegovskikh, V., Park, J. S., & Norwitz, E. R. (2006). Endocrinology of parturition. *Endocrinology and Metabolism Clinics of North America, 35*(1), 173–191.

Snow, C. (2006). Cross-cutting themes and future research directions. In D. August & T. Shanahan (Eds.), *Developing literacy in second-language learners: Report of the National Literacy Panel on Language-Minority Children and Youth* (pp. 631–651). Mahwah, NJ: Erlbaum.

Snyder, H. M., & Sickmund, M. (2006). *Juvenile offenders and victims: 2006 national report.* Washington, DC: U.S. Department of Justice, Office of Justice Programs, Office of Juvenile Justice and Delinquency Prevention.

Snyderman, M., & Rothman, S. (1990). *The IQ controversy.* New Brunswick, NJ: Transaction.

Soan, S., & Tod, J. (2006). Review of dyslexia. *European Journal of Special Needs Education, 21*(3), 354–356.

Sodian, B., Taylor, C., Harris, P. L., & Perner, J. (1991). Early deception and the child's theory of mind: False trails and genuine markers. *Child Development, 62,* 468–483.

Sommer, I. E. C., Ramsey, N. F., Mandl, R. C. W., & Kahn, R. S. (2002). Language lateralization in monozygotic twin pairs concordant and discordant for handedness. *Brain, 125*(12), 2710–2718.

Sontag, L. W., & Richards, T. W. (1938). *Studies in fetal behavior: Fetal heart rate as a behavioral indicator.* Child Development Monographs, *3*(4).

Sorce, J., Emde, R. N., Campos, J. J., Klinnert, M. D. (2000). Maternal emotional signaling: Its effect on the visual cliff behavior of 1-year-olds. In D. Muir & A. Slater, (Eds.), *Infant development: The essential readings. Essential readings in developmental psychology* (pp. 282–292). Malden, MA: Blackwell.

Spelke, E. S., & Owsley, C. (1979). Inter-modal exploration and knowledge in infancy. *Infant Behavior and Development, 2,* 13–27.

Spencer, N. (2006). Explaining the social gradient in smoking in pregnancy: Early life course accumulation and cross-sectional clustering of social risk exposures in the 1958 British national cohort. *Social Science & Medicine, 62*(5), 1250–1259.

Spieker, S. J., et al. (2003). Joint influence of child care and infant attachment security for cognitive and language outcomes of low-income toddlers. *Infant Behavior and Development, 26*(3), 326–344.

Spieker, S., Nelson, D., DeKlyen, M., & Staerkel, F. (2005). Enhancing early attachments in the context of Early Head Start: Can programs emphasizing family support improve rates of secure infant–mother attachments in low-income families? In L. J. Berlin, Y. Ziv, L. Amaya-Jackson, & M. T. Greenberg (Eds.), *Enhancing early attachments: Theory, research, intervention, and policy. Duke series in child development and public policy* (pp. 250–275). New York: Guilford.

Spitz, R. A. (1965). *The first year of life: A psychoanalytic study of normal and deviant object relations.* New York: International Universities Press.

Spitzer, R. L., Gibbon, M., Skodol, A. E., Williams, J. B. W., & First, M. B. (2002). *DSM–IV–TR casebook.* Washington, D.C.: American Psychiatric Press.

Sroufe, L. A. (1979). Socioemotional development. In J. Osofsky (Ed.), *Handbook of infant development.* New York: Wiley.

Sroufe, L. A. (1998). Cited in S. Blakeslee (1998, August 4), Re-evaluating significance of baby's bond with mother, *New York Times,* pp. F1, F2.

Sroufe, L. A. (2005). Attachment and development: A prospective, longitudinal study from birth to adulthood. *Attachment & Human Development, 7*(4), 349–367.

Sroufe, L. A., Bennett, C., Englund, M., Urban, J., & Shulman, S. (1993). The significance of gender boundaries in preadolescence: Contemporary correlates and antecedents of boundary violation and maintenance. *Child Development, 64,* 455–466.

Sroufe, L. A., Waters, E., & Matas, L. (1974). Contextual determinants of infant affectional response. In M. Lewis & L. Rosenblum (Eds.), *The origins of fear.* New York: Wiley.

Stagnitti, K., Unsworth, C., & Rodger, S. (2000). Development of an assessment to identify play behaviours that discriminate between the play of typical preschoolers and preschoolers with pre-academic problems. *Canadian Journal of Occupational Therapy, 67*(5), 291–303.

Stahmer, A. C., Ingersoll, B., & Koegel, R. L. (2004). Inclusive programming for toddlers autism spectrum disorders: Outcomes from the Children's Toddler School. *Journal of Positive Behavior Interventions, 6*(2), 67–82.

Stams, G. J. M., Juffer, F., & IJzendoorn, M. H. van (2002). Maternal sensitivity, infant attachment, and temperament in early childhood predict adjustment in middle childhood: The case of adopted children and their biologically unrelated parents. *Developmental Psychology, 38*(5), 806–821.

Stankoff, B., et al. (2006). Imaging of CNS myelin by positron-emission tomography. *Proceedings of the National Academy of Sciences of the United States of America, 103*(24), 9304–9309.

Stanley, C., Murray, L., & Stein, A. (2004). The effect of postnatal depression on mother–infant interaction, infant response to the still-face perturbation, and performance on an instrumental learning task. *Development and Psychopathology, 16*(1), 1–18.

Stanwood, G. D., Washington, R. A., & Levitt, P. (2001). Identification of a sensitive period of prenatal cocaine exposure that alters the development of the anterior cingulate cortex. *Cerebral Cortex, 11*(5), 430–440.

Stauffacher, K., & DeHart, G. B. (2006). Crossing social contexts: Relational aggression between siblings and friends during early and middle childhood. *Journal of Applied Developmental Psychology, 27*(3), 228–240.

Steele, H. (2005). Editorial. *Attachment & Human Development, 7*(4), 345.

Steele, M., Hodges, J., Kaniuk, J., Hillman, S., & Henderson, K. (2003). Attachment representations and adoption: Associations between maternal states of mind and emotion narratives in previously maltreated children. *Journal of Child Psychotherapy, 29*(2), 187–205.

Steinberg, L., Brown, B. B., & Dornbusch, S. M. (1996). Ethnicity and adolescent achievement. *American Educator, 20*(2), 28–35.

Stemberger, J. P. (2004). Phonological priming and irregular past. *Journal of Memory and Language, 50*(1), 82–95.

Stephenson, R. H., & Banet-Weiser, S. (2007). Super-sized kids: Obesity, children, moral panic, and the media. In J. A. Bryant (Ed.), *The children's television community* (pp. 277–291). Mahwah, NJ Erlbaum.

Sternberg, R. J. (2000). In search of the zipper-rump-a-zoo. *Psychologist, 13*(5), 250–255.

Sternberg, R. J. (2006). The nature of creativity. *Creativity Research Journal, 18*(1), 87–98.

Sternberg, R. J. (2007). A systems model of leadership: WICS. *American Psychologist, 62*(1), 34–42.

Sternberg, R. J., Grigorenko, E. L., & Kidd, K. K. (2005). Intelligence, race, and genetics. *American Psychologist, 60*(1), 46–59.

Sternberg, R. J., & Lubart, T. I. (1995). *Defying the crowd: Cultivating creativity in a culture of conformity.* New York: Free Press.

Sternberg, R. J., & Lubart, T. I. (1996). Investing in creativity. *American Psychologist, 51,* 677–688.

Sternberg, R. J., & The Rainbow Project Collaborators. (2006). The Rainbow Project: Enhancing the SAT through assessments of analytical, practical, and creative skills. *Intelligence, 34*(4), 321–350.

Sternberg, R. J., & Williams, W. M. (1997). Does the Graduate Record Examination predict meaningful success in the graduate training of psychologists? *American Psychologist, 52,* 630–641.

Stevens, B., et al. (2005). Consistent management of repeated procedural pain with sucrose in preterm neonates: Is it effective and safe for repeated use over time? *Clinical Journal of Pain, 21*(6), 543–548.

Stevens, T., Olivárez, Jr., A., & Hamman, D. (2006). The role of cognition, motivation, and emotion in explaining the mathematics achievement gap between Hispanic and White students. *Hispanic Journal of Behavioral Sciences, 28*(2), 161–186.

Stevenson, H. W., Chen, C., & Lee, S. (1993). Mathematics achievement of Chinese, Japanese, and American children: Ten years later. *Science, 259,* 53–58.

Stevenson, J. (1992). Evidence for a genetic etiology in hyperactivity in children. *Behavior Genetics, 22,* 337–344.

Steward, D. K. (2001). Behavioral characteristics of infants with nonorganic failure to thrive during a play interaction. *American Journal of Maternal/Child Nursing, 26*(2), 79–85.

Stifter, C. A., & Wiggins, C. N. (2004). Assessment of disturbances in emotion Regulation and temperament. In R. DelCarmen-Wiggins & A. Carter (Eds.), *Handbook of infant, toddler, and preschool mental health assessment* (pp. 79–103). New York: Oxford University Press.

Stipek, D., & Hakuta, K. (2007). Strategies to ensure that no child starts from behind. In J. L. Aber et al. (Eds.), *Child development and social policy: Knowledge for action, APA Decade of Behavior volumes* (pp. 129–145). Washington, DC: American Psychological Association.

Stipek, D., Recchia, S., & McClintic, S. (1992). *Self-evaluation in young children.* Monographs of the Society for Research in Child Development, 57(1, ser. 226).

Stoel-Gammon, C. (2002). Intervocalic consonants in the speech of typically developing children: Emergence and early use. *Clinical Linguistics and Phonetics, 16*(3), 155–168.

Storch, E. A., et al. (2007). Peer victimization, psychosocial adjustment, and physical activity in overweight and at-risk-for-overweight youth. *Journal of Pediatric Psychology, 32*(1), 80–89.

Stores, G., & Wiggs, L. (Eds.). (2001). *Sleep disturbance in children and adolescents with disorders of development: Its significance and management.* New York: Cambridge University Press.

Straus, M. A. (1995). Cited in C. Collins (1995, May 11), Spanking is becoming the new don't, *New York Times,* p. C8.

Straus, M. A. (2000). Corporal punishment and primary prevention of physical abuse. *Child Abuse and Neglect, 24*(9), 1109–1114.

Straus, M. A., & Field, C. J. (2003). Psychological aggression by American parents: National data on prevalence, chronicity, and severity. *Journal of Marriage and Family, 65*(4), 795–808.

Straus, M. A., & Gelles, R. J. (1990). Societal change and change in family violence from 1975 to 1985 as re-vealed by two national surveys. In M. A. Straus & R. J. Gelles (Eds.), *Physical violence in American families.* New Brunswick, NJ: Transaction.

Straus, M. A., & Stewart, J. H. (1999). Corporal punishment by American parents: National data on prevalence, chronicity, severity, and duration, in relation to child and family characteristics. *Clinical Child and Family Psychology Review, 2*(2), 55–70.

Strayer, F. F. (1990). The social ecology of toddler play groups and the origins of gender discrimination. In F. F. Strayer (Ed.), *Social interaction and behavioral development during early childhood.* Montreal: La Maison D'Ethologie de Montreal.

Strayer, J., & Roberts, W. (2004). Children's anger, emotional expressiveness, and empathy: Relations with parents' empathy, emotional expressiveness, and parenting practices. *Social Development, 13*(2), 229–254.

Streri, A. (2002). Hand preference in 4-month-old infants: Global or local processing of objects in the haptic mode. *Current Psychology Letters: Behaviour, Brain and Cognition, 7,* 39–50.

Stright, A. D., Neitzel, C., Sears, K. G., & Hoke-Sinex, L. (2001). Instruction begins in the home: Relations between parental instruction and children's self-regulation in the classroom. *Journal of Educational Psychology, 93*(3), 456–466.

Strock, M. (2004). *Autism spectrum disorders (pervasive developmental disorders).* NIH Publication NIH-04–5511. Bethesda, MD: National Institute of Mental Health, National Institutes of Health, U.S. Department of Health and Human Services. Available at http://www.nimh.nih.gov/publicat/autism.cfm.

Strohner, H., & Nelson, K. E. (1974). The young child's development of sentence comprehension: Influence of event probability, nonverbal context, syntactic form, and strategies. *Child Development, 45,* 567–576.

Strough, J., Berg, C. A., & Meegan, S. P. (2001). Friendship and gender differences in task and social interpretations of peer collaborative problem solving. *Social Development, 10*(1), 1–22.

Strutt, G. F., Anderson, D. R., & Well, A. D. (1975). A developmental study of the effects of irrelevant information on speeded classification. *Journal of Experimental Child Psychology, 20,* 127–135.

Stunkard, A. J., Harris, J. R., Pedersen, N. I., & McClearn, G. E. (1990). The body-mass index of twins who have been reared apart. *New England Journal of Medicine, 322,* 1483–1487.

Sue, S., & Okazaki, S. (1990). Asian-American educational achievements. *American Psychologist, 45,* 913–920.

Suizzo, M-A. (2004). French and American mothers' childrearing beliefs: Stimulating, responding, and long-term goals. *Journal of Cross-Cultural Psychology, 35*(5), 606–626.

Sukhodolsky, D. G., Golub, A., Stone, E. C., & Orban, L. (2005). Dismantling anger control training for children: A randomized pilot study of social problem-solving versus social skills training components. *Behavior Therapy, 36,* 15–23.

Sulloway, F. J. (2007). Birth order and intelligence. *Science, 316*(5832), 1711–1712.

Sullum, J. (2007, January 25). 10 million missing Chinese girls? *Reason online.* Available at http://www.reason.com/blog/show/118311.html.

Sumner, C. R., Schuh, K. J., Sutton, V. K., Lipetz, R., & Kelsey, D. K. (2006). Placebo-controlled study of the effects of atomoxetine